HISTORICAL MANUSCRIPTS COMMISSION

JP 9

A CALENDAR OF
THE REGISTER OF
WOLSTAN DE BRANSFORD

Bishop of Worcester 1339-49

by

R. M. HAINES

History Master, Westminster School

LONDON
HER MAJESTY'S STATIONERY OFFICE
1966

First published 1966

© *Crown copyright* 1966

Published by
HER MAJESTY'S STATIONERY OFFICE

To be purchased from
49 High Holborn, London w.c.1
423 Oxford Street, London w.1
13A Castle Street, Edinburgh 2
109 St. Mary Street, Cardiff
Brazennose Street, Manchester 2
50 Fairfax Street, Bristol 1
35 Smallbrook, Ringway, Birmingham 5
80 Chichester Street, Belfast 1
or through any bookseller
Price £10 0s. 0d. net

Printed in England for Her Majesty's Stationery Office
by William Clowes and Sons, Limited, London and Beccles

This volume, which has been prepared for the Worcestershire Historical Society, forms No. 4 in the publications of that Society and No. 9 in the *Joint Publication* series of the Historical Manuscripts Commission.

Editor's Acknowledgements

The task of preparing this calendar has been greatly eased by the award made in 1961 by the Leverhulme Trustees, to whom I am most grateful. The Head Master of Westminster generously granted me leave of absence so that I could take advantage of it. Mr. W. A. Pantin read the typescript for the Historical Manuscripts Commission, and I should like to thank him for many useful suggestions. Mr. Neil Ker helped to identify the hands of the register and kindly made a journey to Worcester for that purpose. The initial transcription and a Latin edition of the register were undertaken while working for a research degree of Durham University, and I owe a substantial debt to the exacting standards of my supervisor, Professor H. S. Offler.

Two of my colleagues at Westminster have given substantially of their time and skill: Mr. Ian Ross compiled the map of the diocese, while Mr. F. Dulley read the greater part of the proofs.

Contents

Abbreviations

Introduction

SYNOPSIS

TABLES

The Register

Collation

The register was originally divided into two parts, a practice which began with the sixth register in the Worcester series, that of Bishop Orleton (1327–33). Wolstan's register is the ninth, being now a single volume within vellum boards secured by metal clasps.[1] Bound in are the mediaeval covers, each marked with a large Arabic '9'. That belonging to the original first volume is much mutilated. Its title, *Registrum secundum Wolstani*, puzzled later readers,[2] for it is clearly the initial part.

The two parts are separately foliated. Roman numerals were used in the first, but the folios subsequently received Arabic numeration, apparently in the late fifteenth century. By that time a number of folios had become detached, though some of them were long afterwards discovered among transcripts in the registry. In 1881 these were bound in after the second part by the then registrar, Alfred Hooper, who added a note on the end-paper to that effect. These folios also have Roman and Arabic numerals, but the latter are not continuous with those of the remainder of volume one; in fact they are so muddled as to suggest a chequered career among the documents in the registry.

In 1824 the deputy registrar, Henry Clifton, noted that 'pages' 114, 155 and 185 were missing and that there were two pages marked 121. But he only considered the Arabic numerals. Had he examined the Roman ones as well, he would have seen that there never had been a folio 114, for though the Arabic numerals jump from 113 to 115, as he noted, the corresponding Roman ones are consecutively cxiiii and cxv.[3] Moreover, the accuracy in this respect of the Roman numerals is confirmed by there being no break in the sequence of the subject matter. A similar error can be detected with regard to folio 155, for here too there is really no missing page. As there is a break in both Arabic and Roman numerals, it seems that there was a folio 185. The subject matter is no guide here, but it may be significant that if such a folio did exist it must have been a separate half sheet after the eighteenth quire, and so susceptible to loss. This is not unlikely, both 186 and 187 being separate folios. Two folios are

---

1 The other registers are similarly bound. This was probably carried out under the deputy registrar, Henry Clifton, in the 1820s.
2 'This is quoted as the 2nd volume in the old index but this is the firste' [note on cover].
3 For what follows see Tables 7 and 8.

numbered 121, but the Roman numeration is again consecutive—
cxxi, cxxii.

Clifton did not notice that folio lxxxii had been lost before the
addition of the Arabic numerals. Today there are no further missing
folios until cxlvi (147), at which point there is a gap in the register—
as at present bound—until folio ccxviii (148). Table 7 attempts to
restore the original arrangement and number of folios. The conclu-
sions can only be tentative, for the Roman numerals may not have
advanced consecutively owing to errors of pagination such as are
found among the extant folios. With this proviso it may be calcu-
lated that 37 folios have been lost,[1] no fewer than 35 of them from
the quires which somehow became separated from the body of the
register between the time of its initial pagination and the addition of
the late mediaeval Arabic numerals.

At present the first volume comprises 186 folios (with the fly-leaf),
and 36 more folios bound after the second volume properly belong
to the first. That is, 222 folios survive out of a probable total of 259
(including the fly-leaf). In addition there are seven MS. fragments
which have either been attached to folios or else bound up with them.[2]

The second part of the register presents far fewer difficulties. It is
made up of eighteen folios numbered 2 to 19 in Arabic figures. There
probably never was a folio 1, particularly as the diminutive Roman
numerals[3] run from i to v (i.e. 2–6 Arabic), at which folio they cease.
The *Brevia regia* recorded from folio 5 *verso* to folio 7 *verso* date from
1350 and therefore do not properly belong to Wolstan's register.
Two separate portions of MS. are bound up in this part, though they
would be more in place in the first.

Binding[4]

There are now eighteen quires in the first part of the register varying
from three sheets to seven and from four folios to fourteen.[5] Eight
folios have been cut out and there are two separate ones at the end.
In fact the make-up is very irregular, though seven of the quires do
contain six sheets and twelve folios.

Four further quires, originally in the first volume, are now bound
after the second part and contain eight, eight, sixteen, and four folios
respectively. In the third quire folios clxxix, clxxxvi and clxxxiii are
in the wrong order.[6] Folios clxxxii and clxxxiii form a single sheet,
apparently the centre sheet of a quire containing folios clxxix and

1 Or 38 in the unlikely event of there having been a fo. cclii.
2 Also a 16th century copy (on paper) of part of the Herwynton chantry ordination has
been added after fo. 95.   3 Probably a temporary foliation of a loose gathering.
4 See Table 7.   5 Each quire comprised a number of sheets which were then folded
over to form twice the number of folios.
6 For the calendar the original order has been used. The present order of the folios can
be reconstructed from Table 7.

clxxxvi (also a single sheet) on the outside, but the remaining folios of this quire have been lost.

The second part of the register is made up of two quires of four and eight folios respectively. Two separate folios precede each of these quires and two more complete the volume. The stubs remain, the corresponding six leaves having been cut out.

With the possible exception mentioned above [1] there is no foliation within the quires. There are only two instances of the use of catch-words, one from the folios misplaced after the second part,[2] the other within that part, linking the second quire with the first of the separate leaves which follow.

The arrangement of material

The main divisions of the register are quite clear. In the first part the initial three quires are filled with sundry records of the bishop's consecration and enthronement, appointments and commissions, licences, letters dimissory, and details of the primary visitation of the diocese. The fourth quire is headed: *Hic incipit registrum institucionum, licenciarum, prefeccionum, et appropriacionum ecclesiarum.* This title seems to refer to the entries up to the end of the fifteenth quire (i.e. fo. 147, clxvi), the last entry bearing the date 6 May 1349, three months before the bishop's death. In this section much space is occupied by lengthy entries concerning appropriations, vicarages, and chantries.

In the original arrangement the quires containing the ordination lists followed folio 147. These lists, together with sundry extraneous material, filled some seventy folios, of which about half are missing. Next came three quires (thirty-six folios) of royal writs, interrupted by long entries recording the foundation of Tormarton chantry, the union of Acton Turville and Tormarton churches, and the ordination of the vicarage of the former.

Although such divisions—Introductory; Institutions, Licences, Appointments, Appropriations of Churches; Ordinations; Royal Writs—can readily be seen by cursory inspection, only the second bears a formal heading. With such a variety of material in the first two divisions it must have been difficult to trace an individual entry. There is no roughly contemporary index such as can be found in the registers of Bishops Giffard (1268–1302) and Cobham (1317–27). The notes on the fly-leaf[3] merely give the year A.D. as a guide to searchers. This was usually written at the top of every folio, for within each sub-division the entries are—with some exceptions—in chronological order.

From the standpoint of arrangement and neatness, as of regularity, the second part of the register contrasts markedly with the first, but it is very short and covers only a few months of 1349. The subject matter is carefully divided into five sections, each of them headed.

1 See p. ii, n. 3.   2 fo. clxxxvi (82), which is bound out of order.   3 See text.

They deal respectively with memoranda, ordinations, royal writs, Audience Court proceedings, and institutions. The last section closes with the record of the bishop's death.

Marginal rubrics are to be found regularly throughout the register. Some are of a general character, without indication of the persons or places concerned. But this does not permit an inference that the register is primarily a collection of precedents. For one thing, many marginal entries do include names of persons and places; and for another, some quite cryptic memoranda have detailed marginalia. So far as Wolstan's register is concerned it would appear that the marginalia provided a practical method of tracing individual items. On the whole the mediaeval clerk was not looking for a person as such, but for an entry about him. He was concerned, perhaps, with his orders, or with a licence that the bishop had granted him. The clerk could easily turn to the appropriate section and approximate date and then quickly scan the rubrics for the right type of entry, glancing each time at the body of the entry to see if it concerned the person in question.

The question of the precise function of the register need not detain us further. It was equally a repository of form as of fact, an essential element in ensuring the continuity of administration. One aspect of particular interest ought, however, to be mentioned. It is the special registration of documents from earlier times which had become the subject of current concern. The earliest, dating from Baldwin's episcopate (1180–84), records the ancient endowment of Campden chapel,[1] another the grant of land made (in 1316) by Thomas, earl of Lancaster, in return for the Worcester convent's promise to cele-brate certain anniversaries.[2] The third is the foundation deed of Ripple chantry. This is dated 1320,[3] and although entered in the Liber Albus[4] is not to be found in Cobham's register.

Registration

The register provides no clue as to the organisation responsible for its compilation, nor does it refer to any place or places where current administrative documents were kept or entries written up.[5] Many records of temporary value, and even a number of permanent importance, found no place in it. Anomalies of registration are not infrequent. Sometimes entries are made twice or even more times; occasionally the component parts of lengthy proceedings are recorded individually and again later as elements of a complete process.[6]

Little is known of the office of registrar at Worcester until the second half of the fifteenth century, from which time commissions of appointment can be traced down to the present day. Even the title

1 905.   2 952.   3 969.   4 fo. cxliii et seq.
5 Although documents of lasting importance may well have been kept in the treasury of the cathedral priory. See 905 (rubric).   6 e.g. 772 et seq., 906.

'registrar' is rare in the fourteenth century, but Reynolds, Orleton and Hemenhale are all recorded to have had 'scribes', who doubtless exercised similar functions. Registrar or scribe often enjoyed the status of notary, for the drawing up of 'public instruments' was a prominent feature of administrative and judicial process. Where neither is to be found, it may be that a notary public was doing corresponding work.

It is likely that the person who exercised the functions of registrar was concerned with the actual writing of the register, and to a large extent with its compilation. While neither registrar, nor, until 1349, scribe, finds mention in the present register, two hands can be ascribed to individuals with some degree of confidence.[1] Robert Marny of Bishops Cleeve, a notary,[2] apparently wrote the bulk of the entries prior to 1342. His hand and distinctive sign are to be seen in the first part up to folio 51 *verso*,[3] and some of the earlier ordination lists, as also a substantial section of the royal writs, would seem to be his work.[4] He may also have been engaged on indexing earlier records at the same time. Part of the index to Giffard's register seems to be in his hand, as well as the index to that of Cobham.[5] Marny, who became rector of Halford in 1340,[6] was licensed to be absent for a year's study in 1344.[7] He is not otherwise mentioned in the register after 1341. Perhaps a victim of the plague, he died in March 1349.[8]

The other person who may well have written part of the register is Master William Aleyn, a notary public of Lincoln diocese. He does not occur earlier than July 1349, and his appearance roughly coincides with that of a distinctive hand in the second part of the register responsible for folio 5 *recto* and folios 8 *recto*—19 *verso*. He describes himself as *scriba episcopi*.[9]

The remainder of the register presents difficulties. The predominant hand is one similar to Marny's, lacking his special sign, but often with a distinctive paragraph mark of its own. This could be the hand of Master Thomas Bolevinch of Droitwich. He was acting as a notary for diocesan business in 1343 and his name, surrounded by a roughly drawn rectangular frame, occurs on the dorse of an inserted portion of MS.[10]

A fourth possible scribe is John de Chalveston, rector of South

---

1 In what follows I have received valuable help from Mr. Neil Ker who kindly made a special visit to Worcester to study the hands of the register.
2 He attests two documents: 243, 244.
3 ff. 52r.–53r. are in a hand very like Marny's, but probably not his.
4 ff. cxlvii r. (47) to cl v. (35); the 1341 memoranda on fo. clvi r. (40); probably the lists of those ordained to the first tonsure [clvii] r. (49) to clviii r. (50); ff. ccxviii r. (148) to cc[xx]vi r. (157). The name 'Marny' or 'R. Marny' is added to six entries: 3, 123, 431, 432, 445, 1013.
5 Inf. Neil Ker.   6 381, 382.   7 528.   8 1379.   9 1484.
10 fo. 104 (822). The same name is written in the margin of an entry in the Liber Ruber dated 1344 (fo. 140).

Tawton in Devon and clerk of the bishop's household.[1] Whenever his name appears in the ordination lists[2] a slightly elaborated 'Chalveston' has been written in the margin. But, of course, there could be some other significance.

The Bishop's Early Life and Priorate[3]

Early life

Wolstan de Bransford was probably born in his name-hamlet some two miles to the south-west of Worcester. The date of his birth is unknown, but assuming he adopted a clerical career early in life, it could have been 1284, and may have been a few years before that. It seems correct to identify him as the clerk, son of one John de Bransford, formerly citizen of Worcester, who received letters testimonial from Prior John de Wyke during the 1307–8 vacancy of the see, and who, as deacon, was granted letters dimissory to the priesthood in November 1308 by Bishop Reynolds.[4] It was Reynolds who, on 21 September 1310, at the time of his tardy enthronement, admitted Wolstan as a monk of the cathedral priory, together with Simon Cromp, another future prior.[5]

Wolstan next appears in 1313, when he accompanied his fellow monk, John de Stratford, on a business trip to London in connection with the priory's church of Broadwas,[6] and in the same year there is mention of his receiving rent in the chapter house.[7] In 1315, when the monasteries of Worcester, Gloucester, Llanthony and Cirencester banded together to resist the diocesan official's claim to hospitality during sessions of the consistory court, he was chosen as the Worcester representative.[8]

Election as prior

Following the death of Prior John de Wyke the monks assembled in their chapter house for the election of a successor on 20 October 1317.[9] Forty-one were present[10] and Wolstan, a comparative newcomer, was listed thirty-fourth. Deciding to proceed by way of compromise, the brethren deputed seven of their number to[11]

1 542.   2 1060 (subdeacon), 1061 (deacon), 1066 (priest).
3 Cf. the writer's 'Wolstan de Bransford, prior and bishop of Worcester, c. 1280–1349' in the *University of Birmingham Historical Journal* (1962), vol. VIII, no. 2, pp. 97–113.
4 *Register Sede Vacante* (*W.H.S.*), p. 88 (undated); *Reg. Reynolds* (*W.H.S.*), p. 92.
5 Liber Albus, fo. xlv v. It was comparatively unusual at this time to enter a monastery after ordination as a secular cleric.
6 *Early Compotus Rolls XIIIth cent.* (*W.H.S.*), p. 39.   7 Liber Albus, fo. lviii r.
8 *Cart. S. Petri Glouc.* (*R.S.*), I, pp. 140–46; D. & C. MS. B 1633.
9 The account in the Liber Albus (ff. lxxxiii r. to lxxxiiii v.) is summarised by J. M. Wilson in *Worcester Liber Albus*, 1920, pp. 162–6. Cf. Liber Ruber, fo. 139.
10 Five others were in the infirmary and one, John de Sancto Germano, was absent.
11 Not eight, as Wilson states (*op. cit.*, p. 164). He includes the subprior, Gilbert de Madeleye, in whose name and that of the convent the nominators were appointed.

nominate the final seven[1] whose names were to be sent to the diocesan in accordance with the composition of 1224.[2] Among the latter were a very senior monk, John de Harleye, admitted in 1276 with John de Wyke, and a notable scholar, Richard de Bromwych S.T.P., the precentor, a future prior of Abergavenny, while four others held some official position.[3] The last name was that of Wolstan himself. His inclusion is surprising, for he was relatively young and apparently without experience of office in the priory.

The convent's proctors found Bishop Cobham at St. Mary's hospital, Strood, near Rochester. He delegated two local rectors to enquire into the candidates' qualifications, and later, in London, deputed his brother, James de Cobham, canon of Wells, to make the selection. The canon chose Wolstan, and on the same day, 23 November, Cobham wrote to inform the chapter. A week later, St. Andrew's day, the new prior was installed.[4]

Financial difficulties

Wolstan's priorate, destined to last twenty-one years, spans a troubled period in the monastery's history. The immediate problem was a financial one, but the surviving account rolls are too few to allow of an objective appraisal of the position. The well-known enquiry of 1313, when the monks sought to appropriate Dodderhill church, was based, in accordance with regular practice, on the articles of the priory's own petition. The contentions were doubtless substantially true, though mostly of long standing.[5] All the same, the fact of indebtedness is supported by the Bursar and Cellarer's roll of that time (1313–14), which shows a deficit of over £600,[6] a sum which by 1320–21 had been reduced to £530 8s. 7¼d.[7]

The times were hard. Over and above the ordinary burden of taxation, which was heavy enough on account of wars with Scotland, disturbances in England, and preparations for the Hundred Years' War, other demands were made by the Crown. In 1321 Edward II was asking for men-at-arms to save the Despensers from the wrath of the Marcher barons. The prior replied that he had none and enlarged upon the troubles which beset his house because of the unsettled state of the border.[8] Both Edward II and Edward III

---

1 The 'Roger de Neuwyntone' of Wilson's list (*op. cit.*, p. 164) should be 'Roger de Stevinton'.

2 Between Bp. William de Blois and the then prior and chapter. It is printed in Thomas, *Appendix* 68, pp. 74–6.

3 John de Stratford was almoner, Simon le Botiler, cook; Henry Fouke, subsacrist; and Roger de Stevinton, pittancer.

4 See Wilson, *op. cit.* pp. 165–6; *Reg. Cobham (W.H.S.)*, pp. 1–2.

5 *Worcester Liber Albus*, pp. 124–6; *Reg. Reynolds*, pp. 75–7; printed in Nash, *Worcs.* (1781–2), I, pp. 339–40.

6 D. & C. MS. C. 482. The deficit on the roll is £640 7s. 6¼d. but the editor of *Early Compotus Rolls XIIIth cent. (W.H.S.)* suggests (p. 33 n. 1) that £605 7s. 6¼d. is the correct figure.   7 D. & C. MS. C. 55.   8 *Worcester Liber Albus*, pp. 196–8.

demanded transport for their Scottish campaigns,[1] and in 1332 the latter invoked an aid for the marriage of his sister Eleanor to Reginald, Count of Guelders.

Papal emissaries also sent begging letters. Cardinal Luke de Flisco, in the country as a mediator, asked the priory to provide for one John Rydel, who had lost rectory and goods in the north, and later, on his own behalf, requisitioned a palfrey.[3]

What with procurations, papal and episcopal, expenses at times of visitation, the upkeep of its estates, an exceptionally large number of guests,[4] perennial requests for assistance, and the need to provide for royal corrodians as well as its own servants, it is small wonder that the priory's resources were strained. Litigation was a heavy expense, and proctors had to be maintained at the Curia, the king's courts, the provincial Court of Arches, and elsewhere. But there is a suit which must be considered exceptional even by the standards of the time; one which tested Prior Wolstan's ingenuity, resource and tenacity to the limit.

The case of Alice Conan

In Prior John de Wyke's time Edward II had tried to force the priory to grant a corrody to one Alice Conan. The prior resisted and the matter was dropped. But in 1322 the king revived the demand in favour of Alice, by then lady-in-waiting to the queen. During 1323 Prior Wolstan is said to have argued the case personally in the royal courts. His defence was that the monastery held its lands in free alms and had not been burdened with corrodians until the king had sent Peter d'Avylers nine years previously. The (partly spurious) *Altitonantis* charter of King Edgar,[5] recently confirmed by Edward himself, was produced as evidence. But it was pointed out by the king's lawyers that the charter made no mention of free alms. What is more, it could be shown that the priory had accepted other corrodians since d'Avylers. To the latter point Wolstan replied that he knew it well enough, but the king had promised (in the *Articuli Cleri* of 1316) that he would not again burden religious houses in this way, and his priory had letters patent to that effect. Judgement was given for the prior.

The battle was not to be won so easily. The king continued to cajole, and even to threaten. The prior manœuvred with consummate skill, now pointing out that Alice might be more suitably housed among others of her sex at Nuneaton, now arguing that as the monks held their goods in common he could make no grant

1 *Ibid.*, pp. 96–9, 196–8; *C.C.R.* 1333–37, p. 100; *C.P.R.* 1330–34, p. 446 *et seq.*; *Cal. of Liber Albus*, intro. pp. xvi–xviii, nos. 935–9.
2 *C.C.R.* 1330–33, p. 590; *Foedera* IV, pp. 544–5.
3 *Worcester Liber Albus*, pp. 167–8, 177–8.
4 See *Cal. of Liber Albus*, intro. pp. xlvii–xlviii.
5 For the text, see Eric John, *Land Tenure in Early England*, 1960, pp. 162–7.

without the chapter's assent. In return for a promise that the priory would not be prejudiced thereby, he even offered to make a small grant to Alice from his own funds. All was in vain, for in April 1327 Wolstan was forced to yield in return for the dubious safeguard of letters patent declaring that Alice's pension of £10 a year for life would not be taken as a precedent.[1] For how long this was paid is not known, but as early as 1335 another corrodian, John Ussher, was sent by Edward III to receive such maintenance as John le Treour had enjoyed in Edward I's time.[2]

Financial policy

While remembering the partial nature of the evidence, it is possible to gain some idea of the prior's financial 'policy', if so specific a term can be used.

It would seem that under Wolstan's rule there was an extension of the corrody or livery (*liberacio*) system, for he is recorded to have made thirty such grants, against his predecessor's fourteen.[3] Some, it is true, as in any great household of the time, provided for servants, such as the chief porter and the medical adviser, others for clerks who helped with administrative or legal matters; but a number seem to have been purely financial transactions, providing ready money or extinguishing a debt.[4] This mortgaging of future income for present advantage had grave dangers, and that Wolstan realised the fact is suggested by his attempts, when bishop, to restrict the practice at St. Wulstan's hospital.[5]

The appropriation of churches was an expedient which had more to recommend it from the priory's viewpoint. The initial cost might be high, but the long term gain was substantial. In 1333 Wolstan finally secured Dodderhill church, first appropriated thirty-one years before,[6] and he set in motion the process for acquiring Overbury and its chapels, which was completed after his priorate, in 1346.[7] The combined taxed value of these churches (excluding portions already paid to the priory) was £44.[8]

There is little doubt that the freeing of serfs was accelerated for financial reasons. Certainly Wolstan manumitted a considerable number,[9] so many in fact that Bishop Montacute at his visitation in 1335 called the practice into question. To the implied criticism the

1 The whole case can be followed in *Corrodies at Worcester in the XIVth cent.* (*W.H.S.*), which lists fifty-one letters between 1308 and 1327. There is a detailed *inspeximus* of the proceedings (8 June 1337) in *C.P.R.* 1334–38, pp. 459–60. The final chapter grant is in the Liber Albus (fo. cxxxi r.), and there is a confirmation of this in *C.P.R.* 1327–30, p. 102. Record of the inquisition, dated 12 September 1327 from Worcester, in which a jury found that the priory held its lands in free alms, is in *Original Charters relating to the city of Worcester* (*W.H.S.*), p. 159.
2 *C.C.R.* 1333–37, p. 489. 3 See the indexes to the *Cal. of Liber Albus*.
4 See *Cal. of Liber Albus*, intro. pp. xlix–li. 5 1371, 1373, 1375.
6 Reg. Orleton 2, fo. 53r.–v.; Nash, *Worcs.*, 1, pp. 338–9.
7 *C.P.R.* 1327–30, p. 536; Nash, *Worcs.*, 2, pp. 237–8. 8 *Tax. Eccles.*, p. 217.
9 See *Cal. of Liber Albus*, index s.v. Manumissions.

prior replied that he was merely exercising his well established right.[1]

Lastly there was the acquisition of land, some of it in one of the lost manors, Spetchley. John le Mercer was prevailed upon to surrender his lands in Battenhall—the favourite manor of Prior More in the sixteenth century, Newberne (now Barnes) and Timberdine,[2] in return for a life pension of £26 13s. 4d.[3] There were other negotiations in which John, rector of Harvington by Evesham, figured prominently. He must have known the prior well, for he also came from Bransford and the advowson of his benefice belonged to the chapter.[4] By his agency lands in Spetchley, Alveston, Cropthorne, Timberdine and Northwick, came to the priory, which had secured a mortmain licence permitting such acquisition up to twenty marks' annual value.[5] The same John, in association with Thomas of Evesham, also secured the reversion to the priory of the manor of Crowle Siward.[6]

Spiritual rule

Of the prior's spiritual rule it is not possible to speak with certainty. He seems to have been careful about the qualifications of monks submitted for entry, that is if we can judge fairly from his refusal of a royal nominee because of defects of character, and of an episcopal one for lack of learning. He himself, however, presented for the bishop's approval a candidate who was found to be under age.[7]

Episcopal visitations of the priory do not cast much light here. Cobham was the only bishop to leave injunctions behind him, these being bound up at the end of Montacute's register.[8] They are undated and may well comprise two separate sets, of which the first must belong to the visitation of 1319.[9] Among other matters Cobham sought to make provision for an inventory of the convent's valuables, for the recovery of alienations and loans made by 'R. de Hervynton' while sacrist,[10] the appointment of receivers for the cellarer's office,

---

1 Reg. Montacute 2, ff. 42r., 48r. Cf. *Cal. of Liber Albus*, nos. 1198, 1199 (wrongly dated 1334).
2 All of which lay a short distance to the south and east of Worcester, though now well within its boundaries.
3 *Cal. of Liber Albus*, nos. 1222–5; Habington, *Survey of Worcs.* (W.H.S.), 1, p. 41; *Monasticon* ed. Caley, 1, p. 614 *et seq.*; Nash, *Worcs.*, 2, pp. 326–8. Cf. *V.C.H. Worcs.*, 3, p. 515, and *ibid.* nn. 26–8.
4 Though he secured it by exchange (1320). *Reg. Cobham*, p. 235.
5 *C.P.R.* 1327–30, pp. 343, 450; *ibid.* 1330–34, p. 116; *ibid.* 1334–38, p. 222.
6 *C.P.R.* 1334–38, pp. 130, 182; Reg. Montacute 1, fo. 29r.; *ibid.* 2, ff. 19v. to 20r.; Nash, *Worcs.*, 1, pp. 283–5; Habington, *Survey of Worcs.*, 1, pp. 532–3, 534; *V.C.H. Worcs.*, 3, p. 331, nn. 39, 40.
7 *Cal. of Liber Albus*, nos. 755–6, 763, 1134–7, 1144–5; *Worcester Liber Albus*, pp. 225–6, 229–30.
8 Reg. Montacute 2, ff. 43r.–44r. The writer of this part of *V.C.H. Worcs.* (2, pp. 105–6) gave a mixture of the Gainsburgh and Cobham injunctions as those of Montacute.
9 *Reg. Cobham*, pp. 43–4.
10 Nothing else seems to be known of this monk and his tenure of the sacrist's office.

the imposition of oaths of faithful administration on all officers who had dealings with seculars, the keeping of accounts, and for the exclusion of women and other persons from the monastery, except overnight guests. The other set of injunctions—if it be a separate set—must come from the bishop's second and fragmentary visitation of 1326.[1] It lays down rules for the various obedientiaries.[2]

Such evidence is negative, but the emphasis on administration and accounting does lend support to the general impression gleaned from a variety of sources of an unstable financial position.

On the whole one infers from the Liber Albus, which contains a very large number of Wolstan's letters as prior, that he was an administrator rather than a spiritual man. Diligence and awareness of the needs of the house, whether in purely material matters, or in the field of learning,[3] seemingly provide the keynote to his regimen. But this can be only a tentative conclusion, for the nature of the Liber Albus precludes other than incidental mention of spiritual matters.

Building schemes attributed to the prior

Wolstan de Bransford is best remembered for erecting a bridge over the Teme at his native place (when bishop?), and building the Guest Hall of the priory. Such is the story told by historians of the Worcester bishops from Francis Godwin's time (1615),[4] and which apparently originates in Leland's Itinerary.[5] The tradition may be sound, but it is at present unsupported by written evidence from the fourteenth or fifteenth centuries. Both Browne Willis[6] and Thomas (following him?)[7] ascribe the date 1320 to the hall, but this has been questioned on architectural grounds.[8]

The bridge, of which some masonry from the abutments still remains, was broken down by the Scots at the time of the battle of Worcester (1651).[9] The Guest Hall survived until about 1860, but as the gentlemen of the county could not raise the money needed for its restoration, the fine timber roof was removed to the new church of Holy Trinity, Shrub Hill,[10] and the fabric allowed to deteriorate.

1 Evidence for this visitation is slight, resting mainly on an undated commission which probably belongs to 1326. See *Reg. Cobham*, p. 196. The cathedral priory would have been visited first.

2 There is mention of the corrody granted to John de Broadwas in 1322. Cf. *Worcester Liber Albus*, p. 212.

3 See the correspondence about the return of a monk lecturer printed (from the Liber Albus) in *Chapters of the English Black Monks (Camden Soc.* 3rd ser. XLV), pp. 181–5.

4 *Catalogue of the Bishops of England*, p. 444.

5 1747 (2nd) ed., 8, p. 99 fo. 111b. Green, *Antiquities of Worcester* 1796, 1, p. 192 n. 1, gives Leland as his authority.

6 *An History of the Mitred Parliamentary Abbeys*, 1718–19, 2, p. 262.

7 *Account*, p. 179.

8 Harold Brakspear in *V.C.H. Worcs.* 4, p. 395 n. 35. Such window tracery as remains suggests the latter half of the century. 1320 is also given as the date of building in Lansdowne MS. 1233, no. 58, a late seventeenth century transcript.

9 Hist. MSS. Comm. Rpt. 5, *App.* p. 299.

10 *English Topography, Worcs. (Gentleman's Magazine)*, pp. 88–95.

There is record of the prior's goodwill towards the rebuilding of the nave. He sought licence from Bishop Montacute to reconstruct the small building in the cathedral cemetery which was being used by the stonemasons in the sacrist's employ.[1]

Experience in diocesan affairs

Sede plena, as head of the chapter, the Worcester prior was concerned with certain aspects of diocesan administration. In particular there were processes, such as the alienation of land and property of the see, the appropriation of churches, or the foundation of chantries, which ordinarily required the chapter's confirmation. *Sede vacante* the prior, under the terms of Archbishop Boniface's composition of 1268, exercised spiritual jurisdiction throughout the diocese.[2] In addition, from time to time an individual prior might be employed by a bishop in an *ad hoc* capacity or appointed to serve as a penitentiary.[3]

Wolstan is known to have acted as official *sede vacante* on two occasions: after the death of Bishop Cobham in 1327 and that of Thomas de Hemenhale in 1338. In the earlier instance he was soon elected bishop, and thereafter the subprior exercised the functions of official, as the Boniface composition laid down. In 1338 Wolstan must have assumed the jurisdiction on 21 December, the day of Hemenhale's death. Inexplicably he did not relinquish it on his election as bishop—4 January 1339, for the subprior subsequently acted as his commissary-general.[4] In each case he later exercised the jurisdiction in the capacity of bishop elect and confirmed.

The episcopal elections of 1327 and 1339

It has often been remarked by editors of Worcester records that Wolstan de Bransford was elected by the chapter three or even four times. This is not the case: he was elected only twice.

The earlier occasion was in 1327 during the first week in September. The Crown's assent was given on the 8th of that month and Archbishop Reynolds confirmed the election on 3 October.[5] Meanwhile Pope John XXII had issued bulls translating Orleton from Hereford to Worcester.[6] Before their arrival the temporalities had been restored to Wolstan as bishop elect and confirmed, arrangements being set in motion for his consecration.[7] The archbishop staved off repeated royal injunctions to consecrate, being relieved of the dilemma by his death on 16 November. Instructions were then sent in the king's

1 Reg. Montacute 1, fo. 29v.; 2, fo. 22r. (duplicated). There is no mention of any renewal of the cemetery as stated in *V.C.H. Worcs.* 2, p. 104.

2 See the writer's 'Administration of the Diocese of Worcester *Sede Vacante*, 1266–1350' in the *Journal of Ecclesiastical History* (October 1962), pp. 156–71.

3 Cobham deputed Wolstan to reconcile the polluted cloister at Worcester and made him a penitentiary. *Reg. Cobham,* pp. 13, 21.   4 e.g. R.S.V., fo. 154r.

5 Wilkins, *Concilia,* 2, pp. 537–8; *C.P.R.* 1327–30, pp. 159, 164; Cant. Reg. Reynolds, ff. 206v.–207r.

6 Dated 28 September: *C.P.L.* 1305–42, p. 263; Reg. Orleton 2, ff. 1r.–3v.

7 *Foedera* IV, pp. 314—5; *C.P.R.* 1327–30, pp. 179, 182.

name—Edward III was only fifteen at the time—to the Canterbury prior and chapter, urging them as keepers of the spiritualities to cite the suffragans of the province to effect the consecration without further delay. Despite peremptory warnings to Orleton not to do anything to the Crown's prejudice and efforts to intercept his bulls at the ports,[1] the government, of which Orleton had but recently been a supporter, could do nothing. Both candidates were summoned to the York parliament of February 1328, but there is no record of what happened there. The struggle was over by March, and on the first of that month Adam of Harvington was directed to resume the temporalities, which he then delivered to Orleton.[2] Wolstan retired to the priory where he resumed his former position.

The next two vacancies resulted from translations, and the see was therefore filled by papal provision in each case. It was only after Hemenhale's death, 21 December 1338, that the convent could proceed again to an election. The royal congé d'élire was issued on the 28th, and meeting in chapter the following Sunday the monks appointed the very next day, 4 January 1339, for the proceedings.[3] After the canonical preliminaries, including the reading of the *Quia propter* constitution, they agreed to adopt the method of compromise. According to the *sede vacante* register they chose three compromisers: A. de B., E. de C., and O. de N.[4] On the other hand, a letter sent by Henry Fouke (later sacrist) states that on the advice of Master Thomas de Astleye the monks decided to conduct the election *per viam simplicis compromissi*, nominating Simon Cromp, John of Evesham, John of Westbury, Robert of Weston, and Nicholas de Stanlak, whose unanimous choice fell upon their prior, Wolstan.[5] The discrepancy is puzzling.

On 16 January the king signified to the archbishop's vicar-general, Robert Stratford, bishop of Chichester, that he had assented to the election. Opponents were cited to appear in Maidstone parish church on the next law day after St. Scholastica (10 February). The precise date of the confirmation is not known,[6] but the earliest mandates of the bishop elect and confirmed are dated 16 February from London. The following day the temporalities were restored, and on Palm Sunday (21 March) Wolstan was consecrated in Canterbury cathedral by the bishop of Chichester, being enthroned a week later in his cathedral church by Bernard Sistre, the archdeacon of Canterbury.[7] Thus Wolstan was consecrated twelve years after his initial election.

1 *Foedera* IV, pp. 324–5, 329–30; *C.C.R.* 1327–30, pp. 235, 238–9.
2 *Foedera* IV, p. 331; *C.C.R.* 1327–30, pp. 239, 244; *C.P.R.* 1327–30, p. 245; Reg. Orleton 2, fo. 4r.–v.   3 *R.S.V.*, pp. 256–7, 259, 267 *et seq.*   4 *R.S.V.*, p. 267 *et seq.*
5 *Catalogue of Cathedral Library MSS.* (*W.H.S.*), ed. Floyer & Hamilton, p. 180 F 141.
6 Though Thomas, *Account*, p. 176, gives 20 March as the date, and others have copied him.
7 *C.P.R.* 1338–40, pp. 175, 203; *R.S.V.*, pp. 259–260; *Reg. Bransford*, 21, 24.

The Extent and Divisions of The Diocese

The mediaeval diocese

The diocese which Wolstan ruled included Worcestershire, save for some western parishes lying in Hereford diocese, where they formed part of Burford deanery in the archdeaconry of Shropshire; part of Warwickshire—the remainder forming the archdeaconry of Coventry in Coventry and Lichfield diocese; as well as Gloucestershire east of the Severn.

This area was divided into two archdeaconries, Worcester and Gloucester. The northern archdeaconry comprised eight deaneries,[1] a ninth—Evesham—having passed from the bishop's control by the mid-thirteenth century. In the southern archdeaconry were eleven deaneries.[2]

Exempt jurisdictions

Within the diocese were certain 'exempt' or 'peculiar' jurisdictions: terms used indiscriminately in the register to denote areas entirely—or almost entirely—outside the bishop's authority, as well as those which, though subject to the diocesan, did not fall within the archdeacon's jurisdiction.

Prominent in the former category were the abbot of Evesham's peculiar in the town and vale of Evesham, and the Churchdown jurisdiction of the canons of St. Oswald's, Gloucester. The diocesan had no direct contact with these, and so they are rarely mentioned. Of more recent origin was the exemption of Great Malvern, a cell of Westminster, which Bishop Giffard had conceded in 1283.[3] Also privileged were houses of the Cistercian order—Bordesley, Hailes and Kingswood; the Premonstratensian abbey of Halesowen, and the alien priory of Deerhurst. Their precise relationship to the bishop has not been worked out, but in general the position was that he could not exercise visitation, interfere with their internal affairs,[4] or confirm or quash the elections of their heads. He was acknowledged as diocesan, and at any rate in the case of the Cistercian and Pre-

1 Worcester, Powick, Pershore, Droitwich, Kidderminster, Blockley, Warwick and Kineton.
2 Gloucester, Stonehouse, Dursley, Bristol, Bitton, Hawkesbury, Cirencester, Fairford, Stow, Winchcombe and Campden. At this time, however, Hawkesbury and Bitton are often treated as a single deanery.
3 See *V.C.H Worcs.* 2, pp. 138–141; *Reg. Giffard (W.H.S.)*, intro. pp. xlii–xlvii.
4 But at Deerhurst, according to *V.C.H. Gloucs.* 2, p. 105, Ralph de Ermenovilla was removed by Wolstan and Thomas Graculi [Garculi] put in his place. By composition the bishop's institution of the prior was not to the priory but to the parish church, for Deerhurst was a *prioratus curatus*. See 256–7, 759–61.

monstratensian houses, received a qualified oath of subjection, reverence and obedience from newly elected superiors, usually when he gave them his benediction.[1]

The other category, comprising areas exempt only from archidia-conal jurisdiction, has given rise to some confusion between rural deans and deans of exempt jurisdiction.[2] Most numerous in this class of 'petty archdeaconries' are the episcopal manors. The register mentions the deans of Cleeve, Alvechurch and Tredington, as well as the jurisdictions of Bibury, Blockley, Ripple and St. Helen's, Wor-cester. All these were, or in Bibury's case had at one time been, episcopal churches.[3]

References from a variety of sources[4] enable a composite picture of such jurisdiction to be built up. The dean of jurisdiction was probably appointed by the rector. He could hold chapters, administer correc-tions, and exercise certain testamentary powers. It is likely that he had the assistance of an official and apparitors, and to him were sent episcopal mandates for induction to benefices within his jurisdiction,[5] and for enquiry into their vacancy.[6] Ordinarily such matters lay within the archdeacon's province.

Two entries in the register are of importance in this connection. One is a commission to the dean of Pershore for the sequestration of the goods of John Roger, or Rogers, who had died intestate in Ripple parish. The bishop disclaimed any attempt to usurp the rector's jurisdiction, declaring that he acted because there was no-one to exercise it.[7] The second entry relates to Blockley, where the area of exemption comprised a complete rural deanery. At this time Blockley church was held in commendam by the bishop of Porto,[8] and there seems to have been no suitable arrangement with respect to the jurisdiction. This prompted the bishop to empower the farmer of Blockley, John, rector of Hinton, to administer correction and punishment, to hear and determine ex officio and instance cases, to grant probate of wills, and to exercise rights of coercion and se-questration.[9]

Also exempt from the archdeacon were the collegiate churches of Westbury-on-Trym and Warwick. Robert de Endredeby, dean of the latter church, became involved in a legal dispute with the arch-

1 Although Wolstan's register does not contain any, oaths taken by Cistercian abbots are to be found in Worcester records: e.g. *Reg. Gainsburgh*, p. 114 (Hailes), and *Reg. Cobham*, p. 15 (Kingswood). Examples of episcopal benediction of abbots of Halesowen, a Premonstratensian house, are in Reg. Maidstone, fo. 6v., and Reg. Orleton 2, fo. 41v.
2 e.g. R. A. Wilson in his introduction to *Reg. Reynolds*, p. iv.
3 Bibury had been alienated to the Oseney canons in the middle of the twelfth century.
4 Particularly Reg. Gainsburgh, fo. 15v. [Bredon] and the *Cartulary of Oseney Abbey (Oxf. Hist. Soc.* XCVIII), p. lxxiii and pp. 1–38, nos. 511–48 [Bibury].
5 For an exception, see 1566. In the case of Ripple (571) the mandate is said to have been directed to the official of the *Gloucester* archdeacon. This is either an error for Worcester, or merely an instance of the official being used as a special commissary.
6 e.g. 1485, 1518.   7 180.   8 *C.P.L.* 1305–42, p. 370.   9 129.

deacon of Worcester. In 1343 he was made to forgo his jurisdiction, save in internal choir matters, pending an agreement.[1]

Some of the churches belonging to the cathedral priory had a measure of exemption from the archdeacon, but nothing can be learnt from the register about this.

Archdeaconries

The two archdeaconries formed useful administrative sub-divisions of the diocese. It would be outside the scope of the introduction to detail the powers of archdeacons at this time, as exercised by their permanent 'officials', but the register does throw light on certain of their functions.

Except where exempt jurisdictions were involved, episcopal mandates for enquiry into vacant benefices were sent to the archdeacons' officials.[2] They were required to implement them in the local (ruridecanal) chapter, either at the regular meeting or at one summoned *ad hoc*. The facts of the matter were established by a body of local rectors and vicars, or their proctors.[3] Laymen are not mentioned as participating, nor are the members of the enquiry said to have been sworn, though these conditions seem to have obtained in Norwich diocese.[4] Another type of enquiry—that concerned with the valuation of benefices—was conducted slightly differently, and apparently not in the regular chapter. A sworn jury was empanelled, which included not only beneficed clergy or their proctors, but also laymen.[5] This method was the one usually adopted for the examination of petitions for appropriation,[6] and for the assessment of dilapidations to benefices.[7] In the former case the enquiry was regularly entrusted to special commissaries rather than to the archdeacon's official.

Mandates for induction were almost invariably directed to the appropriate archdeacon or his official,[8] unless the benefice concerned formed part of an exempt area or was in the bishop's collation.[9] Similarly directed were mandates for citing the clergy and representatives of the laity to undergo visitation, although rural deans were entrusted with subsequent citations for correction.[10] To these may be added a steady stream of *ad hoc* mandates, prominent among them being those for the collection of arrears of tenths.[11] It was by such

---

1 556.   2 e.g. 175, 219, 319, 524, 623, 811.
3 It is likely that there was some system of compulsory attendance.   4 819.
5 e.g. 451 (an original return).   6 e.g. 746.   7 e.g. 61.
8 Shortly after Severleye became archdeacon in 1349, mandates for induction to benefices were addressed, not to his 'official', but to his 'commissary'. This could have been because Severleye was a resident archdeacon. See 1431, 1432, *et seq.*, and below, pp. xvii, xx.
9 For exceptions, see p. xv, n. 5, and 241, 465, 1567.
10 See 89. Practice in the diocese varied. Other registers show that warnings of visitation were also sent to individual rural deans in some cases.
11 e.g. 1118, 1122, 1125.

means that the bishop ensured the dissemination of essential information. For instance, the archdeacon of Gloucester was to publish in local chapters and elsewhere the diocesan's revocation of commissions issued to penitentiaries within the archdeaconry.[1] One royal writ of special importance was implemented by summoning the whole body of the clergy to Winchcombe, adjudged to be the centre of the diocese.[2] Another, which required the publication of the Council's ordinances for the regulation of wages at the time of the Black Death, was effected through the usual machinery of the archdeaconries.[3]

Generally speaking the person of the archdeacon was of little consequence from the point of view of diocesan administration, for he was usually an absentee. Robert of Worcester, *Iuris Civilis Professor*, became archdeacon of Worcester in 1337, when he exchanged Meonstoke rectory in Winchester diocese with Bishop Orleton's brother, John.[4] He took virtually no part in the affairs of the see, although he remained archdeacon until the last year of Wolstan's episcopate, when he probably succumbed to the Black Death.[5] His successor, Master John de Severleye, received the collation of the archdeaconry 22 May 1349.[6] He is exceptional in that he was the bishop's chancellor and active in his administration.[7]

Master Roger de Breynton, who had been of consequence in Bishop Orleton's administration, held the Gloucester archdeaconry at the time of Wolstan's election to the see.[8] In 1339 he contemplated exchanging it for the rectory of Old Radnor, in Hereford diocese, where he found employment in the service of Bishops Charlton and Trilleck.[9] In the event he retained possession until 1348 when he successfully negotiated an exchange for Doddington in Ely diocese. Master Richard of Ledbury was instituted in his stead 7 April 1348, but is not mentioned again in the register.[10]

It is not possible to identify any of the archdeacons' officials from the register, but it could be that Master Richard Mahel or Maiel, mentioned as official of the Worcester archdeacon in 1329, 1334 and 1336,[11] continued to exercise the office. He was one of those whom the bishop appointed to receive the canonical obedience of the diocese.[12]

Rural deaneries

It is hard to determine the precise working of rural deaneries, and the register adds little to what is already known from other sources.

1 54.   2 18.   3 1334.
4 Reg. Montacute 1, fo. 27v. For an outline of Robert's career, see Emden, *Biog. Oxon.*, *sub. nom.*
5 He died between 14 and 22 May 1349. Cp. 1410, 1413.   6 1413.
7 See below, pp. xx–xxi.
8 He had held it since June 1331. See Reg. Orleton 1, fo. 31r.; 2, fo. 42r.
9 19 and *Hereford Regs. Charlton*, p. 25; *Trilleck*, pp. 1–2 and *passim*.   10 901–4.
11 Reg. Orleton 2, ff. 11r., 54r.; Reg. Montacute 2, ff. 5r., 36r.; Westm. Abb. Mun. 21262.   12 6.

But it does demonstrate their continued importance in local administration.

As a rule episcopal mandates were directed to rural deans on a territorial basis. Thus the dean of Cirencester was ordered to place the church and chapels of South Cerney under an interdict, the dean of Pershore to cite those in his deanery who had been found culpable at the bishop's visitation, and the dean of Kidderminster to admonish the rector of Clent to reside in his benefice.[1] This was not always the case, however, for not only might the bishop call upon someone other than the rural dean to act within the ruridecanal limits,[2] but also he could make use of the dean in the same manner as any other special commissary.

The office of penitentiary was sometimes conferred on rural deans, though there is only one instance in the present register.[3] The duty of claiming criminous clerks from the secular authorities was regularly imposed on those deans who had lay prisons in their locality. Thus the rural deans of Gloucester, Stow and Worcester received commissions for that purpose.[4] The business of citation was a prominent feature of a dean's activities, and in this work he was assisted by an apparitor appointed, it would seem, by the bishop.[5] The nature of his control over sequestrations is not clear, especially in view of the development of the sequestrator's office, but he was certainly concerned with them.[6]

The Bishop's Officers and 'Familia'

Archdeaconries, rural deaneries, and areas of jurisdiction exempt from the archdeacon, may be regarded as the 'local administration' of the diocese, acting partly on its own initiative, partly in response to episcopal mandates. At the centre, as it were, there had developed a number of specialised offices with important powers, the holders of which exercised authority in all parts of the diocese subject to the bishop.

The diocesan official

Foremost in this 'central administration' was the 'official', or, as he is termed in one instance, the 'official principal'.[7] John de la Lowe, *Iuris Civilis Professor*, held the position for all but a few months of

---

1 94, 103, 135.   2 e.g. 30.   3 53.
4 81, 150, 151; 48, 63. The dean of Gloucester was empowered to act throughout the archdeaconry. The dean of Worcester's commission has no specific limitation. Clearly, however, such commissions mainly concerned the lay prisons at Gloucester and Worcester, and in the case of Stow, that of the abbot of Fécamp's liberty at Slaughter.
5 Episcopal appointments to the office are recorded for Pershore, Dursley and Powick deaneries: 51, 86, 87.
6 e.g. 88, 203. See below, pp. xxi–xxii.   7 1484.

Wolstan's administration. His terms of appointment, as was usual at this time, are couched in general terms. He was to exercise those powers *que ad officialitatis officium in nostra Wygorn' diocesi pertinent*, with the additional *specialis potestas* of enquiring into, correcting, and punishing the faults of the bishop's subjects.[1] Later his judicial competence was extended by other commissions. In November 1339 he was appointed to hear and determine cases involving criminous clerks surrendered by secular judges, with authority to make enquiries about the offences and the character of the clerks concerned, and to arrange for purgation.[2] By another commission of the same date he was directed, in conjunction with the sequestrator, Henry de Neubold, to take cognisance of the *comperta* arising from the bishop's recent visitation of the Worcester archdeaconry. For this purpose he received powers of enquiry, correction and punishment. As these had already been granted to him as official, there was a clause declaring that it was not the bishop's intention thereby to revoke the earlier commission.[3] He was also included in later commissions of this kind.[4]

We learn little of the official's activity by virtue of such judicial commissions, and they represent only a part of his activities. Essentially he was the bishop's right hand man, active in every sphere of administration. The register obviously does not tell the full story, but he features prominently all the same. He was present at the appointment of deputies for the collection of debts due to the see (16 October 1339),[5] and witnessed the letters patent empowering John de Walton and Philip le Yonge to act as episcopal proctors at the Curia (12 December 1339).[6] He acted as the bishop's special commissary for the election of a prioress of Pinley in 1342, and attended the election proceedings of the abbot of Tewkesbury five years later.[7] In 1344 he was sent to secure the cathedral chapter's assent to the appropriation of Clent with Rowley to Halesowen abbey.[8] He appended the seal of his office to the submission made by Adam of Harvington's executors, and was present in Hartlebury chapel when Henry de Lench swore on behalf of the abbot of Pershore and each of his fellow monks, one by one, to observe the details of Adam's chantry.[9] In the same year, 1346, he is recorded to have been present at the resignation of the rector of St. Swithin's, Worcester.[10] In short, he was involved in the manifold activities of the see's administration, remaining active until his death, probably from the plague, shortly before 1 July 1349.[11]

The chancellor and commissary

The chancellor, nominally the custodian of the episcopal seals, was seemingly appointed by their formal transfer to him.[12] One of his

1 23: 19 September 1339. 2 101: 26 November 1339.
3 104: 26 November 1339. 4 536 (undated), 567 (22 January 1343).
5 96. 6 243. 7 485, 943. 8 526. 9 906. 10 755.
11 1484. Cf. Emden, *Biog. Oxon.*, *sub nom.*
12 For this, see *Reg. Gainsburgh*, fo. 22v., p. 75.

perquisites was the fee charged when documents were sealed.[1] In practice few diocesan chancellors were resident at this time, and so they took little or no active part in administration.

John de Severleye, Wolstan's chancellor, was initially no exception to the general rule. His appointment is not entered in the register and there is no mention of his holding the office until 1342. In the early part of the episcopate he was continuing his studies, receiving licences of absence in 1339, 1340 and 1341 (for two years).[2] He was empowered by a commission of 10 December 1342[3] to hear and determine suits belonging to the bishop's audience and to impose correction and punishment on those found guilty at the recent visitation.[4] He was associated with other legal officers in another commission for correction issued in January 1343.[5]

The court of audience, which went with the diocesan as he travelled from place to place, was the chancellor's usual sphere of action. But the only proceedings of that court in the register took place at Hartlebury a short time before Wolstan's death, when John de Severleye presided, not *ex officio*, but by virtue of a general commission *in omnibus causis et negociis*. This is dated 4 October 1342, slightly earlier than the one mentioned above, and gave Severleye powers of enquiry, correction and punishment, with the right to take cognisance of matrimonial cases.[6] The suits in this very interesting and unusual court record were mainly such as lay within the competence of the archdeacon. It is true that bishop and archdeacon had concurrent jurisdiction in lesser causes, but it could be significant that Severleye was at the time archdeacon of Worcester as well as chancellor. He might for convenience have drawn archidiaconal suits into the audience court.

Severleye was appointed proctor for the parliaments of 1343 and 1344, and for the councils of 1344 and 1346.[7] In 1345 he is to be found witnessing an oath at Bredon,[8] and in the following year the election decree of the master of Billeswick hospital.[9] But if the register be the criterion, his activities were few until 1348.

The wide span of Severleye's employment suggests the career administrator. Under Wolstan's successor, John Thoresby, he is mentioned as official, and as joint vicar-general with the prior of Llanthony.[10] In 1352 he exchanged his Worcester archdeaconry for Buxted rectory in Chichester diocese.[11] The year following he was among those present at Reginald Bryan's profession of obedience to

---

1 Instances are hard to come by, but there is a list of fees for one of the Longdon processes in Westm. Abb. Mun. 21262. The chancellor at that time (Robert de Worth) received £2, his clerk 3s. 4d., and his squire 2s.

2 223, 334, 429. The first allowed him to remain *in scolis litterarum:* no specific reasons are given in the others.   3 566.   4 See below, p. xxxi.

5 567. See below, pp. xxii–xxiii, xxxi.   6 1330, 1365.   7 1192, 1217, 1208, 1258

8 726.   9 728.   10 Reg. Thoresby, ff. 2r., 9r., 12r., 26r. *et seq.*

11 *R.S.V.*, pp. 200–201.

the see of Canterbury.[1] He is described as canon of Chichester in 1336, when he was one of those deputed by Archbishop Islep to take cognisance of cases pending in the peculiar of South Malling, the dean of which had died.[2] Between 1353 and 1355 he was acting as Auditor and Commissary of the archbishop's court.[3]

The sequestrator, receiver, and commissary-general

One of the most important developments in the central adminstration was the emergence, during the thirteenth century, of the office of sequestrator. Its origin is bound up with the bishop's claim to the fruits of vacant benefices, but the fourteenth century sequestrator regularly exercised testamentary powers, and those of correction and punishment.

There are two commissions for the appointment of Master Henry de Neubold as sequestrator, the first issued before the bishop's consecration. Both are in the same form, simply granting powers of probate and the oversight of executors' administration, together with such other powers as were known to belong to the office.[4]

The sequestrator acted throughout the diocese, except where areas of exempt jurisdiction precluded his doing so. As we have seen, the deans of 'petty archdeaconries' probably had some rights over wills, this certainly being the case at Blockley,[5] but the extent of their rights is not clear. At Barnsley, which lay within the jurisdiction of Bibury, the dean's action in granting probate of the rector's will was described by the diocesan official, for reasons unknown, as *nullius penitus esse firmitatis, tanquam facta per eum ad quem eadem facere non pertinuit.*[6]

Other exceptions to the sequestrator's authority arose from the archbishop's prerogative jurisdiction. By virtue of this, the archbishop himself, and *sede vacante* the prior, claimed probate of the wills of all noble persons throughout the province, as well as of those who held goods in more than one diocese.[7] When, in 1349, the prior of Canterbury, acting during the vacancy following Stratford's death, committed his powers to the bishop for the probate of Hugh le Despenser's will, Wolstan replied that he could do nothing as the executors had not produced the will, nor had they even attempted to do so.[8]

But although testamentary matters were a prominent aspect of Henry de Neubold's work, he also acted as the bishop's commissary-general,[9] with powers to correct and punish faults brought to light at

1 Churchill, *Cant. Admin.*, 2, p. 132. Bryan was bp. of Worcester 1352-61.
2 Churchill, *Cant. Admin.*, 1, p. 77.
3 *Ibid.* 1, p. 491. Cf. *ibid.* 1, pp. 140, 491n.; 2, p. 243. See also Emden, *Biog. Oxon., sub nom.*   4 8 (16 February 1339), 26 (30 March 1339).
5 129. See above, p. xv.   6 425.   7 1338.   8 *Ibid.*
9 Or legal officer. The term varies in meaning, so that it is impossible to determine the precise nature of the legal powers enjoyed by Neubold.

visitation,[1] and as collector of all the pensions and procurations due
to the diocesan.[2]

His duties were further extended by *ad hoc* commissions. Following
the bishop's visitation in 1339 of the priory of the Holy Sepulchre at
Warwick, he was deputed to enquire into its condition and to report
his findings.[3] Much later, in 1345, he examined the proposed appropriation of Aston Cantlow church to Maxstoke priory, and subsequently secured the Worcester chapter's assent to the union.[4] He was
also associated with the dean of the Christianity of Warwick[5] in the
custody of the fruits of that church,[6] though normally one would
have expected him to act *ex officio* in such matters. In April of 1346 he
and his clerk Ralph witnessed the oath of indemnity sworn by the
newly instituted rector of the church of St. Philip and St. Jacob,
Bristol.[7] Three years later he was deputed to ascertain whether the
portion assigned to Pillerton vicarage reached the estimated amount.[8]
Thus, although seldom recorded as a witness of administrative acts,
he was in various ways constantly engaged in episcopal business.

Henry de Neubold was in fact concerned with the see's administration for much longer than a single episcopate. Under Bishop
Montacute he had been auditor of causes,[9] also sequestrator and
commissary-general.[10] After Wolstan's death he continued in
Thoresby's service and followed John de Severleye as official and
vicar-general.[11]

The adjutor and special commissary

By a commission of 1 July 1339 Master Hugh de Penebrugg was
appointed adjutor or special commissary, a title which appears to be
unique in the fourteenth century diocese.[12] Master Hugh was authorised to act in causes, whether brought *ex officio* or at the instance of
parties, which were heard *coram episcopo*, that is, in the bishop's
audience court. It would seem then that Hugh was the assessor of the
commissary-general, although no-one is mentioned as holding such
office at the time of his appointment. In the body of the commission
is the express declaration that it was not intended that there should
be any encroachment upon the jurisdiction of the official or commissary-general.

Hugh's judicial functions were extended by a commission of
January 1343 in which he was associated with the official, chancellor

---

1 As corrector he was associated with other legal officers in commissions of 1339 (104),
?1342–3 (536) and 1343 (567).
2 913.   3 118.   4 746–748.
5 This term was used of the rural deans of Worcester, Warwick, Gloucester and Bristol.
6 749.   7 795.   8 1335.
9 Reg. Montacute 2, ff. 42r., 48r.
10 Reg. Montacute 2, ff. 15r., 17r. He was later commissary-general of Bp. Bryan (1352–
61). See Emden, *Biog. Oxon.*, *sub nom.*
11 Reg. Thoresby, ff. 42v., 44r.   12 65.

(or commissary-general) and sequestrator, in the punishment of
faults arising from visitation.[1]

The special commissary was frequently in attendance on the
bishop, was active in a variety of business, particularly judicial, and
his name occurs often in the register.[2]

A temporary 'commissary-general'

On 16 February 1339 Wolstan, then bishop-elect, empowered
Master William de Bergeveny to hear and determine causes in the
consistory courts of the city and diocese, and to exercise all episcopal
jurisdiction.[3] This has the appearance of a temporary arrangement
to ensure continuity of consistorial activity, pending the appointment
of an official, and also of administration generally. By another
commission of the same date Master William was deputed, together
with three others, to receive the canonical obedience of the clergy of
the diocese.[4]

Although William had been associated with the cathedral priory,[5]
and was to be ordained by Wolstan,[6] his recorded activities in the
diocese are few. But this is hardly surprising, for in 1341 he was regent
doctor in Theology at Oxford, and was elected chancellor of the
university in that year and again in 1343.[7]

Occasional legal advisers and lesser officers

The official, the sequestrator, the adjutor, and the chancellor,
constituted the core of the bishop's central administration. That they
were all legal officers serves to emphasise the diocesan's preoccupation with judicial matters, though it should be remembered that it is
seldom easy to disentangle administrative from judicial process.

Whereas these officers provided the legal knowledge essential for
the everyday conduct of affairs, there were others to whom the bishop
might turn, either because they were men of particular distinction, or
merely out of personal friendship.

Master Thomas de Astley, for whose brother the bishop made
provision,[8] may fall into the category of advisers who were also
friends. So too may Master Thomas de Lench, the dean of St.
Mary's, Warwick, whose procuration Wolstan remitted *de gracia
speciali* and out of personal regard.[9] To John de Lech, *Iuris Canonici
Professor*, he granted an annual pension of £6 13s. 4d., for past

1 567. See below, p. xxxi.
2 e.g. 3, 96, 243, 244, 794, 1013, 1054. These activities are not recorded by Emden, *Biog.
Oxon.*, s.v. Penebrigge *alias* Barewe.   3 7.   4 6.
5 He carried news of Hemenhale's death to the king. *R.S.V.*, p. 259.
6 1004 (subdeacon), 1008 (deacon).
7 *Snappe's Formulary*, (*Oxf. Hist. Soc.* lxxx) pp. 80, 81, 325. His distinguished career is
summarised by Emden, *Biog. Oxon.*, s.v. Bergeveney.
8 84. The *inspeximus* and confirmation of this grant is in C.P.R. 1350–54, p. 396. For
Astley's part in the 1339 election proceedings, see above, p. xiii.   9 115.

counsel and that to be given in the future.[1] None of these men is known to have taken part in the administration, but it is likely that the bishop sought their advice on specific occasions.

Of less exalted status, but in much closer contact with the diocesan, were a number of clerks, some of whom occupied lesser offices. The scribe or registrar, whose position has been touched on above,[2] must have been in regular attendance. Important in a more domestic sphere was John de Chalveston, who acted as clerk of the bishop's household.[3] The steward of the household, William de Salwarp, was apparently a man of some local standing.[4] He was a proctor in the 1343 parliament and witnessed grants from the episcopal manors of Henbury and Alvechurch.[5] The receiver, Master John Botoner, was a frequent witness of administrative processes.[6] In September 1342 he rendered account of his financial activities, and was given full acquittance after audit.[7] The following January he received another discharge, this time for £100 which had been sent to him by an episcopal servant, John de Wych.[8] His financial province was altogether wider than that of the sequestrator, for it extended to all the sums due to the bishop from both spiritualities and temporalities, while the latter seems, in this instance at least, to have been responsible only for regular pensions and (visitatorial?) procurations.[9]

A person frequently in attendance on the bishop was Nicholas de Stanlak, who became a monk of the cathedral priory when Wolstan was prior. The register records his being present or officially acting as a witness on five occasions.[10] In 1340 he was associated with John de Preston as proctor for the choice of a Worcester prior.[11] The following year he occurs as the bishop's penitentiary, possibly in a personal sense,[12] in which case he may have been Wolstan's chaplain, although John de Rippon is the only person so entitled in the register.[13]

Other clerks, such as Henry de Winchcombe,[14] William de Preston,[15] and John de Dumbleton,[16] witnessed isolated acts, but their names are too infrequent to suggest any close association with the bishop's *familia*.

1 113. He had had extensive administrative experience in Winchester, Bath & Wells, and Hereford dioceses before becoming Official of the Court of Canterbury in 1348. See Emden, *Biog. Oxon.*, s.v. Lecche *alias* Loveryng de Northlech.
2 See pp. v–vi.
3 542. It is just possible that he was also concerned with writing part of the register. See pp. v–vi.
4 If the identification be correct, it was he who secured mortmain licences for the foundation of chantries at Salwarpe (in 1347) and Hindlip (in 1356). These schemes seem to have been abortive, but some salt workings were given to Westwood priory. See *V.C.H. Worcs.* 2, pp. 150, 258; 3, pp. 209–10, 401; 4, pp. 136, 182.
5 1192; 111, 120, 121.   6 e.g. 243, 244, 245, 677, 726, 764.   7 541.   8 555.
9 And in addition such sums as were derived from his other duties. See above, pp. xxi–xxii.   10 3, 244, 432, 521, 755.   11 290.   12 3.
13 1562.   14 503, 594.   15 245, 594. Rector of Hethe, Lincoln diocese.
16 521. Rector of Sedgeberrow.

Parliamentary and Curial proctors

Parliamentary proctors were commonly drawn from the bishop's administrative staff: exceptionally they had no other connection with the diocese. Robert de Chikewell, who represented the bishop at the parliament of January 1340,[1] falls into the latter category. He was reappointed for the second (March) session,[2] and again for the third (July),[3] this time jointly with Thomas de Evesham.[4]

There is no record of a summons for the important parliament which first met in April 1341. John de Severleye and William de Salwarp were deputed proctors for the 1343 parliament, and John de Stoke, rector of Saintbury, John de Thoresby (the future bishop), and Severleye again, for that of 1344.[5] The last three were also appointed for the council of 1344, and John de Severleye and John de Stoke for that of 1346.[6]

In December of the first year of his episcopate Wolstan deputed Master John de Walton and Master Philip le Yonge to act for him in the Curia.[7] Philip took advantage of his position to claim the vicarage of Bromsgrove, in the patronage of Worcester priory. Thereupon the bishop associated Richard de Thormerton, a canon of Westbury, with the other proctor, to prosecute a suit against him.[8] At a later date a similar incident was to involve the bishop in more serious consequences.[9]

The remuneration of episcopal officers

There is a particularly close relationship between the holders of benefices in the bishop's collation and his administrative staff. The existence of patronage of this kind may indeed be said to have made administration possible, for without this resource a bishop would have found it hard to maintain his staff. Wolstan is only known to have granted one pension to a secular clerk,[10] though doubtless his *familiares* had liveries of which we learn nothing from the register.

The correlation between episcopal benefice and episcopal clerk is so striking that it is worth examining in detail.[11] The official, John de la Lowe, received the collation of Bredon in 1341, retaining the benefice until his death in 1349.[12] The chancellor, John de Severleye, held Billesley, not in episcopal collation, at the time of Wolstan's promotion, but resigned it in 1349 on becoming archdeacon of Worcester.[13] The sequestrator, Henry de Neubold, received the collation of Weston-on-Avon in 1341, following the resignation of

1 106.   2 283.   3 137.
4 Who farmed the bishop's church of Hillingdon (Middx.). See 139.
5 1192, 1217.   6 1208, 1258.   7 243.   8 244.
9 See below, pp. xlix–l.   10 See above, pp. xxiii–xxlv.
11 Unless otherwise stated all the benefices mentioned were in the bishop's regular collation or had come to him by devolution.
12 435.   13 1413.

Hugh de Penebrugg, the adjutor, who had himself been instituted the previous year.[1] Neubold remained rector until after the bishop's death. Penebrugg's resignation of Weston was made so that he could assume Hartlebury, John le Botoner, the bishop's receiver, being the commissary for his induction.[2] Botoner himself received Halford rectory, to which he was inducted in the person of his proctor, Thomas Bolevinch, early in 1340.[3] Not long afterwards he exchanged it with Robert Marny, who was possibly the registrar,[4] for the rectory of Naunton-on-Cotswold.[5] He resigned Naunton in 1349 and moved to Ely diocese as vicar of Wisbech.[6] But Robert Marny seems to have lost Halford for a time, John Bate of Cleeve being instituted in 1341.[7] However, he recovered the benefice in the following year, though in August 1344 he exchanged it for Eastleach, in the patronage of Great Malvern priory.[8] He probably died in March 1349, for his successor was instituted on the 20th of that month.[9]

Naunton church, left vacant by Botoner's removal to Wisbech, was collated to the bishop's *scriba*, William Aleyn.[10] Two days later, 6 August 1349, Aleyn secured the more valuable rectory of Withington and vacated Naunton.[11] The mandate for his induction to Naunton had been directed to John de Rippon, the bishop's chaplain, who himself received the collation of Halford, Neubold being one of the inductors.[12] Thomas Bolevinch, possibly one of the scribes of the register,[13] received St. Peter's, Warwick, of which the presentation had lapsed to the bishop.[14]

The comprehensiveness of the system, which provided for so many episcopal clerks, can be clearly seen, while the inter-relation of proctors, inductors, and persons instituted serves to emphasise the close-knit character of the bishop's *familia*. That the administration's gain was the parishes' loss would not be gainsaid, but at least it was a system which Wolstan used with moderation, allowing no pluralism[15] or nepotism. This was in marked contrast to what had happened under one of his predecessors, Orleton, during whose regime both abuses had been rife.

Temporal officers

By nature the register provides comparatively little information about the bishop's temporalities, although the appointments of officers are often recorded. The manors were distributed among all three counties of the diocese, and there were also lands at Hillingdon in Middlesex and a London house in the Strand.

1 390, 357.   2 389.   3 241.   4 See above, p. v.
5 381-2.   6 1562.   7 446.   8 646.
9 1379.   10 1562.   11 1566.   12 1563.
13 See above, p. v.   14 744-5.
15 With the sole exception of Robert de Chikewell, one of his parliamentary proctors (see above, p. xxv). A notable pluralist, he yet received Hampton, an episcopal rectory in 1341 (410).

As steward of his temporalities in the counties of Worcester and Warwick the bishop appointed Peter de Groete, whom he had once described as his particular friend.[1] It was no doubt this Peter de Groete who witnessed the charters in favour of John de Peyto junior, John de Stoke, and Thomas de Henley.[2] The Groetes, father and son, both named Peter, acquired Pirton Foliot manor in 1340, and later, other Worcestershire lands.[3]

Appointed steward of the Gloucestershire temporalities was William de Cheltenham, who was annually to have clothes and sustenance for himself and his horses *prout decet*, together with £6 13s. 4d. from the reeve of Salt Marsh [Henbury].[4] William had a house at Pucklechurch and was licensed to have an oratory there in 1342.[5] He was a prominent man in the county. Together with Thomas de Berkeley he was directed to enquire into the assaults on collectors of a tenth and fifteenth, to arrest such as were guilty, and to lodge them in gaol.[6] In 1344 he served on a commission of *oyer* and *terminer* set up to investigate riots at Hereford,[7] and on other commissions was associated with Lord Berkeley and Thomas de Berkeley of Coberley.

The hundred of Oswaldslow was in the main a fairly compact area round Worcester, in which the bishop enjoyed the privileges of a franchise, in particular the return of writs.[8] In 1343 Thomas le Somery was appointed bailiff under the same conditions as his predecessors.[9] As he had been given the office for life by Hemenhale,[10] he must have been dispossessed, unless the new commission was merely a confirmation. Further difficulty arose in 1349 when two appointments were made, the first on 27 June of Richard de Bromwich, the second, three days later, of Thomas atte Mulle.[11]

The manors of Stratford and Hampton, including the episcopal property in Stratford town, had a separate bailiff, Adam de Styventon, who was appointed 5 April 1339. He was to hold the lesser courts and the hundreds of Pathlow and *Gilpuc*.[12] But the following August John de Peyto was granted Stratford manor at an annual rent of £60 and also the profits of the bishop's hundred and liberties (excepting Hampton) in the county of Warwick.[13]

1 33; *R.S.V.*, p. 257.   2 80, 111, 120, 121.
3 *V.C.H. Worcs.* 3, pp. 269, 384n.; 4, p. 335. A Peter de Groete was acting as sheriff of Worcester in 1347 (*C.P.R.* 1345–48, p. 383), and the name occurs frequently in lists of members for Worcester city and of knights of the shire. See Nash, *Worcs.*, 1, pp. xxvi. xxix.
4 67.   5 467.   6 *C.P.R.* 1343–45, pp. 514–5.   7 *Ibid.*, pp. 419–20.
8 The register contains one writ addressed to the sheriff (1124) for the levying of distraints notwithstanding the franchise, presumably because of the bailiff's default.
9 565; *C.C.R.* 1343–46, p. 202.
10 *C.P.R.* 1338–40, p. 90: 14 June 1338. An *inspeximus* and confirmation of the prior and chapter's letters dated 21 March.
11 1331, 1332.   12 31.
13 80. A pardon by fine of five marks for not having licence for this grant is in *C.P.R.* 1338–40, p. 329.

William de Netherton was appointed (1340) custodian of the bishop's house or houses in the parish of St. Mary-le-Strand, as well as receiver of all rents there and elsewhere in London.[1] Wolstan may not have stayed in the house, apart from a short period while bishop-elect, and it was no doubt leased. We know that Sir Robert Parving, chief justice of the King's Bench and sometime treasurer, died there in 1343,[2] and that John Thoresby, the future bishop of Worcester, made use of the house when keeper of the Chancery rolls,[3] and later as keeper of the Privy Seal.[4]

Another layman closely associated with the bishop, though he appears not to have held office, was Hugh de Cookseye. In an un-dated document, probably of 1339, he was granted £2 annual rent and a robe from the proceeds of Hanbury manor in consideration of past and future service, counsel, and aid.[5] Hugh was a member of the well known family which held the manor of Great Cooksey in Upton Warren, as well as other property in Worcestershire.[6]

Aspects of Administration

Visitation

In the matter of visitation Wolstan has claim to be the most diligent of the fourteenth century bishops of Worcester. Not only did he carry out a primary visitation far more thorough than any other of which record survives, but also second and third visitations, though evidence of the last is fragmentary. It is unusual at any time to find the triennial rule observed, and Wolstan's personal preoccupation with each visitation makes this instance the more remarkable. Only for part of one, the third, is he known to have made use of com-missaries.

The regular practice, which the register confirms, was for the bishop first to visit his cathedral chapter, as bound by canon law,[7] and then the Worcester archdeaconry. The other archdeaconry was left until later, being on the whole much more cursorily dealt with.

Some features of this primary visitation deserve to be stressed. Although he spent reasonable time in the Worcester archdeaconry, Wolstan seems of set purpose to have given particular attention to that of Gloucester. Moreover, instead of following the customary arrangement of visiting a deanery in one or two churches, he often

1 140.   2 *C.C.R.* 1343–46, pp. 97, 225.   3 *Ibid.*, p. 473, and cf. p. 480.
4 668.   5 74.
6 Hugh succeeded his brother Walter before 1333 and died in 1356; his wife, Edward le Botiler's daughter Denise, died 1376–7. See *V.C.H. Worcs.* 3, p. 232. Hugh witnessed the grant to John de Peyto (80) and the oath sworn by Sir William Corbet (2).
7 *Sext* 3, 20, c. 1.

did so in three, four, or even five. How he allotted his time is not known, but it would be just to assume that a visitation in several churches provided greater opportunities for detailed examination.

The register contains four entries concerned with preliminary arrangements for the visitation of the northern archdeaconry: the formal intimation to the Worcester monks of his intention to visit them on 14 October,[1] a corresponding warning to the convent of Little Malvern,[2] a mandate to the official of the archdeacon suspending his jurisdiction for the time being and directing him to cite the clergy and representatives of the laity at the dates and places named,[3] and a full itinerary.[4]

The bishop visited the archdeaconry in two stages. The first, occupying seventeen days, lasted from 14th until 30th October. In that period he covered some 120 miles, visiting four deaneries, two hospitals, and four other religious houses, including the cathedral priory. After a brief interval the visitation was completed in the sixteen days between 3rd and 19th November. Wolstan covered roughly the same mileage as in the earlier stage, visiting the other four deaneries, the episcopal churches of Stratford and Hampton, and nine religious houses.

For the Gloucester archdeaconry there is only one entry in the register, the itinerary. This shows the bishop's plan to have been both extensive and very detailed. The itinerary falls into three stages. The first of these, from 7 February to 13 March 1340, involved the deaneries of Campden, Stow, Fairford, Cirencester, Stonehouse and Winchcombe. This was the most strenuous part of the business. For five weeks the bishop was almost continuously on the move. In thirty-six days he slept at no fewer than twenty-nine places and covered about 150 miles, many of them among hilly Cotswold country, and at the most unfavourable season.

There followed an interval during which the bishop returned to Hartlebury, whence he moved to Alvechurch for the Easter festival. By 14 May he was at Bredon, preparatory to launching the second stage of the visitation. Meanwhile he visited the nearby churches of Tewkesbury and Deerhurst. The real work began on 22 May and continued until 2 June, during which time Wolstan was occupied with the deaneries of Gloucester, Dursley, Hawkesbury and Bitton.

Before dealing with the Bristol deanery the bishop spent just over a fortnight at his conveniently placed manor of Henbury, presumably recuperating from the rigours of travelling. After spending the 19th and part of 20th June at St. Augustine's abbey he returned to Henbury, whence he journeyed daily to Bristol for the visitation of the town's numerous churches and religious houses.

Two days of apparent inactivity followed—24 and 25 June. On the

1 85.   3 89.
2 90.   4 102.

26th the bishop turned northwards again and the itinerary ends with his dedication of Eastington church on the 29th.

The total mileage covered during this primary visitation, in both archdeaconries, could not have been less than 500, and may have been substantially more.[1]

Long before the process was complete the machinery of correction had been set in motion. The bishop could barely have settled in at Hartlebury after his circuit of the Worcester archdeaconry when he issued a commission (26 November 1339) to the official and sequestrator for this purpose.[2] It was followed up by a mandate to the dean of Pershore for the citation of offenders to receive correction and answer questions.[3] It could be that this was entered as an exemplar, and that corresponding mandates were sent to the other rural deans.

Action must have been taken in various matters as a direct consequence of visitation, though the fact is not always stated. The rectoral fruits of Chedworth, appropriated to the Norman abbey of Lyre, were sequestrated by reason of *comperta* and *detecta*,[4] and it was information laid before the bishop as visitor which gave rise to a licence for the prioress of St. Bartholomew's hospital to lease a dormitory which was no longer needed.[5] We may suspect that arrangements for the appointment of coadjutors at Frampton Cotterell[6] and Turkdean,[7] and the citation of the absentee rectors of Campden and Kidderminster,[8] also stemmed from visitatorial *detecta*.

Only one set of injunctions to a religious house has been entered in the register, that concerning St. Augustine's, Bristol.[9] There is nothing novel about these injunctions, and the reassuring phrases with which they close are common form, though doubtless the bishop, himself a monk, was fully in sympathy with their compassionate tone. More serious were the defects at the priory of the Holy Sepulchre, Warwick. The sequestrator was instructed to make thorough enquiry into the economic state of the house and its administration, and given power to suspend officers guilty of squandering the priory's resources.[10]

The second visitation was clearly on a much smaller scale, but in any case it is incompletely reported in the register. Warnings of the bishop's intention to hold visitation were sent to the cathedral priory and the official of the Worcester archdeacon on the same day, 3 October 1342.[11] The chapter was to receive the diocesan on the first juridical day after All Saints—Monday 4 November, and the

1 Not including the journey to and from Hartlebury following the temporary interruption of visitation on 13 March.

2 104.   3 103.
4 138.   5 326.
6 132 and cf. 45.   7 131, 133.
8 123, 135.   9 116.
10 118.   11 530, 531.

archdeaconry immediately thereafter. The itinerary contained in the official's mandate only covers the period from 5 to 11 November, and the deaneries of Worcester, Powick, Droitwich and Kidderminster.[1] But a mandate for the citation of offenders in the Pershore deanery[2] and a commission to John de la Lowe and Henry de Neubold to impose correction there,[3] both undated, suggest that other parts of the archdeaconry were visited.

On the other hand a different arrangement could have been adopted, for the bishop announced his intention of visiting the religious houses of Alcester and Wroxall on 22 and 25 January 1343, and at the primary visitation both had been included in the Warwick deanery. Support is lent to the idea of a later visitation of this deanery by the bishop's presence at Arrow on 21 January, and at Hampton on 1 February.[4] This would mean a partial reversal of the normal order of visitation, since a fragmentary itinerary for the Gloucester archdeaconry shows that the bishop planned to visit Campden deanery from 28 to 30 November, at which point the scribe turned to a new folio and apparently omitted the remainder of the progress.[5] There is no satisfactory evidence of the resumption of visitation in this archdeaconry during the following year.

There are two commissions for the correction of the *comperta*, in addition to the one mentioned above for Pershore deanery. The first, dated 10 December 1342, is really a general commission for John de Severleye to hear extraconsistorial cases, but with the addition of a clause empowering him to deal with matters arising from the visitation.[6] The second commission, issued 22 January 1343, is a joint one for the four principal legal officers—the official, chancellor, sequestrator and adjutor.[7]

Even less information has been given for the third visitation. There are no mandates for the Worcester prior or for either archdeacon, but there is a fragment of the *progressus*, though this was crossed out after only four days had been entered.[8]

The visitation began as usual in the chapter house at Worcester. The following day, 8 November 1345, the bishop dined at the priory and went on to Hartlebury for the night. His commissaries, together with a notary, stayed in the priory and on the next morning visited the churches of the city and neighbourhood in the mother church of St. Helen. The entry seems contradictory at this point, but it may be that some of the outlying churches were visited on the same day by the bishop himself. On the last day of the itinerary, 10 November, the bishop visited various churches of West Worcestershire in Astley

1 The prior of Dudley probably produced his titles at this time. See 537.
2 535.   3 536.
4 533, 534; 496, 494.   5 532.
6 566.   7 567.
8 751.

church, returning to Hartlebury for the night. Apart from these details, the only entries which refer to the 1345 visitation are an acquittance for procuration paid by Halesowen abbey on behalf of Clent church, and Abbot Hereward's chantry ordination, which in 1346 mentions the recent visitation of Cirencester abbey.[1]

A fourth visitation should theoretically have begun in 1348, but there is no evidence of it in the register. An air of finality is given by the fact that Henry de Neubold, the corrector-general and collector of procurations, received his acquittance in November of that year.[2]

Benefices: collation, licences for absence, exchanges

It is a common assumption that in the case of benefices in episcopal patronage the usual arrangement of presentation by the patron, followed by admission and institution by the ordinary, was replaced by simple collation. But the present register shows that this was not invariably so, a distinction being regularly made between the actual 'conferring' of the benefice and institution.[3]

An unexpected feature of Wolstan's administration is revealed by an analysis of dispensations for absence from benefices. These are surprisingly few for the length of the episcopate: altogether 112, involving something over 162 years.[4] With one exception mentioned below, they fall into three classes: those for study, absence, and attendance upon persons of note. Sometimes the right to farm a benefice is conferred at the same time, while separate licences to farm imply additional rectoral absence.

The largest category is that of licences for study, there being forty-five involving over sixty-three years. Twenty-eight of these are for a single year, and only four were conceded for three or more. It would seem that the monk-bishop was deliberately restricting such absences, possibly because he felt less sympathy with the aspirations of secular clerks than had Cobham or Reynolds before him.[5] On the other hand, Wolstan did license seven incumbents to attend heads of religious houses, though only for eight years in all.[6]

The bishop's powers of dispensation did not extend to vicars, but he did allow (*quantum de iure possumus*) Hugh, perpetual vicar of Henbury, to visit the shrine of Our Lady at Walsingham.[7]

Full details of the licences are in Table 4, but it may be useful to give a summary at this point.

1 753, 835,   2 913.
3 e.g. 241. The form used is as follows: *Ecclesiam de . . . nostre diocesis vacantem et ad nostram collacionem pleno iure spectantem tibi conferimus intuitu caritatis, teque rectorem cum suis iuribus et pertinenciis universis canonice instituimus in eadem.* Cf. 744–5.
4 In a comparable period Cobham granted 212, involving 280 years.
5 Cobham granted 155 such licences (217 years) over a decade, Reynolds 78 (146 years) in half that time.
6 Such licences are comparatively rare in other Worcester registers.
7 328.

DISPENSATIONS FOR ABSENCE FROM BENEFICES
1339–1349

Type	Number of licences	Approx. time involved in years
Study[1]	45	+63
Absence	34	+52
Attendance	21	+24
Farm	11[2]	23
Pilgrimage	1	—
Totals:	112	+162

The practice of exchanging benefices becomes common in most English dioceses from about the second decade of the fourteenth century. Once the process had been established there is little evidence of its regulation by the ordinaries. At Worcester there is a substantial increase in exchanges during Cobham's episcopate (1317–27), when just under fifty were effected.[3] The present register contains sixty-three,[4] forty-six of which involved benefices outside the diocese.

Exchanges certainly increased the mobility of incumbents and the possibility of migration to other dioceses. But the unequal value of benefices suggests that some other consideration must at times have entered into transactions of this kind. There is an instance in the register of one party to an exchange taking an oath to indemnify the bishop to the extent of 15s., apparently for legal or administrative expenses incurred with respect to the other party.[5]

EXCHANGES OF BENEFICES

Year	Within diocese	Outside diocese	Total exchanges	Institutions involved[6]	Total recorded institutions
1339	3	4	7	10	27
1340	3	7	10	13	38
1341	2	4	6	8	35
1342	2	2	4	6	26
1343	—	7	7	7	23
1344	3	5	8	11	38
1345	1	1	2	3	22
1346	1	3	4	5	17
1347	1	5	6	7	15
1348	1	8	9	10	36
1349 to 6 Aug.	—	—	—	—	217[7]
	17	46	63	80	494

1 In accordance with the constitution *Cum ex eo, Sext* 1, 6, c. 34.
2 In addition, 8 of the licences for study, 9 of those for 'absence', and 3 of those for attendance, also permitted the farming of the benefices concerned.
3 E. H. Pearce (*Thomas de Cobham*, p. 92) suggests that there were over 50. The present writer can trace 46.
4 Some others, e.g. 19, 73, 122, were not carried out.   5 896.
6 i.e. within the diocese.   7 See the tables on pp. li–lii.

It is difficult to determine the underlying factors which gave rise to so marked a development, though occasionally the reasons given by individual exchangers at the time of the preliminary enquiry in the deanery have been recorded.[1]

The number of exchanges fluctuated from year to year, with peaks in 1340, 1344 and 1348. In one year only, 1345, does the number of institutions by this means fall much below a quarter of the total of recorded institutions; generally it lies between a quarter and a third. The Black Death brought the practice to a temporary halt, for it became easy to move to other benefices as they fell vacant.

Chantries

There are detailed ordinations of thirteen chantries in the register; in fact they form the most prominent of the classes of document entered. One such is the Ripple ordination, dating from Bishop Cobham's time (1320) but not to be found in his register.[2] This had to be inspected by Wolstan owing to an unusual difficulty about presentation which the founder had not foreseen.[3] In addition there is a copy of a twelfth century foundation deed of St. Katherine's chapel, Campden.[4] The endowment was provided by one Gondevill *pro salute anime mee et antecessorum meorum*, and the scribe had no hesitation in describing it as a chantry.[5]

The establishment of a chantry was a complicated, if somewhat stereotyped, process. The founder was above all anxious that his wishes would be honoured in perpetuity. For this purpose a sufficient endowment was essential.[6] The usual method was to grant lands and rents of a certain value, together with a sum of money and sundry essential goods and chattels. All had to be handed on unimpaired to each successive chaplain. If there were more than one chaplain the endowment was regularly assigned to a *custos* or warden, with the obligation to provide for his colleagues. It was important too that there should be definite rules for the presentation of chaplains, with rights devolving upon second, or even third parties, in case of failure to present. Finally the founder drew up detailed ordinances concerning the conduct of the chaplains, the scope of their duties, and the circumstances in which they might be removed. Frequently the bishop was exhorted to make full enquiries at times of visitation, which may indicate some contemporary faith in the efficacy of such reformatory methods.

1 654 provides an exceptionally detailed instance.
2 969. It is entered in the Liber Albus. See *Cal. of Liber Albus*, intro. pp. xxxvii–xxxviii.
3 970.
4 *Temp.* Bishop Baldwin, 1180–84.
5 905. Technically speaking a chantry was a special Mass offered for the founder's salvation.
6 In 1341 two Gloucester chantries were united by the bishop because of the paucity of their endowments. See 119.

The various stages in the formal process of foundation can be readily distinguished in the entry for the Berkeley chantry in Coberley church.[1] This is entitled *ordinacio* in the marginal rubric, though that word has a more specialised meaning noted below. The entry is in the form of the bishop's *inspeximus* and confirmation of the whole process, dated 5 July 1340 from Blockley. Included are letters patent of the founder, dated 9 November 1337, which constitute the actual *fundacio* and themselves contain the royal mortmain licence of 23 May 1336, the *dotacio* or transfer of the endowment to the chaplain and his successors (9 November 1337), as well as the *ordinacio*—the precise details of Masses, observances and other regulations imposed by the founder. The bishop's function was two-fold: to approve, ratify and confirm—so far as he could—the foundation, grant and ordination, and to inhibit anyone, by threat of excommunication, from maliciously infringing them. It was customary for the Worcester chapter to add its confirmation, though this is not always recorded in the register.[2]

The later foundation at Coberley[3] exhibits an elaborate precaution. The ordination document was produced in four copies, one each for the warden of the chantry, the rector of Coberley, the prior and convent of Little Malvern, and the diocesan. In the case of the chantries within the monasteries of Cirencester and Pershore, proposals were submitted for the bishop's definitive ordination.[4] But as a general rule the matter was not left to the bishop.

Thomas de Berkeley, the third baron and eighth feudal lord of Berkeley,[5] was responsible for no less than six chantries, though four of them were in the name of his chaplain, William de Syde.[6]

The four 'Syde chantries'[7] were founded respectively in Syde church, and in the chapels of St. Katherine, Cambridge, within Slimbridge parish; St. Maurice, Newport, in that of Berkeley; and St. John the Baptist, Wortley, in that of Wotton-under-Edge. Only at Newport was provision made for more than one chaplain. There

---

1 154.
2 It is doubtful whether either episcopal or capitular confirmation was essential to the legality of a chantry foundation, but the wise founder would clearly seek episcopal approval at least. Many foundations were never registered.
3 834.   4 835, 906.
5 He succeeded his father Maurice in 1326. He received back the Berkeley lands confiscated for the latter's opposition to the Despensers, and was later acquitted of complicity in Edward II's murder at Berkeley castle. He married, firstly, Margaret fourth daughter of Roger Mortimer, and secondly, Catherine daughter of John Cliveden of Charfield. After fighting in Scotland and France—at Crecy, Calais and Poitiers—he died in 1361. Dugdale, *Baronage*, 1, pp. 355–359; G.E.C. *Complete Peerage*, 2, pp. 127–30.
6 In 1340 he was licensed to choose a confessor and to serve, or have served, oratories within St. Augustine's abbey, Bristol and Berkeley castle (240). He was the mandatory for the induction of chantry priests at Over and Wortley (1000), and presented a chaplain to Over (1462). On the Patent Rolls (*C.P.R.* 1343–45, p. 194) is recorded an exchange of lands granted to him by Thomas lord Berkeley.
7 658–661.

Robert de Sodynton, the *custos*, was to be helped by a *capellanus secundarius*. Apart from the differences which this entailed, the four ordinations are *mutatis mutandis* the same, forming parts of a single scheme.[1]

The chaplains were in each case required to pray specifically for the good estate of the founder (William de Syde), of Thomas lord Berkeley, Maurice de Berkeley (his brother),[2] Maurice de Berkeley (son of Thomas),[3] John Maltravers,[4] Reginald de Cobham and his wife Joan,[5] Richard de Cestre,[6] and William de Cheltenham,[7] during their lifetime, and for their souls after death. In addition they were to pray for the souls of those already dead: the founder's parents and relatives, John and Margaret Giffard,[8] Margaret de Berkeley,[9] and John de Wylington and his wife Joan.[10] Such names are an apt commentary on the strength of the Berkeley connection and its pro-Lancaster complexion.

In each of the Syde ordinations cattle, growing crops, and money, were set aside for the day to day needs of the priests, their enumeration providing some useful economic details.

1 The mortmain licences are all dated 5 May 1343 (*C.P.R.* 1343-45, pp. 23, 32). An earlier licence (19 May 1341), at the instance of Maurice de Berkeley (brother of Thomas), was for a foundation at Cam (*C.P.R.* 1340-43, p. 306: cf. *ibid.* p. 185). There is no mention of this in the register.

2 He served frequently and with honour in Scotland and France (Dugdale, *Baronage*, 1, pp. 355-6). In 735 he is termed 'lord of Uley' (Gloucs.).

3 He succeeded his father in 1361, dying in 1368, it was said from the effect of wounds received at Poitiers. Dugdale, *Baronage*, 1, pp. 359-60; G.E.C. *Complete Peerage*, 2, p. 130.

4 Apparently the younger of that name. He had followed Lancaster's cause and fought at Boroughbridge. After his return to England with Isabella and Mortimer in 1326 he was associated with Thomas lord Berkeley in the custody of Edward II. Sentenced to death in 1330, he fled abroad and remained there until 1345 when he received a safe conduct to attend parliament. In 1351 his outlawry was annulled and his lands were fully restored in the following year. His first wife, Millicent, whom he married about 1313, was the daughter of Maurice lord Berkeley (ob. 1326). *D.N.B.* XXXVI, pp. 6-7; G.E.C. *Complete Peerage*, 8 pp. 581-5.

5 Cobham of Sterborough married Thomas lord Berkeley's daughter Joan. Prominent both as soldier and ambassador in France, he was several times appointed Admiral of the West. In 1361 he died of the plague. His wife survived him for eight years and bequeathed her body for burial in St. Mary Overy, Southwark. Dugdale, *Baronage*, 2, pp. 67-8. G.E.C. *Complete Peerage*, 3, p. 353.

6 Who he was is not clear, nor his connection with the Berkeleys.

7 One of the bishop's stewards. See above, p. xxvii. In the Newport ordination a Robert Groundy followed Cheltenham.

8 Giffard of Brimpsfield was a prominent Gloucestershire landholder, who died seized of the manors of Brimpsfield, Rockhampton, Syde and Badgeworth. Captured after Boroughbridge (1322) he was hanged and quartered at Gloucester. In 1327 his widow, Margaret, was trying to recover Syde, which had passed to the elder Despenser and then to the Crown. Dugdale, *Baronage*, 1, p. 501; G.E.C. *Complete Peerage*, 5, pp. 797-9; *Rotuli Parliamentorum Anglie . . . inediti* (*Camden Soc.* 3rd ser. LI), pp. 154-6.

9 First wife of Thomas lord Berkeley.

10 The Wylingtons had held the manor of Yate (Gloucs.) since 1208. John also joined Lancaster's rebellion, but resumed his lands under Edward III. Joan presented to Hill Croome in 1342, being then a widow. See 478; Dugdale, *Baronage*, 2, p. 142; Banks, *Baronia*, 1, p. 461.

CHANTRY ENDOWMENTS

	SYDE	£	s.	d.	CAMBRIDGE		£	s.	d.
Oxen	2 + 1 horse	1	10	0	4		2	13	4
Sheep	90	6	15	0	–		–	–	–
Wheat	7 acres	1	1	0	13 acres		2	12	0
Barley	11 acres	1	7	6	–		–	–	–
Dredge	7 acres		14	0	–		–	–	–
Oats	12 acres		18	0	8 acres 1 rood			13	1½
Beans	–	–	–	–	5 acres			12	6
Money	4 marks	2	13	4	4 marks		2	13	4
Total value		£14	18	10			£9	4	3¼

	NEWPORT (2 chaplains)	£	s.	d.	WORTLEY	£	s.	d.
Oxen	6	4	0	0	4	2	0	0
Sheep	–	–	–	–	–	–	–	–
Wheat	18 acres	3	12	0	11½ acres	2	6	0
Barley	–	–	–	–	½ acre		1	3
Dredge	1 acre		2	0	6 acres		12	0
Oats	18 acres	1	7	0	18 acres	1	7	0
Beans	14 acres	1	15	0	1 acre		2	6
Money	8 marks	5	6	8	4 marks	2	13	4
Mares	3	1	4	0	–	–	–	–
Total value		£17	6	8		£9	2	1

The two chantries established in Thomas lord Berkeley's own name were at Over chapel, in Almondsbury parish, and St. Augustine's abbey, Bristol, which had been founded by his ancestor, Robert FitzHarding. These were almost exclusively devoted to the spiritual welfare of Lord Berkeley himself and of his first wife, Margaret.

A feature of the foundations within Slimbridge, Berkeley, Wotton and Almondsbury parishes, is the evident intention that chantry priests should supplement the parochial clergy by ministering in outlying chapels. There is special emphasis on this in the Newport ordination.[1]

At Coberley, in the church of St. Giles, two chantries were established by another Thomas de Berkeley, whose family formed a junior branch of the original owners of Berkeley, ousted by Robert Fitz-Harding.[2]

1 660.
2 The third Roger de Berkeley lost his lands because of his adherence to Stephen and never recovered Berkeley. The senior line was continued in the Berkeleys of Dursley. Thomas de Berkeley of Coberley was a prominent man in Gloucestershire. In 1342 he received exemption for life from serving on assizes, recognitions &c., but in 1345 made a visitation of the royal hospital of St. Bartholomew in Bristol, and in 1346 served on a commission *de walliis et fossatis*. In many commissions he was associated with his more powerful namesake of Berkeley and other knights of the shire. *D.N.B.* IV, p. 340 *et seq.*; *C.P.R.* 1340–43, p. 534; *ibid.* 1343–45, p. 514; *ibid.* 1345–48, pp. 101, 186, 466, 472; *ibid.* 1348–50, pp. 165, 169, 235, 239–40.

4

Thomas first secured a mortmain licence in 1336[1] but the details of the chantry were not drawn up officially, nor the grant made, until November of the ensuing year. The bishop's confirmation was given three years after that, 5 July 1340.[2] Then, in 1345, Thomas paid a fine of forty marks for a further alienation. This time he planned a more ambitious chantry with a *custos* and two chaplains, who were to minister in the newly erected south chapel, which still contains the tomb of Sir Thomas with recumbent effigies of himself and his wife Joan.[3] The ordinances provide detailed regulations for the community life which the chaplains were expected to lead in a house called *Beverlee*. The foundation appears to have been a separate one which did not absorb its predecessor.

Even more ambitious was the chantry founded by John de la Riviere, lord of Tormarton, and patron of the church there and at neighbouring Acton Turville.[4] His tomb lies in the chancel at Tormarton, and on it is the matrix of his monumental brass. He must have been depicted supporting a church or chapel, a device taken to indicate a founder.[5] An entry in Montacute's register shows that he did build a chapel dedicated to Our Lady adjoining the church and established a chantry there in 1336.[6] But it is with a later, apparently separate, foundation that the present register is concerned.

There are two mortmain licences for this on the patent rolls. The earlier, dated 1340, permitted the alienation of a messuage and two carucates of land to a chaplain who was to celebrate Mass in the Lady Chapel, while the other, of 1343, allowed the appropriation of Acton Turville church to the chantry *custos*, William Edward.[7] Acton was taxed at only £4 6s. 8d.[8] but the chantry itself was valued at as much as 100 marks (£66 13s. 4d.) in a papal confirmation of 1348.[9]

There are two ordinations in the register, the first probably resulted from the earlier mortmain licence and may therefore belong to 1341,[10] while the second, in the form of the bishop's letters patent

1 *C.P.R.* 1334–38, p. 268.   2 154. See above, p. xxxv.

3 His second wife. His first was also named Joan and her anniversary was likewise to be kept by the chaplains. See 834.

4 The family had suffered for rebellion against Edward II and had been dispossessed by FitzAlan, earl of Arundel. The latter was executed in 1326 and the Riviere lands were restored in the first year of Edward III's reign. Like the Berkeleys John de la Riviere was prominent in the affairs of the county. In particular he acted as one of the overseers of the Statute of Westminster II. Rudder, *A New History of Gloucestershire*, 1779, p. 773 et seq.; *C.P.R.* 1343–45, p. 78

5 Haines, *Manual of Monumental Brasses*, 1861, 1, p. cxxiv (illustration); 2, p. 70.

6 *quamdam cantariam capelle Beate Marie quam idem miles erexit ecclesie subscripte contiguam.* Reg. Montacute 1, fo. 27r.

7 *C.P.R.* 1340–43, p. 9; *ibid.* 1343–45, p. 44.

8 *Tax. Eccles.*, p. 240. For the appropriation, see 1212.

9 *C.P.L.* 1342–62, pp. 300–1. Tormarton church itself, which virtually became part of the endowment, was taxed at £10 13s. 4d. (*Tax. Eccles.*, p. 221).

10 449.

incorporating the founder's petition, is dated 1 May 1344.[1] This latter embodies the final stage of the founder's plans, whereby Tormarton church became incorporated as a perpetual wardenship (*perpetua custodia*), the former rector becoming the *custos* of the chantry with the obligation of permanent residence. This was virtual appropriation.[2]

In addition to the warden there were to be four chaplains to celebrate Mass; two clerks, one in deacon's and the other in sub-deacon's orders, to serve the church; and three choristers. The arrangements for church services are carefully prescribed, but there is no parallel to the precise regulations at Coberley for the common life outside the church. A similar arrangement was intended, for the chaplains and others were to live in the same house and the warden was to dispense graded stipends to them. But most remarkable is the enumeration of vestments with elaborate details of the liturgical colours.

THE TORMARTON VESTMENTS

Colour	Occasion	With or without cope and tunicles
	High Altar	
Violet	Vigils	Without
Red	Easter and solemn feasts of martyrs and apostles	With
Green	Christmas and solemn feasts of confessors	With
White	Five feasts of Our Lady and other solemn feasts of virgins	With
Black	Anniversaries and burials of the founder and other named persons	—
	Altar in the Lady Chapel	
White	Masses of Our Lady on vigils	Without
White (more costly)	Sundays and other common feasts	—
Black	Requiem Masses	

Nave Altars of St. Anne & St. Joachim
Two pairs of vestments, one for each altar, for the use of untitled priests wishing to celebrate Mass.

The Broadwas chantry, in contrast to all the foregoing, was founded by a secular clerk, Master John de Bradewas. His identification presents some difficulty, because there appear to have been at

1 1211.
2 The difference being that the advowson was retained by the patron and not assigned to the chantry warden. At Stratford, in 1336, the advowson was so transferred by the founder, Archbishop Stratford (Reg. Montacute 1, ff. 50r.–51r.). In both instances the chantry foundation had the effect of increasing the number of parochial clergy.

least two other clerks of the same name.[1] It would seem, however, that he is the John de Bradewas who earlier held the benefices of Himbleton,[2] Sedgeberrow, Suckley and Tetbury in succession,[3] and who had a distinguished administrative career, not only in the priory's service,[4] but also as sequestrator of Bishops Reynolds, Maidstone and Cobham.[5] Towards the end of his active career, in 1322, he and John, son of Margery de Housele, were granted corrodies and the use of St. Oswald's chamber in Worcester priory in return for 200 marks and ten quarters of wheat.[6] It was this Margery, surnamed Drew, and her sons John and William, for whom, among others, the two Broadwas chantry priests were directed to pray.[7]

The ordination itself must date from 1344, as the founder presented the chantry priests for institution in December of that year.[8] Their Masses were to be celebrated in the newly built chapel of Our Lady, which remains as a separately gabled structure to the south of the nave, to which it is connected by an arcade of two bays.

John de Bradewas had died by 1349 when the prior of Worcester presented to the chantry, thereby exercising a right which devolved upon him only after the founder's death.[9]

Another secular clerk to found a chantry at this time was Master Adam de Herwynton [Harvington], but his interests were far from being confined to the Worcester diocese, though he had been Orleton's vicar-general[10] and attorney,[11] and clearly owed much of his advancement to him[12]. In Gainsburgh's register he occurs twice as chamberlain of the Exchequer,[13] and he also served Edward III's government, being presented to Tredington in 1328 as a royal clerk.[14] At his death in 31 March 1344 he was a prebendary of Hereford besides holding the Compton Mordack prebend in St.

1 A Master John de Bradewas witnessed the resignation of the vicar of Brimpsfield in 1344 (594), and the following year is mentioned as rector of Sedgeberrow and a notary public (726). This person was ordained successively acolyte, subdeacon and deacon during Wolstan's episcopate (692, 1060, 1061). The earl of Warwick petitioned the pope for a dispensation to enable John to study civil law for seven years (C.P.P. 1342–1419, p. 101: in 1345). Another John de Bradewas, priest, was instituted to the vicarage of St. Andrew's, Pershore, in 1340, but he is not termed *magister* (308).

2 *Reg. Giffard*, p. 540 (1301).

3 For a time he held Sedgeberrow *in commendam* with Himbleton. Suckley he exchanged for Tetbury, resigning the latter on its appropriation in 1331. *Cal. of Liber Albus*, nos. 456, 564, 629; *Reg. Reynolds*, pp. 149, 150; Reg. Orleton 1, fo. 25r.; *Reg. Cobham*, p. 229.

4 For the many references to him in the Liber Albus and the Sede Vacante register, see the indexes to the printed calendars *sub nom.*

5 *Reg. Reynolds*, pp. 2, 11–12; Reg. Maidstone, fo. 36v.; *Reg. Cobham*, pp. 4, 44, *passim*. He is not mentioned by Emden.

6 *Cal. of Liber Albus*, no. 948.

7 684.   8 682–3.   9 1515.

10 Reg. Orleton 1, ff. 3v., 6r., 39r.; *ibid.* 1, fo. 40v.; *ibid.* 1, fo. 27r. and 2, fo. 53r.

11 *C.P.R.* 1330–34, p. 373.

12 He was also Orleton's vicar-general at Hereford, and received his canonry at that time. *Hereford Reg. Orleton*, pp. 209, 374, 375.

13 Reg. Gainsburgh, pp. 214, 230.

14 *C.P.R.* 1327–30, p. 347.

Mary's, Warwick, to which he had been presented by the earl of Warwick.[1]

The chantry had been planned as early as 1332, when Adam was granted licence to alienate to the abbot and convent of Pershore, a messuage, toft, a carucate and a half of land, twelve acres of meadow, four of pasture, and 40s. rent in Pershore.[2] These lands were held for life by Ellen, widow of Hugh le Porter, and were to be conveyed only after her death.[3]

Although the chantry was founded in a monastic church, it was to be served by two secular priests, who were to live in a house named *le Porters*, doubtless after the family of Ellen and Hugh. Very careful precautions were taken to ensure its continuance. In return for the endowment worth £10 a year, and an additional 143 marks (£95 6s. 8d.) transferred by Adam's executors, the monks were to shoulder the financial responsibilities of the chantry and the celebration of the founder's anniversary. All thirty-one of them individually swore (by proxy) to maintain the chantry, and each future monk was to take the same oath at his profession.

The entries concerning this chantry provide one of the more glaring examples of the duplication which occurs in the register. The full process, dated 27 February 1346,[4] contains recensions of several documents, four of which are entered elsewhere.[5]

The latest of the chantries was likewise established in a monastery, St. Augustine's abbey, Cirencester. But this time the abbot himself, William Hereward, was the founder.[6]

There are two entries concerned with the Hereward chantry: the convent's submission to the bishop's ordination, dated 3 October 1346, and the ordination itself, sealed by Wolstan at Hartlebury eight days later.[7] In the submission the various benefactions and excellences of the abbot are first recited, and then the precise rents which he had granted for specific purposes. These had apparently been increased meanwhile, for slightly larger sums are interlineated in the later document.[8]

Here too a secular clerk was to celebrate the Masses, although a canon was to be warden of the chapel and had to house him within the monastery precincts. An exceptional feature was the concession by the bishop of a forty days' indulgence to all who furthered the project by prayer or in other ways.

Before leaving the subject of chantries some general points may be

---

1 Both Guy de Beauchamp (ob. 1315) and his son Thomas were to be commemorated by the chantry priests.
2 *C.P.R.* 1330–34, p. 250. 3 *C.P.R.* 1338–40, p. 518.
4 906. 5 772, 773, 774, 885.
6 He was abbot 1335–52. 7 835, 836.
8 The patent rolls also record a licence for Robert Hereward to alienate to the abbey a large amount of property, including 49 messuages and four shops in Cirencester. *C.P.R.* 1345–48, pp. 40–1: 28 January 1346.

worth noting. The Gloucestershire families of Berkeley, Berkeley of
Coberley, and de la Riviere, were responsible for three quarters of
the twelve chantries founded during Wolstan's episcopate. Abbot
Hereward's chantry brings the Gloucestershire total to nine, but in
Worcestershire there were only the secular clerks' foundations at
Broadwas and Pershore, while Warwickshire had none at all.

Apart from Tormarton, which had an exceptional establishment
of ten persons, the chantries were on a small scale. Seven provided for
one chaplain, those of Newport, Pershore and Broadwas for two, and
the later Coberley foundation for three. Some founders clearly had a
concern beyond their own salvation and that of a small number of
named persons; they wished to extend the cure of souls by providing
help for the parochial clergy.[1]

Lastly, there are many indications in the ordinances of the widespread cult of the Virgin and of its strong influence upon the minds
of the founders.

Appropriations

Seven appropriations of churches to monastic houses are recorded in
the register, and one to a chantry foundation. But this is not the
complete picture; other sources show that three further churches,
Pillerton,[2] Overbury[3] and Newbold Pacey,[4] were also appropriated.
This total of twelve is the highest for any decade in the half century.[5]

The rectories of Tanworth, Aston Cantlow and Yardley, formed
part of the endowment of the earl of Huntingdon's newly established
priory at Maxstoke.[6] In 1331 Sir William de Clinton, as he then was,
had established a secular college with a warden and chaplains in the
parish church of St. Michael, Maxstoke.[7] He refounded it in 1336 as
a priory of Augustinian canons regular, having secured a mortmain
licence for the alienation of £40 in land and rent, as well as the
advowsons of Maxstoke and Long Itchington.[8] A charter of foundation, dated 10 March 1337, made provision for a prior and twelve
canons.[9] In 1345 there were nineteen canons, and two years later
apparently twenty.[10]

Early in 1340 the earl secured the advowson of Tanworth from

1 Cf. Dr. Wood Legh's critical remarks on the motives of chantry founders in *Church Life in England under Edward III*, p. 114 *et seq.*
2 Liber Albus, fo. clxxvii r.–v.
3 *Liber Pensionum (W.H.S.)*, pp. 18–19; Nash, *Worcs.*, 2, pp. 237–8.
4 *Liber Pensionum*, p. 13; *C.P.L.* 1342–62, p. 224.
5 Between 1300 and the end of 1349 36 churches were appropriated.
6 321, 750, 838.
7 Dugdale, *Baronage*, 1, p. 530, mentions five priests. In *C.P.R.* 1334–38, pp. 309–10, there are said to have been six.
8 *C.P.R.* 1334–38, pp. 309–10, 318.
9 See the *inspeximus* and confirmation in *C.P.R.* 1338–40, p. 26: 4 March 1338. Printed in *Monasticon* ed. Caley, 6, pp. 524–6.
10 746, 750, 838.

the prior of Kenilworth, as well as a release of rights of presentation by the earl of Warwick.[1] The appropriation document was drawn up in June of the same year, a vicarage portion of £13 6s. 8d. being reserved.[2]

The actual process of appropriation is more fully recorded in the case of Aston Cantlow. Having obtained royal licence to alienate the advowson and to appropriate the rectory,[3] the earl petitioned the bishop on his priory's behalf. This petition is incorporated in the mandate of 23 June 1345, directing Henry de Neubold to enquire as to the validity of the priory's contentions and the adequacy of the vicarage.[4] This he was to do by journeying to Aston Cantlow and laying the articles of the petition before a jury of local clerks and laymen, whose depositions were to be taken down and sent to the bishop.[5] The bishop, having decided the fitness of appropriation,[6] commissioned Henry de Neubold to secure the assent of the Worcester prior and chapter. Attached to his commission was a schedule containing the articles of the petition and the proofs given by the jury.[7] Neubold placed the facts before the chapter and after discussion secured the required consent. Details of these proceedings were recorded in his return to the bishop, dated the following day.[8] The bishop's seal was appended to the appropriation document on 4 October and that of the Worcester chapter on the 6th.[9] Papal confirmation was added in 1348.[10] But before the union could take effect the rectory had to become vacant by death or cession. William did resign in the earl's house at Southwark on 24 August 1345, while the appropriation was *sub judice*, but for some reason a successor was instituted three weeks later.[11]

There are two entries in Yardley's case, the bishop's appropriation decree (3 May 1347) and the chapter's confirmation (22 June 1347).[12] Royal licence for alienation of the advowson and appropriation had been secured in the previous year.[13] The pope confirmed the arrangement in 1350.[14]

The remaining appropriations, apart from that of Acton Turville, which has been dealt with in connection with the Tormarton chantry,[15] were for the support of well established religious houses.

John Botetourt, lord of Warley, received licence in 1340 to transfer the advowson of Clent church with Rowley chapel to the Pre-

1 *C.P.R.* 1338–40, p. 436: 8 March 1340.   2 321.
3 *C.P.R.* 1343–45, p. 476.
4 746. A vicarage was already established: see 685.   5 *Ibid.*
6 'Manifest poverty' was the criterion laid down by Cardinal Ottobon.
7 747.   8 748. 22 September 1345.   9 750.
10 *C.P.L.* 1342–62, p. 285. Papal confirmation was not essential, nor was it generally sought.
11 742, 743.   12 833, 838.
13 *C.P.R.* 1345–48, p. 135.
14 *C.P.L.* 1342–62, p. 333.
15 See above, pp. xxxviii–xxxix.

monstratensian abbey at Halesowen.[1] The appropriation decree is dated 31 May 1344.[2] This includes an unusually comprehensive petition which, among other things, mentions a recent fire in Halesowen and the serious decline in offerings at the head of St. Barbara.

The Benedictine monks of St. Werburgh, Chester, had in 1332 received licence to appropriate Campden, of which they already held the advowson, but the appropriation decree was not drawn up until 10 July 1340.[3] The petition stresses the abbey's losses from inundation of the Wirral peninsula, the troubles in Wales, and the ruinous state of the fabric.

The Augustinian abbey of Lilleshall was likewise in possession of the advowson of Great Badminton, and acquired a licence to appropriate in 1340.[4] The decree in the register is undated and contains only one specific reason for the deterioration of the house's finances, the claims of travellers on its hospitality, there being no towns nearby.[5]

The entry recording the appropriation of a moiety of Moreton Daubeney church to the hospital of St. John, Warwick, also bears no date. It must have been effected prior to 14 December 1340, when the brethren agreed to pay an annual indemnity of forty pence to the bishop.[6] The royal licence for alienation was not granted until 1345.[7] The other half of Moreton Daubeney was appropriated to the hospital in the time of Bishop Bryan.[8]

In cases of appropriation a pension was generally reserved to the diocesan because of the loss of those fruits which came to him at times of vacancy. Thus at Tanworth the vicar had to pay an annual sum of 13s. 4d., and the appropriators of Clent one of £1 6s 8d.[9] The vicar of Kidderminster was under obligation to pay 13s. 4d. to the bishop and the same sum to the Worcester prior, who suffered corresponding losses *sede vacante*, while the appropriator of Moreton Daubeney paid forty pence to each.[10] The payment of these indemnities is not always recorded in the register.

Much criticism, both in the fourteenth century and in later times, has been levied against the practice of appropriation. But some qualification should be made. Where, as at Tormarton, a church was appropriated to a chantry, the parochial needs were almost certainly better catered for, though Tormarton's gain may have been Acton Turville's loss.[11] Even in the case of monastic appropriation, the matter was not as clear-cut as might appear. Rectors could readily acquire licences to be absent for long periods, and some may have

1 *C.P.R.* 1338–40, p. 443. Botetourt's charter is in *Monasticon* ed. Caley, 6, p. 929: 4 April 1340. Cf. 1204.
2 681. Cf. 526.   3 *C.P.R.* 1330–34, p. 261; 329.
4 *C.P.R.* 1338–40, p. 521.   5 450. Cf. 451.
6 108, 148.   7 *C.P.R.* 1343–45, p. 553.
8 Reg. Bryan. fo. 91r.   9 157, 160; 681, 753.
10 108, 148.   11 See pp. xxxviii–xxxix.

left their benefices licence or no, the rector of Clent providing an apt example of this.[1] In such case the serving of a parish by an endowed instead of a stipendiary vicar, by a priest who was sworn to residence, may have had much to recommend it. It would be hard to maintain that those rectoral tithes which became diverted to monastic uses had formerly been devoted exclusively to parochial ones. There were too many rectors whose interests, and indeed persons, lay elsewhere than in their parishes.

Whether an individual diocesan was in favour of the secular clerk enjoying the greater tithes, or the monastic foundation, must have depended on his background—and most bishops were secular clerks. Wolstan, as a monk-bishop, was clearly in favour of supporting monastic institutions and his real feelings doubtless coincided with those expressed in the formal preamble to the Aston Cantlow appropriation.[2] This attitude is one with the parsimonious granting of licences for rectoral absence. But whatever his attitude, there is no evidence that an individual diocesan could materially affect the trend towards appropriation. There were too many powerful outside interests involved, and once such a process became well established there was little that even a vigorous bishop could do to curb it.[3]

Vicarages

The bishops of Worcester at this time were careful to fulfil their obligation to ordain vicarages in appropriated churches. Wolstan was no exception. Only at Moreton Daubeney, not fully appropriated until 1359, is there no trace of a vicarage.

Of the seven vicarage ordinations in the register, four concern churches appropriated during the episcopate—Tanworth,[4] Campden,[5] Great Badminton,[6] and Acton Turville.[7] The remainder are re-ordinations of existing vicarages at Kidderminster, Standish and Wellesbourne. There are no ordinations for Aston Cantlow, where a vicarage was already established, Clent with Rowley, or Yardley. But in the last two cases the defects of the register are supplied by other sources.[8]

1 Nicholas Jobinol was ordered to reside in 1340 (135) and was clearly a thorn in the bishop's flesh (538, 540). He was apparently made to vacate Clent, but the clerk with whom he exchanged it could not have been resident either (568). The rector of Campden was also absent in 1340 (123).
2 *Pastoralis officii solicitudo continua requirit, et mentem nostram velut cotidiana instancia stimulat et inducit, ut illis potissime sub iugo regularis observancie constitutis, nostre liberalitatis dexteram uberius extendamus, quibus iuxta status sui decenciam proprie non suppetunt facultates.* (750).
3 As Bishop Cobham had found.
4 160, 325. The latter is dated 11 March 1342.   5 595.
6 159: 29 December 1342.
7 1213: undated (?1344).
8 The Clent ordination (undated) is in *Monasticon* ed. Caley, 6, p. 929 (from a MS. in the possession of the then Baron Dudley). The Yardley vicarage (also undated) is in Nash, *Worcs.*, 2, pp. 482–3 from Liber Albus fo. 203.

Kidderminster had been appropriated to the sisters of the leper hospital of Maiden Bradley in 1335 by Bishop Montacute, who had ordained a vicarage in the following year.[1] Because of disputes with the vicar, John de la Doune, the convent submitted a compromise arrangement to the diocesan. In a separate submission the vicar agreed to abide by the latter's decision. The re-ordination, which incorporates both submissions, is dated 18 December 1340.[2]

A similar dispute between the monks of St. Peter's, Gloucester, and Master Walter of Evesham, vicar of their church at Standish, led to the ordination of a vicarage in 1348. A public instrument was drawn up in the presence of the abbot, prior, and thirty-four monks, all duly assembled in their chapter house. After inspection of this document the bishop formally approved it on 23 September.[3] Lands at Standish had been in the abbey's possession since Saxon times,[4] and the bishop confirmed a document of 1202 which recorded the abbot's restitution of the manor to the almoner of his house.[5]

Wellesbourne provides another instance of ancient appropriation. Roger, earl of Warwick (ob. 1153) had granted it to Kenilworth priory and Henry I had added his confirmation.[6] The vicarage ordination is dated 15 October 1348, and once again was a consequence of disagreement between vicar and appropriator.[7]

The vicarage documents are of great interest, but as the details are given fully in the text they need not detain us here. Only at Tanworth and Campden is there mention of additional clergy. At the former the vicar had to find a parochial chaplain when he was not himself officiating, as well as a clerk to give daily assistance. The vicar of Campden had to find a parish priest when unable to say Mass himself, also a secondary priest and a deacon for daily ministrations. The Campden vicarage, though rated at £20, was apparently thought to have been insufficient. At any rate, in 1343 the bishop of Lincoln was deputed by the pope to confirm or alter the amount at his discretion.[8]

Religious houses[9]

In the ordinary course the bishop was concerned with those monasteries subject to his jurisdiction only at times of visitation, or of the election of their heads.

The present register contains a very large number of entries about elections, and the process at Tewkesbury in 1347 must surely be one of the most fully recorded.[10]

1 Reg. Montacute 1, ff. 20v.–21v.; *ibid.* ff. 24v.–25r.
2 153.   3 945.
4 *Monasticon* ed. Caley, 1, p. 550.   5 837.
6 Dugdale, *Baronage*, 1, p. 67; *Monasticon* ed. Caley, 6, pp. 219, 228.   7 950.
8 *C.P.L.* 1342–62, pp. 186–7.   9 See Table 2 for elections.
10 926–943.

At Pershore there seems to have been serious dissension among the monks. William de Herwynton resigned as abbot 26 September 1340, but the bishop recalled him a month later to curb the ensuing maladministration in both spiritualities and temporalities.[1] The election which followed brought the double candidature of Thomas de Pyriton, supported by fifteen monks, and Robert de Lutlynton, who had thirteen votes. Wolstan quashed both elections as uncanonical, deprived the monks of their powers for that turn, and himself appointed Pyriton.[2]

William de Sherborne's election as abbot of Winchcombe (1340) was likewise quashed,[3] so too was that of the prioress of the Cistercian nunnery at Cookhill (1349).[4] The bishop's official took the same course at Studley (1349).[5] But in all three cases the elect was eventually appointed.[6]

It was perhaps knowledge of what had happened at Pershore and Winchcombe that prompted the Tewkesbury monks to take every precaution. Some experienced secular clerks were invited to be present and John de la Lowe, the official, gave advice and guidance at each stage of the proceedings.

Legal action was taken to remove the prior of St. Mark's hospital, Billeswick. The bishop had licensed the master, Ralph de Tetbury, to be absent for a year while on pilgrimage to the shrine of St. James [of Compostella]. Other brethren were appointed to administer the affairs of the house meanwhile.[7] But Ralph failed to return. A suit against him was heard in the Court of Canterbury and terminated with his deprivation.[8]

At another hospital, St. Wulstan's, Worcester, the bishop apparently deprived one Robert de Merston of the office of preceptor. On 13 June 1341 he had deputed the Worcester prior to receive a certain Peter Fraunceys as brother of the hospital. Five days later the newcomer was appointed preceptor and immediately inducted.[9] Robert's deprivation is only known because he ventilated his grievances at the Curia to such effect that the archbishop of Canterbury was commissioned to make enquiry and to reinstate him if injustice could be proved.[10]

Wolstan's Episcopate

A resident diocesan

The register owes its value partly to the number and variety of the records it contains, partly to the light it throws upon one of the most

1 141, 352, 353.   2 361 *et seq.*   3 296–302.   4 1434.   5 1504.
6 This was regular practice when the election was quashed *propter vitium formae.*
7 75–77.   8 787.   9 406, 408, 409.
10 *C.P.L.* 1342–62, p. 70: 13 April 1343.

conscientious bishops of the time. Wolstan was a local man, whose interests were confined to his native diocese and who believed in performing his episcopal functions in person. After his return from London as bishop elect and confirmed he is not known to have left its confines, except perhaps on one occasion, Archbishop Stratford's provincial council held at St. Paul's in October 1342.[1] Even then, dates in his register make this doubtful, and certainly preclude more than a brief absence. No other bishop who had held the see since Giffard's death in January 1302, with the possible exception of Montacute,[2] could claim anything like as much.

Ill-health

Physical infirmity, though there is no sign that it impeded the bishop's journeyings through his diocese, especially at times of visitation, was his reason for not attending secular parliaments and councils. Because cf it the king, in 1340, excused him from all such attendance, in consideration of a promise to celebrate the anniversary of Edward II in St. Peter's abbey, Gloucester, so long as he was able.[3] The exemption was renewed two years later,[4] and in 1346 the bishop's continued infirmity was pleaded by his proctor at the council summoned by the archbishop to St. Paul's.[5] In the light of this the record of Wolstan's widespread industry is the more remarkable.

Ordinations

The diligence with which the bishop exercised the office of visitation[6] is equally evident in his holding of ordinations. Many bishops of the time were content to celebrate orders in the chapels of their manor houses, or at best in a small circle of churches convenient for themselves rather than for the candidates, who often had to travel long distances. Wolstan's method, which is of a pattern with his other work, shows a more pastoral concern.

The bishop is known to have held forty-three ordinations,[7] though twelve of them involved ten persons or less. Of the eighteen in which fifty or more orders were conferred, and for which a locality is given,[8] eight took place in the Gloucester archdeaconry. This is an unusually high proportion, which would have been higher had not the last five ordinations been held at Hartlebury between December 1348

1 His name is among those given as present in Lyndwood, *Provinciale, Const. Prov.*, p. 43.
2 Who held the see for a relatively short time and about whose activities much less can be gleaned.
3 *Foedera* V, p. 191; *C.P.R.* 1338–50, p. 546.
4 *Foedera* V, p. 310; *C.P.R.* 1340–43, p. 431.
5 780.   6 See above, p. xxviii *et seq.*
7 The lists are defective for the years 1339–42, part of 1344, and for 1347 and 1348. For one of the 43—the ordination of 11 March 1340—no list of those ordained has survived. See Table 5.
8 Ordination lists for ?1342 and 18 December 1344 are only partial.

and the bishop's death the following August. By that time Wolstan's physical state must have prevented any other course.

There is nothing to suggest that orders were celebrated other than by the bishop himself, even at the very end of his life. Exactly two months before he died Wolstan conferred 171 orders. All this at a time when the busy diocesan often made use of a 'suffragan', usually an Irish bishop or one with a title *in partibus infidelium*.

The Dunclent affair

The even tenor of the episcopate was disturbed by the bitter attack of a secular clerk, apparently a native of the diocese, who resented the bishop's resisting his provision to the episcopal rectory of Tredington.

The story is a long one, and only an outline can be given here. It really begins with the royal presentation to Tredington in 1327 of Master Henry de Clyf.[1] This was by virtue of the see's vacancy and the king's right of *regale*. A series of presentations of royal clerks followed,[2] culminating in 1344 with that of Thomas de Baddeby.[3] The bishop fought the claim in the courts, but the King's Bench decision against him did not settle the matter.[4] There appeared another claimant, Thomas Dunclent, who had a provisory bull. At the Curia he had been acting as the cathedral priory's proctor,[5] and was not without powerful friends at home.[6] It was rumoured that his associates were preparing to carry off the tithes and other profits by means of an armed raid. The sheriff, Peter de Groete, was instructed to make proclamation against those who threatened this breach of the peace. But the warning went unheeded, the fruits being duly carried off. A further writ commanded the sheriff to attach the persons of those responsible and to lodge them in the Tower.[7] Dunclent emerged victorious. In August 1348 those concerned in the disturbances were pardoned, the presentation of Baddeby was revoked, and the papal nominee's position was acknowledged.[8] Meanwhile he had secured a papal indult which enabled him to remain at a university for three years without the obligation of taking deacon's orders.[9]

This struggle clarifies some otherwise mysterious happenings. John Bodeman[10] and Thomas Dunclent are recorded to have brought

1 *C.P.R.* 1327–30, pp. 205, 232.
2 *C.P.R.* 1327–30, p. 347 (Adam de Herwynton); *ibid.* 1338–40, p. 175 (John de Charnelles).
3 *C.P.R.* 1343–45, p. 349; 1214.   4 *C.P.R.* 1343–45, p. 419; 1215.
5 Liber Albus, fo. clxxxix r.
6 See, for instance, *C.P.P.* 1342–1419, pp. 6, 59, 65, 191.
7 *C.P.R.* 1343–45, pp. 419, 589; *ibid.* 1345–48, pp. 171, 313, 322, 383.
8 *C.P.R.* 1345–48, p. 447; *ibid.* 1348–50, p. 220.
9 *C.P.L.* 1342–62, p. 301. Cf. *C.P.P.* 1342–1419, p. 199.
10 Nothing seems to be known of his part in the affair. He could have been Dunclent's proctor.

a suit against the bishop in the Curia, alleging his disobedience to the Holy See. This must refer to Wolstan's resistance to Dunclent's Tredington claim. The case involved a summons to Avignon, but early in 1345 Edward III wrote to Clement VI on the bishop's behalf, pointing out that such was his age and infirmity that were he to obey the citation he might well die on the way. The royal proctors at the Curia were instructed to assist those of the bishop in avoiding the demand for personal attendance.[1]

The diocese and the Hundred Years' War

The first decade of the French war roughly coincides with Wolstan's episcopate. Its main effect on the diocese, as seen through the register, was a heavy burden of taxation. The triennial tenth of 1337, which proved extremely difficult to collect,[2] was followed by annual tenths in 1338[3] and 1340.[4] In 1342 another tenth was conceded, a royal clerk, William de Neuwynham, being sent to secure some anticipation of the agreed dates of payment and to borrow additional sums. The bishop could not agree to such anticipation on behalf of the diocese, though he made concessions for his own part *licet in hoc graviter onerati*, and the abbots of Pershore and Evesham did likewise.[5] A further triennial tenth was granted in 1344, followed by a biennial tenth two years later.[6]

But the levying of tenths was not the only burden. In 1338, after the king's brief experiment in the establishment of monopolistic conditions for the sale of wool,[7] a moiety of the crop was demanded from the clergy, and this was followed in 1347 by a loan of wool.[8] In addition there were the papal nuncios' demands for procuration, the collection of which was alternatively permitted and forbidden by the king.[9] On one occasion Edward III planned to divert the procurations to his own use as a forced loan, a plan which Archbishop Stratford countered by suggesting to the bishops that they should retain a corresponding part of the royal tenth.[10] This incident provides an interesting sidelight on the dispute between king and archbishop, which led to Stratford's resignation of the Great Seal and subsequent indictment.[11] In 1342 Wolstan was called upon for a personal 'loan' of a hundred marks, and for a further two hundred four years later.[12] In 1347 his temporalities were assessed for an aid on account of the knighting of the Prince of Wales.[13]

1 *Foedera* V, pp. 438–9; Thomas, *Appendix*, pp. 115–6.
2 17, 29, 142, 1118, 1122, 1125.   3 1115, 1123.
4 1142.   5 1046–1048.
6 1231, 1292, 1298.   7 See *History* N.S. XXXVII, pp. 8–24.
8 1115–1117, 1123, 1127, 1290.   9 1255, 1291, 1322.
10 323, 1140, 1145, 1146.
11 For which see G. T. Lapsley, 'Abp. Stratford and the Parliamentary Crisis of 1341' (in *Crown, Community and Parliament*, pp. 231–272).
12 *Foedera* V, pp. 346–7, 491.   13 *C.C.R.* 1346–49, p. 231.

The more spiritual aspect of the Church's contribution to the war—the offering up of prayers for its successful outcome—is also reflected in the register. After Edward III had sailed for France in July 1338 a writ directed the bishop to see that Masses were celebrated, the word of God expounded, and devout processions, hymns, vigils and other pious works performed for the triumph of his armies.[1] News of the naval victory of Sluys in June 1340 reached Wolstan at Blockley. At once he gave orders for a general thanksgiving throughout the diocese. With Edward's departure for Brittany two years later there arrived a further writ, accompanied by Archbishop Stratford's grant of a forty days' indulgence to all those, duly penitent and shriven, who assisted at the offering of prayers and Masses asked for by the king. Subsequent writs demanding the diocese's suffrages for the favourable outcome of hostilities were received in 1345 and 1346.[4]

The Black Death

The weight of taxation was as nothing compared with the terrifying blow which fell early in the Winter of 1348. Northwards from the port of Bristol crept the Black Death, leaving a trail of vacant vicarages and rectories behind it. Judging from the number of institutions it must have arrived about November. Between December and April of the following year it was taking a fairly constant toll of incumbents, becoming really virulent during the months of May, June and July, and the first week of August. From then onwards the depressing story is continued in the folios of the *sede vacante* register.[5]

The tables which follow show the ravages of the plague among the beneficed clergy, including priests of perpetual chantries.

The second table shows that at the height of the plague recorded deaths accounted for some 78% of total institutions. There is no

COMPARATIVE FIGURES OF INSTITUTIONS[6]

Month	1348	1349
January	3	13
February	3	12
March	2	14
April	2	14
May	0	39
June	2	45
July	1	67
August	1	13 [1st–6th only]
	14	217

1 1131.   2 1144.   3 1045, 1171.
4 1245, 1270.   5 *R.S.V.*, p. 223 *et seq.*
6 See the table on p. xxxiii for details of institutions in other years.

INSTITUTIONS 1 APRIL– 6 AUGUST 1349

| Month | Total | Death | Cause of vacancy | | Another benefice assumed |
			Resig.	None given	
April	14	13	0	1	0
May	39	30	4	5[2]	2
June	45	36	3	6	1
July	67	52[1]	10	5	5
August 1st–6th	13	8	4	1[3]	4
	—	—	—	—	—
Totals	178	139	21	18	12
	—	—	—	—	—

question of any widespread desertion of cures, but it became relatively easy to resign one benefice and assume another without going through the process of exchange.[4]

In Worcester itself the ordinary burial places proved inadequate, and on the bishop's instructions the lay cemetery in the cathedral precincts was abandoned for the churchyard of St. Oswald's hospital.[5]

The royal ordinances for the regulation of wages and prices were delivered to the bishop in July 1349. On the 3rd he instructed the Worcester prior to publish them in the cathedral and set in motion the machinery of the archdeaconries to like purpose.[6] The episcopal manors suffered heavily from loss of tenants and stock alike. After the bishop's death the royal escheators could collect so little rent that commissions were set up to test the accuracy of their returns.[7] The incoming bishop, Thoresby, sued Wolstan's executors for a thousand marks' dilapidations and a hundred pounds' worth of stock.[8]

Wolstan's achievement

It was then, on a lugubrious note that the episcopate closed, the bishop carrying out his duties though bedridden in his castle-manor of Hartlebury, where he breathed his last on 6 August, having instituted two rectors that very morning at sunrise.

Our sources are objective, but they are sufficient to outline the figure of a conscientious diocesan, who at a time when the maxim *qui facit per alium facit per se* was operative in almost every sphere of church activity, contented himself with the *minutiae* of administration and the pastoral care of his flock.

A monk, with the predilections of his order, he favoured monastic appropriation and the regular life, but at the same time avoided some harmful assumptions of the secular clerk, all too ready to

1 Including one prebend.
2 Including one prebend.
3 This refers to Blockley, a newly created vicarage.
4 See pp. xxxiii–xxxiv.
5 999.   6 1334.
7 *V.C.H. Worcs.* 4, p. 448.   8 Thomas, *Account*, p. 179.

advocate courses which benefited the higher reaches of the administration while denuding the parishes of the more intelligent men. He was not convinced of the value of the Schools as a training ground for parochial clergy and kept a close eye on the number and duration of licences for study. Pluralism was unknown among his officers, in marked contrast to the nepotism and benefice accumulation which Orleton had encouraged. No contemporary would have censured him had he entrusted much of the work of visitation to commissaries, as the busy Cobham did, or had he, like Reynolds, left most of his ordinations in the hands of suffragan bishops, or even, like most of his recent predecessors, spent a substantial part of his time outside his diocese. He did none of these things.

Within the limitations of his day—and it would have been difficult for an individual bishop to step beyond them—he was a good diocesan; not learned, but a careful administrator, and one who must have known his flock as well as any fourteenth century bishop. Of Wolstan de Bransford Edward III could write with enthusiasm: *inter alios prelatos regni nostri Angliae justus pius et honestus, ac Deo et sanctae Romanae ecclesiae devotus et obediens sit, et semper fuerit reputatus.*[1]

1 *Foedera* V, p. 438.

Note on Editorial Method

It was not possible to have the register published *in extenso*, and the next best thing appeared to be a calendar which would give, as nearly as possible, all the essential information contained in the text. Those entries which were merely noted in the original are classed as Memoranda, even when this description is not used in the MS. The calendar varies from a near translation to a brief summary of entries in common form, but all the names of persons and places have been included and particular attention has been given to administrative details.

Place-names, except when part of a personal name, have been rendered in modern spelling. The MS. reading accompanies doubtful renderings, and this is also the case when the form is unusual or remote from the modern one. Where identification fails the MS. form is given in italics. Variants follow the modern form in the index.

The entries are numbered and only institutions and letters dimissory have been taken out of the text and placed among the tables at the end. On Mr. Pantin's advice a number of the more interesting documents, particularly chantry endowments, have been printed in full after the tables. Although this has entailed some repetition, it does maintain the unity of the English calendar.

A Calendar of the Register of Wolstan De Bransford Bishop of Worcester 1339—1349

Volume 1

1 *Undated*

Form of appointment of a religious as a penitentiary, with reservation to the bishop of cases not ordinarily within the scope of a general commission.

2 *23 April [1339] Hartlebury*

Memorandum of the receipt at Hartlebury of the archbishop's [1] mandate for enquiry into the detention of the goods of Thomas de Hemenhale, the late bishop [1337–8]. On the following day [24 April] the archdeacons were directed to execute the mandate and to certify what they had done by 14 May.

3 *13 February 1341 Hartlebury*

Memorandum of the oath sworn before the bishop by William Corbet, knight, of Chaddesley,[2] that from that time he would not know carnally Alice Alewy of [Droit]wich, and would abstain from her company.[3] He also swore to treat his wife with marital affection and to behave as a husband ought. If convicted of a breach of these conditions he promised to pay £40 to the bishop's alms. Present were Hugh de Cokeseye, John Aleyn of [Droit]wich, John de Stone, Ds. Nicholas de Stanlak, the bishop's pentitentiary; and M. Hugh de Penebrugg, rector of Hartlebury.   R. Marny [4]

4

Some contemporary index notes referring mainly to appropriations, vicarages and chantries.

1 John Stratford, 1333–48.
2 For his career see *V.C.H. Worcs.* 3, p. 38. He was allegedly in his eighties in 1351.
3 Corbet had already abjured Alice in Bp. Orleton's time. See Reg. Orleton I, fo. 26r.
4 Robert de Marny of Bishops Cleeve, a notary public.

5 *17 February 1339*
Introductory rubric to the register of the bishop elect and confirmed.[1]

6 *16 February 1339 London*
Commission for Br. Simon Cromp and Br. John de Westbury, monks of Worcester, and M. Richard Mayel and M. William de Bergeveny, clerks, jointly and severally, to receive the canonical obedience of all ecclesiastics, both religious and secular, of the city and diocese of Worcester, with the power of canonical coercion.

7 *16 February 1339 London*
Commission for M. William de Bergeveny, clerk, to hear, take cognisance of, and terminate all causes and suits moved or to be moved in the consistories of the city and diocese of Worcester, and to exercise all episcopal jurisdiction, with the power of canonical coercion.

8 *16 February 1339 London*
Commission for M. Henry de Neubold, clerk, to seek out and receive the proofs of the wills of all those dying in the city and diocese of Worcester, to approve and insinuate them,[2] to commit to executors the administration of the goods of both testate and intestate, and to do everything else known to pertain by right or custom to the office of sequestrator in the city and diocese.

16 *18 February 1339*
Memorandum that the bishop received in London the mandate of Peter, cardinal priest of St. Praxedis, and Bertrand, cardinal deacon of St. Mary in Aquiro, nuncios of the apostolic see, for the collection of their procurations. On 19 February he deputed the abbot of Cirencester to execute the mandate.

17 *2 March 1339 Hillingdon*
Mandate to M. Henry de Neubold, the diocesan sequestrator. He is to execute a royal writ received by the bishop elect in London on 21 February and to certify what he has done by Easter [28 March]. The writ, dated 20 February and tested by R. de Sadyngton at Westminster,[3] declares that the abbot and convent of Cirencester, collectors of the triennial tenth,[4] are still burdened with the following

---

1 The style used by the bishop until his consecration. Cf. 20.
2 Professor Jacob (*Reg. Chichele* 2, p. x) renders the three stages *probacio, approbacio,* and *insinuacio,* as 'proving, declaration of validity, registration'.
3 It is not in *C.P.R.* Cf. 1118 below.   4 Granted in 1337.

sums for the first year: 4s. for the pension of the abbot of Cormeilles in Olveston church, 13s. 4d. for the prebend in Westbury formerly held by Peter de Leycestr', 20s. for the rector of Rockhampton, 3½d. for the abbot of Fountains' portion in that church, 2s. 6d. for the prior of Bradenstoke's portion in Dodington church, 1s. 4d. for the portion of Bitton in Wapley, 6s. 8d. for the rector of Aston Somerville, 8d. for the portion in Todenham church formerly held by Richard de Ware, 12d. for that of the abbot of Bordesley in Campden church, 5s. 4d. for that of the bishop of Worcester in Down Ampney vicarage, 3s. 8d. for Lower Swell church, and 2s. 8d. for Tytherington church. The bishop is to see that the collectors are paid, but if any of the indebted clerks have acquittances they are to appear at the Exchequer in 15 days of Easter [i.e. 11 April] and the levying of money from their goods is to be stayed meanwhile.

RETURN:
The writ was received so late that nothing could be done.

18 *5 March 1339 Hillingdon*

Mandate instructing the archdeacon of Worcester, in accordance with the terms of a royal writ, dated 16 February, requesting help against the French, to call together the clergy of his archdeaconry on the Monday after Palm Sunday [i.e. 22 March] in the parish church of Winchcombe, being about the centre of the diocese. A similar mandate was sent to the archdeacon of Gloucester.[1]

19 *24 February 1339 Farnham*

Commission for M. Richard de Sydenhale, archdeacon of Shropshire, and Ds. Walter Carles, canon of Hereford, special commissaries of Thomas [Charlton], bp. of Hereford [1327–44], to examine the reasons for the proposed exchange of benefices between Ds. Roger de Breynton, archdeacon of Gloucester, and Bartholomew Tyrel, rector of Old Radnor, Hereford diocese; to authorise the exchange, and to admit Roger's resignation of the archdeaconry and to confer it on Bartholomew. Bartholomew's induction and oath of canonical obedience are reserved to the diocesan.[2]

20 *27 March 1339*

Introductory rubric to the register of the bishop, now consecrated.[3]

21 *21 March 1339*

Memorandum of the bishop's consecration at Canterbury on Palm Sunday.

1 Printed in Wilkins, *Concilia* 2, pp. 654–5.
2 The exchange was not carried out. See 901–4.
3 Cf. 5.

22 *28 March 1339*

Memorandum of the bishop's enthronement in Worcester cathedral on Easter Day by Bernard Sistre, archdeacon of Canterbury.

23 *19 September 1339 Hartlebury*

Commission for M. John de la Lowe, Professor of Civil Law, rector of Heckfield (*Heghfeld*), Winchester diocese, to act in all matters pertaining to the office of the officiality in the diocese of Worcester, with the special power of enquiring into, correcting, and punishing the excesses of the bishop's subjects.

24 *21 March 1339* [1] *Canterbury*

Commission of Robert [Stratford], bp. of Chichester [1337–62], vicar-general of John [Stratford], abp. of Canterbury [1333–48], absent *in remotis*, authorising the archdeacon of Canterbury to install Wolstan [de Bransford], whose election he has confirmed and whom he has consecrated.

But the archdeacon said that he did not wish to do anything by virtue of the commission, declaring his competence to act in his own right.

25 *30 March 1339 Spetchley*

Licence for two years granted to John de Honesworth for the celebration of Mass (*divina . . . facere celebrari*) by a suitable priest in an oratory within his house of *Walbrok* in Halesowen parish; but only in a low voice and to the exclusion of parishioners and others, apart from guests. On great feasts he is to attend the mother church and the priest must first take an oath to indemnify the rector or vicar.

26 *30 March 1339 Spetchley*

Commission for Henry de Neubold to grant probate of wills and to act as sequestrator. [2]

27 *31 March 1339 Spetchley*

Delegation to the prior of Little Malvern of the bishop's powers as sole executor for the provision of John Rich, a poor priest of the diocese, to an ecclesiastical benefice with or without cure in the presentation of the prior and convent of Great Malvern. The letters of provision, together with the bishop's own process, are being sent by Rich's hand for the prior's inspection and subsequent return to the bearer.

1 Received at Kempsey 26 March (marginal rubric).
2 In the same form as the commission issued by the bishop elect. See 8.

28 *2 April 1339*

Memorandum that the bishop committed the office of penitentiary to Br. Ralph Courteys of the order of Preachers in the same form in which his predecessor, Walter,[1] had been accustomed to commit it.

29 *3 April 1339 Spetchley*

Mandate to the official of the archdeacon of Gloucester. He is to cite the dean of Campden to appear on 9 April before the bishop's commissary in St. Nicholas' church, Gloucester, to answer for his contempt and disobedience in failing to certify his action in response to the mandate of M. Henry de Neubold, the sequestrator, whom the bishop empowered to levy certain arrears of the triennial tenth, namely 6s. 8d. for the rector of Aston Somerville, 8d. for M. Richard de Ware's portion in Todenham church, and 12d. for the abbot of Bordesley's portion in Campden church.[2]

30 *3 April 1339 Spetchley*

Mandate to the rectors of Haselor and Alcester, and to the vicar of Beoley. Because the bishop has received a complaint from the abbot and convent of Alcester that certain persons unknown have cut down their woods, they are to declare publicly in their churches, and elsewhere at the request of the religious, that the malefactors are to make restitution within a certain term under pain of greater ex-communication, which in default they are to promulgate at such times and places as they think fit. They are also to discover the offenders' names and to cite them to appear before the bishop or his commissary to answer articles touching the salvation of their souls and their canonical correction, and to receive salutary penance.

31 *5 April 1339 Spetchley*

Appointment during pleasure of Adam de Styventon as bailiff of the bishop's manors of Old Stratford, Hampton-on-Avon, and Stratford town, in the county of Warwick, with the right to hold the bishop's little courts together with the hundreds of Pathlow (*Path'*) and *Gilpuc*[3] in the same county, and to deal with everything affecting the bishop's profit within the said manors, saving *le Lawedayes* and the lands to be sold.

32 *4 April 1339 Spetchley*

Appointment during pleasure of Peter de Penebrugg as constable of

1 14th century predecessors of this name were Reynolds (1308–13) and Maidstone (1313–17).
2 See 17.
3 Dugdale (*Warwickshire* 1765 ed., p. 448) mentions a court of this name being held in the hundred of Pathlow.

the bishop's castle at Hartlebury. He is to receive what former constables were wont to receive for the office.

33 *6 April 1339 Spetchley*

Appointment of Peter de Groete of Worcester as steward of all the bishop's temporalities in the counties of Worcester and Warwick, with full power to do everything known to pertain to the office. He is to receive during the bishop's life, and his own satisfactory execution of the office, gowns and appropriate sustenance for himself and his horses, together with £8, payable in equal instalments at Michaelmas [29 September] and the Annunciation [25 March].

34 *9 April 1339 Spetchley*

Mandate to the dean of Cleeve. Although Richard le Chapman of Cleeve, lately deceased, lawfully made a will and appointed executors, to whom the administration of his goods was committed in form of law, certain persons have removed and hidden such goods, to the peril of their souls, the perturbation of the executors, and the pernicious example of others. After due canonical warning the dean is to declare excommunicate, in all churches or chapels within his jurisdiction,[1] all who fail within 15 days to restore the goods or to pay what they owe, and is also to discover the names of the offenders. He is to certify the bishop's Official as to the execution of the mandate.

35 *10 April 1339 Spetchley*

Commission, until revoked, for Ds. William de Strattone, canon of Oseney resident at Bibury, to exercise the office of penitentiary in the county of Gloucester, with reservation to the bishop of cases not ordinarily within the scope of a general commission.

36 *6 May 1339 Hartlebury*

Memorandum that Br. Richard de Sharpmore of the order of Preachers, residing in the Warwick house, was appointed a penitentiary in the same form.

37 *10 April 1339 Worcester*

Licence for Thomas de Newynton to have Mass (*divina officia*) celebrated by a suitable priest in an oratory within the ambit of his house at Naunton Beauchamp, without prejudice to the offerings and other rights of the parish church.

1 Cleeve, an episcopal manor, was exempt from archidiaconal jurisdiction.

38 *12 April 1339 Worcester*

Letter from the subprior, Nicholas Morice, and the convent of the cathedral priory, recalling the vacancy caused by the bishop's consecration and nominating seven monks, Brothers Robert de Clyfton, the precentor; Simon le Botiler, the hosteler; Henry Fouk, the infirmarian; John de Westbury, John de Leye, William de Birlyngham, and Roger de Bosbury; from whom, in accordance with the composition between Bishop William de Blois [1218–36] and the then prior and convent,[1] the bishop is to choose the new prior. Brothers John de Evesham and John de Muchilneye are appointed proctors with power to depute substitutes and to take any lawful oath on the convent's behalf.

39 *Undated*

Appointment by the bishop of Simon le Botiler as prior of Worcester in accordance with the terms of the composition.[2]

40 *13 April 1339 Worcester*

Mandate to the subprior and convent of Worcester informing them of the bishop's choice of Simon le Botiler as prior and of his induction and installation. They are to treat him with all due reverence and to render obedience.

41 *24 April 1339*

Memorandum of the commission for William de Beckeford, rector of Holy Trinity, Bristol, to act as a penitentiary.

42 *24 April 1339 Hartlebury*

Commission for Ds. William de Beckeford and Ds. Walter, rectors respectively of Holy Trinity and St. Philip's, Bristol, to secure from the king's justices all clerks indicted for felony or apprehended for other crimes, and to take charge of them, with power of canonical coercion.

43 *1 May 1339 Hartlebury*

Commission for M. Richard de Legh, vicar of Standish, to exercise the office of penitentiary among his parishioners, with the exception of certain cases.[3]

---

1 Drawn up in 1224.   2 Cf. 92–93.

3 *corruptoribus monialium et casibus in quibus sentencia excommunicacionis incurritur ab homine vel a iure, et eciam pendentibus vel descendentibus ex iudicaria potestate, ac aliis in quibus requiritur dispensacio pontificalis exceptis.* This form was used by Reynolds at Canterbury. See Churchill, *Cant. Admin.* I, p. 124 n. 3.

44 *3 May 1339 Hartlebury*

Memorandum that the dean of Warwick[1] was ordered to cite Ds. Thomas Ruel, rector of St. Michael's, Warwick, and John de Gayton, to appear before the bishop or his commissary on the next juridical day after St. Dunstan [19 May] to answer a charge of assaulting John Geryn.

45 *4 May 1339 Hartlebury*

Appointment of Philip de Weston, priest, as coadjutor to Ds. John de Wilthon, rector of Frampton Cotterell, who has long suffered from bouts of madness which render him incapable of exercising control over the spiritualities and temporalities of his cure. Nothing belonging to the church is to be alienated without the coadjutor's consent; he is to have drawn up on the testimony of trustworthy persons an inventory of the rector's goods; and must give an account of his administration when called upon.[2]

46 *6 May 1339 Hartlebury*

Memorandum of the letter (*littera citatoria*) sent to the dean of Kineton for the citation of Thomas Basset of Warwick to appear before the bishop or his commissary on the next juridical day after Holy Trinity [30 May] to answer articles to be preferred against him *ex officio*.

47 *7 May 1339 Hartlebury*

Memorandum of the licence for Henry de Bradeweye to have Mass (*divina officia*) celebrated in an oratory within the ambit of his house at Broadway.[3]

48 *15 May 1339 Bredon*

Commission for the dean of Stow to secure the persons of criminous clerks from the royal justices.[4]

49 *13 May 1339 Kempsey*

Mandate to the dean of Worcester. The bishop has learned from the grievous complaint of the parishioners, that on Ascension Day [6 May], while the clergy and laity were processing round Hallow churchyard, unknown evildoers entered the church and stole a leather-bound breviary,[5] contrary to the wish of the parishioners, its

1 Probably the rural dean.
2 Cf. 132.
3 *Ut supra in ii folio*. Apparently a reference to 37, two folios back.
4 Form as in 42.
5 *quoddam portiforium nigro vitulino piloso corio coopertum.*

guardians, thereby committing sacrilege and with their aiders and abettors incurring *ipso facto* the sentence of greater excommunication. The dean is to see that the sentence is pronounced[1] in all the churches of the Worcester deanery, on Sundays and festivals during Mass, when the greater part of the people is present. He is also to discover the names of those responsible and to send them with details of what he has done to the bishop or his commissary general.

50 *19 May 1339 Bredon*

Licence for Beatrice, wife of Sir John de Bisshopesdon, knight,[2] to choose as confessor for two years a discreet and suitable priest, able to absolve her and to enjoin salutary penance even in cases reserved to the bishop by right and custom.

51 *18 May 1339*

Memorandum of the grant during pleasure to Hugh de Groete of the office of apparitor in Pershore deanery.[3]

52 *19 May 1339 Bredon*

Memorandum that the office of penitentiary was committed, until revoked, to Br. John Mangeaunt, prior of St. Peter's Gloucester, Professor of Canon Law.

53 *19 May 1339 Bredon*

Memorandum that a commission was granted in the same form to Ds. Walter Marny, rector of St. John's, Gloucester.

54 *28 May 1339 Bredon*

Mandate to the official of the archdeacon of Gloucester. As the bishop has revoked, and does by his present letters revoke, all commissions of the office of penitentiary granted by his predecessors in the archdeaconry, the official is to declare the fact publicly in the chapters and other meetings within the archdeaconry,[4] and to see that rectors, vicars and parish priests do likewise in their parishes, inhibiting their parishioners from having recourse to those who are no longer able to absolve them.

1 *pulsatis campanis, cruce erecta, candelis quatuor cruci affixis, accensis, et in signum perdicionis eorum de cruce depositis, extinctis, et in terram proiectis.*
2 He had been a knight of the shire in the 1314 parliament at York and held lands at Waresley from the Beauchamp family. His wife survived him and is mentioned in 1374. See Nash, *Worcs.* I, p. xxvi; *V.C.H. Worcs.* 3, pp. 19n., 25, 384; *ibid.* 4, p. 20.
3 As official *sede vacante* (Prior) Bransford had already appointed Hugh to this office (26 December 1338). He was influenced by his special friendship for Peter de Groete. See *R.S.V.*, p. 257 and 33 above.
4 ... *in capitulis in dicto archidiaconatu per vos celebrandis et aliis convocacionibus inibi faciendis* The phrase is common form.

55 *6 June 1339 Bredon*

Memorandum that the office of pentitentiary was committed, until revoked, to Br. Roger de la Lee of the Friars Minor, residing in their Coventry house.

56 *7 June 1339 Bredon*

Letters patent of the bishop's obligation, on account of his recent elevation, to pay 100 shillings' pension to Robert de Kyngestone, king's clerk, nominated by Chancery writ,[1] in two equal instalments at St. Michael [29 September] and Easter, until such time as he be provided with a competent benefice.

57 *16 June 1339 Bredon*

Commission for R[obert Wyville], bp. of Salisbury [1330–75], to carry out an exchange of benefices between M. John Usk, rector of Hanbury, in the bishop of Worcester's collation, and William de Herwynton, rector of Portland, Salisbury diocese.

58 *23 June 1339 Stoneham*

Certification by the bishop of Salisbury of his execution of the above commission. After examination and approval of the reasons for the exchange, he has authorised it, accepted the resignation of M. John, and conferred Hanbury church on M. William, reserving to the diocesan his induction and oath of obedience.

59 *24 June 1339 Elstow*

Letters dimissory issued by Simon de Islep, canon of Lincoln, vicar-general of the bishop of Lincoln [Henry Burghersh, 1320–40], enabling the nuns of Studley priory to receive consecration or benediction from any catholic bishop, he being empowered by the same authority to admit their profession.

60 *27 June 1339 Bredon*

Letters testimonial to the effect that in the chapel of the bishop's manor, Margery de Berchesdon and Agnes de Pyrie, nuns of Studley, Lincoln diocese, after exhibiting the above letters dimissory, received consecration or benediction at the hands of the bishop, who admitted their profession.

61 *30 June 1339 Bredon*

Mandate to the official of the archdeacon of Gloucester. The bishop has learned from Ds. William Tippare, vicar of Cold Aston, that Ds.

---

1 *C.C.R.* 1339–41, p. 105.

Robert Abraham his immediate predecessor, now deceased, left unremedied numerous defects in the chancel, the books and ornaments of the church, and in the house. The official is to go to the church as soon as possible, and after summoning the executors, if there be any, he is to estimate the value of such defects by means of a jury of clerks and laymen who are in a position to know, and to sequestrate the goods of the deceased to that amount until such time as he receive further instructions. He is to certify the bishop of his action, giving details of the goods sequestrated, their value, and the names of the jurors.

62 *12 July 1339*

Memorandum that the bishop[1] appointed M. Ralph de Holbech, canon of Lichfield, to take cognisance of and to terminate the suit between the warden of the Friars Minor of Lichfield of the one part, and Richard Fordeyne, Ds. Adam de Eyton, Ds. William de Burwey, Ds. Peter Cave, chaplains, Richard Valeis, John Lille, Ds. William Bryd and Ds. Richard Blake, chaplains, of the other; to absolve the transgressors from sentence of excommunication and to enjoin salutary penances.

63 *12 July 1339 Bredon*

Commission for the dean of Worcester and the dean of the jurisdiction of St. Helen's, Worcester,[2] to secure criminous clerks from the king's justices or from any other secular power.[3]

64 *18 July 1339 Bredon*

Commission to the dean of Kineton. Because the bishop has imposed purgation on Ds. Richard Ireys, rector of Dry Marston, who has been gravely defamed of the rape of Alice Praers, and wishes to spare him labour and expense, the dean is to admit [his purgation][4] with the eighth hand[5]—a body of upright and legal men of his own condition having genuine knowledge of the matter.

65 *1 July 1339 Bredon*

Commission to M. Hugh de Penebrugg. He is empowered, with the right of canonical coercion, both to act in all causes and legal

---

1 As conservator of the privileges of the Franciscan order within the province of Canterbury. See 107.
2 An episcopal church exempt from archidiaconal jurisdiction.
3 The form differs from that in 42, and there is no specific mention of the subsequent custody of the clerks.
4 This would seem to be what was intended, although the rubric runs: *Commissio ad examinandum testes in purgacione rectoris de Drye Merston.* Usually the rural dean merely published the intended purgation (e.g. 100), the judicial process being reserved to one of the bishop's legal officers.
5 i.e. His own oath was supported by the oaths of seven compurgators.

business moved or to be moved in the bishop's court, whether *ex officio* or at the instance of parties, and to enquire into, correct and punish the excesses of his subjects; and he is appointed adjutor or special commissary. It is not the bishop's intention to derogate thereby from the jurisdiction of the Official or commissary-general.

66 *21 July 1339 Bredon*

Dispensation for John de Tyso, priest. The bishop has received his petition showing that in 1338, shortly after St. Peter ad Vincula [1 August], in Tysoe, he had laid violent hands, not without some provocation, upon Robert Jenecok, priest, whom he had wounded in the arm to the drawing of blood with a knife he was carrying. Becoming penitent he made satisfaction to Robert, and before celebrating Mass (*divina*) besought the bishop's predecessor, Thomas de Hemenhale [1337–8], that, as he could not go to the Holy See at the time without manifest danger of death, owing to the notorious perils of land and sea,[1] he might receive absolution in accordance with the constitution covering the case.[2] Bishop Hemenhale acceded to his request and granted absolution provided that once the danger had passed and there was no lawful impediment John presented himself at the Holy See to give satisfaction, as required by the constitution. In order, therefore, to prevent defamation of the petitioner, or the raising of objection to his orders or to his assumption of an ecclesiastical benefice, the bishop has had letters patent sealed in witness of the above.

67 *29 April 1339 Bredon*

Appointment of William de Cheltenham as steward of all the bishop's temporalities in the county of Gloucester, with full power to do everything known to pertain to the office. He is to receive annually robes and appropriate sustenance for himself and his horses, and 10 marks [£6 13s. 4d] from the bishop's reeve of Salt Marsh [Henbury], to be paid in equal instalments at the Nativity of St. John the Baptist [24 June], St. Michael [29 September], Christmas, and the Annunciation [25 March].

68 *29 July 1339 Bredon*

Memorandum of the licence for two years permitting John de Cheltenham to have Mass (*divina officia*) celebrated by a suitable priest in his oratories at Woodcroft and Charlton, without prejudice to the offerings and other ecclesiastical rights of parish churches.

1 Apparently a reference to the outbreak of hostilities with France.
2 *Decretum*, Causa 17, Qu. 4, C. 29: *Si quis suadente diabolo*. Cf. *Extra* 5, 39, c. 26.

69 *1 August 1339 Alcester*

Memorandum of the grant of a similar licence for three years to M. William de Adelmynton within his oratories at Whitefield and Admington.

70 *1 August 1339 Alcester*

Memorandum of a similar licence for Emma Wilkynes within her oratory of Wood Bevington (*Wodebynynton*).

71 *1 August 1339 Alcester*

Licence for John de Wotton, rector of Elmdon, Coventry & Lichfield diocese, to solemnise matrimony in Oversley chapel, within the bishop's diocese, between Henry de Braylesford and Beatrice le Botiler, provided that the banns are duly called and that there is no other canonical impediment, and without prejudice to the offerings and other rights of the parish church.

72 *Undated*

Mandate to the dean of Pershore. The bishop has received the complaint of Celestra, wife of Richard Hayl, that unknown evildoers have falsely and maliciously defamed her among reputable persons (*bonos et graves*), among whom she was not previously defamed, by imputing to her incontinency with sundry priests, so that she has had to purge herself of the crime before the bishop's commissary *ad hoc*. All such defamers have incurred the sentence of greater excommunication decreed by the Council of Oxford.[1] The dean is to see that they are pronounced excommunicate with the usual ceremonies,[2] on Sundays and festivals during Mass, both in the church of St. Andrew, and, at the request of Celestra, in neighbouring churches.

73 *24 July 1339 Bredon*

Commission for [Henry Burghersh], bishop of Lincoln [1320–40], or his vicar-general in spirituals, to examine the proposed exchange of benefices between Geoffrey de Upton, rector of Eton next Windsor, Lincoln diocese, and M. Thomas Powys, rector of Holt, and should he approve the reasons, on the basis of an enquiry held by the archdeacon of Worcester's official, to admit and institute Geoffrey to Holt, his induction and oath of canonical obedience being reserved to the diocesan.

1 Summoned by Langton in 1222. *Const. Prov.*, p. I: tit. *Item excommunicamus.*
2 See 49.

74 *Undated*

Indenture of the grant to Hugh de Cokeseye,[1] for the bishop's lifetime, of 40s. annual rent together with a robe, or 20s. in lieu. The
rent is to be taken from the episcopal manor of Hanbury in equal
instalments at Michaelmas [29 September] and Easter, the robe at
Christmas. Should the rent fall into arrears he is empowered to levy
distraints on the manor. The bishop also quitclaims to Hugh his
right of the rent of saltworks in [Droit]wich,[2] which the latter holds
for life by grant of Bishop Hemenhale [1337–8] made with the assent
and confirmation of the prior and chapter.

75 *29 July 1339 Bredon*

Licence for Br. Ralph [de Tetbury],[3] master of St. Mark's, Billeswick next Bristol, to visit, in fulfilment of his vow, the shrine of St.
James [of Compostella] *in statu humili*, and to be absent for a year
from Michaelmas next [29 September]. He is not to wander in other
places, and should he accomplish his pilgrimage in a shorter time is
to return without delay to his cure. In the meantime arrangements
are to be made for the temporalities of his house and the cure of
souls.

76 *29 July 1339 Bredon*

Commission for Br. John de Stok of St. Mark's [hospital], Billeswick
next Bristol. Because of the licence granted to Br. Raph [75], and
with his express consent, he is to administer the temporalities of the
house during Ralph's absence. Both ministers and other brethren are
to obey him in such matters.

77 *29 July 1339 Bredon*

Similar commission for Br. J[ohn] de Stokelond[4] to exercise the
cure of the spiritualities.

78 *27 July 1339 Cirencester*

Memorandum of the commission for R[obert Wyville], bp. of
Salisbury [1330–75], to carry out the exchange of benefices between
John de Carltone, vicar of Laverstock, Salisbury diocese, and M.
Henry de Lodelowe, rector of Hatherop.

1 A member of the family which held the manor of Great Cooksey in Upton Warren as
well as other lands in Worcestershire. Hugh succeeded his brother Walter before 1333
and died in 1376–7. *V.C.H. Worcs.* 3, p. 232, and *ibid.* index *sub nom.*
2 *in toto illo redditu . . . pro bulleriis quatuor plumborum aque salse simul cum salinis et vinstalstide
in villa de Wych.* The editor of the *Red Book of Worcester* (*W.H.S.*) suggests (p. 183 n. 1)
that *vinestal* may be a corruption of the Norman word *windas*, a windlass. In E.P.N.S.
Worcs. (p. 360 s.v. Finstall), the suggested meaning is 'a place for heaping firewood'.
3 See 781 *et seq.*
4 He became master of the hospital in 1346. See 781 *et seq.*

6

79 *12 August 1339 Wick-by-Worcester*
Commission for Brothers Nicholas Moryce, subprior of the cathedral priory, and Henry Fouk, infirmarian, to admit the profession of Agnes Groos as a nun of Whiston.[1]

80 *12 August 1339 Wick-by-Worcester*
Indenture of the grant for life to John de Peyto, junior,[2] of the bishop's manor of Stratford-on-Avon, with all its accustomed liberties and appurtenances, saving knights' fees, advowsons of churches, and the advowson of the newly founded chantry in Stratford church,[3] at a rent of 60 pounds of silver payable in equal instalments at St. Michael [29 September], St. Andrew [30 November], the Annunciation [25 March], and the Nativity of St. John the Baptist [24 June]. The bishop also grants all his hundreds and liberties in the county of Warwick with their profits and appurtenances, except the liberty of Hampton. John is to allow the levying of distraints on all his Warwickshire lands in the event of non-payment of the rent. He also undertakes not to alienate the manor without the bishop's assent and that of the Worcester prior and chapter, on pain of re-entry by the bishop or his successors. He is to maintain the manor &c. at his own cost in at least as good a state as he received it. Witnesses: Ds. John de Sapy, knight, Hugh de Cokeseye, John de Grafton, Peter de Groete, John Worthyng, John de Middelmor, Richard de Clodesale and others.

81 *28 August 1339 Alvechurch*
Memorandum of the commission for Ds. Walter Marny, dean of Gloucester, to secure criminous clerks from the king's justices or any other secular judges throughout the Gloucester archdeaconry.

82 *11 September 1339 Hartlebury*
Memorandum of the licence for M. John de Trilleck, rector of Bredon and prebendary of Westbury, to have an oratory within his prebendal house.

83 *11 September 1339 Hartlebury*
Memorandum of a similar licence granted for one year to Robert de Longedon within his houses of Hill (*Hulle*) and *Olbed*.[4]

1 Printed in Nash, *Worcs.* I, p. 217.
2 He was pardoned for receiving the grant without royal licence. *C.P.R.* 1338–40, p. 329 (28 October 1339).
3 Originally founded by Bp. (later Abp.) John Stratford in 1332, who refounded it four years later on a larger scale,
4 Apparently identical with the *Holibed* in Castle Morton parish of 277.

84 *7 September 1339 Hartlebury*

Letters patent acknowledging the bishop's obligation to pay William de Asteleye,[1] brother of M. Thomas de Asteleye,[2] for life, five marks' [£3 6s. 8d.] annual pension in equal instalments at Michaelmas [29 September] and the Annunciation [25 March], together with a robe, or 20s. in lieu, at Christmas, from the episcopal manor of Kempsey. In the event of non-payment he may levy distraints. Moreover, with his famulus and horse, William is to receive honourable entertainment whenever he visits the bishop.

85 *22 September 1339 Hartlebury*

Letter to the Worcester prior and chapter announcing the bishop's intention to carry out visitation, ordering them to recall absent monks, and citing them to appear before him in their chapter house on the Thursday after St. Denis [i.e. 14 October].

86 *26 September 1339 Hartlebury*

Memorandum that the office of apparitor in Dursley deanery was granted to Thomas le Brut of Dursley.

87 *27 September 1339 Hartlebury*

Memorandum that the office of apparitor in Powick deanery was granted to Roger Strech of Stratford.

88 *26 September 1339 Hartlebury*

Memorandum that Ds. William de Stiveclyve, vicar of Tetbury, took an oath of canonical obedience to the bishop, who relaxed the sequestration imposed by his predecessor on apostolic authority and instructed the dean of Stonehouse to restore the fruits and profits received meanwhile.

89 *30 September 1339 Hartlebury*

Mandate to the archdeacon of Worcester's official informing him of the bishop's intention to visit the clergy and people of the archdeaconry, and first of all the deaneries of Worcester, Powick, Kidderminster and [Droit]wich at the following times and places: Friday after St. Denis [15 October] in the cathedral church—the churches of the city and the neighbouring churches of St. John's Wick, Wichenford, Grimley with Hallow chapel, Claines and Warn-

---

1 *C.P.R.* 1350–54, p. 396, has an *inspeximus* and confirmation of this grant, dated 27 January 1353.

2 After Hemenhale's death the Worcester monks are said to have adopted the method of compromise for the election of the new bishop (Bransford) *de consilio magistri Thome de Astleye. Catalogue of MSS.* p. 180, *App.* F 141.

don; Saturday [16 October], the remaining churches and chapels of the Worcester deanery; the following Wednesday [20 October], the deanery of Powick—the churches of Powick, Suckley, Acton Beauchamp, Leigh, Upton on Severn, Hanley, Great Malvern, Madresfield, and Clevelode, in Powick church, and Thursday [21 October] in Longdon church, Longdon itself and the rest of the churches and chapels of the deanery; the Monday following [25 October], the deanery of Kidderminster—the churches of Kidderminster, Wolverley, Hartlebury, Elmley Lovett, Doverdale, Chaddesley with its chapel(s), [Bel]broughton, Broom and Churchill, in Kidderminster church, and Tuesday [26 October] in Hales[owen] church, Hales[owen] itself and the remaining churches of the deanery; Friday [29 October], in the deanery of Droitwich—Tardebigge, Beoley, Northfield and its chapel, Bromsgrove with its chapels of [King's] Norton and Grafton, Alvechurch, and Stoke [Prior] with its chapel, in Tardebigge church, and Saturday [30 October] in Dodderhill church, Dodderhill itself and the remaining churches and chapels of the deanery. The official is to cite all heads of religious houses [within the four deaneries], portionists, pensioners, and others holding churches in *proprios usus*, pensions, portions, or benefices in plurality contrary to law, as well as deans, rectors, vicars, parochial or chantry chaplains and others celebrating Mass, clerks and ministers of each church, chapel or oratory, and those having oratories, whether exempt from archidiaconal jurisdiction or not, and from each parish four, and from each chapel three trustworthy parishioners likely to have knowledge of things requiring correction and reformation, who are to be chosen not by the rectors and vicars but by the official himself. All these are to appear before the bishop to show their titles, privileges, muniments, dispensations, letters of appropriation &c., ordinations of vicarages and letters of orders, to undergo visitation, and to receive the bishop's canonical mandates in accordance with the canons and constitutions. By the custom of the diocese, from the time of his receipt of the bishop's mandate the official is not to hold chapters, to make corrections, or to issue letters of purgation, until the completion of the visitation. In a schedule attached to his letters of certification he is to include the names of those cited, of all holders of appropriated churches, portions, pensions, benefices in plurality, oratories and chantries, of non-resident holders of benefices, those farming their churches, parish priests and others celebrating Mass, and of the parishioners chosen from each church or chapel.

90 *30 September 1339 Hartlebury*

Letter to the prior and convent of Little Malvern, warning them of the bishop's intended visitation on the Thursday after St. Luke [i.e.

21 October], and directing them to appear before him in their chapter house on that day.[1]

91 *5 September 1339 Hartlebury*

Memorandum that the bishop empowered Ds. Robert de Stavertone, portionist of St. Nicholas' church, Warwick, and the dean of Kineton, to receive criminous clerks from the royal justices, bailiffs, or others having secular power.

92 *13 April 1339 Worcester*

Letter to Simon le Botiler, monk of Worcester, informing him of his appointment as prior,[2] and committing to his care the spiritualities and temporalities of the cathedral priory.

93 *13 April 1339 Worcester*

Mandate to the subprior and convent of Worcester, giving details of Botiler's appointment and ordering them to obey him.[3]

94 *6 October 1339 Hartlebury*

Mandate to the dean of Cirencester. The bishop having personally reconciled the churchyard of South Cerney, which had been polluted by the violent spilling of blood, is entitled by the custom of the church of Worcester to levy £2 14s. 6d. as fees—including those of his ministers. The dean is to warn all concerned to make payment within four days of his monition, and in default to lay the church and its chapels under an interdict, no-one being allowed to celebrate Mass there on pain of greater excommunication *ipso facto*.

95 *7 October 1339 Hartlebury*

Memorandum of the licence for the abbot of St. Peter's, Gloucester[4] and his fellow monks, to celebrate Mass, or to have it celebrated by a suitable chaplain, in an oratory within their manor of Prinknash.

96 *16 October 1339 Worcester*

Public instrument attesting the appointment by the bishop, within a chamber of his palace, of Masters Hugh de Seton, Robert de Tresk and John de Walton, clerks, as his special proctors and agents for the collection of all debts due to the church of Worcester, the recovery of money paid without due cause (*indebite*) by the bishop's predecessor,

1 Printed in Nash, *Worcs.*, 2, p. 150.
2 The actual words of appointment are in 39. Simon is described as free and legitimate, more than 30 years old, in priest's orders, and professed of the order of St. Benedict in the church of Worcester.
3 A different form of 40.
4 Adam de Staunton, 1337–51. Cf. 97.

Thomas de Hemenhale [1337–8], or by anyone else, and the impugning of all instruments &c. concerned with the church's liability. The bishop pledges himself to honour the actions of his proctors. Present were Masters John de la Lowe, Professor of Civil Law, William de Burgeveny and Hugh de Penebrugg.

97 *29 November 1339*

Memorandum that a licence for two years was granted to Br. Adam de Staunton, abbot of Gloucester, permitting him to have a suitable priest as confessor, with power to absolve him even in reserved cases and to enjoin salutary penance.

98 *30 November 1339 Hartlebury*

Memorandum of the admisson and institution of Br. Thomas de Mammesfeld, canon of Oseney, a priest of Lincoln diocese, to the custody and cure of Bibury church and its adjacent chapels, to which he had been presented by the abbot and convent of Oseney, the appropriators. The letter for induction was sent to the parish priest of Bibury.[1]

99 *30 November 1339*

Commission for the parish priest of Bibury to induct the above Br. Thomas de Mammesfeld.

100 *5 November 1339 Broadway*

Mandate to the dean of Winchcombe. The bishop has received the petition of John de Abbotesbury and John de Felipeston (near Blandford, Dorset), clerks, for admission to purgation. They claim to have been falsely and maliciously defamed of the robbery of William Garcom', cellarer of Winchcombe, at *Beggerescy* on Michaelmas eve [i.e. 28 September] 1336, for which were indicted before R. de Foxcote, lately sheriff of Gloucestershire, at the tourn held 3 October following at Holford, and lodged in Gloucester prison. Later they were claimed as clerks and removed to the episcopal gaol, where they have since been detained. The dean is to have proclamation made in the vulgar tongue at Mass on Sundays and festivals, in all the churches of the deanery, that opponents of such purgation should appear before the bishop or his commissary on the second juridical day after St. Katherine [25 November], assigned for the clerks' final purgation.

101 *26 November 1339 Hartlebury*

Commission empowering the Official to hear and determine criminal causes moved or to be moved against clerks indicted for felony or

1 Bibury was exempt from archidiaconal jurisdiction.

apprehended for other crimes, and freed by the king's justices in accordance with canonical sanctions; to bring accusations against such clerks *ex officio* or at the instance of those desiring to do so; to enquire into the crimes and as to the repute, conduct and conversation of the clerks; to admit their purgation in form of law at such times and places as he may appoint; and to do everything else required, with power of canonical coercion. The Official is to send details of his proceedings to the bishop.

102 *The bishop's visitation of the Worcester archdeaconry in 1339* [*14 October–19 November*][1]

Date October	Details of churches visited &c.	Visitation held in	Dined	Stayed the night
Th. 14	Worcester cath. chapter. Procuration for bp. and his *familia* in food and drink for two days and a night	Chapter house	Worcester priory	The priory

DEANERY OF WORCESTER[2]

Fr. 15	Churches of the city [and neighbourhood]	The cathedral		The palace
Sat. 16	All the [remaining] churches of the deanery	The cathedral		The palace
Sun. 17	Dedicated the altar of All Saints, Worcester			The palace
Mon. 18 St. Luke	Priory of Whiston, St. Oswald's hosp., [Worcester]	[The priory & hospital]		The palace
Tues. 19	St. Wulstan's hosp., Worcester	The hospital		

DEANERY OF POWICK
October

Wed. 20	Powick and many other nearby churches. Procuration 4 marks	Powick church	Powick	*Ibid.*
Th. 21	Longdon and neighbouring churches. Procuration 4 marks	[Longdon church]	Longdon	*Ibid.*
Fr. 22	Little Malvern priory	[The priory]		
Sat. 23	Dedicated altar at Upton on Severn		Spetchley	*Ibid.*
Sun. 24	Astley priory. Procuration 5 marks, half of which the bp. remitted *de gracia sua* to the prior	[The priory]	Hartlebury	*Ibid.*

1 For convenience this itinerary (cf. 117) is given in tabulated form. The days, but not the dates, are given in the original. Further details of the churches visited are in 89.
2 In the MS. the rubric *Decanatus Wyg'* follows the entry for Friday.

Date	Details of churches visited &c.	Visitation held in	Dined	Stayed the night
DEANERY OF KIDDERMINSTER				
October				
Mon. 25	Kidderminster and neighbouring churches	[Kidderminster church]	Clent	*Ibid.*
Tues. 26	Hales[owen] and many neighbouring churches. Procuration 4 marks	Halesowen church	Clent	*Ibid.*
Wed. 27	Dedicated altar at Hagley		[Bel]broughton	*Ibid.*
Th. 28 SS. Simon & Jude	Dedicated altar at [Bel]broughton		Northfield	*Ibid.*
DEANERY OF [DROIT]WICH				
Fr. 29	Tardebigge and many neighbouring churches. Procuration 4 marks	Tardebigge church	Hanbury	*Ibid.*
Sat. 30	Dodderhill and many other churches of the deanery	Dodderhill church		
DEANERY OF PERSHORE				
November				
Wed. 3	Pershore and neighbouring churches	St. Andrew's, Pershore	Cropthorne	*Ibid.*
Th. 4	Cropthorne and many other churches of the deanery	Cropthorne church		
DEANERY OF BLOCKLEY				
Fr. 5	Deanery of Blockley	[Blockley church]	Blockley	*Ibid.*
DEANERY OF KINETON				
Sat. 6	Wolford and many neighbouring churches. Procuration 4 marks	Wolford church	Honington, in prior of Coventry's manor	*Ibid.*
Sun. 7	Dedicated altar at Cherrington		Tredington	*Ibid.*
Mon. 8	Eatington and many other churches of the deanery	Eatington church	Lambcote, in prior of Kenilworth's manor	*Ibid.*
STRATFORD AND HAMPTON				
Tues. 9	Stratford and Hampton with their chapels	Stratford church	Hampton	*Ibid.*
Wed. 10	Dedicated altars at Barford and Sherborne		Hampton	*Ibid.*

Date	Details of churches visited &c.	Visitation held in	Dined	Stayed the night
DEANERY OF WARWICK				
November				
Th. 11 St. Martin	St. Mary's, Warwick. Procuration 4 marks	St. Mary's	Priory of Holy Sepulchre	*Ibid.*
Fr. 12	Priory of Holy Sepulchre. Procuration 4 marks.	[The priory]		
	Hospitals of St. John & St. Michael, Warwick	[The hospitals]	Budbrooke rectory	*Ibid.*
Sat. 13	Priories of Pinley and Wroxall. Procuration of 4 marks remitted to them	[The priories]	Rowington, in abbot of Reading's manor	*Ibid.*
Mon. 15	Wootton Wawen and many other neighbouring churches. Procuration 4 marks. Dedicated altar at Oldberrow	Wootton church	Oldberrow, in the abbot of Evesham's manor	*Ibid.*
Tues. 16	Studley priory. Procuration 4 marks	The priory	Kinwarton	*Ibid.*
Wed. 17	Alcester abbey. Procuration 4 marks.	[The abbey]		
	Alcester and many other nearby churches	Alcester church	Weethley	*Ibid.*
Th. 18	Cookhill priory	[The priory]	Fladbury	*Ibid.*
Fr. 19	Pershore abbey. Procuration 4 marks	[The abbey]		

103 *6 December 1339 Hartlebury*

Mandate to the dean of Pershore. During his visitation of the deanery the bishop found certain matters requiring correction. The dean is to see that all those named in an attached schedule are cited to appear before him or his commissary on Tuesday after the Conception of Our Lady [i.e. 14 December] in St. Andrew's church, Pershore, to undergo correction according to the nature of the *comperta*[1] and to answer questions about them. The bishop is leaving for the present many things which he intends to amend later on.

104 *26 November 1339 Hartlebury*

Commission to the official and to M. Henry de Neubold, the sequestrator. Because the bishop is prevented by urgent business from proceeding personally to the final correction of *comperta* in the Worcester archdeaconry, they are empowered to take cognisance of

---

1 The *detecta* were disclosures made at the time of visitation. From them the *comperta* were deduced by the bishop and his clerks.

and to deal with such *comperta*, to enquire into them, and to impose correction and punishment, with the right of canonical coercion. The bishop does not intend by the present commission to revoke that already conceded to the Official.[1]

105 *2 November 1339 Worcester*

Letters patent of the bishop's obligation, on account of his consecration by Robert [Stratford], bp. of Chichester [1337–62],[2] to pay 100s. annual pension to Richard de Twyverton, the crucifer of the archbishop of Canterbury and nominated by him in letters patent, until such time as he be provided with an acceptable benefice. The sum is to be paid in equal instalments at Christmas and St. John the Baptist [24 June], with rights of distraint on all the bishop's goods in case of default.

106 *9 January 1340 Hartlebury*

The bishop excuses himself for lawful reasons[3] from attendance at the Parliament summoned to Westminster in the octave of St. Hilary [i.e. 20 January] and appoints the bearer of the letter, M. Robert de Chigewell, canon of London, as his proctor, with the right to appoint a substitute.

107 *6 January 1340 Hartlebury*

Commission by the bishop, as conservator, jointly with the bishops of Winchester and London, of the privileges of the Friars Minor, to the sacrist of the cathedral priory. He is to take cognisance of, proceed with, and determine the matter of the notorious injuries inflicted on the warden and friars of Shrewsbury by M. Thomas de Beruhill, clerk; Ds. William Hoby, Ds. John de Overtone, Ds. William Neuport, Ds. Thomas de Dene, chaplains; and Ds. William Pope, vicar of St. Alkmund the King, Shrewsbury.

108 *Undated Hartlebury*

Appropriation of a moiety of Moreton Daubeney church. The bishop has received the petition of the master and brethren of St. John's hospital, Warwick, to the effect that the fruits, rents and profits of their hospital are so slender as to be insufficient for their own support, that of guests, and of the sick and infirm poor, and for the sustaining of other burdens; that their house was so lavishly built in times past by pious founders that they have to expend a great part of their resources on its upkeep and repair, and will have to do so in the

1 Apparently a reference to the Official's commission of appointment (23) which includes powers of enquiry, correction and punishment.
2 See 24.
3 His visitation of the southern archdeaconry was to begin on 7 February. See 117.

future; that the hospital is in a public place and in a well-known town, and is burdened by the reception of men from many parts of the world, especially founders' heirs and descendants, both at times of the county court (*comitatus*) and whenever people assemble for the justices or other public purposes, as well as by housing the sick and infirm poor; that it has suffered so many calamities of the times— mortality of cattle, heavy exactions and tallages, extortions of enemies, and other adversities, that unless salutary remedy be forth-coming there must be a fall in the number of brethren, a lessening of charity and hospitality, and a decline of divine worship. The bishop, having established the truth of the above by a thorough enquiry, and after consultation with the cathedral prior and chapter, with their assent grants that the hospital may hold the moiety of Moreton Daubeney *in proprios usus*, as petitioned. On the death or cession of the present rector the brethren are to have possession, but with reserva-tion of an adequate vicarage, to be ordained by the bishop or his successor. Once in possession they are to pay half a mark [6s. 8d.] annually at the Annunciation [25 March], of which the diocesan and the chapter are to receive equal portions as recompense for the emoluments which they would otherwise have enjoyed, either *sede plena* or *sede vacante*, whenever the church became vacant.

109 *7 January 1340 Winchcombe*

Petition of Br. Richard [of Idbury], abbot of Winchcombe [1315–40], to be relieved of his office.[1]

110 *12 January 1340 Hartlebury*

Licence for Br. Richard [of Idbury], abbot of Winchcombe, to resign his office.[2]

111 *3 February 1340 Hanbury*

Charter embodying the grant to Ds. John de Stok', rector of Saint-bury, of a piece of arable land within the bishop's manor of Hanbury by Droitwich and stretching as far as the park at Feckenham. He is to pay 10s. rent in equal instalments at Easter and Michaelmas [29 September]. Witnesses: Peter de Groete, Ds. William de Sallewarp, Geoffrey Bate, Osbert Spelly and others.

112 *11 February 1340 Didbrook*

Commission for the abbot of Pershore [William de Herwynton, 1307–40] to absolve Henry de Harleye, deceased, from the sentence

1 He resigned on 22 March (284) and provision was made for him in May (318).
2 *Nos considerantes vos in huiusmodi postulacione aut utilitatem monasterii vestri predicti aut salutem propriam attendisse . . .*

of excommunication imposed by the bishop, provided that he showed signs of penitence before his death.

113 *13 January 1340 Hartlebury*

Grant to M. John de Lech, Professor of Canon Law, the bishop's clerk, by reason of his faithful help and counsel in the past, and for its future continuance, of ten marks' [£6 13s. 4d.] annual pension, until such time as he be promoted to an acceptable benefice. The sum is to be paid to him, or to anyone bearing his letters of acquittance, in equal instalments at St. John the Baptist [24 June] and Christmas, on pain of distraint.

114 *9 February 1340 Winchcombe*

Memorandum of the commission for Henry [Burghersh], bishop of Lincoln [1320–40], or his vicar-general in spirituals, to carry out the exchange of benefices between M. John Trillek, rector of Bredon, and M. John de Orletone, rector of Witney, Lincoln diocese.

115 *Undated*[1]

Letters patent declaring that the remission of one mark of the four paid as procuration at the time of the bishop's visitation by M. Thomas Lench of [Droit]wich, dean of the collegiate church of St. Mary, Warwick, was made of special grace and for reasons of personal affection to an individual and not to the whole college. It is not, therefore, to be taken as a precedent.

116 *Undated*

Injunctions for the abbot and convent of St. Augustine's abbey, Bristol, drawn up by the bishop as a result of his recent visitation.[2]

Since, according to both laws,[3] it is not enough to make statutes unless there be someone to uphold them, and obedience is better than sacrifice,[4] no canon, young or old, is to leave the cloister without licence of his superior (*prelati sui seu custodis ordinis*). He who does so is to be confined to the cloister for the next three days, and is to sit there reading the psalter.

Negligence in the performance of the divine work is to be deplored, so everyone not justly excused must be present at both day and night Hours, at Masses, and in chapter. Should anyone be absent without lawful cause approved by the chapter president (*prelatus capituli*), he is to be confined to the cloister for an equivalent period. In the case of officers, they are to say as many psalters or to undergo as many disciplines as the president shall determine.

1 The bishop visited the college on 11 November 1339. See 102.
2 The bishop visited the monastery 19–20 June 1340. See 117.
3 i.e. Civil and Canon.   4 I Samuel 15, 22.

By both laws the revealer of counsel is adjudged faithless. Accordingly, no-one is to disclose the counsel of the chapter to any secular person, on pain of deprivation of office, and of being excluded from chapter discussion as infamous and traitorous for as long as the president and brethren consider appropriate.

The evangelist teaches that he who offers a gift at the altar should first be reconciled to his brother;[1] no-one is to vilify his brethren or to provoke them to anger or strife, and no-one who has offended his brother by angry word or deed ought to approach the altar until reconciled. He who presumes to do so is to have only bread, beer and vegetables for the next three Fridays, and if he repeat the offence, the penalty may be increased by the abbot or the prior.

In the nature of things, he who is engaged in many tasks gives less attention to each. The *frater obedienciarius* who is put down for the greater Mass[2] must serve the convent every day of his week, and so if he has an office he may appoint a substitute for that period.

Since to read and not understand is accounted negligence, that the brethren by practice may better comprehend what they utter, their conversation while at work or at other lawful time is to be in Latin or French, under penalty to be prudently regulated by the president.

The above articles and penalties contain nothing new, but for their souls' salvation the bishop urges the canons to observe the statutes of their own general chapter.

Christ's poor must nowhere be defrauded of their due portion, and it is not fitting that this be increased beyond measure. Alms are to be collected in full by the almoner, and faithfully distributed according to the constitutions of the Fathers.

Holiness becomes the house of the Lord,[3] and therefore it should not lie in ruins. The sacrist is to see that the church is properly roofed, a burden he has borne *ab antiquo*.

The bishop does not bind the brethren to the observance of his injunctions by sentence of excommunication, as he sees other visitors have done, because he does not wish to imperil their souls, and he trusts that the penalty (*pena arbitraria vel ordinaria*) he intends to impose on any who disobey will suffice. He will not appoint an outside corrector this time, preferring to conceal their faults and crimes than to publish them. In any case, God be praised, he has found more things worthy of commendation than of correction.[4]

The injunctions are to be read once a year in chapter.

1 Matthew 5, 23–4.
2 The hebdomadarian sang the High Mass daily during his week of office.
3 Ps. 94, 6.
4 But the conciliatory sentiments of this paragraph are common form, which Cobham also used in his undated injunctions to Little Malvern priory. *Reg. Cobham*, p. 156.

117 *The bishop's visitation of the Gloucester archdeaconry in 1340* [*7 February–29 June*][1]

Date	Details of churches visited &c.	Visitation held in	Dined	Stayed the night
[DEANERY OF CAMPDEN]				
February				
Mon. 7	Beckford and some nearby churches. Procuration of . . . marks from the then prior[2]	Beckford church	Dumbleton rectory	*Ibid.*
Tues. 8	Dumbleton and nearby churches. Dedicated altar at Alderton	Dumbleton church	Winchcombe	*Ibid.*
Wed. 9	Winchcombe abbey.	The abbey	*Ibid.*	*Ibid.*
Th. 10	Two days' stay at the convent's expense. Proc. in food and drink			
Fr. 11	Didbrook and nearby churches. Procuration 4 marks	Didbrook church	Stanway	*Ibid.*
Sat. 12	Wickham and other nearby churches	Wickham church	Broadway	*Ibid.*
Mon. 14	Campden and other nearby churches	Campden church	Ebrington	*Ibid.*
Tues. 15	Dedicated high altar of Todenham church. Procuration in food and drink		[Todenham]	*Ibid.*
DEANERY OF STOW				
Wed. 16	Longborough and many nearby churches. Procuration 4 marks	Longborough church	Broadwell, in the abbot of Evesham's manor	*Ibid.*
Th. 17	Stow and many nearby churches	Stow church	Bourton	*Ibid.*
Fr. 18	Rissington and many nearby churches	Rissington church	Great Barrington, in the prior of Llanthony's manor	*Ibid.*
DEANERY OF FAIRFORD				
Sat. 19	Eastleach and three nearby churches	Eastleach church	*Benynton*	Lechlade priory
Sun. 20			Lechlade priory	Fairford rectory
Mon. 21	Hatherop and some nearby churches	Hatherop church	Coln St. Aldwyn	*Ibid.*

1 For convenience this itinerary is given in tabulated form. The days, but not the dates, are given in the original. Cf. p. 21 n. 1.

2 There was an Augustinian priory at Beckford, but no specific mention is made of its visitation.

Date	Details of churches visited &c.	Visitation held in	Dined	Stayed the night
Tues. 22	The bishop rested the whole day at Bibury[1]			
Wed. 23	Sherborne and some nearby churches	Sherborne chapel	Sherborne, in abbot of Winchcombe's manor	*Ibid.*

DEANERY OF CIRENCESTER

Date	Details of churches visited &c.	Visitation held in	Dined	Stayed the night
Th. 24	Farmington and many nearby churches	Farmington church	Northleach, in abbot of Gloucester's manor	*Ibid.*
Fr. 25 St. Mathias	Hampnett and many nearby churches	Hampnett church	Chedworth	*Ibid.*
Sat. 26	Rendcombe and many nearby churches	Rendcombe church	Ampney Crucis	*Ibid.*
Sun. 27	Dedicated high altar at Siddington[2]		Cirencester	*Ibid.*
Mon. 28	Cirencester abbey. Procuration in food and drink	The abbey	*Ibid.*	*Ibid.*
Tues. 29	Cirencester abbey Corrections	The abbey	Sapperton	*Ibid.*

DEANERY OF STONEHOUSE

March

Date	Details of churches visited &c.	Visitation held in	Dined	Stayed the night
Wed. 1	Rodmarton and many nearby churches. Dedicated high altar at Rodmarton	Rodmarton church	Tetbury	*Ibid.*
Th. 2	Cherrington and some nearby churches	Cherrington church	Avening	*Ibid.*
Fri. 3	Minchinhampton and some nearby churches	Minchin-hampton church	Minchin-hampton	*Ibid.*
Sat. 4[3]	Horsley and Nympsfield churches, chapel of house of Kinley[4]	Horsley church	Horsley	*Ibid.*
Sun. 5	Reconciled churchyard at Kingscote		Horsley	*Ibid.*
Mon. 6	Kings Stanley and four nearby churches. Dedicated altar of Stroud chapel	Kings Stanley church	[Leonard] Stanley *Monachorum*	*Ibid.*

1 The usual *vis'* of the MS. has been altered to *ivit.*
2 *Sodynton Mar'. Petr'* crossed out.
3 *die Gregorii* interlined in a later hand.
4 A college of secular priests.

Date	Details of churches visited &c.	Visitation held in	Dined	Stayed the night
Tues. 7	Stonehouse and many nearby churches	Stonehouse church	Standish, in almoner of Gloucester's manor	Ibid.
Wed. 8	St. Peter's abbey, Gloucester. Procuration in food and drink	The abbey	Ibid.	Ibid.
Th. 9	Gloucester abbey. Corrections. Two days stay at the convent's expense	Ibid.	Ibid.	Ibid.

DEANERY OF WINCHCOMBE

Date	Details of churches visited &c.	Visitation held in	Dined	Stayed the night
Fr. 10	Leckhampton and other churches	Leckhampton ch.	Cheltenham	Ibid.
Sat. 11	Ordinations held in Cheltenham church,[1] and visitation of that and other churches	Cheltenham ch.	Prestbury, in the prior of Llanthony's manor	
Sun. 12	Dedication of altar at Elmstone		Bishops Cleeve	Ibid.
Mon. 13	Bishops Cleeve church and chapel(s)	Bishops Cleeve ch.	Ibid.	Ibid.
May Th. 18	Tewkesbury and Deerhurst churches	Deerhurst ch.	Bredon	Ibid.

DEANERY OF GLOUCESTER

Date	Details of churches visited &c.	Visitation held in	Dined	Stayed the night
Mon. 22	Llanthony priory	The priory	Ibid.	Ibid.
Tues. 23	Procurations in food and and drink. Stay of two days			
Wed. 24	Church of St. Mary before the abbey gate, Gloucester. Churches of the town and those of Harescombe, Pitchcombe, Brookthorpe, Matson, Hartpury, Ashleworth	St. Mary's ch.	Longney, in the abbot of Pershore's manor	
Fr. 26	Longney, Arlingham, Frocester, Fretherne, Moreton [Valence] with chapel, Standish with chapel(s), Haresfield.	Longney ch.	Slimbridge rectory	Ibid.

1 The list of those ordained is not in the register.

Date	Details of churches visited &c.	Visitation held in	Dined	Stayed the night

DEANERY OF DURSLEY

Sat. 27	Cam with chapel, Frampton-on-Severn, Slimbridge, Uley, Coaley, Berkeley with chapels. Dedication of Stinchcombe chapel.	Stinchcombe chapel	Cam rectory	*Ibid.*
Sun. 28	Dedication of altar at Nibley chapel		Wotton [under-Edge] rectory	
Mon. 29	Wotton with chapel(s), Rockhampton, Thornbury with chapel(s), Newington, Beverstone with Kingscote chapel, Lasborough, Ozleworth	Wotton ch.	Hawkesbury rectory	*Ibid.*

DEANERY OF HAWKESBURY AND BITTON

Tues. 30	Hawkesbury with chapel(s), Boxwell with chapel(s), Weston Birt and other nearby churches	Hawkesbury ch.	Great Sodbury, with the vicar	Cod-rington, in Roger Kantok's manor
Wed. 31	Wapley and other churches	Wapley ch.	Puckle-church rectory	*Ibid.*
June Th. 1	Pucklechurch and other churches	Pucklechurch ch.	*Ibid.*	*Ibid.*
Fr. 2	Iron Acton and other churches	Iron Acton ch.	Henbury	*Ibid.*

DEANERY OF BRISTOL

Mon. 19	St. Augustine's abbey, Bristol, where the bp. stayed two days and made corrections	The abbey	*Ibid.*	*Ibid.*
Tues. 20	Hospital of St. Mark [Gaunt's], Bristol	The hospital		Henbury
Wed. 21	Priory of St. James [cell of Tewkesbury]. Hospitals of St. Bartholomew and St. Mary Magdalene	The priory The hospitals	Henbury	*Ibid.*
Th. 22	Holy Trinity and other churches of the town	Holy Trinity ch., Bristol	Henbury	*Ibid.*
Fr. 23	Collegiate ch. of Westbury, Henbury, Winterbourne, Stoke Gifford, Filton, Clifton	Westbury on Trym	Henbury	*Ibid.*

7

Date	Details of churches visited &c.	Visitation held in	Dined	Stayed the night
Mon. 26	Almondsbury, Horfield, Littleton, Olveston, Elberton, Tockington, Weston, Oldbury, Berkeley	Almondsbury ch.	Olveston rectory	*Ibid.*
Tues. 27	Dedication of the churchyard of Oldbury chapel		Berkeley	*Ibid.*
Th. 29 SS. Peter & Paul	Dedication of Eastington church			

118 *Undated*

Mandate to M. Henry de Neubold, the sequestrator. Repeated allegations have reached the bishop from trustworthy persons that all is not well with the priory of the Holy Sepulchre, Warwick, and with the affairs (*condiciones*) of the prior and regular officers. Desiring to know the facts, he requires the sequestrator to go in person to the priory, to summon all concerned, and to make diligent enquiry, by means of the regulars themselves and of others—even seculars— staying with them, as to the state of the house and the affairs of the prior and other canons, especially those of officials and administrators of the common goods. He is to bring back his findings or, failing that, to send them by letters under his seal. Adequate food and drink is to be provided from the goods of the house for canons engaged in the day or night offices. But if the prior, cellarer, or any other administrator of such goods be widely suspected of waste, he is to be suspended from administering them until the matter has been thrashed out before the bishop.

119 *20 March 1341 Hartlebury*

Union of two Gloucester chantries. The late William de Sondhurst, citizen of Gloucester, and Ds. John de Sondhurst, chaplain, out of devotion and for the salvation of their souls and those of their progenitors, parents and benefactors, and of all the faithful living and departed, founded two perpetual chantries in the churches of Holy Trinity and St. John, Gloucester, and endowed them adequately by the standards of the time. Subsequently, however, the rents became so diminished by men's malice that now it is impossible to find suitable chaplains willing to accept titles in the chantries, as their joint income barely suffices for the proper support of one priest. The bishop, therefore, deploring the decline of divine worship and wishing to prevent its utter extinction, desiring moreover to implement as far as possible the founders' wishes, by pontifical authority, and with the consent of Hugh de Chywe, citizen of Gloucester, the present patron, joins the two chantries, and directs that the chaplain presented to the diocesan in future shall exercise his office for the souls of those named by the founders in the churches of Holy Trinity and St. John by alternate years.

120 *18 April 1340 Alvechurch*
Charter confirming the grant to Thomas de Heneleye and John, his elder son, of the virgate of land with appurtenances which John Ruddok and Isabella, his wife, held in the episcopal manor of Alvechurch. It is to be held of the bishop by Thomas and John, and the lawful heirs of John, or failing them by John's brother, John, and his lawful heirs, or if there be none, by Joan, his sister, and her heirs, and in their default is to revert to the bishop. An annual rent of 15s. is to be paid in equal instalments at the four usual terms for all service and exactions, saving suit of the bishop's court of Alvechurch and royal service. Witnesses: John de Beauchamp, Thomas Blancfront, William de Salewarp, Peter de Greote senior, Peter ate Chaumbre, and others.[1]

121 *20 May 1348 Alvechurch*
Charter[2] confirming the grant to Thomas de Heneleye and John, his elder son, of a messuage, curtilage and croft which Richard Robert held of the bishop in the manor of Alvechurch, lying between the land of the above Thomas and that of John Gerveyse, as well as of a parcel of meadow in *Longemedewe* between Thomas's meadow and that of Ds. John Blauncfront and Alan le Taillour. All these are to be held by Thomas and John, and the lawful heirs of John [&c. as in 120], at an annual rent of 2s., to be paid in equal instalments at the four usual terms for all service and other obligations (*pro omni servicio, consuetudine, exaccione et demanda*), saving suit of the bishop's court at Alvechurch and royal service. Witnesses: Ds. John de Beauchamp, knight; Roger Blauncfront, Ds. William de Sallewarp, Peter de Greote, John atte Chaumbre and others.

122 *23 March 1340 Hartlebury*
Memorandum of the commission for Ralph [of Shrewsbury], bishop of Bath & Wells [1329–63], to carry out the exchange of benefices between Ds. John Jeoly, rector of Saltford, Bath & Wells diocese, and Ds. John de Strengeston, vicar of Bitton, on the basis of an enquiry held by the archdeacon of Gloucester's official.

123 *9 April 1340 Hartlebury*
Memorandum that the bishop admonished the rector of Campden, in the person of his proctor, Robert de Campden, to make personal

1 Cf. 124.
2 Described in the marginal rubric as being *in forma ampliori*.

residence in his church *sub pena iuris*. Present were J. de la Lowe and
J. de Preston. R. Marny.[1]

124 *18 April 1340 Alvechurch*

Charter confirming a grant of land to Thomas de Heneleye.[2]

125 *11 April 1340 Hartlebury*

Letters patent acknowledging the receipt of 30s. from the abbot and
convent of Evesham, the appropriators of Ombersley church.[3] This
is for the next term of St. Michael, being an annual pension due to
the bishop by way of indemnity.[4]

126 *24 April 1340 Alvechurch*

Commission for Robert [Wyville], bishop of Salisbury [1330–75], to
carry out the exchange of benefices between Ds. John de Manesergh,
rector of Tormarton, and Ds. John de Astweyt, rector of Brightwalton, Salisbury diocese, on the basis of an enquiry held by the
archdeacon of Gloucester's official.

127 *24 April 1340 Alvechurch*

Letters patent of Robert de Kyngestone, king's clerk, acknowledging
the receipt of the Michaelmas [29 September] 1339 and Easter
[16 April] 1340 instalments of his annual pension of 100s.[5]

128 *22 April 1340 Alvechurch*

Charter embodying the grant to John de Strete, his heirs and
assigns, of the custody of the land and tenement(s) in Henbury in
Salt Marsh and Redland of John, son of Edmund du Seler of Bristol,
heir of John du Seler, Edmund's father, which are in the bishop's
hand by reason of John's minority, and also of his marriage, provided
he be not disparaged. Should John die under age, John de Strete,
his heirs and assigns, may retain custody of the above until there
be an heir of lawful age.

129 *15 May 1340 Bredon*

Commission, until revoked, for the farmer of Blockley church,[6] M.
John, rector of Hinton, to correct and punish the excesses of the

1 Robert Marny of Bishops Cleeve, a notary.
2 The entry is scored out. It is a duplicate of 120, except that the sister is called Alice
  and not Joan.
3 It was appropriated in 1326. See *Reg. Cobham*, p. 199.
4 Cf. 147. The original was in the form of an indenture: the bishop's seal was appended
  to one part, that of the abbot and convent to the other.
5 See 56.
6 Held *in commendam* by John, bishop of Porto. *C.P.L.* 1305–42, p. 370.

bishop's subjects within the exempt jurisdiction of Blockley; to hear, take cognisance of, and terminate all causes and suits moved or to be moved within the jurisdiction, whether *ex officio* or at the instance of parties; to seek out and receive proofs of the wills of those dying within it, to approve and insinuate them,[1] to commit to executors the administration of the goods of both testate and intestate, to hear the accounts of their administration, and to grant letters of acquittance; with the power of canonical coercion and of lawful sequestration.

130 *10 June 1340 Henbury*

Memorandum of the commission for the deans of Warwick and Kineton, and Ds. Robert de Staverton, portionist in St. Nicholas' church, Warwick, to secure criminous clerks from the king's justices and other secular judges.

131 *20 June 1340 Henbury*

Memorandum of the commission for Ds. Thomas Neel of Rodbourne, a priest of Salisbury diocese, to administer the spiritualities and temporalities of Turkdean vicarage and to act as coadjutor to the vicar, until the bishop should determine otherwise.[2]

132 *24 June 1340 Henbury*

Memorandum of a similar commission for Ds. Henry, vicar of Great Sodbury, to act as coadjutor to the rector of Frampton Cotterell.[3]

133 *1 July 1340*

Memorandum that the bishop deputed Ds. Thomas Neel to act as coadjutor to the vicar of Turkdean, and enjoined the vicar, on his obedience and under penalty of excommunication, to admit Thomas and to show him all his goods so that an inventory could be made.[4]

134 *29 June 1340 Withington*

Mandate to the dean of Dursley. Although the chapel of Alkerton, which is in Eastington parish and well known to be subject to that church, has been suspended by the fault of its parishioners, the hearing of Mass and partaking of the sacraments—except in lawfully excepted cases—being in consequence forbidden there, it has come repeatedly to the bishop's ears that the parishioners of the chapel refuse to go to Eastington for Mass or the sacraments, in contempt of their mother church and to the injury of the rector, the peril of their souls, and the pernicious example and scandal of many persons. In

1 Cf. p. 3 n. 2.   Cf. 133.   3 Cf. 45.   4 Cf. 131.

order, therefore, that by depriving them of the communion of neighbouring churches, these ill-disposed persons, being put to shame, may return to the unity of their mother church, the dean is to inhibit the rectors of [Leonard] Stanley (*monachorum*), King's Stanley, Moreton [Valence], Wheatenhurst, Nympsfield, and the vicars of Frocester, Stonehouse, Standish and Frampton, and any others at the request of the rector of Eastington, from admitting the parishioners of Alkerton to Mass or other ecclesiastical sacraments, on pain of being charged with disobedience and contempt.

135 *3 July 1340 Blockley*

Mandate to the dean of Kidderminster. Although, according to the canons, he who assumes the rule of a parish church must reside there in person,[1] the bishop learns that Nicholas Jobinol, purporting to be rector of Clent and Rowley, does not do so. He therefore orders the dean to warn the said Nicholas, in person if he can be found within Kidderminster deanery, otherwise through his proctor, or if he has not appointed one, by public citation in [Clent] church in the presence of his acquaintances and friends, that he is to reside personally within 15 days, and that if he does not obey, the bishop will take proceedings against him. The dean is to signify within eight days the date of the mandate's receipt and the manner and form of his monition.

136 *4 July 1340 Blockley*

Memorandum that the bishop, as sole executor deputed by the Holy See to provide Robert Waltres of Iccomb, poor clerk, with a competent benefice in the patronage of Deerhurst priory, committed his powers to the rectors of Aston Somerville, Toddington, Dumbleton and Hinton. He did not thereby revoke the commission of S[imon], formerly bishop of Worcester [1334–7], and now of Ely [1337–45], to the abbot of Winchcombe.

137 *3 July 1340 Blockley*

Memorandum that the bishop appointed Master R. de Chigewell and Ds. Thomas de Evesham, jointly and severally, as his proctors for the parliament to be held at Westminster on the Wednesday after the Translation of St. Thomas the Martyr [i.e. 12 July].[2]

138 *1 July 1340 Withington*

Memorandum that custody of the sequestration of the fruits, profits, and offerings of Chedworth rectory, appropriated to Lyre Abbey

---

1 *Sext* I, 6, c. 14 *Licet canon.*
2 The third session of the 1340 parliament. Reference is made to 106 for the form of the document.

[Normandy], which was imposed by reason of the *comperta* and *detecta*[1] of the bishop's recent visitation, was granted to Ds. Richard de Stowe, chaplain, of Chedworth;[2] Richard ate Stile of Chedworth, and Richard Parkar of Sherborne.

139 *1 September 1340 Hartlebury*

Letters patent declaring that by the bishop's grant at the time of his consecration, and in return for a sum of money, Ds. Thomas de Evesham has collected and retained all the fruits, offerings and profits of Hillingdon church, London diocese, from that time until the present, and is entitled to do likewise until the Annunciation [25 March 1341]. The bishop, on his own behalf and that of his executors, accordingly quitclaims to Thomas all such fruits &c.

140 *1 September 1340 Hartlebury*

Appointment of William de Netherton as custodian of the bishop's houses (*hospicii sive domorum nostrarum*) in the parish of St. Mary-le-Strand in the suburb of London, and as receiver of all his rents in the city and suburb, with powers of distraint. He is to receive, during satisfactory performance of his office, what others were wont to receive under the bishop's predecessors.

141 *21 October 1340 Alvechurch*

Appointment of Br. William de Herwynton, formerly abbot of Pershore,[3] to administer the spiritualities and temporalities of that house because of their mismanagement.

142 *2 November 1340 Alvechurch*

Commission to the abbot and convent of Cirencester. As the bishop learns from the letters and register of his predecessor T[homas de Hemenhale],[4] they were appointed collectors in the Gloucester archdeaconry of the triennial tenth granted by the clergy of the Canterbury province in St. Bride's church, London.[5] Although the greater number of those beneficed in the archdeaconry have paid the tenth, some have not. The collectors are therefore given full power, by means of ecclesiastical censure and the sequestration of the fruits of benefices, to exact such arrears, as well as to proceed summarily against the recalcitrant and to punish them. The bishop reserves to himself the relaxation of their coercive measures and absolution from sentence.

1 See p. 23 n. 1.
2 *de Stowe* is interlineated and an alternative reading would be 'chaplain of Chedworth'.
3 The entry is printed in Nash, *Worcs.* 2, p. 255. The abbot had resigned in September. See 351–3.
4 Bishop 1337–8.   5 In 1337.

143 *2 November 1340 Alvechurch*

Memorandum of the commission for Ds. William, perpetual vicar of Eatington, to act as a penitentiary among his parishioners.

144 *2 November 1340 Alvechurch*

Memorandum of another commission in the same form for the vicar of Wolverley.

145 *27 October 1340 Alvechurch*

Memorandum that the bishop relaxed the interdict imposed until Christmas on Wootton Wawen church for non-payment of the procuration due for his visitation.

146 *9 November 1340 Alvechurch*

Memorandum that the bishop relaxed the interdict imposed on Tewkesbury parish church and its chapels for non-payment of procuration for two reconcilations of the churchyard there.

147 *11 April 1340*[1]

Indenture of the abbot and convent of Evesham's obligation to pay 30s. annually to the bishop and his successors, by reason of their appropriation of Ombersley church and the consequent loss of the profits which would have accrued to the diocesan at times of its vacancy.[2]

148 *14 December 1340 Hartlebury*

Similar indenture whereby the master and brethren of St. John's hospital, Warwick, acknowledge their obligation to pay 40d. annually at the Annunciation [25 March] by the hand of the cathedral sacrist, because of the appropriation of a moiety of Moreton Daubeney church [v. 108].

149 *15 December 1340 Hartlebury*

Letters patent acknowledging payment of the above 40d. for the next term of the Annunciation [i.e. 25 Mar. 1341].[3]

150 *20 January 1341 Hartlebury*

Memorandum of the commission for Ds. Walter Marny, rector of St. John's, Gloucester, and dean of the Christianity of that place, and Ds. William, rector of St. Aldate's there, jointly and severally,

1 The bishop's seal was appended to the other part at Hartlebury on 12 April. Cf. p. 34 n. 4.
2 Printed in Nash, *Worcs.* 2, p. 227.
3 In the form of an indenture and *mutatis mutandis* as 125.

to claim criminous clerks from the royal justices and other secular authorities.[1]

151 *13 May 1341 Hartlebury*

Memorandum that the office of penitentiary was committed for two years to the vicar of Painswick, with the exception of certain cases.[2]

152 *20 June 1341 Blockley*

Memorandum of the commission for Ds. Walter Marny, rector of St. John's, Gloucester, and Richard, perpetual vicar of St. Owen's there, jointly and severally, to claim criminous clerks.[3]

153 *18 December 1340 Hartlebury*

Letters patent of the bishop's re-ordination of Kidderminster vicarage. Bishop Simon [de Montacute, 1334–7] appropriated Kidderminster church to the leper hospital of Maiden Bradley, Salisbury diocese,[4] with reservation of an adequate portion, which he later assigned to a vicar.[5] Dispute subsequently arose between the sisters of the hospital and Ds. John de la Doune, the perpetual vicar, as to the sufficiency of the portion, the parties eventually agreeing to submit to the bishop's ordination. The submission[6] of the prior, Henry, and of the Augustinian convent of Maiden Bradley follows. John de la Doune, the present vicar, alleged that the portions were insufficient for the necessary burdens of the vicarage, while the convent contended that they were large enough in common years, bearing in mind the church's resources. After long dispute, they have agreed, by the mediation of upright men, trustworthy parishioners, and other mutual friends with knowledge of the resources and burdens of the church, that a new ordination should be made by the diocesan. The present vicar and his successors are to have the manor of Hurcott, where the rectors formerly lived, with the houses, buildings, closes [&c.] pertaining to it, being within the church's demesne, together with all fruits, profits, offerings, obventions, greater and lesser tithes, which M. John de Careslegh, the last rector, received, or ought to have received; except the tithes of corn and hay which the convent has received *ab antiquo* from lands and meadows between Stour and Severn within the parish, all tithes from their demesne lands of Oldington and Burlish lying in the parish, and those from

1 Cf. 152.
2 *corruptoribus monialium, fractoribus parcorum, et casu periurii in assisis, exheredacionibus et indictamentis exceptis.* Cf. p. 8 n. 3.
3 Cf. 150.
4 In 1335. Reg. Montacute I, ff. 20v.–21r.; Liber Albus ff. clix v.–clx v.
5 In 1336. Reg. Montacute I, ff. 24v.–25r.
6 Dated 11 December 1340 from Maiden Bradley.

the assarts and newly tilled lands (*novales*), comprising less than an acre, which lie between Stour and Severn and are commonly called the *Burgaieries*—all of which are reserved to the convent. Excepted also are the tithes from the parks of Trimpley and Eymore, which the convent recently granted to the Worcester chapter as compensation for the emoluments mentioned below. The vicars are to pay 20 marks yearly [£13 6s. 8d.] in the convent's manor of Oldington from the above fruits [&c.], *nomine simplicis beneficii* and on account of the appropriation, in four equal instalments at Christmas, Easter, the Nativity of St. John the Baptist [24 June] and Michaelmas [29 September], starting next Christmas. The remaining fruits [&c.] are for the vicar's support, being by general consent adjudged adequate for hospitality and other burdens. But he is bound to pay annually at Michaelmas one mark each to the diocesan and the Worcester chapter, as recompense for the emoluments which they would have received at times of the church's vacancy had the appropriation not been made. The vicar is to pay the procurations of cardinals, legates, or papal nuncios, and all additional charges, as well as episcopal, archidiaconal and other burdens (*onera*), both ordinary and extra-ordinary, including the repair of the chancel to the extent of 40d. yearly—the convent being responsible for expenditure in excess of that sum, provided that the 20 marks be paid in full. The vicars are to swear, both in the convent's chapter house immediately after their presentation, and before the bishop at the time of their institution, that they will pay the 20 marks, and also the two marks due to the bishop and chapter, and will faithfully observe all the above. Should the oath be omitted through negligence at the time of his institution, the vicar is to swear it before the bishop at some other time. In default of payment the goods of the vicarage are to be sequestrated, on the convent's complaint, by the bishop's authority or that of the archdeacon or his official. The prior and convent reserve the right of re-entry into Hurcott and of taking restraints and keeping them at Oldington until all arrears, and expenses consequent upon such non-payment, shall have been discharged. They bind themselves to observe the above on pain of distraint to be levied by the diocesan on their house, the church of Kidderminster, and all their movable and immovable goods. By unanimous assent they submit to the bishop's ordination in the above form. John de la Doune, vicar of Kidderminster, likewise submits to the bishop's ordination and taxation of his vicarage.[1]

The bishop, therefore,[2] wishing to reconcile the parties and mindful of the parishioners' souls, accepts the submissions, in so far as they accord with the canons, and by diocesan authority ordains that

1 Dated from Hartlebury, 14 December 1340.
2 *Hic incipit ordinacio* in margin. The bishop's ordination merely reiterates the provisions of the priory's submission.

John de la Doune and his successors in the vicarage are to receive everything contained in the convent's submission and to make the payments enumerated therein. He reserves to himself the right to supply omissions in the ordination and to interpret doubtful or obscure points, saving always the right, dignity and custom of the church of Worcester.

154 *5 July 1340 Blockley*

Inspeximus and confirmation of the ordination of a chantry at Coberley by Ds. Thomas de Berkeley of Coberley. A royal licence, dated 24 May 1336 from Woodstock,[1] has permitted the alienation in mortmain of a messuage, two tofts, four virgates of land and two marks of rent in Coberley, to a chaplain who is to celebrate Mass daily in St. Giles' church, Coberley, in honour of Our Lady and for the souls of Thomas de Berkeley, his ancestors, and all the faithful departed. By a charter dated 9 November 1337 from Coberley, and witnessed by Ds. Walter, then rector of Coberley, John Delkeston, Henry de Brocworth, John Lohaut,[2] William de Solers, and others, Thomas de Berkeley has granted the above to Ds. Walter de Bradeweye, chaplain, and his successors, to whom the two marks' rent is to be paid in equal instalments at the four usual terms—one mark each from the tenements of William Clocleford and Walter le Walkar. The founder having presented Walter [de Bradeweye] to the chantry at the altar of Our Lady,[3] has procured his institution by the diocesan. In future he and his heirs are to make presentation, but if this is not done within a month the right is to pass to the rector of Coberley, and after a further month to the bishop or, *sede vacante*, the Worcester prior. The chaplains are to reside and to minister in accordance with the ordination, and are to take an oath to that effect at the time of their institution. If any chaplain should fail to reside or to celebrate for a fortnight, unless there be just cause, the patron is to present another without delay. The chaplains are to be in the parish church on festivals, and on feasts of nine lessons are to minister with the other [clergy] at Matins, Mass and Vespers, unless lawfully prevented. They are to say the office of the dead for the souls mentioned below on the days required by the ordinal of the Sarum Use. On Sundays they are to celebrate Mass of the Holy Trinity, on Thursdays that of the Holy Spirit, on Tuesdays that of St. John the Baptist, and on the other days Mass of Our Lady, for the founder's welfare and for his soul after death, for the souls of his father and mother, those of the chantry's benefactors, and of all the faithful departed. In all their Masses the chaplains are to say for the founder the collect which begins *Omnipotens sempiterne Deus miserere*

1 Cf. *C.P.R.* 1334–38, p. 268. 2 *Lovat* below.
3 The ordination proper begins at this point.

famulo tuo Thoma &c., and after his death that beginning *Omnipotens sempiterne Deus cui nunquam sine spe misericordie supplicatur*—with mention of his name. On the anniversary of his death they are to say the office of the dead with nine psalms and lessons and as many responses. They are to be content with their portion, and are not to accept money from anyone else for the celebration of Mass. If a chaplain be convicted of so doing, he is to be removed. Should a chaplain become so old or infirm as to be unable personally to celebrate the Masses, he may say such private prayers as he can and have two Masses celebrated each week, one for the souls of the above persons, the other a Mass of Our Lady. He is not to be removed because of his disabilities. The founder wishes his heirs to see that the ordination is adhered to and, so far as he can, lays them under obligation to repair the buildings, should this become necessary through no fault of the chaplains. At times of visitation the bishop is to enquire into all the above and is to remove delinquent chaplains if their faults demand it. The founder expressly forbids the infringement of his ordination by any heir, relative, or other person, on pain of divine judgement at the last day. Witnesses: Ds. Walter, then rector of Coberley, John Delkeston, Henry de Brocworth, John Lovat, William de Solers, and others. Dated 9 November 1337 from Coberley. The bishop, therefore, commending the pious desire of Thomas de Berkeley, approves, ratifies and confirms the foundation, grant and ordination (*fundacio, dotacio, et ordinacio*) of the chantry, and inhibits anyone, under pain of greater excommunication, from maliciously infringing them or impeding the chaplains' enjoyment of their rights and portions.

155 *4 June 1342 Henbury*

Memorandum of the appointment of Ds. Roger de Charingworth, priest, as coadjutor (*coadiutor seu curator*) to the rector of Oldbury. He was to take charge of the rector's person and of the church, both in spiritualities and temporalities, until his powers were revoked.

156 *6 July 1342 Henbury*

Letters patent of the right of the abbot and convent of Glastonbury, Bath & Wells diocese, to receive 50 shillings' pension from Puckle-church parish church, they having produced their muniments at the time of the bishop's visitation.

157 *25 March 1343 Alvechurch*

Acquittance for Ds. Robert de Folwode, perpetual vicar of Tanworth, in respect of 13s. 4d. paid by him to the bishop for the year 1342, as laid down in the taxation and ordination of his vicarage.[1]

1 See 160.

158 *28 July 1343 Bidford*

Letters patent of Thomas de Poleye, rector of Barwell, Lincoln diocese, appointing Peter de Bunynton his proctor for the resignation of Quinton church in Worcester diocese. At the request of Thomas, whose seal is not widely known, the dean of the Christianity of Warwick has attached the seal of his office.

159 *29 December 1342 Hartlebury*

Ordination of Great Badminton vicarage. The bishop appropriated the church of Badminton to the Augustinian convent of Our Lady at Lilleshall, Coventry & Lichfield diocese, with reservation of a suitable portion for a perpetual vicar.[1] He now ordains the vicarage, assigning to it the following fruits, profits, rents and obventions. In the first place there are reserved to the religious the appropriated church, its demesne lands, and the tithes of sheaves of every kind from the vill and lands of Badminton, as well as the tithe of hay from the demesne and the vill, together with the whole tithe of wool and lambs and the pension, said to be as much as 10s., allegedly due from Oldbury church—if they can recover it.[2] The vicar and his successors are to have all the greater and lesser tithes, offerings and obventions from the neighbouring vills of Oldbury and Didmarton which belong to Badminton church, as well as such fruits, tithes, offerings, rents and obventions from those places, which in Badminton parish itself are reserved to the religious. The latter are to have a house built appropriate to the vicar's status, together with a dovecot as good as that now at the rectory house, and are to put the vicar who first has the cure of souls in possession of them. The religious are not to be held liable to pay tithes to the vicar for lands or other goods which they have or may have in the future within the vill of Badminton. But they are to pay to the vicar, as part of his portion, half a mark [6s. 8d.] annually at the Invention of the Holy Cross [3 May]. The vicars are to sustain all ordinary burdens, save the repair and rebuilding of the chancel, while the religious are to bear the extraordinary ones, together with the pensions due to the bishop and the cathedral chapter because of the appropriation.

160 *18–19 March 1342 Maxstoke & Tanworth*

The diocesan's copy[3] of a tripartite indenture embodying the ordination of Tanworth vicarage. The bishop appropriated Tanworth church to the prior and canons regular of the Augustinian house of Maxstoke, Coventry & Lichfield diocese, with reservation of a

1 See 450, 451.
2 Cf. *Tax. Eccles.*, p. 220b, where the pension is valued at 8s. 6d.
3 Sealed by the vicar of Tanworth and the Maxstoke canons. See below.

vicarage which he estimated at 20 marks [£13 6s. 8d.].[1] He now assigns the vicarage. The vicars are to have the house or messuage which the rectors formerly had, with its appurtenances in Tanworth. They are to receive the tithe of calves, piglets, goslings, eggs, foals, wool, milk, cheese, wax, honey and bees, gardens, curtilages, fisheries, fish, dovecots, mills, flax and hemp, both brushwood and other timber (*silve tam cedue quam non cedue*),[2] trees, fruits and pastures; excepting the tithe of the house in Tanworth parish belonging to the religious, and the fodder for their animals there. The vicars are also to have the great and small tithes of the parish; except those of corn of hay, which the canons are to have because of the appropriation, together with the messuage and curtilage adjoining the churchyard, until now occupied by the parish priests and known to be in the church's gift. But to the vicars is assigned the tithe of hay from the demesne meadows of the earl of Warwick, known as *Wodemedwe, Parkmedwe, Redefordemedwe, Rowmedwe, Lytemedwe, Stokmedwe, Burymedwe, Lutylheynesmedwe, Muchelheinesmedwe, Holumedwe, Southcroftesmedwe, Knolleburymedwe, Astonmedwe, Roundemedwe,* and all the other demesne meadows now in the earl's possession, as well as that from the meadows called *Wodardesmedwe, Tornoresmedwe, Longemedwe and Rudlingesmedwe*—which tithe is estimated at four cartloads of hay a year. They are also to have live and dead mortuaries, all offerings, obventions, annals, trentals, herbage and trees within the churchyard, and everything else belonging to the altarage of the church. The prior and canons are to be liable for the payment of pensions and for all other burdens, both ordinary and extraordinary. The vicars are to find a parish chaplain when they are themselves unable or unwilling to minister there daily, the bread and wine for the divine ministry—including that for the parishioners at Easter and other times when they are accustomed to communicate, as well as the lights (*cera*) commonly placed round the high altar, and they are to keep the lamp burning in the chancel. As compensation for this last the vicars are to receive an annual rent of 2s. 6d. from the lands and tenements of Thomas Wystan originally granted for this purpose. The vicarage must also discharge the annual pension of 13s. 4d., due to the bishop by way of indemnity, to be paid in the cathedral church at the Annunciation [25 March], as laid down in the appropriation. Vicar, canons, and diocesan are each to have a copy of the indenture sealed by the other two parties. The prior and convent of Maxstoke give consent and append their common seal to this [the bishop's] part of the indenture. Robert de Folewode, perpetual vicar of Tanworth, likewise accepts the ordination for himself and his successors, and appends his seal.[3] Dated from the

---

[1] See 321.   [2] *Silva caedua* is defined in the constitution *Quamquam ex solventibus* attributed to Abp. Stratford and glossed by Lyndwood, *Provinciale*, p. 190.

[3] Each of these two parties appended a *subscripcio* in the same form to the copy retained by the other.

chapter house at Maxstoke, 18 March, and from Tanworth, 19 March 1342.

HERE BEGINS THE REGISTER OF INSTITUTIONS, LICENCES, APPOINTMENTS, AND APPROPRIATIONS OF CHURCHES

161 *30 March 1339 Spetchley*

Licence for John de Horssleye, subdeacon, rector of Clent, to study for a year at a *studium generale* within the realm, provided that meanwhile his church be properly served, the cure of souls be not neglected, and that he appoint a suitable proctor to answer to the ordinaries.[1]

162 *3 April 1339*

Memorandum that letters dimissory for all holy orders were granted to John de Hanley, having the first tonsure. [See 163].

163 *3 April 1339 Spetchley*

Dispensation for John de Hanleye [see p. 432]. He has petitioned for appropriate remedy in that being young, simple, and ignorant of the law, and unaware, moreover, that he was sinning, he had received the first tonsure from the bishop of Bath, without licence of his own diocesan. The bishop ratifies and confirms the order, and, so far as he can, dispenses John from any disability he may have incurred. No-one is to object on such account to his free exercise of the ministry appropriate to the order.

166 *6 April 1339*

Memorandum of the licence for Godfrey de Stratford, subdeacon, rector of St. Andrew's, Worcester, to study until Michaelmas [29 September].

167 *9 April 1339*

Memorandum of a similar licence for Nicholas de Drokenesford, acolyte, rector of Pirton. It was for one year, during which time he was neither required to take further orders, except that of subdeacon, nor to reside.

168 *12 April 1339*

Memorandum of the licence for Roger Abraham, rector of Fretherne, to attend (*insistere in obsequiis*) John de Sapy, knight, for one year.

---

1 *Proviso tamen quod ecclesia tua predicta interim debitis non fraudetur obsequiis et animarum cura in eadem nullatenus negligatur, ac in ipsa procuratorem dimittas ydoneum et sufficientem qui ordinariis respondeat loco tui.*

169 *22 April 1339 Hartlebury*

Memorandum that M. Hugh de Penebrugg, *organum vocis domini constitutus*, received Ds. Ralph de Staunton's resignation of Coughton vicarage.[1]

170 *22 April 1339 Hartlebury*

Memorandum that M. Hugh likewise received Ds. John de Bisshopeston's resignation of the perpetual chantry in St. Helen's, Worcester.[2]

173 *26 April 1339 Hartlebury*

Memorandum of the licence for Philip de Gosynton, priest, rector of St. Swithin's, Worcester, to study for a year.

174 *26 April 1339 Hartlebury*

Memorandum that letters testimonial as to the orders of subdeacon, deacon and priest, were conceded to John Sharp of Nottingham, after inspection of Thomas de Cobham's register.[3]

175 *28 April 1339 Hartlebury*

Mandate to the official of the archdeacon of Gloucester. The prior and chapter of Worcester have presented Robert de Warsleye, priest, to the vacant church of Harvington, claiming that such presentation belongs to them. The official, in the full chapter of the place summoned *ad hoc*, is to hold an enquiry by a sufficient number of rectors and vicars into the vacancy and patronage of the church, and as to the status, age, orders and character of the person presented. At the instance of the presentee he is to send the result, with the names of the witnesses, to the bishop.[4]

176 *27 April 1339 Boddington*

Presentation by John de Bures, lord of Boddington, of Ds. John de Holeweye, chaplain, the bearer, to the vacant church of Kemerton. The bishop is asked to admit him *intuitu caritatis*.

1 Exchanged for a chantry in St. Helen's, Worcester. Cf. 170.
2 Exchanged for Coughton. Cf. 169.
3 He had been ordained on letters dimissory of the archbishop of York. See *Reg. Cobham*, pp. 164, 175, 194, 215.
4 *Quocirca tibi mandamus . . . quatenus an dicta ecclesia vacat, et si sic, qualiter et a quo tempore cepit vacare, quis sit eius verus patronus et quis ultimo presentavit ad eandem, an sit litigiosa, pensionaria, vel porcionaria, et si sic, cui vel quibus et in quanto, et an dictus presentatus sit liber et legitimus et in qua etate ac quibus ordinibus sit constitutus, ac de condicionibus et meritis persone eiusdem, an beneficiatus alibi existat, ac de ceteris articulis debitis et consuetis in hac parte, in pleno loci capitulo ob hoc vobis [MS. 'nobis'] celebrato per rectores et vicarios in numero sufficienti inquisicionem facias diligentem.*

177 *27 April 1339*

Memorandum of a mandate to the archdeacon of Gloucester's official for enquiry into the vacancy at Kemerton.

178 *30 April 1339 Hartlebury*

Letters to John de Holeweye, priest, admitting and instituting him as rector of Kemerton, to which he had been presented by John de Bures, knight, on the vacancy caused by the death of Ds. John de London.

Memorandum that John de Holeweye took the oath of obedience in the usual form and that the mandate for his induction was sent the same day.

Mandate to the archdeacon of Gloucester's official for the induction of the above John.

179 *29 April 1339 Hartlebury*

Mandate to the dean of the jurisdiction of Ripple (*iurisdiccionis nostre de Rippel*).[1] Ds. John Salemon of Ripple has presented Walter Hatherich, priest, to the chantry in Ripple church formerly held by John Hoghges. The dean is to hold a thorough enquiry into the vacancy of the chantry, its value, the details of its ordination,[2] the circumstances and character of the presentee, and as to the person who last made presentation.[3]

180 *29 April 1339 Hartlebury*

Commission to the dean of Pershore. Ds. John Rogers (*Rogeri*), chaplain, recently died intestate in the parish of Ripple, and there is no-one there to exercise the rector's jurisdiction in the matter. The bishop, therefore, being unwilling that the goods of the deceased should be unjustly taken, desiring rather, as behoves his office, that proper provision be made in the interests of the dead man's soul, orders the dean to sequestrate all goods within the diocese which belonged to the deceased at the time of his death, and to keep them in safe custody until he receive further instructions. Details of the goods and their value are to be sent to the bishop. The dean is to inform all whom it concerns that it is not the bishop's intention to usurp the rector of Ripple's jurisdiction, but merely to supply the defect on this occasion.

1 An episcopal manor exempt from the archdeacon's jurisdiction.
2 See 969.
3 *Quocirca tibi mandamus quatenus vocatis vocandis tam super vacacione dicte cantarie, curaque spectante ad eam, in quibusque porcionibus consistat, ac valore annuo earundem, qualiter, per quem, a quo tempore fuerit ordinata, necnon etate, natalibus, conversacione, ordinibus ac meritis persone ad eam presentate, et quis ultimo presentavit ad eam, inquisicionem facias diligentem.*

182 *2 May 1339*

Memorandum that letters testimonial as to the order of subdeacon were conceded to John Buttere of Ombersley, after inspection of Bishop Hemenhale's register.[1]

185 *7 May 1339 Hartlebury*

Memorandum that letters testimonial as to the order of priest were conceded to Nicholas de Hartlebury, after inspection of the same register.[2]

186 *8 May 1339 Hartlebury*

Memorandum of the licence for Ds. William Brescy, rector of Miserden, to study for a year at a *studium generale* within the realm. At the end of that time he was to give an account of his stay.[3]

187 *7 May 1339 Hartlebury*

Memorandum that letters testimonial as to the order of subdeacon were conceded to John de Baggepathe of Brickhampton (*Brynghampton*), Worcester diocese, after inspection of Bishop Hemenhale's register.[4]

188 *10 May 1339 Hartlebury*

Memorandum that letters testimonial as to the order of subdeacon were issued to William de Snoweshulle after inspection of the same register.[5]

189 *10 May 1339 Hartlebury*

Memorandum that letters testimonial as to the order of deacon were issued to Robert Mareschal of Ledbury, Hereford diocese, after inspection of the same register.[6]

190 *17 May 1339 Bredon*

Memorandum of the licence for M. Thomas de Lench of [Droit]-wich, dean of the collegiate church of St. Mary, Warwick, and in minor orders, to attend any *studium generale* for a year.[7]

1 Reg. Hemenhale, fo. 29r.
2 *Ibid.* fo. 32v.
3 *Voluit eciam dominus quod in fine anni de huiusmodi sua mora et usu studii sibi fidem &c.* Cf. 193.
4 Reg. Hemenhale, fo. 28v.
5 *Ibid.* fo. 35r.
6 *Ibid.* fo. 35v.
7 *Salvis ecclesie cathedralis Wyg' iuribus et ecclesie collegiate predicte consuetudinibus et statutis.*

191 *28 May 1339 Bredon*

Memorandum of the licence for M. John Trillek, priest, rector of Bredon, to leave his church for lawful reasons for five years. He was to appoint a vicar and to give an account of his absence at the end of that term.

192 *28 May 1339 Bredon*

Memorandum of the licence for Ds. Adam de Legh, priest, rector of St. Michael's, Gloucester, to be absent for one year.

193 *22 May 1339 Bredon*

Memorandum of the licence for Ds. William Brescy, rector of Miserden, to study in England for a year, and during that time to farm his church to an ecclesiastic (*alicui viro ecclesiastico*).[1]

194 *1 June 1339 Bredon*

Memorandum of the licence for M. Richard de Preyeres, sub-deacon, rector of Pucklechurch, to study in England for one year.

197 *23 June 1339 Stoneham*

Letters of [Robert Wyville], bishop of Salisbury [1330–75], collating Hanbury church, in the diocesan's patronage, to M. William de Hervynton, formerly rector of Portland, by reason of an exchange with M. John de Usk.

198 *15 June 1339 Oxford*

M. William de Hervynton, rector of Portland, Salisbury diocese, appoints Adam le Boteler, clerk, his lawful proctor to exchange Portland for any other ecclesiastical benefice, to resign it for that purpose, to obtain possession of another benefice, to accept such benefice and to receive institution to it on his behalf, to take the oath of canonical obedience and any other lawful oath, and to do everything else necessary in the circumstances, with power to appoint a substitute. At William's request the chancellor of Oxford University appended his seal.[2]

On the same day,[3] having received the oath of canonical obedience from William's proctor, the bishop wrote to the dean of [Droit]wich for his induction.

199 *26 June 1339 Bredon*

Mandate to the dean of [Droit]wich for the induction of the above M. William to Hanbury.

1 Cf. 186.
2 Hervynton is mentioned in 1338 as a regent doctor in Civil Law at Oxford. *Snappe's Formulary*, p. 77.
3 *Sic.* In fact it was 26 June.

200 *3 July 1339*

Memorandum that the bishop wrote to the official of the Gloucester archdeacon for the holding of an enquiry into the vacancy of Little Sodbury church, to which John de Bretonia, priest, had been presented by Jordan of Little Sodbury.

201 *7 July 1339 Bredon*

Memorandum of the licence for Ds. Hugh de Babenton, priest, rector of St. Stephen's, Bristol, to leave his church and to attend the abbess of Shaftesbury for a year from Michaelmas next [29 September].

202 *8 July 1339 Bredon*

Memorandum of the licence for M. Richard de la Felde, rector of Witley, to farm his church to a suitable person for two years.

203 *9 July 1339 Bredon*

Memorandum that the bishop relaxed until 19 July the sequestration of the rector of Dry Marston's goods, imposed on his authority by the dean of Campden. The dean was to allow the rector to dispose of them freely, but at the end of the term the sequestration was to be reimposed failing other instruction.

204 *12 July 1339 Bredon*

Memorandum that the bishop heard, examined and discussed, on the authority of [William Melton], archbishop of York [1317–40], the reasons for the exchange of benefices between William Barneby, warden (*custos*) of the chapel or hospital of Longbridge by Berkeley, and Ds. Thomas de Baldene, priest, warden of the chapel of Our Lady at Norton, York diocese. Finding them to be true and lawful, the bishop approved, consented to, and authorised the exchange, received the resignations of the parties, and admitted William to Norton chapel, to which he had been presented by Hugh de Hastyng, knight, but reserved to the archbishop his induction and oath of canonical obedience. He also appointed Thomas de Baldene to Longbridge chapel, in his collation for that turn. Mandate for the latter's induction was sent to the official of the Gloucester archdeacon.

206 *9 August 1339*

Memorandum of the licence for Ds. John le Bor, vicar of Dodderhill, to farm his vicarage to Ds. Adam de Boreford, priest, for a year from Michaelmas [29 September].

208 *9 August 1339*

Memorandum of the licence for Ds. John de Wycombe, rector of Lasborough, to leave his church.

209 *29 August 1339*

Memorandum of the licence for Ds. John Haym, rector of Stow, to attend Ds. William de Everdone, rector of Fladbury, for one year.

210 *2 September 1339 Hartlebury*

Memorandum of the licence for Peter FizWaryn, rector of Tortworth, to study for a year at a *studium generale* within the realm.

211 *22 September 1339 Hartlebury*

Memorandum of the licence for Ds. Richard de Tadynton, rector of Weston-on-Avon, to leave his church for two years from Michaelmas [29 September].

212 *22 September 1339 Woodford*

Letters of [Robert Wyville], bishop of Salisbury [1330–75], to John de Carlton, priest, instituting him on the diocesan's authority to Hatherop church, to which he had been presented by the abbot and convent of St. Peter's Gloucester, by reason of an exchange with M. Henry de Lodelowe for Laverstock vicarage, in the bishop's own diocese and patronage.

213 *25 September 1339 Hartlebury*

Memorandum that the bishop wrote to the official of the Gloucester archdeacon for John de Karlton's induction to Laverstock [*sic*].

214 *26 September 1339 Hartlebury*

Memorandum of the licence for M. Roger de Astone, Professor of Civil Law, to farm his prebend of Moreton and Whaddon [in Hereford cathedral] for three years.

215 *28 September 1339 Hartlebury*

Memorandum of the licence for Ds. Robert de Clyfton, rector of St. Michael's, Worcester, to attend Lady Isabella de Clare[1] for a year.

---

1 Maurice de Berkeley (ob. 1326) married secondly Isabella, daughter of Gilbert de Clare, the son of Richard de Clare, earl of Gloucester, and of his first wife Alicia, daughter of Guy, earl of Angouleme. Isabella was born 10 March 1263 and is said (G.E.C. *Complete Peerage* 2, pp. 128–9) to have died without issue in 1333 (7 Edw. III). But the Isabella de Clare in 269 below is termed *domina de Berkeley*.

216 *29 September 1339 Hartlebury*

Memorandum of the licence for Thomas de Astmede, rector of Horton, to study for one year.

219 *16 October 1339 [Worcester]*

Memorandum of the commission for the archdeacon of Gloucester's official to enquire into the vacancy of Combe Baskerville church, the reasons for its exchange with Knightwick, the right of presentation to it and the person who last presented, and as to the orders, character, and conversation of Ds. William de Clifford, whom M. Philip de Ullingwyk had presented. If the enquiry found for the presentee, the official was to admit, institute and induct him, saving the right, custom and dignity of the cathedral church.

220 *16 October 1339*

Memorandum of the licence for Godfrey de Stretford, rector of St. Andrew's, Worcester, to study for a year at a *studium generale*,[1] in accordance with the constitution *Cum ex eo*.[2]

221 *15 October 1339 Worcester*

Memorandum of the licence for Ds. Thomas de Shirebourn, rector of Sapperton, to remain in a place of learning, *vel alibi dumtamen in loco honesto*, for two years, and to farm his church to any suitable person for that period.

222 *12 September 1339*

Memorandum of the licence for M. William de Herwynton, rector of Hanbury by Droitwich, to study for a year in accordance with the constitution *Cum ex eo*.[3]

223 *18 October 1339 Worcester*

Memorandum of the licence for M. John de Severleye, rector of Billesley, to study *in scolis litterarum ubi viget studium generale* for one year.

224 *23 October 1339 Upton*

Memorandum of the licence for Ds. William Marchal, rector of Dorsington, to remain *in scolis litterarum . . . vel alibi dumtamen in loco honesto* for one year.

---

1 From an unnamed feast. The words *tempore confeccionis* are crossed out and *festo* is interlineated.
2 *Sext* I, 6, c. 34.
3 *Sext* I, 6, c. 34. Cf. 197–8.

225 *6 November 1339 Honington*

Memorandum of the licence for Ds. Richard Deyvill, rector of Evenlode, to study in a *studium generale* in England for one year from Michaelmas last [29 September] and to farm his church for that period.

227 *10 November 1339 Hampton*

Memorandum that the bishop, on the authority of [Roger Northburgh], bishop of Coventry & Lichfield [1322–58], approved the exchange between Henry de Schulton, priest, rector of Stretton-on-Fosse, and John de Wentebrygg, clerk, rector of Southam, Coventry & Lichfield diocese. He admitted and instituted Henry to Southam church (patrons: prior and conv. of Coventry), and John to Stretton (patron: John de Leycestre). After receiving John's oath of canonical obedience, the bishop wrote to the dean of Blockley for his induction.

228 *12 November 1339 Warwick*

Memorandum that the bishop, on the authority of [Robert Wyville], bp. of Salisbury [1330–75], approved the exchange between Ds. Peter de Lench, priest, rector of Church Lench, and Ds. Robert de More, vicar of Chirton, Salisbury diocese. He admitted and instituted Peter to Chirton vicarage (patrons: prior and conv. of Llanthony by Gloucester), and Robert to Church Lench (patron: Thomas de Beauchamp, earl of Warwick). The mandate for Robert's induction was sent to the official of the Worcester archdeacon.

229 *6 November 1339 Blockley*

Letter to Simon Cromp, monk of Worcester, informing him of his appointment as prior, on the death of Simon le Botiller, and committing to his care the spiritualities and temporalities of the priory.[1]

230 *6 November 1339 Blockley*

Mandate to the subprior and convent of Worcester. The bishop has chosen Br. Simon Cromp as prior from among the seven monks presented to him [cf. 38] and has committed to his care the administration of the priory's spiritualities and temporalities [229]. They are to obey the new prior's canonical and lawful mandates.

On the same day the bishop wrote to the archdeacon of Worcester for the prior's induction.

1 Cf. 38–40, 92–93.

231 *15 November 1339 Rowington*

Letters patent of the appointment, until the bishop ordains other-wise, of Br. Richard Colys, monk of Worcester, as sacrist of the cathedral church.

232 *15 November 1339 Rowington*

Mandate to the prior and convent of Worcester, informing them of Colys' appointment as sacrist and directing them, on their obedience, to allow him to exercise the office and to dispose of those things pertaining to it. Without delay they are to deliver up the keys and everything else which by custom belongs to the office.

233 *23 November 1339 Hartlebury*

Memorandum of the licence for Ds. Robert de Warsley, rector of Harvington [by Evesham], to attend the prior of Worcester for a year.

234 *25 November 1339 Hartlebury*

Memorandum of the licence for Ds. Richard, rector of St. Martin's, Worcester, to leave his church for three years and to farm it for that period to M. Robert, archdeacon of Worcester.[1]

238 *7 December 1339 Hartlebury*

Memorandum of the licence for Ds. Thomas de Oxon, rector of Little Rissington, to study for a year in a [*studium generale*], *vel alibi dumtamen in loco honesto.*

240 *9 January 1340 Hartlebury*

Memorandum of the licence for Ds. William de Syde, priest, to choose a suitable priest as confessor and to celebrate Mass (*divina officia*), both in person and by a suitable chaplain, in his oratories within St. Augustine's abbey, Bristol, and Berkeley castle.[2]

241 *30 December 1339 Hartlebury*

Letter to John Botoner, priest, conferring on him the church of Halford, in episcopal collation, and instituting him as rector, saving to the diocesan and his successors the right, custom and dignity of the cathedral church.[3]

---

1 The marginal rubric runs: *Licencia studendi et ecclesiam ad firmam dimittendi.* In the entry itself *studio insistere litterarum ubicumque viget studium generale* has been crossed out and *ab ecclesia sua predicta licite valeat absentare* interlineated.

2 William de Syde was Thomas lord Berkeley's chaplain.

3 Marginal rubric: *Collacio et institucio rectoris ecclesie de Halford.* Ordinarily the term *collation* was reserved for benefices in the bishop's patronage, *institution* being used in all other cases. But this distinction is not maintained in the present register.

19 January 1340

Mandate to the archdeacon of Worcester's official[1] for the induction of John in the person of his proctor, M. Thomas Bolvynch of [Droit]wich.

242 *5 March 1340 Horsley*

Memorandum of the commission for Br. Richard de Bradel', monk of Kingswood, to exercise the office of penitentiary.

243 *12 December 1339 Hartlebury*

Letters patent of the appointment, jointly and severally, of Masters John de Walton and Philip le Yonge, clerks of Hereford and Worcestor dioceses respectively, to act as the bishop's proctors in the Roman Curia. In testimony thereof the bishop has had the letters written down and published by a notary. The proxy is to remain in force for two years.

Subscription of R[obert] de Marny of Bishops Cleeve, clerk of Worcester diocese, notary public by apostolic authority. He was present during the proceedings, together with Masters J[ohn] de la Lowe, Hugh de Peneb[rugg], and John Botoner, clerks and witnesses to the above, and at the bishop's command wrote and published the letters, adding his customary sign.

244 *15 May 1340 Bredon*

Letters patent of the appointment, jointly and severally, of Richard de Thormerton, canon of Westbury, and John de Walton, clerks, as the bishop's proctors (*procuratores, negociorum gestores, et nuncios speciales*) for prosecuting the case in the Roman Curia against M. Philip le Yonge, calling himself vicar of Bromsgrove. This has arisen from certain processes touching the bishop and his church, involving suspension, interdict or excommunication, which at the instance of Philip have been effected on apostolic authority.

Notarial subcription of Robert de Marny of Bishops Cleeve, notary public by apostolic authority. Witnessed by Br. Nicholas de Stanlak and Masters Hugh de Penebrugg and John Botoner, clerks.[1]

245 *6 May 1341 Loxley*

Memorandum that in Loxley church the underwritten parishioners[3] swore on the Holy Gospels, in the bishop's presence, to render to the Worcester prior and chapter and to the office of chamberlain there,

1 It was unusual for the mandate for induction to a benefice in the bishop's collation to be directed to the archdeacon's official.
2 Cf. 243.
3 The schedule of names is not recorded.

arrears of an annual sum of 18s. due at the Purification [2 February] but unpaid for three years. Half of the money was to be paid at the Nativity of Our Lady [8 September], the other half at St. Andrew [30 November]. The parishioners also swore to make payment at each subsequent Purification. Present were Masters John de la Lowe, John de Peyto senior, John Botoner, Ds. William de Preston and Ds. Thomas de Vaston, priests, and Ds. William, vicar of Eatington.

246 *15 January 1340 Hartlebury*

Memorandum of the licence for Nicholas de Drokenesford, deacon, rector of Pirton, to attend M. John de Gadesdene until Michaelmas and from then until the same feast in the following year, and to farm his church to any suitable person.

247 *13 January 1340 Hartlebury*

Memorandum of the licence for Margaret, widow of Richard Bikerton, to have Mass (*divina*) celebrated in an oratory within her house at *Hilyngwyk*.

248 *23 January 1340 Hartlebury*

Memorandum that the bishop approved the exchange between Ds. John de Merston, rector of St. Alban's, Worcester, and Ds. Hugh Straddel of Gloucester, vicar of Tibberton. He admitted and instituted John to Tibberton (patrons: prior and conv. of Worcester), *prestito per eum prius iuramento de residencia corporali in dicta vicaria facienda*, and Hugh to St. Alban's rectory (patrons: abbot and conv. of Evesham). Mandate for their induction was sent to the archdeacon of Worcester's official.[1]

250 *6 February 1340 Sedgeberrow*

Memorandum of the licence for Leonard de Lucy, rector of Cherrington to study for a year at a *studium generale* within the realm.

251 *8 February 1340 Alderton*

Memorandum of the licence for John Besemancel to have a chaplain to celebrate Mass (*divina*) in an oratory within his house at Alderton.

252 *13 February 1340 Broadway*

Memorandum of the licence for Ds. Henry Morys, rector of Daylesford, to farm his church for three years from last Michaelmas [29 September].

1 Cf. 204.

253 *13 February 1340 Broadway*

Memorandum that the bishop, on the authority of Gaucelinus, bishop of Albano, Pope Benedict XII's penitentiary, dispensed Nicholas, son of Richard le Taillor of Childs Wickham, from the defect of illegitimacy (*super defectu natalium quem paciebatur inter solutum genitus et solutam*).

255 *14 February 1340 Ebrington*

Memorandum of the licence for Thomas Boteller, knight, to have for two years a chaplain or chaplains to celebrate Mass (*divina*) within his manors of Badminton and Weston sub-Edge.

256 *9 December 1339 St. Denis, Paris*

Presentation by Guy, abbot of St. Denis, of Br. Ralph de Ermenovilla, the bearer, whom he has appointed prior of Deerhurst. In accordance with the composition arising out of the dispute between the bishop's predecessors Godfrey Giffard [1268–1302] and Walter Cantilupe [1237–66] and the then abbot, Matthew, the abbot of St. Denis should present the new prior to the bishop, not by reason of the priory but of the parochial cure attached to it.[1] The abbot requests the admission of Br. Ralph to the parish church in accordance with the composition, Br. John de Vetolio having been recalled because of infirmity and for other lawful reasons.

257 *8 February 1340 Winchcombe*

Letter to Br. Ralph de Ermenovilla admitting and instituting him to the cure of Deerhurst parish church, in accordance with the composition [of 1269] between Godfrey Giffard, sometime bishop of Worcester [1268–1302], and Matthew, formerly abbot of St. Denis.

258 *8 February 1340 Winchcombe*

Mandate to the dean of Winchcombe for the induction of the above Br. Ralph.

259 *21 February 1340 Fairford*

Memorandum of the commission for Br. Walter de Stowe, a friar of Lechlade, to exercise the office of penitentiary for a year among the parishioners of Lechlade church.[2]

---

1 An earlier composition was confirmed by Cantilupe in 1265 (*Reg. Giffard*, p. 10), the other dates from 1269 (*ibid.*, p. 37; Liber Ruber, fo. lxxxvi v.). In 1312 Reynolds, at the instance of the prior of Deerhurst, had published *ad memoriam futurorum* all the admissions, institutions and oaths of obedience recorded in Giffard's register. See *Reg. Reynolds*, p. 40.

2 *Corruptoribus monialium et casu periurii in assisis, exheredacionibus et indictamentis ubi vertitur causa sanguinis dumtaxat exceptis.* Cf. 43, 151.

260 *22 February 1340 Fairford*

Memorandum of the commission for M. Stephen, rector of Fairford, to act as a penitentiary among his parishioners.

261 *24 February 1340 Sherborne*

Memorandum of the similar commission for Br. Thomas de Mammeshull, canon of Oseney, to act among his parishioners at Bibury.

262 *24 February 1340*

Memorandum that the bishop admitted Br. William de Bourz, from the Gloucester house of the order of Preachers, to hear the confessions of the bishop's subjects within the limits of that house and to enjoin salutary penances, in accordance with the *constitucio novella* which begins *Super cathedram.*[1]

263 *28 February 1340 Cirencester*

Memorandum of the licence for Ds. Nicholas Weston, rector of Littleton, to leave his church for one year and to attend the abbot of Malmesbury.

264 *28 February 1340 Cirencester*

Memorandum of the licence for Ds. Ralph de Wylynton, knight, to choose a chaplain as confessor.

265 *28 February 1340 Cirencester*

Memorandum of the licence for Ds. John de Carlton, rector of Hatherop, to farm his church for one year to Walter, parochial chaplain of Coln St. Aldwyn.

266 *28 February 1340 Cirencester*

Memorandum that the bishop admitted witnesses who successfully proved that John Richemon of Ampney St. Mary had been ordained deacon to the title of patrimony in the conventual church of Winchcombe on Saturday in Embertide, the eve of Holy Trinity 1324,[2] by Br. Robert [le Petit], bishop of Clonfert, on the authority of Bishop Thomas de Cobham.

---

1 Incorporated in *Clement* 3, 7, c. 2 *Dudum*. See also *Extrav. Commun.* 3, 6, c. 2.
2 i.e. 9 June 1324. In fact the ordination was held on Trinity eve [5 June] 1322. See *Reg. Cobham*, p. 125 *et seq.*

267 *3 March 1340 Minchinhampton*

Memorandum of the licence for John de Anseleye, knight, to have Mass (*divina*) celebrated by suitable chaplains in the oratories of his manors of Minchinhampton and Down Hatherley.

268 *4 March 1340 Horsley*

Memorandum of the commission for Ds. Henry Costantyn, vicar of Great Sodbury, to hear the confessions of all the bishop's subjects within the deanery[1] of Hawkesbury and Bitton, to enjoin salutary penances, and to absolve them even in cases reserved to the bishop, but with certain exceptions.[2]

269 *5 March 1340 Kingscote*

Memorandum of the licence for Br. Henry de Wotton, from the Bristol house of Friars Minor, to hear the confessions of Isabella de Clare, lady of Berkeley,[3] and of her family, to enjoin upon them salutary penances, and to grant absolution except in certain cases.[4]

270 *5 March 1340 Horsley*

Memorandum of the licence for Ds. Simon Basset, knight, to have Mass (*divina*) celebrated by a suitable chaplain within his manor of Uley.

271 *6 March 1340 [Leonard] Stanley (monachorum)*

Licence for Henry de Clyfford and his wife Matilda to have Mass (*divina*) celebrated by suitable priests for two years within an oratory in their manor of Daneway (*Deneweye*) in Bisley (*Byleslegh*) parish.

272 *6 March 1340 [Leonard] Stanley*

Memorandum of the licence for Margery Bartram to have Mass (*divina*) celebrated in an oratory within her house at Alderton for two years.

273 *7 March 1340 Standish*

Memorandum of the similar licence for Robert Dabitot within his manor of . . .[5]

1 Or *deaneries*. MS. *decanat'*.
2 *corruptoribus monialium, fractoribus* [*parcorum*] *et maneriorum suorum et casu periurii in assisis, exheredacionibus et indictamentis &c.* Cf. 43, 151, 259.
3 See 215.
4 *corruptoribus monialium et fractoribus parcorum suorum et casu periurii in assisis &c.*
5 Blank in MS. The duration of the licence is also omitted.

274 *8 March 1340 Gloucester*

Memorandum of the licence for Ds. Maurice de Berkeley[1] to have Mass (*divina*) celebrated by six priests in his oratory at Uley for two years.

275 *8 March 1340 Gloucester*

Memorandum of a similar licence granted to Henry de Brocworth (*sub forma predicta*).

276 *8 March 1340 Gloucester*

Memorandum of the similar licence granted for two years to William de Mathesdene within his oratory at Brockworth.

277 *11 March 1340 Prestbury*

Memorandum of the similar licence granted for two years to Robert de Longedon within his oratories of Longdon and *Holibed* in Castle Morton parish.[2]

278 *15 March 1340 Winchcombe*

Memorandum of the licence for Ds. James, rector of Eckington, to leave his church for three years and to farm it to Ds. Richard Spelly during that period.

279 *25 October 1339 Kidderminster*

Letter to Isabella de Fokerham, nun of the Benedictine house of Wroxall. Because of the vacancy caused by Agnes de Broy's resignation, and by virtue of the faculty granted to him,[3] the bishop appoints and institutes Isabella as prioress, committing to her custody both the spiritualities and temporalities, but reserving pontifical and archidiaconal rights and the dignity of the cathedral church.

280 *25 October 1339 Kidderminster*

Mandate to the official of the Worcester archdeacon for the induction and installation of Isabella de Fokerham as prioress of Wroxall. He is to see that the sisters of the house render due obedience to her, restraining the recalcitrant by ecclesiastical censure.

1 Brother of Thomas lord Berkeley (the third baron) and son of Maurice de Berkeley (see p. 51 n. 1). He is called *Maurice de Berkeley of Uley* in 735 (witness list).
2 Cf. 83. *Holibed* survives in *Hollybed Common* (E.P.N.S. *Worcs.*, p. 214), but in 1340 Castle Morton was a chapelry of Longdon.
3 By the subprioress and convent, though the phrase has been omitted. Cf. 281.

281 *Undated*[1]

Letters patent declaring that the bishop's appointment of the prioress of Wroxall, made by the authority and with the unanimous consent of the subprioress and convent, would not prejudice the nuns' rights of free election at future vacancies.

282 *22 March 1340 Hartlebury*

Memorandum of the licence for Ds. Peter de Mountfort, knight, to choose a suitable priest as confessor.

283 *22 March 1340 Hartlebury*

Memorandum of the appointment of M. Robert de Chikwell, canon of London, as the bishop's proctor in the parliament summoned to Westminster for 29 March,[2] *ut supra in procuratorio proximi parliamenti &c.*[3]

284 *22 March 1340 Winchcombe*

Letter from Richard de Iddebury, abbot of Winchcombe, asking to be relieved of his office and dignity for lawful reasons.

285 *24 March 1340 Hartlebury*

Letter informing the king that the bishop had received the abbot of Winchcombe's resignation on 22 March, and considering it to be in the interests of the monastery and of Br. Richard's welfare, had accepted it on the 23rd and absolved the abbot from his cure and rule.

286 *25 March 1340 Hartlebury*

Memorandum of the appointment of a penitentiary[4] in the deanery of Pershore, certain cases being excepted.[5]

288 *1 April 1340 Hartlebury*

Memorandum that the diocesan received a certificate, dated from Belvoir 24 March 1340, to the effect that Henry [Burghersh], bishop of Lincoln [1320–40], had carried out the exchange of benefices between M. John Trillek, rector of Bredon, and M. John de Orlton, rector of Witney, Lincoln diocese. He had collated Bredon, in the diocesan's collation, to Orlton, in the person of his proctor John de Beautr', clerk.

1 Probably as above, 25 October.
2 The second session of the 1340 parliament.
3 A reference to 137.
4 Unnamed.
5 The cases are those in 268 with the addition of *percussoribus clericorum*.

On the same day [1 April] the rector of Strensham was ordered to induct Orlton.

289 *12 April 1340 Hartlebury*

Mandate to the dean of Campden. The bishop has learned from the prior and convent of Winchcombe that on the vacancy caused by Br. Richard de Iddebury's resignation,[1] they canonically elected Br. William de Shirebourn, a fellow monk, as abbot, and they now seek confirmation of such election. The dean is therefore to make citation either by name (*nominatim*), if any come forward, otherwise publicly (*generaliter . . . palam et publice*) in the conventual church, that any opponent or co-elect is to appear before the bishop or his commissaries on 24 April to propound objections and to proceed as laid down by the canons. The term is adequate, though shortened because of the manifest danger of the situation.[2] The dean is to certify the bishop or his commissaries of his execution of the mandate and is to send the names of those cited, if any.

290 *21 April 1340 Worcester*

Letter from the convent of the cathedral priory. Owing to the death of Prior Simon Crompe[3] on 10 April, the monks on the 21st nominated seven of their number for presentation to the bishop: Brothers Nicholas Morice, the subprior; Henry Fouk, the infirmarian; John de Westbury, the precentor; John de Evesham, Bachelor in Theology; Robert de Weston, the cellarer; John de Leye and William de Birlingham. Brothers Nicholas de Stanlak and John de Preston junior are being sent as special proctors.[4]

291 *Undated*

The bishop appoints John de Evesham as prior of Worcester in accordance with the composition.[5]

292 *22 April 1340 Hartlebury*

Letter to John de Evesham, monk of Worcester, informing him of his appointment as prior and committing to his care the spiritualities and temporalities of the priory.[6]

293 *22 April 1340 Hartlebury*

Memorandum that the bishop wrote to the subprior and convent of Worcester, informing them of John de Evesham's appointment and ordering them to render him obedience.[7]

---

1 See 284–5.
2 In the event the election was quashed (295 *et seq.*), but the phrase is common form.
3 Appointed in 1339. See 229.
4 Cf. 38.   5 Cf. 39.   6 Cf. 92.   7 Cf. 40, 93, 230.

294 *22 April 1340 Hartlebury*

Mandate to the official of the Worcester archdeacon. He is to put John de Evesham in possession of the cathedral priory and to assign him a stall in choir and a place in chapter.

295 *18 April 1340 Hinton*

Certification by the dean of Campden of his execution of the bishop's mandate concerning the abbot of Winchcombe's election.[1] As no co-elect or opponent came forward whom he could cite by name, he caused public citation to be made in the conventual church of Winchcombe and the chapter house there, in the presence of the prior and convent.

296 *24–26 April 1340 Alvechurch*

Judicial proceedings (*acta*) concerning the election of Br. William de Shyrebourn as abbot of Winchcombe, held before the bishop in Alvechurch parish church. The elect appeared personally, the abbot and convent by Brothers William de Gloucester and William de Elmeleye. The dean of Campden's certificate [295] was read; pronouncement was made at the entry to the chancel and at the church doors that all opponents were to come forward; the alleged election of Br. William was declared by M. William le Boys, rector of Twyning, examiner general of the Court of Canterbury;[2] a decree was published prohibiting further objection to the election or the person of the elect; the election decree and other instruments were produced on behalf of the prior and convent, for whom appeared two *instructores*, Brothers Walter de Tewkesbury and Robert de Aldrynton, monks of Winchcombe, and five witnesses: Thomas ate Halle of Sherborne, Henry Veysy of the same, Ralph Bryd of Admington, John Hikkes of the same, and Walter de Snowsulle of Sherborne, who, on being admitted and sworn, were precluded from bringing forward additional evidence; the examination of the witnesses was committed to M. Hugh de Penebrugg and M. Henry Tankard, and the following Wednesday appointed for further proceedings. On that day the parties appeared as before, the witnesses' attestations were published, and lengthy discussion of them and of the election decree took place, after which by the consent of the parties the case was concluded and the bishop pronounced definitive sentence.

297 *[26 April 1340]* *Alvechurch*

The bishop, on the advice of his legal assessors,[3] declares void the election of William de Shirebourn and deprives the prior and con-

---

1 See 289.   2 He is not in Churchill's list: *Cant. Admin.* 2, p. 240.
3 *de iuris peritorum nobis assidencium concilio.*

9

vent of their right of election in this instance, on the grounds that
the election contravened the *forma compromissi*,[1] was in other ways
uncanonical, and that the prior and convent had knowingly approved it.

298 [*26 April 1340*] *Alvechurch*

The bishop, having quashed the election of William de Shirebourn,
appoints him abbot of Winchcombe.[2]

299 *26 April 1340 Alvechurch*

Letter to Br. William de Shirebourn informing him of the quashing
of his election and of his subsequent appointment as abbot, and
committing to his care the spiritualities and temporalities of the
monastery.

300 *14 May 1340 Bredon*

Mandate to the archdeacon of Gloucester or M. John de la Lowe, the
Official, for the induction and installation of William de Shyrebourn
as abbot of Winchcombe.

301 *26 April 1340 Alvechurch*

Mandate to the prior and convent of Winchcombe, informing them
of Shyrebourn's appointment and ordering them to render him due
obedience.

302 *Undated*

Letter to the king requesting the restoration of the temporalities of
Winchcombe Abbey.

307 *3 May 1340 Alvechurch*

Memorandum that after he had seen the certificate of [Robert
Wyville], bishop of Salisbury [1330–75], giving details of his execution of the commission for the exchange of the churches of Tormarton
and Brightwalton, Salisbury diocese, and had inspected Ds. John de
Astweyt's letter of institution [to Tormarton], the diocesan received
the latter's oath of canonical obedience and ordered the dean of
Hawkesbury and Bitton to induct him.

1 One of the three canonical methods of election laid down in *Extra* 1, 6, c. 42 *Quia
propter*, the other two being the *via scrutinii* and the *via inspiracionis*.
2 *In nomine patris et filii et spiritus sancti, auctoritate nostra diocesana et iure nobis devoluto in hac
parte, prefati monasterii de Wynch' eligimus et preficimus in abbatem, ipsique monasterio pro-
videmus canonice de eodem.*

309 *4 May 1340 Alvechurch*

Memorandum of the licence for M. Thomas de Lench of [Droit]-wich, dean of the collegiate church of St. Mary, Warwick, to farm his deanery until All Saints [1 November].

310 *10 May 1340 Hartlebury*

Memorandum of the licence for John Huwet of Rowley to have Mass (*divina*) celebrated *submissa tamen voce* in an oratory within his grange of Blakeley for a period of three years.

313 *29 May 1340 Hawkesbury*

Memorandum of the licence for Ds. John de Lughteburgh, rector of Rodmarton, to leave his church for two years.

315 *31 May 1340 Pucklechurch*

Memorandum of the licence for Ds. Thomas Thornhulle, rector of Shipton Moyne, to leave his church until Michaelmas [29 September] and for a year thereafter, and to attend Robert Selymon, knight.

317 *8 June 1340*

Memorandum of the licence for Ds. William de Treswell, rector of Salwarpe, to be absent for a year.

318 *19 May 1340 Bredon*

Provision for Br. Richard de Iddebury, formerly abbot of Winch-combe. The bishop has received the prior and convent of Winch-combe's letter dated 4 March, declaring Iddebury's labours on the monastery's behalf, his intention—of which the bishop has been informed—to resign his office because of age,[1] and requesting that provision be made for him, having regard to the resources of the house. They promise to abide by the terms of the award (*ordinacio, disposicio et provisio*), each of the monks having sworn individually to do so (*submissio, promissio, iuramenti prestacio*). The bishop, therefore, determines that Br. Richard, in recompense for his labours on the monastery's behalf and the benefits he has bestowed upon it, and because of his former dignity, is to have a chamber in the infirmary with the buildings next to it. He is to receive daily three monks' loaves of the accustomed weight (*antiqui ponderis*), two loaves for trenchers (*trenchours*), and four jugfuls (by common measure) of the better ale. From the abbot's kitchen he is to have meat or fish as the abbot, either raw or cooked as he prefers, as well as fish from the conventual kitchen and, like the abbot, cheese when he wants it,

1 Iddebury's letter in the register is dated 22 March. See 284-5.

or half a wey annually. For his chamber he is to receive yearly five pounds of wax, twelve pounds of Paris (*paris'*) [1] candles, and fuel as required. He may choose a chaplain at will—after the abbot's chaplain has been chosen—and his chaplain is to enjoy the same perquisites as the latter. He may also have a squire,[2] a servant [?],[3] and a groom,[4] who are to be treated as their counterparts in the abbot's household.[5] In addition to the common portions from the *camera* and the pittancer, he is to receive an annual sum of £10, payable during his lifetime from the common goods of the monastery in equal instalments at or within ten days of the four usual terms: St. John the Baptist [24 June], St. Michael [29 September], Christmas and the Annunciation [25 March]. The bishop enjoins Abbot William [de Shyrebourn], Thomas de Hereford, the prior—*here followed the names of all the monks* [6]—to observe the above as they had sworn to do, on pain of excommunication.[7] For Br. Richard's greater security the abbot and monks are to ratify the ordination and to bind themselves by oath to uphold it. The bishop reserves the right to supply defects in his ordination and to interpret doubtful points. The abbot and convent append their ratification (*ratificacio, promissio, iuramenti prestacio et consignacio*), dated 20 May from Winchcombe.

319 *8 June 1340 Henbury*

Memorandum of the commission for the official of the Worcester archdeacon, or his *locum tenens*, to hold an enquiry—without awaiting the full chapter of the place [8]—into the vacancy of St. Andrew's church, Droitwich, the right of patronage there and that of the presentor for the occasion, and into the life, character, birth, orders and age of William Beste, priest, presented by the prior of Deerhurst, the alleged patron. If the enquiry found for the presentee, the official was to admit and institute him, to receive his oath of canonical obedience, and to carry out his induction.

321 *17 June 1340 Henbury*

Letters patent of the appropriation of Tanworth church. The bishop has received a petition from William de Clynton, earl of Huntingdon. The earl had founded and endowed a house of Augustinian canons regular at Maxstoke in Coventry archdeaconry [Coventry & Lichfield diocese], for the salvation of his own soul, those of his ancestors,

1 Cf. Liber Albus, fo. 214: *sex libras candelarum parisien'*.
2 Or donzel (*domicellus*).   3 homo de *mest*[*aria?*].   4 *garcio*.
5 Squire and groom were specifically entitled to receive clothes and food.
6 The scribe did not bother to record them in the register.
7 He pronounced the threefold canonical warning in advance, thus rendering contraveners *ipso facto* excommunicate.
8 Cf. 175.

and of all the faithful departed. Immediately afterwards the number of canons was increased,[1] so that now the original endowment no longer suffices for their needs, for their special obligation of hospitality —it being well known that the house is near a public highway, the erection of new buildings and the repair of old ones, and for the support of other recent burdens. He therefore asks the bishop to relieve the canons' necessities by appropriating to them the parish church of Tanworth, the advowson of which he has already granted. The bishop, approving the worthy and holy intention of the earl for the increase of divine worship, and having regard to the fervour of devotion which has kindled in him so worthy a design, has found, after careful discussion with the Worcester chapter, that the first endowment is now clearly inadequate, and that the other reasons advanced are true and lawful. Therefore, after invocation of the Holy Spirit, and with the express consent of the chapter, having summoned all interested parties—everything else being as required by law, he has decreed the appropriation of the church to the canons, to be held by them in perpetuity to their own uses. On the cession or death of the present rector the religious may lawfully take possession of the fruits and profits of the church, saving a suitable portion— estimated at 20 marks [£13 6s. 8d.]—which is to be assigned by the diocesan to a vicar who is to exercise the cure of souls. The bishop reserves the right, dignity and honour of the church of Worcester, and also an annual pension of two marks of silver and one stone of wax due *ab antiquo* from the church to the monastery of Kenilworth.

322 *1 October 1340 Hartlebury*

Licence for Brothers William de Lobbenham, Professor of the Sacred Page, Matthew de Gloucester, John de Soutborn, Robert de Abyndon, Robert de Burmynton and John of Worcester, priests of the Carmelite house at Bristol, to preach publicly the word of God to the bishop's subjects, to hear the confessions of those wishing to be confessed, to absolve them and to impose salutary penances, in accordance with the constitution *Super cathedram*[2] and by virtue of a special papal privilege granted to the bishop.

323 *30 May 1340 Lambeth*

Private letter from [John Stratford], archbishop of Canterbury [1333–48], received at Eastington 30 June together with a royal charter of the liberties of the English Church and a writ for the levying of a tenth granted by the clergy.[3] The archbishop, as a

---

1 In 1331 Sir William de Clinton, as he then was, established a secular college in Maxstoke parish church. It was refounded as a priory of canons regular in 1336. See the introduction, p. xlii *et seq.*
2 *Clement* 3, 7, c. 2.   3 Marginal rubric.

result of his efforts to restore the position of the Church (*circa reformacionem status ecclesie Anglie*), has procured after great labour a royal charter granting fuller liberties—as was determined unanimously in the last convocation of the clergy of Canterbury province.[1] The king is sending the charter by the bearer of the present letter.[2] The archbishop urges the bishop to deposit it safely in his cathedral so that the Church may enjoy such fuller liberty in times to come. Moreover, he has learned that the king intends to take the cardinals' procurations for the present year from the collectors by way of loan—and by force if necessary, which would greatly prejudice both himself and his suffragans. He has suggested to the king that on this occasion as much of the tenth should be kept in the hands of the collectors as is received in the king's name from the procurations. In this way the cardinals can be satisfied and the threatened danger averted. He counsels the bishop to do this.

324 *19 June 1340*

Memorandum that after he had seen the certificate of [Simon de Montacute], bishop of Ely [1337–45], giving details of his execution of the commission for the exchange of the churches of Suckley and Little Gransden, Ely diocese, and had inspected Ds. John de Weston's letter of institution [to Suckley], the diocesan received the latter's oath of canonical obedience and wrote to the archdeacon of Worcester's official for his induction.

325 *11 & 13 March 1342*

The prior and convent of Maxstoke's copy of the Tanworth vicarage ordination, sealed by the bishop at Hartlebury 11 March, and by Robert de Folewarde, the vicar, at Tanworth 13 March.[3]

326 *28 June 1340 Berkeley*

Letter to Eleanor, prioress of St. Bartholomew's hospital, Bristol, and the sisters of the place. In view of the lawful reasons brought forward during his recent visitation and the petition presented to him at that time, the bishop grants the sisters special licence to lease for sixty years to J. Fysshwer and his wife, and to their son J., the ancient dormitory of their hospital in which the sisters used to lie when there were both brethren and sisters, as well as a plot nearby called *Lowynesmede*, next to the burial ground of their house, 80 feet long and 12 feet wide. They may build appropriately on these sites to the profit and advantage of the hospital, and are to pay an annual rent of five shillings.

1 This met 27 January 1340. A tenth was granted on conditions: see 1142.
2 The clerical petitions were conceded in the fourth statute of the 1340 parliament. See Stubbs, *Const. Hist.* 2, p. 383; Tout, *Chapters* 3, p. 105. Harriss, 'The Commons' Petitions of 1340', *E.H.R.* LXXVIII, pp. 625–654.
3 Cf. 160.

327 *22 May*[1] *1340 Henbury*

Memorandum of the licence for Ds. William Briscy, rector of Miserden, to leave his church for a year and to farm it for that period to a suitable person.

328 *16 June 1340 Henbury*

Licence, in so far as lies within the bishop's power,[2] for Ds. Hugh, perpetual vicar of Henbury, to leave his church[3] and to visit the shrine of Our Lady of Walsingham, his parents and friends. Meanwhile his church is not to be defrauded of its due services, nor the cure of souls neglected, and a suitable proctor, able to answer to the bishop and other ordinaries, is to be appointed. As a protection against slanderous tongues (*morsus detrahencium*) the bishop has caused the letters to be issued patent under his seal.

329 *10 July 1340 Blockley*

Appropriation of Campden church. The bishop has received a petition from the abbot and convent of St. Werburgh, Chester, Coventry & Lichfield diocese. In it they allege that as their monastery is near a seaport they have to bear heavy and insupportable burdens —magnates and poor men staying in their house while awaiting a passage, as well as various tallages and imposts. Since the foundation of the monastery they have lost by inundation and the sea's irresistible force more than thirty carucates of land from the vills and manors of Bromborough, Eastham, Whitby and Ince,[4] stretching ten miles along the shore and inland for more than half a mile—an irreparable loss of £100 a year, and one which increases daily. Moreover, various manors in Wales—Broughton, Dyserth and Holywell church, have been irrecoverably lost owing to the wars between the English kings and the princes of Wales, while most of the monastic church and the entire tower are so obviously decayed that anyone ministering there hazards his life. For all these reasons the monks are seeking help to support burdens for which their resources are inadequate. The bishop, having learned the truth of the above by an enquiry, and with the consent of the Worcester chapter, grants and assigns to the monastery *in proprios usus* the church of Campden, which is already in the monks' patronage and from which they have formerly received an annual pension of ten shillings. On the cession or death of the present rector they can take possession on their own authority,

---

1 Apparently an error for *June*.
2 *tibi quantum de iure possumus*. The bishop's dispensatory powers were not considered to extend to vicars. Athon discusses the point in his gloss ad ver. *Residentiam* (*Const. Othonis*, pp. 26–7).
3 The duration of the licence is not stated, a blank being left in the MS.
4 In the Wirral peninsula.

saving the rights of the diocesan, the church of Worcester, and the archdeacon. The bishop reserves from the fruits of the church a suitable portion—estimated at £20—for the support of a vicar. Such portion is to be ordained by himself or his successors and may be increased should this prove necessary.[1] The vicar is to be presented by the abbot and convent for institution and induction by the diocesan.

335 *24 July 1340*

Memorandum of the licence for the rector of Alcester to be absent for a year.

336 *27 July 1340 Bredon*

Memorandum of the licence for Ds. William Beste, rector of St. Andrew's Droitwich, to leave his church and to attend Hugh le Despenser.[2]

337 *28 July 1340 Fladbury*

Memorandum of the licence for Ds. William de Wodemonton, rector of Bagendon, to leave his church from Michaelmas next [29 September] until the same feast in 1341, and to farm it for that period.

338 *30 July 1340 Kempsey*

Memorandum of the licence for Ds. Adam Esgar, rector of Haresfield, and Roger de Stanford, rector of St. Helen's Worcester, to attend Thomas [Charlton], bishop of Hereford [1327–44], for two years.

339 *30 July 1340 Kempsey*

Memorandum of the licence for Ds. Roger, rector of Fretherne, to be absent for one year and to attend John de Sapy, knight.

340 *3 August 1340 Hartlebury*

Memorandum that on the authority of Simon de Islep, vicar-general of [Henry Burghersh], bishop of Lincoln [1320–40], then *in remotis*, the diocesan approved the exchange of benefices between Thomas de Oxon', rector of Little Rissington, and Thomas de Ippewell, rector of Wood Eaton, Lincoln diocese. He admitted and instituted Thomas de Oxon', by his proctor M. Robert de Crissale, to Wood Eaton (patrons: abbot and conv. of Eynsham), ordering the archdeacon of Oxford or his commissary to induct him, and likewise

1 See 595.
2 Son of Hugh le Despenser the younger. No term is given.

Thomas de Ippewell to Little Rissington (patrons: abbot and conv. of Oseney), sending the mandate for induction to the Gloucester archdeacon or his official.

341 *6 August 1340 Hartlebury*

Memorandum of the diocesan's approval on the same authority [v. 340] of the exchange between Ds. John Davy of Dodford, rector of Oxhill, and Ds. John de Baynton, vicar of Dodford, Lincoln diocese. The bishop admitted and instituted Davy to Dodford vicarage (patrons: prior and conv. of Luffield), with the obligation of residence, and John de Baynton to Oxhill (patron: William de Kaynes, kt.), directing the Worcester archdeacon's official to induct the latter.

342 *14 August 1340 Wick-by-Worcester*

Licence[1] for Robert de Hasele, rector of Dyrham, to leave his church for two years and to remain in the Court of Canterbury on the business of the prior of Lewes, as well as to farm his church meanwhile to any suitable person. At the end of the term he is to give proof *in forma iuris* of his prosecution of the prior's affairs.

343 *16 August 1340 Worcester*

Memorandum of the licence for Roger de Asswelle, rector of Acton Turville, to leave his church for two years and to farm it to William de Walton, chaplain, for that period.

344 *29 August 1340 Hartlebury*

Memorandum of the licence for M. John de Severleye, rector of Billesley, to leave his church for one year.

345 *4 September 1340 Hartlebury*

Memorandum of the licence for Peter FizWaryn, subdeacon, rector of Tortworth, to study in England for one year.[2]

346 *15 September 1340 Hartlebury*

Memorandum of the licence for Ds. John Wodekoc, rector of Fulbrook, to leave his church for two years.

1 Subject to the usual conditions: *proviso tamen quod ecclesia tua predicta debitis non defraudetur obsequiis et animarum cura in eadem minime negligatur, quodque procuratorem ydoneum ibidem dimittas qui nobis et aliis ordinariis tuis ceterisque quorum interest respondere valeat vice tua.*
2 Subject to the usual provisos. See above.

347 *13 April 1340 Hartlebury*

Letters patent of the bishop's induction of the abbot and convent of Evesham to Ombersley church, the appropriation of which had been effected by Bp. Thomas [de Cobham] [1] and confirmed by Pope John XXII, the abbey receiving an annual pension as a sign of possession.

348 *11 September 1340 Bosbury*

Letter of Thomas [Charlton], bishop of Hereford [1327–44], reciting the diocesan's commission dated 2 September from Hartlebury, for the exchange of benefices between Ds. Roger de Stanford, rector of St. Helen's Worcester, and Ds. Richard called *Clerk*, rector of Rock, Hereford diocese. After examination and approval of the reasons for exchange, he accepted the parties' resignations, collated St. Helen's (in the diocesan's patronage) to Richard, in the person of his proctor, Ds. William de Kentles, and instituted him as rector, with the reservations made in the commission. [2]

12 September 1340

Memorandum that the diocesan wrote to the dean of Worcester for the induction of Richard called *Clerk* or his proctor, whereupon the proctor took the oath of canonical obedience.

350 *25 September 1340 Hartlebury*

Memorandum of the licence for M. Thomas de Bradewell, rector of Coln St. Dennis, to study for two years. [3]

351 *24 September 1340*

Letter from William de Herwynton, abbot of Pershore, asking licence to surrender his office on account of old age and bodily infirmity.

352 *26 September 1340*

Letter from Abbot William de Herwynton formally resigning his office, having received the bishop's licence to do so. [4]

353 *27 September 1340 Hartlebury*

The bishop informs the prior and convent of Pershore that he has received Herwynton's resignation and at the instance of Ds. Adam de

1 In 1326. *Reg. Cobham*, p. 199.
2 The oath of canonical obedience and induction.
3 *dumtamen ecclesia sua predicta debitis obsequiis et pauperes eiusdem ecclesie sue parochiani congruis elemosinis arbitrio dicti patris canonice moderandis interim non fraudentur, ac hospitalitas &c., procuratoremque &c., fructusque ecclesie sue predicte in domibus rectorie integraliter reponi faciat &c.*
4 See 351.

Herwynton, his own very dear friend, whom the abbot had sent to urge his suit, has accepted it, considering this to be in the interests of the monastery and of the abbot's welfare.

354 *17 September 1340 Bredon*

Memorandum that the bishop dispensed John Wodelond of Withington from the defect of illegitimacy, by authority of Gaucelinus, bishop of Albano, the papal penitentiary.

355 *3 October 1340 Hartlebury*

Memorandum of the dispensation in accordance with the constitution *Cum ex eo*[1] for M. Thomas de Astmede, rector of Horton, to study at a *studium generale* for two years.

356 *11 October 1340 Hartlebury*

Memorandum of the licence for Ds. Henry de Bradewas, rector of Weston Birt, to leave his church for one year.

358 *3 November 1340 Alvechurch*

Memorandum of the licence for Ds. John Kyniot, rector of Clifford, to study for one year.

360 *6 November 1340 Alvechurch*

Memorandum of the licence for Ds. Hugh de Babeton, rector of St. Stephen's Bristol, to attend the abbess of Shaftesbury until Michaelmas next [29 September 1341].

361 *Undated*[2]

Certification by the archdeacon of Worcester's official of his execution of an episcopal mandate, dated 31 October from Alvechurch, for the citation of opponents of the election of T. de Pyriton,[3] cellarer of Pershore abbey, which followed upon the resignation of William de Herwynton.[4] On Friday after All Saints [i.e. 3 November] he went to the abbey church, but not finding R. de Lutlynton, the co-elect, or any proctor of his, he was unable to cite him personally. He did make public citation that Lutlynton and any others who wished to oppose the election were to appear before the bishop or his commissaries on the Thursday after St. Leonard [i.e. 9 November].

1 *Sext* I, 6, c. 34.
2 It was probably dated 3 November.
3 *Ut supra in proclamacione abbatis de Wynch'*. See 289.
4 See 351 *et seq.*

362 *Undated* [1]

Mandate to the official of the Worcester archdeacon for the further citation of R. de Lutlynton—in person if he can be found, otherwise openly in the conventual church of Pershore and among his acquaintances and friends—to appear in Hartlebury parish church on the Tuesday after St. Martin [i.e. 14 November].

363 *29 September 1340 Hartlebury*

Memorandum of the licence in accordance with the constitution *Cum ex eo* [2] for Godfrey de Preston, rector of St. Andrew's Worcester, to study for two years. [3]

364 *29 September 1340 Hartlebury*

Memorandum of the licence for Ds. Adam de Legh to study for two years. [4]

365 *Undated*

Certification by William de Herwynton, Professor of Laws, rector of Hanbury by [Droit]wich, of his execution of a mandate for the citation of Robert [de Lutlynton]. [5] He has found the co-elect and cited him by name.

366 *9 & 14 November 1340 Alvechurch*

Judicial proceedings (*acta*) concerning the contested election of Brothers Thomas de Pyriton and Robert de Lutlynton as abbots of Pershore, held before the bishop in the chapel of his manor of Alvechurch. Pyriton appeared in person, Lutlynton did not appear, although properly summoned. Adam de Opton acted as proctor for Pyriton's electors—the prior, and Brothers William de Herwynton, Henry de Staunton, W. de Cleobury, Roger de Clyve, W. Baret, J. Colewall, William Porter, Henry de Besford, J. de la Hay, Robert de Wotton, Robert de Clyfton, Philip de Stone, J. de Clehangre, W. de Brerhull and J. de Leygrove. Those who elected Lutlynton did not appear. The elections were published by M. W[illiam] de Herwynton, Professor of Civil Law, rector of Hanbury; the official of the Worcester archdeacon's certificate of citation [361] was produced; pronouncement was made at the manor gate that all who wished to oppose Pyriton's election should put forward their objections, and as no-one appeared all future objection was precluded. On Pyriton's

---

1 Probably dated 10 or 11 November as the previous mandate had been returned and the date appointed for the proceedings [9 November] had clearly passed.
2 *Sext* I, 6, c. 34.
3 A sign in the margin refers back to a similar one above 355.   4 Cf. 192.
5 *Ut supra in proxima littera usque ad verbum*—a reference to 362.

behalf were produced certain articles and his election decree, and on the king's part, his licence to elect and consent to the election, as well as seven other instruments sealed with the monastery's common seal and a public instrument under the hand of a notary. Two *instructores*, Brothers W. Baret and J. Colewall, were brought forward, and also four witnesses: Brothers W. Porter and J. de la Hay, monks of Pershore, and M. William Adelmynton and Master J. Kinytel of *Wych*, clerks. When these had been admitted and sworn, the Tuesday after St. Martin [i.e. 14 November] in Hartlebury church was appointed for further proceedings. On that day Herwynton's certificate of citation [365] was read and Br. Richard de Lych appeared as proctor for Lutlynton's electors, with the request that his election be confirmed. Lutlynton did not appear and was declared contumacious, being thereby precluded from taking further part in the proceedings. The [witnesses'] attestations were published and after lengthy discussion of them and of the election decree, and with the consent of the elect and his electors, the bishop proceeded to definitive sentence. Having thoroughly examined the processes of the elections, that of Pyriton made by way of scrutiny by the prior and 15 monks, and that of Luttleton by 13 other monks, he finds that both contravened the form of the General Council;[1] he therefore declares them void and deprives the chapter of their right of election for the occasion.

367 *Undated*[2]

The bishop, having quashed both elections at Pershore, appoints Thomas de Pyriton as abbot.[3]

368 *14 November 1340 Hartlebury*

Letter to the king giving details of the Pershore election and requesting restitution of the abbey's temporalities.

369 *19 November 1340 Hartlebury*

Inspeximus and confirmation of letters of the archdeacon of Worcester's official, dated 20 July 1340 from Kidderminster, declaring that, as the bishop's special commissary, he had admitted and instituted Ds. John de la Doune, priest, to the vicarage of Kidderminster, vacant by the death of Master J. Karsleye[4] and in the patronage of the hospital of Maiden Bradley, Salisbury diocese. The bishop also confirms other letters of the official certifying John's induction.[5]

1 The IVth Lateran. Cf. 297.
2 Probably 14 November.
3 Cf. 298.
4 Karsleye (Careslegh) had in fact been the rector. Cf. 153.
5 Marginal rubric: *Littere testimoniales institucionis et induccionis vicarii de Kydermunstre.*

370 *1 September 1340 Berkhamstead*

Writ of *ne admittas*. The bishop is not to admit anyone to the vacant church of Whatcote, the advowson of which is the subject of a suit in the king's court between Robert le Wolf and John de Morhalle.

371 *23 November 1340 Hartlebury*

Memorandum of the bishop's receipt of a royal writ, dated 15 November from Westminster, informing him of the recovery by John de Morhalle and his wife, Amicia, of the right of presentation to Whatcote, and directing him to admit a suitable person, notwithstanding the opposition of Robert le Wolf.

373 *24 November 1340 Hartlebury*

Memorandum of the dispensation for Thomas de Morhall to study for one year in accordance with the constitution *Cum ex eo*.[1]

374 *14 November 1340 Hartlebury*

The bishop informs Br. Thomas de Pyriton of his appointment as abbot of Pershore.[2]

375 *26 November 1340 Hartlebury*

Mandate to the archdeacon of Worcester or his official for the induction and installation of Thomas de Pyriton as abbot of Pershore.[3]

376 *26 November 1340 Hartlebury*

Letter to the prior and convent of Pershore directing them to obey their new abbot.[4]

377 *28 November 1340 Hartlebury*

Commission for the prior of Worcester to examine and admit three clerks—Richard de Hengsceseye, John Troubrugg and Robert de la Lee—whom, in accordance with custom, he had presented to the bishop for admission to the monastic order in the church of Worcester.

378 *6 December 1340 Hartlebury*

Memorandum that, as all the conditions for a lawful exchange were in being, the bishop admitted and instituted Ds. Richard de Billesleye, priest, to Hawling rectory (patrons: abbot and conv. of

1 *Sext* I, 6, c. 34.   2 See 365 *et seq.*
3 Cf. 300.   4 Cf. 301.

Winchcombe) and Ds. Robert Belde of Stratford, priest, to the vicarage of Great Barrington (patrons: prior and conv. of Llanthony by Gloucester). He ordered the official of the Gloucester archdeacon or his *locum tenens* to induct them.

380 *16 December 1340 Hartlebury*

Memorandum of the licence for Ds. John de Sevenhamton, rector of Didmarton, to leave his church for a year and to attend the prior of Bath.

383 *18 December 1340 Hartlebury*

Memorandum that the bishop wrote to the dean of Stow for the induction of M. John [Botoner] to Naunton and to the dean of Kineton for that of Robert [Marny] to Halford.[1]

384 *2 January 1341*

Memorandum that the bishop, at the presentation of Ds. Peter de Lonuceio Alerynelni, who had been empowered to act by John, abbot of St. Peter of Castellion, Conches, in Evreux diocese, admitted Br. John de Silvaneto to the church and priory of Wootton Wawen, vacant by the resignation of Br. John de Lotoveris, and instituted him as prior. After receiving his oath of canonical obedience the bishop wrote to the archdeacon of Worcester's official for his induction.

385 *6 January 1341 Hartlebury*

Memorandum of the licence for Ds. Philip de Warleye, rector of Wickwar, to leave his church until Michaelmas [29 September].

386 *6 January 1341 Hartlebury*

Memorandum of the licence for M. Henry de Ombresl', rector of Welford, to choose a priest as confessor.

388 *16 January 1341 Hartlebury*

Memorandum that the bishop, on his own authority and by virtue of the commission of Ds. Bernard Umentis canon of St. Emilion, proctor, vicar-general in England, and *ad hoc* commissary of Raymond, cardinal deacon of New St. Mary's [St. Francesca Romana], the dean of Salisbury, examined and approved the exchange between John Crowe, rector of the chapel of St. Nicholas, Earley, in the decanal jurisdiction of Sonning, Salisbury diocese, and Roger Colicote,

1 See *Institutions* 381, 382.

vicar of Lower Swell. The bishop instituted Roger to Earley chapel (patron: Humphrey de Rokele) and John de Lower Swell (patrons: abbot and conv. of Notley)—after the latter had taken an oath of residence in accordance with Ottobon's constitution. The archdeacon of Gloucester or his commissary was ordered to induct John.

395 *9 March 1341 Hartlebury*

Memorandum of the licence for Ds. Robert Aylwy, priest, rector of Badminton, to attend the earl of Lancaster[1] for one year and to leave his church.

396 *9 March 1341 Hartlebury*

Memorandum of the licence for Ds. Yvo de Edenham, rector of Daglingworth, priest, to study at a *studium generale* in England for a year and to farm his church for that time.[2]

397 *25 March 1341 Hartlebury*

Memorandum that Br. Simon de Barton, abbot of Hulton, received benediction in the bishop's chapel, by letters dimissory of [Roger Northburgh], bishop of Coventry & Lichfield [1322–58].

398 *12 April 1341 Hartlebury*

Memorandum of the licence for Ds. Philip de Gosynton, rector of St. Swithin's Worcester, to leave his church for a year and to farm it.

400 *18 April 1341 Hartlebury*

Memorandum that, at the presentation of the abbot and convent of St. Taurin, Evreux diocese, the bishop admitted and instituted Br. Ralph de Valle, monk of that monastery, to the wardenship (*custodia*) of Astley priory, and appointed him prior. Ralph took the oath of canonical obedience and swore that he would pay the portions due to the vicar at the appointed times and would respect the other rights of the vicarage, which had been anciently ordained. The official of the Worcester archdeacon was ordered to put him in possession of the priory.

401 *22 April 1341 Hartlebury*

Memorandum of the licence for M. Richard de Billesleye, rector of Hawling, to remain in a place of learning, or elsewhere *dumtamen* [*in*]

---

1 Henry, earl of Lancaster and Leicester (ob. 1345), the brother of Thomas, earl of Lancaster (exec. 1322).
2 *Ita tamen quod in fine dicti anni de mora sua et usu studii fidem faciat dicto patri in forma iuris.*

loco honesto, until Michaelmas [29 September] and from then until the same feast in the following year, as well as to farm his church.

404 *27 April 1341 Avignon*

Bull of Pope Benedict [XII] received at Blockley 30 May.[1] Hugh le Despenser, lord of Tewkesbury, son of Hugh le Despenser [the younger], deceased, and Elizabeth Montacute, daughter of William de Montacute, earl of Salisbury, of Worcester and Salisbury dioceses, have petitioned the pope, with the king's support, to remove the impediment to their proposed marriage, so that the former quarrels between Hugh le Despenser [the younger] and the earl, and their friends and relatives, may be quieted thereby. The impediment arises from the fact that Giles de Badlesmere, the late husband of Elizabeth, was related to Hugh in the third degree of consanguinity. The pope, therefore, desiring the welfare and peace of all, orders the bishop, should he find this to be so, to dispense the parties by apostolic authority.

405 *31 May[2] 1341 Blockley*

The bishop, as sole executor of the above papal letters, after observing the lawful process, grants dispensation for Hugh le Despenser and Elizabeth Montacute to marry.

406 *13 June 1341 Blockley*

Memorandum that the prior of Worcester was empowered to receive Ds. Peter Fraunceys of Worcester, priest, as a brother of St. Wulstan's hospital there, and to induct him in the habit worn *ab antiquo* by the brothers.[3]

407 *Undated*

Form of letter to be sent to the king's chancellor for the capture of an excommunicate.

408 *18 June 1341 Hampton Bishop*

Memorandum that the bishop appointed Ds. Peter Fraunceys of Worcester as preceptor of the hospital of St. Wulstan there, which belonged to his presentation *pleno iure*, committing to him during pleasure the care of the spiritualities and temporalities.[4]

1 Marginal rubric. See *C.P.L.* 1305–42, p. 553.
2 MS. *xxxii* [*sic*] *die Maii*.
3 See 408–9.
4 It appears that the bishop had dispossessed Robert de Merston, the former precentor, who later ventilated his grievances at the Curia. *C.P.L.* 1342–62, p. 70, and see *Introduction*, p. xlvii.

10

409 *18 June 1341 Hampton*

Memorandum that the Worcester prior was ordered to induct the above Peter, to receive his lawful obedience in the bishop's name, and to enjoin the brothers of the hospital to obey him.

412 *26 June 1341 [Blockley]*

Memorandum of the licence for Ds. Walter Dastyn, knight, to have Mass (*divina*) celebrated in oratories within his manors of Dumbleton and Wormington.

413 *29 June 1341 Blockley*

Memorandum that the diocesan, on the authority of [Thomas Charlton], bishop of Hereford [1327–44], approved the exchange between Ds. William Wyring', rector of St. Aldate's, Gloucester, and Ds. Henry de Wygemore, rector of Little Cowarne, Hereford diocese. He admitted and instituted William to Cowarne (patrons: abbot and conv. of St. Peter's, Gloucester) and Henry to St. Aldate's (patron: prior of Deerhurst), and ordered the archdeacon of Gloucester or his official to induct the latter.

414 *8 July 1341 Blockley*

Memorandum that the executors of the will of Ds. Walter de Morton, deceased, formerly rector of Hampton Bishop, rendered account of their administration before the bishop, who discharged them from their duties.

415 *29 July 1341 Withington*

Memorandum that the bishop granted dispensation to Robert Fraunceys, acolyte, who without letters dimissory had received the first tonsure from Roger [Mortival], bishop of Salisbury [1315–30], and had subsequently been advanced to all lesser orders by Bishop Robert [Wyville] of that diocese [1330–75].

416 *29 July 1341 Withington*

Memorandum that the bishop ordered the official of the Worcester archdeacon to induct Ds. John de Flete to Suckley church, for which he had exchanged the wardenship (*custodia*) of *Sydingburnbrok* hospital, London diocese,[1] and to which he had been presented by the king who held the temporalities of Newent priory by reason of the war with France. On the diocesan's authority he had been admitted and instituted as rector by Ralph [Stratford], bishop of London [1340–54].

1 Near Brentwood, Essex. See Tanner, *Notitia*, p. 135.

417 *26 July 1341 Westbury*

Certification by the dean of Westbury that in accordance with the bishop's mandate, dated 21 July from Withington,[1] he had gone in person to the conventual church of St. Augustine, Bristol, on the feast of St. James [25 July], and both in the choir and elsewhere cited opponents of the election [of Br. Ralph de Assch] to come forward. As none did so, he made general citation in accordance with the tenor of the mandate. His own seal not being widely known, he had appended that of the deanery of Bristol.

418 *31 July–2 August 1341 Withington*

Judicial proceedings (*acta*) concerning the election of Br. Ralph de Assch as abbot of St. Augustine's, Bristol, held before the bishop in Withington parish church.[2] The elect appeared personally, the prior and convent in the person of M. Robert de Netlynton. The dean of Westbury's certificate was read [417]; pronouncement was made at the church doors and at the entry to the chancel that all opponents were to come forward; the decree of the alleged election, four notarial instruments, and nine other sealed documents were produced on behalf of the elect and the prior and convent, for whom appeared two *instructores*, Brothers Walter de Schaftebury and William Axe, and one witness, Br. William de Iweleye, canons of the monastery, who, on being admitted and sworn, were precluded from bringing forward further evidence. The Thursday after St. Peter ad Vincula [i.e. 2 August] at the same place was appointed for the publication of the attestations and for further proceedings. On that day the parties appeared as before, the attestations were published, the business of the election was set forth by M. Robert [de Netlynton], and the elect and the prior and convent were forbidden to produce further proofs. After discussion of the [election] decree, the attestations, and the process, the bishop with the consent of the parties proceeded to confirm the election.[3]

419 *31 July 1341 Withington*

Confirmation of the election of Br. Ralph de Assch, canon of St. Augustine's Bristol, as abbot of that house, he having been canonically elected.

420 *2 August 1341 Withington*

Letter to Queen Philippa informing her of the confirmation of Assch's election and asking that she do what pertains to her in the matter.

1 The original recited the convent's request for confirmation but the entry merely refers back to 289 (*Ut supra in proclamacione abbatis Wynchecombie*).
2 Cf. 296.
3 The scribe began the confirmation but recommenced it on the dorse of the folio.

421 *2 August 1341 Withington*

Letter to Br. Ralph de Assch recalling his election by way of scrutiny [1]
on the death of John Snow, the last abbot of St. Augustine's Bristol,
informing him of its confirmation, and committing to his care the
administration of the temporalities and spiritualities of the house.

422 *30 August 1341 Withington*

Mandate to the prior of St. James's Bristol for the induction of Br.
Ralph de Assch, whose election the bishop has confirmed and on
whom he has bestowed benediction.

423 *3 August 1341 Withington*

Memorandum of the licence for M. Roger de Midelton, rector of
Boxwell, to leave his church for one year and to attend the abbot of
Cirencester. [2]

424 *5 August 1341 Withington*

Memorandum of the licence for Ds. William Brescy, rector of
Miserden, to leave his church for a year and to farm it for that
period.

425 *9 August 1341 Withington*

Memorandum that the will of Thomas de Rysele, rector of Barnsley
chapel, was proved before the Official, acting as the bishop's special
commissary. He committed the administration to Simon, the rector's
brother, and to John Nenur, the executors named in the will.
Probate before the dean of Bibury and his grant of administration
were declared null as having been made without authority (*tanquam
facta per eum ad quem eadem facere non pertinuit*). [3]

429 *29 August 1341 Withington*

Memorandum of the licence for M. John de Severleye, rector of
Billesley, to leave his church for two years.

430 *29 August 1341 Withington*

Memorandum of the licence for Warin Trussel, knight, and his wife
Matilda, to have Mass (*divina*) celebrated in an oratory within their
manor of Billesley for two years.

---

1 See p. 64 n. 1.
2 William Hereward, 1335–52.
3 Testamentary powers undoubtedly belonged to the dean of the exempt jurisdiction of
Bibury and it is not clear why the official intervened in this instance.

431 *2 September 1341 Withington*

Memorandum that the bishop admitted and instituted Ds. Geoffrey ate Cherche of Great Waltham to Barnsley church, in the person of his proctor Ds. William de Preston, rector of Hethe, and at the presentation of Humphrey Bo[h]un, earl of Hereford and Essex, lord of Brecon. After the proctor had taken the oath of canonical obedience, the dean of Bibury, warden of the exempt jurisdiction of that place, was directed to carry out the induction. The rector had appointed William de Preston his proctor for securing the benefice on 1 September. Present as witnesses were M. Peter de Avebury and Ds. Thomas de Vascon, rector of St. Nicholas', Worcester. Marny.[1]

432 *2 September 1341 Withington*

Memorandum that the bishop revoked his injunction (*monicio*) to Ds. Thomas, rector of Cam, to reside in his church in accordance with the Canons. Present were Brothers Thomas de la Lee and Nicholas de Stanlak, monks of Worcester. Marny.[2]

433 *3 September 1341 Withington*

Memorandum of the dispensation in accordance with the constitution *Cum ex eo*[3] for M. Geoffrey de Welleford, subdeacon, rector of Bishampton, to study for five years.

436 *12 September 1341 Withington*

Memorandum of the licence for M. Thomas de Bradewell, rector of Coln St. Dennis, to leave his church for two years from Michaelmas next [29 September].

439 *11 October 1341 Alvechurch*

Memorandum that the bishop, on the authority of Roger [Northburgh], bishop of Coventry [1322–58], approved the exchange between M. Richard Praers, rector of Pucklechurch, and Ralph de la Rode, rector of Hodnet, Coventry & Lichfield diocese. He admitted and instituted Ralph, by his proctor M. John de Midelton, to Pucklechurch (patron: Ralph [of Shrewsbury], bp. of Bath [1329–63]), and Richard to Hodnet (patrons: prior and conv. of Shrewsbury). The official of the Gloucester archdeacon was ordered to induct the former.

440 *12 October 1341 Alvechurch*

Memorandum that the bishop approved the exchange between Ds. William de Heyberar, vicar of Frocester, and Ds. Henry de Wygemor,

---

1 See p. 2 n. 4.   2 *Ibid.*   3 *Sext* I, 6, c. 34.

rector of St. Aldate's Gloucester.[1] After receiving their resignations he admitted and instituted William to St. Aldate's (patron: prior of Deerhurst) and Henry to Frocester (patrons: abbot and conv. of St. Peter's, Gloucester). The official of the Gloucester archdeacon was ordered to induct them.

442 *21 October 1341 Hartlebury*

Memorandum that the bishop approved the exchange between Ds. Stephen de Greneburgh, vicar of Feckenham, and Ds. John ate Grene, rector of Stanton. He admitted and instituted Stephen to Stanton (patrons: abbot and conv. of Winchcombe) and John to Feckenham (patron: the king, the temporalities of Lyre Abbey being in his hand on account of the war with France). The official of the Worcester archdeacon was ordered to induct the latter, the official of the Gloucester archdeacon the former.

448 *30 December 1341 Hartlebury*

Memorandum of the dispensation in accordance with the constitution *Cum ex eo*[1] for Clement de Weston, acolyte, rector of St. Martin's Worcester, to leave his church for two years and to farm it for that period.

449 *Undated* [1341?][3]

Letters patent of the bishop's ordination of Tormarton chantry. John de la Rivere, lord of Tormarton and patron of the church, wishing to increase divine worship and the number of those ministering there, assigned and appropriated to the church and its rector a messuage and two carucates of arable land in Tormarton for the support of four chaplains (apart from the rector) to celebrate Mass, two clerks—one in subdeacon's and the other in deacon's orders—to serve the church continually and to sleep there at night, and three choristers. He has asked the bishop to make regulations for them. In the morning, at an hour varying with the season, bells are to be rung for Matins. On non-festival days one bell is to be rung for a long period, then, after an interval, another for half as long as the first, and finally, after a correspondingly shorter interval, two bells are to be rung together for a short period. On solemn festivals the second and third rings, and on Sundays and ordinary feasts all three, are to be made with two bells, with the same intervals as above. The bells are to be rung in the same manner for Vespers. Immediately

---

1 Which he had only recently received in exchange for Little Cowarne. See 413.
2 *Sext* I, 6, c. 34.
3 There is another ordination (1211) dated 1 May 1344. The present one has been crossed out and *vacat* written in the margin. It has many details not in the other entry and appears to be an earlier arrangement.

the ringing ceases the chaplains, clerks and choristers, in white surplices and black almuces, are to be in the quire ready to sing Matins and, as they think fit, either to say or sing all the canonical hours, though these are to be sung (*dicantur cum nota*) on the greater festivals. There are to be three Masses. The first, of Our Lady, is to be sung with three collects—of Our Lady, for the living, and for the departed. The second is to be a said requiem for the souls of those named below, with three collects—for the departed, for peace, and for the living. The third, the Mass of the day, is to be sung with three collects—of the day, for the living, and for the departed. Until these services are finished the ministers, save for good reason, are not to leave the church or remove their robes. On the days appointed by the Sarum Use, after the first bell has been rung for Vespers and until the end of the peal, prayers are to be said for the souls of John, the founder, and his wife Margaret—after death, and for those of John's father and mother, his ancestors and descendants, the patrons of the church and other benefactors, the chantry chaplains, and all the faithful departed. Vespers and Compline are to be sung daily. On the day of the founder's burial, on his anniversary and those of his wife, father and mother, and of all the patrons of the church, there are to be prayers and solemn sung Masses for the departed with nine lessons, copes and tunicles being worn except at Easter time. The curfew is to be rung every evening with a single bell. On feasts of Our Lady, particularly the Assumption [15 August], the divine office is to be celebrated with special solemnity. The rector is to be resident and to exercise the spiritual cure with the chaplains, or through one of them deputed for the purpose. When present at the offices he is to wear a white surplice and an almuce with black fur or silk, according to the season. He is to pay graded stipends to the chaplains, clerks and choristers, the payments being sufficient to procure competent ministers. He is also to be responsible for the vestments and other ornaments. Five sets (*paria*) of vestments have been provided for the high altar: violet for non-festival days, red for Easter and solemn feasts of martyrs and apostles, green for Christmas and solemn feasts of confessors, white for the five feasts of Our Lady and other solemn feasts of virgins, and black for anniversaries.[1] In the Lady Chapel are three sets: a white one for Masses of Our Lady on non-festival days, a more costly set for Sundays and other common feasts, and a third set in black for requiem Masses.[2] For the nave altars of St. Anne & St. Joachim there are two sets of vestments with towels and altar cloths for the use of untitled priests wishing to celebrate Mass. A gilded box holds a gold cross with a particle of wood from Christ's cross and a crystal jar containing a drop of the Virgin's milk, as well as other relics. Also provided are two silver-gilt

1 The red, green and white sets having a cope and tunicles.
2 All apparently without cope and tunicles.

morses for the copes, three chalices, three corporals, two missals, two graduals, two breviaries with musical notation, ten surplices and ten almuces. All these have been given to the church by the founder, and for their repair and replacement he has granted a hundred rams (*arietes*) to the rector, who is to pass on the same number to his successors. The rector is also to keep a light burning in the chancel and every Good Friday during the founder's lifetime, and after his death on his anniversary, he is to distribute a halfpenny loaf and a herring to each of a hundred poor persons in memory of the founder and those named above. For greater security the bishop decrees that the rector, and his successors at the time of their admission, are to swear to carry out the obligations laid upon them, under penalty of paying 100s. each to the cathedral church, the bishop, the archdeacon of Gloucester, and the patron of Tormarton church. Should a chaplain, clerk, or chorister have to be replaced, and the rector fail to do this within a month, then the bishop or his official is to supply the defect. A minister found guilty of neglect is to be punished by the ordinary and may be removed from office. That the rector and chaplains may the more readily perform their duties, they are forbidden to serve the patron of the church or any other person. The bishop declares that his ordination, made with the consent of the rector and patron, is to endure for all time, with reservation to himself and his successors, to the prior and chapter *sede vacante*, the archdeacon of Gloucester, and the bishop's ministers, of canonical obedience, procurations, pentecostals, and of everything else due to them. The bishop's seal and those of the rector and patron are appended.

450 *Undated*[1]

Letters patent of the appropriation of Great Badminton church. The petition of the abbot and convent of Lilleshall, Coventry & Lichfield diocese, alleges that their house, being remote from towns, is so burdened by hospitality to both rich and poor, that frequently things intended for the daily sustenance of the canons are diverted to guests who arrive unexpectedly. Because of this it is impossible to maintain the established number of canons except in poverty, especially as the English church is daily vexed by more than its usual oppressions. They therefore ask that the parish church of Great Badminton, in their patronage, be appropriated to them. The bishop, after enquiry by a sworn jury of clerks and laymen, and with the help of lawful documents, has found the convent's allegations justified and its petition reasonable and conducive to piety. In the presence of the canons' proctor, Jordan de Puyelesdon, and with the consent of the cathedral prior and chapter, he formally appropriates the church, saving the rights and dignity of the church of Worcester and of the

1 Probably 1341 or 1342. See 159, 451.

archdeacon of the place. On the death or cession of the present rector the canons may take possession by authority of the appropriation. A suitable portion, to be assigned by the bishop or his successors, is reserved for a perpetual vicarage, from which the vicar will be able to pay episcopal and other dues.

451[1] *4 September 1342 Badminton*

Certification by the official of the Gloucester archdeacon of his execution of the bishop's mandate, dated 4 September 1342 from Hartlebury, for the valuation of Great Badminton rectory, appropriated to Lilleshall abbey. In accordance with the mandate he went to Badminton church on 4 September[2] and held an enquiry by a sworn jury comprising the rectors of Dodington and Acton Turville, the vicar of Hawkesbury, the proctors of other absent rectors and vicars, and Walter North, William Red, David Crouk, Robert Bonde, Robert Forthey, John Vernon, Roger Kyng, Adam Pobenild, laymen and parishioners of the church. The enquiry found that in common years the demesne land is worth 20s., the rectory dovecote 4s., the tithe of corn in Badminton £6 13s. 4d., of barley £3 9s. 8d., of dredge £2 10s., of pulse 10s., of oats 2s., of hay from the demesne and township £2 13s. 4d., and of wool and lambs 30s. The offerings, obventions and anniversaries amount in common years to £1 6s. 8d., the lesser tithes of calves, foals, piglets, dovecots, mills, geese, cheese and milk to 15s., the live and dead mortuaries to 13s. 4d., while *chircheschot* is worth 7s. 6d. The tithe of hay and other lesser tithes in Oldbury and Didmarton belonging to Badminton church are worth £4 13s. 4d.[3]

461 *13 April 1342*

Memorandum that the bishop approved the exchange between Ds. Richard de Hatherleye, vicar of St. Owen's Gloucester, and Ds. Simon Tankard, rector of St. Mary's-in-the-South there. He admitted and instituted Richard to St. Mary's (patrons: prior and conv. of Llanthony by Gloucester) and Simon to St. Owen's (in the same patronage). The official of the Gloucester archdeacon was ordered to induct them.

466 *2 June 1342 Henbury*

Memorandum of the licence (until revoked) for Thomas de Shrygg to have an oratory within his house *Schrigg* in Pucklechurch parish.

1 This is the original return addressed on the dorse to the bishop.
2 It hardly seems possible that the enquiry could in fact have been held on the same day.
3 The total value is £25 18s. 2d. In 1291 (*Tax. Eccles.*, p. 220) the church was assessed at £13 6s. 8d. with a further portion of 8s. 6d. from Oldbury.

467 *14 June 1342 Henbury*

Memorandum of the licence (until revoked) for William de Cheltenham to have an oratory in his house at Pucklechurch.

468 *2 June 1342*

Memorandum of the licence for Walter Whyt and Isabella his wife to have an oratory in their house should either or both be incapacitated by illness.

469 *2 June 1342 [Henbury]*

Memorandum of the commission for Matthew, vicar of Berkeley, to exercise the office of penitentiary.

470 *15 June 1342 Henbury*

Memorandum of the licence for Roger Tortele and Juliana his wife to have an oratory at Bristol.

471 *28 June 1342*

Memorandum of the licence (during pleasure) for William de Tedyrhynton to have an oratory at St. Chloe (*Senkeleye*).

473 *14 July 1342*

Memorandum that the bishop empowered M. Robert de Endredeby [1] and Robert de Staverton [2] to receive criminous clerks from the justices.

474 *3 August 1342*

Memorandum of the licence for Ds. Robert de Burghton to leave his church [3] [for a year] and to farm it *eodem anno durante*.

476 *3 August 1342 Overbury*

Memorandum that Br. Giles Boyn, canon of St. Barbara, proctor in England of the prior and convent of St. Barbara,[4] presented himself to the bishop and showed his proxy.

480 *21 September 1342*

Memorandum of the special licence for Ralph de la Rode, rector of Pucklechurch, to leave his church for a year.

1 Dean of St. Mary's, Warwick.
2 Portionist of St. Nicholas's, Warwick. See 91, 130.
3 Ripple.
4 Ste. Barbe-en-Auge.

483 *11 October 1342*

Memorandum of the licence for Ds. Adam, rector of Barford, to farm his church for a year. He is to provide a suitable proctor &c.

485 *21 August 1342 Pinley*

Judicial proceedings (*acta*) concerning the election of Amicia de Hynton as prioress of Pinley, which were held in the church of Pinley priory before John de la Lowe, rector of Bredon, the bishop's special commissary *ad hoc*. Amicia, the elect, appeared in person, the sub-prioress and convent through John Tankart of Warwick. The official of the Worcester archdeacon's certificate showed that no opponents had come forward but that general citation had been made. The usual citation was made at the entry to the quire, M. Henry Tankard produced the election decree, and all were prohibited from objecting further to the election or person of the elect. Four instruments and the election decree were brought forward on the convent's behalf, and two *instructores*, Alice de Hales and Isabella de Langeleye, nuns of the place. After they had been examined and their attestations published, the commissary at length proceeded to his sentence of confirmation.

488 *7 November 1342 Worcester*

Resignation of Abbots Morton rectory by Henry Coleman.[1] Having been newly instituted to Wolverley church, an incompatible benefice, he is resigning Abbots Morton as the law requires, but with reservation of his right to resume it should Wolverley prove to have been canonically collated to someone else on apostolic or other authority.[2] At his request the dean of Worcester has appended the seal of his office.

491 *7 November 1342*

A duplicate of 488.

492 *31 December 1342 Hartlebury*

Memorandum that the bishop discharged the prior and monks of Dudley to whom, at the time of his visitation, he had assigned a day for exhibiting their title to Dudley church and to a pension of six marks [£4] from that of Northfield. [Cf. 537].

493 *14 January 1343*

Memorandum that the bishop granted licence *quatenus de iure potuit* for Ds. William, perpetual vicar of Tirley, to be absent until Quad-

---

1 According to 487 (see *Institutions*) Nicholas de Poywek was instituted to Abbots Morton 8 Nov. 1342 on the death of M. John de Walcot. There is no record of Coleman's institution.
2 As allowed in *Sext* 3, 4, c. 20.

ragesima Sunday [2 March] on legal business concerning himself and his vicarage.[1]

494 *1 February 1343 Hampton Bishop*

Memorandum of the special licence for Ivo de Edenham, rector of Daglingworth, to be absent for a year on his own affairs, provided that his church be not deprived of its services or the cure of souls neglected, and that he appoint a suitable proctor.

498 *24 March 1343 Alvechurch*

Memorandum that the bishop granted Thomas [de Custon] letters dimissory to all holy orders and licensed him to leave his church[2] for a year.

503 *1 May 1343 Hartlebury*

Memorandum that the bishop admitted and instituted John Payn, priest, to Whichford, on the presentation of John Mouhon, knight, and directed the official of the Worcester archdeacon to induct him. Payn swore to indemnify the bishop for any action which might arise from the resignation of Baldwin de Mouhon, the last rector. The resignation was sealed with Baldwin's own seal and that of Tredington deanery, and evidenced by a letter of credence from the earl of Lancaster. The proceedings (*acta*) took place in the presence of M. John de la Lowe, Henry de Wynchecumbe and Henry Strode.

506 *5 June 1343 Hartlebury*

Memorandum that the bishop admitted and instituted Br. William Provot, monk of St. Taurin, Evreux diocese, to the wardenship (*custodia*) of Astley priory, to which he had been presented by the abbot and convent of St. Taurin. The official of the Worcester archdeacon was ordered to induct him. Immediately after his institution and oath of obedience the prior swore to pay the portions due to the vicar of Astley without delay or fraud.

507 *8 June 1343 Hartlebury*

Memorandum of the dispensation for Ds. William de Bourtham, rector of *Kymenhale* portion in Leigh church, to study at a *studium generale* for three years from St. Peter ad Vincula [1 August]. During that time he was to surrender his portion to Ds. Thomas Chyrchleynch, priest.

---

1 *pro prosecucione iuris sui et ipsius vicarie et defensione sui status . . . ita tamen quod ydoneum procuratorem loco sui in ipsa vicaria dimittere[t] qui vices suas in omnibus gereret in eadem.*
2 Severn Stoke. See *Institutions* 497.

508 *8 June 1343 Hartlebury*

Memorandum of the dispensation for Hugh de Monynton, acolyte, rector of St. Stephen's Bristol, to leave his church for a year, provided that during that time he proceed to the order of subdeacon in accordance with the Boniface constitution.[1]

510 *24 May 1343 Hartlebury*

Memorandum of the licence for M. William de Bosco, rector of Twyning, to be absent from his church as long as he remains in the service of Robert [Stratford], bishop of Chichester [1337–62].

511 *2 June 1343*

Memorandum of the licence for Hugh de Brandeston to have [Mass] celebrated in his manor of Lapworth.

512 *2 June 1343*

Memorandum of the similar licence (until revoked) for Thomas de Morton Folet in his house there.

513 *16 June 1343*

Memorandum of the similar licence for Thomas Aumondisham in his manor of Southam in Bishops Cleeve parish.

514 *11 July 1343*

Memorandum of the licence for M. Robert de Chikwell, rector of Hampton Bishop, to leave his church for two years.

515 *20 June 1343 Cofton*

Resignation of John Chastilion, rector of Northfield with Cofton chapel. Because his own seal is not well known he has had appended that of Droitwich (*Wych*) deanery.

516 *1 August 1343 Henbury*

Memorandum of the admission and institution of M. Peter Malet, by his proctor Nicholas Hogges, to Barnsley rectory (patron: Humphrey Bohun, earl of Hereford & Essex, lord of Brecon), by reason of an exchange with Spettisbury, Salisbury diocese.

517 *29 August 1343 Hartlebury*

Memorandum of the admission and institution of M. William, called Loveryng, of Northleach, in the person of his proctor M. John

1 *Sext* 1, 6, c. 34 (Boniface VIII).

de Lech,[1] to the rectory of Withington (in the bishop's collation), by reason of an exchange for Woodchurch (patron: John [Stratford], archbishop of Canterbury [1333–48]).

520 *8 November 1343 Hartlebury*

Memorandum of the admission and institution of Walter le Whyte of Bristol, clerk, to St. Stephen's rectory, Bristol, vacant by the resignation of Hugh de Monynton[2] in accordance with the chapter *Si beneficia*.[3] Patrons: abbot and conv. of Glastonbury. Mandate for induction was sent to the official of the Gloucester archdeacon.

521 *8 November 1343 Hartlebury chapel*

Memorandum of the oath sworn before the bishop, in the presence of Thomas Bolevynch, notary public, by the above Walter. In the event of legal action[4] following from his institution to St. Stephen's, he promised to indemnify the diocesan. And if the bishop and his council should feel there was no other way to avoid injury of this kind, Walter was to resign the benefice. Witnesses: M. John de la Lowe, rector of Bredon, Nicholas de Stanlak, monk of Worcester, and Ds. John de Dombleton, rector of Sedgeberrow.

522 *6 October 1343 Withington*

Memorandum of the licence for William Brescy, rector of Miserden, to be absent from Michaelmas last [29 September] until the same feast in 1345 and to farm his church. This is to enable him to serve [Richard de Bury], bishop of Durham [1333–45], at whose instance the licence was granted.

523 *10 September 1343 Hartlebury*

Memorandum that the bishop admitted and instituted Br. William de Knytcote as warden (*ad custodiam magisterium et regimen spiritualium et temporalium*) of St. Michael's hospital, Warwick, on the presentation of Thomas de Beauchamp, earl of Warwick. The dean of the Christianity of Warwick was ordered to induct him.

524 *27 November 1343 Tetbury*

Certification by the official of the Gloucester archdeacon of his execution of an episcopal mandate, dated 13 November from

---

1 *In personam magistri Johannis de Lech, racione Johannis Lech procuratoris predicti magistri Willelmi literatorie et sub manu publica constituti. Qui procurator posuit verba sua in ore predicti Johannis de Lech tanquam vocem organis sui.*
2 See 508.
3 *Sext* 3, 4, c. 20.
4 *si contingeret . . . episcopum . . . per quemcumque provisum apostolicum qualitercumque inbrigari, implacitari seu vexari.*

Hartlebury, for enquiry, in a full chapter to be held in the ordinary course, into the vacancy of Brimpsfield vicarage, to which Roger de Haketo, prior of Brimpsfield, had presented William de Hildesleye. In a chapter held on 27 November in Tetbury church, he conducted an enquiry by the rectors of Kings Stanley, Eastington, Elkstone, Edgeworth, Cowley, Cherrington, Woodchester and Syde, the vicars of Stonehouse, Tetbury and Bisley, and the proctors of other absent rectors and vicars.[1] This found the vicarage to be vacant, that it became so with the death of Ds. John de Prestbury on the Sunday after St. Leonard [i.e. 9 November], that Roger de Haketo is the true patron and presented the above John on the last occasion, that the church is free from litigation and not burdened with a pension or portion, and that the presentee is legitimate, of good life and honest conversation, 30 and more years of age, a priest, and not beneficed elsewhere.

526 *17 January 1344 Hartlebury*

Commission to M. John de la Lowe, Professor of Civil Law, the bishop's Official. The abbot and convent of the Premonstratensian house of Halesowen (*Hales*), for the reasons set out in an attached schedule, have petitioned for the appropriation to them of Clent church with Rowley chapel, of which they are patrons. The bishop has satisfied himself as to the truth of their allegations by means of an enquiry held by the Official, but because churches should not be alienated without the consent of the chapter, he orders him to go personally to Worcester to discuss the matter with the chapter and to secure its consent.

527 *19 January 1344 Hartlebury*

Commission to the prior of the Holy Sepulchre, Warwick, and to the dean of St. Mary's collegiate church there. Nicholas Mariote, Simon de Merhston, Henry Bobbi, John de Alicestre senior and John de Alicestre junior, brothers of St. John's hospital, Warwick, have informed the bishop of their election of Br. Philip de Besford as master and warden and have requested its confirmation. The commissaries are to examine such election and if lawful to confirm it.[2]

528 *18 January 1344 Hartlebury*

Memorandum of the licence for M. Robert Maremy,[3] rector of Halford, to study for a year in a *studium generale* in England.

1 All beneficed clergy of Stonehouse deanery.
2 See 579, 580.
3 *Marony* in margin. The usual form is *Marny*.

530 *3 October 1342 Withington*

Warning to the prior and convent of Worcester of the bishop's intention to hold a further visitation. They are to recall any absent monks and to appear before him on the next juridical day after All Saints [i.e. 4 November].

531 *3 October 1342 Withington*

Mandate to the official of the Worcester archdeacon. The bishop intends to visit the clergy and people [of the archdeaconry] as follows: on Tuesday after All Saints [i.e. 5 November], the city churches in the cathedral, the hospitals of St. Oswald & St. Wulstan in their respective houses; on Wednesday [6 November], also in the cathedral, the churches of Hindlip, Warndon, Bredicot, Spetchley, Pirton, Severn Stoke, Kempsey, Tibberton, Wick, Claines, Aston Bishop,[1] and their chapels;[2] also on Wednesday, in Powick church, Powick, Hanley, Great Malvern, Madresfield and Clevelode churches;[3] on Thursday [7 November], in Dodderhill church, those of Dodderhill, Elmbridge, [Droitwich] St. Andrew, [Droitwich] St. Nicholas, [Witton] St. Mary, [Witton] St. Peter, Salwarpe, Martin [Hussingtree], Hampton [Lovett] and Hadzor; on Friday [8 November], in Tardebigge church, those of Tardebigge, Beoley, [Kings] Norton, Northfield, Cofton [Hacket], Bromsgrove, Grafton, Upton [Warren], Stoke [Prior], Aston, Hanbury and Alvechurch;[4] on Saturday [9 November], in Halesowen church, those of Halesowen, Yardley, Dudley, Clent, Rowley, Swinford, Pedmore, Hagley; on Monday [11 November], in Kidderminster church, those of Mitton, [Bel]broughton, Broom, Churchill, Chaddesley, Stone, Rushock, Elmley Lovett, Doverdale, Hartlebury, Wolverley, Kidderminster.[5] The official is to cite all rectors, vicars and parish priests of churches and chapels subject to diocesan jurisdiction, all other priests celebrating there, and four or six trustworthy men from each parish, according to its size, so that from them may be learned the truth about the bishop's subjects, the condition of the churches, and other articles to be put by the bishop and his clerks. All having appropriated churches or portions, pensions or tithes from churches other than their own, and rectors holding benefices with cure in plurality, are to be cited to produce evidence of their right to do so.

532 *Undated*[6]

Certificate from the official of the Gloucester archdeacon reciting the bishop's mandate,[7] received 15 November, for summoning the clergy

---

1 i.e. White Ladies Aston.   2 The above being in Worcester deanery.
3 In Powick deanery.   4 In Droitwich deanery.
5 In Kidderminster deanery.
6 It must have been dated between 15 and 28 November 1342.
7 *Littera melior ad citandum clerum et populum pro visitacione subeunda.* The entry stops short at the end of the mandate, which is undated.

and people [of his archdeaconry] to undergo visitation at the following times and places: on Thursday after St. Katherine [i.e. 28 November] in Didbrook church, the churches of Didbrook, Kemerton, Alderton, Dumbleton, Wormington, Toddington, Stanway; on Friday [29 November], in Childs Wickham church, those of Childs Wickham, Stanton, Buckland, Broadway, Willersey, Hinton, Aston Somerville; on Saturday [30 November], Beckford church.[1] The official is to cite all heads of religious houses, portionists [&c.],[2] as well as deans, rectors [&c.], clerks and holy water bearers (aquebaiulos)[3] from every church, chapel, or oratory—at least one clerk from each, and from every parish four, and from every chapel two or three trustworthy parishioners . . . [&c. as in 89].

533 *Undated*

Warning to the abbot and convent of Alcester of the bishop's intention to visit them on the Wednesday after St. Wulstan [i.e. 23 January 1343].[4]

534 *8 January 1343 Hartlebury*

Similar warning [in Old French] to the prioress and convent of Wroxall of the bishop's intended visitation on the Saturday after St. Vincent [i.e. 25 January].

535 *Undated*

Mandate to the dean of Pershore. He is to cite all those whose faults were brought to light at the recent visitation of the deanery to appear before the bishop or his commissary.[5]

536 *Undated*

Commission to M. John de la Lowe and M. Henry de Newebold, rectors respectively of Bredon and Weston. The bishop has recently visited Pershore deanery, but is prevented by pressure of business from carrying out final correction. They are empowered, jointly and severally, to take cognisance of and to proceed with all *comperta* and the causes and suits arising from them, to terminate all such, and to impose correction and punishment.

1 The scribe turned to a new folio at this point and it may be that he omitted the latter part of the itinerary.
2 With a few variants the entry follows 89.
3 This word interlined. For the appointment of such 'parish clerks', see Lyndwood, *Const. Prov.*, p. 21.
4 Cf. 90.
5 The form is the same as in 103.

537 *Undated*[1]

Letters patent to the effect that the prior of Dudley produced evidence of his house's title to Dudley church and to a pension from that of Northfield.

538 *10 January 1343 Hartlebury*

Letters patent acknowledging the payment by Ds. Nicholas Jobynol, rector of Clent with Rowley chapel of five marks [£3 6s. 8d.] out of the ten due to be paid by Pentecost [1 June] because of the expenses in which he had involved the bishop by bringing unjust actions against him in divers courts.[2]

539 *8 November 1342*

Memorandum that ten marks [£6 13s. 4d.] were paid to the proctor of M. Richard de Thormerton as pension due from the bishop.

540 *9 January 1343*

The agreement with Jobynol.[3] Nicholas [de Jobynol], rector of Clent, was absolved by the bishop on taking an oath to obey the Church. He renounced the inhibitions and appeals which he had brought or had sought to bring against the bishop and his commissaries. He promised to pay ten marks [£6 13s. 4d.] towards the expenses incurred by the bishop. He is to be admitted to purgation with the eighth hand[4] before Quadragesima Sunday [2 March] on account of the charges against him. Meanwhile, he is to see that the abbot and convent of Halesowen, by way of exchange, pension, or other suitable means, are enabled to present to his benefice, as was determined by the bishop on the advice of the lord of Dudley.[5]

541 *29 September 1342 Withington*[6]

Letters patent of the bishop's receipt through his auditors of the final account of M. John le Botoner, his receiver. This was for the sums, derived from both spiritual and temporal profits, delivered to Botoner by the bishop, his bailiffs, reeves, ministers, or others, from the beginning of the world until the drawing up of the present document. The bishop grants acquittances for himself, his executors, and successors.

542 *1 October 1342 Withington*

Letters patent of the bishop's receipt through his auditors of the final account of John de Chalveston, clerk of his household (*clericus*

---

1 But see 492.   2 See 540.   3 Cf. 538.
4 i.e. with the aid of seven compurgators.
5 For the exchange, see 568.   6 Cf. 555.

hospicii nostri), for all the incomings, outgoings and expenses during his whole period of office.

543 *29 September 1343*

Memorandum of the licence for M. Peter Malet, rector of Barnsley, to leave his church and to study for two years.

544 *20 September 1343*

Memorandum of the similar licence granted for one year to Ds. Thomas Stephans, rector of Winstone.

545 *15 October 1343 Withington*

Memorandum of the licence for M. John de la Lowe, rector of Bredon, to farm his chapel of Cutsdean for three years.

548 *14 September 1343*

Memorandum of the licence for M. Thomas de Bradewell, rector of [Coln] St. Dennis,[1] to leave his church for a year.

549 *19 October 1343*

Memorandum of the licence for Eleanor, formerly wife of John de Chyltenham, to have Mass [*divina*] celebrated within Cheltenham parish.

552 *13 January 1345 Hartlebury*

Memorandum of the licence for Ds. Henry, rector of Pillerton, to leave his church and to farm it to John de Bourton, clerk.[2]

555 *17 January 1343 Hartlebury*

Further letter of acquittance[3] for M. John le Botoner, the bishop's receiver, on account of £100 which the bishop, through his servant John de Wych, had delivered to him on the Sunday after St. Frideswide [i.e. 20 October 1342].

556 *4 February 1343 Hampton Bishop*

Memorandum that on the Tuesday after the Purification, in Hampton church, M. Robert de Endredeby, dean of the collegiate church of St. Mary, Warwick, swore on the Gospels in the presence of the bishop's special commissaries, Masters John de la Lowe and Hugh de

---

1 See 436.   2 Cf. 696.   3 Cf. 541.

Penebrugg, *pro tribunali sedentibus*, that he would exercise no archidiaconal jurisdiction in the town of Warwick until the suit or disagreement between the archdeacon of Worcester and himself had been settled by amicable arrangement or judicial award. Exception was made of his jurisdiction over the canons with respect to the *regimen chori* and the manner of assembling for divine worship. He also swore that should he exercise jurisdiction contrary to his oath, he would pay £20 to the bishop *ad augmentum elemosine sue*. The proceedings (*acta*) took place in the presence of M. Thomas Bolvynch, notary public and William de la Lowe.

559 *8 May 1344*

Memorandum of the licence for Ds. William de la More, rector of Churchill, to be absent for two years.

560 *9 May 1344*

Memorandum that Robert of Gloucester, William Murymouth and John de Southam, monks of Tewkesbury, were ordained acolytes at Hartlebury.

562 *26 April 1343 Wiveliscombe*

Certification by Ralph [of Shrewsbury], bishop of Bath & Wells [1329–63], of his execution of the diocesan's mandate, dated 3 March from Monks Stanley,[1] for the exchange, in accordance with the findings of an enquiry held by the official of the Gloucester archdeacon, between M. Thomas de la Felde, rector of Oake, Bath & Wells diocese, and Roger de Middeltone, rector of Boxwell.[2]

563 *26 April 1343 Wiveliscombe*

Letters of institution. The bishop of Bath & Wells informs M. Thomas de la Felde that on the diocesan's authority he has admitted and instituted him to Boxwell church, at the presentation of the abbot and convent of St. Peter's Gloucester.[3]

564 *6 June 1343 Hartlebury*

Certification by the bishop, in response to a royal writ *super bastardia* and after holding an enquiry, that Geoffrey, son of Geoffrey de la Mar' of *Makeseye*, is legitimate.[4]

1 Cf. 73.   2 See 563.   3 See 562.
4 The entry in *C.P.R.* 1343–45 (p. 267) is dated 15 June 1344, and the bishop is said to have returned the writ in the octave of Trinity (15 June in 1343, 6 June in 1344). The defendants in a land dispute before the justices alleged that Geoffrey de la Mare was a bastard.

565 *1 October 1343*[1] *Withington*

Letters patent [in old French] of the appointment of Thomas le Somery as bailiff of the bishop's franchise of Oswaldslow.

566 *10 December 1342 Hartlebury*

Commission to M. John de Severleye, the bishop's chancellor. He is empowered to hear, take cognisance of, and to terminate all causes and suits, present or future, which pertain to the bishop's audience outside his consistory court, with authority to punish and to correct the *comperta* of the recent visitation. [2]

567 *22 January 1343 Alcester*

Commission to Masters John de la Lowe, John de Severleye, Henry de Newbold and Hugh de Penebrugg, rectors respectively of Bredon, Billesley, Weston-on-Avon and Hartlebury. Owing to pressure of business the bishop is unable to proceed personally to the final correction of *comperta* arising from his recent visitation in various parts of the diocese. They are empowered, jointly and severally, to take cognisance of and to proceed with all *comperta* and the causes and suits arising from them, to terminate such, and to impose correction and punishment. [3]

568 *10 September 1343 London*

Certification by Roger [Northburgh], bishop of Coventry & Lichfield [1322–58], of his execution of the diocesan's mandate, dated 29 August from Hartlebury, for the exchange between Nicholas Jobinol of Dudley, rector of Clent with Rowley and M. John de Northwell, clerk, rector of Kingswinford, Coventry & Lichfield diocese. [4]

569 *Undated*

Memorandum that the official of the Worcester archdeacon was ordered to induct the above John after he had taken the oath of canonical obedience in the person of his proctor.

570 *15 October 1343 Potterne*

Certification by Robert [Wyville], bishop of Salisbury [1330–75], of his execution of the diocesan's mandate, dated 6 October from Withington, for the exchange between Ds. Robert de Burton, rector

1 An entry in *C.C.R.* 1343–46 (p. 202), dated 3 December 1343, records the restoration to Somery of this bailiwick. See intro. p. xxvii.
2 Cf. 1330.　　3 Cf. 536.
4 Jobinol had been ordered to vacate the benefice (540).

of Ripple (patron: the bp. of Worcester), and Ds. John de Ryvers, prebendary of Netherbury in Salisbury cathedral.

571 *Undated*
Memorandum of the mandate for the official of the Gloucester archdeacon[1] to induct the above John.

572 *3 January 1342 Hartlebury*
Letters patent of the grant to Walter atte More, Matilda his wife, and William their son, of a messuage and virgate of land in Salt Marsh within the bishop's manor of Henbury. They are to hold the same, jointly and severally, for their lives, or for the life of the survivor, at a rent of 26s. 8d., payable in equal instalments at the four usual terms, with the obligation of suit at the bishop's court and hundred of Henbury every three weeks, two appearances at *Le Lawedaye* of Henbury, royal service, and payment of heriot on the deaths of Walter, Matilda and William. Should the rent be in arrears for half a year, the bishop for the time being is to have the right of re-entry. After the death of all the tenants the messuage and virgate are to revert to the bishop and his successors. Witnesses: John de Trie[?],[2] John de Weston, Thomas de Gydeford, John de Brokenburwe, Richard de Sautemareys, William de Stok, Walter de Eyton and others.

573 *18 April 1343 Mortlake*
The king, as custodian of the land and heir of John Giffard, tenant in chief, presents his clerk, Henry de Ingelby, for institution to Weston sub-Edge church.[3]

574 *6 September 1343 Hanslope*
Presentation by Thomas de Beauchamp, earl of Warwick, of Br. William de Knytecote for institution as warden of St. Michael's hospital, Warwick.[4]

575 *25 November 1343 Eaton*
Certification by Thomas [Charlton], bishop of Hereford [1327–44], of his execution of the diocesan's commission, dated 13 November from Hartlebury, for the exchange, in accordance with the findings of an enquiry to be held by the official of the Worcester archdeacon,

1 Ripple was an episcopal manor, and in such cases it was usual to direct the mandate to someone other than the official of the archdeacon within whose territory the place lay. The Gloucester official seems here to have been a special commissary. See intro., p. xv, n.5.
2 Or *Tree*.
3 *C.P.R.* 1343–45, p. 14. He was instituted 7 May (504), but resigned before 10 October (518, 576).
4 Instituted 10 September (523).

between Ds. John de Uppynton, vicar of Kinlet, Hereford diocese, and Ds. John de Portes, vicar of Stone.

576 *15 September 1343*
Presentation by the king of his clerk John de Codynton for institution to Weston sub-Edge.[1]

577 *20 December 1343 Sutton Coldfield*
Presentation by Thomas de Beauchamp, earl of Warwick, of Ds. Nicholas Walwyn, priest, for institution to Hindlip church.

578 *20 December 1343 u.s.*
Identical letter of presentation to Hindlip church in favour of Simon de Chalveston.

579 *17 January 1344 Warwick*
Certification of the election of a master of St. John's hospital, Warwick. Brothers Nicholas Mariote, Simon de Merston, Henry Bubbi,[2] John de Alicestr' senior and John de Alicestr' junior, declare that on the resignation of Brother Henry, the last master or warden, and with the licence of their patron, Thomas de Beauchamp, earl of Warwick, they elected Br. Philip de Besford, priest, as their new head. They now present him to the bishop for consecration (*munus consecracionis impartiri*).[3]

580 *19 January 1344*
Commission for the examination and confirmation of the above election. [Duplicate of 527].

581 *20 October 1343 Gimingham* [?][4]
Mandate for the collection of the cardinals' procurations. John [Stratford], archbishop of Canterbury [1333–48], informs the bishop that Br. Andruinus, prior of Collonges [?] (*de Colungiis*), the representative in England of P.,[5] bishop of Palestrina, and A.,[6] bishop of Tusculum, cardinals and apostolic nuncios to France and England,[7] has ordered that 500 gold florins of Florence be paid to him as expenses for the 250 days spent on the cardinals' business in the dioceses of the province. The sum is to be delivered to him in London by the Purification [2 February], the archbishop being empowered to enforce payment from the clergy of his province. In the Council at St. Paul's [October 1342] the archbishop, with the consent of his suffragans, had paid £10 from his own resources to Br. Geoffrey[8] de Crannford,[9] an Augustinian Hermit, whom the cardi-

---

1 Instituted 10 October (518). Cf. 573.   2 *Bobbi* in 527, *Bobby* in 580.
3 Cf. 527, 580, 602.   4 MS. *Gymingham*.
5 Peter IV des Prez.   6 Annibal de Ceccano.
7 For the negotiation of a truce. This was signed at Malestroit in January 1343.
8 Wrongly called *Ralph* the first time he is mentioned in the entry.
9 *Crantfeld* in 596.

nals had sent initially. At the same time the method of levying the money to pay both Geoffrey and future nuncios was discussed. It was agreed that a farthing in the pound should be levied on all benefices and ecclesiastical goods assessed for the tenth. Should the sum be greater than that required, after allowing for the expenses of collection, the surplus was to be kept by the archbishop to defray future charges of the kind. The bishop, therefore, is to see that the money from his diocese is collected by St. Hilary [13 January] and delivered to the dean of St. Paul's in his house in London on the morrow of the Conversion of St. Paul [i.e. 26 January].[1]

582 *5 December 1343 Hartlebury*

Mandate to the official of the Worcester archdeacon[2] for the collection, in accordance with the above mandate [581], of a farthing in the pound of ecclesiastical benefices, both exempt and non-exempt.

583 *20 January 1344 Hartlebury*

Letter informing the archbishop of the execution of his mandate for the collection of procuration [581]. Attached were schedules of the contributors' names and of the sums paid.[3]

585 *13 February 1344*

Memorandum of the licence for M. William de Lech, rector of Withington, to absent himself and to study for two years from Michaelmas last [29 September] until the same feast in 1344 [*sic*].

587 *18 September 1343*

Memorandum of the licence for Agnes Austyn of Salford to have Mass (*divina*) celebrated in an oratory within her house there, provided that the priest take an oath before the rector of the place.

588 *17 November 1343*

Memorandum of the licence for Ds. Adam, rector of Barford, to farm his church to Ds. John, rector of Orsett, London diocese, from Michaelmas last [29 September] until the same feast in 1345.

589 *1 April 1344 Hartlebury*

Memorandum of the licence for M. Thomas de Clypston, acolyte, to study for one year. He was also granted letters dimissory to the order of subdeacon.

---

1 Details of the levy are given by W. E. Lunt, *Financial Relations of the Papacy with England 1327–1534*, (1962), pp. 636–639.
2 The rubric indicates that a similar mandate was sent to the official of the other archdeacon.
3 Not recorded in the register.

590 *28 March 1345*

Memorandum of the licence for the abbot and convent of Gloucester to farm South Cerney church to Robert, its perpetual vicar, for three years.

594 *6 January 1344 Hartlebury*

Resignation of William de Hyldisleye, perpetual vicar of Brimpsfield, in the presence of Ds. William de Preston, rector of Hethe in Lincoln diocese, Ds. Henry de Wynchcombe, and M. John de Bradewas.[1]

595 *23 April 1343 Hartlebury*

Letters patent of the ordination of Campden vicarage. The bishop has appropriated the church to the abbot and convent of St. Werburgh, Chester, with reservation of a vicarage estimated at £20.[2] The vicar is to have the house or messuage that the rectors had before appropriation, though its granges are reserved to the abbot and convent. He and his successors are to receive the tithe of calves, piglets, lambs, goslings, eggs, foals, wool, milk, cheese, wax, honey and bees, gardens, curtilages, fisheries, fish, dovecots, mills, flax and hemp, both brushwood and other timber, trees, fruits and pastures, from the whole parish; all the great and lesser tithes, except those of any kind of grain; as well as the tithe of hay from *Litlemuchy* meadow in Broad Campden and from the demesne meadows of the lords of Campden, commonly called *Eorlesmore, Sturte, Alphatehomme* and *Overhomme*—the monks being entitled to the tithe of the remaining hay in the parish. The vicars are also to have live and dead mortuaries and all offerings, obventions, annals, trentals, herbage and trees within the churchyard, and everything else belonging to the altarage of the church.

The monks are to be liable for all pensions and other burdens, both ordinary and extraordinary, present and future. But the vicars are to find a parish chaplain when they are themselves unable or unwilling to officiate in the church, and one secondary priest and a deacon to minister there daily, and are to pay four marks' procuration to the diocesan at his triennial visitation. The bishop reserves to himself and his successors the right to alter or add to the ordination if necessary.

596 *26 January 1344 London*

Gilbert,[3] dean of St. Paul's, collector of the procurations of Andruinus, prior of Collonges [?], and of Br. Geoffrey de Crantfeld, an Augustinian Hermit, acknowledges the receipt at the hands of

---

1 See 524, 525.   2 See 329.
3 de Bruera (1336/7–1353).

M. John de Severleye, rector of Billesley, of £7 6s. 8½d. from ecclesiastical and temporal benefices in the diocese.[1]

597 *6 February 1344 Hartlebury*

Mandate to the [rural] dean of Warwick. Laymen who carry off or dispose of offerings in churches or chapels, their porches or churchyards, on whatever pretext, unless with the consent of the ecclesiastical persons to whom such offerings belong, and for sufficient and lawful cause approved by the diocesan, are *ipso facto* excommunicate by reason of a decree of the provincial council last held at St. Paul's.[2] Despite this, the bishop has learned that certain persons unknown carried off 49 wax candles which were burning before the altars and statues in Ipsley church on the feast of the Purification [2 February]. The dean is to see that at Mass on Sundays and festivals all those concerned in the removal, detention or disposal of the candles are declared excommunicate in Ipsley church and others throughout the deanery. He is not to cease from such denunciation until he receives further instructions from the bishop. He is also to discover the names of the malefactors and to cite both them and objectors to the denunciation to appear before the bishop or his commissary in Hartlebury church on the next juridical day after St. Peter in Cathedra [22 February], the former to show cause why they should not be declared excommunicate by name, the latter to give reasons for their objection (*reclamacio*).

598 *17 January 1344 Wiveliscombe*

Commission of Ralph [of Shrewsbury], bishop of Bath & Wells [1329–63], authorising the diocesan to carry out the exchange between William de Pillardynton, rector of Duntisbourne, and Walter de Retford, rector of White Staunton, Bath & Wells diocese.

599 *19 February 1344 Hartlebury*

Appointment of Br. Richard de Hadleye, a monk of the cathedral church, to exercise the office of guardian of the feretories of SS. Oswald and Wulfstan, recently vacated by Br. William Mose because of old age.[3]

600 *5 March 1344 Hartlebury*

Commission to the abbot of St. Peter's Gloucester and the prior of St. Oswald's there. Thomas de Bruton, perpetual vicar of Tytherington, summoned before the bishop to answer for crimes and faults

1 See 581–3.
2 In October 1342. See Lyndwood, *Const. Prov.*, p. 45: *Immoderate temeritatis.*
3 There were two such tumbaries, the other being appointed by the chapter. It had been agreed in 1224 that the bishop and convent should divide the offerings between them. See Thomas, *Appendix*, p. 76.

discovered at his visitation, has submitted himself and his rights in the vicarage to the bishop's determination. Unable to deal further with the matter himself, the bishop empowers the commissioners, jointly or severally, to accept the vicarage should it be freely surrendered, otherwise to deprive Thomas for the faults which he has confessed, details of which can be sent if need be under the episcopal seal. They are to inform the patron of the vacancy.

601 *5 March 1344 Hartlebury*

Commission to the prior of St. Bartholomew's, Bristol, the dean of the place, the abbot of St. Peter's Gloucester and the prior of St. Oswald's there, or any one of them. Should the enquiry which the bishop is sending under the seal of the official of the Gloucester archdeacon find for the presentee, and there be no other canonical objection, they are to admit, institute, and induct Ds. Adam ate Halle, deacon, to Painswick vicarage, at the presentation of the prior and convent of Llanthony by Gloucester.

602 *23 February 1344 Warwick*

Certification by Br. William, prior of the Holy Sepulchre, Warwick, and Robert de Enderdeby, dean of St. Mary's collegiate church, of their execution of the bishop's mandate for the examination and confirmation of Br. Philip de Besford's election as prior of St. John's hospital, Warwick.[1] On the authority of the commission they had summoned any co-elect or opponent of the election to appear before them. None having done so, they examined the merits of the person elected, of the electors themselves, and the form of the election. They found that Br. Philip had been lawfully elected by the above-named brothers,[2] who exercised the right both by common law and special apostolic privilege, and that the consent of the patron, Thomas de Beauchamp, earl of Warwick, both to the election and the person elected, had been duly obtained. They therefore confirmed such election and committed the administration of the spiritualities and temporalities to the elect.

605 *28 January 1344 Westminster*

The king, as custodian of the lands of Brimpsfield priory, in his hand by reason of the French war, presents his clerk William de Hildesley for institution to the vicarage of Brimpsfield.[3]

608 *8 March 1344 Hartlebury*

Memorandum of the commission (during pleasure) for Br. John de Pyriton, a canon of Cirencester, to exercise the office of penitentiary within Cirencester deanery, except in reserved cases.

1 See 527, 579, 580.　　2 See 527, 579.　　3 See *Institutions* 604.

611 *21 February 1344*

Memorandum of the licence for Katherine de Sapy to have as her confessor for a year Ds. Roger de Aldryntone, chaplain of St. Mary's Redmarley.

614 *27 October 1343 Withington*

Memorandum of the licence for William Brisci, rector of Miserden, to be absent from his church from Michaelmas last *usque ad idem tempus* [*sic*].

615 *28 November 1343*

Memorandum of the dispensation, in accordance with the chapter *Cum ex eo*,[1] for Ds. Robert Tromon, rector of Quinton, to attend the Schools.

619 *22 March 1344 Burton by Beverley*

Certification[2] by William [Zouche], archbishop of York [1342–52], of his execution of the diocesan's mandate, dated 13 March from Hartlebury, for the exchange of benefices, in accordance with the findings of an enquiry held by the commissary of the Worcester archdeacon, between Ds. William de Northwell, rector of Owston, York diocese, and Ds. John de Northwell, canon of Southwell, prebendary of Northwell in that church, and rector of Clent with Rowley. The archbishop has instituted William de Northwell to Clent with Rowley (patrons: the abbot and conv. of Halesowen) in the person of his proctor, William de Rutton, clerk of York diocese.

620 *31 March 1344 Hartlebury*

Memorandum of the oath of obedience taken by the above William in the person of his proctor, and of the mandate sent to the archdeacon of Worcester's official for his induction.

623 *27 April 1344 Campden*

Certification by the official of the Gloucester archdeacon of his execution of an episcopal mandate, dated 26 April from Pershore, for enquiry, in a full chapter to be held in the ordinary course, into the vacancy of Aston Somerville rectory, to which Geoffrey de Aston Somervill had presented Alan Janekynes, chaplain. Should this find for the presentee he was to institute and induct him. Accordingly, in a chapter held in Campden church, he conducted an enquiry by the rectors of Willersey, Aston sub-Edge, and Buckland; the vicars of

1 *Sext* 1, 6, c. 34.
2 Received by the bishop at Hartlebury on 31 March.

Beckford, Campden, Didbrook and Stanway; and the proctors of absent rectors and vicars.[1] This found the church to be vacant by the resignation of William Somerville on 26 April last [627], that Geoffrey de Aston Somervill, the true patron, has the right to present, and that Hawysa, at the time lady of Aston Somerville, now wife of Geoffrey, presented the above William on the last occasion. It also found the church to be free from litigation and not subject to a pension or portion, and the presentee of honest conversation, aged 30 and more, in priest's orders, and not beneficed elsewhere. He has therefore instituted and inducted such presentee.

624 1 May 1344

Alan Janekynes, rector of Aston Somerville, resigns his church into the bishop's hands.

627 26 April 1344 Pershore

Acceptance by the bishop of William de Aston Somervill's resignation of the same church.[2]

629 8 May 1344 Hereford

John Reesz, canon of Hereford, vicar-general in spirituals of John [Trillek], bishop elect and confirmed of Hereford [1344–60], who is absent from his diocese, grants a faculty and special licence to the bishop for the consecration of an altar in St. Guthlac's church, Hereford,[3] unless it be already consecrated.

630 29 April 1344 Farnham

Faculty granted by John [Trillek], bishop elect and confirmed of Hereford [1344–60], to the prior and brethren of the order of Preachers in Hereford, for the reconciliation by any catholic bishop of that place within their close where they are wont to celebrate the divine offices, it having been polluted by the spilling of blood.

637 12 July 1344 Droitwich

Resignation of Richard Bartelam, rector of the chapel of Shell next Hanbury. Because his own seal is not widely known he has had that of Droitwich (*Wych*) deanery appended to his letter.

1 All beneficed clergy of Campden deanery.
2 Janekynes was instituted on 27 April [v. 623], John de Aston on 5 May [*Institutions*, 628].
3 St. Guthlac's priory was a cell of St. Peter's Abbey, Gloucester.

639 *22 July 1344*

John le Meyr, perpetual administrator of Shell, resigns that chapel
into the bishop's hands by reason of an exchange with the vicarage
of St. Peter's, Witton next Droitwich.[1]

640 *22 July 1344 Alvechurch*

Memorandum that the bishop approved the exchange between John
called *le Meyr*, perpetual administrator of Shell chapel, and William
called *le Child*, perpetual vicar of St. Peter's, Witton next Droitwich.[2]
He admitted and instituted John to St. Peter's (patrons: the prior
and conv. of Studley) and directed the official of the Worcester
archdeacon to induct him.

642 *30 July 1344 Droitwich*

Robert Payn, rector of Martin [Hussingtree], proctor of William
Child, rector of Shell, resigns the chapel into the bishop's hands,
realising how dangerous and difficult is the exercise of the cure of
souls. Because his own seal is not widely known he has had that of
Droitwich (*Wych*) deanery appended to the document.

643 *15 July 1340*[3] *Glasshampton*

William le Child, vicar of St. Peter's Witton, appoints Robert Payn
his proctor, with special power to exchange his vicarage with John le
Meyr for Shell chapel, and to receive institution and corporal
possession of the latter. The seal of Droitwich (*Wych*) deanery is
appended.

644 *22 July 1344*

Robert Payn, as proctor of William le Child, resigns St. Peter's
vicarage, Witton, because of an exchange for Shell chapel.

645 *13 July 1344 Alvechurch*[4]

Memorandum of the oath sworn within the bishop's manor by Ds.
Robert Payn, rector of Martin [Hussingtree], and John le Meyr of
Droitwich, to indemnify the bishop in the event of legal action being
taken against him by the pope because of his presentation to St.
Peter's vicarage, Witton. Witnesses: Thomas Bolevinch and M.
Stephen Ally, clerks.

1 See 637, 640 *et seq.*
2 *per modum et formam quarundam inquisicionum ex utraque parte captarum et in hac parte factarum.*
3 An error for *1344.*
4 See 642.

647 *3 August 1344 Hereford*

Commission of John Rees, canon of Hereford, vicar-general in spirituals of John [Trillek], bishop elect and confirmed of Hereford [1344–60], for the carrying out of an exchange of benefices between John de Gurdewalle, perpetual vicar of Mamble, Hereford diocese, and Thomas Aleyn, rector of St. Clement's Worcester.[1]

652 *24 August 1344 Withington*

Commission to the official of the Gloucester archdeacon. He is to admit, institute and induct Ralph de Brantyngham, clerk, to the church of Siddington by Cirencester, at the king's presentation, the lands of Monmouth priory[2] being in his hands by reason of the war with France.

654 *9 August 1344 Rock*

Certification by the archdeacon of Shropshire's official of his execution of the bishop's mandate, dated 4 August from Hartlebury, for enquiry into the vicarage of Mamble, because of the proposed exchange between John de Curdewall,[3] its perpetual vicar, and Thomas Aleyn, rector of St. Clement's Worcester.[4] In full chapter held *ex causis legitimis et probabilibus* in Rock church on the Monday after St. Oswald [i.e. 9 August], he conducted the enquiry by Roger de Stanford, Richard Nouwel, John de Horsuet, John de Glynton and Geoffrey de Abbedal, rectors respectively of Rock, Nene Sollars, Stanford, Stockton and Abberley, and by Richard Carles and Robert Morys, the vicars of Cleobury Mortimer and Lindridge. The enquiry found the vicarage not vacant but filled by John Curdewall, the vicar. The abbot and convent of St. James', Wigmore, are the true patrons, who last presented and have the right to do so at future vacancies. The church is not litigious, subject to a pension or portion, or taxed. Ds. Thomas Aleyn, the presentee, is free and legitimate, of praiseworthy life and honest conversation, 27 years of age or more, in priest's orders, and in possession of another benefice with cure—St. Clement's church, Worcester. The reasons for exchange are, on John de Curdewall's part, that he is unable to remain in Mamble for fear of death or bodily injury at the hands of his deadly enemies in the district; on Thomas's part, that the corruption of the air in the city [Worcester] is harmful to his constitution (*corrupcionem aeris . . . compleccioni sue contrarii*), and that he is excessively burdened by the constant incursion of relatives from Droitwich. The official is returning the enquiry under the seal of his officiality.

1 See 654.   2 A cell of St. Florence near Saumur in Anjou.
3 Gurdewalle in 647.
4 The bishop's mandate contains a recension of the Hereford vicar-general's commission (647).

658 *5 July 1343*[1] *Hartlebury*

Episcopal confirmation of William de Syde's ordination of a per-
petual chantry in the parish church of Our Lady, Syde, to be served
by a suitable chaplain. The king, by letters dated 5 May 1343 from
Westminster,[2] has licensed the alienation of one messuage, two
virgates of arable, and one acre of wood, with appurtenances in
Syde. William de Syde has granted these by charter to Ds. Ralph
Cole, chaplain, and his successors, who are to celebrate Mass of Our
Lady daily for the welfare of the founder and of Thomas, lord of
Berkeley, Maurice de Berkeley, Maurice de Berkeley,[3] John
Mautravers, Reginald de Cobham, his wife Joan, Richard de Cestre,
William de Chiltenham, and of all the founder's relations, friends
and benefactors, as well as for his soul after death, for the souls of all
the above, and for those of the founder's father and mother, brothers,
sisters and relations, for the souls of John Gyffard, Lady Margaret
Gyffard, Lady Margaret de Berkeley, John de Wylinton, Joan his
wife, for those of all the founder's friends and benefactors, and for the
souls of all the faithful departed. William de Syde[4] has presented the
above chaplain to the bishop and secured his admission, institution
and induction. He is to continue to present during his lifetime, and
thereafter the lord of Berkeley for the time being. Should either fail
to present a suitable chaplain within a month, the abbot of St.
Augustine's Bristol is to do so for that turn, and after a further month,
the bishop, or *sede vacante* the prior. The chaplain and his successors
are to reside in the chantry and to minister daily in accordance with
the founder's ordination. Should any fail to do so for the space of a
fortnight, another chaplain is to be presented, unless there be some
just and reasonable cause approved by the diocesan. The chaplains
are to be in the parish church daily for Mass, Matins and the Hours,
chanting and ministering with the other ministers of the church,
unless prevented by lawful cause. Every day they are to recite the
office of the dead for the souls of those mentioned above, that is the
Placebo and *Dirige* with the commendation. At each Mass they are
to say for the founder and all the above, while they live, the collect
Deus qui caritatis dona with the appropriate secret and post-communion,
and, for their souls after death, the collect *Fidelium Deus* or *Omnipotens
sempiterne Deus cui nunquam sine spe*, together with the secret and post-
communion. They are to celebrate the anniversary of the founder's
death by saying the office of the dead and a Mass on the morrow.
They are to be content with their portion and are not to receive

1 William de Syde's letters patent are dated 20 June 1343 from Syde. The Worcester
  prior and chapter added their confirmation on 10 July.
2 *C.P.R.* 1343–45, p. 32.
3 Maurice de Berkeley the elder was Thomas lord Berkeley's brother. Thomas had a
  son Maurice who succeeded him in 1361 and died in 1368.
4 The ordination proper begins at this point.

anything from anyone else for the celebration of Mass. They are to serve no-one, save God alone; to live chastely and honestly, to avoid markets and taverns, to take no part in unlawful trading, and to shun frivolities, public entertainments, and all dubious gatherings. The chaplain for the time being is not to farm out his portion, save for a term of years, and then only at its true value and with the founder's consent, or after his death, that of the lord of Berkeley. Should he offend in this, he is to be removed and the portions taken into the founder's hand, or that of the lord of Berkeley, until another chaplain be appointed. The buildings, closes, and other appurtenances of the chantry are to be kept in repair. For their upkeep the founder has given goods to the value of £14 18s. 10d.; one horse and two oxen worth 30s., 90 sheep worth £6 15s., seven acres of wheat worth 21s., eleven acres of barley worth 27s. 6d., seven of dredge worth 14s., and twelve of oats worth 18s., together with four marks [£2 13s. 4d.] in money. All of this is to be passed on to each succeeding chaplain, under the view of the lord of Berkeley, who is to see that the chaplain carries out the temporal provisions of the ordination. At the time of his institution the chaplain is to swear before the ordinary to observe all the above, and annually on the feast of the Assumption [15 August] he is to publish the ordinances at Mass, or some other appropriate time, in the people's presence. In the event of his becoming so aged or infirm as to be unable to celebrate Mass in person, he is to recite the Lord's Prayer daily and other private prayers, together with the *Placebo*, *Dirige* and commendation, the seven [penitential] psalms, the fifteen [gradual] psalms, and the Litany. He is to have two Masses celebrated each week by a suitable chaplain, one of Our Lady for the founder and all the above while living, the other for the souls of those departed. He is by no means to be removed because of such age or infirmity. The bishop, or his vicar, is to make enquiry at his visitation, and at other times, as to whether everything has been done according to the ordination. Should there be notable defects or crimes he is to punish the offender according to their gravity. Witnesses: Thomas de Berkeley of Coberley, John de Acton, Walter de Cirencestre, John de Elkeston, Thomas de la Mare of Rendcombe, John de Alspath, Thomas de Berton of Eycote and others. Syde, 20 June 1343. The bishop, therefore, confirms the chantry by his ordinary authority, so far as lies in his power.[1]

Prior John [of Evesham] and the cathedral chapter add their confirmation. Worcester, 10 July 1343.

659 *5 July 1343*[2] *Hartlebury*

Confirmation of William de Syde's ordination of a perpetual chantry

1 See 154.
2 The ordination of this, as of the other Syde chantries, is dated 20 June 1343, the prior and chapter's confirmation, 10 July 1343.

12

in St. Katherine's chapel, Cambridge, in Slimbridge parish.[1] The
founder has received royal licence to alienate a messuage, a virgate
of arable and 50s. rent with appurtenances in Berkeley, Cam and
Slimbridge.[2] These he has granted to Ds. Walter atte Forde,
chaplain, and his successors, who are to celebrate Mass of Our Lady
daily for the founder's welfare [&c. as in 658]. The chaplains are to
be in Slimbridge parish church, ministering and chanting with the
other ministers; that is to say, at Christmas and the Epiphany, at
Matins and Mass; on the Purification, Ash Wednesday and Palm
Sunday, at Mass; on Maundy Thursday, Good Friday, the vigil of
Easter and Easter Day, at Matins and Mass; on the vigil and day of
Pentecost, at Mass; as well as on all other feasts at which the parishioners are obliged by right or custom to make offerings (offere tenentur).
For the upkeep of the chantry the founder has given goods worth
£9 4s. 3½d.: four oxen worth £2 13s. 4d.; 13 acres of wheat worth
£2 12s.; five acres of beans worth 12s. 6d.; eight acres one rood of oats
worth 13s. 1½d.; and four marks [£2 13s. 4d.] in money. The ordination is to be read annually on the feast of All Saints [1 November] in
Slimbridge church. The bishop is to make enquiries at his visitation,
and should he discover any notable shortcomings, such as wastage of
the goods and substance of the chantry or the crime of incontinence,
he is to correct and punish the offender, or to remove him altogether.
Witnesses: Thomas de Bradeston, John de Acton, Peter Corbet,
Simon Basset, knights, John Sergeant and others. Berkeley, 20 June
1343.

660 *5 July 1343*[3] *Hartlebury*
Confirmation of William de Syde's ordination of a perpetual chantry
in St. Maurice's chapel, Newport, in Berkeley parish.[4] The founder
has received royal licences to alienate two messuages, two virgates of
arable and 100s. rent with appurtenances in Berkeley, Wotton,
Alkington and Hill next Berkeley.[5] These he has granted to Ds.
Robert de Sodynton, chaplain, the warden (*custos*) of St. Maurice's
chapel, Newport, and to one other chaplain, who are to celebrate
Mass daily for the founder's welfare [&c. as in 658, but with the
addition of Robert Groundy after William de Chiltenham]. He has presented
the said Robert to the bishop as warden of the chantry (*sub nomine*

---

1 The same form was used in all the Syde chantries. This entry is therefore similar to 658
and only the differences of detail have been included in the following summary.
2 C.P.R. 1343–45, p. 32. 5 May 1343.
3 The founder's ordination is dated 20 June 1343, the prior and chapter's confirmation
10 July, as in the other Syde chantries.
4 The form is the same as that for the other Syde chantries (*see* 658) with the variants
found in 659 (including Robert Groundy's name). In addition there are the verbal
differences arising from the fact that there were two chaplains in this case. They were
both bound to reside and to minister in the same manner as a single chaplain.
5 C.P.R. 1343–45, p. 23. 5 May 1343.

custodis), has had him admitted, instituted and inducted, and has provided[1] for a second chaplain. The chaplains are to live, eat and sleep under the same roof, on equal terms (*absque inconvenienti personarum distinccione*). Because the founder desires that both wayfarers, tillers of the soil, and other workers, should hear Mass daily to the honour of Almighty God, one of the chaplains, at the warden's discretion, is to celebrate in the early morning, the other at about the third hour in Summer and the sixth in Winter. The warden is to provide the second chaplain with food, clothing, and other necessaries. He is also to be chiefly responsible for the administration and care of things belonging to the chantry. On the death or retirement of the second chaplain the warden, with the founder's consent, or after his death, that of the lord of Berkeley, is to appoint another within six months. For the upkeep of the chantry the founder has given goods worth £17 6s. 8d.: three mares worth 24s.; six oxen worth £4; 18 acres of wheat worth £3 12s.; 14 acres of beans worth £1 15s.; one acre of dredge worth 2s.; 18 acres of oats worth 27s.; and eight marks [£5 6s. 8d.] in money. At the time of their institution the wardens are to swear before the ordinary to observe the ordination, and are to have it read out in Berkeley church every year on the feast of All Saints [1 November]. Witnesses: Thomas de Bradeston [*&c. as in 659*].

661 *5 July 1343*[2] *Hartlebury*
Confirmation of William de Syde's ordination of a perpetual chantry in St. John the Baptist's chapel, Wortley, in Wotton parish.[3] The founder has received royal licence[4] to alienate one messuage, one virgate of arable and 50s. rent with appurtenances in Wotton. These he has granted to Ds. Walter atte Forde, chaplain, and his successors. For the upkeep of the chantry the founder has given goods worth £9 2s. 1d.: four oxen worth £2; 11½ acres of wheat worth £2 6s.; half an acre of barley worth 1s. 3d.; one acre of beans worth 2s. 6d.; six acres of dredge worth 12s.; 18 acres of oats worth 27s.; and four marks [£2 13s. 4d.] in money. The ordination is to be read annually in Wotton church on the feast of All Saints [1 November]. Witnesses: Thomas de Bradeston [*&c. as in 659, except that John Chaussy replaces John Sergeant*].

662 *28 September 1345 Blockley*
Appointment (until revoked) of Ds. Alexander de Welleby, priest, rector of Eaton Hastings, Salisbury diocese, as *iconomus* of Deerhurst church. From public report, as well as expert enquiry, the bishop has learned that Deerhurst parish church has long been without a lawful

1 *Ordinavi.* This could mean that he actually appointed him.
2 The founder's ordination is dated 20 June 1343, the prior and chapter's confirmation 10 July, as in the other Syde chantries.
3 This entry is the same *mutatis mutandis* as 659.
4 *C.P.R.* 1343–45, p. 23. 5 May 1343.

defender because of the absence of the prior of the place,[1] and that the cure of souls has been grievously neglected. To remedy this he is appointing Ds. Alexander collector of the fruits, obventions, and profits of the church, and their lawful administrator or *yconomus*. He is to exercise the cure by means of a suitable chaplain of his own choosing.

667 *1 January 1346 Hartlebury*

Letters patent declaring the validity of the evidences produced by the abbot and convent of St. Augustine's, Bristol. During the bishop's recent visitation of the diocese,[2] he had ordered the religious to show their title to the appropriated churches of Ashleworth, Berkeley, Wapley and Almondsbury, and to those of St. Nicholas, St. Leonard, All Saints, and St. Augustine the less, within the town of Bristol, as well as to all their pensions and portions within the diocese. On the day appointed they had exhibited before the bishop's commissary apostolic letters, charters of various princes and temporal lords, letters of the bishop's predecessors and of the Worcester chapter, as well as sundry other muniments. Full and trustworthy information as to their continued possession of such churches and portions from time beyond memory was also received. In view of which, and in response to the petition of the canons, the bishop dismissed them from his examination.

668 *20 March 1346 London*

Public instrument attesting the appointment by M. John de Irford, clerk of Lincoln diocese, allegedly rector of Oddingley in Worcester diocese, of Robert de Thoresby and Philip de Ravendale, clerk, as his proctors, jointly or severally, for the exchange of his church with that of Rudbaxton, St. David's diocese. The proceedings took place in the house of M. John de Thoresby, canon of Lincoln, Keeper of the Privy Seal, within the parish of St. Mary-le-Strand, London diocese.[3] Present as witnesses were Ds. John de Brygham and Ds. Matthew de Asschton, rectors of Meopham and Foston (Canterbury and Lincoln dioceses respectively). William de Swafeld, clerk of Lincoln diocese, notary public by apostolic authority, drew up the instrument and added his accustomed mark.

669 *14 December 1345 Worcester*

Public instrument whereby, in the house of Peter the notary public within the city of Worcester, Ds. John de Chalkeford, rector of

1 Deerhurst was an alien priory, since *c.* 1059 a cell of St. Denis.
2 Apparently a reference to the third visitation in 1345, for which there is little information.
3 This was the London house of the Worcester bishops. See *C.C.R.* 1343–46, pp. 473, 480.

Rudbaxton,[1] appointed M. Peter de Bynbrok, rector of All Saints',
Worcester, his lawful proctor, with special power to exchange
Rudbaxton church for that of Oddingley. Present as witnesses were
Walter Boterole, Simon de Aruwe and Peter the notary, clerk of
Worcester diocese,[2] who drew up the instrument and appended his
seal.

670 *Undated* [3]

Commission of Henry [of Gower], bishop of St. David's [1328-47],
authorising the diocesan to carry out the exchange between John de
Chalkeford, rector of Rudbaxton (patron: John de Byton, Master of
Slebach),[4] and M. John de Irford, rector of Oddingley. He is to
institute the latter to Rudbaxton if the enquiry to be made by the
official of the archdeacon of St. David's finds for the presentor and
presentee.[5]

673 *22 November 1344 Hartlebury*

Commission for Br. Nicholas Morice, subprior of the cathedral
monastery, to admit the profession of Agnes Corbet as a nun of
Whiston by Worcester.

674 *6 November 1344 Buckden*

Certification by Thomas [Bek], bishop of Lincoln [1342-47], of his
execution of the diocesan's mandate, dated 21 October from Bredon,
for the exchange, in accordance with the findings of an enquiry held
by the official of the Gloucester archdeacon, between William Bryscy,
rector of Miserden (patron: the king as custodian of the land and
heir of Edmund, earl of Kent),[6] and John de Bymbrok, rector of
Shoby, Lincoln diocese.

675 *10 November 1344*

Memorandum of the oath of obedience taken by John de Bymbrok
and of the mandate sent to the official of the Gloucester archdeacon
for his induction.

676 *24 November 1344 Hartlebury*

Memorandum that the prior and convent of Kenilworth paid four
marks [£2 13s. 4d.] to the bishop, by way of procuration, for the

1 See 668.
2 In his subscription he calls himself *Petrus Ricardi* [*sic*] *Beaugrant*.
3 The entry is unfinished and was probably contained on the next folio, now missing.
4 A preceptory of the Knights Hospitallers near Haverfordwest.
5 See 668-9.
6 A brother of Edward II who was executed in 1330 after rebelling against Mortimer.

Michaelmas term of 1344, such sum being payable every three years on account of their appropriation of Bidford church.[1]

677 *27 November 1344 Hartlebury*

Letter of Thomas de Colne Rogeri, chaplain, dated 27 November from Broadwas, resigning the chantry which M. John de Bradewas, clerk, had recently founded in the church of St. Mary Magdalene, Broadwas. The bishop accepted the resignation in his manor of Hartlebury. Present as witnesses were M. Simon de Clare, rector of Elmley Lovett, and M. John le Botoner.

679 *3 October 1343 Avignon*

Papal dispensation for Baldwin de Mohun. Gaucelinus, bishop of Albano, has received the petition of Baldwin de Mohun, rector of Whichford, declaring that before coming of lawful age he had been instituted on the presentation of his uncle, a layman, and in due time, had been advanced to the priesthood on the title of his church. Now of lawful age and ready to resign the church, he has humbly asked the Holy See for remedy. Gaucelinus, as papal penitentiary, authorises the bishop, should he find the facts to be as alleged (*si est ita*), to absolve Baldwin, subject to appropriate penance and temporary suspension from the exercise of his orders, and after resignation of the church and restoration of its fruits. The bishop may then grant dispensation for him to exercise such orders again and to take up any benefice, including the original one.

680 *24 April 1344 Hartlebury*

Memorandum that M. Ralph le Whyte of Brailes, proctor of the above Baldwin, appeared before the bishop, who absolved his lord, enjoining as salutary penance that Baldwin should for eight consecutive days recite the seven penitential psalms together with the Litany. He suspended him for a month from the execution of his orders, and granted dispensation for his admission to any ecclesiastical benefice, including Whichford, should he be presented again.

681 *31 May 1344 Blockley*

Letters patent of the appropriation of Clent church with its chapel of Rowley. The bishop has received a petition from the abbot and convent of the Premonstratensian house of Hales[owen]. Although their conventual church and other essential buildings were in ancient times sumptuously built by pious founders, they have become so ruinous because of age and decay that their imminent collapse is

1 See Liber Albus, fo. lxxi v, and cf. 899 below.

feared, the religious being unable to assemble with safety for divine worship either in nave or quire. The number of canons has so increased that the original resources no longer suffice, and it is common knowledge that the monastery is near the public highway and therefore burdened with numerous guests, rich and poor. Certain churches, rights and possessions given to the monastery by the liberality of the faithful have been lost owing to the power of the magnates, whom they have been unable to resist, while their remaining arable lands are for the most part sterile. Although in the past much of their sustenance was derived from the offerings of pilgrims at the head of St. Barbara, virgin and martyr, these have now ceased owing to the scarcity of money, the lukewarmness of devotion, and the various oppressions of the people. Moreover, because of a recent fire in their houses and those of their tenants in Halesowen, besides various oppressions, exactions and other adversities, the canons' resources have been seriously depleted. For these reasons they ask the bishop to appropriate to them the church of Clent with Rowley chapel, which is in their patronage. The bishop, therefore, having learned the truth of the allegations by means of an enquiry, and knowing it to be pleasing to God to help the oppressed, particularly the religious, has decreed, after diligent, serious, and solemn discussion with the cathedral prior and chapter, and with their consent, that the church is to be appropriated to the canons. On the death or cession of the present rector the religious may lawfully take possession of the church and chapel. A suitable portion, estimated at £10, is reserved for a vicarage to be established by the bishop or his successors. By means of this the vicar, who is to be presented by the canons, may support the burdens imposed upon him by the bishop's ordination or that of his successors, saving always the dignity, custom and honour of the bishop, the cathedral church, and the archdeacon. As recompense for the fruits which would have accrued to the diocesan at vacancies and other times, the bishop, with the express consent of the religious, reserves a pension of two marks [£1 6s. 8d.], to be paid annually at Michaelmas [29 September], once they are in possession of the church.

684 *Undated*

Inspeximus and confirmation of the charter of M. John de Bradewas, clerk, for the foundation of a chantry in the church of St. Mary Magdalene, Broadwas.[1] By authority of a royal licence, with the consent of the Worcester prior and convent, patrons of the church, that of its rector, and all others concerned, M. John de Bradewas, for the increase of divine worship, has granted lands and tenements in free alms to God, Our Lady His mother, St. John the Baptist,

---

1 Nash, *Worcs.*, 1, p. 140 *et seq.*, gives a transcript.

St. John the Evangelist, to St. Mary Magdalene and St. Paul the Apostle, patrons of the church, and to Ds. Thomas de Colne Rogeri and Ds. Walter de Bradewas, chaplains. The chaplains are to celebrate Mass daily in the newly built chapel of St. Mary the Virgin.[1] During his lifetime the founder is to present the above Thomas and Walter and their successors for institution by the ordinary. After his death the prior of Worcester is to present. Should the prior fail to make presentation within a month, then the bishop or his vicar is to do so before the expiry of a further month, but without prejudice to the prior's right at subsequent vacancies. *Sede vacante*, the ordinary[2] is to present within two months, saving the bishop's future right. But if, owing to the prior's negligence, the chantry should be without suitable chaplains for two months, the collation is to devolve permanently on the diocesan, or whoever may be exercising his jurisdiction. The chaplains are to celebrate Mass in turn, or by alternate weeks, in honour of the Virgin, and with her office, for the welfare of King Edward and Queen Philippa, that of Wolstan, bishop of Worcester, Prior John of Evesham and the Worcester convent, the founder, William de Bradewas, William de Kyllesby, Peter de Groete, Margery[3] de Housele, John and William, her sons, Henry and Matilda, the founder's father and mother, his brothers, sisters, relations and benefactors, and all the faithful departed. Mass is to be celebrated with collect, secret and communion for the founder, during his lifetime, and with another collect, secret and communion for the king, queen and all the above. After the founder's death it is to be celebrated for his soul, with collect, secret and communion, as for a priest, and likewise for the others named, after their deaths. If, owing to illness or for other sufficient reason, the above offices cannot be performed, after four days a chaplain or chaplains must be found for this purpose. Except on double feasts the chaplains are to say the *Placebo, Dirige* and commendation daily for the founder and the others mentioned, and for his and their souls after death. They are to be present as often as possible at Matins and the canonical Hours with the other chaplains and clerks of the church. A priest guilty of incontinence or other excesses is to be corrected by the ordinary. Should he be defamed a second time for a sin of the flesh, and be convicted or unable to purge himself, another chaplain is to be admitted in his place. Every year the chaplains are to find five pounds of wax for five candles and one lamp. These are to burn at appropriate times in the chapel of Our Lady and are to be renewed at the Annunciation [25 March]. On All Souls Day [2 November]

1 The chapel is a separately gabled structure divided from the south-eastern part of the nave by an arcade of two bays.
2 i.e. The Worcester prior.
3 Surnamed Drew (*Dreu*) in the mortmain licence which follows.

five shillings, or bread or corn to that value, are to be distributed to the poor, under the supervision of the rector and other trustworthy men of the parish. After the founder's death this sum is to be distributed on his anniversary, for his soul and those of all the above. Whenever the chaplains fail to obey the ordination they are to pay 20s. towards the fabric of the cathedral church, under compulsion of the ordinary. On the founder's anniversary they are to say the *Placebo* and *Dirige*, and to sing Mass at the altar of Our Lady in the chapel for his soul and those of the others. In addition to the lands the founder has given the chaplain ten marks [£6 13s. 4d.] and all growing crops. Each of them is to leave five marks to his successor together with his share of the following property:[1] eight working oxen, a wagon, cart and plough with accoutrements, a harrow, chest, cask, vat(?),[2] barrel, brass pot, plate, pitcher, gridiron, axe, a basin with washing bowl, a table with trestles, a form, a table-cloth with napkin, a cup, a mortar and pestle, a ladder, winnowing fan, bushel, sack and basket. He is also to leave one half of all other movable goods, and if necessary either he or his executors is to be compelled to do so by the ordinary. All goods, rents or profits from the chantry lands and tenements are to be used in common, and without waste, by the chaplains, who are to reside permanently in Broadwas. Every year, on the feast of All Saints [1 November], the ordinances are to be published by them in the church, in the presence of all the people. An oath to observe them fully and faithfully is to be taken by every chaplain at the time of his admission. The founder warrants against all men their possession of the chantry lands, tenements, rights and appurtenances. Witnesses: John le Nower of Wichenford, William de Abyndon, Thomas de Abyndon of Wichenford, John le Jeuene of Cotheridge, Thomas Godewyne of Doddenham, and others. Dated 22 March 1344 from Broadwas. *There follows a recension of the royal licence.* The king permits John de Bradewas, clerk, to alienate a messuage, 82 acres of arable land, seven of meadow, and ten of wood, with appurtenances in Cotheridge, held of him in chief, and a messuage, 18 acres of arable, and three of meadow, with appurtenances in Doddenham, Ankerdine and Broadwas, not so held, for the support of two chaplains who are to celebrate Mass daily in the church of St. Mary Magdalene, Broadwas.[3] Dated 1 March 1344 from Westminster.[4] The bishop, therefore, approving the praiseworthy desire of M. John de Bradewas, ratifies and confirms the above articles by pontifical authority. Wishing to ensure their inviolable observance, he inhibits anyone from infringing them under penalty of greater excommunication;

---

1 *de quolibet . . . melius quod habebit tempore vacacionis.*   2 MS. *cunem* or *cuvem* (? for *cuvam*).
3 The names of the beneficiaries are given in full, as above.
4 *C.P.R.* 1343–45, p. 215. There are two earlier licences: *ibid.* p. 49 (23 May 1343), and *ibid.* 1338–40, pp. 477–8 (21 April 1340).

such sentence to be pronounced, if need be, by the dean of Worcester for the time being, at the instance of M. John de Bradewas or that of the chantry chaplains.

685 *21 December 1344 Auckland*

Certification by Richard [of Bury], bishop of Durham [1333–45], of his execution of the diocesan's commission, dated 3 November from Hartlebury, for the exchange, in accordance with the findings of an enquiry held by the official of the Worcester archdeacon, between Antony Fossour, vicar of Aston Cantlow, and Thomas de Normanton, vicar of Bedlington, Durham diocese.

Accordingly the diocesan wrote to the archdeacon's official for Thomas's induction to Aston Cantlow.

692 *6 February 1345 Hartlebury*

Memorandum that the bishop, in Hartlebury chapel, ordained Simon de Geynesburgh, rector of Winchfield, Winchester diocese, to the order of acolyte, by letters dimissory of his diocesan. He also ordained to the same order, M. Thomas Belamy, rector of Broadwell, and M. John de Bradewas, rector of Sedgeberrow.

693 *7 February 1345 Hartlebury*

Memorandum that the bishop admitted Brothers John de Grosseleye and William de Lodelowe, of the Augustinian order of Hermits, to preach and hear confessions within the diocese in accordance with the constitution *Super cathedram*.[1]

696 *13 January 1345 Hartlebury*

Memorandum of the licence for Ds. Henry, rector of Pillerton, to leave his church and to farm it to John de Bourton for three years.[2]

701 *20 February 1345*

Memorandum that the bishop ordained as acolyte M. Walter de Evesham, who swore obedience to him and his successors, and to his Official and ministers.

704 *27 January 1345*

Memorandum of the licence for Ds. Robert[3] de More, rector of Churchill, to farm his church for three years to John son of William de Shareshull, clerk.

---

1 Incorporated in *Clement* 3, 7, c. 2 *Dudum.*   2 Cf. 552.
3 *Recte* William.

705 *10 January 1345*

Memorandum of the licence for Walter de Clodeshale, rector of Pedmore, acolyte, to attend a *studium generale* in England for a year from Michaelmas last [29 September 1344].

706 *7 March 1345 Hartlebury*

Licence for John de Harewell, rector of Whichford (*Wicheueford*), to attend Hugh of Audley, earl of Gloucester, for a year, and to receive the fruits of his church as though resident. During that time it is to be properly served by a chaplain and other suitable ministers, and a permanent proctor is to be appointed at the outset to answer for episcopal rights and other burdens, both spiritual, temporal and legal.[1] Also, at the peril of his conscience, the rector is to come to the help of the poor of his parish. Otherwise the licence is to be void.

708 *7 March 1345*

Memorandum of the above licence.

709 *9 March 1345*

Memorandum of the licence for M. Luke, rector of Honington, to study for three years in accordance with the Boniface composition.[2]

710 *28 March 1345*

Memorandum of the similar licence, but for two years, granted to M. Peter Gros of Worcester, rector of Suckley.

714 *10 October 1344 Avignon*

Papal dispensation for William Elys. Gaucelinus, bishop of Albano, writes that he has received a petition on behalf of William Elys of Horsham in Martley parish, and of Juliana his wife, to the effect that in ignorance of any impediment they had contracted a marriage *in facie ecclesie*, after due publication of the banns, and had consummated it. Subsequently they had learned privately that William's mother was godmother to Juliana at her confirmation by the ordinary, and as great scandal might arise were they to separate (*si divorcium fieret inter eos*), they have humbly asked the Holy See for remedy. Gaucelinus, as penitentiary, and by authority of a special mandate delivered *viva voce* by the Pope, empowers the bishop, should the facts be as alleged (*si est ita*) to dispense the parties so that they may remain lawfully married and their children be accounted legitimate.

1 *iura episcopalia et alia onera eidem incumbencia in spiritualibus et temporalibus, causisque et negociis, per procuratorem ydoneum continue commorantem . . . agnosci facias prout decet.*
2 *Sext* 1, 6, c. 34.

715 *17 March 1345 Hartlebury*

Memorandum that in accordance with the tenor of the above letters the bishop dispensed William and Juliana after receiving information from sworn and trustworthy men.

718 *26 March 1345*

Memorandum of the licence for M. Thomas Belamy, subdeacon, rector of Broadwell, to study for a year, without obligation to proceed to further orders during that time, in accordance with the constitution *Cum ex eo*.[1]

719 *14 March 1345 Farnham*

Commission from John [Trillek], bishop of Hereford [1344–60], for the induction of M. John de Lech to the prebend of Inkberrow, which he had collated to him together with a canonry of Hereford. These had been resigned by Ds. John de la Chambre by reason of an exchange for the church of Mapledurham with Petersfield chapel, Winchester diocese.

720 *30 March 1345 Hartlebury*

Memorandum that the bishop admitted and instituted the above M. John de Lech, in the person of his proctor M. William de Lech, to the prebend of Inkberrow, and directed the official of the Worcester archdeacon to induct him.

721 *26 April 1345 Hartlebury*

Certification by the bishop of his execution of the mandate of Thomas [Bek], bishop of Lincoln [1341–47], for the institution and induction of John de Blockeleygh to South Luffenham church, to which he had been presented by Thomas de Beauchamp, earl of Warwick. Having examined the certificate of an enquiry sent under the bishop of Lincoln's seal, and finding no canonical impediment, he instituted John in the person of his proctor, William de Sotton.

725 *6 March 1345 Bredicot*

Letters patent of William Byrkeby, clerk, lord of the manor of Bredicot, declaring the grant on behalf of himself and his heirs to Walter de Dunstaple, clerk, of five marks [£3 6s. 8d.] yearly for life.[2]

726 *21 May 1345 Bredon*

Memorandum that in the bishop's manor the above Walter de Dunstaple swore, in the presence of Masters John de Severleye,

1 *Sext* i, 6, c. 34.   2 Rubric: *Titulus Walteri de Dunstable.*

John le Botinere and John de Bradewas, notary public, rectors respectively of Billesley, Naunton on the Wold, and Sedgeberrow, that he would never bring a suit against the bishop or his successors by virtue of the chapter *Cum secundum apostolum*[1] on account of his ordination as subdeacon at Hartlebury on Holy Saturday.[2]

728 *17 July 1345 Bredon*

Memorandum of the licence for Edmund Hakelute, his wife, and M. Thomas Hakelute, to hear Mass (*divina*) for one year in an oratory at Crookbarrow within the parish of St. Peter's Worcester.

729 *19 July 1345 Henbury in Salt Marsh*

Memorandum of the licence granted until revoked to Elias de Filton and Emma his wife for celebration *in loco honesto*.

730 *16 August 1345*

Memorandum of the licence for Ds. William de Syde to have Mass celebrated (*celebrandi et audiendi divina*) in a chapel at Kings Weston within Henbury parish.

732 *26 August 1345 Henbury*

Memorandum of the licence for Walter Broun de Leonhales, priest, rector of St. Werburgh's, Bristol, to be absent for a year.

733 *26 August 1345 Henbury*

Memorandum of the licence granted to John Uphovere for celebration in the same parish [*sic*] during the infirmity of himself and his wife.

735 *30 June 1345 Bredon*

Inspeximus and confirmation of the ordination of a chantry in St. James's chapel, Over, by Thomas lord Berkeley.[3] A royal licence, dated 12 March 1345 from Westminster,[4] has permitted the alienation in mortmain of a messuage and two virgates of land in Over to a chaplain, who is to celebrate Mass daily in the chapel there for the souls of the said Thomas, Margaret his late wife, and all the faithful departed. By a charter dated 20 May 1345 from Berkeley, Thomas de Berkeley, son of Maurice de Berkeley, knight, has granted the above to Ds. William de Cope of Tetbury and his successors. The founder

1 *Extra* 3, 5, c. 16. This laid an obligation on bishops to support those whom they ordained without adequate title.
2 Cf. 1063, where he is said to have been ordained to the title of Holy Trinity hospital, Bridgnorth.
3 Cf. 154 which is in the same form.
4 *C.P.R.* 1343–45, p. 442.

has presented William to the bishop,[1] who has instituted him. In future presentation is to be made by himself or his heirs. But should this not be done within a month, the right is to pass to the abbot of St. Augustine's Bristol, and after a further month, to the bishop, or *sede vacante*, the Worcester prior, saving the right of the founder or his heirs to present at subsequent vacancies. The chaplains are to reside and to minister in accordance with the ordination, and are to take an oath to that effect at the time of their institution. If any chaplain should fail to reside or to celebrate for a fortnight, unless with just cause, the patron is to present another without delay. The chaplains are to be in Almondsbury parish church where they are to minister with the other [clergy] at Matins and Mass on the feasts of Christmas, the Epiphany [6 January], and the Purification [2 February], and at Mass[2] on Ash Wednesday, Maundy Thursday, Good Friday, Holy Saturday, Easter Day and the eve and day of Pentecost. They are to say the office of the dead daily, that is, the *Placebo* and *Dirige* with the commendation, for the souls mentioned above. In each of their Masses they are to recite the collect *Deus qui caritatis dona* with the secret and post-communion for the founder, his relations and bene-factors, during their lifetime, and for his friends, relations and bene-factors who have died, the collect *Fidelium Deus* or *Omnipotens sempiterne Deus cui nunquam sine spe* with the secret and post-com-munion. On the day of the founder's death and on his anniversary they are to say the office of the dead with Mass on the morrow. They are to be content with their portion, and are not to accept money from anyone else for the celebration of Mass.[3] . . . Witnesses: Maurice de Berkeley, lord of Uley, the founder's brother, Maurice de Berkeley, his son, Thomas de Bradeston, Simon Basset, Peter Corbet, knights, and others. The bishop, approving the above, confirms the ordination.[4]

736 *16 August 1345 Henbury in Salt Marsh*

Licence for Ds. Peter, rector of Nympsfield. In view of the damage done by fire to his rectory house, through no fault of his own, the bishop permits him to leave his church for four years, so that he can study at a university, and to farm it to the prior of Horsley. During that time it is to be properly served, there is to be no neglect of the cure of souls, the rectory buildings are to be rebuilt from the rev-

1 The ordination proper begins at this point.
2 But the phrase seems not quite right, and the scribe may have intended to record an arrangement more like that in 659.
3 From this point the provisions are virtually the same as in 154, though with verbal differences. There is an additional clause (cf. 659) forbidding the alienation of the chantry portion, except for a life term, at its true value, and with the consent of the founder or his heirs—under penalty of re-entry by the latter.
4 As in 154.

enues (*iuxta discrecionem et possibilitatem a Deo tibi datas*), and a suitable proctor appointed to answer to the ordinaries and others concerned.

739 *26 August 1345*

Memorandum of the licence for Ds. Walter Broun, rector of St. Werburgh's, Bristol, to be absent for one year. [Duplicate of 732.]

741 *11 September 1345 Withington*

Memorandum of the licence for M. Thomas de Bradewelle, rector of Coln St. Dennis, to be absent for two years.

743 *24 August 1345 Southwark*

Public instrument drawn up by John, called *Wallensis*, clerk of Lincoln diocese and notary public by apostolic authority, testifying to the resignation of William Savage, clerk, rector of Aston Cantlow.[1] The proceedings took place in the house of William de Clynton, earl of Huntingdon, near to that of the bishop of Winchester in Southwark, in the presence of the above earl, of William de Setonham, knight, M. Godfrey Froumont, Ds. Henry de Sodynton, and Ds. Thomas de Merston, clerks, and of Richard de Lambeth and William de Caythorp.

744 *Undated*

The bishop collates[2] to M. Thomas Bolwynch, clerk, the church of St. Peter, Warwick, which to the great peril of the parishioners' souls, had been vacant for longer than the time allowed by the canons.[3]

745 *1 August 1345 Bristol*

Memorandum that within the monastery of St. Augustine the bishop instituted[4] the above Thomas Bolwynch and wrote for his induction to the official of the Worcester archdeacon or his *locum tenens*, to M. Robert de Staverton, portionist of St. Nicholas' church, Warwick, and to Ds. John de Tyso, parish priest of Billesley.

746 *Undated[5] Aston Cantlow*

Execution of an episcopal mandate dated 23 June 1345 from Bishops Cleeve. The bishop has received a petition of the prior and convent

1 The entry includes a recension of the letter of resignation addressed to the bishop.
2 Rubric: *Collacio ecclesie Sancti Petri Warr'*. This is of interest because it shows that sometimes (cf. 241) collation and institution (n. 4 below) were treated as distinct processes. See intro. p. xxxii.
3 The right of collation devolved on the bishop after four months if the patron were a layman, after six if he were an ecclesiastic.
4 Rubric: *Institucio ecclesie Sancti Petri Warrewich*. Cf. n. 2 above.
5 Allegedly *ut supra*, i.e. 23 June, but this seems unlikely, if not impossible. Cf. 748.

of Maxstoke, Coventry & Lichfield diocese, as follows. William de Clynton, earl of Huntingdon, had founded *de novo*[1] their house of Augustinian canons regular and endowed it with his goods. Four canons and a prior constituted the initial foundation, but the earl urged them to increase that number. On the strength of his promise to greatly augment their resources, they expanded to twenty. Although the earl has given them certain temporal goods and the patronage of Aston Cantlow church, their total revenues are insufficient to support so many canons. Because of this they ask for the above church to be appropriated to them, saving the portion of the vicarage already established there. The bishop directs Henry de Neubold to enquire by means of a sworn body of trustworthy men, both laymen and clerks, into the truth of the above and as to the adequacy of the vicarage portion. Henry de Neubold certifies that he has duly executed the bishop's mandate and appends the depositions of the jurors.[2]

747 *15 September 1345 Withington*

Mandate for M. Henry de Neubold, rector of Weston-on-Avon, to secure the consent of the Worcester prior and chapter to the appropriation of Aston Cantlow church.[3]

748 *22 September 1345 Gloucester*

Certification by Henry de Neubold of his execution of the above commission. On the feast of St. Matthew [21 September] he went personally to the cathedral chapter and after lengthy discussion secured its consent.

749 *9 September 1345 Withington*

Mandate to M. Henry de Neubold, the bishop's sequestrator, and to the dean of the Christianity of Warwick. It has been the custom of the Worcester diocese, time out of mind, for the diocesan to have the disposal of the fruits and obventions of all vacant ecclesiastical benefices. The bishop has learned that since 24 August Aston Cantlow church has been vacant owing to the resignation of Ds. William Savage the last rector.[4] He therefore declares the fruits sequestrated, and directs the commissaries to keep them so until otherwise instructed. By St. Matthew [21 September] they are to inform him of their proceedings and of the amount and nature of the fruits they have found.

1 In 1331 Sir William de Clynton, as he then was, established a secular college. Five years later he refounded it as a priory of canons regular. Dugdale, *Baronage*, 1, p. 233; *C.P.R.* 1334-38, pp. 309-10, 318.
2 These are not recorded in the register.
3 Cf. 526.   4 743.

750 *4 October 1345 Blockley*

Letters patent of the appropriation of Aston Cantlow church. The bishop has received a petition of the prior and convent of Maxstoke. William de Clynton, earl of Huntingdon, at the time of his first foundation of their house had provided for only four canons regular and a prior, though intending to increase that number later. It was at his instance that the bishop appropriated to them the parish church of Tanworth.[1] The number of canons has now been increased to nineteen, and the resources of the original foundation of almost fourteen years previously[2] no longer suffice for their upkeep, the maintenance of hospitality, and the support of the burdens laid upon them. They request the bishop to appropriate to them Aston Cantlow church, the advowson of which their founder acquired anew and granted to them. The bishop, having ascertained the truth of the above by means of an enquiry held for that purpose, appropriates the church with the express consent of the Worcester chapter. On the death or cession of the present rector the religious may take the fruits for their own use, saving the vicar's portion. The cathedral prior and chapter add their confirmation. Worcester, 6 October.

751 *A portion of the itinerary for the bishop's third visitation of the Worcester archdeaconry, 7–10 November 1345*[3]

Date	Details of churches visited &c.	Visitation held in	Dined	Stayed the night
Mon. 7	Worcester priory	Chapter House	The priory	The priory
Tues. 8	*Idem.*		*Idem.*	Hartlebury (The commissaries and notary in the priory)

DEANERY OF WORCESTER

| Wed. 9 | *By the bp.'s commissaries:* Worcester: churches of St. Helen, St. Peter the Great, St. Nicholas, St. Andrew, St. Swithin, All Saints, St. Clement, St. Martin, St. Alban, Wick with the chapel of St. John, Claines, Aston Bishop, Tibberton, | St. Helen's church and rectory | Hartlebury | *Ibid.*[4] |

1 321.   2 i.e. 1331.   3 For convenience this is given in tabulated form. Cf. 117.
4 There seems to be an error here. The commissaries are said to have conducted the visitation in St. Helen's church, but the entry concludes: *in rectoria Sancte Elene et prandit et pernoctavit in manerio suo de Hertlebur'*. It may be that the bishop himself visited some of the churches listed, possibly those from Wick onwards.

13

Date	Details of churches visited &c.	Visitation held in	Dined	Stayed the night

DEANERY OF WORCESTER (contd.)

Wed. 9 (contd.)	By the bp.'s commissaries (contd.): Kempsey with chapel[s], Ombersley, Hindlip, Warndon, Bredicot, Spetchley, Pirton, Severn Stoke			
Th. 10	By the bishop: Astley, Witley, Shrawley, Shelsley, Holt, Martley, Areley, Knightwick, Cotheridge, Kenswick, Broadwas, Grimley with the chapel of Hallow, Wichenford chapel.	Astley church	Hartlebury	Ibid.

753 *16 December 1345 Hartlebury*

Letters patent acknowledging the receipt from the abbot and convent of Halesowen of four marks [£2 13s. 4d.], due by way of procuration from their church of Halesowen for the bishop's visitation of 1345, and of a further two marks for the Michaelmas term of that year on account of their appropriation of Clent church with Rowley chapel.[1]

754 *24 January 1346 Liddington*

Commission of Thomas [Bek], bishop of Lincoln [1342–47], authorising the diocesan to carry out the exchange between Ds. Philip de Gosynton, rector of St. Swithin's, Worcester, and Ds. William de Preston, rector of Hethe, Lincoln diocese, in accordance with the findings of an enquiry to be held by the official of the archdeacon of Oxford.

755 *29 January 1346 Hampton Bishop*

Resignation of St. Swithin's church, Worcester, by John Ryppon, priest, of York diocese, proctor of Ds. Philip de Gosynton, the rector, by reason of an exchange with Hethe church, Lincoln diocese. The resignation was made and read out in the presence of M. John de la Lowe, Nicholas de Stanlake, John Botoner, and others.

757 *26 March 1345 Hartlebury*

Memorandum of the licence for Thomas Belamy, rector of Broadwell, to be absent for a year.

1 681.

759 *26 November 1345 St. Denis, [Paris]*

Giles, abbot of St. Denis, informs the bishop that he has removed Br. Thomas Garculi, formerly prior of Deerhurst, at his own wish and in the interests of the monastery, and is appointing him to a more acceptable position. For institution to Deerhurst parish church, thereby left vacant, he presents the new prior, Br. John Godelli, the bearer of his letter.[1]

760 *26 November 1345 St. Denis*

Public instrument drawn up by Ralph, called *du Pile*, clerk of Amiens diocese, notary public by apostolic authority, testifying to the resignation of Br. Thomas Garculi, prior of Deerhurst. Present as witnesses were Nicholas de Mondevilla, subprior, Peter called *de Pailli*, third prior, John de Monte Archiis, cantor, Aubyn de Trelabille, precentor,[2] Gerard called *de Marcheis*, infirmarian, Philip de Pulcro Puteo, monks of St. Denis, and M. Stephen Raymund, secular clerk, licentiate in both laws.

761 *17 February 1346 Cropthorne*

The bishop informs the above Br. John Godelli [759] of his institution to the cure of Deerhurst church.

762 *17 February 1346 Cropthorne*

Mandate to the official of the Gloucester archdeacon for Godelli's induction in accordance with the composition between Matthew, formerly abbot of St. Denis, and bishop Godfrey Giffard.[3]

764 *Undated*

Resignation of John de Wyttelfordbrugg, rector of Northfield church with Cofton chapel. Witnesses: John Botyner and Ds. Henry Kynges of Winchcombe.

770 *2 April 1346 London*

Letters patent of Ralph de Brantyngham, rector of Kirkby Thore, Carlisle diocese, declaring that he has assumed the church of Kirkby Thore and totally renounced that of Siddington, of which he was lately rector. The royal presentee to Siddington[4] is to be free of any interference from himself or those acting on his behalf. At his request John de Offord, dean of Lincoln, has added his seal.[5]

1 Cf. 256.   2 MS. *preceptor.*   3 Cf. 257.
4 John Edwart. See *Institutions* 771.
5 Offord was royal chancellor at the time.

772 *25 February 1346 Pershore*

The abbot and convent of Pershore appoint Br. Robert de Luttelton their proctor for the foundation of Adam de Herwynton's chantry.[1]

773 *25 February 1346 Pershore*

Letters patent of the abbot and convent of Pershore reciting the grant of lands and money by Adam de Herwynton for the establishment of a chantry.[2]

774 *27 February 1346 Bredon*

Submission of Adam de Herwynton's executors to the bishop's ordination of the above chantry.[3]

775 *12 April 1346 Hartlebury*

Presentation to the Herwynton chantry. Hugh de Cokesheye, William de Herwynton, Robert de Alvreston, Roger de la Felde, Thomas de Sloghtre, executors of the last will and testament of Adam de Herwynton, lately deceased, present Ds. John de la Felde and Ds. John de Diclesdon of Gotherington, priests, for institution to the chantry in the chapel on the south side of the nave of Pershore abbey in which Herwynton lies buried.[4]

778 *18 April 1346 Hartlebury*

Commission for the cathedral prior, the archdeacon of Worcester, the Official, and the chancellor. The bishop has received letters from the king and from John [Stratford], archbishop of Canterbury [1333–48], which he is sending for their inspection. The king, for the greater safety of the realm, which is threatened by invasion, for the defence of the Church, the confounding of his enemies, and the wider prosecution of his rights, has determined with the consent of the peers and magnates to cross the sea, which cannot be done without the help of many armed men and at great expense. In view of the king's request and that of the archbishop for the anticipation of the terms of the last year of the recently granted triennial tenth,[5] he has summoned the clergy of the diocese to appear in the cathedral church on 20 April, as will be seen more clearly in the royal letters and his own certifications. As he is prevented by urgent business from being present in person, he charges them to expound the royal letters to the clergy on the day appointed, and on such further days as may prove necessary, and to secure their assent to the king's demands. They are to inform him of their proceedings, of the clergy's decision, and of the names of those who give their assent.

---

1 See 906.   2 *Ibid.*   3 *Ibid.*   4 See *Institutions* 776.
5 It was granted in 1344. See 1218, 1231.

785 *29 March 1346 Billeswick*

Notarial instrument drawn up by John de Chaille.[1] Br. John de Stokelonde, precentor and president of St. Mark's hospital, and Brothers William de Cler', Geoffrey de Hemy[n]gton, Nicholas de Bristoll, Robert de Trillek, William Achard, Robert de Westbury and Richard Fraunceys, came together in their chapter house on 29 March. After reading letters patent of the official of the Court of Canterbury, from which it appeared that it was open to them to elect a new master, they appointed 5 April for that purpose. Arrangements were made for the recall of their absent brethren Ralph de Tettebury, John de Stoke and Richard de Yate. Present as witnesses were Walter de Oterhampton, clerk, and Nicholas called 'Kyard', *litteratus*.

786 *6 April 1346*

Notarial instrument drawn up by John de Chaille attesting the process by which the consent of Br. John de Stokelonde to his election was secured.[2] Brothers William de Cler', Geoffrey de Hemyngton, Nicholas de Bristoll, John de Stoke, Richard de Yate, William Achard, Robert de Westebury and Richard Fraunceys, in the presence of the above notary and of William de Malmesbury and Walter de Oterhampton, clerks, acting as witnesses, appointed Br. Robert de Trillek their proctor to acquaint Br. John de Stokelonde with his election and to secure his consent. Before the ninth hour of the same day, in the choir of the hospital of St. Katherine the Virgin next Bedminster, Bath & Wells diocese, and in the presence of the above notary and of Brothers William Godewyn, master of the hospital, John de Greynton, Richard de Oxingdon, Peter de Scheftesbury and John de Hampton Meysi, as well as of M. William de Clerewelle, clerk, and other witnesses, Br. Robert de Trillek appeared before the elect and presented to him the process of election with the request that he give his consent. The elect replied in writing that he needed time for consideration. About the hour of Vespers the proctor appeared again and repeated his request in the presence of the notary, the brethren of St. Katherine's hospital, and of Robert Gyen and John de Strete, *litterati*. This time John de Stokelonde delivered his written consent to the proctor.

787 *13 March 1346 London*

Mandate from the official of the Court of Canterbury addressed to the Worcester Official, the official of the archdeacon of Gloucester, and the [rural] deans of that archdeaconry. There had come before his court a suit between the brethren of St. Mark's hospital and Br. Ralph de Tettebury concerning the latter's removal from the

1 See 781.   2 Rubric: *Requisicio et prestacio consensus.*

mastership. After production of the libel, contestation of the suit, and various other processes, the parties agreed to submit to his arbitration. He has declared Ralph de Tettebury to be deprived of the mastership and the brethren of the hospital free to elect someone in his place, while reserving to himself the right to make provision for Ralph from the hospital's goods, as required by the terms of the submission. The commissaries are to publish the sentence at such times and places as they think fit and as the brethren of the hospital may request.

788 *5 April 1346 Billeswick*

Letter of the president, Br. John de Stokelonde, and other brethren of St. Mark's Billeswick, deputing five of their number to act as compromisers.[1] The dean of Bristol appended his seal at their special request.[2]

789 *5 April 1346 Billeswick*

Letters of the above compromisers[3] appointing Br. William Achard, one of their number, to elect Br. John de Stokelonde in their name and to publish such election.

790 *8 April 1346 Billeswick*

Letters patent[4] of the appointment by the brethren of St. Mark's[5] of Brothers William de Cler' and Geoffrey de Henyngton as proctors and *instructores* in the matter of Stokelonde's election. They are to give details of the proceedings before the bishop or his *locum tenens*, to deal with matters arising from them, and to take any oath that may be necessary.

791 *8 April 1346 Billeswick*

Letters patent[6] of the appointment by the brethren of St. Mark's[7] of Br. John de Stoke and M. Robert de Nettelton, clerk, as their proctors for securing the bishop's confirmation of Stokelonde's election.

792 *24 April 1346 Bristol*

Judicial examination by the prior of St. James's Bristol, the bishop's commissary *ad hoc*, of the election process.[8] In the parish church of

1 See 781.   2 He did the same in 789–791.
3 Rubric: *Littera super potestate eligendi et publicandi eleccionem.*
4 Rubric: *Procuratorium instructorum.*
5 As given at the beginning of 781, discounting the proctors themselves.
6 Rubric: *Procuratorium ad prosequendum eleccionem.*
7 As enumerated at the beginning of 781, excepting John de Stoke himself.
8 Rubric: *Attestaciones super instruccione negocii.*

St. James on the Monday following *Quasi modo geniti*,[1] the morrow of St. George the Martyr,[2] the commissary, after the recitation of his commission, received the certificate of the dean of Bristol, which was likewise read out. From the latter it appeared that the dean had cited any co-elect or opponent of Stokelonde's election to appear before the bishop or his commissary. No-one coming forward, the elect and the proctor of St. Mark's presented themselves, and the latter's proxy was read. Further citation was made, again without result, whereupon all such opponents were declared contumacious and precluded from interfering in the proceedings. The commissary then began his examination. He first received the oaths *de veritate dicenda* of the *instructores*, Brothers William de Cler' and Geoffrey de Hemyngton, and of John Fychet and Roger le Brewer, the witnesses, and then personally and by John de Chaille, the notary, examined them carefully with respect to the election itself and the various articles handed to him by the convent's proctor. Their attestations were as follows. Br. William de Cler' asserted that the brethren first heard of the vacancy from the mandate of the official of the Court of Canterbury. It arrived on 29 March and at the hour of Vespers they met in their chapter house and appointed 5 April for the election. He intended to prove certain articles. Firstly, that Br. John de Stokelonde was a freeman, legitimate, and at the time of his election professed of the order of St. Augustine in that house (St. Mark's) and in priest's orders. *Item*, that he was so at the time of the election, both before and after it, and by common repute. *Item*, that all the brethren at the election were professed to the same Rule and observance and were in priest's orders. *Item*, that they were so long before and subsequently. *Item*, that the whole election procedure was lawfully carried out on a single occasion (*uno contextu*)—between dawn and the sixth hour[3] on 5 April. *Item*, that John de Chaille, by whose hand all the public instruments were drawn up, was for the whole time a *tabellio* and notary public, and generally taken for such. All the above articles he declared to be true. He had known the father and mother of the elect during their lifetime. They were free tenants of the manor of Stockland, of which the brethren of St. Mark's are lords, and they were living together in matrimony long before John de Stokelonde's birth. Br. Geoffrey de Hemyngton, aged sixty or more, when examined on the articles said the same as William de Cler'. John Fychet and Roger le Brewer, both aged fifty and more, when questioned on the first article replied as Br. William had done, except that they only knew of Stokelonde's profession and priesthood by hearsay.

---

1 The Sunday after Easter. 2 i.e. 24 April, the day after the feast.
3 In his notarial subscription (781) John de Chaille declared that it had taken place *inter solis ortum et horam nonam*.

793 *Undated*

The bishop confirms the election[1] of John de Stokelonde as master of St. Mark's Billeswick and commits the temporalities and spiritualities of the house to his care.

794 *27 April 1346 Hartlebury*

The bishop's definitive sentence in favour of John de Stokelonde's election, delivered within Hartlebury castle in the presence of Masters John de Severleye, Hugh de Penebrugg, Robert de Nettelton and John de Chaylle, notary public.

795 *22 May 1346 Hartlebury*

Memorandum of the institution of Richard le Smale, clerk, to the church of St. Philip and St. Jacob, Bristol, at the presentation of his brother, John le Smale. He swore to pay any expenses which might be incurred by the bishop in the event of litigation. Witnesses: M. Henry de Neubold and Ralph, his clerk.

801 *2 February 1346 Hartlebury*

Memorandum of the licence for M. Thomas de Aysschton, subdeacon, to study for one year in accordance with Ottobon's constitution.[2]

803 *20 March 1346 Hartlebury*

Memorandum of the licence for Ds. Philip de Merston, rector of Broughton Hacket, to be absent for a year, provided that he remain in the service of John Handlowe, knight.

810 *14 November 1346 Hereford*

Commission of Stephen [of Ledbury], dean of Hereford, and the chapter there, authorising the diocesan to carry out the exchange between Ds. William le Beste, rector of St. Andrew's [Droit]wich, and Walter de la Brok, vicar of Marden, within the jurisdiction and patronage of the Hereford dean and chapter.

811 *7 November 1346 Elmbridge*

Certification by the official of the archdeacon of Worcester of his execution of the bishop's mandate, dated 3 November from Hartlebury, for enquiry into the above church of St. Andrew, to which the king had presented Walter de la Broke, vicar of Marden, because of a proposed exchange and on account of the temporalities of Deer-

1 Rubric: *Sentencia eleccionis.*
2 Boniface's constitution *Cum ex eo* (*Sext* 1, 6, c. 34) was probably intended.

hurst priory, in his hand by reason of the war with France. In accordance with the mandate, the official held an enquiry in the full chapter of the place celebrated in the ordinary course on the Tuesday after All Saints [i.e. 7 November] in Elmbridge chapel.[1] The enquiry was conducted by means of the rectors of Upton Warren, Martin [Hussingtree], Hadzor and St. Mary's Witton, the vicars of Bromsgrove, Beoley, Dodderhill and St. Peter's Witton, and the proctors of other rectors and vicars of the deanery. It found that the presentation belongs to the king, but that the prior of Deerhurst last presented William le Beste, who is now the incumbent. The church is not litigious, nor portionary, but subject to a pension of 6s. 8d. payable to the prior. The presentee is free and legitimate, of good life and honest conversation, aged 35 and more, in priest's orders, and not beneficed elsewhere. The reasons put forward for the exchange are that the air of Droitwich does not suit William de Beste,[2] and— [on Walter de Broke's side] [3]—that on assuming the rectory of St. Andrew's he will be able to fulfil his desire to attend a university once he has obtained the bishop's licence.[4]

817 *17 April 1347 Stow*

Certification by John de Resyndon, rector of Yeovil, Bath & Wells diocese, and Thomas, rector of Little Rissington, dean of Stow, of their execution of the bishop's mandate dated 13 April from Hartlebury. By means of an expert and discreet enquiry they examined the reasons why Alice Maidegod of Stow, widow, wished to take the vow of chastity. Having found them to be sincere and appropriate, they bestowed benediction on Alice in accordance with their commission. They append their seals and that of the deanery of Stow.[5]

818 *9 September 1346 Reepham*

Certification by the official of the archdeacon of Norwich of his execution of the mandate of William [Bateman], bishop of Norwich [1344–55], dated 2 September from Terling, for enquiry into the proposed exchange of Sparham church, to which William de Clynton, earl of Huntingdon, had presented M. Nicholas Janiny, rector of Hampton Bishop.[6] In accordance with the mandate the

1 A chapelry of Dodderhill.
2 *aer ville de Wych non est compaciens sanitati Willelmi de Beste.*
3 A phrase has slipped out of the MS.
4 *Cum adeptus fuerit eandem ecclesiam . . . posset, licencia et dispensacione vestris legitime primitus obtentis, scolas quod multum affectat, ubi viget studium universale, adire et addiscere et ad augmentum cultus divini fructus facere uberiores.* As a vicar he could not have realised his ambition.
5 *sigilla nostra una cum sigillo officii decanatus de Stowe.*
6 The form is somewhat different from that in use at Worcester and contains the clauses: *quibusque de causis et inter quas personas fiet permutacio memorata,* and *an dictus presentatus pluralis existat et in quo.*

official held an enquiry in a full chapter summoned for that purpose[1] in the church of Our Lady at Reepham. It was conducted by means of M. John de Brecham, rector of a moiety of Reepham church; Gilbert, rector of Foxley; Simon, rector of Swannington; and by John, son of Hugh of Sparham, Roger Anot and John Unfrey of the same place, Peter Waleys of Booton, and Robert Martyn of Lyng, laymen. All say, under oath (*iurati*), that William de Clynton has the right of presentation because of his wife Juliana's dower, she having the patronage of Sparham after the death of her husband, John de Hastyng, knight.[2] The said earl, by right of this dower, last presented Ds. Simon de Geynesburgh, now rector. The jurors are unaware of the reasons for the exchange, nor do they know the names of the parties, except from the bishop's own mandate. The church is not litigious or subject to a pension, but a portion consisting of two [parts of the] sheaves taken as tithes (*duas garbas decimales*) from certain lands within Sparham parish in the fee of Robert de Malteby, knight, is received by the prior and convent of the cathedral church of Holy Trinity, Norwich—the third sheaf going to the rector. It is estimated to be worth 25 marks [£16 13s. 4d.].[3] The jurors know nothing of the life, character, orders or age of the presentee, nor whether he is a pluralist or subject to any other canonical bar. There is no canonical objection to the presentor.

819 *17 September 1346 London*

Commission of William [Bateman], bishop of Norwich [1344–55], authorising the diocesan to carry out the above exchange in accordance with the finding of the enquiry held by the official of the archdeacon of Norwich.

820 *22 January 1347 Worcester*

Memorandum of the licence for John de Oxon', rector of St. Andrew's, Worcester, to be absent for one year.

821 *22 January 1347 Worcester*

Memorandum of the licence for Ds. Nicholas, rector of Abbots Morton to leave his church for one year from the feast of St. Mathias the Apostle [24 February].

822 *20 August 1347 Hartlebury*

Commission for William [Zouche], archbishop of York [1342–52], to carry out the exchange between Ds. Walter de Wetewang,

1 The bishop directed him to do so, even though it was harvest time—*tempore messium non obstante*.
2 Juliana, daughter and heir of Sir Thomas de Leyburne, widow of John lord Hastings of Abergavenny, married secondly Thomas le Blount, and finally William de Clinton.
3 Apparently an answer to the question about the value of the portion. According to the *Taxatio* (p. 82b) Sparham itself was assessed at £16 13s. 4d., the portion at £2 13s. 4d.

prebendary in the collegiate church of Westbury of that prebend held immediately before him by M. John de Trillec, which is in the bishop's patronage and diocese, and Ds. John de Melborn, canon of York and prebendary of Wetwang in that church.

823 *23 September 1346*

Resignation of Sparham church, Norwich diocese, made by William Curteys of Gainsburgh, chaplain, as proctor of the rector, Ds. Simon de Geynesburgh.[1]

824 *23 September 1346*

Similar resignation of Hampton Bishop church by Nicholas de Allesleye as proctor of M. Nicholas Janyny.[2]

826 *25 January 1347 Leominster*

Certification by John [Trillek], bishop of Hereford [1344–60], of his execution of the diocesan's commission, dated 4 January from Hartlebury, for the exchange between M. Philip de Ullyngwyk, rector of Knightwick, in the patronage of the prior and convent of Worcester, and Ds. Philip Drym, rector of Ullingswick, Hereford diocese.[3]

828 *12 October 1345 Blockley*

Letter to Br. John of Leominster reciting the privilege, dated 22 July 1342 from Villeneuve, Avignon diocese,[4] whereby Pope Clement VI granted the bishop's petition that he should be allowed to choose two able monks of Worcester, capable of profiting from the Schools, to be supported there from the goods of his *mensa* or bishopric, and this notwithstanding their subjection to the prior. The bishop informs Br. John that he is choosing him in accordance with the privilege and is sending him to a *studium* until such time as he recalls him.

831 *12 September 1347*

Memorandum of the licence for Henry, rector of St. Michael's Worcester, to farm his church for a year to any suitable person.

832 *19 June 1347 Hartlebury*

Memorandum of the commission for the prior of Worcester[5] to receive the profession of Richard Moreys and Walter de Froucestr' as monks of the cathedral church.

1 See 818, 819, and *Institutions* 825.   2 *Ibid.*   3 See *Institutions* 827.
4 XI Kal. Aug. 1 Clement VI. Clement's coronation was 19 May 1342, but in *C.P.L.* 1342–62, p. 70, this licence is dated 1343.
5 John of Evesham.

833 *22 June 1347 Worcester*

Letters patent of the Worcester prior and chapter confirming the bishop's appropriation, dated 3 May from Hartlebury, of Yardley church to the prior and convent of Maxstoke, who had been granted the advowson by William de Clinton, earl of Huntingdon.[1]

834 *24 September 1347 Withington*[2]

Letters patent of Thomas de Berkeley of Coberley declaring his foundation in honour of the Holy Trinity, Our Lady, and St. Giles, abbot and confessor, of a chantry to be served by three priests—a warden (*custos*) and two suitable chaplains—in the church of St. Giles, Coberley, for the welfare of himself and his wife Joan, and for their souls after death, for those of his ancestors and heirs, the benefactors of the chantry, and all the faithful departed. This has been done with the consent of the king, the rector, and all others concerned. The royal licence, dated 17 March 1345 from the Tower of London,[3] permitted the alienation to the chaplains of thirteen messuages, two tofts, 34 virgates of land and two of wood, with appurtenances in Coberley. These the founder has granted by charter to Ds. Henry Averay,[4] chaplain, warden of the chantry of Our Lady at Coberley, and his successors. They comprise a messuage and three virgates called *Eldresfeldeslond*, a toft and three virgates called *Baillifslond*, and various lands held in bondage: a messuage and two virgates by Thomas Jannes; a messuage and two virgates by William Lutesone; a messuage, toft, and three virgates by Robert Jannes; a messuage and two virgates by Alice Willes, Thomas le Holdare, Thomas Elyot, Philip Jones and Thomas Jones respectively; a virgate by John Fyppes; two virgates by Thomas Murival; a messuage and two virgates each by John Colynes, Henry le Mule-ward, Richard Jones and Henry Brouning; together with the persons of all the above, their goods, chattels and broods (*sequele*). Witnesses to the charter were John Giffard of Leckhampton, and Thomas Botiler, knights, Ds. William, rector of Minchinhampton, Ds. Walter, rector of Coberley, John de Elkeston, and others.

Henry Averay,[5] a secular priest instituted and inducted by the diocesan on the founder's presentation is to be warden of the chantry. With him are to be two secular chaplains, whom the founder is to appoint during his lifetime. At future vacancies caused by the death or cession of the warden the more suitable of the chap-

1 Printed in Nash, *Worcs.*, 2, p. 482. The petition is *mutatis mutandis* as in 746 (cf. 321), but the final number of canons is left vague as *magnum numerum*.
2 The letters patent are undated. This must be the date and place of the bishop's *inspeximus* and confirmation. Cf. 154.
3 *C.P.R.* 1343–45, p. 449. By fine of 40 marks.
4 In the MS. blank spaces were left here and elsewhere, the warden's name being filled in afterwards.
5 The founder's ordination begins at this point.

lains is to be presented in his place by the founder, and after his death, by the rector of Coberley, or, if the rectory be vacant, by the prior of Little Malvern, and if the priory be vacant likewise, by the subprior. Such presentation is to be made within a month, after which the bishop is to choose one of the chaplains for that turn, or *sede vacante*, whoever has the right of collation to benefices. Should neither make presentation within the month, then *sede plena* the archbishop of Canterbury is to choose from the chaplains, or *sede vacante* the prior of Holy Trinity, Canterbury, but without prejudice to the rights of the others at future vacancies. At both his institution and induction the warden is to take an oath—in the presence of the rector of Coberley, and his parishioners should they wish to be there—to observe the chantry ordinances himself, to see that they are observed by others, to reside continually with the chaplains, unless absent on chantry business, and in the place appointed by the founder and the house built by him—which are to be known as *Beverlee*, and also to maintain and defend the rights of the chantry. With him he is to have two chaplains able and willing to serve the chantry, whom he is to provide with food and drink: that is, bread made from finely sieved wheaten flour, good ale—six flagons of the better quality brewed from a bushel of barley, and vegetables. On non-festival days they are to sit down together for two meals, dinner and supper, each of one course. On festivals they are to have two courses, one consisting of two parts of salted meat from store with one part of fresh meat—a proportion likewise to be observed with regard to fish on days of abstinence,[1] while the other course is to be plain and sufficient rather than sumptuous. In addition, each chaplain is to have two marks, payable in equal instalments at the Annunciation [25 March] and St. Peter ad Vincula [1 August], for clothes, surplices, and all other necessities. At the times of their admission the chaplains are to swear to obey the warden's lawful commands. After the founder's death they are to be chosen by the warden who is not to remove them except for reasonable cause. The remaining resources, after deduction of the above expenses and those of the warden's *familia*, are to be put to the uses of the chantry. The warden is to provide for the chaplains such wine and light as may be necessary for the celebration of the divine services. Both warden and chaplains are to have access to Coberley church at appropriate times and are to keep the keys of the door to the new chapel built by the founder. The lands and property of the chantry are not to be alienated in fee, or for a term of life or of years—even by consent of the majority, with the exception of rented houses and bondages which may lawfully be let for a term in the usual way for the chantry's profit. Under penalty of excommunication no corrody,

---

1 This seems to be the meaning of the phrase: *et idem volo ceteris diebus quibus a carnibus abstinent in exhibendis piscibus observari.*

livery or pension is to be sold or given to anyone. Should the warden be guilty of incest, adultery, or extravagance, or be found incapable or unworthy, he is to be summarily removed by the bishop, or *sede vacante* by the prior and chapter, and someone else instituted in his stead. In the event of one of the chaplains being guilty of the above offences, or proving otherwise unsuitable or negligent, the warden is to remove him instantly. But should he fail to appoint a successor within a month of the amoval, death or cession of a chaplain, the warden is to be deprived *ipso facto* and another instituted in his place. To prevent any interruption in the celebration of Masses during the month in which the warden fails to appoint a chaplain, the rector of Coberley, or if the church be vacant, the prior of Little Malvern, is to present one for that turn. The warden and chaplains are to have a decent tonsure with their ears standing free from the hair and a large crown. Their clothes are to be of one colour; either blue, plain or a mixture, or russet, which should be neither too dark nor too light. They are to wear an over-tunic without openings (*super-tunica clausa*) and reaching to the ankles, as is seemly. On ferial days, and at other times when working, they may wear shorter tunics, but these are to be closed. The price of the cloth is not to exceed two shillings. The warden and chaplains are to behave as befits priests, to live together, to dine at the same table, and to sleep in the house provided. Women are not to stay there or to serve in the household. Every day the warden and chaplains are to come together in the most convenient place to say Matins and the canonical hours. But on Sundays and other feast days these offices are to be said or sung—as may be agreeable to the rector—in the parish church, with the warden and chaplains clothed in surplices. The *Placebo*, *Dirige* and commendation are likewise to be recited daily in accordance with the Use of Sarum. The warden and chaplains are each to celebrate Mass daily: one a Mass of Our Lady—to be sung on Saturdays—in the chapel adjoining the church, or elsewhere within the church if more convenient; another, of the Day, with commendation of the above persons and souls; the third, of Requiem, for the founder's welfare and that of his wife, Joan, for their souls after death, as for those of the founder's ancestors, heirs, the benefactors of the chantry, and of all the faithful departed. After the founder's death they are to keep his anniversary with solemn ringing of bells. The day before, after Vespers, they are to sing the *Placebo* and *Dirige*, and on the morrow—the Anniversary itself—they are to sing Mass together in as solemn a manner as they can. They are to observe in the same way the anniversaries of the founder's father, and, after her death, of the founder's wife, Joan, and of Joan, his former wife. Every day after Matins and the canonical Hours each is to say for the faithful departed the psalm *De profundis* with the *Pater Noster* and *Ave*, together with the usual prayers and afterwards the words: *Anima domini Thome fundatoris nostri et anime uxoris suarum parentum et heredum benefactorumque nostrorum et omnium fidelium defunctorum per Dei misericordiam in pace requiescant.* These words are also to be said by each after his Mass, and by one of them daily after Grace at table. At the time of their admission the chaplains are to promise to execute their office faithfully, to maintain the rights and liberties of the chantry, and to be personally resident. If the warden be prevented by sickness or age from performing his office, the rector, or (during vacancies) the prior of Little Malvern, is to present one of the chaplains to the bishop as coadjutor, with the obligation to exercise the office and to render an account of his custodianship. The warden, meanwhile, may have a competent servant, who is to be provided with necessaries from the chantry goods, and if these suffice, another chaplain is to be admitted to celebrate the third Mass. Because the chaplains are to be considered permanent (*ut perpetui*), in the event of one of them being unable to celebrate his Mass on account of sickness or age, the warden is to provide him with food, and from his salary and other goods of the chantry another suitable chaplain is to be maintained. No warden instituted to the chantry should be inducted by proxy. Immediately after induction, and before assuming the administration of the chantry goods, he is to compile an inventory in the presence of the rector of Coberley. This is to comprise chalices, books, vestments, ornaments, and anything else provided there for the divine offices, as well as the names of debtors, the amount of their debts, all vessels of silver, tin or copper, and other utensils, as well as horses, oxen, draught animals (*affri et iumenta*), cows, sheep, pigs, and other stock, carts, ploughs, and anything else belonging to the chantry or to be assigned to it in the future. The inventory is to be in the form of a tripartite indenture; one part for the rector, another for the warden, the third for the chaplains. Nothing is to be alienated, destroyed or carried off. On the contrary, the warden should strive to increase by his industry the talent entrusted to him. Priests who neglect to oppose, as they are bound, any defrauding of the chantry, are to lose their stipends for the period during which they permitted it without contradiction. On the death, cession, or deprivation of the warden, all the fruits and profits are to be fully converted to the chantry's use and their administration is to pass automatically to the priest who has served the chantry longer, until such time as a new warden be inducted and an inventory made as described above. Neither the sequestrator nor any other minister of the ordinary is to enter upon any part of such goods by reason of the vacancy or on any other pretext. The administrator himself is not to act until an inventory has been made, and for the period of the vacancy must keep a written account of receipts and expenditure. This, after taking an oath to render faithful account, he is to surrender to the warden within a month of his induction. Drunkenness and insobriety,

14

leading as they do to feebleness of mind and wantonness, are to be shunned by all, particularly ministers of God. The warden and chaplains, therefore, are not to frequent taverns, and the latter are expressly forbidden to visit such places without the warden's licence. Should warden or chaplain infringe any article of the above ordination he is to be punished as perjured and removed from the chantry, and likewise in cases of dilapidation. To keep the details in mind and leave no excuse for ignorance, either the warden or one of the chaplains, in the presence of the others, is to read out the ordination (*fundacio, dotacio et ordinacio*) in Coberley church on the vigils of the five feasts of the Virgin and on that of St. John the Baptist.[1] On the Friday following such recitation the warden is to summon both chaplains to a convenient place and is there to correct and punish them according to their faults. The present letters have been prepared in quadruplicate: one part is to be kept by the warden and his successors, another by the rector of Coberley, a third by the prior and convent of Little Malvern, and the fourth by the bishop. Infringement of the ordination by any heir or relative of the founder, or by any other person, is expressly forbidden on pain of divine judgement at the Last Day.[2]

835 *11 October 1346 Blockley*

Letters patent of the foundation of Abbot Hereward's chantry in Cirencester abbey. During the bishop's recent visitation, Prior Reginald de Schypton and the rest of the convent came before him in the chapter house, where, on behalf of the abbot, Br. William de Hereward, were set forth the various works which he had performed for the benefit of the house. By his provident care he had relieved the monastery of the debts which encumbered it at the time of his promotion, and before. The conventual church, which threatened to become ruinous in many places, he had repaired and largely rebuilt or strengthened. At immense cost and labour he had secured the erection of essential buildings (*domos*), both within the monastery precincts and in the manors beyond. Moreover, he had gained confirmation of those rights and liberties generously granted at the monastery's foundation by kings and others, or belonging to it by ancient custom, which had been impugned by malicious persons, and had procured definition of certain points in the foundation charter which some considered doubtful or obscure.[3] Besides all this, he had

1 The five feasts are the Purification (2 February), the Annunciation (25 March), the Assumption (15 August), the Nativity (8 September) and the Conception (8 December). The Nativity of St. John falls on 24 June.
2 At this point the list of witnesses and the dating clause are omitted (cf. 154). See p. 140 n. 2.
3 See the royal *inspeximus* and confirmation, dated 1 July 1336, printed in *Monasticon* ed. Caley, VI, pp. 177–8.

acquired annual rents of £4, £3 and 30s.:[1] assigning the first to the newly built chapel of Our Lady towards the increase of divine worship, the second to the pittancer's office for the canons' more ample daily provision and an increased pittance (*ad uberiorem procuracionem cotidianam fratrum . . . et ipsorum ampliorem quietem*), and the last to the almonry for the benefit of the poor. In view of these acts it was urged that the abbot's name should be specially remembered by present and future canons. The bishop, having examined the matter with the aid of letters, royal charters and other documents, has found the details to be true. With the consent of the abbot and prior, who have agreed to abide by his arbitration, and after diligent discussion with them and others, he has undertaken the burden of drawing up the ordination, considering it right that the abbot should receive due reward for the permanent benefits he had bestowed on the monastery. He therefore ordains that there is to be a secular chaplain in the Lady Chapel, suitably trained in singing, who is to be present at the daily Mass of Our Lady clothed in a surplice, and is to sing and in other ways minister there. Immediately afterwards he is himself to celebrate Mass at the chapel altar for the abbot's welfare, while living, and for his soul after death, for the welfare of all the brethren or canons of the monastery, present and future, and for the souls of the founder, those of the kings of England and the monastery's benefactors, those of the present king and queen and their children, and of the abbot's father and mother and all the faithful departed. The canon who is warden (*custos*) of the Lady Chapel is to make available, by means of the goods given to the chapel by the abbot, both an adequate place within the precincts for the chaplain to live in, and also food, drink, clothing and other necessaries, up to the value of £3 a year. After the abbot's death his anniversary is to be kept by the canons in the same way as the anniversaries of abbots Henry, Adam and Richard.[2] During the abbot's lifetime the almoner is to make an annual distribution to the poor at the Assumption [15 August] of 20s. 8d. more than the usual amount. After his death this is to be done on his anniversary. The pittancer, in consideration of the above grant to his office, is to provide annually at the Assumption a pittance worth 20s. From that sum he is to furnish a quart of ale to each of the canons and brethren, and what is not spent on ale is to be used for a food pittance. After the abbot's death such pittance is to be distributed on his anniversary. The abbot, prior and convent on being apprised of the above arrangements approved and accepted them for themselves and their successors. The bishop inhibits anyone under penalty of

1 These amounts have been altered from £3 6s. 10d., £2 16s. 7d., and 25s. 3d. respectively. The original sums are unaltered in the convent's submission (836).
2 The previous three abbots were named Henry de Hampnett, Adam Brokenberwe and Richard de Charlton.

greater excommunication from infringing them. The abbot, prior and convent append their common seal. To ensure that the above be observed with greater fervour and devotion, the bishop grants a forty days' indulgence to all his parishioners, being truly penitent and contrite, or others whose diocesans approve and accept such indulgence, who give of their goods, make special effort to ensure the observation and implementation of the above, or lend their support by counsel, aid, or good-will, and who pray devoutly for the abbot's welfare during his lifetime, or for his soul after death, and recite the Lord's Prayer and Hail Mary with pious intention.

836 *3 October 1346 Cirencester*

Submission of the abbot, prior and convent of Cirencester, relating the abbot's merits and agreeing to abide by the bishop's arbitration.[1]

837 *26 February 1347*[2] *Hartlebury*

Inspeximus and confirmation of the grant of Standish manor to the almonry of Gloucester abbey. The bishop has inspected the letters of his predecessor, Bishop Mauger [1200–12], to the following effect. Thomas [Carbonel], abbot of Gloucester [1180–1212], on the diocesan's advice and that of the entire convent of Gloucester, has restored to God and the abbey almonry for the use of Christ's poor, the whole manor of Standish with its appurtenances—tithes, rents and profits, saving to the cellarer the ancient payments (*assise*) on the anniversary of Abbot Serlo [1072–1105] and those in malt. The almoner is to have full disposal of the manor in the interests of the poor. It is not to be put to other uses, either wholly or in part, except at times of exceptional need and with the consent of the entire convent. Excepted are four marks [£2 13s. 4d.] payable annually to Abbot Thomas and his successors, in equal instalments at Christmas and Easter, for their private alms. Sentence of excommunication is pronounced against those who infringe the grant. Given in the chapter house at Gloucester on the feast of St. Mary Magdalen [22 July] 1202. Witnesses: Bishop Mauger, Robert, abbot of Winchcombe [1194–1221], and many others. The bishop, however, bearing in mind that there is no heavier penalty in God's Church than excommunication, that men of the present age are more prone to sin, and that the old enemy directs particular attention to the religious, with the express consent of Abbot Adam [de Staunton][3] and the convent, revokes the former penalty and replaces it by one more suitable. In future the whole of what is due from Standish manor is to be paid weekly by the almoner to the subalmoner, who is to expend

1 See 835.
2 Also sealed by the convent on the following Thursday, 1 March.
3 1338–51.

it undiminished on the poor: for the fine bread in baked loaves (*pro assisa panis coci in pane furnito*), 5¼ bushels of wheat, that is, 34 quarters and 5 bushels a year; for the coarse bread in baked loaves (*pro assisa panis fulberti in pane furnito*), 4 quarters and one bushel of pulse, amounting to 214½ quarters a year. The almoner is also to give away annually towards Christmas (*contra Natale*) 90 yards of woollen cloth, to be distributed among 30 poor persons—three yards apiece. Should almoner or subalmoner be found negligent, either during the bishop's visitation or at some other time, the religious are to pay 100s. towards the fabric of the cathedral church, as they have expressly agreed. The bishop judicially (*diffinitive et sentencialiter*) imposes such penalty upon them in the person of their proctor, M. William de Bergeveny, clerk. One part of the present indenture, to which the bishop's seal is appended, is to remain in the convent's possession, the other, with the convent's common seal, is to be kept by the bishop.

838 *3 May 1347 Hartlebury*

Letters patent of the appropriation of Yardley church to Maxstoke Priory.[1]

840 *Undated*[2]

Resignation of St. Laurence's church, Rowington, by Gilbert de Aston, its perpetual vicar, on account of old age.[3]

841 *12 July 1339*[4] *Bredon*

Inspeximus and confirmation of letters of Simon [de Montacute], formerly bishop of Worcester [1334–37], now of Ely [1337–45], addressed to Br. Nicholas de Upton, monk of Little Malvern, and dated 29 December 1336 from Bredon. These record how, following his election as guardian (*custos*) of his priory's temporalities in Ireland, Br. Nicholas had come before the bishop in his manor at Bredon, together with the prior of Little Malvern [Hugh de Pyribrok, 1326–60] and Adam de Bekkeford, the subprior, and given proof of perpetual and lawful impediment, in that he was unable to cross the Irish Sea without hazarding his life. To this declaration the prior and subprior agreed, whereupon the bishop absolved Br. Nicholas from his obligation.

---

1 See 833, which is allegedly the Worcester chapter's confirmation of this document. In fact there are many verbal differences. The *magnum numerum* of 833 becomes *ad vicenarium* (cf. 746).

2 Probably October 1347. See *Institutions* 839.

3 *Quia discursis adolocencie (sic) mee temporibus transacta cum sudore temporum curricula produxerunt ad senium.*

4 An attached portion of MS. out of chronological order.

842 *14 March 1348 Towcester*

Certification by John [Gynewell], bishop of Lincoln [1347–62], of his execution of the diocesan's commission, dated 2 March from Hartlebury, for the exchange, in accordance with the findings of an enquiry to be held by the official of the Gloucester archdeacon, between Ds. John de Rediswell, vicar of Broadwell, Lincoln diocese and Thomas de Eggesworth, rector of Winstone (patron: John de Allespath).

843 *25 March 1348 Hartlebury*

Memorandum of the oath of obedience taken by John de Rideswell and of the mandate sent to the official of the Gloucester archdeacon for his induction to Winstone.

845 *17 November 1347 St. Katherine next Lincoln*

Commission of John [Gynewell], bishop of Lincoln [1347–62], authorising the diocesan to carry out the exchange between Ivo, rector of Daglingworth, and Robert, rector of Oving, Lincoln diocese, in accordance with the findings of an enquiry which he is sending for inspection and wishes to have returned by Ivo's hand as soon as possible.

846 *Undated*

Robert de Upthon resigns his church of Oving into the bishop's hands.

847 *Undated*

Ivo de Endenham likewise resigns Daglingworth church.

28 November 1347 Hartlebury

Memorandum of Robert's institution to Daglingworth and of the certification of the above commission (845).[1]

848 *16 January 1348 Hartlebury*

Letter to the prior of the Holy Sepulchre, Warwick. The bishop through his special commissary, M. John de la Lowe, had imposed penance on Br. Richard de Kekyngwik, a canon of the priory, for certain faults (*demerita*), in the hope of relaxing it subject to his good behaviour. He now commands the prior to allow Richard to enjoy the same freedom as his brethren (*gaudere liberis permittatis habenis*). But in the event of his returning to dissolute life the penance is to be reimposed at once.

1   This memorandum was tacked on to the original entry.

849 *25 November 1347 Hartlebury*

Memorandum of the licence concerning non-residence and orders granted to Ds. Walter de Clodeshale, subdeacon, rector of Pedmore. He may study for a year.

850 *18 December 1347*

Memorandum that on his own authority and that of Robert [Wyville], bishop of Salisbury [1330–75], the bishop admitted and instituted John Borgh, rector of Shenington, to Sherston church, Salisbury diocese. On the same day he admitted and instituted John Gerad,[1] rector of Sherston, to Shenington church, and a mandate for his induction was sent to the official of the Gloucester archdeacon.

851 *2 December 1347 Ramsbury*

Commission of Robert [Wyville], bishop of Salisbury, for carrying out the above exchange in accordance with the findings of an enquiry to be held by the official of the archdeacon of Wiltshire.

855 *29 November 1347*[2] *Hartlebury*

Memorandum that the diocesan carried out an exchange of the benefices of Daglingworth and Oving in accordance with the bishop of Lincoln's commission. Mandate for induction to Daglingworth was sent to the official of the Gloucester archdeacon.

858 *4 January 1348 Ramsbury*

Certification by Robert [Wyville], bishop of Salisbury [1330–75], of his execution of the diocesan's commission, dated 11 December from Hartlebury, for an exchange, in accordance with the findings of an enquiry held by the official of the Gloucester archdeacon, between Ds. John Harpele, vicar of Preston, and Ds. Robert Douwale, vicar of Winkfield, Salisbury diocese.

865 *[4 January 1348]*

Exchange of the benefices of Preston and Winkfield (Salisbury diocese).[3]

866 *29 January 1348 Old Temple, London*

Commission of John [Gynewell], bishop of Lincoln [1347–62], authorising the diocesan to carry out the exchange between M.

---

1 *Jerad* in the following entry.
2 *Penultimo die Novembris.* But cf. 847, where the date is given as 28 November.
3 So far as it goes, this entry is a duplicate of 858. The scribe completed the bishop's commission, but then started another entry on the dorse of the folio.

Thomas de Clypston, rector of Compton Wyniates, and Robert le Ferour of Grantham, rector of Great Ponton, Lincoln diocese, in accordance with the findings of an enquiry to be held by the official of the archdeacon of Lincoln. He is to admit and institute Thomas to Ponton (patron: Ds. John de Langebergh, canon of Salisbury and prebendary of Grantham Borialis in the same).[1]

868 *8 February 1348 Grantham*

Certification by the official of the archdeacon of Lincoln that he has executed the bishop of Lincoln's mandate, dated 29 January from the Old Temple, London, and received by him 3 February, for enquiry into the above exchange and the vacancy of Great Ponton church, to which M. John de Langebergh, canon of Salisbury, has presented M. Thomas de Clypston. In compliance with the mandate, he held an enquiry in the chapter of the place on 8 January[2] by a sworn jury comprising William, Walter and Lambert, rectors respectively of Denton, Little Ponton and Belton; Henry, Robert and Gilbert, vicars respectively of Grantham Borealis, Grantham Australis and Honington; and John, parish chaplain and proctor of Ds. William, rector of Stroxton. The enquiry found the presentee to be of good life and honest conversation, free and legitimate, but in what orders is not known. Ds. John de Langebergh is the true patron by reason of his prebend and last presented Robert Ferour, who is still the incumbent. The reason for the exchange, so far as the presentee is concerned, is that he has relatives, acquaintances and friends in the neighbourhood of Great Ponton, and considers that he would profit God's Church more by living and working among them than among strangers.[3] The church is not litigious, but is subject to an annual pension of ten marks [£6 13s. 4d.], payable to the prebendary of Grantham Borealis, and is taxed at 25 marks [£16 13s. 4d.].

869 *4 January 1348*

Exchange of the benefices of Preston and Winkfield (Salisbury diocese).[4]

870 *15 January 1348*

Memorandum of the oath of obedience taken by Robert Douwale and of the mandate sent to the official of the Gloucester archdeacon for his induction [to Preston].[5]

1 See *Institutions* 867, 868 and 876.
2 *Sic* for *February*.
3 *habet . . . consanguineos notos et amicos inter quos affectat stare et conversare et inter quos magis credit proficere in ecclesia dei quam alibi inter extraneos et ignotos.*
4 A duplicate of 858. Cf. 865.
5 See 858, 869.

871 *3 March 1348 Ramsbury*

Commission of Robert [Wyville], bishop of Salisbury [1330–75], authorising the diocesan to carry out the exchange between M. Peter FilzWaryn, rector of Tortworth, and Ds. John de Stokes, rector of Lytchett Matravers, Salisbury diocese, in accordance with the findings of an enquiry to be held by the official of the archdeacon of Dorset.

872 *2 April 1348 Milborne*

Certification by the official of the archdeacon of Dorset that he has executed his diocesan's mandate, dated 3 March from Ramsbury, for enquiry[1] into the above exchange and the vacancy of Lytchett Matravers church, to which John Mautravers the son, has presented M. Peter FilzWaryn. The official finds that John Mautravers is the true patron and last presented Ds. John de Stokes. The presentee is free and legitimate, of good life and honest conversation, and in priest's orders. The chapter knows nothing of the reasons for the exchange.[2]

875 *28 August 1348 Henbury*

Commission to the official of the archdeacon of Gloucester and the dean of Gloucester. The diocesan has received letters of John [Trillek], bishop of Hereford [1344–60], dated 27 August from Ledbury, informing him of the collation to M. William de Herewynton, priest, of the canonry in the church of Hereford, with the prebend of Moreton and Whaddon in Worcester diocese, which became vacant on the recent death of M. Richard de Chaddesley, and asking him to arrange for Herewynton's induction to the prebend. The commissaries are to carry out the induction, either jointly or severally, and to certify that they have done so *sub sigillo autentico nobis noto.*

879 *September 1348(?)*

Renunciation by Thomas de Baddeby of his claim to Tredington church(?).[3]

885 *9 April 1346 Pershore*

The abbot and convent of Pershore appoint Br. Henry de Lench their proctor for approving the chantry ordinances drawn up by the bishop.[4]

---

1 *nichil de fama vel opinione set de certitudine omnium premissorum ac eciam aliarum dicti negocii circumstanciarum nobis rescribentes, de quibus vos et loci capitulum in omnem eventum si dampnum accederet aut postmodum forsan assercioni vestre contrarium apparuerit volueritis (sic) respondere.*
2 See *Institutions* 873, 874.   3 This entry is almost entirely illegible.
4 Duplicated in 906 *q.v.*

886 *4 July 1347 Salisbury*

Letters patent of John de Camera, precentor and canon of Salisbury, and president of the chapter there, to the effect that he has executed the mandate[1] of William de Nassyngton, Official, and Robert de Worth, canon of Salisbury, vicars general in spirituals of Robert [Wyville], bishop of Salisbury [1330–75], for the installation of Ds. William de Farlegh, clerk, presented by the king to the prebend of Horton on account of the recent vacancy of the see, and instituted by the vicars in the person of his proctor M. Richard de Hyda.

887 *4 July 1347 Salisbury*

Letter of the above vicars general notifying Ds. William de Farlegh of his admission and institution by proxy to the prebend of Horton, and exemplifying the commission, dated 1 June from Sonning, whereby they are empowered during the bishop of Salisbury's absence from his diocese, to enquire into, correct, and punish the excesses of his subjects, to institute and induct those presented to benefices, with or without cure, and to deprive beneficed clerks as the law requires.

888 *12 July 1347 Hartlebury*

Mandate to the official of the Gloucester archdeacon, reciting letters of the above vicars general,[2] dated 4 July from Salisbury, and directing him to induct William de Farlegh to the prebend of Horton and such of its rights and appurtenances as lie within the diocesan's jurisdiction.

889 *10 July 1347 Wellington*

Certification by Ralph [of Shrewsbury], bishop of Bath & Wells [1329–63], of his execution of the diocesan's commission, dated 2 July from Hartlebury, for the exchange, in accordance with the findings of an enquiry held by the official of the Gloucester archdeacon, between Ds. William de Clyfford, rector of Combe Baskerville, and M. John Stilligo, rector of Sparkford, Bath & Wells diocese.

890 *15 July 1347*

Memorandum that the official of the Gloucester archdeacon was ordered to induct the above John [to Combe Baskerville].

891 *9 July 1347 Hartlebury*

Appointment of Ds. Thomas, priest, rector of Lancaut, Hereford diocese, as coadjutor to Ds. Richard, rector of St. Helen's Worcester,

1 Of the same date and place.
2 Cf. 886, 887.

whom the bishop has learned both from the testimony of trustworthy persons and by common repute, is so impeded by age and bodily sickness as to be unable to exercise the cure of souls and other spiritual and temporal functions of his office without a helper. The coadjutor is under obligation to exercise his office faithfully, to draw up a true inventory, and to render honest accounts, as he has sworn to do before the bishop. The rector is not to alienate any of the goods of the church without his consent.

On the same day the bishop wrote to the rector of St. Helen's ordering him on his obedience to admit the coadjutor and to allow him to exercise his office.

892 *16 July 1347 Hartlebury*

Licence for the abbot of [St. Werburgh's] Chester[1] to farm for three years the church of Campden, appropriated to his monastery, provided that meanwhile the burdens incumbent upon it be properly supported.

893 *Undated* [1346]

The bishop excuses himself from attendance at a council summoned to St. Paul's. [Duplicate of 780.]

894 *8 September 1347 Hartlebury*

Letters patent of the manumission of John de Fladebury, son of Robert Pule of that place.

895 *9 September 1347 Tintern*

Certification by John [Pascal], bishop of Llandaff [1347–61], of his execution of the diocesan's mandate for the exchange between M. Peter Malet, rector of Barnsley, and Ds. Nicholas Hogges, rector of Marchergeryn, Llandaff diocese, who had been presented for institution to Barnsley by Humphrey de Bohun, earl of Hereford and Essex, lord of Brecon.

896 *11 September 1347 Hartlebury*

Memorandum that the above Nicholas took the oath of canonical obedience and swore to indemnify the bishop for outgoings of 15s. on Peter Malet's account.[2]

---

1 William de Bebington, 1324–49.
2 *iuramentum corporale de salvando dominum indempnem pro exitibus de xv solidis currentibus versus Petrum Malet.*

897 *Undated* [*October 1347*]

Resignation of Rowington vicarage. [Duplicate of 840.]

899 *15 October 1347 Alvechurch*

Letters patent acknowledging payment by the prior and convent of Kenilworth of four marks [£2 13s. 4d.], due for the Michaelmas 1347 term on account of the three-yearly procuration for Bidford church, appropriated to their monastery.[1]

900 *3 November 1347 Hartlebury*

Memorandum of the above payment to the bishop.[2]

901 *30 January 1348 London*

Commission of Thomas [de Lisle], bishop of Ely [1345–61], authorising the diocesan to carry out the exchange between Ds. Roger de Breynton, archdeacon of Gloucester,[3] and M. Richard de Ledebury, rector of Doddington, in the diocese of Ely and the patronage of its bishop.

902 *7 April 1348*

Resignation of the archdeaconry of Gloucester by Roger de Breynton, in the person of his proctor William de Mere, by reason of the above exchange.

903 *7 April 1348*

Similar resignation of M. Richard de Ledebury, through his proctor, Thomas de Ledebury.

904 *7 April 1348 Hartlebury*

Memorandum of the process of the above exchange which took place before the bishop in the chapel of Hartlebury castle. The prior of Worcester and the sacrist were directed to induct and install M. Richard de Ledebury.

905 *Undated* (1180 X 1184)

Charter whereby Gondevill, for the salvation of his soul and those of his forebears, grants three hides of land in Westington,[4] in free alms

1 Cf. 676.
2 The discrepancy in dates is puzzling. The rubric runs: *Alia acquietancia pro priore et conventu de Kenilworth.*
3 The exchange he planned in 1339 did not take place. Cf. 19.
4 Rubric: *Ordinacio cantarie capelle Beate Katerine de Campeden que est sub cera in thesauro ecclesie cathedralis Wygorn.*

(*imperpetuam et puram elemosinam*) and quit of all secular claim and service, to the chapel of St. Katherine the Virgin, which he has founded in his *curia* of Campden; that is, half a hide which William Ailwy holds, a virgate which Hardyng' holds, a virgate which Levi holds, a virgate which Alfred holds,[1] a virgate which William Collynge*s* holds, a virgate which Walter son of Gunnild' holds, a virgate which Alfred son of Ralph holds, a virgate which William son of Walter holds, a virgate which *Averd'* son of *H[er?]urb'* holds, a virgate which his *son* Amphrey holds [?],[2] a virgate which Geoffrey Hathe holds, and two messuages in the vill of Campden before the gate of his (Gondevill's) court, from Serlo's messuage to the demesne [?] of Herbert; saving the tithes belonging to the mother church. With the counsel and assent of clerks and laymen he has appointed two priests to minister in the chapel, each of whom is to have one and a half hides for his prebend, rendering a pound of incense each year to the mother church. This was done in the presence of Baldwin, bishop of Worcester [1180–84],[3] by the wish of Osmund the rector (*persona*), so that the chapel might enjoy full liberty. Because of this concession he also gives in free alms to the mother church of the manor of Campden the tithes of four mills, which it had not had before. The chaplains of the chapel are to be presented by his heirs. After presentation to the bishop and institution by him, they are to swear fealty to the rector [and] that they will not usurp[4] offerings, tithes, or anything else belonging to the mother church. They must also swear to be resident, except when with the bishop's licence, or at the lord's wish, they are allowed to be absent temporarily for good reason. The founder's heirs are to present only priests who will serve the chapel assiduously and in their own persons. Witnesses: Baldwin, bishop of Worcester, Simon Luvel, archdeacon, Richard Luvel, William son of Robert Osmund of Campden, William de Baton', Ralph de Welneford, Alfred, William Caperon, Richard, Eustace de Horsynton, the brothers Robert, William and Andrew, Robert the marshal, Roger the cook, Robert Waleys, Gilbert, Gilbert the clerk, Adam the clerk, Geoffrey of Ireland, and others.

906 *27 February 1346 Bredon*

Letters patent of the bishop's ordination of Ds. Adam de Herwynton's chantry in Pershore Abbey. Adam de Herwynton, recognising the nature of human frailty, how there comes an end to this life for every creature high or low, and desiring by works of piety to prepare for the

---

1 *Huerel* inexplicably follows this phrase: *et virgatam quam Aluered tenet Huerel, et virgatam . . .*
2 The MS. has *quam Amfrid' fil' suam* (*sic*) *tenet.*
3 Archbishop of Canterbury 1185–90.
4 The MS. has *fidelitatem iurare debea[n]t persone matris ecclesie quod nichil de oblacionibus . . .* But *fideliter* was probably intended and could have been in the original, which the scribe seems to have experienced some difficulty in deciphering.

day of the final harvest, trusting, moreover, to the efficacy of prayers for God's mercy—among other works of piety, out of the goods given him by God made provision for the foundation of a perpetual chantry of two secular priests in the conventual church of Pershore. In the event of the diocesan lending his authority and consent to the project, he wished the chaplains to offer daily the sacrifice of their lips (*domino offerent vitulos labiorum*) for the soul of Guy de Beauchamp, lately earl of Warwick, for the souls of Adam's father and mother, his relations and benefactors, and for those of all the faithful departed, as well as for the welfare of Thomas, earl of Warwick, and the lady Katherine his wife, during their lifetime, and for their souls after death. The abbot and convent of St. Edburgh and Adam de Herwynton petitioned that in view of the latter's grant to the monastery of lands and tenements in the town and fields of Pershore, producing an annual rent of £10, the above chantry should be celebrated at the expense of the religious at the altar in the south of the nave of the conventual church within the chapel where Adam de Herwynton now lies buried, and that his anniversary should be kept by the whole convent. For the maintenance of the anniversary, Hugh de Cokeseye, M. William de Herwynton, Robert de Alvreston, Roger de la Felde and Thomas de Sloghtre, the executors of the last will and testament of Adam de Herwynton, transferred 143 marks [£95 6s. 8d.] to the abbot and convent, who converted them to their own uses. In return for which lands and money the monks by letters patent acknowledged their obligation to sustain the chantry and anniversary. Adam de Herwynton having died before the completion of the above plan, his executors wish to carry it to a conclusion. The abbot and convent, by letters patent dated 25 February 1346 from Pershore, have submitted to the bishop's decree in the matter, declaring the endowment sufficient for the support of the burdens imposed. The executors have made a submission in the same terms by letters dated 26 February[1] 1346 from Bredon and sealed by the Official, their own seals not being widely known. In view of the above, the bishop, approving Adam de Herwynton's pious intention, and bearing in mind how profitable it is, both for the living and the dead, to have prayers directed to God, accepts the submissions of the parties. By enquiry he has found the above lands and money sufficient for the upkeep of the chantry and anniversary, and the lands and tenements most useful and profitable, considering the site of the abbey. By virtue of the submissions and of the consent given by Adam de Herwynton in his lifetime, and with the counsel of men learned in the law, he has proceeded to ordain a perpetual chantry and anniversary. There are to be two secular priests bound to celebrate, at about the first hour of each day and at the altar in the chapel

1 27 February in 774.

where Herwynton lies buried, two requiem Masses for the souls of the founder and those others named above, unless on greater feasts they should wish to celebrate the office of the day, in which case they are to make special commemoration of the same souls. Initially the two priests are to be presented to the bishop by letters patent of the executors, and within two months of the present ordination. At subsequent vacancies the religious, or the greater part of them, are to present within a month. Should the priests be found suitable the diocesan is to institute and induct them without delay. At their institution they are to swear to uphold the chantry ordination. From the monastery's resources they are to receive nine marks [£6] a year, in equal instalments at Christmas, the Annunciation [25 March], the Nativity of St. John the Baptist [24 June] and St. Michael [29 September]. They are to live together in the house built for their use within the messuage called *le Porters* in Pershore, which is to be attached to their *mensa* in perpetuity. The abbot and convent are to be responsible for its repair and maintenance, and are also to provide books, a chalice, vestments, lights, candles, bread and wine, for the celebration of the above Masses. Annually on the day of Herwynton's death, 31 March, they are to keep his solemn anniversary, each monk in his Masses remembering Herwynton's soul with compassion (*visceribus compassionis*) among those of other benefactors. Lest this should be done merely from fear of enforcement of the ordination, on that day forty shillings are to be distributed equally among the monks, except that, as in other similar distributions, the abbot and prior may receive larger portions. To obviate neglect of the chantry and anniversary owing to the passage of time, and to prevent any infringement of the ordination, the bishop imposes the burden of its support on the abbot and convent by decree, and in the presence of M. John de la Lowe, William de Adelmynton, Ds. John de Rypon, chaplain, John de Aula of Pershore and Br. Robert de Lutleton, the monks' proctor specially deputed for the purpose, condemns the religious, present and future, to sustain such burden under penalty of greater excommunication, to be incurred *ipso facto* should they attempt anything to the prejudice of the above, whether directly or indirectly, openly or in secret. Should the chantry cease for eight days owing to the malice of the abbot or any of the religious, on each such occasion the convent is to pay thirty shillings to the bishop's alms.

During episcopal visitation of the abbey, and at such other times as may seem expedient, enquiry is to be made, even on oath, as to the circumstances of the chantry and anniversary. To give permanent force to the ordination, the present abbot and each of the monks individually are to take an oath to support it, and every future monk is to do likewise at the time of his profession. By their letters patent, dated 25 February from Pershore, the abbot and convent appoint

Br. Robert de Lutleton, their fellow monk, as proctor for presenting their submission to the diocesan and accepting his ordination. In witness of all the above the bishop appends his seal.[1]

Memorandum that subsequently, 12 April, the executors and Br. Henry de Lench, the monks' proctor for taking the oath, came before the bishop in his chapel at Hartlebury. There, in the presence of M. John de Severle and M. John de la Lowe, the proctor took separate oaths on behalf of Br. Thomas, the abbot, and each of the monks, William de Brerhulle, prior, William Baret, John de Colewell, William le Porter, Henry de Besford, Henry de Staunton, Andrew de Lega, John de Hay, William de Clebury, John de Longedon, Robert de Wotton, John Dapetot, Philip de Stone, Richard de Lychfeld, Robert de Lutleton, William de Rudmarleygh, John de Lydeneye, William de Strengesham, John de Wyrcestr', John de Clehungre, Richard de Blockeleye, William de Beauchamp, John de Leygrove, Richard de Teukesbury, John de Clanefeld, Richard de Haukesbury, William de Ledene, William Folevill and William de Grafton. Finally, Henry de Lench took the oath on his own behalf.

The abbot and convent's letters patent, dated Palm Sunday [9 April] 1346 from Pershore, and to which the dean of Pershore appended the seal of his office, recite the bishop's foundation of the chantry and the appointment of Br. Henry de Lench as proctor for taking the oath.

907 *25 April 1348*[2] *Hartlebury*

Episcopal confirmation of Thomas de Berkeley's ordination of a perpetual chantry in St. Augustine's abbey, Bristol.[3] In pursuance of a royal licence[4] Thomas de Berkeley has granted two messuages and twenty shillings' rent in Bristol to William de Underlith, chaplain, who is to celebrate Mass (*divina*) daily for the welfare of the founder while living, for his soul after death, for the soul of his late wife, Margaret, and for those of all the faithful departed. He has presented the above chaplain to the bishop and secured his admission, institution and induction. Should he, or after his death his heirs, fail to make presentation within a month, the abbot of St. Augustine's is to do so for that turn, and if he also fail to present, the bishop, or *sede vacante* the prior, is to do so, saving the rights of the founder and his heirs at future vacancies. The chaplain and his successors are to be resident and to minister daily in accordance with the ordination.

1 The ordination proper ends at this point.
2 Thomas de Berkeley's charter is dated 20 April from Berkeley. The Worcester prior and chapter added their confirmation on 27 April. See below.
3 The entry follows 658 closely.
4 The licence is not recited in the charter, as was common. It is in *C.P.R.* 1348–50, p. 49, dated 8 April 1348, and supersedes an earlier one for a messuage and 40s. rent.

Should any fail to do so for a fortnight, another chaplain is to be appointed [&c. as in 658]. Every day the chaplain and his successors are to recite the office of the dead for the above mentioned souls, that is the *Placebo* and *Dirige* with the commendation. At each Mass they are to say for the founder, during his lifetime, the collect *Deus qui caritatis dona* with the appropriate secret and post-communion. After his death they are to say for his soul, that of his wife Margaret, and for those of all the faithful departed, the collect *Fidelium Deus* or *Deus cui proprium misereri* with secret and post-communion. On the anniversary of his death, and that of his wife Margaret, they are to say the office of the dead in full and a Mass on the morrow. They are to be content with their portion, to avoid undesirable places, and to maintain the chantry buildings.[1] At the time of his institution the chaplain is to swear to observe all the above, and annually on the feast of St. Augustine [28 August], or at some more suitable time, the present instrument is to be published in the abbey before all the people. Should a chaplain become so aged or infirm as to be unable to celebrate Mass in person, he is to recite the Lord's Prayer daily and other private prayers [&c. as in no. 658—gravity]. Witnesses: Maurice de Berkeley, the founder's son, Ds. Thomas de Bradeston, Ds. John de Acton, Ds. Simon Basset, William de Chiltenham, and others. Berkeley, 20 April 1348

Prior John [of Evesham] and the cathedral chapter add their confirmation. Worcester, 27 April 1348.

909 *27 August 1348 Henbury*

Memorandum of the licence for Ds. Walter Mucheldevere, rector of Cam (*Chamme*), to be absent for two years.

910 *30 September 1348*

Memorandum of the licence for M. William de Coleford, rector of Kemerton, to study for a year at a *studium generale* in England.

911 *29 August 1348 Henbury*

Resignation by William Edward of the wardenship (*custodia*) or rectory of Tormarton chantry and of the cure of souls of that parish.

Memorandum that the resignation was read out at Henbury in the bishop's presence and admitted by him. Present as witnesses were Ds. John de la Ryver', knight, M. John de Severleye and M. Walter de Beggeworth, notary public by apostolic authority.

912 *3 November 1348 Hartlebury*

Memorandum that in the presence of M. John de Severleye, the bishop's commissary, Ds. Thomas, rector of Beverstone, swore to

---

1 As in 658, but without mention of any specific provision for such upkeep.

15

indemnify the bishop for losses incurred in the king's court (*pro exitibus contra dictum patrem in curia regis currentibus*) on account of a writ against the said Master [*sic*] Thomas issued at the instance of a certain M. Robert Cornwaleys, rector of Uley.

913 *5 November 1348 Hartlebury*

Letters patent to the effect that M. Henry de Neubold, rector of Weston-on-Avon, the bishop's sequestrator general, who also exercised a general commission (*commissarius generaliter . . . deputatus*) to correct and punish excesses of the bishop's subjects brought to light at any of his visitations, and a specific one as collector and receiver of certain pension and procurations,[1] appeared before the bishop, and after rendering a faithful account of all the sums received by reason of his offices, was granted full acquittance.

916 *19 October 1348 Hartlebury*

Memorandum of the admission and institution of Peter de Avenynge, priest, to the chantry of Our Lady in Minchinhampton church, and of his oath to observe the chantry ordinances. Should Ds. William de Presbury, or any subsequent rector, fail to make presentation to the chantry within a month of its vacancy, the bishop is to do so, or *sede vacante* the prior. Should both be negligent, the archbishop is to provide a suitable person. The official of the Gloucester archdeacon was directed to induct the above Peter.

926 *10 September 1347 Ripple*

Formal pronouncement, declaration and confirmation by the bishop of the election of Thomas de Leghe, prior of Tewkesbury, as abbot of that house.

Memorandum that the above took place in the parish church of Ripple in the presence of John de More, notary public, M. John de la Lowe, M. John de Severley, and others.

927 *20 August 1347 Tewkesbury*

Letter of the subprior, Br. Peter de Bradeweye, and of the convent of Tewkesbury, deputing nine of their number to act as compromisers for the election of an abbot.[2] Present as witnesses were M. Stephen de Northeye, M. William de Aysschton, John de la More, clerk, notary public, and others.

928 *30 August 1347 Dover*

Letter of Hugh le Despenser, lord of Glamorgan and Morgannou, patron of Tewkesbury abbey (*nostre advocacionis*), informing the

---

1 *ad levandum colligendum et recipiendum quascumque pensiones et procuraciones in dicta nostra diocesi nobis quomodolibet debitas collector specialiter deputatus.*

2 See 940.

bishop of his consent to the election of Thomas de Leghe as abbot and asking him to do what pertains to his office in the matter.

929 *29 August 1347 Tewkesbury*

Letters patent of the appointment by the subprior, Peter de Bradeweye, and by the convent of Tewkesbury, of their fellow monks, John Marcle and John de Teukysbury, as proctors for securing the bishop's assent to Thomas de Leghe's election.

930 *Undated*[1]

Protestation by Br. Thomas de Leghe, prior of Tewkesbury, on his own behalf and that of the whole convent, to the effect that no excommunicate or other unauthorised person is to take part in the election at Tewkesbury. The voices of any such who may later be found to have done so are to be disregarded.

931 *20 August 1347 Tewkesbury*

Letters patent of the appointment by the compromisers[2] of William de Baddeseye, one of their number, to elect Thomas de Leghe in their name. Present were M. Stephen de Northeye, M. William de Asshoton and John de la More, clerk, notary public.

932 *4 August 1347 Calais*

Licence of Hugh le Despenser for the election of an abbot by the convent of Tewkesbury, Br. John de Saltford and Br. John de Teukisbury having brought news of Abbot John de Cotes' death.

933 *13 August 1347 Tewkesbury*

Letters patent of the prior and convent of Tewkesbury. Following the death on 22 July of Abbot John de Cotes and his burial on the 31st, and having obtained licence to elect a successor from their patron, Hugh le Despenser, Br. Thomas de Leghe, prior, and Brothers Walter de Bristoll, John Besmancel, John de Aston, Peter de Bradeweye, Thomas de Colewell, Adam de Rodeberwe, Richard de Ledebury, cellarer, William Widecombe, sacrist, John de Saltford, Robert de Stolton, almoner, John de Beodeford, precentor, Thomas de Cannynges, James de Longedon, cook, William Whiscard, John Marcele, John Neubury, William Baddeseye, chamberlain, William Marleberewe, William de Gloucester, John de Tewkesbury, Richard de Gloucester, John de Evesham, John Stone, William de Bristoll, John Absolon, Walter de Schallingford, Alexander Atforton, Richard Circestre, Thomas Wilcote, Robert de Gloucester, William

---

1 Cf. 936.   2 See 927.

Murymouth and Richard Wilforton, came together on 10 August in the chapter house. They agreed upon the morning of Monday after the Assumption [i.e. 20 August], in the chapter house, for the time and place of the election. Brothers John de Stradhull, Simon de Weston and William de Putteleye being absent, Ds. John Baylyf, priest, was deputed to inform them of the arrangements for the election and to cite them to appear. Present as witnesses were William de Asshton, rector of Atherstone, Ds. John Baylyf and Ds. John Fairford, priests.

934 *13 August 1347 Tewkesbury*
Similar letters patent of the appointment of John Widecombe, priest, to cite the absent monks William de Campeden, Robert de Ragon, Roger Noreys, Thomas de Chesterton and Richard de Hampslap.[1]

935 *20 August 1347 Tewkesbury*
Letters patent of Br. William de Baddeseye's appointment by the subprior and convent of Tewkesbury to publish the election of Thomas de Leghe to the clergy and people. Present as witnesses were M. Stephen de Northeye, M. William de Asshton and John de la More, notary public.

936 *20 August 1347 Tewkesbury*
Letters patent of the appointment by the same of their prior, Thomas de Leghe, to warn all excommunicated and other unauthorised persons to take no part in the election.[2] Present as witnesses were M. Stephen de Northeye, William de Asshton,[3] and others.

937 *21 August 1347 Tewkesbury*
Letters patent of the appointment by the same of Brothers John de Aston, John de Saltford and William de Badeseye, jointly or severally, to apprise Thomas de Leghe of his election and to secure his assent.[4]

938 *9 September 1347 Tewkesbury*
Certification by the archdeacon of Gloucester's official of his execution of the bishop's mandate, dated 5 September from Hartlebury, for the citation of opponents of Thomas de Leghe's election to appear before the bishop or his commissary in the parish church of Ripple on the Monday after the Exaltation of the Holy Cross [i.e. 17 September]. Finding no co-elect or opponent of the election, he made general citation.

---

1 *Mutatis mutandis* as in 933, and with the same witnesses.   2 Cf. 930.
3 Sometimes (e.g. 935) entitled *magister*.   4 Witnesses as in 935.

939 *Undated*[1]

Petition of the convent of Tewkesbury's proctor for the bishop's confirmation of Thomas de Leghe's election.

940 *26 August 1347 Tewkesbury*

Notarially attested decree of the Tewkesbury election, addressed to the bishop. The canons provide that a regular church should not lie vacant for longer than three months.[2] When, therefore, the monastery of Tewkesbury became vacant with the death on 22 July of Abbot John de Cotes, the monks, after his burial on the 31st and the arrival of Hugh le Despenser's licence to elect a successor, agreed upon 20 August for the election, and meanwhile cited those of their house who were absent.[3] On the appointed day, when all who were entitled to be present and who could come were assembled, the word of God was expounded, the hymn *Veni Creator* solemnly sung, and the constitution *Quia propter*[4] read out. After lengthy discussion the brethren agreed to proceed by way of compromise. Accordingly, they empowered Brothers Thomas de Leghe, prior, Richard de Ledebury, cellarer, John de Straddul, prior of Cranborne,[5] Robert de Stolton, almoner, James de Lon[ge]don, cook, William de Baddeseye, chamberlain, William de Marlebergh, Walter de Schalyngford and Thomas de Wytlecote, to elect an abbot before nightfall.[6] The compromisers then drew apart and after much discussion cast their votes—with the single exception of the elect himself—for Thomas de Leghe, the prior. Thereupon one of the compromisers, William de Baddeseye, elected the abbot on his own behalf and that of the whole convent.[7] The monks, save Thomas de Leghe who remained silent, approved the election. Solemnly chanting the *Te Deum laudamus* they bore him to the principal altar of the monastery and placed him upon it, according to custom. At once William de Baddeseye published the election to the clergy and people,[8] who were there in great number. Subsequently, on 21 August, John de Aston, John de Saltford and William de Baddeseye, as proctors of the convent presented the election to the elect in the infirmary chapel and besought his consent.[9] On 22 August they renewed their request and the elect, not wishing to resist the divine will, gave his assent. In view of the above the convent ask the bishop to give his confirmation and to impart benediction to the elect.

Notarial subscription of John de la More, clerk of Exeter diocese, notary public by apostolic authority, who together with the witnesses, M. Stephen de Northeye and M. William de Aysshton, rectors

1 Cf. 926, 929. 2 *Extra* 1, 6, c. 41. 3 See 933, 934.
4 *Extra* 1, 6, c. 42. 5 Dorset. A cell of Tewkesbury.
6 See 927. 7 See 931. 8 See 935.
9 See 937.

respectively of Fairford and Atherston, was present throughout the above process.

941 *20 August 1347 Tewkesbury*

Public instrument attesting the details of the Tewkesbury election. On 20 August, following the celebration of Mass of the Holy Spirit in the quire and the summons to the chapter, Thomas de Leghe, prior of Tewkesbury, and the other 39 monks of the monastery—Brothers Walter de Bristoll, John Besemansel, John de Aston, Peter de Bradeweye, subprior, Thomas de Colewell, Adam de Redelegh,[1] William de Campeden, prior of Bristol,[2] Richard de Ledebury, cellarer, William de Wydecombe, sacrist, John de Straddul, prior of Cranborne,[3] John de Saltford, John de Stolton, almoner, John de Bydeford, precentor, Thomas de Cannynges, James de Longedon, cook, William Whyscard, John de Marcle, subcellarer, William de Putteleye, John de Neuwebury, Roger Noreys, Robert Ragon, William de Baddeseye, chamberlain, William de Marlebergh, third prior, William de Glouc[estr'], John de Teukysbur', Richard de Gloucestr', John de Evesham, John de Stone, Thomas de Chesterton, Richard de Hampslap, William de Bristoll, John Absolon, Walter de Schalyngford, Alexander de Atforton, Richard de Cirencestr', Thomas de Wylecote, Robert de Gloucestr', William Murymouth and Richard de Wylfurton, assembled in the chapter house before the first hour of the day for the election. There Br. Walter de Schalyngford expounded the word of God and the prior and monks solemnly chanted the hymn *Veni Creator Spiritus*, whereupon M. Stephen de Northeye junior, clerk, read out the convent's letters patent to the effect that the date and place of the election had been fixed and Ds. John Baylyf, chaplain, deputed to summon the absent Simon de Weston.[4] John Baylyf certified on oath that he had carried out the citation and handed the convent's letter to Simon, who had read it through. The latter was publicly summoned at the door of the chapter house, but without effect. Br. William de Baddeseye then read a letter from Hugh le Despenser, the monastery's patron, sealed with red wax, which showed that licence for the election had been granted. Immediately afterwards he recited the constitution *Quia propter*.[5] The prior and monks asked seculars, that is, M. John de la Lowe, Professor of Civil Law, rector of Bredon, M. Stephen de Northeye, rector of Fairford, M. William de Asshton, rector of Atherstone and Stephen de Northeye junior, clerk, to remain for the whole process of election as witnesses, but with the protestation that this did not mean they were there as of right. After this, Master John

1 An error for *de Rodebergh* or *Rodeberwe* (Rodborough). Cf. 933.
2 St. James's Bristol, a cell of Tewkesbury.
3 Dorset. Another cell of Tewkesbury.
4 See 933.   5 *Extra* 1, 6, c. 42.

asked if all were present who should be. The prior and monks replied that they were all there except Brother Simon. Master John then asked whether all were in Holy Orders and professed of the order of St. Benedict in the monastery. The prior and many others replied that they were. After Brother Simon had been repeatedly summoned at the door of the chapter house, the prior, at the express wish of his brethren, pronounced him contumacious and declared that the election should continue notwithstanding his absence. The prior proceeded to warn all excommunicated and other unauthorised persons to take no part in the election.[1] The prior and monks then discussed which form they should adopt. Master John propounded the forms laid down at the Council[2] and suggested that the safest was the way of compromise, whereupon the monks decided to proceed by that method. Master John stated that the wish of each monk should be clearly known, so the prior and 39 monks individually gave their assent.[3] Next they discussed the names of those whom they might wish to have as compromisers, and eventually chose nine.[4] Master John had the names written down and read out, each monk individually assenting to them. He then suggested that it would be useful for the convent to consider the actual form of the compromise, adding, among other things, that its duration should be limited. He proposed a particular form which, at the convent's express wish, was written down and read out.[5] To this each assented and the document was sealed with the common seal. The monks then agreed that the subprior, Peter de Bradeweye, who after the prior was their president and had the first voice among them, should transfer their power to the nine compromisers. Acting on his own behalf and by authority of the convent's *viva voce* mandate, he conferred the power of election on the compromisers and undertook to accept their choice.[6] The latter accepted the charge and retired to a certain *locutorium* on the south side of the chapter house, together with the notary and witnesses. There they discussed the possibility of electing someone from among themselves or from the rest of the convent. Eventually Richard de Ledebury, the cellarer, named Thomas de Leghe, the prior, and at once the remaining compromisers—save Thomas himself—cast their votes in the same direction. After which the compromisers, by special mandate which was put into writing, empowered William de Baddeseye to elect Thomas as abbot.[7] They returned to the chapter house where, in the presence of the subprior and the rest of the monks, William de Baddeseye gave an account of their proceedings and made solemn pronouncement of the election at about the ninth hour and before nightfall. The monks, apart from

1 See 930.   2 See p. 64 n. 1.
3 The way this was done both in this instance and in those which follow was for the prior
  to be asked first and then for him to put the question to each of the other monks.
4 The names are as in 940.   5 927.
6 Either their unanimous choice or that of a majority.   7 See 931.

Thomas de Leghe, unanimously approved and ratified the election and by written mandate authorised William de Baddeseye to publish it.[1] Chanting the *Te Deum laudamus* they carried the elect to the principal altar of the church and laid him upon it. Standing by the side of the altar William de Baddeseye published the election in the vulgar tongue in the presence of a large number of clergy and people. On Tuesday 21 August, in the presence of the notary and witnesses, the proctors of the subprior and convent, Brothers John de Aston, John de Saltford and William de Baddeseye, went to the chapel of the infirmary. There they found the elect, to whom they showed their mandate and had it read out in his presence.[2] They then formally presented the election and asked for the elect's consent. He replied that he wished to consider the matter. On the Wednesday, 22 August, the proctors returned and in the presence of the notary and witnesses again besought the elect to agree to the election. This he finally did. Present at the above proceedings were Masters Stephen de Northeye and William de Aysshton, rectors respectively of Fairford and Atherstone, together with many other witnesses.

Notarial subscription of John de la More, clerk of Exeter diocese, notary public by apostolic authority.

942 *Undated*

Articles which the proctor of the Tewkesbury convent proposes to prove before the bishop or his commissary with respect to the election of Thomas de Leghe as abbot; first, that the abbey is conventual, regular, and ordinarily ruled by an abbot, and is known to be so in the diocese of Worcester and especially in Tewkesbury; *item*, that Br. John de Cotes was the last abbot and publicly accepted as such; *item*, that Br. John died on 22 July 1347; *item*, that by his death the monastery became vacant and continued to be so; *item*, that the body of Abbot John was buried on 31 July; *item*, that Hugh le Despenser, lord of Glamorgan and Morgannou, is patron of the monastery; *item*, that all the above facts are well known in Tewkesbury and neighbourhood; *item*, that the monastery being vacant and licence having been duly obtained, the monks assembled[3] on 13 August in their chapter house and appointed 20 August for the election, and because Simon de Weston and others were absent, they deputed John Baillif, priest, to cite them; *item*, that the monks assembled for the election in the morning, after Mass of the Holy Spirit and the ringing of the bell for chapter; *item*, that all the monks there were lettered, aged 25 or more, professed of the order of St. Benedict in the monastery, in Holy Orders, of good reputation, and entitled to take part in the election; *item*, that Br. Thomas de Leghe was at the time of his

1 See 935.   2 See 937.   3 They are enumerated as in 933.

election, as before and after it, monk and prior of the monastery, one of the community, professed of the Order of St. Benedict, 30 years of age and more, in priest's orders, legitimate, circumspect and provident in both spiritual and temporal affairs, adequately lettered, of praiseworthy life and character, and generally held to be so; *item*, that at the time of the election, as before and after it, the convent comprised 41 monks, to whom as a body the election of an abbot belongs; *item*, that Ds. John Bailiff certified on oath that he had cited Br. Simon de Weston; *item*, that Br. Simon, although summoned at the door of the chapter house on the day of the election and long awaited, did not appear; *item*, that by the custom of the monastery, when the abbot is dead or absent, the prior by virtue of his office presides over the convent and has the first voice in capitular deliberations and acts; *item*, that in the absence of both the abbot and prior the subprior presides by reason of his office; *item*, that John de la More who was present during the process of election and who wrote it down in public form, is a clerk and notary public by apostolic authority and generally held to be such in Tewkesbury and neighbourhood.

943 *Undated*

Additional articles to be proved on behalf of the Tewkesbury convent after the examination of those given above.[1] The proctor intends to prove that when the prior and monks assembled in chapter, Walter de Schalyngford expounded the word of God, the *Veni Creator Spiritus* was sung, and M. Stephen de Northeye junior, clerk, publicly read out letters fixing the day of the election and the mandate for John Baillyf, chaplain, to cite absentees; *item*, that William de Baddeseye recited letters patent of Hugh le Despenser granting licence to elect, and that he then read publicly the constitution *Quia propter*;[2] *item*, that the convent asked seculars, Masters John de la Lowe, Professor of Civil Law, Stephen de Northeye senior, William de Aysshton and Stephen de Northeye junior, clerks of Worcester diocese, who were in the chapter house at the time, to remain for the election process as witnesses, but without right in the election; *item*, that Br. Simon was frequently cited at the door to the chapter house at the first hour of the election day, and when he did not appear, the prior declared him contumacious and decreed that the election should continue none the less; *item*, that by virtue of the convent's special mandate the prior read out a protestation in the form annexed to the present article, beginning *In Dei nomine amen*;[3] *item*, that the prior and the other 39 monks discussed which form of election they should adopt and eventually determined to proceed by way of compromise; *item*, that they then decided upon nine compromisers;[4] *item*, that they

1 Rubric.　　2 *Extra* 1, 6, c. 42.　　3 See 930.　　4 See 927, 940.

finally agreed upon a particular method of compromise;[1] *item*, that subsequently Br. Peter de Bradeweye, the subprior, transferred the power of election to the compromisers; *item*, that the nine compromisers accepted the charge and withdrew to a *locutorium* near the chapter house, where their choice eventually fell upon the prior, Thomas de Leghe; *item*, that the compromisers deputed Br. William de Baddeseye to elect Br. Thomas;[2] *item*, that the compromisers returned to the chapter house and through William de Baddeseye communicated to the subprior and convent their proceedings; *item*, that Br. William then published the election;[3] *item*, that the election was approved by the rest of the monks, the *Te Deum laudamus* chanted, and the elect placed upon the principal altar of the monastery; *item*, that Br. William de Baddeseye, standing by the side of the altar, published the election to the clergy and people; *item*, that on Tuesday 21 August, Brothers John de Aston, John de Saltford and William de Baddeseye, the proctors of the subprior and convent, presented the election to the prior, who asked for time to consider the matter;[4] *item*, that on the following Wednesday the proctors again sought his consent, which was duly given.

944 *16 March 1348 Hartlebury*

Memorandum that the bishop admitted two friars of the Augustinian order, Roger Fillode and Richard de Byrmyngham, to hear confessions.

945 *23 September 1348 Withington*

Inspeximus and confirmation of the ordination of Standish vicarage by the abbot and convent of St. Peter's, Gloucester.[5] The bishop has inspected a public instrument to the effect that on 28 July, Brothers Adam de Staunton, abbot, Stephen de Ayssch, prior, John de Bolynghop, Robert de Oxeneford, John Toky, refectorer, Walter de Ore, precentor, John Kylpek, Peter de Brocworth, Warin de Ayssch, almoner, Richard Heed, chamberlain, Nicholas de Breuton, master of the chapel, Andrew Munede, Thomas de Horton, sacrist, John Longeneye, Walter de Hadenham, John le Palmare, Walter de Hertysleye, John de Crykelade, William de Clopton, infirmarian, Henry de Blockelegh, subsacrist, Thomas de Cheltenham, master of the town,[6] John de Hulle, subalmoner, Reginald de la Boure, hosteler, John de Weston, John de Bevyrleye, subcellarer, Richard Walynton, Henry de Wotton, John de Lech, subchaplain, Henry de Fayrford, William de Foxcote, Nicholas de Sterchysden, William de Neuwent, John de Poywyk and William de Rodleye, constituting the convent of St. Peter's, Gloucester, came together in the presence

1 See 927, 940.   2 See 931.   3 See 940.   4 See 937.
5 Dated from Gloucester, 2 August 1348.   6 *Magister ville.*

of a notary and witnesses for the ordination of Standish vicarage. This was on account of the many disagreements between the convent, appropriators of Standish, and M. Walter de Evesham and his predecessors, perpetual vicars of the church, as to the sufficiency of the vicarial portion, more particularly because for the most part such portion had not been separate but intermingled with that of the rectors. To obviate future disputes the convent, with the vicar's express consent, by virtue of his submission, and in his presence, have ordained the vicarage. The vicar and his successors are to have at Little Haresfield near Standish a house (*mansum*) with garden and curtilage and three adjacent crofts, one virgate of arable land with hedges and ditches, and two and a half acres of meadow—as did former vicars. At Upper *Hoxlyng* they are to have two tenements with gardens and adjacent crofts, and five acres of arable in the field which John Huwe and Benedict ate Pyrie hold of the vicar of Standish, as they have done of previous vicars; at Ruscombe by Randwick, a house (*mansum*) with outbuildings (*cum eius domibus*), gardens, crofts, closes and pastures, as well as four acres of arable and other appurtenances which the vicars formerly held, but with the exception of the better grange with the adjacent barton, commonly called *Bernhay*. This last is specially reserved to the religious for the storage of their tithes (*pro decimus garbarum suarum decimalium retinendis*).

At Saul the vicars are to have six acres of arable, and at Hardwicke at least 32 acres, which their predecessors enjoyed. They are not to receive any tithes of wheat, rye, barley, oats,[1] legumes, lentils, beans, peas, or any kind of corn from the above lands or others within the parish, but are to manage as best they can without receiving or paying tithes (*absque decime cuiuscunque recepcione . . . et sine decime solucione modo quo poterunt meliori*). They are to have grass and hay from the four churchyards of Standish, Randwick, Hardwicke and Saul, as well as all lesser tithes (*minute seu minores*) of flax, wool, animals, or anything else within the parish borders, excepting tithes belonging to the courts or manors of Standish and Pitchcombe, even if the animals from these manors feed or bed down wholly or in part within the parish. They are to receive all tithes of mills, apart from the abbot's mills, and every kind of offering, whether alive or dead, together with dead mortuaries, live mortuaries being reserved to the religious. Every year the abbot and convent are to pay to the vicar in Standish parish church £15 5s. in equal instalments at the three terms of St. Michael [29 September], the Annunciation [25 March] and the Nativity of St. John the Baptist [24 June]. The religious lay themselves, their successors, and all their spiritual goods under obligation to make this payment. All the remaining fruits, obventions, oblations and profits not specifically granted to the vicars are to belong to the rectors. The vicars, with the help of other suitable

1 The MS. has *nuprotilionis*(?) at this point.

persons, are to exercise the cure of souls both in the mother church and its chapels, to discharge all the due and accustomed episcopal and archidiaconal burdens, to keep a lamp (*mortariolum vel lampadem*) burning at night in the mother church, to maintain appropriate hospitality, and to be responsible for the rebuilding and repair of a third of the chancel of Standish church, as well as the whole of the chancel at Hardwicke. They should not bear any other burdens. To that part of the indenture remaining in the vicar's hands was appended the common seal of the convent, to that remaining with the religious, the seals of the vicar and the office of the deanery of Gloucester, the latter at the vicar's request. The above proceedings took place in the chapter house at Gloucester in the presence of witnesses, Masters John de Lynchelade and William de Bergeveny, *iuris periti*, and Ds. John Pyrie, rector of Staunton. Robert de Rodmerton, clerk of Worcester diocese, notary public by apostolic authority, was present throughout and set down the proceedings in public form. The bishop, finding the above ordination, taxation or limitation of the vicarage to have been made not collusorily but in good faith, at the petition of the parties and in their presence judicially declares it appropriate and sufficient, and authorises, ratifies and confirms it, condemning the religious, in the person of their proctor, Br. Thomas de Horton, to make the annual payment assigned to the vicar and his successors, under penalty of paying double the amount of the default to the fabric of the cathedral church.[1]

946 *30 May 1348 Hartlebury*

Memorandum of the licence for M. Richard de Ledebury, archdeacon of Gloucester, to choose confessors able to absolve him and enjoin salutary penance, and also to celebrate Mass (*divina*), personally or by means of suitable priests, in oratories and other appropriate places within the diocese, whenever he happens to be staying within its borders.

947 *11 May 1348 Hereford*

Commission of William de Herwynton, vicar-general in spirituals of John [Trillek], bishop of Hereford [1344–60], for the carrying out of an exchange between Ds. William de Baggesouere, perpetual vicar of Clifford, Hereford diocese, and Ds. William Heritage, vicar of Staverton.[2] He acts by virtue of the bishop of Hereford's commission, dated 29 April 1348 from Whitbourne, appointing him vicar-general in spirituals[3] with power to accept resignations of benefices, whether

1 The entry concludes with a recension of Thomas de Horton's proxy, dated 2 August 1348 from Gloucester.
2 See *Institutions* 948, 949.
3 He is described as official and Professor of Civil Law.

arising from exchange or any other cause, to approve the reasons for exchanges, to receive presentations to benefices with or without cure, to enquire into vacancies with the accustomed articles, to admit, institute and induct to benefices, to accept oaths of canonical obedience, to confirm or annul elections, to ordain vicarages *de novo* in the bishop's name, or to augment those found to be insufficient, and to do everything else known to pertain to the office of vicar.

950 *15 October 1348 Hartlebury*

Letters patent of the ordination of Wellesbourne vicarage.[1] In times past there has been contention between the prior and convent of Kenilworth, Coventry & Lichfield diocese, the appropriators of Wellesbourne, and the vicars of that church, with respect to the vicarial portion and the manner of obtaining it. To settle such conflict and to avoid the spiritual danger which many have incurred as a consequence of the collection of the tithes and their division, agreement has been reached between Ds. Peter de Salle, perpetual vicar of Wellesbourne and the religious. The latter are to have all tithes of woods, underwoods and sheaves belonging to the church within the parish, except those from the crofts in the vill of Wellesbourne Hastings,[2] and Nether Walton, all of which were formerly enclosed by hedges and ditches, though now only some of them are. These tithes are to belong to the vicars as before. Excepted also are tithes in Upper Walton anciently assigned to the chaplain of the chapel there. The religious are to receive the whole tithe of hay from the tithes of the lords of Walton and Wellesbourne Mountford, and Roger de Bisshopesdon. Should any of these lords subsequently acquire or resume possession of land within Wellesbourne parish from which the vicar has been accustomed to receive tithes of hay, such tithes are to belong to the vicar even though the lands constitute the lord's demesne. All other ecclesiastical emoluments belonging to the church are to go to the vicars, tithes of the convent's manor within the parish and the increase of their animals alone excepted. The vicar is to have the whole of the house in which he now lives, and in which his predecessors lived, together with a messuage and half a virgate of glebe by the churchyard, free of all exaction, service, rent, heriot, or other secular burden, and of the payment of tithes. He is also to receive annually from the convent's barn at Wellesbourne three cartloads of white straw, one at each of the feasts of All Saints [1 November], the Purification [2 February], and Easter, or instead, three shillings payable in instalments at the same terms, whichever the religious choose. With regard to the ordinary and extraordinary

1 The church was given to the Kenilworth canons by Roger de Newburgh, earl of Warwick and Henry I confirmed the grant. It was probably appropriated anciently. Cf. Dugdale, *Warwickshire* 1, p. 572.
2 *Wellesburn' Straunge*.

burdens, it is agreed that the vicar is to pay archidiaconal procuration and synodals, to find the bread and wine for celebrations, and also the accustomed lights at and around the high altar, while all other burdens are to be sustained by the religious. The bishop, after examination of the above arrangements, finds them to have been ordained for the utility of the church concerned and the salvation of souls, and consequently confirms them by his ordinary authority.

952 *18 March 1316 Worcester*

Letters patent of Prior John de Wyk and the Worcester chapter. In return for a messuage and buildings lying next to the bishop's manor in the vill of Westm[inster], formerly held by Robert le Coupare, and which Thomas, earl of Lancaster, has given to Walter de Maidenestan [Maidstone], bishop of Worcester [1313–17], and his successors in perpetual alms, the convent has unanimously agreed to celebrate the anniversaries of Edmund, late earl of Lancaster and Leicester, son of King Henry III, and his wife Blanche, sometime queen of Navarre, which fall on 4 June and 4 May respectively. The *Placebo* and *Dirige* are to be observed in accordance with the custom of the church by the ringing of the greater bells and with four lighted candles on the high altar, followed on the morrow by a Mass for the souls of Edmund and Blanche and those of all the faithful departed. Further, in consideration of the benefit derived from the devotion of Thomas, earl of Lancaster, and Robert Holland (*de Holandia*) to the church of Worcester and to Walter [Maidstone] its bishop, the convent admits them as *fratres speciales*, participants in all the prayers, vigils, almsgiving and other good works (*beneficia*) of the monks and their successors, which by the Saviour's clemency they may be deemed worthy to perform. After their deaths, when their names have been notified to the convent, the same shall be done for them in the church as for the other brethren, and in addition their anniversaries kept like those of Edmund and Blanche. Such anniversaries may be anticipated or postponed according to the custom of the church by the precentor's decision. The convent also desires that a certain annual rent of 24s. which the bishops were wont to receive for the above messuage with appurtenances by right of the church of Worcester be cancelled and the earl and his heirs accounted discharged as well of arrears as of the principal rent.

953 *28 July 1348*

Memorandum of the enquiry into the vacancy of Tarrington vicarage, Hereford diocese, by M. Thomas de Dumbleton, rector of Stoke Edith; Walter, perpetual vicar of Wellington, dean of Weston; William, vicar of Dilwyn; Robert, vicar of Burghill; Master Hugh, vicar of Dormington; Roger, vicar of Weston [Beggard]; Richard, vicar of Bodenham; and Hugh, vicar of Brinsop; incumbents of [Weston] deanery assembled on the Monday after St. James the Apostle [i.e. 28 July] in the cathedral church of Hereford. The enquiry found that the vicarage was full, Ds. John de Rondelesham being the vicar; that the prior and convent of Monmouth were the true patrons, although for that turn the king, because the priory's temporalities were in his hand on account of the war with France, had presented Ds. Walter de la Broke, rector of St. Andrew's Droitwich, who wished to exchange benefices;[1] that the vicarage was subject to a pension of 12s. payable to the priory, but not litigious or taxed; and that the presentee was of good life and honest conversation, and in priest's orders.

969 *27 August 1320 Bredon*

Inspeximus and confirmation by Thomas [de Cobham], bishop of Worcester [1317–27], of the ordination of a chantry at Ripple by John Salemon of Stratford, clerk. The founder has received royal licence to assign two messuages, 48 acres of arable land, 12 of meadow, and three of pasture, with 12s. annual rent and appurtenances in Ripple, to two chaplains who are to celebrate in the church there. By virtue of such licence and with the consent of Ds. Walter de Bedewynde, rector of Ripple, he has granted to God, Our Lady, and to Ds. Philip Camd' of Twyning, chaplain, and his successors, a messuage, 24 acres of arable land and five of meadow in *Russheleye* and *la More*, together with 11s. 9d. annual rent for messuages and tenements in Ripple formerly held by Alan de Rippel, clerk, made up as follows: from John the miller 1s. 10d., John *in Angulo* 1s. 10d., William Gerveis 8d., Osmer Bogge 1s. 6d., Alice Symkyn 6d., Richard *in Angulo* 8d., Alice daughter of Marth[a] Aleyn 6d., Robert Faber 1s., Thomas *in Angulo* 1s. 4d., Agnes atte Stayre 1s. 2d., John Ormes 6d. and Alice Stabald 3d. The chaplain and his successors are to celebrate Mass daily for the good estate of the founder while living and for his soul after death, for the souls of his father John, his mother Leticia, his sisters Alice, Amice, Christine and Joan, and all his ancestors, heirs, relations, friends and benefactors, also for the good estate of Bishop Thomas de Cobham, and for his soul after death, as for the souls of his ancestors, relations and friends, for the souls of John de Sapi and Sybil his wife, their ancestors, heirs and relations; for the souls of Walter de Beauchamp, his wife Alice, their sons Walter, William and Giles, their daughter Petronilla, and all their heirs, relations and friends; for the souls of Simon de Crombe, his ancestors, heirs, relations and friends, and for those of all the faithful departed. The founder ordains[2] that the chaplain

1 See *Institutions* 954.   2 The ordinances proper begin at this point.

be presented by himself to the bishop, or *sede vacante* the prior, for admission and institution to the chantry, and after his death, by Henry Beneid, chaplain of the other chantry, and his successors. A priest native to Ripple, who is otherwise suitable and unbeneficed, is to be preferred to outside persons. Should Henry Beneid, or any successor of his, fail to make presentation within a month, the right is to devolve for that turn only on the bishop, or *sede vacante* the prior. Each chaplain admitted to the chantry is to swear to maintain all the above and to serve in person, unless prevented by reasonable and inevitable cause, and then for the duration of such impediment he is to have another suitable chaplain to do what pertains to the chantry—so far as his [? its] resources allow. The chaplain ought to be in Ripple church with the other chaplains and clerks for Matins and the canonical Hours, and is to undergo visitation and correction by the rector and ordinary like other priests of the church. During the founder's lifetime the chaplain is to say at Mass one collect with secret and post-communion for his welfare, and another, likewise with secret and post-communion, for all those mentioned above. After his death the chaplains are daily in their Masses to say for his soul, with individual mention, a collect with secret and post-communion, and for the souls of the above and all the faithful departed Mass is to be celebrated with prayers of special intention. The chaplain is to live chastely and honestly for the praise of God and Our Lady and for his soul's perpetual salvation. Should he be defamed a second time after correction for carnal sin, and be convicted or unable to purge himself, he is to be deprived of the chantry by the ordinary and another chaplain instituted in his stead. In the event of a priest being defamed of incontinence with a particular woman, he is to shun her company and suspected places under heavy penalty. The priest is to provide three pounds of wax a year for two candles before the altar of St. Peter in Ripple church, which are to be renewed at Christmas and the Assumption [15 August]. After the founder's death the priest is to distribute five shillings to the poor on his anniversary, or corn or bread of that value should he consider it better for them. At the same time he is also to distribute in a similar manner the value of heriots, escheats, reliefs, fines, amercements, and all other profits of the above tenements beyond the fixed annual rent already mentioned. During the founder's lifetime this is to be done on the feast of All Souls [2 November]. Every anniversary he is to sing the *Placebo* and *Dirige* and a Mass at the altar of St. Peter for the founder's soul, the souls of those named above, and those of all the faithful departed. Because the founder, in addition to the above lands and tenements, has given five marks [£3 6s. 8d.] to Ds. Philip for his support during the first year, he requires him at the end of his life, or at his cession or deprivation, to transfer the same sum to his successor, under compulsion of the ordinary if need be. Hay meadows (*prata crescencia*), trees and hedges are not included in this sum. Philip, as every future chaplain, is to leave to his successor the following principal household goods, in each case the best article in his possession at the time of vacancy: a waggon or cart, a plough with accoutrements, a harrow, chest, barrel, vat, cask, a wine vessel (*tina*), a brass pot, plate, pitcher, gridiron, a table, a form with trestles, a napkin, towel, washing bowl, basin, ladder, winnowing fan, sack, a bushel for measuring corn and a basket. Under pain of divine judgement and vengeance the founder inhibits any of his relatives or kinsmen from impeding the chantry or infringing its articles in any way. He has sealed the above with his seal and also that of the deanery of Ripple *ad maiorem evidenciam*. Witnesses: William de Beauchamp, John de Sapi and Simon de Crombe, knights; Nicholas Russel, William Dabetot, John de Hulle, Robert de Sestaneslade, Richard Felip, and others, a.d. 1320.[1] The bishop [Cobham], approving John Salemon's pious intention, ratifies and confirms the ordination by diocesan authority, saving the rights, rents and services due to himself and his successors and to the lords of the fee. To further safeguard the ordination he excommunicates *in genere* all those who in future maliciously infringe its provisions.

970 *4 November 1348 Hartlebury*

Memorandum that, on hearing of the death of John Salemon, the founder of the chantries copied above, and of that of Ds. Walter Hatherych, chaplain, who last held one of them at Salemon's presentation, and because the other also lay vacant, the bishop conferred that formerly held by Hatherych on Ds. John de Hardres, chaplain. But before orders could be given for his induction, a certain Henry Thomas, priest, intervened with a presentation to the other chantry, which he alleged had been made by Hatherych, and sought to be admitted. After discussion as to the validity of the presentation, Thomas renounced his right, if such he had, into the bishop's hands. The bishop then conferred the chantry on him for that turn, declaring that the collations made in such unusual circumstances (*in casu tam mirabili*) were not intended to be prejudicial to the founder's ordination which he wished to remain in full force.[2]

973 *17 December 1348 Whitbourne*

Certification by John [Trillek], bishop of Hereford [1344–60], of his execution of the diocesan's commission, dated 8 December from

---

1 At this point there is a recension of the mortmain licence mentioned above, dated 14 August 1319 from Hartford Bridge, Northumberland. *C.P.R.* 1317–21, p. 388, and cf. *ibid.* p. 389.

2 Salemon did not envisage the possibility of his dying at about the same time as both chantries fell vacant.

16

Hartlebury, for the exchange, in accordance with the findings of an enquiry to be held by the official of the Worcester archdeacon, between Ds. Robert Payne, rector of Martin [Hussingtree] (patron: Walter de Pyrie), and Ds. Robert Morys of Worcester, vicar of Lindridge, Hereford diocese.

Memorandum that on 18 December the above Robert took the oath of canonical obedience.

997 *27 March 1349*

Memorandum that the bishop appointed Matilda de Luttelton prioress of the house of St. Mary Magdalene, Bristol,[1] and instituted her.[2] Immediately afterwards a letter for her induction was sent to the dean of Bristol.

998 *15 April 1349 Hartlebury*

Licence for John de Preston and Richard de Hadleye, monks of the cathedral church, to hear the confessions of those of the bishop's subjects wishing to come to them, to absolve all such even in cases specially reserved to the bishop, and to enjoin salutary penance upon them.

999 *18 April 1349 Hartlebury*

Mandate to the dean of Worcester. The unheard of mortality at the present time has brought an immense increase in the number of those buried in the cathedral cemetery, which has become inadequate. In view of this, the bishop has decided to allow the use of the church-yard of St. Oswald's hospital. The dean is to inform the sacrist and all others whom it may concern that burials belonging to the cathedral church may take place at St. Oswald's at the discretion of the sacrist.[3]

1000 *21 March 1349 Bristol*

Certification by William de Syde, clerk, that he has carried out the bishop's mandate for the admission, institution and induction of William de Veye, priest, to Over chantry, and of John atte Mulle, priest, to that of Wortley.

1001 *11 May 1349 Hartlebury*

Appointment of Br. Nicholas de Hogschawe, a monk of the cathedral church, as guardian of the feretories of Saints [Oswald and Wulfstan].

1002 *26 May 1349 Hartlebury*

Memorandum that in the chapel of Hartlebury castle Br. John de Alyncestre junior, of St. John's hospital, Warwick, who had been

1 An Augustinian priory.
2 The actual words of the *prefeccio* and *institucio* are given.
3 Printed in Nash, *Worcs.*, 1, pp. 226–7.

elected master of that house, resigned the office because of a defect in the proof of his election process and for other reasons. The bishop thereupon appointed him master.[1]

1003 *26 May 1349*
The bishop by his ordinary authority appoints Br. William de Salopia, priest, professed in the habit of St. Oswald's hospital by Worcester, as master or preceptor of that house.

Ordination Lists

Abbreviations:

A. & C.	abbot (or abbess) and convent
D. & C.	dean and chapter
P. & C.	prior (or prioress) and convent
l.d.	letters dimissory
r.	rector
to t.	to the title
v.	vicar
*	the clause 'de quo reputavit se esse contentum' whether given in full or abbreviated in the MS.
†	the clause 'quem esse docuit' whether in full or abbreviated in the MS.

1004 *27 March 1339 Orders celebrated by the bishop in Kempsey parish church on Holy Saturday.*

Acolytes

Br. Walter de Wynferton, monk of Worcester.
Br. Thomas de Burton ⎫
Br. William de Wyke ⎬ Friars Minor of Worcester.
Br. William de Alvedeleye ⎭
Richard Golsmyt of Gloucester, Worc. diocese.
John de la Chaunbr' of Worc. diocese.
Laurence Jacob of St. David's diocese, by l.d.

Subdeacons

Br. William de Holte ⎫
Br. John de Poiwyke ⎬ monks of Worcester.
Br. Roger de Munstruworth ⎭

---

1 The actual words of the resignation and appointment are given.

[*Subdeacons continued.*]

M. William de Bergeveny of Llandaff diocese, by l.d. to t. of the bishop.

Br. Walter de Hyde.

Deacons

Br. Nicholas Hayl ⎱ monks of Kingswood, Worc. diocese.
Br. Henry de Clyve ⎰

Br. Nicholas de Thenelesford of Worc. diocese.

Br. John de Optone of Worc. diocese.

M. Hugh de Staunton, to t. of the house of the scholars of Merton, Oxford, Lincoln diocese, by l.d. of the bishop of Lincoln's vicar.

M. Richard Clehangre of Hereford diocese, by l.d. to t. of the scholars of Merton, Oxford.

M. Reginald de Strattone of Salisbury diocese, by l.d. to t. of Merton, Oxford.

M. John de Lullynton of Lincoln diocese, by l.d. to t. of the nuns of St. Michael next Stamford.

William le Walssh, r. of St. Laurence's, Warwick, Worc. diocese, to t. of his church.

Nicholas Simond of Marston, Worc. diocese, to t. of St. Wulstan's hospital, Worcester.

Philip Landowe of St. David's diocese, by l.d. to t. of the D. & C. of Hereford.

Robert de Teynton, r. of Great Rissington, Worc. diocese, to t. of his church.

Priests

Br. Roger Broun, monk of Winchcombe, Worc. diocese.

Br. Resus de Multone.

Br. Henry de Ʒyppeswych of St. Wulstan's hospital, Worcester.

M. Walter Chaundos, r. of *Or'*, Salisbury diocese, by l.d. to t. of his church.

Robert son of Robert ate Welle of Walesby, Lincoln diocese, by l.d. to t. of the house of Wellow.

Richard de Billesleye, v. of [Great] Barrington, Worc. diocese, to t. of his vicarage.

Stephen Barry, v. of Almondsbury, Worc. diocese, to t. of his vicarage.

John de Malgarsbury of Worc. diocese, to t. of the A. & C. of Bruern.

Bartholomew de Wyncote of Worc. diocese, to t. of the A. & C. of Bordesley.

Peter son of Reginald le Mercer of Warwick, to t. of the house of St. Sepulchre, Warwick.

Robert Vilers, r. of Tackley, Lincoln diocese, by l.d. of the vicar of the bishop of Lincoln to t. of his church.

Martin de Mildenhale of Norwich diocese, by l.d. to t. of the prior of the church of Our Lady, Ixworth.

Richard de Russhoc of Hereford diocese, by l.d. to t. of the P. & C. of Ivychurch.

William le Blak of Upton, Worc. diocese, to t. of patrimony.

1005 *4 May 1333 Gloucester*

Coln Rogers.[1] Letter of manumission conceded of grace to Walter, son of Henry atte Iate, at a court held on Tuesday after the Invention of the Holy Cross 1333, enabling him to learn letters and to proceed to Holy Orders without claim. Should he return to the mechanical arts at any future time, he is once more to be of servile condition and a bondman, together with all his goods, chattels and brood (*sequela*). In witness whereof the seal of the cellarer's office was appended to this enrolment.

1006 *17 April [1339?] Spetchley*

Memorandum that the bishop ordained the above Walter to the first tonsure after inspection of his letter of manumission.

1007 *3 May [1339?] Hartlebury*

Memorandum that the bishop ordained Hugh de Leemustre of Hereford diocese to the first tonsure by letters dimissory of Ds. Robert de Henle, canon of Hereford, vicar-general in spirituals of Thomas [Charlton], bishop of Hereford [1327–44], then *in remotis*.

1008 *22 May 1339 Orders celebrated by the bishop in the conventual church, of Tewkesbury on the eve of Trinity Sunday.*[2]

Memorandum that sentence of excommunication was brought against those ordained at this ordination who were not examined or admitted by the examiners appointed by the bishop.

Acolytes

M. Walter de Mersston.
Walter de Caunpeden.
William de Redyng'.
Thomas Tailor of Lechlade.
John le Mulleward of the same.
Robert le Capeter of the same.
Robert de Bourton.

John Stonhewer of Gloucester.
Geoffrey Reygnald of
 Rowington.
John Parker of Aston.
Thomas Caperon.
John Kene of Yardley.
Robert de Cronemer.

1 A manor belonging to Gloucester Abbey.
2 *Die sabbati Quatuor Temporum in vigilia Sancte Trinitatis.*

[Acolytes continued.]

John ate Welle of Brockhampton.[1]

Thomas Coyfistar of Cirencester.

John de Ticlewardyn.

John le Deye of Bredon.

Peter Matteshale of Cirencester.

John Sely of the same.

Nicholas, son of Richard de Grossemonte, by l.d.

Thomas Payn of Kinnersley, Hereford diocese, by l.d.

John Randulf of Pershore.

Richard Faber of the same.

Henry le Pledor of Birlingham.

John Tursceint.

John Wyot of *Scenton* [or *Stenton*].

Geoffrey Crysp of Horsley.

Walter Godeswayn.

Robert Aldesworth.

Edmund de Berkeleye.

Richard Clent.

Henry Umfrey of Sherborne.

John Arderne of Cirencester.

Nicholas Henton.

John Hynton.

John le Smyt of Bredon.

Thomas Haukyn of Kempsford.

Richard Luttulton.

William le Marechal of Bishops Cleeve.

William de Bokeland.

John Haveryng of Fairford.

Thomas de Bortone.

William Hok of Standish.

Thomas Mogge of Defford.

John Bryhtwy of Sherborne.

John de Honybounrne [*sic*].

Walter de Bokelond.

John de Lutteleton.

John Huwet.

Walter ate Ʒate of Coln.

Henry de Lenchwyk.

William Cok.

Richard de Alveston.

Reginald le Pope.

Nicholas Gautron.

Richard le Cok of Cirencester.

Henry Fabri of Broad Rissington.

Richard Fryk of Norton.

Nicholas Haukere of Norton.

William Geffrey of Kempsford.

John (de Bokelond) Williames.

William Wygeput of Cirencester.

William Crassoun of Foxcote.

Henry Lucas of Quinton.

John Fort' of Pershore.

Nicholas ate Yate of Compton-in-Henmarsh.

Thomas Starel of Wolverton.

Thomas Bertram of Great Rissington.

Richard Kenlegh of Worcester.

William Fraunceys of Dodington.

John Canon of Gloucester.

Thomas Pordhomme of Lechlade.

Robert Aldernam of Besford.

John Adam of Besford.

Richard de Welegh of Broad Campden.

William,[2] son of Ralph le Yonge of Burford, Hereford diocese, by l.d. of his bishop's vicar.

Richard Cademan of Warwick.

John de la Halle of Shrewley.

Hugh Simond of Westcote.

Hugh le Hopare of Shrewley.

Geoffrey Holles of Westcote.

John Kyng'.

Walter le Smyt'.

Thomas Pleystede.

---

1 MS. *Brokhampton*.   2 MS. *Willelmi*.

Thomas de Doudeswelle.
Roger Colas.
John Bury.
Simon Marny.
John Gernon.
John Bate.
Richard Deye.
Simon Thormerton.
John Lynton.
William de Baudynton.
John Sley.
John Wykewone.
Henry Portere.
Richard Averey.
Robert Grevile.
John ate Orchard.
Richard Bovynton.
Thomas Torkeden.
William ate Hay.
John Capel.
Laurence Stanncomb.
John Whelare.
M. Thomas de Alston.
Edmund Noreys.
John Oldeswelle.
William Vannar'.
Robert Crissp.
Robert Bisshop.
Helias Haket.
Henry Clerk of Evesham.
William de Bladyngton.
Stephen de Oxon'.
John Lyngeyn.
Robert Cornere.
John Whytteneye.
Peter de Doddelegh.

John Samon'.
Richard Sumpter.
Thomas de Charlecote.
Richard Colyns.
Thomas de Rysyndon.
John de Astone.
Robert de Mersston.
Nicholas le Cok of Walton.
Philip de Rysyndon.
Thomas de Stok.
John de Bodynton.
William Caple of Hereford
diocese, by l.d. of the Hereford
vicar.
Walter de Bokenhull of Hereford
diocese, by l.d. of the vicar.
Roger Holyn of Hereford
diocese, by l.d. of the vicar of
the bishop of Hereford.
Gilbert Stanshawe.
Richard de Stannton.
John Pireman.
Thomas Potel of Hereford
diocese, by l.d. of the vicar of
the bishop of Hereford.
Alan de Bercheston.
George de Umfrevill, r. of
Middle Chinnock, Bath &
Wells diocese, by l.d.
John Hereward of Cirencester.
John Erchebaud.
John le Clerk of Cowley.
John de Bury.
Roger Colas of Bristol.
Hugh, son of Robert Simond of
Alvington.

Acolytes Religious:
Br. Henry de Akenton, monk of Bordesley.
Br. William de Leomunstr', monk of Wenlock.
Br. Walter le Maunce3.
Br. Richard de Wyhst of St. John's hospital, Ludlow, by l.d.
Br. John de Covyntr' of the order of Minorites.
Br. John le Mareschal of Lydney, Hereford diocese, by l.d. of his
bishop's vicar.
Br. Thomas le Wolf' of Hereford diocese, by l.d. of the vicar.

Subdeacons

John Alewy, to t. of St. John's hospital, Lechlade.*
Robert Sotemay, to t. of St. Michael's hospital, Warwick.*
William Cofton, to t. of patrimony.*†
William Lovede of Harvington [by Evesham], to t. of the A. & C. of Bordesley.*
Thomas Savagesbury of [Droit]wich, to t. of patrimony.
Reginald ate Hethe, to t. of the A. & C. of Bordesley.*
Richard Welyfed, to t. of patrimony.
John le Whyte of Compton in the exempt jurisdiction of Church-down, to t. of the P. & C. of Little Malvern by l.d. of the bishop [*sic*] of York.*
Robert Geraud of Stratford, to t. of St. Sepulchre's hospital, Warwick.*
Henry Prouhomme of Lechlade, to t. of St. John's hospital there.*
Henry Alfred of Sherborne, to t. of the A. & C. of Bruern.*
John Colyns of Southrop, to t. of St. John's, Lechlade.*
John Kyniot of Shell, to t. of patrimony.
John Grene of [Droit]wich, to t. of patrimony.
Henry in the Hurne of Ripple, to t. of St. John's hospital, Lechlade.*
Stephen le Whyte of Withington, to t. of St. John's hospital, Lechlade.*
Henry de Welneford of Stourton, to t. of the A. & C. of Bruern.*
William Kokes of Kings Norton, to t. of the house of the Holy Trinity, Thelsford.
Richard Willies of Gossington, to t. of patrimony.
John le Whyte of Withington, to t. of the A. & C. of Bruern.*
John Haym of Daylesford, to t. of the A. & C. of Bruern.*
John Evenelode, to t. of Cold Norton priory.*
William Burel of Wootton, Lincoln diocese, to t. of the A. & C. of Godstow by l.d.
Elias Perkyns of Dudley, to t. of patrimony.*
Nicholas Bowyar of Gloucester, to t. of the A. & C. of Dore.*
Thomas de Chyrlench, to t. of the A. & C. of Bordesley.
Walter Dodynton, to t. of patrimony by l.d. of the vicar of the bishop of Hereford.
Stephen de Aula, to t. of Philip de Salso Marisco in four marks' [£2 13s. 4d.] annual rent.
Walter Cademan of Warwick, to t. of the house of Stoneleigh.*
Giles de Asston, to t. of Cold Norton priory.*
Robert le Tailour of Eastleach, to t. of St. John's hospital, Lechlade.*
Thomas de Val, to t. of the A. & C. of Bordesley.*
William Chese, to t. of St. John's hospital, Lechlade.*
William Richard of Himbleton, to t. of the bishop's grace. T. R. Derlyng' [*sic*].

William ate Wode of Chaddesley, to t. of patrimony. *Consulatur dominus pro digito.*

Richard le Clerk of Batsford, to t. of the nuns of Nuneaton priory.*

John de Sodbury of Worcester, to t. of St. Wulstan's hospital there.*

William Benetham of Northleach, to t. of patrimony.*

William de Tydynton, to t. of patrimony.*

Henry Pydes of Wotton.

John Sley, to t. of patrimony.*

Robert de Byrchesleye, to t. of the A. & C. of Pershore.*

John Sergeaunt of Norton, to t. of the A. & C. of Bordesley.*

Thomas Grey of Sudeley, to t. of the A. & C. of Bruern.*

Richard Loveryng, to t. of St. John's hospital, Lechlade.*

John de Otyndone, to t. of the A. & C. of Oseney.*

William Pesshoun of Almondsbury, to t. of patrimony.

Thomas Lewelyn of Gloucester, to t. of the A. & C. of Alcester.*

Robert de Westhrop of Cherrington,[1] to t. of Mottisfont priory.*

William Parys of Oddington, to t. of the A. & C. of Bruern.*

John Pydes of Wotton, to t. of the nuns of Kington.*

John Mulleward of Southrop, to t. of St. John's hospital, Lechlade.*

William Molendinarius of Rowington, to t. of the A. & C. of Bordesley.*

Thomas de Bayngrove, to t. of the house of St. Oswald, Gloucester.*

William le Gardiner of Bishops Cleeve, to t. of patrimony.*

William Dalby of Winchcombe, to t. of the house of Bruern.*

Ralph Simondes of Willersey, to t. of patrimony.*

Hugh Dobyn, r. of Lassington, York diocese, by l.d. to t. of his church.

Richard Lylye of Wormington, to t. of patrimony.*

John Glasiere of Cirencester, to t. of St. John's hospital, Lechlade.*

John Seebryht of Hereford diocese, to t. of the perpetual chantry of Our Lady in Awre church, by l.d.

William Dillyng of Exeter diocese, to t. of St. John's hospital, Shrewsbury, by l.d.*

John le Heybere of Gloucester, to t. of the house of Flaxley.*

John Corbet of Earthcott, to t. of an annual pension of four marks [£2 13s. 4d.].*

Walter Baret of Dumbleton, to t. of patrimony.*

Richard Kempeleye of Hereford diocese, to t. of patrimony by l.d.*

Thomas Ashforde of Ludlow, Hereford diocese, to t. of patrimony by l.d. of the vicar.

John Bartlot of Worcester, to t. of the P. & C. of Great Malvern.*

Richard son of Alexander de Lanton, of Hereford diocese, to t. of patrimony by l.d. of the vicar.*

John Louwheʒate of Ledbury, to t. of patrimony by l.d. of his diocesan's vicar.*

1 MS. *Chiryton.*

[*Subdeacons continued.*]

Robert Hayward of Llantwit, Llandaff diocese, to t. of an annual rent of 50s. by l.d.

Walter le Palmare of Hennor, Hereford diocese, to t. of an annual rent by l.d.

Simon de Ketelby of Lincoln diocese, to t. of the hospital of St. Lazarus at Burton next Melton Mowbray by l.d.

William Ricard of Dillington, Lincoln diocese, to t. of Bushmead priory by l.d.*

Richard Staneweye of Cranborne, Salisbury diocese, to t. of Tarrant abbey by l.d.

William de Hamenassh of Hereford diocese, to t. of patrimony by l.d. of the vicar.*

Simon de Drayton of Hereford diocese, to t. of patrimony by l.d.*

William Whyteleye, to t. of patrimony.*

William de Inteberwe, to t. of the house of Tewkesbury.

Henry Lescy of Quinton, to t. of patrimony.*

John Lutekene of Lechlade, to t. of St. John's hospital there.*

William Wymark' of Hereford diocese, to t. of patrimony by l.d. of the vicar.*

Nicholas de Drokenesford, r. of Pirton, to t. of his church.

William Spark of Bishops Cleeve, to t. of patrimony.*

William de Malmeshull of Hereford diocese, to t. of the dean of Hereford by l.d. of the vicar.

John Partrych, to t. of St. John's hospital, Lechlade.*

Roger Kyrkeby super Wreck of Lincoln diocese, to t. of the A. & C. of Croxton by l.d. of the vicar.*

Hugh Celle of Longdon, to t. of the A. & C. of Eynsham.*

William de Osberston, r. of Stanford, Salisbury diocese, to t. of his church by l.d.

John Despense, to t. of patrimony.*

John Colet of Besford, to t. of patrimony.*

William Cobald of Kempsford, to t. of St. John's hospital, Lechlade.*

William Durynton of Salisbury diocese, to t. of the house of Amesbury (*Ambreslegh*).*

John de Haddeleye of Norwich diocese, to t. of Holy Trinity priory, Bridgnorth, by l.d.

Walter de Bradewas, to t. of the bishop's grace.

William de Mersstone, to t. of patrimony.*

John le Mason of Leach St. Andrew [Eastleach Turville], to t. of St. John's hospital, Lechlade.*

Robert Penedok, to t. of the A. [*sic*] & C. of Great Malvern.*

Richard Kyde of Hereford diocese, to t. of the dean of Hereford, by l.d. of the vicar.*

William Clyve, to t. of the A. & C. of Bordesley.*

Ds. Henry Oskerwell, r. of Askerswell, Salisbury diocese, by l.d. to t. of his church.

Thomas Same of Norwich diocese, to t. of the house of Rewley next Oxford by l.d.*

Subdeacons: Religious

Br. Thomas de Dodecote ⎱
Br. Laurence de Lekforde ⎰ canons of Oseney.

Br. John Gelemyn ⎱ of Warwick.
Br. Richard Oky ⎰

Br. Richard de Aylesbury ⎱
Br. Thomas de Walesford ⎰ of the order of Preachers.

Br. Laurence de Glouc' ⎱
Br. Richard de Broedon ⎬ monks of Malvern.
Br. John de Leye ⎰

Br. Richard de Tettebury ⎱
Br. Roger Redyng' ⎰ monks of Bruern.

Br. Thomas Borthone ⎱
Br. William Wyke ⎪
Br. William Alvedeleye ⎬ Friars Minor of Worcester.
Br. Hugh de Markeleye ⎪
Br. Richard de Kydermustr' ⎰

Br. Walter de Wynfreton, monk of Worcester.

Br. Ralph de Swanewych, of the order of Carmelites.

Deacons

M. William de Bergeveny, by l.d.

John Henrys of Littleton, to t. of patrimony.*

John de Anneford, to t. of the prior of the hospital of St. John of Jerusalem.

Walter Austyn of Norton, to t. of patrimony.*

Thomas son of John Colles of Westcote, to t. of the A. & C. of Bruern.*

William son of William le Baylyf of Quinton, to t. of the master and convent of Holy Trinity, Thelsford.*

Thomas Robyns of Iccomb, to t. of the A. & C. of Bruern.*

John Brevill of Leckhampton, to t. of the A. & C. of Bruern.*

John Beale of Longdon, to t. of the A. & C. of Pershore.

Ralph de Ulenhale, to t. of patrimony.*

Adam le Yonge of Kersoe, to t. of the A. & C. of Halesowen.

Giles Polle of Tewkesbury, to t. of patrimony.*

Robert ate Watre of Whichford, to t. of the A. & C. of Oseney.

John de Masynton, to t. of the A. & C. of Dore.*

Robert son of John le Taillour of Leckhampton, to t. of the A. & C. of Bruern.

John Suede, to t. of a papal provision affecting the A. & C. of Winchcombe.*

[*Deacons continued.*]

John Noble, to t. of the master of St. Mark's, Billeswick.*

Robert de Bevynton, to t. of the A. & C. of Bordesley.*

William Holeweye of Beckford, to t. of the P. & C. of Studley.

Alexander son of Walter de Stodleye, to t. of the A. & C. of Bordesley.*

John Bayngrove of Aston Somerville, to t. of the A. & C. of Bruern.*

John Jurdan of Codrington, to t. of patrimony.*

John Pleystede of Badgeworth, to t. of the prioress of Our Lady of Usk.

Henry Hardyng' of Strensham, to t. of patrimony.*

Thomas le Smyt of Great Compton, to t. of the A. & C. of Oseney.

William son of William Aleyn of Upton, to t. of patrimony.*

Thomas Marmioun, to t. of patrimony. He swore to remain in the Schools for a year.*

Thomas Goschorn of Tredington, to t. of patrimony. He swore to remain in the Schools for a year.

Walter Crowe of Cirencester, to t. of St. John's hospital, Lechlade.

William son of Gilbert Bakester of Studley, to t. of patrimony. He swore to remain in the Schools for a year.

Walter Croweleye of Ullenhall, to t. of patrimony.*

Giles de Grafton, to t. of the A. & C. of Bruern.*

Nicholas de Hampstede of Snitterfield, to t. of patrimony.*

Roger de Henleye, to t. of patrimony.*

John Goffe of Stow, to t. of the A. & C. of Pershore.*

John Scotard, to t. of patrimony.*

John Bisleye of Gloucester, to t. of the A. & C. of Alcester.*

Thomas de Botyndon, to t. of the P. & C. of St. Frideswide's, Oxford. He swore to remain in the Schools for a year.

John de Turkedene, to t. of patrimony.*

John le Bedel of Marston Meysey, to t. of St. John's hospital, Lechlade. He swore to remain in the Schools for a year.*

Walter son of Gilbert de Longeneye, to t. of St. Bartholomew's, Gloucester.

Peter Rose of Sheriffs Lench, to t. of the A. & C. of Bordesley.

John Lode, to t. of patrimony.*

Stephen Genis of Naunton [or Newington],[1] to t. of the prior of St. Oswald's, Gloucester.

John Blondel of Adlestrop, to t. of the A. & C. of Bruern.

William Welsch of Rodmarton, to t. of patrimony.*

John Hale of Campden, to t. of St. John's hospital, Lechlade. He swore to remain in the Schools for a year.*

William de Pipplynton, to t. of patrimony. He swore to remain in the Schools for a year.*

John Wolny of Great Barrington, to t. of the A. & C. of Bruern.*

Richard Babmynton, to t. of the A. & C. of Bruern.*

1 MS. *Newynton.*

William ate Wele of Norton, to t. of St. John's hospital, Lechlade.*
John Butter' of Ombersley, to t. of patrimony.*
John Wilkyn of Little Barrington, to t. of the A. & C. of Bruern.*
William Wygemor of Hasfield, to t. of patrimony.*
Thomas Chylyene of Ampney, to t. of the P. & C. of Bradenstoke.*
Richard Coteroft of Chedworth, to t. of St. John's hospital, Lechlade.*
Walter Smalcombe of Cherrington,[1] to t. of the A. & C. of Bruern.*
John de Seynebury, to t. of the A. & C. of Bruern.*
William Odde of Uckington, to t. of the A. & C. of Evesham.*
Henry Cergeaunt of Kings Norton, to t. of the A. & C. of Bordesley.*
Thomas de Diclesdon, to t. of the P. & C. of Brecon.*
Walter de Otyntone, to t. of the A. & C. of Bruern. He swore to remain in the Schools for a year.
William Kronnok of South Cerney, to t. of St. John's hospital, Lechlade. He swore to remain in the Schools for a year.*
Richard Skymere of Welford, to t. of the A. & C. of Bordesley.*
Geoffrey Bovetoun of Chedworth, to t. of the A. & C. of Bruern.*
Walter Saltere of Tewkesbury, to t. of the P. & C. of Cold Norton.*
William Dirvasale of Compton Verney (*Comtonmurdak*), Coventry & Lichfield diocese, to t. of the P. & C. of Studley by l.d.
Thomas Voulare of Bristol, to t. of the P. & C. of Maiden Bradley.*
Roger Wilkyns of Welford, to t. of the A. & C. of Bordesley.*
William Rych of Haseley, to t. of patrimony.*
Geoffrey Murival of Hereford diocese, to t. of patrimony by l.d.*
John Tondy of Pinvin, to t. of patrimony.*
Nicholas Hawe of Wotton [or Wootton][2] to t. of the A. & C. of Dore.*
William Baker of Wellesbourne, to t. of the minister of Holy Trinity, Thelsford.*
John Mulleward of Cowley, to t. of the P. & C. of Studley.*
William Boreford of Shipton, to t. of St. John's hospital, Lechlade.*
Henry Wyhlde of Meysey Hampton, to t. of the hospital of St. John of Jerusalem.*
Robert de Chyryton, to t. of St. John's hospital, Lechlade.*
John ate Welle of Wick, to t. of patrimony.*
William Snowsull of Campden, to t. of St. John's hospital, Lechlade.*
Roger Zelimon of Blockley, to t. of the P. & C. of Maiden Bradley.*
William de Weston, to t. of the P. & C. of Ivychurch.*[3]
William Fonteyne of Winchcombe, to t. of the A. & C. of Bordesley.*
John de Cirencestr', r. of Stratton, to t. of his church.
John de Coldastone, to t. of patrimony.*
William le Cran of Dursley, to t. of patrimony.*
William Bate of Bengeworth, to t. of the A. & C. of Bordesley. He is to remain for a year in the Schools.*

1 MS. *Chyreton.* 2 MS. *Wotton.* 3 MS. *monasterii Edere* [Ederosi].

[*Deacons continued.*]

John Henry of Guiting, to t. of patrimony. He is to remain for a year in the Schools.*

John Baggepathe of Brickhampton (*Bryhthampton*), to t. of the A. & C. of Bordesley.*

William Pepir of Wawensmoor, to t. of the A. & C. of Bordesley.*

Richard Coteler of Hereford diocese, to t. of patrimony by l.d.*

John Heynes of Uckington, to t. of patrimony.*

Simon Josep of Coates, Lincoln diocese, to t. of St. John's hospital, Newport Pagnell, by l.d.

John Noth of Newent, Hereford diocese, to t. of patrimony by l.d.*

John Pope of Great Barrington, to t. of the A. & C. of Bruern. He is to remain in the Schools for a year without taking further orders.*

Richard Burgeys of Fladbury, to t. of the A. & C. of Bruern.*

William Bailyf of Norton next Bredon, to t. of patrimony.*

Philip Toukere of Exeter diocese, to t. in the possession of the registrar (*penes registr'*) of the bishop of Exeter by l.d.*

Henry Cone of Aston [or Ashton],[1] Salisbury diocese, to t. of St. John's hospital, Lechlade, by l.d.*

Thomas de Berneston of York diocese, to t. of the A. & C. of Godstow by l.d.*

John Blangfront of London diocese, to t. of the chapel of *La Maudeleyne, Miden'* [*sic*] diocese, by l.d.*

John Metke of Chirton, Salisbury diocese, to t. of the P. & C. of St. *Wandregesile*, Upavon, by l.d.

John le Mere of Eton, Lincoln diocese, to t. of the A. & C. of Oseney by l.d. He swore to remain in the Schools for a year.*

Thomas ate Barre of Chippenham, Salisbury diocese, to t. of the P. & C. of Maiden Bradley by l.d.*

James Haket of Hereford diocese, to t. of patrimony by l.d. of the vicar.*

John Oliver of Chippenham, Salisbury diocese, to t. of the P. & C. of Ivychurch (*monasterii Ederosi*) by l.d.*

Roger Kayham of Hereford diocese, to t. of patrimony by l.d.*

Robert Flemmyng of Lichfield & Coventry diocese, to t. of the prior and brethren of St. John's hospital [Lichfield?] by l.d.*

John le Hert' of Thornbury, Hereford diocese, to t. of patrimony by l.d. of the vicar.*

Roger de Ledebury of Hereford diocese, to t. of patrimony by l.d.

Thomas Eode of Weston, Lincoln diocese, to t. of the house of Snelshall by l.d.

John ate Hasshe of Fladbury, to t. of patrimony.*

Thomas de Saham of Norwich diocese, by l.d.*

1 MS. *Asston*.

Deacons: Religious

Br. William Mounserel, monk of Bruern, by l.d.
Br. Robert de Cudelynton ⎱ canons of Oseney by l.d.
Br. John de Redyng' ⎰
Br. Adam Sharpmor ⎱ of the order of Preachers, presented by the
Br. John Worthyn ⎰ prior of the Warwick convent.
Br. Robert Mukelton, monk of Fountains, by l.d.
Br. Gerard de Fonteyne ⎱ monks of Wenlock, Hereford diocese.
Br. Richard de Lodelowe ⎰
Br. John Lubury of the order of Preachers, *per priorem tunc presentem.*
Br. Walter de Poywyke, monk of Great Malvern.
Br. Hugh de Shyrebourne, monk of St. Peter's, Gloucester.
Br. John de Kyrketon of the Worcester convent of the order of Preachers.
Br. Walter de Hyde.
Br. William Feryme, canon of Cirencester.
Br. John de Groete, canon of St. Augustine's, Bristol.
Br. Richard de Blockeleye, monk of Pershore.
Br. Richard de Sutton
Br. Nicholas de Hampton ⎱
Br. John de Medebourne ⎬ monks of Abingdon, by l.d.
Br. John de Dumbelton ⎰

Priests

John Reynald of Hatherop, to t. of the prior and brethren of Lechlade.*
John Palmare of Shoulton, to t. of the prior and brethren of Lechlade.*
Walter le Clerk of Evington (*3evynton*), to t. of patrimony.*†
John Scorre of Netherton, to t. of patrimony.*†
William Love of Longdon, to t. of patrimony.*†
Adam Hopkyns of Clopton, to t. of the P. & C. of St. Frideswide the Virgin, Oxford.*
Randolf son of Robert de Fulwode of Tanworth, to t. of the A. & C. of Bordesley.*
Walter le Tailour of Weston, to t. of the minister and brethren of Thelsford.*
Hugh de Asteleye of Ullenhall, to t. of patrimony.*†
William Fevere of Beckford, to t. of the A. & C. of Bruern.*
Henry Martyn of Combrook, to t. of patrimony.*†
Walter Hogges of *Staunton*, to t. of the A. & C. of Bruern.*
Thomas Forch of Grafton, to t. of patrimony.*†
John Malle of Naunton [or Newington],¹ to t. of the A. & C. of Bruern.*

1 MS. *Neuwynton.*

[*Priests continued.*]

John Boulers *receipt sub spe gracie domini quia titulus suus remanet penes registrum.*

William Bruggemon of Coln St. Dennis, to t. of patrimony.*†

Thomas de Upcote, to t. of patrimony.*†

Richard Cogges, to t. of the A. & C. of Bruern.*†

Walter le Carpenter of Oddington, to t. of the P. & C. of Cold Norton.*

William ate Yate of Wickhamford, to t. of the A. & C. of Bordesley.*

John Henrys of Bourton, to t. of the A. & C. of Bruern.*

John Caprych of North Moreton, Salisbury diocese, to t. of the house of Dorchester.*

Walter le Rock of Buckland, to t. of the A. & C. of Bordesley.*

John de Leomustre of Bristol, to t. of St. Wulstan's hospital, Worcester.*

William Ballard of [Droit]wich, to t. of patrimony.*†

John de Malleye of Hereford diocese, to t. of patrimony by l.d.*†

Richard de Leytenhale of Hereford diocese, by l.d. to t. of patrimony.*†

John de Bodenham, r. of Little Wormington, to t. of his church.

John Ernald, to t. of patrimony.*†

John Heyr of Compton, to t. of the prioress & convent [*sic*].

Richard Gernvyll, r. of St. Peter's, Bristol, to t. of his church.

Thomas Raulyns of Aston [or Ashton],[1] to t. of the P. & C. of Studley.*

John son of Simon de Walynton, to the chantry in Chelmscote chapel.*

Ralph son of John Jones of Dodwell, to t. of the P. & C. of Studley.*

John Henrys of Poden, to t. of patrimony.*†

John Mile of Kington [or Kineton],[2] to t. of patrimony.*†

John Tylare of Bromsgrove, to t. of the A. & C. of Bordesley.*

John Dilaman of Sutton, to t. of the prior & canons of Cold Norton.*

John son of Walter Siward, to t. of patrimony.*†

Adam Anketyl, to t. of patrimony.*†

Roger Roberd, to t. of the monastery of Our Lady, Boxgrove.*

Robert son of William Bythestrete, to t. of the A. & C. of Bruern.*

Walter de Muthe, to t. of patrimony.*†

Walter Stauwart, to t. of patrimony.*†

Peter de Hulle, to t. of the house of Lechlade.*

Thomas de Teukesbur', to t. of St. James' next London.*

John le Frenshe, to t. of patrimony.*†

John Peckere of Salisbury diocese, to t. of St. John's, Lechlade, by l.d.*

John Parlebeen, to t. of Henry de Umfrevill.*

---

1 MS. *Asston.*   2 MS. *Kyngton.*

William ate Welde of Sherborne, to t. of patrimony.*†

William West of Aston [or Ashton],[1] to t. of St. Wulstan's hospital, Worcester, by l.d.*

Nicholas Freman of Badsey, to t. of the A. & C. of Bordesley.*

John son of Hugh de Holte, to t. of St. Wulstan's hospital, Worcester.*

Peter Copcy of Newport Pagnell, to t. of St. John the Baptist's hospital.*

1009 *1 April 1340 Orders celebrated by the bishop in the parish church of Kidderminster.*[2]

Memorandum that sentence of excommunication was brought against those ordained at this ordination who were not examined or admitted by the examiners appointed by the bishop.

Acolytes

John Bradewas.

Richard DamEmme.

Thomas Dygon of Doverdale.

John Taillor of Acton.

John Braas of [Droit]wich.

John Selewey of Farmington.

William Pebmor of Kidderminster.

Robert Bolrak' of Kidderminster.

Richard Pope of Over Eatington (*Everetyndon*).

Simon de Pilardynton.

Nicholas de Kent.

Roger de Arleye.

William Taillor of Kidderminster.

John Midewynter of Pillerton.

Richard ate Welle of Lapworth.

Robert Baner of Hatherop.

John Wattes of Farmington.

Walter Moreyn of Gloucester.

John Dypel of Bromsgrove.

William Dypel of [Droit]wich.

Robert de Henleye.

Thomas Don of Coln [St.] Aldwyn.

William Stodley of Kidderminster.

Thomas Griffyn of Bromsgrove.

Robert Holbarwe.

John Hudecote.

Adam Canon of Handley[?],[3] Salisbury diocese, by l.d.

Geoffrey de Langeleye of [Hereford][4] diocese, by l.d. of the vicar-general.

Subdeacons

John le Webbe of Gloucester, to t. of the A. & C. of Flaxley.*

William son of Henry le Eyr, to t. of the A. & C. of Bordesley.*

John son of William Archebaud of Cirencester, to t. of the A. & C. of Cirencester.*

Nicholas Janes of Down Ampney, to t. of the prior of St. John of Jerusalem.*

Thomas Hauky of Kempsford, to t. of the prior of St. John of Jerusalem.

1 MS. *Asston.*   2 *Die Sabbati qua cantatur officium 'Scicientes'.*

3 MS. *Hondlaw.*   4 Illegible owing to damp.

17

[*Subdeacons continued.*]

John Wolde of Worcester, to t. of the P. & C. of Little Malvern.*
John Janemon, to t. of the P. & C. of St. Frideswide's, Oxford.*
William Moryce, to t. of the bishop's grace.
Thomas Balle of Tredington, to t. of the A. & C. of Bordesley.*
Walter Godefrei of Harvington [near Evesham], to t. of the A. & C. of Bordesley.*
John son of Robert le Mason of Bengeworth, in the jurisdiction of the abbot of Evesham, to t. of the A. & C. of Bordesley by l.d. of the aforesaid abbot.*
Richard le Somyter of Gloucester, within the jurisdiction of Church-down, York [diocese], to t. of the P. & C. of St. Oswald's by l.d.
William son of John ate Grene of Paxford, to t. of the A. & C. of Bordesley.*
Gilbert Averyng of Fairford, to t. of St. John of Jerusalem.*
Thomas son of Robert Deyster of Warwick, to t. of the P. & C. of St. Sepulchre, Warwick.*
Thomas Smythes of Ilmington, to t. of the A. & C. of Alcester.*
Walter Nok' of Fairford, to t. of the prior of St. John of Jerusalem.*
James de Wyverdeleye, to t. of patrimony sufficiently proven.*
Nicholas le Taillor of Childs Wickham, to t. of the A. & C. of Hailes.*
William Colne of Preston-on-Stour, to t. of the A. & C. of Bordesley.*
John Symmes of Compton, to t. of the A. & C. of Oseney.*
Robert Persone of Rowington, to t. of the A. & C. of Bordesley.*
William le Spenser of Ombersley, to t. of the A. & C. of Bordesley.*
William Odeler of Kidderminster, to t. of the A. & C. of Bordesley.*
Robert son of Thomas ate Brugg of Alcester, to t. of the A. & C. of Bordesley.*
Nicholas de Abbelench, to t. of the A. & C. of Bordesley.*
John de Wodecomb, to t. of the chantry of William de Boun.*
Adam Heethey, to t. of patrimony.*†

Deacons

William Lovede of Harvington [near Evesham], to t. of the A. & C. of Bordesley.*
Richard Wylifed, to t. of patrimony.*†
Gilbert Stanshawe, to t. of the A. & C. of Tewkesbury.*
John Deyer of Newent, Hereford diocese, by l.d. of the vicar-general to t. of patrimony.*†
Nicholas Bowyar of Gloucester, to t. of the A. & C. of Dore.*
William de Derby of Ashford, Canterbury diocese, by l.d. to t. of the house of St. Sepulchre, Warwick.
William Spark of Bishops Cleeve, to t. of patrimony.*†

Henry Tresoderon, Exeter diocese, by l.d. to t. of the P. & C. of Bodmin, of the order of St. Augustine.*

Robert Sotemay of Warwick, to t. of St. Michael's, Warwick.*

John de Otyndon, to t. of the A. & C. of Oseney.*

William Bentham of Northleach, to t. of patrimony sufficiently proven.*

Walter Bradewas, to t. of the bishop's grace.

Priests: Religious

Br. Richard de Tettebury ⎱
Br. Roger de Redyng' ⎰ monks of Bruern.

Br. John de Acton, monk of Bordesley.

Priests: Beneficed (Promoti)

Eustace Hathewy, r. of Minsterworth, Hereford diocese, by l.d. of the vicar-general.

Roger de Stanford, r. of St. Helen's Worcester, to t. of his church.

Priests: Unbeneficed (Non Promoti)

Richard le Clerk of Batsford, to t. of the P. & C. of Nuneaton.*

William de Woditon of Coventry & Lichfield diocese, to t. of Holy Trinity, Bridgnorth (*Bruggenorht*) by l.d.*

John Whyte of Compton, in the jurisdiction of Churchdown, by l.d. [of the archbp.] of York, to t. of the prior of Little Malvern.*

John Croxton, v. of Bloxham, Lincoln diocese, by l.d.[1]

Walter Dodyton of Hereford diocese, by l.d. of Richard de Sidenhal the vicar-general to t. of patrimony.*†

Richard son of John Jakes of Kempley, Hereford diocese, to t. of patrimony by l.d. of Richard de Sidenhal the vicar-general.

William Pebmor of Kidderminster, to t. of the P. & C. of Dodford.*

William Hardyng of Marston *Sicca*, to t. of patrimony.*†

Simon de Drayton of Hereford diocese, by l.d. of the vicar-general to t. of patrimony.*†

John ate Grene, to t. of patrimony.*†

William de Coftone, to t. of patrimony.*†

William Yonge of Hereford diocese, by l.d. of the vicar-general to t. of patrimony.*†

William Coterel of Hereford diocese, by l.d. of the vicar-general to t. of patrimony.*†

John Bele of Longdon, to t. of the A. & C. of Pershore.*

Nicholas Hampstede of Snitterfield, to t. of the prior of St. Sepulchre's, Warwick.*

John de Bodrynton, to t. of patrimony sufficiently proven.*

1 His name should be in the earlier list of those already promoted.

[Priests: Unbeneficed (Non Promoti) continued.]

Simon de Ketelbury of Lincoln diocese, to t. of St. Lazarus of Burton by l.d. of Simon de Islep.*

Roger de Kirkeby super Wrekk of Lincoln diocese, to t. of the A. & C. of Croxton by l.d. of M. Simon de Islep, the vicar.

John Heyberar of Gloucester, to t. of the A. & C. of Flaxley.*

John Toudyn of Pinvin, to t. of patrimony.*†

John Herrys of Littleton, to t. of patrimony.*†

Thomas Lewelyn, to t. of the A. & C. of Alcester.*

John son of Henry Johns of Turkdean, to t. of patrimony.*†

Reginald de la Heth, to t. of the A. & C. of Bordesley.*

John de la Lode, to t. of patrimony.*†

Adam de Creddesho, to t. of the A. & C. of Halesowen.*

William Wygem[or] of Hasfield, to t. of patrimony.*†

William ate Wode of Chaddesley, to t. of patrimony.*†

1010 *15 April 1340 Orders celebrated by the bishop in Alvechurch parish church on Holy Saturday.*

Subdeacon

Robert de Wynnesbury, r. of Little Barningham, Norwich diocese, by l.d. to t. of his church.

Deacon

John Archebaud of Cirencester, to t. of the A. & C. of Cirencester.*

Priests

Br. John de Leomustr' ⎫
Br. John de Hereford ⎬ monks of Worcester.
Br. John de Poywyk ⎭

1011 *26 May 1341 Hartlebury*

Memorandum that the bishop, in accordance with the letters of Gaucelinus, bishop of Albano, Pope Benedict XII's penitentiary, dispensed John Waters of Coln, acolyte, from the defect of illegitimacy, thus enabling him to proceed to all Holy Orders and to hold a benefice even though with cure of souls.

1012 *26 May 1341 Hartlebury*

Similar dispensation for John Chestr' of Bibury, clerk.

1013 *26 August 1341 Withington*

Memorandum that those named below appeared in person before the bishop and confessed that on St. Laurence's day last [10 August] they had broken into his park at Penne by Henbury in Saltmarsh. They asked to be absolved from the sentence of greater excommunication which the bishop had brought against them. After swearing to abide by the mandates of the Church, the bishop absolved them and enjoined such salutary penance as appears below. Present were Masters John de la Lowe, Hugh de Pene[brugg] and Peter de Avebur', with many others.

Names of those breaking into the park at Penne:
Nicholas Poyntz: enjoined to say fifty *Aves*.
John de Brokenbregh: to say fifty *Aves*.

Nicholas ate More John de Hagkeley Nicholas son of Poyntz	Because they discharged arrows each is to offer his bow and arrow on the high altar of Our Lady, Worcester.
John Chamberleyn John de Weston senior Thomas de Hagh' John de Weston junior John de Hagh' William Batelyne Hugh Poyntz Nicholas de Hakkel' Walter Sonyter John de Robyndon Edward le Bagh' Robert Hatheweye John Jankynes	All of these are to offer a candle containing five pounds of wax at the high altar of Holy Trinity church, Bristol. R. Marny T'[1]

1014 *29 August 1341 Withington*
Memorandum that on the authority of Gaucelinus, bishop of Albano, papal penitentiary, the bishop dispensed John, called Neuman, of Norton, Lincoln diocese, from the defect of illegitimacy, thus enabling him to be promoted to all orders and to hold an ecclesiastical benefice, even with cure of souls, provided that he perform the residence such benefice may require.

1015 *14 February 1344*
Memorandum that the bishop granted licence of absence from his church of Eastleach St. Martin[2] to M. Thomas de Asschton, clerk, with obligation to proceed only to the subdiaconate meanwhile, in accordance with the constitution *Cum ex eo*.[3]

1017 *6 August 1343*
Memorandum of the licence (granted until revoked) for John Horncastel to have an oratory in his house at Bristol within the parish of St. Nicholas.

1 A reference to R. de Marny, a notary public.   2 *Recte* St. Andrew.
3 *Sext* 1, 6, c. 34.

1018 *7 August 1343*

Memorandum of the licence (granted until revoked) for Roger de Lemesey, knight, to have Mass celebrated (*celebrandi*) in his manor of *La Lee* within Henley parish.

1019 [*1343?*]

Carmelite friars of Gloucester licensed to preach and to grant absolution:

Prior Br. Nicholas de Insula.

Br. Thomas de Heymisham.

Br. John de Dodebrugg.

Br. William Pershore.

Br. Adam Hope.

Br. Thomas Lemustre.

[Remainder of folio blank]

1020 *20 May 1339 Bredon*

Memorandum that the bishop ordained Simon de Thormarton to the first tonsure.

1021 [*1339?*][1] *List of those ordained to the first tonsure.*

Richard de Guyting.

John le Dyare.

Thomas de la Chirchheye.

Robert Trappe.

John Lucas.

Walter Dyare.

Walter Graundon.

Richard Cok.

John Wytewelle.

John Stonhouse of
    Cirencester.

Nicholas Pulter.

Robert de Southserneye.

Richard Crok'.

Thomas Robes.

Henry Warener.

Thomas Goderust.

John Aylford.

John de Cirenc'.

Ralph de Cirenc'.

Richard Coyfstere.

Nicholas Kynny.

Richard le Smyht.

John Loveday.

Thomas Dounton.

John Beneth.

Walter le Neuew.

William Porter.

Thomas Baroun.

Robert Taillor.

John Body.

Richard Hamond.

William de Northfeld.

Thomas Gros.

John Piddle.

Richard Sned.

Simon de Hosyntre.

John Halt.

Henry Cleangr'.

Thomas Sennampton de
    so & so [*sic*].

Thomas Ledene.

Adam le Manns.

John Stacy.

1 It is possible that this ordination took place at Bredon as in 1020 above.

William Frebern.

William Andreu of Taynton (*Teynton*), the prior's bondman, who showed a letter of manumission.

William de la Sale of Honeybourne.

William Lilye of Wormington.

Thomas Corlegh of Hockley (*Haukelegh*).

William de Grovehurste.

John Colyns.

Robert Laurens, illegitimate (*illeg'*).

Thomas Willekyn.

Walter Haylyn.

John Heylyn.

John Job.

William Baldwyne.

Stephen Rolves.

Simon de Morton.

William Gorney.

Nicholas de Apperle.

Peter Aleyn.

William Norman.

William ate Haseles.

William de Seynebury.

Thomas le White.

Thomas le Maister.

Robert Sones.

John le Wodeward.

John son of John de la Mare.

Henry le Wodeward.

John Wyther.

Henry Daniel.

John Neucome.

Walter de Clyvelode.

Robert de Karenc'.

Richard Pek.

William Roberd.

Andrew de Staunton.

William de Somerforde.

Walter Laschulle.

William de Somerforde.

William de la Hale.

Walter Priour.

Richard Couelegh.

Stephen Broun.

William Blount.

Thomas de Chasteltone.

Richard Folyot.

Henry Fyppes.

Robert Janekyns.

Robert Culne.

John Colyns.

John Bradeweye.

Robert Grant.

William le Soutere.

Thomas le White of Elmley, manumitted by a letter of his lord, the earl of Warwick.

John le Peyntor of Winchcombe.

William Noble of Batsford.

Robert de Bradewas.

John Michel of Strensham.

Simon de Aumeneye.

William de Aldrynton.

William de la Haye.

Richard de Shirlegh.

William de Morton.

William de Couele.

William de Quenton.

William Poty.

John de Hope.

Thomas Freman.

Henry Colet.

Walter Frankelyn.

Richard Wykewane.

William Prune.

John de Acton.

William Colyns.

John Usk of Bentham.

Thomas Bryd.

William Walton.

William Foliot.

John Peyntor.

John Goldsmyt.

Robert le Walkere.

Thomas ate Yate of Dursley.

Robert Weylond.

William ate West yate.

John Clement.

[*Ordained to first tonsure.*]
William de Malgarsbur'.
John Colly.
John Taillor of *Lench'*.
Walter Beale.
John Husser of Stottesden,
    Hereford diocese, by l.d. of
    the vicar-general.
Thomas Golde.
John Broumon.
John de Worthyn.
John de Clyfford.
John Mep of [Droit]wich.
Michael de Bladynton.
John de Combrok.
William Rondolf of *Aylesford*.
John de Kyngton.
Henry Taillor of Wickham.
John Harpor.
Robert de Dumbleton.
William Wattes of Naunton
    [or Newington] [1]
John de Dumbleton.
John de Quentone.
Philip Vynour.
Richard de Malverne.
John de Newynton.
John de Sheldon.
Thomas de Clopton.
Nicholas de Schotrive.
John Brangwayn.
John Stannford.
William de Honyborn.
Richard de Bradewelle.
William Hickeman.
William Aldesworth.
William Persone of Stratford.
William Micel.
Henry Goldecote.
Richard Denes.
John de Honyborn.
Ralph son of Ralph.
John Montagu.
John Hyckeman.
John Noryce.

1 MS. *Newynt'*.

Nicholas Geraud.
Helias de Mulcote.
John Belgeloyn junior.
Adam Clynton.
Stephen le Frent.
Vincent Freman of Inkberrow.
Simon Savage.
John Aleyse of Rissington.
John de Swelle.
John Scryveyn.
Roger de Hudecote.
Richard Gabbe.
John Bryd.
William Leukenore.
John Brevel.
John Botiller.
Walter de la Bolde.
William Hopere.
Nicholas Passour.
John de Whitfeld.
Walter de Whitfeld.
Robert de Todyntone.
William de Eltyngton.
John de Arlemede.
Robert Topas.
Philip Passour.
William de Broke.
Richard Hewes.
John Dean.
Simon de Newynton.
John Pete.
John Adams.
John Wrenford.
William Mersh.
John Wilchere.
William Hathiel.
Robert Lucas.
John de Dumbelton.
Thomas de Northfelde.
Thomas de Wittewell.
Roger de Bradeford.
Walter Smythos.
Richard Pacy.
John de la Hulle.
William Tursteyn.

Peter Gillyng.
Henry le Freke.
Richard le Freke.
Philip Dabitot.
John ate Halle.
Richard le Whelare.
Robert Munkes.
William Rondulf.
William Janekyns.
William Newe.
Walter de Sanford.
David Bonevill.
Walter Bonevill.
William Bonevill.
John de Bristoll'.
John Mulleward of Shirley.
Nicholas Bolde.
Nicholas le Taillor.
Richard Eggard.
Thomas de Fairford.
John Devenych.
Robert Wenrych.
John Hobbes.
Andrew Rok.
John Mareschal of *Chaddl'*.
Robert Taillor of Longborough.
Alan Hokkes.
Robert Plounte.
Geoffrey Welesalle.
Ralph Rosun of Windrush.
Thomas ate Halle.
Geoffrey Bonlur.
Thomas Pieres.
John Wilkyn.
William Snow.
John de Bannebury.
Robert de Aston.
Robert le Palmer.
Robert Loveryng.
Robert Polham.
Robert Stowell.
Robert Doudeswell.
Robert Gibbes.
Robert ate Hasele.
Henry Howes.
Thomas Edward.

John ate Watr'.
John Martyn.
Henry Welny.
William Monk.
John Lucas.
Thomas Everlee.
John Romeyn.
John Gardiner.
John Lutekene.
William Colne.
Henry Patyn.
William Cok.
Henry Beseby.
John Beneyt.
Thomas Wyrcestre.
Thomas Mordak.
John Witteslade.
John Brachel.
Robert Mordak.
Richard Mareschal.
John Spyring.
William Mulleward.
Walter Patyn.
Thomas Mulleward.
Henry de Bristoll'.
William de Stannford.
John Frankelyn.
Robert Halford.
Robert Halford [*bis*].
John Halford.
William Rokele.
Simon Martyn.
John Fayrford.
John Aldeworth.
Richard de Barre.
John de London.
Thomas Roger.
John ate Roche.
John Pomyes.
John Jolyf.
William Honte.
Reginald West.
Robert Nichol.
Theobald de Alveston.
William Dyer.
Richard ate Hulle.

[*Ordained to first tonsure.*]
Henry Bawet.
Thomas Squies.
William Salford.
John Stub.
Walter Brounyng.
William Felawe.
Robert Wedebrugg.
Henry Palte.
John de Wedebrugg.
John Brounyng.
John de Alre.
John le Taillor.
John Boteler.
Ralph de Nortthote.
John Noble.
Walter Tanner.
Walter Waltres.
John ate Nachssh.
John Heyward.
William Kenewrek.
Richard Wayfer.
John Mannsel.
Thomas Hallye.
John Baldewych.
Henry Burdon.
John de Loutheburgh.
Edward de Amundesham.
Walter Whyte.
Peter Ingham.
John Jolyf.
John Dene.
John Bakster.
Walter Smyth of Churcham,
    by l.d.
Walter Smyth [*bis*].
Edmund Masyndon.
Robert Eweyn.
Adam Maysmor.
Thomas Godrych, of Hereford
    diocese, by l.d.
John Heyford of Barrington.
Richard ate Bergh.
John Fort.
Richard Peytevyn.
John Peytevyn.

John Boyville.
Thomas Munstreworth.
John Hukkele.
Thomas Hukkele.
John Tappe.
Stephen Broun.
Edward Broun.
Thomas Passemer.
Stephen Passemer.
Richard Hunte.
John Clerk.
Walter Sherberd.
John Prestebury.
John Bourton.
Eugene ate Bathalle.
William Paunteleye.
Thomas Brokworth.
William Tuffele.
Thomas Wodehous.
John Couele.
John Pendok.
Walter Tuffele.
Richard Whyte.
Richard Wyneyorod.
John Clyve.
Gilbert Talbot.
Richard Maysmor.
William Baget.
William Jordan.
Adam Sampson.
Thomas de Mumham.
John ate Pulle.
John Walkere.
Henry de Staunton.
William Gunny.
Richard Mulleward.
John de Baldenale.
John Aleyn.
John Stone.
Richard Braʒ.
Nicholas Lodesmor.
John Gosgrave.
William Daniel.
John Brachel.
Thomas Colles.
Walter ate Halle.

Thomas son of Henry Clerk.
Robert Dalman.
John Bannebury.
John ate Rok.
Thomas ate Well.
Thomas Pekke.
Stephen Willecok of
    Eldersfield.
Richard Bodyn.
John Vauxz.
J. Persone of Barnsley.
Philip de Baudinton.
John Brag.
John Boun.
Thomas Bocton.
Geoffrey Wariner of Tetbury.
Walter Linton of Hereford
    diocese, by l.d.
Nicholas Puttes.
Robert Barbast.
Roger de Doudeswell.
Richard le Yonge of
    Siddington.
William Irlona.
John Clement.
John Avebury.
Henry Avebury.
William Mulleward.
John Bagge.
John ate Yate.
John Buttok.
John Clencham.
Thomas Cotes.
Peter Sudgrove.
Richard Broun.
William Cannyngg.
Peter Houchon.
Richard Wynchecomb.
Robert Daglyngworth.
Henry Hamptenet.
John Gilmyng.

Nicholas Heryng.
William de Pole.
Richard ate Halle
Richard ate Hyde.
Nicholas Colne.
Nicholas Wytteneye.
John Monk.
William Brokenbergh.
Thomas Basset.
William Kyngescote.
William de Weleye.
James Page.
Geoffrey de Horsleye.
Hugh de Rodbergh.
Edmund Gurney.
John de Strode.
Henry Clyfford.
John de Newelonde.
Thomas Loker'.
John Matheu.
William Hukkefar'.
John Doppyng.
Thomas Wych.
John Gilberd.
Henry de Rodbergh.
Walter Oldelond.
William Taillor.
John Litle.
Robert Clavill.
William Rodbergh.
John Rodbergh.
William Middelton.
William Dodebrugg.
Adam son of Reginald de
    Kingscote.

On the feast of the Purification
(? *pur'e*) 1348:[1]
Helyas de Wynnecote.

On the morrow of the feast:
John de Smyth of *Sal[e?]*[2]

1024 *11 October 1341 Alvechurch*
Memorandum that the bishop admitted to the monastic habit of the
cathedral church of Worcester John de Lodelowe and Richard
Blaket, clerks, presented to him by the prior and chapter.

1 New style. The Purification falls on 2 February.   2 MS. torn. Saul?

1025 *18 May 1343 Westminster*

Royal writ informing the bishop that Margaret, formerly wife of William Skay of Weston Birt, has recovered the presentation to Weston Birt church in a suit in the king's court against Joan, formerly wife of John de Wylinton. He is to admit Margaret's suitable presentee. Tested J. de Stonore. Roll ccliii Manes'.

1042 *Undated [1342?] Part of ordination list.*

[Subdeacons]

John son of Henry de Stanton, to t. of the P. & C. of Cold Norton.
John Scheptone, to t. of the prior of St. John of Jerusalem in England.
William le Chartar' of Kibworth, Lincoln diocese, by l.d. of the Lincoln official *sede vacante*.

Deacons

Br. Thomas Peverel ⎫
Br. Richard Botiler ⎪
Br. Elias de Actone ⎬ of the order of Carmelites.
Br. Stephen de Oxon' ⎭
Br. Thomas Edwards ⎫
Br. John Bruges   ⎬ of the order of Preachers.
Br. Robert de Northeye of St. John's hospital, Lechlade.
Br. John de Clone of the order of Minorites.
Br. Nicholas de Biriton, canon of Haughmond, by l.d.
Br. Matthew de Devenan of the order of Minorites.
Br. Thomas de Perschor, canon of Llanthony priory next Gloucester.
Br. John de Hulton of the order of St. Augustine, [Droit]wich.[1]
Br. William de Bradeleye, monk of Kingswood.
Walter Baret of Dumbleton, to t. of Henry de Bradeweye.
Stephen de Estenoner of Hereford diocese, by l.d. to t. of the D. & [C] of Hereford.
Stephen de Wemme of Coventry & Lichfield diocese, to t. of St. Giles' hospital, Shrewsbury, by l.d.
John Hyndelupe, to t. of the prior of Llanthony by Gloucester.
M. Giles de Stanneford, canon of Hereford, by l.d. to t. . . . .
John Petit, r. of Harrington, Lincoln diocese, to t. of his church by l.d. of the Lincoln official *sede vacante*.
M. Thomas de Astmede, r. of Horton, to t. of his church.
Richard Hanifeld of Bristol, to t. of the brethren of the Kalendaries.
Thomas oye Eche of Norton to t. of St. Sepulchre, Warwick.
John Stivenes of Willersey[?],[2] to t. of Our Lady of Keynsham.
Nicholas Bartelot of Welford, to t. of the A. & C. of Cirencester.
John Kyniot of Shell, to t. of patrimony.*

1 This must refer to the house of Austin friars.
2 MS. *Wyllareye*.

Robert le Taylour of Eastleach, to t. of St. John's, Lechlade.

John Attehull of Little Barrington, to t. of the P. & C. of Cold Norton.

John Haym of [D]aylesford, to t. of the A. & C. of Bruern.

Adam son of Reginald, son of Adam de Kyngescote, to t. of the A. & C. of Kingswood.

Henry Wynton,[1] to t. of patrimony.*

Philip de Medewelegh of Coventry & Lichfield diocese, to t. of Holy Trinity hospital, Bridgnorth.

John son of Stephen de Grosso Monte of Llandaff diocese, by l.d. to t. of patrimony.*

John de Suytbury, to t. of St. Wulstan's hospital, Worcester.

Philip de Sobbur', to t. of the abbot of Lilleshall.

William a Bovetoune of Horsley, to t. of the abbess of Godstow.

Thomas de Walton of Coventry & Lichfield diocese, to t. of the nuns of Chester [?],[2] by l.d.

Robert de Bokehull of Hereford diocese, by l.d. to t. of the D. & C. of Hereford.

Roger Weppe of Hereford [diocese?],[3] by l.d. to t. of the P. & C. of Bradwell.

John son of Nicholas Schad, to t. of the A. & C. of Alcester.

Henry son of Thomas Hobkynes of Grafton, to t. of the house of Kington.

William Chantecler of Bretforton, to t. of the P. & C. of Studley [by l.d.][4] of the A. & C. of Evesham.

Richard Bonamy of Beckford, to t. of the P. & C. of Little Malvern.

Stephen de Wemme of Coventry & Lichfield diocese, to t. of St. Giles' hospital, Shrewsbury, by l.d.

William Huymon of Dudley, to t. [sic].

Priests

Br. Ralph de Swanwyk ⎫
Br. John de Sotyrton ⎪
Br. John Compton ⎬ of the order of Carmelites.
Br. Walter Begworth ⎭

Br. Griffin de Pola ⎫
Br. Richard de Haukesbur' ⎪
Br. Thomas de Barton ⎬ of the order of Minorites.
Br. Nicholas Walay ⎪
Br. Henry Tour ⎭

Br. Richard de Hamslape.

Br. William Gyʒen.

Br. John Clanefeld.

1 Later interlineation of 's' to read *Wynston*.
2 MS. *Sestr'*. 3 MS. *Herefordenc'*.
4 MS. *ad titulum*. Bretforton lay within the exempt jurisdiction of Evesham Abbey.

[*Priests continued.*]

Br. Richard de Teukesbur'.

Br. John Cerne
Br. William de Dodton'   } of the order of St. Augustine.

Br. Robert de Wygorn', monk of Eynsham, Lincoln diocese, by l.d. of the Lincoln official *sede vacante*.

Br. John de Wilton, of the order of Preachers.

Br. William de Schyrugg, of the order of Minorites.

Br. Hugh de Wodestok, canon of Oseney, Lincoln diocese, by l.d. of the official of Lincoln *sede vacante*.

Br. Richard de Disscheby
Br. William de Sodynton   } canons of Maxstoke, by l.d.

Br. Richard Lyvet, monk of Alcester.

M. William de Herwynton, rector of Hanbury next [Droit]wich, to t. of his church.

Roger de Wolvardeleye, to t. of patrimony.*

Walter Godefrey, to t. of the A. & C. of Bordesley.

Thomas son of William le Taylour of Lechlade, to t. of the P. & C. of Llanthony.

John de Reynham of Upton, to t. of patrimony.*

William Wyxi of Dursley, to t. of patrimony.*

Geoffrey Beton of Chedworth (*Sheddeworth*), to t. of the A. & C. of Bruern.

John Glasiar' of Cirencester, to t. of St. John's, Lechlade.

Geoffrey de Langeleye of Hereford diocese, to t. of patrimony by l.d.*

William Dyngell, v. of Berkswich, Coventry & Lichfield diocese, by l.d.

Roger de Ledebury of Hereford diocese, to t. of patrimony by l.d.

William Cobald, to t. of St. John's hospital, Lechlade, to t. of the A. & C. of Bordesley.[1]

Robert son of Thomas atte Brugge of Alcester, to t. of the abbot of Bordesley.*

Richard de Aylysbury of Salisbury diocese, by l.d. to t. of St. John's, Lechlade.

Thomas de Savagebury of [Droit]wich, to t. of patrimony worth 40s. a year.

Thomas Marmion of [Droit]wich, to t. of patrimony.*

John Corbed of Earthcott, to t. of patrimony.*

Henry Proudomne of Lechlade, to t. of the hospital there.

John Bury of Olveston, to t. of patrimony.

John le Mason of Eastleach St. Andrew [Turville], to t. of St. John's hospital, Lechlade.

John de Lecch'.

John Symmes of *Nigra* Compton, to t. of the A. & C. of Oseney.

1 *Sic.* Cf. p. 184.

John Jannemon, to t. of the P. & C. of St. Frideswide's, Oxford.
Henry Neuman of Woodstock, Lincoln diocese, by l.d. of Walter de Stauren', the official *sede vacante*, to t. of Rewley next Oxford.
John atte Halle of Little Witley, Worc. diocese, to t. of patrimony.*
Robert Tebertone of Hereford diocese, by l.d. to t. of the perpetual vicarage of St. Katherine, Hereford.
John Sibile of Kibworth, Lincoln diocese, to t. of St. John's hospital, Northampton, by l.d. of the Lincoln official *sede vacante*.
Henry de Wodewart, of Hereford diocese, by l.d. to t. of St. Katherine's hospital, Ledbury.
John de Nanskylly of Exeter diocese by l.d. to t. of the P. & C. of Bodmin.*

1043 *28 August 1342*[1] *Orsett*

Mandate of Ralph [Stratford], bishop of London [1340–54].[2] He has received the archbishop's letter, dated 23 August from Otford, which contains a recension of the royal writ[3] accusing the French of breaking the truce negotiated at the instance of Pope Clement VI, enlarging upon the perils of strife on the Scottish border, declaring the king's intention of mounting an expedition against France,[4] and calling upon the archbishop to summon a council. On the archbishop's authority he cites the diocesan to appear in St. Paul's church, London, on the third juridical day after St. Faith [6 October], to discuss the contents of the royal mandate. He directs him to summon representatives of the clergy of his diocese[5] and to certify the archbishop of his proceedings, attaching a schedule of the names of those cited.

1044 *28 August 1342*[6] *Orsett*

Further mandate of Ralph [Stratford], bishop of London. In his letter of 23 August from Otford the archbishop has declared his intention to summon a provincial council[7] in order to publish those remedies devised at the last London council[8] for the correction of excesses, the reformation of morals, and the preservation of the

1 Received by the bishop 7 September.
2 In his capacity of dean of the Canterbury province.
3 Dated 15 August from the Tower. It is printed in *Foedera* V, pp. 338–9.
4 He sailed for Brittany early in October and was absent for three years.
5 In the usual form: *Prior vestre ecclesie cathedralis, abbatesque et priores alii electivi sub se plenum conventum habentes, necnon archidiaconi personaliter, quodlibet autem capitulorum, conventuum et collegiorum predictorum per unum, clerusque predictus per duos sufficientes procuratores et ydoneos . . .*
6 Received by the bishop on the same day as the previous mandate.
7 Rubric: *Littera domini episcopi London' pro concilio convocando generali.*
8 Cf. 323, 1142.

liberty and immunity of the church,[1] as well as to discuss certain articles deferred until the next council and other arduous matters which have recently arisen to the detriment of the state of the Church and clergy. Because certain bishops absented themselves without cause from the previous council, the archbishop will not have any excused on this occasion unless for some essential reason to be declared and proved at the council, on pain of canonical punishment for contumacy. By the authority of the archbishop's mandate the diocesan is summoned to appear personally in St. Paul's church on the Monday after the Translation of St. Edward [i.e. 14 October]. He is likewise to cite representatives of the clergy of his diocese,[2] and to inform the heads of exempt churches, other than mendicants, so that they also may be present without prejudice to their privileges, which the archbishop has no wish to infringe.

1045 *28 August 1342*[3] *Orsett*

Further mandate of Ralph [Stratford], bishop of London.[4] He has received a letter from the archbishop, dated 23 August from Otford, containing a recension of the king's writ *Terribilis in iudiciis*[5] with its request for the prayers of the province in support of his expedition to France and of the army sent against the Scots. In response to the royal plea the archbishop requires all bishops, throughout their cities and dioceses, to have Masses devoutly celebrated, sermons preached, processions held, and other devotions offered to God for the safety of the king and his companions and the successful prosecution of his rights. Hoping by God's mercy to stimulate further the minds of the faithful, and trusting to the prayers and merits of Our Lady, St. Thomas the glorious martyr, and all the saints, he has granted forty days' indulgence to all those who, being truly penitent and confessed, carry out the above during the royal journey. To this indulgence he wishes the comprovincial bishops to add their own. On the archbishop's authority the diocesan is directed to implement the mandate and to certify the archbishop of his actions in the matter by Christmas.

1046 *20 October 1342*[6] *Kennington*

Royal writ for the anticipation of payment of a tenth. The king thanks the bishop for the annual tenth conceded by him and the

---

1 The constitutions ascribed to Stratford are printed in Lyndwood, *Const. Prov.*, p. 43 *et seq.* Bp. Wolstan is listed among those present at the council.
2 As on p. 205 n. 5, but with *si eis utile videatur* added after *archidiaconi*.
3 Received by the bishop on the same day as the previous mandate.
4 Rubric: *Littera ad orandum pro pace.*
5 Dated 12 August from the Tower of London. It is printed in Rymer, *Foedera* V, p. 339, where it is dated 20 August.
6 Received at Worcester 4 November.

other clergy of the Canterbury province. Because of his urgent need, however, the archbishop and other prelates were asked at the end of the last royal council at Westminster to anticipate the terms arranged for payment, so that it could be levied at Christmas and Pentecost [1 June 1343]. To this they consented, provided that it should prove agreeable to the bishop and others who were absent. He now asks the bishop for his willing assent and urges him to summon the clergy of his diocese so that they can be persuaded to give theirs also. Tested by Edward, duke of Cornwall and earl of Chester, the king's son and guardian of the realm.

1047 *30 November 1342 Kennington*

Royal writ for the appointment of collectors of a tenth. The bishop is to appoint collectors without delay to implement the grant of a tenth made at the last congregation of the clergy in St. Paul's, London, and payable in equal instalments at the Annunciation [25 March] and the Nativity of St. John the Baptist [24 June]. The collectors are to pay the money at the appointed terms, or at earlier ones should the clergy be agreeable. Their names are to be sent to the Treasurer and barons of the Exchequer, together with information about the anticipation of the terms, should this be conceded. They are to send the names of those paying the tenth before the agreed terms and to deliver the money to the king without delay. (Tested as above.)

1048 *Undated*

The bishop's reply to the Treasurer and barons of the Exchequer. On the authority of the above writ he has appointed the abbot of Winchcombe in the Gloucester archdeaconry, and the prior of Great Malvern in that of Worcester, to levy, collect, and grant acquittances for the tenth. Although he urged the clergy with all his might to anticipate the terms of payment, he could not bring them to do so. He gladly agrees to such anticipation for his own portion, and recently informed the king of his consent. But after he had done so, the king, by means of letters carried by Ds. William de Neuwynham, clerk, sought the loan of a certain sum of money for expediting his affairs. Because he could not accede fully to that request, as he still cannot, he now grants, though heavily burdened thereby, that whatever sum he would have paid at the appointed terms, he will discharge before any of them. This is to assist the king's expedition, which he earnestly hopes may be successful. The abbots of Evesham and Pershore have agreed to do the same for their portions. But the bishop wishes it to be known that the clergy of the diocese, both religious and others, consider it settled that the last term of payment will be the feast of St. Peter ad Vincula [1 August], as laid down at the council.

18

1049 *21 December 1342 Orders celebrated by the bishop in Hartlebury parish church on the Saturday in Embertide.*[1]

Acolytes: Religious

Br. John de Lodelowe ⎫
Br. Richard Blaket ⎬ monks of Worcester.
Br. Thomas de Bramdesford, of the order of Minorites.
Br. John de Stouwe, monk of Bordesley.

Acolytes: Secular (Non religiosi)

Peter de Pygre.
Roger de Ippesleye.
Thomas de Gloucestr'.
Roger de Astone.
John de Beruwe.

Subdeacons: Religious

Br. Philip de Stockton, of the order of Minorites.
Br. William Hore', monk of Shrewsbury.
Br. Peter Yrenmonger.
Br. William Rudyng'.
Br. John de Wadbaruwe.
Br. John de Uptone.

Subdeacons: Secular

Peter de Celario of Bayonne diocese, by l.d. to t. of patrimony.*†
Ralph West of Overbury, Worc. diocese, to t. of patrimony.*†
John Bladyntone of Stanton [or Staunton],[2] Worc. diocese, to t. of the A. & C. of Bordesley and of Ds. William de Somervill *ad omnes.*[3]*
Richard atteWelle of Lapworth, Worc. diocese, to t. of the D. & C. of the collegiate church of St. Mary, Warwick.
William Champeneye of Beoley,[4] Worc. diocese, to t. of the A. & C. of Alcester.*
Robert Penne of Lichfield & Coventry diocese, by l.d. to t. of the A. & C. of [St. Mary] in the Meadows (*de Pratis*), Leicester.
John Knyt of Adlestrop, Worc. diocese, to t. of the P. & C. of Ivychurch.
Richard Salcombe of Painswick, Worc. diocese, to t. of the P. & C. of Great Malvern.
Ralph Deuwy of Aston, Worc. diocese, to t. of the house of St. Frideswide next Oxford, Lincoln diocese.

1 *Die Sabbati Quatuor Temporum.*
2 MS. *Stanton.*
3 Part of an interlineated phrase. *Ad omnes* [*sacros ordines*] is usually used of letters dimissory, but must refer here to the title.
4 MS. *Beleoley.*

Deacons: Religious

Br. Richard Hulle.   Br. John de Grete.
Br. Robert de Stratton.   Br. Richard Brokerst.
Br. John Troubrugge.

Deacons: Secular

William Carter of Kibworth, Lincoln diocese, to t. of the P. & C. of Caldwell by l.d.

William Osbern of Gloucester, Worc. diocese, to t. of the A. & C. of Flaxley.

Richard Aleyn of Warwick, to t. of the house of St. Sepulchre, Warwick.

John in the Lone of Lapworth, Worc. diocese, to t. of the P. & C. of St. Frideswide's next Oxford.

John Pardoner of Alcester, Worc. diocese, to t. of the A. & C. of Alcester.

Elias de Strengesham of Worc. diocese, to t. of patrimony.*†

William de L[aneley]e,¹ r. of Preston-on-the-Weald Moors, to t. of his church by l.d.

Henry Lessy of Quinton, Worc. diocese, to t. of patrimony.*

Thomas Aleyn son of Robert Aleyn of [Droit]wich, Worc. diocese, to t. of his church aforesaid [St. Clement's, Worcester].

*Priests: Religious*²

Br. John de . . . . .[monk of] Great Malvern.
Br. William . . .
Br. Andrew de Whytechyrich.
Br. William att. . .gham.
Br. Roger de . .astr' of the order of St. Augustine.
Br. William . . .oston.
Br. Thomas C. .nbe.
Br. John B. .rton.

*Priests: Secular*³

John de Sancto Dionisio of the parish of St. Denis Backchurch (*de Garschurch*), London diocese, an exempt jurisdiction, by l.d. of the archbishop of Canterbury to t. of the A. & C. of *Ponte*.⁴*

Charles de Bosmevile of Coventry & Lichfield diocese, to t. of the P. & C. of Henwood by l.d.

Richard Wykewane of Worc. diocese, to t. of the A. & C. of Bordesley.

1 He should probably be among the subdeacons and with the Christian name 'Roger'. A 'Roger de Laneleye, r. of Preston' is later ordained deacon and priest. See pp. 243, 247.
2 The MS. has suffered from damp and the following entries are not fully legible.
3 The MS. has *Non religiosi* crossed out and *Seculares alias dictum* interlineated. The term *non religiosi* is rarely used in the remainder of the lists.
4 Apparently Robertsbridge, Sussex (*de Ponte Roberti*).

[*Priests: Secular continued.*]

Thomas de Oneslowe, r. of Heanor (*Havemer*), Coventry & Lichfield diocese, to t. of his church by l.d.

Walter Wille. . of Condicote, Worc. diocese, to t. of the hospital of St. John of Jerusalem *per altum priorem.*

Peter de K. .ete of Salisbury diocese, to t. of the P. & C. of Little Malvern.[1]*

Richard Bonamy of Beckford, Worc. diocese, to t. of the P. & C. of Little Malvern.

Thomas Blythe.

William Prestone.

William Morice.

Ralph Ouwyn of Exeter diocese, by l.d. to t. of the P. & C. of Bodmin.*

Henry Grafton.

1050 *8 March 1343 Orders celebrated by the bishop in Cheltenham parish church during the first week of Lent.*

Acolytes: Religious

Br. William de Bourton ⎫
Br. John Slymbrugge   ⎬ canons of Bristol.
Br. Richard Leygrove ⎭

Br. Peter de Lodebrok ⎫ Friars Minor.
Br. Peter Holybrond   ⎭

Acolytes: Secular

Nicholas Poywek'.	John Duncan.
Walter le Marchal.	William Bate.
William de London'.	John Hale.
William Bonde.	Geoffrey de Slouthr'.
Thomas de Brayles.	John de Grosso Monte.
Nicholas Dynggald.	John de Asschton.
William Cok of Driffield.	John Batyn.
William Haynes.	Peter de Besilles.
John Hergast.	Thomas de Bemynton.
Gilbert le Taylor.	Richard de Torltone.
John de Frompton.	Thomas Usk.
William Lodyntone.	James Undeslowe.
Henry Bampti of Barrington	John Underhulle.
(*Byrmington*).	Thomas Wynston.
Robert Hulles.	

1 An entry has been crossed out here. It was the same as that for Henry Lessy in the list of secular deacons above.

Subdeacons: Religious

Br. William Tressham ⎫
Br. John de Beole ⎪
Br. Thomas de Oxon' ⎬ canons of Cirencester.
Br. Peter de Lynham ⎭

Br. John de Cheltenham ⎫
Br. Walter de Prestbury ⎬ monks of Hailes.

Br. John de Evesham ⎫
Br. Alexander de Atforton ⎬ monks of Tewkesbury.
Br. Richard de Cirenc' ⎭

Br. Richard Payn, of Kingswood.

Br. John de Dumbelton ⎫
Br. Thomas de Malmeshull ⎬ monks of Winchcombe.

Subdeacons: Secular

Richard de Ketteford of Hereford diocese, to t. of the D. & C. of Hereford by l.d.

John son of Thomas Henr' of Halford, to t. of the A. & C. of Combe.

Peter Pyngnerey of Bayeux diocese, to t. of the A. & C. of St. Augustine's, Bristol.

John Wawepel, to t. of the P. & C. of *Sotleye* [Studley].

John Edden of Barton (*Berton*), to t. of the prior of St. John of Jerusalem.

Solomon Roger' of Barnsley, to t. of the P. & C. of Monkton Farleigh [?] (*Farnleye*).

William Cogan, r. of Hartest, Norwich diocese, to t. of his church.

Richard Broun of Acton Turville, to t. of John de la Revere, knight.

John Kyng' of Winchcombe, to t. of his patrimony.*

William Adam of Broad Campden, to t. of the A. & C. of Alcester.

Deacons: Religious

Br. Henry de Swyndon, monk of Winchcombe.

Br. Thomas de Rodbourne ⎫
Br. William de Cleve ⎪
Br. Robert Wayfer ⎬ monks of Malmesbury.
Br. Roger de Axebrugg ⎭

Br. David Pabuer junior.

Br. William de Ende, of Kingswood.

Br. Richard de Dumbelton.

Deacons: Secular

Richard Sacumbe of Painswick, Worc. diocese, to t. of the P. & C. of Great Malvern.

Peter de Celario, to t. of patrimony.*

Nicholas Wynont of Cirencester, to t. of the abbess of Godstow.

William Champeneye of Beoley, to t. of the abbot [*sic*].[1]

1 Of Alcester. See pp. 208, 220.

[*Deacons: Secular continued.*]

Stephen son of John Roberts of Lower Swell, to t. of patrimony.*

Nicholas atte Hoke of Standish, to t. of patrimony.*

John son of John le Bulker' of Great Compton, to t. of the A. & C. of Oseney.

John de Chidwell of Great Rissington, to t. of the house of St. John of Jerusalem.

Philip son of Philip Nichol of Rycote, to t. of the hospital of St. John of Jerusalem by l.d. of the bishop of Lincoln.

Walter Hows of Dorn, to t. of his patrimony.

Robert de Pilton of Salisbury diocese, by l.d. to t. of St. John's hospital, Cricklade.

Thomas de Castello of Marshfield, Worc. diocese, to t. of the A. & C. of Our Lady, Keynsham.*

Priests: Religious

Br. Ralph Moniassch.

Br. John de Eynesham.

Br. Thomas de Perschor', of Llanthony.

Br. John Doddeleye, of the order of Carmelites.

Br. Robert of the house of Lechlade.

Br. John de Sotton of the order of Minorites.

Br. Laurence de Minstreworthe.

Br. John de Weston.

Br. Walter de . . .mouthe.

Priests: Secular

Philip de Sobbury, to t. of the house of Lilleshall.*

William de Bovetoun of Horsley, to t. of the A. & C. of Godstow.

John Walteres of Coln St. Aldwyn, to t. of the hospital of St. John of Jerusalem.

John Colet of Besford, to t. of patrimony.*

Robert de Bradewater, to t. of the A. & C. of Godstow.

Richard le Nywe of Coleshill, to t. of the prior and brethren of St. John's, Lechlade, by l.d. of the bishop of Salisbury.

Robert de Marcle of Hereford diocese, to t. of the D. & C. of Hereford by l.d.

Richard Aleyn of Warwick, Worc. diocese, to t. of St. Sepulchre's, Warwick.

Llewelyn son of John de Wynston, by l.d. of Henry, bishop of St. David's, to t. of the P. & C. of Craswall.

John Partrich of Hallow, to t. of St. John's hospital, Lechalde.

Nicholas Bartelot of Welford, to t. of the A. & C. of Alcester.*

William Chauntecler of Bretforton, by l.d. of the abbot of Evesham, to t. of the P. & C. of Studley.

Adam son of Reginald, son of Adam de Kyngescote, to t. of the A. & C. of Kingswood.

Henry Wilde of Meysey Hampton, to t. of the hospital of St. John of Jerusalem.

John de Colthaston, to t. of his patrimony.[1]*

Thomas Aleyn of [Droit]wich, r. of St. Clement's Worcester, to t. of his church.

Thomas Steph. . . of Edgeworth, r. of Winstone, to t. of his church.

John de Maneby, to t. of the A. & C. of Tewkesbury by l.d. of the archbishop of York.

Walter de Walford of Worcester diocese, to t. of his patrimony.*

John Pydes, to t. of the P. & C. of Kingston (*Kyngeston*).[2]

1051 *29 March 1343 Orders celebrated by the bishop in the chapel of his manor at Bredon.*[3]

Acolytes: Secular

Geoffrey ap Pr'. Adam Samson of Bishops Cleeve.
John de Westmoncote. John le Kok of Cirencester.
Simon Beruwe. Elias de Hamptone.

Subdeacons: Religious

Br. John Stoke, monk of Bordesley.
Br. John de Bereford ⎱
Br. Richard Walynton ⎰ monks of Gloucester.
Br. Richard Haukesbury ⎱
Br. William de Ledene ⎰ monks of Pershore.

Subdeacons: Secular

Henry Kynges of Winchcombe.
John Riche of Ragley, Worc. diocese, to t. of the A. & C. of Bordesley.[4]
M. Thomas de Asshton, r. of Eastleach St. Andrew,[5] to t. of his church.

Deacons: Religious

Br. John de Chiltenham ⎱
Br. Walter de Prestbury ⎰ monks of Hailes.
Br. John Lamver ⎱
Br. Henry Portescu ⎰ Carmelites.

---

1 *Ricardus Aleyn de Warr'* crossed out. 2 *Recte* Kington. Cf. p. 183.
3 *Die Sabbati qua cantatur 'Scicientes'.* 4 But cf. p. 316 5 But cf. 1015.

[*Deacons: Religious continued.*]

Br. Thomas de Malmeshull   ⎫
Br. John de Dombelton   ⎬ monks of Winchcombe.
                        ⎭

Deacons: Secular

Philip Kyng' of Winchcombe, to t. of patrimony.*

Peter Pingnereȝ of Bayeux diocese, to t. of the A. & C. of St. Augustine's, Bristol.

Thomas de Wychiford, r. of Sheinton, to t. of his church.

Priest: Religious

Br. Philip de Stocton, of the order of Minorites, Worcester.

Priest: Secular

John Pardoner of Alcester, to t. of the house of Alcester.*

1052 *12 April 1343 Orders celebrated by the bishop in Hartlebury parish church on Holy Saturday.*

Subdeacons

Nicholas de Poywek, r. of Abbots Morton, Worc. diocese, to t. of his church.

John de Walton of Tewkesbury, to t. of the A. & C. of Evesham. [1]

John Balle of Worc. diocese, to t. of the A. & C. of Alcester.

Deacons

Roger de Aston, r. of Fonthill Gifford, Salisbury diocese, to t. of his church.

Br. William de Ketteryng, monk of Ramsey, Lincoln diocese, by l.d.

Henry Kyng of Winchcombe.

Richard Vachan of Crickhowell, St. David's diocese, to t. of the A. [*sic*] & C. of St. John the Baptist, Llanthony Prima, of the Augustinian order.*

Priests

Thomas de Wydchiford, r. of Sheinton, Coventry & Lichfield diocese, to t. of his church.*

Br. Adam de Sotton, monk of [Bury] St. Edmunds, Norwich diocese, by l.d. of his abbot, privileged and exempt.

William de Sotton of Lincoln diocese, by l.d. to t. of the house of the scholars of Merton Hall, Oxford.

John de Borewell, r. of Middleham, York diocese, to t. of his church by l.d.

---

1 MS. *Evesham,* but this should be *Eynesham* (Eynsham). See pp. 216, 220 and *Index* s.v. 'Walton'.

1053 *7 June 1343 Orders celebrated by the bishop in Hartlebury parish church on the eve of Trinity Sunday.*

Acolytes: Religious

Br. William de Stoke, canon of Halesowen.
Br. Thomas de Marleberge.

Br. William Mees.
Br. John Frater.
Br. John Wantyngg.

Acolytes: Secular [1]

Richard de Quenyntone, r. of Stow.
Richard Houald of Warwick.
Richard Troket of Yardley.
Hugh Bathecote of [Droit]wich.
William de Quynton.
Robert de Halyes of Norton.
John Poleyn.
Thomas Raulyn of Warwick.
William Benge.
Richard Asschelyn of [H]ynkeley.
Henry Raggel. . of the same.
Thomas P. . . . . de H[athe]rop.
John . . . . . of Gloucester.
M. Henry . . . . , Hereford diocese, by l.d.

Subdeacons: Religious

Br. Thomas . . . . .
Br. William . . . . .

Br. Simon de . . . .
Br. Richard de W[?]. . . .

Subdeacons: Secular

William son of Adam . . . .efelde of Kings Norton, to t. of the A. & C. of Bordesley.*
John le Leche of Twyning, Worc. diocese, to t. of the prior and brethren of St. John's, Lechlade.*
John son of Robert de Gopeshull next Tewkesbury, Worc. diocese, to t. of the A. & C. of Eynsham.*
John de Vale of Wootton Wawen, to t. of his patrimony.*†
John Wodestoke of Stratford-on-Avon, to t. of the P. & C. of Studley.
Richard Poywek of Dumbleton, Worc. diocese, to t. of his patrimony.
John de Wylcote of Worc. diocese, to t. of the A. & C. of Alcester.
William Lee of Broad Marston, to t. of the A. & C. of Alcester.

1 The MS. has been affected by damp at this point.

Deacons: Religious

Br. Peter le Yrenmonger.
Br. John de Stok.
Br. William Ledene
Br. Richard Haukesbury   } monks of Worcester.[1]

Deacons: Secular

Nicholas Poywek, r. of Abbots Morton, to t. of his church.
John Bornhard of Worc. diocese, to t. of the A. & C. of Oseney.
Richard atte Welle of Lapworth, Worc. diocese, to t. of the collegiate church of St. Mary, Warwick.
Adam atte Hulle of Kings Norton, to t. of the hospital of St. John of Jerusalem.*
John son of John le Walton of Tewkesbury, to t. of the A. & C. of Eynsham.[2]
John Balle of Tredington, Worc. diocese, to t. of the A. & C. of Alcester.
Thomas Doul of Bromsgrove, to t. of his patrimony.*
John de Hothoun of York diocese, by l.d. to t.*
Nicholas Wychiford of Hereford diocese, r. of Chetton, to t. of his church.
John Schypton of Southwick, Worc. diocese, to t. of the house of St. John of Jerusalem.*

Priests: Religious

Br. John de Greothe
Br. Walter de Poyweke   } monks of Great Malvern.
Br. John de Scheyntone
Br. John de Alicestre.
Br. John de Stapelford.
Br. John de Chyltenham, monk of Hailes.
Br. John de Stourbrugg.

Priests: Secular

Roger de Aston, r. of Fonthill Gifford, Salisbury diocese, by l.d. to t. of his church.
John Bulker of Great Compton, to t. of the A. & C. of Oseney.
John Schad of Admington, Worc. diocese, to t. of the A. & C. of Alcester.
John Kyng' of Winchcombe, to t. of his patrimony.†
Peter de Celario of Bayeux[3] diocese, by l.d. to t. of his patrimony.
Peter Pygner' of Bayeux diocese, by l.d. to t. of the A. & C. of St. Augustine's, Bristol.
Robert Penne of Lichfield (*Lych*) diocese, by l.d. to t. of the A. & C. of Leicester.

1 *Recte* Pershore.
2 MS. *Eynesham.* Cf. pp. 214 n.1, 220.
3 MS. *Baioc'* (Bayeux), but *Baionens'* (Bayonne) may have been intended as on p. 208.

John in ye Lone of Lapworth, Worc. diocese, to t. of the house of St. Frideswide.

William Richard of Himbleton, Worc. diocese, to t. of the bishop's grace.

William Okleye of Worc. diocese, to t. of his patrimony.*

Henry Kyng' of Winchcombe.

1054 *20 September 1343 Orders celebrated by the bishop in Bishops Cleeve parish church on the Saturday in Embertide after the feast of the Exaltation of the Holy Cross.*

Acolytes: Religious

Br. Thomas de Farndon, monk of Hailes.
Br. Philip de Stok ⎱
Br. William de Holwey ⎰ Minorites.
Br. Roger Clodishale.
Br. John de Aston.

Acolytes: Secular

William Cokkes.
John Ewayn.
Walter de Quenton.
John de Kent.
Adam Toly.
Thomas Mile.
William Ekklessale.
John Godefrey.
John Mason.

Thomas Stok.
Thomas Der[by] of Bristol.
Walter Ha. . . . .
William Clifton.
Roger Fre[n?].
Stephen de Rouwynton.
Thomas Lapeȝat.
Henry atte Ȝeate.

Subdeacons: Religious

Br. John de Walton.
Br. Thomas de Stanton, monk of Hailes.
Br. Robert Croxham.
Br. William de Stoke.
Br. William Borden.
Br. John de Slymbrugg.

Br. Richard de Leygrave.
Br. William Cok'.
Br. John Wydehull.
Br. Robert Loughteburgh.
Br. John de Lynton.
Br. Henry de Polton.
Br. Walter Schalingford.

Subdeacons: Secular [1]

John . . . of Worc. diocese, to t. of patrimony.*†
William Eweyn, portionist in the church of St. Nicholas, Warwick, to t. of his portion.

1 Part of this entry affected by damp.

[*Subdeacons: Secular continued.*]

John Underhull, to t. of patrimony.*†
John de Alderton, to t. of the prior of Cold Norton.*
Simon de Southcerneye, to t. of the house of Oseney.*
Robert Jordan of Marshfield, to t. of the A. & C. of Keynsham.
Thomas Veysi, to t. of the P. & C. of Wroxton.
Ralph Boner of *Boudon* [? Bourton nr. Banbury], Lincoln diocese, by l.d. to t. of the P. & C. of Chacombe.*
John de Kendale, r. of Caldecote, Norwich diocese, to t. of his church by l.d.
John Cromhale, to t. of the prior and brethren of the Calendaries, Bristol.
M. Richard de Quenton, r. of St. Edward's church, Stow, to t. of his church.
William Cokebele of Brailes, to t. of the [A] & C. of Stoneleigh.
John Lyngayn of Worc. diocese, to t. of the [A. & C.] of St. Augustine's, Bristol.
Robert le Taylour, r. of St. [Peter's?] by Worcester castle, to t. of his church.[1]
Thomas Payn of Huntingdon . . . . to t. of his patrimony.*[2]

Deacons: Religious

Br. Thomas de Salop.   Br. John Upton.
Br. Thomas de Fulford.   Br. John de Evesham.
Br. Richard Chaddisle.   Br. Richard de Cirencestr'.
Br. John Mason.   Br. Alexander de Peneb'.
Br. William Derby.   Br. William de Redingge.
Br. John Wystowe.

Deacons: Secular

John Gopishull of Upton, to t. of the monastery of Eynsham.*
Philip de Alyncestr', r. of Little Compton, to t. of his church.
William Pynnock of Salford, Lincoln diocese, by l.d. to t. of the house of Eynsham.
William Adam of Broad Campden, to t. of the A. & C. of Alcester.
John Lech' of Twyning, to t. of the prior and brethren of Lechlade.*
Thomas Camvyle of Birmingham (*Byrmyncham*), to t. of patrimony.*
Henry Laurenc' of *Clopton*, to t. of patrimony.*
John son of Adam le Taylour of Fulwell, Lincoln diocese, by l.d. to t. of the P. & C. of Daventry.*
John Waupol of Pendock, to t. of Studley priory of the Augustinian order.

1 q. . . . . .*ewangel' corporaliter per eundem iuravit quod aliqua matri. . . . . . .sua predicta non faceret per se nec per aliquem alium presbiterum permittere faceret celebrari. Testibus Hugone de Pen[ebrugg], [Johanne] de Severleye.*
2 'William Scheynton, r. of Merthyr, Llandaff diocese, by l.d. to t. of his church', crossed out.

Henry de Axebrugg' of Bristol, to t. of patrimony.*

Richard Broun of Acton, to t. of Ds. John de la Ryver'.

John son of Thomas Henry of Halford, to t. of the A. & C. of Combe.

John Ryche of Ragley, Salisbury[1] diocese, to t. of the house of Bordesley.*

William de Schynton, r. of Merthyr, Llandaff diocese, by l.d. to t. of his church.[2]

Priests: Religious

Br. William Rydeleye.

Br. John Grenbergh.

Br. Adam de Warsope.

Br. William de Wodeton.

Br. John de Bredon.

Br. Richard de Haukesbury.

Br. Roger de Hereford
Br. William de Cirencestr' } monks of Worcester.
Br. Thomas de Barndisle
Br. Richard de Henxeye

Br. Richard de Dombelton, monk of Hailes.

Priests: Secular

Nicholas de Wycheford of Hereford diocese, by l.d. to t. of his church of Chetton.*

M. John Hothum of York diocese, by l.d. to t.*

Thomas de Castello of Marshfield, Worc. diocese, to t. of the monastery of St. Mary, Keynsham.*

Robert Noreys of Honington, Worc. diocese, to t. of the P. & C. of Wroxton.

M. William de Haukesworth of York diocese, by l.d. to t. of the house of scholars of St. Mary's, Oxford.[3]

Nicholas atte Holte of Standish, Worc. diocese, to t. of his patrimony.

Walter Hewes of Dorn, Worc. diocese, to t. of his patrimony.*

John Balle of Tredington, Worc. diocese, to t. of the A. & C. of Alcester.

Richard de Payneswick of Worc. diocese, to t. of the P. & C. of Great Malvern.

Simon de Derlingescote of Worc. diocese, to t. of the P. & C. of Wroxton.

John Spence of Kidderminster, Worc. diocese, to t. of his patrimony.*

William Ros of Oxford, Lincoln diocese, by l.d. to t.

1 Error for 'Worcester'. See p. 213.
2 Cf. p. 218 n.2.
3 MS. *ad titulum domus scolarum Beate Marie Oxon.*

[Priests: Secular continued.]

Henry Frankeleyn of Stanton [or Staunton],[1] Worc. diocese, to t. of
the A. & C. of Alcester.

Robert Sage of Penkridge, Coventry & Lichfield diocese, by l.d.

Robert de Rodecote of Worcester, to t. of his patrimony.*

William Michel of Marlcliff, Worc. diocese, to t. of the A. & C. of
Bordesley.

Thomas son of Richard Trug' of Charlecote, to t. of the house of
Thelsford.

Henry Lessy of Quinton, Worc. diocese, to t. of patrimony.*

John son of John de Walton of Worc. diocese, to t. of the A. & C. of
Eynsham.

Elias Mosard of Strensham, to t. of his patrimony.

John Teberay of Coventry & Lichfield diocese, to t. of the nuns of
Henwood, by l.d.

William Osbern of Gloucester, Worc. diocese, to t. of the A. & C. of
Flaxley.

Roger Selyman of Blockley, to t. of the P. & C. of Maiden Bradley.

William Champeneye of Beoley, Worc. diocese, to t. of the A. & C.
of Alcester.

Thomas de Astmede, r. of Horton, to t. of his church.

William de Stouwe, to t. of patrimony.

John Bournhart, to t. of the house of Oseney.

Nicholas Poywek, r. of Abbots Morton, to t. of his church.

1055 *20 December 1343 Orders celebrated by the bishop in Hartlebury
parish church on Saturday in Embertide.*

Acolytes[2]

Br. Stephen de Alcestr' of the Cistercian order.

M. Walter le Wytthe, r. of St. Stephen's Bristol, to t. of his church.

Robert de Merston.

Henry Cassy of [Droit]wich.

Robert Wylmy [? Wyburn] of Stratford.

John Ragoun.

M. Thomas de Chipston, r. of Compton Wyniates.

Subdeacons: Religious

Br. John de Lodelowe ⎫
Br. Richard Blaket ⎭ monks of Worcester.

Br. John de Stanton ⎫
Br. Roger Tryllek ⎬ Preachers.
Br. Ralph Bey(r?)el ⎭

---

1 MS. *Stanton.*   2 *Acolit' religios'* in margin.

Br. Philip de Stok' ⎫
Br. John de Wystanston ⎬ Minorites.
Br. Roger Clodeshale ⎪
Br. William Holeweye ⎭

[Two folios are missing. The rest of this ordination list has been lost.]

1056 *20 March 1344 Orders celebrated by the bishop in the chapel of his manor at Hartlebury.*[1]

Subdeacons: Secular

Robert de Etyndon, acolyte, of Worc. diocese, to t. of the prior, prioress and convent of Westwood.
William de Hocyndon, r. of St. Alban's Worcester, to t. of his church.
Richard Sparry of Clent, Worc. diocese, to t. of his patrimony.
John de Lynchelade, r. of Ludgershall, Lincoln diocese, to t. of his church by l.d.

Deacon: Religious[2]

Br. Richard Franceys, of the house of St. Mark, Bristol.

Priests: Secular

Walter Broun, r. of St. Werburgh's Bristol.
William Averay, called 'of Kings Sutton', of Lincoln diocese, v. of Castle Bytham, by l.d.

1057 *3 April 1344 Orders celebrated by the bishop in Hartlebury parish church on Holy Saturday.*

Acolytes

Br. William Doget of the order of Carmelites.
Richard Poyweke.
John le Boys son of Robert le Boys.

Subdeacons

Peter son of William Piersson of *Dorlington*,[3] perpetual v. of Kineton [*Kyngton fori*], to t. of his vicarage.
John Boyloun, r. of the second portion in Bisley church, to t. of his portion.
Edmund de Clynton, r. of Sutton, Norwich diocese, by l.d. of the bishop elect and confirmed of Norwich, to t. of his church.
John le Bray of Quinton, Worc. diocese, to t. of the A. & C. of Alcester.

1 *Die Sabbati qua cantatur officium 'Scicientes'.*
2 MS. *Diaconi religiosi* [*sic*].
3 For Dorsington?

Deacons

John le Ʒonge of Coventry & Lichfield diocese, by l.d. to t. of the P. & C. of Wombridge.*

John Hars of Holt, Worc. diocese, to t. of the dean of the king's free chapel of St. Martin-le-Grand, London.*

Reginald de Caynton, r. of Biddulph, Coventry & Lichfield diocese, by l.d. to t. of his church.

John de Lynchelade, r. of Ludgershall, Lincoln diocese, by l.d. to t. of his church.

Walter son of John de Meneʒate of Shelsley Kings, Worc. diocese, to t. of the P. & C. of Newland in Sherwood (*de novo loco in Schyrwode*), York diocese.*

Priests: Religious [*sic*]

Br. Richard de Arderne of the order of Carmelites.

John de Tymmor, r. of a moiety of Egginton church, Coventry & Lichfield diocese, by l.d. to t. of his moiety.

1058 *29 May 1344 Orders celebrated by the bishop in Campden parish church on the eve of Trinity Sunday.*

Acolytes: Religious

Br. Simon de Brocworth   ⎫
Br. Adam de Dauntesheye   ⎬ of [Llanthony next] Gloucester.
                             ⎭

Br. Fulk de Lacy of the order of Preachers, Warwick.

Br. *Garn'* [1] Longespy of the order of Minorites, Worcester.

Br. John Lynton.

Br. Henry Polton.

Br. Richard Franceys.

Br. William de la Felde.

Br. Philip de Button.

Br. John de Whystanton.

Br. Philip de Stoke.

Br. Thomas de Staunton.

Br. William de Bradeleye.

Br. William de Lende.

Br. Walter de Cirencestr'   ⎫
                             ⎬ of Bruern.
Br. John de Schyrton   ⎭

Acolytes: Secular

M. Thomas Staunton of Hereford diocese, by l.d. of John Rez, vicar-general of Thomas[2] Trynlek, bishop elect and confirmed.

William Colyns of Mickleton.

1 *Garinus* for Warin?
2 *Recte* John.

Henry de Broughton.
Richard Palmere of Mickleton.
John de Wlmeston.
Henry de Caldecote.
John de Blockelegh.
Simon Royse.
Reginald Godefrey.
William atte Halle of Shenington.
Thomas Laurenc' of Weston.
William Raulyn of Stratford.
William Horseleye.
William Watcote.
Thomas Whyther.
William de Etyndon.
William Wylicote.
William Wattes of Naunton [or Newington].[1]
John le Taylour.
John Dalby of Winchcombe.
Thomas Robyns of Nether Eatington (*Nethyretyndon*).
John Lithethurne.
Thomas de Lithethurne.
Richard Bertram, r. of Shell.

Subdeacons: Religious

Br. John de Lydȝate, canon of Kenilworth.
Br. William de Kedermunstre, monk of Shrewsbury, by l.d.
Br. William de Mews ⎱ of the order of Minorites.
Br. John de Hodynton ⎰
Br. John de Borneby of the order of Preachers.
Br. John de Berkeleye ⎱ of Llanthony next Gloucester.
Br. Richard de Chyriton ⎰
Br. Thomas de Wilcote ⎫
Br. Robert de Gloucestr' ⎬ monks of Tewkesbury.
Br. William de Eton ⎪
Br. Richard de Wilferton ⎭

Subdeacons: Secular

William Roberd of South Littleton, Worc. diocese, to t. of the P. &
C. of St. Frideswide's, Oxford.*
John atte Were of Worc. diocese, to t. of his patrimony.*† He swore
to attend the Grammar Schools with diligence for two years before
proceeding to higher orders.[2]

1 MS. *Neuwynton.*
2 *Et iste admissus iuravit tactis sacrosanctis ewangeliis per biennium excerciturum scolas gramaticales
cum diligencia antequam ascendat ad ordines superiores.*

19

[*Subdeacons: Secular continued.*]

Henry le Palmere of Alderminster, Worc. diocese, to t. of the P. & C. of Studley.*

William son of Richard Jecob of Worc. diocese, to t. of the A. & C. of Pershore.*

Roger Dod of Eatington, Worc. diocese, to t. of the prior and canons of St. Peter's, Dunstable.*

Robert de Halford son of John de Evnelode, to t. of the A. & C. of Oseney.*

Nicholas son of John de Southam of Warwick, Worc. diocese, to t. of the D. & C. of St. Mary's collegiate church, Warwick.*

Richard son of John Gregory of Moreton, Worc. diocese, to t. of the A. & C. of Abbotsbury.*

Nicholas Bosevyle of Wickham, Worc. diocese, to t. of the A. & C. of Bordesley.*

Walter atte Ʒate of Coln Rogers, Worc. diocese, to t. of the P. & C. of Farleigh.*

John Bonsyre of Toddington, Worc. diocese, to t. of his patrimony.

Geoffrey de Broughton of Coventry & Lichfield diocese, by l.d. to t. of the prioress of Nuneaton.

John le Caluwe of Charlecote, Worc. diocese, to t. of the P. & C. of St. Frideswide's, Oxford.*

William Plomer of Bengeworth, Worc. diocese, to t. of the A. & C. of Wroxton.*

John Schoriot of Minchinhampton, Worc. diocese, to t. of the P. & C. of Usk, Llandaff diocese.*

Richard de Marteleye, Worc. diocese, to t. of the house of St. John, Shrewsbury.*

Richard le Taylour of Weston-in-Henmarsh, Worc. diocese, to t. of the house of St. Sepulchre, Warwick.

Henry Thomasson of Nether Eatington, Worc. diocese, to t. of the house of Craswall.

Roger Chastelion, r. of Woodborough, Salisbury diocese, by l.d.

Nicholas de Acton Burnel of Coventry & Lichfield diocese, to t. of St. John the Baptist's hospital, Shrewsbury.

John Wattes of Farmington, Worc. diocese, to t. of his patrimony.

Deacons: Religious

Br. Thomas de Schrevenham ⎱ canons of Kenilworth, by l.d.
Br. Henry de Quenton ⎰

Br. John de Stouwe, monk of Bruern, by l.d. of the bishop of Lincoln.

Br. Richard Billyng' of the order of Preachers, Gloucester.

Br. Henry de Seggesbaruwe, monk of Hailes.

Br. Richard de Oldebury, of Kingswood.

Deacons: Secular

John Sadelere of the exempt jurisdiction of Evesham, to t. of the A. & C. of Bordesley, by l.d. of the abbot of Evesham.*

William Whette of Rissington, Worc. diocese, to t. of his patrimony.*

John Saundres of South Littleton in the exempt jurisdiction of Evesham, by l.d. of the abbot to t. of his patrimony.*

William Janne of Bretforton, Worc. diocese, in the exempt jurisdiction of Evesham, by l.d. of the abbot to t. of the A. & C. of Bordesley.

Henry Bloxham of Swalcliffe, Lincoln diocese, by l.d. to t. of his patrimony.

John Grenehull of the exempt jurisdiction of Evesham, to t. of the P. & C. of Studley.

William Fylet of Hereford diocese, to t. of the A. & C. of Buildwas by l.d. of the vicar-spiritual (*vicar' spiritual'*) of Hereford.*

John son of John le Mason of Minchinhampton, Worc. diocese, to t. of the perpetual chantry of Aston, Hereford diocese.

John son of Ralph de Bladynton, Worc. diocese, to t. of the A. & C. of Bordesley.*

William Holte of the exempt jurisdiction of Evesham, by l.d. of the A. & C. to t. of patrimony.*

Robert Tromwyne, r. of Quinton, Worc. diocese, to t. of his church.*

William Hodynton, r. of St. Alban's Worcester, to t. of his church.*

John de Walton, r. of Sper[nall], to t. of his church.*[1]

Peter son of William Person, v. of Kineton, Worc. diocese, to t. of his vicarage.

M. Edmund le Botyler, r. of a moiety of Malpas, Lichfield & Coventry diocese, to t. of his church.

John Underhull of Worc. diocese, to t. of his patrimony.*

John le Grant of Bibury, Worc. diocese, [to t.] of the A. & C. of Oseney.

John le Freman of Lower Slaughter, Worc. [diocese, to t.] of the A. & C. of Eynsham.*

John Syde of Gloucester, Worc. diocese, to [t. of the P. & C.] of St. Oswald's, Gloucester.*

Robert de Etyndon of Worc. diocese, to t. of the prior, prioress & convent of Westwood.*

John Ground of *Wilcote*,[2] Worc. diocese, to t. of the A. & C. of Alcester.*

John Cromhale of Worc. diocese, to t. of the prior and brethren of the Calendaries, Bristol.*

John Boner of Little Wormington, Worc. diocese, to t. of his patrimony.*

Robert Kene of Northway (*Northeye*), Worc. diocese, to t. of the P. & C. of St. Oswald's, Gloucester.

---

1 MS. damaged by damp here and below.   2 Willicote (Gl.)?

[*Deacons: Secular continued.*]

Thomas Dodde of Worc. diocese, to t. of his patrimony.*

John son of Richard Tyleman of Winchcombe, Worc. diocese, to t. of his patrimony.*

Henry Humfray of Sherborne, Worc. diocese, [to t. of his patrimony].*

Thomas son of Henry Geffrey of Over Eatington (*Ovyretynd'*), Worc. diocese, to t. of his patrimony.

William Cockes [? Cookes] of Alcester, Worc. diocese, to t. [of the P. & C.] of Studley.

John Myntemor of Winchcombe, Worc. [diocese], to [t.] of the A. & C. of Eynsham.

[Two folios are missing and the rest of this ordination has been lost.]

1059 *Undated*[1] *Celebration of orders.* [*Initial entries on missing folio.*]

Subdeacons: Secular

Roger Poure, r. of Weston-on-Trent, Coventry & Lichfield diocese, to t. of his church by l.d.

Robert son of John le Mer of Monyhull (*Molenhulle*), Worc. diocese, to t. of the A. & C. of Tewkesbury.

Robert de Gervennith of Norwich diocese, by the bishop's grace.

Robert Erchebaud of Cirencester, Worc. diocese, to t. of his patrimony.*

William Bromley of Coventry & Lichfield diocese, to t. of St. John's Shrewsbury by l.d.

Deacons: Religious

Br. Walter de Bedeston ⎱
Br. Thomas Rodberwe ⎰ monks of Malmesbury.

Br. William de Cirenc' ⎱
Br. John de Schipton ⎰ monks of Bruern.

Br. John de Barwe, monk of Little Malvern.

Br. Roger de Clodeshale of the order of Minorites.

Br. Adam Tryllek ⎱
Br. John Mazon   ⎰ of the order of Carmelites.

Deacons: Secular

M. Thomas de Stannton, canon of Hereford, by l.d. to t.[2]

M. John de Gotham of York diocese, by l.d. to t. [of his church] of Gotham.

M. Robert de Mildeltone[3] of York diocese, by l.d. of the archbishop of York [to t.] of Merton Hall, Oxford.

---

1 Probably 18 December 1344.   2 *sue prebende* crossed out.   3 For 'Mideltone'.

Thomas de Welynghop of Hereford diocese, to t. of the dean of Hereford Cathedral by l.d. of M. William de Herwynton.

William Oppedich of Worc. diocese, to t. of the bishop.

John Coriot of Hampton, Worc. diocese, to t. of the prioress of Usk (*Hysok'*).

John Neubolde Oppestoure, to t. of the abbot of Bordesley, Worc. diocese.

John Warniete of Stafford, Coventry & Lichfield diocese, by l.d. to t. of St. John's hospital, Stafford.

John Braye.

Richard Bartlam, r. of Shell, Worc. diocese, to t. of his [chapel].

Thomas Cherington of Lichfield & Coventry diocese, by l.d. to t. of St. John's hospital, Shrewsbury.

William Asteleie of Worc. diocese, to t. of the bishop.

Priests: *Religious*

Br. Robert atte Lee.

Br. Thomas Ragoun.

Br. John Tour.

Br. Henry Lichfield.

Br. John de Stouwa.

Br. Nicholas de Solihulle.

Br. John Boreford.

Br. John de Bevyrleie.

Br. Richard de Wylynton.

Br. William de Lenthale.

Br. John Bengworthe.

Br. John de Upton.

Br. William de Kidermunstr'.

Br. Matthew de Pesschawe.

Priests: *Secular*

M. Edmund le Boteler, r. of a moiety of Malpas, to t. of his church by l.d.

Robert Tromon, r. of Quinton, to t. of his church.

John Colynton of Coventry & Lichfield diocese, by l.d. of Bishop Roger to t. of the prior of Cold Norton.

Thomas Dod of Great Barrington, to t. of patrimony. Worc. diocese.

Nicholas de Acton, r. of Acton, Coventry & Lichfield diocese, by l.d. to t. of his church.

Ralph de Patyngham of Coventry & Lichfield diocese, by l.d. to t. of Lilleshall abbey.

William Carter of Kibworth (*Kubbeworth*), [Lincoln][1] diocese, by l.d. to t. of the house of Caldwell.

William Martelene of Worc. [diocese to t.] of the house of St. John, Shrewsbury.

M. Hugh de M. . . . . . , [r.] of Ditcheat (*Dichezate*).

1 MS. torn here and below.

1060 *19 February 1345*[1] *Orders celebrated by the bishop in Hartlebury parish church on Saturday in the first week of Lent.*[2]

Acolytes: Religious

Br. John Camme.
Br. Henry de Elmeleye.
Br. John de Oxon' of Flaxley, Hereford diocese, by l.d.
Br. William Goldon of the order of Minorites, Gloucester.
Br. Roger de Birmyncham of the Augustinian order, Maxstoke.

Acolytes: Secular

Richard Kymmesford of Longdon, v. of Marshfield, Worc. diocese.
John Carpenter of *Otyndon*.[3]
William atte . . . .
Robert Honder . . . . of Alderminster.
Adam . . . .worth . . . . .orden.
Nicholas de . . . . . diocese, by l.d.
John Bradele.
Walter . .blond [?Blond].
William Bos. .h.d. . .
William de Coldhast.
John [T?]alwoode.
John Hychecokes de . . .

Subdeacons: Religious

Br. Richard de Stre[ngesham]
Br. John de Te[ttebury]
Br. John de Dayl[esford]   } monks of Worcester.
Br. Thomas de . . . .

Br. William . . .
Br. William . . .   } monks of Pershore.

Br. Thomas[?]
Br. Nicholas   } canons of Maxstoke.
Br. Hugh

Subdeacons: Secular

Walter . . . . v. of Standish, to t. of his [church].
Hugh de Greyby . . . . . r. of [*Ruyton*], Coventry & Lichfield diocese, by l.d.
Hamo de . . . . of the church of . .Brereton. . . . by l.d.
CHALVESTON[4] John de Chalv[eston], [r.] of South Tawton, [Exeter diocese], by l.d.

1 This side of the folio has suffered badly from damp and is in part illegible.
2 *Die Sabbati Quatuor Temporum in prima ebdomada Quadragesime.*
3 *Recte Etyndon* for Eatington. Cf. pp. 240, 243.
4 Marginal rubric. Attention is regularly drawn to this name whenever it occurs. It may be that Chalveston had some part in writing the register. See intro. pp. v–vi.

John de Bradew[as], r. of Sedgeberrow, ...de &c.
John Rychese de [Wych]. . . . .
Thomas Swon of [Brailes]. . . . .[to t. of the P.] & C. of Wroxton.
Robert de Byton of Hereford diocese, by l.d. to t. of patrimony.*
Roger called Ippesley of Worc. diocese, to t. of Ds. William de Salwarp.
John son of William Boner' of Killingworth, Lincoln diocese, by l.d. to t. of the A. & C. of Sulby.*
Roger de Clyve of Lichfield diocese, by l.d. [to t. of] the A. & C. of Combermere.*
John Daniel of Adlestrop¹ (*Alderthrop*), Worc. diocese, to t. of the P. & C. of St. Frideswide's, Oxford.*
Thomas Mogge of Defford, Worc. diocese, to t. of patrimony.*
John Morys, to t. of his patrimony.*
Geoffrey de Catton', r. of Oddingley, to t. of his church.*

Deacons: Religious

Br. Simon de Tamworthia, monk [*sic*] of Maxstoke.
Br. John de Banwelle of the order of Minorites.

Deacons: Secular

Walter inthedene of Quenington, Worc. diocese, to t. of the prior of St. John of Jerusalem.*
John Muleward of Chaddesley, Worc. diocese, to t. of the prior of St. John of Jerusalem in England.*
Richard le Tayllour of Weston-in-Henmarsh, Worc. diocese, to t. of the P. & C. of Wroxton.
John de Stratford of Worc. diocese, to t. of the P. & C. of Studley.*
Richard son of John Gregory of Moreton Daubeney, Worc. diocese, to t. of the P. [*sic*] & C. of Abbotsbury.*
Robert Halford of Worc. diocese, to t. of the A. & C. of Oseney.*
John le Marschal of Barton-in-Henmarsh, to t. of the P. & C. of St. Frideswide's, Oxford.*
John Osebarn of Chastleton, Lincoln diocese, to t. of the A. & C. of Oseney.*
Robert de Ʒarnemouth, Norwich diocese, to t. of the bishop's grace.
Walter le Newe of Northway, Worc. diocese, to t. of the prior & priory of St. Margaret outside the town of Marlborough.*
Richard Lovot of Northway, Worc. diocese, to t. of the prior & brethren of St. John's hospital by the bridge in Lechlade.*
William son of William Jacob of Alderminster, Worc. diocese, to t. of the P. [*sic*] & C. of Pershore.*
Henry Palmare of Alderminster, Worc. diocese, to t. of the P. & C. of Studley.*

¹ Perhaps 'Alderton'.

Priests: Religious

Br. John de Longeney, monk of Flaxley, Hereford diocese, by l.d.
Br. John de Stanley, monk of Flaxley, Hereford diocese, by l.d.
Br. Giles Martyn of the order of Minorites, Worcester.

Priests: Secular

M. Philip Godham, r. of Gotham, York diocese, by l.d.
Thomas Veysy of Tysoe, Worc. diocese, to t. of the P. & C. of Wroxton.*
Henry Thomassone of Nether Eatington, Worc. diocese, to t. of the P. & C. of Wroxton.
John Hars of Holt, Worc. diocese, to t. of the dean of the king's free chapel of St. Martin-le-Grand, London.
John le Freman of Lower Slaughter, Worc. diocese, to t. of the A. & C. of Eynsham.*
John Coriot of Minchinhampton, Worc. diocese, to t. of the prioress of Usk.*
John Braye of Quinton, Worc. diocese, to t. of the A. & C. of Alcester.*
John Neubold uppe Stoure, to t. of the A. & C. of Bordesley.*
Walter atte Ʒate of Coln Rogers, Worc. diocese, to t. of the P. & C. of Farleigh.*
Roger Dot of Eatington, to t. of the P. & C. of St. Peter's, Dunstable.*
Richard Sparry of Clent, Worc. diocese, to t. of his patrimony.*
William de Hastleye, Worc. diocese, ordained by the bishop's grace.
Ralph Hementys of Stoke (*Stok'*), Hereford diocese, by l.d. to t. of patrimony.*

1061 *12 March 1345 Orders celebrated by the bishop in the chapel of his manor of Hartlebury.*[1]

Subdeacons: Religious

Br. William Guldon
Br. William de Wytheleye   } of the order of Minorites.
Br. John de Stanleye

Subdeacons: Secular

Richard de Longedon, v. of Marshfield, to t. of his vicarage.
John de Westmancote of Worc. diocese, to t. of the P. & C. of Little Malvern.
Robert called 'de Haulegh' of Campden, Worc. diocese, to t. of his church of *Burnyd*.

1 In margin.

Deacons: Secular

Peter Besyle, r. of Didmarton, to t. of his church.

John Rycheyse of [Droit]wich, to t. of his patrimony.*†

Geoffrey Catton, r. of Oddingley, to t. of his church.

M. Walter de Evesham', v. of Standish, Worc. diocese, to t. of his church.

Thomas Mogge of Defford, to t. of his patrimony.*†

M. John de Bradewas, r. of Sedgeberrow, to t. of his church.

CHALVESTON.[1] John de Chalveston, r. of South Tawton, Exeter diocese, by l.d. to t. of his church.

Deacons: Religious

Br. John de Bradenham of the order of Minorites.

Br. John de Berkele ⎫
Br. Simon de Brocworth ⎪
                        ⎬ canons of Llanthony next Gloucester.
Br. Richard de Cheriton ⎪
Br. Adam de Danteseye ⎭

Priests: Religious

Br. Henry de Swyndon, monk of Winchcombe.

Br. Robert Woderoue of the order of Minorites.

Br. William de Lenthale, monk of Gloucester.

Priests: Secular

William Robert of South Littleton, Worc. diocese, to t. of the P. & C. of St. Frideswide's, Oxford.

John le Mareschal of Barton-in-Henmarsh, Worc. diocese, to t. of the monastery of St. Frideswide, Oxford.

Roger le Baxter of Wixhill (*Wyggingshull*), Coventry & Lichfield diocese, to t. of the house of Henwood.*

John de Stretford of Worc. diocese, to t. of the P. & C. of Studley.*

Robert de Ʒervennich, by l.d. to t. of the bishop's grace.

1062 *27 March 1345 Memorandum that the following were ordained acolytes by the bishop in his chapel at Hartlebury on Easter Day:*

Peter Gros of Worcester, r. of Suckley.

William de Pylkynton, r. of Swillington, York diocese, by l.d.

Robert Beralt of Defford, Worc. diocese.

1063 *26 March 1345 Orders celebrated by the bishop in Hartlebury parish church on Holy Saturday.*

Subdeacons: Secular

William Adam, v. of Shebbear (*Schestbear'*), Exeter diocese, by l.d. to t. of his vicarage.*

1 In margin.

[*Subdeacons: Secular continued*]

John Hylle of Brixton, v. of Walkhampton, Exeter diocese, to t. of his vicarage by l.d.*

Thomas Mareschal of Lechlade, of Worc. diocese, to t. of the house of St. John of Jerusalem.*

Nicholas Phelippes of Southrop, Worc. diocese, to t. of St. John's hospital, Lechlade.*

Thomas Belamy, r. of Broadwell, Worc. diocese, to t. of his church.*

Walter de Dunstaple of Lincoln diocese, to t. of the prior & brethren of Holy Trinity hospital, Bridgnorth (*Brugg'*), by l.d.

Walter de Clodeshale, r. of Pedmore, Worc. diocese, to t. of his church.*

Deacons: Religious

Br. William Folvyle, monk of Pershore.

Br. William de Grafton.

Deacons: Secular

John Mayel of Tenbury (*Temdebury*), Hereford diocese, by l.d. of M.

William de Herwynton, vicar-general of John, bishop of Hereford, acting *in remotis*, to t. of his patrimony.*†

Roger called 'Ippesley', to t. of Ds. William de Salwarp.*

Priests: Secular

John de Chamberne, v. of Landkey, Exeter diocese, by l.d. to t. of his vicarage.*

William son of Adam atte Felde of Kings Norton, Worc. diocese, to t. of the A. & C. of Bordesley.*

Walter de Evesham, v. of Standish, Worc. diocese, to t. of his vicarage.*

Thomas Mogge of Defford, to t. of his patrimony.*†

John de Ruydon, r. of [North] Kilworth (*Kenelingworth rabat3*), Lincoln diocese, by l.d. to t. of his church.*

Stephen son of Ralph Schorn of Croft, Lincoln diocese, by l.d. to t. of the P. & C. of the house of St. Michael outside Stamford.*

1064 *21 May 1345 Orders celebrated by the bishop in Tewkesbury Abbey on the Saturday in Embertide after Pentecost.*[1]

Acolytes: Religious

Br. John de Southorle.

Br. Philip Craft.

Br. William de Leye.

1 *Die Sabbati Quatuor Temporum in septimana Pentecostes.*

Br. William de Fechyrby.
Br. John Compton, monk of Gloucester.
Br. William de Leye, monk of Hailes.

Acolytes: Secular
Walter Stratford super Abonam.
Thomas Chesterton of Prestbury.
John Hope.
Roger Tettebur'.
William called 'Thomas' of Wotton-under-Edge (*Wotton under Hegge*).
William Pedus of Wotton-under-Edge.
Philip Benet of *Kynton*.[1]
William Bonde of Wotton-under-Edge.
William le Yonge of Morton.
William le Walkere of Wotton-under-Edge.
John de Coumbe of Wotton-under-Edge.
John Flemyng of Upton.
Richard Philippes of Luddington (*Lodynton*).
John atte Forde.
John de Ilmedon.
Gilbert Derlyng of Winchcombe.
Richard le Honte of *Benyngton*.[2]
Thomas Cok of Farmington (*Thormerton*).
John Astelyn of Ragley.
Ralph Stonhous of Cirencester.
Robert Albast of Wellesbourne.
Roger atte Lane of Wellesbourne.
Richard Wodeford of Broadwell.
Ralph Schyre, by l.d.
Thomas Notclyve of Pershore.
Richard Crossonn of Little Barrington.
Walter Watherel of Painswick.
William Mountford of Aston-on-Carrant.
Richard de Todenham.
Robert Caperonn of Horsley.
John Derlyng of Fairford.
William Muleward of Windrush.
Walter Chapelyn of Quenington.
William Walkare of Quenington.
Walter Capel of Berkeley.
Robert Pokok of Bristol.
Thomas de Syde.
John Coupare of Greatworth, Lincoln diocese.
Henry Goldecote.

1 Both 'Kington' and 'Kyneton' are to be found fairly near Wotton.
2 Bevington, Gl.? Cf. Binton (*Bevyngton*), Wa.

[Acolytes: Secular continued]

Robert de Brailles.
Richard Halle of Brailes.
John Clech of Bewdley (*Beauleu*).
Richard Bokelont.
Thomas de Hampton.
Nicholas Lyffe of Cropthorne.
John Dervel of Wick (*Wyk*).
John Barbour of Pershore.
Richard Schyrleye of Yardley.
Richard Brystowe of *Wotton*.
Richard de Aylmeston of Hereford diocese, by l.d. of William de
Hervynton, vicar-general of John, bishop of Hereford.
Walter Rag of Temple Guiting.
Walter de Merston Boteler.
John Lench of [Droit]wich.
Richard Wilkenes of Broadwell.
John Aleyn of Newbold.
John Cotes of Winchcombe.
John Ibetas of *Wotton*.
Laurence de Aston Underegge.
Richard Smetʒher of Fiddington.
Roger Bate of *Benhale*.[1]
John Richemon of Shenington.
Richard Lokkesleye.

Subdeacons: Religious

Br. John Camme.
Br. Henry Volde.
Br. John de Oxenford, monks [*sic*] of St. Mary's, Flaxley, of the
Cistercian order. By l.d. of M. William de Herwynton, vicar-general
of John, bishop of Hereford, absent *in remotis*.
Br. Hugh de Saundrynton ⎫
Br. Robert de Wetton   ⎬ canons of Cirencester.
Br. Richard de Bensynton ⎭
Br. Thomas de Marlebergh of Great Malvern.
Br. Thomas de Aston, monk of Kingswood, Worc. diocese.
Br. Henry de Felde Elmelegh [*sic*] of the Cistercian order, monk of
St. Mary's, Flaxley, Hereford diocese, by l.d. of M. William de
Herwynton [&c. as above].

Subdeacons: Secular

Ds. John Bret, r. of Cheam, Winchester diocese, to t. of his church,

1 Cf. Beanhall, Wo.

by l.d. of the archbishop of Canterbury by reason of the exempt jurisdiction immediately subject to him.[1]

John Stillego, r. of Sparkford, Bath & Wells diocese, to t. of his church. He swore that by St. Peter ad Vincula (1 August) he would produce letters of his institution and induction. By l.d. of the bishop of Bath & Wells.

M. Luke de Herdeburgh, r. of Honington, Worc. diocese, to t. of his church.

M. John Lovecok of Aston-on-Carrant, perpetual v. of Arlingham, Worc. diocese, to t. of his vicarage.

Nicholas le Moy of Bourton, Worc. diocese, to t. of the P. & C. of the monastery of St. Frideswide.

Walter Turkeden, diocese, to t. of the A. & C. of Oseney monastery.

William called 'atte Halle' of Shenington, Worc. diocese, to t. of the P. & C. of Wroxton.

Geoffrey Henrys of Horsley, Worc. diocese, to t. of the P. & C. of Bruton.

William le Vey of Syde, Worc. diocese, to t. of the A. & C. of St. Augustine's, Bristol.

Richard Arnald of Hereford diocese, by l.d. of William de Herwynton, vicar-general of John, bishop of Hereford, absent *in remotis*, to t. of his patrimony.†

William Hauthorn of Eatington, Worc. diocese, to t. of the P. & C. of St. Frideswide's monastery, Oxford.

Walter Wyther of Worc. diocese, to t. of the P. & C. of Llanthony Prima.*

Adam Dod of Eatington, Worc. diocese, to t. of the P. & C. of Caldwell.*

Simon le Mariner of Eldersfield, Worc. diocese, to t. of the P. & C. of St. Oswald's, Gloucester.*

Geoffrey Crisp of Horsley, Worc. diocese, to t. of his patrimony.*

William Willenton, Worc. diocese, to t. of the master & brethren of St. Oswald's hospital, Worcester.*

Robert Ward of Wyre Piddle, Worc. diocese, to t. of his patrimony.*

Hugh ate Mulle of Ampney, Worc. diocese, to t. of the P. & C. of St. Oswald's, Gloucester.

William Hechecokes of Holdfast, Worc. diocese, to t. of his patrimony.*

John Faukes of Quenington, Worc. diocese, to t. of the prior of the hospital of [St. John] of Jerusalem in England.

John Sedare of Haddenham, Lincoln diocese, to t. of the A. & C. of (?) Thame (*Came*) by l.d.*

Richard Heyward of Rowell (*Rowelle*), Worc. diocese, to t. of the P. & C. of St. Frideswide's monastery, Oxford.*

1 For those parishes immediately subject to the abp., see Churchill, *Canterbury Administration*, I. p. 83 *et seq.*

[Subdeacons: Secular continued.]

Richard Nicholes of Kempsford, Worc. diocese, to t. of the P. *[sic]* & C. of Godstow.

John Taverner of Cardiff, Llandaff diocese, by l.d. to t. of his patrimony.* He is not to be ordained to further orders until he has produced *(reportaverit)* a better title.

John Stokwell of *Morton*, Worc. diocese, to t. of his patrimony.* He is not to be ordained [&c. as above].[1]

Richard son of Stephen de Wichforde of Worc. diocese, to t. of Br. Philip de Tame, prior of St. John of Jerusalem.*

Philip Tyrel of Tewkesbury, Worc. diocese, to t. of Ds. John de Hanslape by the bishop's grace.*

John son of William le Swon of Hardwick in Eldersfield, Worc. diocese, to t. of his patrimony.*†

William Palmere of Bretforton, by l.d. of the A. & C. of Evesham to t. of the A. & C. of Bordesley.*

Robert le Somenour of Windrush, Worc. diocese, to t. of patrimony.*

John son of Robert de Berkeleye, Worc. diocese, to t. of his patrimony.

Deacons: Religious

Br. Robert de Hynkeleye, monk of Sandwell[2] priory, Coventry & Lichfield diocese, by l.d.

Br. William de Bysscheleye, monk of Great Malvern.

Br. Henry de Wotton, monk of Gloucester.

Br. John Lech ⎫
Br. John Sauleye ⎬ monks of Gloucester.

Br. Roger Wentebrigge ⎫ monks of Coventry, Coventry & Lich-
Br. John de Wotton ⎬ field diocese, by l.d.

Br. Hugh de Iburton of Flaxley, Hereford diocese, by l.d.

Br. William Witleye of the order of Minorites, from the Worcester convent.

Deacons: Secular

Thomas Montestevens of Bristol, Worc. diocese, to t. of Roger Turtle.*

Nicholas de Wykewone of Worc. diocese, to t. of the A. & C. of Bordesley.*

Richard[3] Erchebaud of Cirencester, to t. of patrimony.†

M. William de Heghtredebur' of Salisbury diocese, by l.d. to t. of the warden *(custos)*, scholars and brethren of the house of the scholars of Merton in the University of Oxford.*

M. Richard de Longedon, v. of Marshfield, to t. of his vicarage.

John Daniel of Adlestrop, Worc. diocese, to t. of the P. & C. of St. Frideswide's, Oxford.

1 Cf. p. 241.
2 MS. *Stanwell.*
3 *Recte* Robert. Cf. pp. 226, 243.

William Drake of Llandaff diocese, by l.d. to t. of Thomas Bangdrip, lord *de la Splotte*, which the bishop of grace admits on this occasion. William took an oath to produce letters of his bishop by the feast of the Assumpton [15 August] which would testify to the truth of his title.

Roger Chastelyn, r. of Barcheston, Worc. diocese, to t. of his church.

John de Westmoncote of Worc. diocese, to t. of the P. & C. of Great Malvern.

Roger atte Nelme of Dursley, Worc. diocese, to t. of his patrimony.

Robert son of John le Mer of Monyhull [1] (*Mokynhull*), Worc. diocese, to t. of the A. & C. of Tewkesbury.*

Thomas de Wolvirton, Coventry & Lichfield diocese, to t. of the house of St. John, Shrewsbury, by l.d.*

Simon Schory of Blockley, to t. of the P. & C. of Ravenstone.*

Walter son of Reginald le Heyward of Frilford (*Firlyng ford*), Lincoln diocese, by l.d. to t. of the A. & C. of Bordesley.

William Aliam [Adam], v. of Shebbear (*Schestbear'*), Exeter diocese, to t. of his vicarage by l.d.*

John Hille of Brixton, v. of Walkhampton, Exeter diocese, to t. of his vicarage by l.d.*

John Hopere of *Staunton*, Worc. diocese, to t. of the P. & C. of Cold Norton.*

Thomas Swon of Brailes, Worc. diocese, to t. of the P. & C. of Wroxton.*

Thomas Marschal of Lechlade, Worc. diocese, to t. of the prior of St. John of Jerusalem by the bishop's grace.*

Walter Cok of Coln St. Aldwyn, Worc. diocese, to t. of the prior of the hospital of St. John of Jerusalem in England.*

Priests: Religious

Br. William de Stoke, canon of Halesowen [*Halesoweyn*], Worc. diocese.

Br. Adam Trillek of the order of Carmelites.

Br. Richard Payn, monk of Kingswood monastery, of the Cistercian order, Worc. diocese.

Br. John Witbarwe, monk of Little Malvern, Worc. diocese.

Br. Simon de Segrave
Br. Adam Rodeborne
Br. Walter Budeston
Br. Walter Camme
Br. Thomas Rodberwe

} monks of Malmesbury, Salisbury diocese, presented by their abbot by virtue of a privilege accorded to the monastery by the apostolic see.

Br. John de Stone of the order of Hermits of St. Augustine from the convent of Warrington (*Werynton*).

1 Cf. p. 226.

Br. William de Tresham
Br. Peter de Lynham
Br. John de Beouleye } canons of Cirencester.
Br. John Berkeleye

Br. Simon de Brocworth
Br. Richard de Chirynton
Br. Adam Danntesheye } canons of Llanthony next Gloucester.
Br. John Berkeleye

Br. John de Evesham, monk of Tewkesbury.

Priests: Secular

John Richardes of Sherborne, Worc. diocese, to t. of the prior of the hospital of St. John of Jerusalem.*

Geoffrey de Weston, v. of Beckford, Worc. diocese, to t. of his vicarage.

Peter Besylles, r. of Didmarton, Worc. diocese, to t. of his church.

John Calewe of Charlecote, Worc. diocese, to t. of St. Frideswide's priory, Oxford.*

Richard son of John Gregory of Moreton Daubeney, Worc. diocese, to t. of the P. [*sic*] & C. of Abbotsbury.*

John Edden of Barton (*Berton*), Worc. diocese, to t. of the prior of the hospital of St. John of Jerusalem.*

John Wattes of Farmington, Worc. diocese, to t. of patrimony.*

John Schipton of Southwick, Worc. diocese, to t. of the hospital of St. John of Jerusalem.*

Richard Bertlam, r. or administrator of Shell, Worc. diocese, to t. of his chapel.

Hamo, r. of Brereton, Coventry & Lichfield diocese, by l.d. to t. of his church.

John le Graunt of Bibury, Worc. diocese, to t. of the A. & C. of Oseney.*

Aumary (*Almaricus*) le Boteler, r. of Kingston Seymour, Bath & Wells diocese, by l.d. to t. of his church.

M. Walter Beggesworth, r. of Mathon, Worc. diocese, to t. of his church.

John Muleward of Castlett, Worc. diocese, to t. of the P. & C. of St. John of Jerusalem in England.*

Walter Newe of Northway, Worc. diocese, to t. of the P. & C. of St. Margaret's outside the town of Marlborough.*

Walter Itheden of Quenington, Worc. diocese, to t. of the prior of St. John of Jerusalem.*

Thomas le Duk' of Gloucester, within the jurisdiction of Churchdown, by l.d. of the archbishop of York to t. of the P. & C. of St. Oswald's, Gloucester.

William Updich of Bristol, Worc. diocese, to the bishop's title.*

Richard Lovet of Northway, Worc. diocese, to t. of the prior of St. John's hospital by the bridge in Lechlade.*

Roger called 'Ippesleye' of Worc. diocese, to t. of William de Salwarp.*

1065 *18 February 1347 Acolytes ordained on the Sunday before the feast of the Chair of St. Peter [22 February].*

John atte Nelme of Southam.
William Blout of Prestbury.

1066 *24 September 1345 Orders celebrated by the bishop in Campden parish church on the Saturday of Embertide in September.*[1]

Acolyte: Religious

Br. Robert Tryllowe of the order of Preachers.

Acolytes: Secular

Thomas de Leynch Rondulf.   John Gardyner of Kempsford.
John Massy of Quenington.   William Loveryng of
Thomas Massy of Williamstrip.   Farmington.
Walter Chyne of Adlestrop.   John Sampson.
John Pechesleye.   Richard Baroun.
John Hindemon of Aston sub-   Nicholas Margrete of
   Edge.   Saintbury.
Simon Edwart of Thornbury.   Roger Syde of Gloucester.

Subdeacons: Religious

Br. John Wydewyle of the order of Preachers, Warwick.
Br. John de Aston Cantelou, monk of Bordesley.
Br. William Beoulu of the order of Preachers.
Br. Robert de Stouwe, monk of Bruern, of the Cistercian order.

Subdeacons: Secular

M. Peter Gros of Worcester, r. of Suckley, to t. of his church.
Richard de Maiysmor of Worc. diocese, to t. of the house of St. Bartholomew, Gloucester.*
Walter Averey of Adlestrop, Worc. diocese, to t. of the prior of Ivychurch, Salisbury diocese.*
Richard Horlar of Broadwell, Worc. diocese, to t. of Ivychurch, Salisbury diocese.*
Thomas Derby of Bristol, to t. of the P. & C. of the church of the apostles SS. Peter and Paul, Taunton.*

1 *Die Sabbati Quatuor Temporum mensis Septembris.*

20

[Subdeacons: Secular continued.]

Richard de Swelle Inferiori son of Laurence de Condicote to t. of the A. & C. of St. Mary's, Missenden.*

Simon de Tormerton of Worc. diocese, to t. of Ds. John de la Ryvere, knight, which the bishop approved.*

William Heyne of Tysoe, Worc. diocese, to t. of the P. & C. of Chacombe.*

William Jolyf of Rollright (*Roulondifryth*), Lincoln diocese, by l.d. to t. of the P. & C. of Wroxton.

Richard de Hampslap of Tanworth, Worc. diocese, v. of Kempsford, to t. of his vicarage.

Richard son of Nicholas de Eton of Warwick, to t. of his patrimony.*†

John Carpenter of Eatington,¹ to t. of the P. & C. of St. Frideswide's monastery, Oxford.

John de Blocklegh, r. of South Luffenham, by l.d. to t. of his church.

John Clement of South Cerney, to t. of the house of St. John, Lechlade.*

Richard le Clerk of Willersey, to t. of the A. & C. of Alcester, admitted by the bishop's grace. He swore to remain continuously at the Schools for two years and not to proceed to further orders during that time without dispensation.

Roger de Domfreston of Coventry & Lichfield diocese, by l.d. to t. of St. John's hospital, Shrewsbury.

Deacon: Religious

Br. Hugh de Bereford of the order of Preachers, Warwick.

Deacons: Secular

M. Robert de Wygorn', archdeacon of Worcester, to t. of his archdeaconry.

John Webbe of Gloucester, to t. of the A. & C. of Flaxley monastery.*

John Faukes of Quenington, to t. of the hospital of St. John of Jerusalem.*

Nicholas Phelippes of Southrop, Worc. diocese, to t. of St. John's hospital, Lechlade.*

Richard Haywart of Rowell, Worc. diocese, to t. of the P. & C. of St. Frideswide's, Oxford.

John son of Robert de Berkeleye, to t. of patrimony.†

Simon de Southcerneye of Worc. diocese, to t. of the A. & C. of Oseney.*

William Gardiner of Kempsford, to t. of the P. & C. of Amesbury.

Walter Torkeden of Worc. diocese, to t. of the A. & C. of Oseney.

William le Vey of Syde, Worc. diocese, to t. of the A. & C. of St. Augustine's, Bristol.

1 MS. *Etyndon*. Cf. pp. 228, 247.

William le Plomer of Bengeworth, to t. of the P. & C. of Wroxton.
Geoffrey Henr' of Horsley, to t. of the P. & C. of Bruton (*Boruton*).*
John Sale of Moreton Daubeney, Worc. diocese, to t. of the P. & C. of *Swelleshale*.*[1]
William Hychcokes of Holdfast, Worc. diocese, to t. of his patrimony.†
John Lovecok of Aston-on-Carrant, v. of Arlingham, to t. of his vicarage.
John de Stocwell of *Morton*, Worc. diocese, to t. of his patrimony.†
Geoffrey Crysp of Horsley, Worc. diocese, to t. of his patrimony &c.
Richard son of Stephen de Wycheford, to t. of Br. Philip de Tame, prior of St. John of Jerusalem.*

Priests: Religious

Br. Thomas de Schrevenham ⎫
Br. John Lidiȝard   ⎬ canons of Kenilworth.
Br. Henry de Quenton   ⎭
Br. William de Grafton, monk of Pershore.
Br. William Valon   ⎫ of the order of Preachers.
Br. Thomas Evyrischawe   ⎭

Priests: Secular

CHALVESTON. John de Chalveston, r. of South Tawton, Exeter diocese, to t. of his church.
Roger Chasteleyn, r. of Barcheston, to t. of his church.
William son of Richard Jacob of Alderminster (*Aldreston*), Worc. diocese, to t. of the A. & C. of Pershore.
Henry le Palmere of Alderminster, Worc. diocese, to t. of the P. & C. of Studley.
John son of Henry le Schephurde of *Stanton*, to t. of the prior & canons of Cold Norton.
Nicholas de Southam of Worc. diocese, to t. of the collegiate church of St. Mary, Warwick.
Walter Cok of Coln St. Aldwyn, to t. of the prior of St. John of Jerusalem.*
John Rycheyse of [Droit]wich, to t. of his patrimony.*†
William Cokkes of Alcester, to t. of the P. & C. of Studley.*
Thomas Croume, v. of St. Leonard's Bristol, to t. of his vicarage.*
Robert son of John le Mer of Monyhull (*Mokenhull*), Worc. diocese, to t. of the A. & C. of Tewkesbury.*
Thomas de Mersch of Worc. diocese, to t. of the P & C. of Cold Norton.*
Nicholas Bosevyle of Wickham, Worc. diocese, to t. of the A. & C. of Bordesley.*

1 There is no house of this name in Knowles & Hadcock, *Medieval Religious Houses* (1953). Possibly *Snelleshale* (for Snelshall Priory, Bucks.) was intended.

[*Priests: Secular continued.*]

Richard de Longedon, v. of Marshfield, to t. of his vicarage.

Thomas le Swon of Brailes, to t. of the P. & C. of Wroxton.

Robert de Halford of Worc. diocese, to t. of the A. & C. of Oseney.

Richard Poyweke of Worc. diocese, to t. of his patrimony.*†

John Osbern of Chastleton, Lincoln diocese, by l.d. to t. of the A. & C. of Oseney.

Richard Taylour of Weston in Henmarsh, to t. of the P. & C. of Wroxton.

Ralph West of Overbury, to t. of his patrimony.*†

John de Westmancote of Worc. diocese, to t. of the P. & C. of Little Malvern.*

1067 *17 December 1345 Orders celebrated by the bishop in the chapel of Hartlebury Castle on Saturday in Embertide.*

Subdeacons: Religious

Br. William de Steresden of the order of Preachers.

Br. John de Poleye

Br. Robert de Weston

Br. John de Baxterleye   } monks of Merevale, Coventry & Lichfield diocese, by l.d.

Br. Thomas de Hausteleyed

Br. Hugh de Weston

Br. Richard de Conventre   } monks [*sic*] of Lilleshall, by l.d.

Br. William Asttele, canon of Halesowen (*Hales*).

Br. William de Inteberewe of the order of St. Augustine.

Subdeacons: Secular

John Enston of Winchcombe, perpetual v. of Hatherley, Worc. diocese.*

Richard de Clyve of Worc. diocese, to t. of his patrimony.*

Henry de Haukesherd of Coventry & Lichfield diocese, to t. of the P. & C. of Trentham Priory.*

Simon Snow of Hanbury, Worc. diocese, to t. of the D. & C. of Hereford.

Thomas de Syde of Worc. diocese, to t. of the A. & C. of St. Augustine's, Bristol.

John Caluwe of Elmley Lovett, Worc. diocese, to t. of the A. & C. of Halesowen.*

Deacons: Religious

Br. William Lantherne

Br. John Wydemyle

Br. John de Croft   } of the order of Preachers.

Br. William de Hurst

Br. John de Aston of the order of Minorites.
Br. Peter Herde.
Br. William de Tynburhongel, Coventry & Lichfield diocese.
Br. John de Aston, monk of Bordesley.
Br. Thomas de Scheynton ⎫
Br. Walter de Campeden ⎬ monks of Merevale.
Br. Robert de Kerby ⎭

Deacons: Secular

John de Blockelegh, r. of South Luffenham, Lincoln diocese, by l.d.
Roger de Umfreston of Coventry & Lichfield diocese, to t. of St. John's Shrewsbury.*
Roger de Lanleye, r. of Preston-on-the-Weald Moors, Coventry & Lichfield diocese, by l.d. to t. of his church.
John de Lanleye of Coventry & Lichfield diocese, to t. of the house of Wombridge.*
John atte Were of Farmington, Worc. diocese, to t. of his patrimony.*
Richard de Hamslap of Tanworth, v. of Kempsford, to t. of his vicarage.
John Carpinter of Eatington,[1] Worc. diocese, to t. of the prior of St. Frideswide's, Oxford.
William atte Ʒate of Slimbridge, Worc. diocese, to t. of a pension of four marks or patrimony.
John Stilligo, rector of Sparkford, Bath & Wells diocese by l.d.

Priest: Religious

Br. John de Atherston, monk of Merevale.

Priests: Secular

Thomas de Wybaston of Coventry & Lichfield diocese, by l.d. to t. of the house of Lilleshall.*
Richard Heyward of Rowell, Worc. diocese, to t. of the P. & C. of St. Frideswide's.*
M. John Lovecok of Aston-on-Carrant, v. of Arlingham, to t. of his vicarage.
Richard Aleyn of [Droit]wich, to t. of his patrimony.†
Robert Erchebaud of Cirencester, Worc. diocese, to t. of patrimony.
Richard son of Stephen de Wycheford, to t. of Br. Philip de Tame, prior of St. John of Jerusalem.*

1068 *9 March 1343 Acolytes ordained by the bishop in his chapel at Withington.*

Br. Richard de Haukesbury ⎫
⎬ monks of Pershore.
Br. William Lydene ⎭

1 MS. *Etyndon.* See p. 240 n.1.

1069 *11 March 1346 Orders celebrated by the bishop in Hartlebury parish church on the Saturday of Embertide in the first week of Lent.*[1]

Acolytes: Religious

Br. Geoffrey Lambert ⎱
Br. Richard de Forde ⎰ of the order of Carmelites.

Br. Thomas Wanertre ⎱
Br. Thomas Bosedone ⎰ of the order of Friars Minor.

Acolytes: Secular

Nicholas son of Alan de Doddeleye.
John atte Mulle of *Wilmeston*.
William atte Pole of Dudley.
John Rotteley junior of Tysoe.
Nicholas Frankeleyn of Barcheston.
John in the Hoerne of Preston-on-Stour.
John Gorgan of Rissington (*Rusyndon*).
Thomas de la Lowe of Hampton Lovett.
Thomas Birmyngham of Dudley.
John Rotteley senior of Tysoe.
Walter Aylemer of Cirencester.
Nicholas Pule of Craycombe (*Craucombe*).[2]
Walter le Ram of Fladbury.
Thomas Pymme of Tysoe.
Richard ȝely of Norton.
William Waryn of Alscot.
John Pupplynton senior.
John Pupplynton junior.
Alexander Derhurst.
William Couk of Peopleton.
John Wariner of Peopleton.
John Hugon of Fladbury.
Adam Karles, r. of the third portion of St. Nicholas' church, Warwick.

Subdeacons: Religious

Br. Thomas de Leye.
Br. Thomas de Salop.
Br. Richard de Doddeleye.
Br. Thomas de Bannebur'.
Br. Richard de Cherhull.
Br. Warin de Longusperey.
Br. Roger Wrighinton.

Br. John de Aylesbur' of the order of Minorites.
Br. Thomas de Coule.
Br. John de Brackele, by l.d.
Br. George de Hamptonet, by l.d.

1 *Die Sabbati Quatuor Temporum in prima ebdomada Quadragesime.*
2 In Fladbury.

Subdeacons: Secular

John le Cok of Cleeve, Worc. diocese, to t. of the A. & C. of Eynsham.*

Richard son of Simon Dragon of [Droit]wich, to t. of his patrimony.*†

Henry de Herlaston of Coventry & Lichfield diocese, by l.d. to t. of the master and brethren of the Maison Dieu (*domus Dei*), Dover.

Henry le Vissher of Gloucester, Worc. [diocese], to t. of the house of St. Bartholomew there.*

John Frankeloyn of Quinton, Worc. diocese, to t. of the A. & C. of Alcester.*

William Watekote of Worc. diocese, to t. of the house of the P. & C. Wroxton.*

John son of Robert le Taylour of Tysoe, Worc. diocese, to t. of the P. & C. of Wroxton.*

John Bele of Prestbury, Worc. diocese, to t. of his patrimony.*

Robert Honynton of Worc. diocese, to t. of the house of Bicester.

Thomas Colemon of Worc. diocese, to t. of the A. & C. of Eynsham.*

Richard le Coupare of Coventry & Lichfield diocese, by l.d. to t. of the A. & C. of Hulton.*

William Henr' of Coventry & Lichfield diocese, by l.d. to t. of the P. & C. of Trentham.*

James son of John Hobbes of Bushley (*Bissheleye*), to t. of his patrimony.*

Adam de Bradewell of Worc. diocese, to t. of the monastery of St. Mary, Merton.*

Robert de Henynton of Worc. diocese, to t. of the P. & C. of Bicester.*

Thomas Sybille of Woollashill, Worc. diocese, to t. of patrimony.*

Thomas Basset of Lichfield, Coventry & Lichfield diocese, to t. of St. John the Baptist's, Lichfield.

Matthew le Wodare of Worc. diocese, to t. of the P. & C. of Little Malvern.

William Thorald of Warwick, r. of Ashow (*Assheso*), Coventry & Lichfield diocese, by l.d.

Elias atte Croye of Minchinhampton, Worc. diocese, to t. of the P. & C. of Llanthony next Gloucester.

Deacons: Religious

Br. John de Vyse.

Br. Thomas Marleberge of Great Malvern.

Br. Gilbert de Brayles of Lincoln diocese, by l.d.

Br. John Burbache.

Br. Richard Fayrclogh.

Br. Thomas de Brannseford.

Richard de Strengesham.[1]

Stephen de Tettebur'.

John de Flore.

Thomas de Roddeleye.

Br. Thomas de Bokyngham.

1 Richard and the next three ordinands are not entitled *Frater*.

Deacons: Secular

Philip Tyrel of Worc. diocese, to t. of the house of Lechlade by the bishop's special grace.

Simon Snow of Worc. diocese [to t.] of the D. & C. of Hereford.

Adam Laurence of Pendock, Worc. diocese, to t. of the house of Llanthony Prima.

Walter Weer' of Worc. diocese, to t. of the house of Llanthony Prima.

John son of William le Swon of Eldersfield, Worc. diocese, to t. of patrimony.

Henry Haukeshert of *Ston'* (Stone?), Coventry & Lichfield diocese, by l.d. to t. of the priory of Trentham.*

Richard de Mayesmor of Worc. diocese, to t. of the prior & brethren of St. Bartholomew's, Gloucester.*

Robert le Somenour of Windrush (*Wenrich*), Worc. diocese, to t. of his patrimony.

Walter Averey of Adlestrop (*Tadelesthorp*), to t. of the monastery of Ivychurch.*

Simon de Tormerton of Worc. diocese, to t. of Ds. John de Ryver', knight.*

Richard de Chantmond of Bishops Cleeve, Worc. diocese, to t. of patrimony.*

John Odynton of Worc. diocese, to t. of the A. & C. of Oseney.*

Thomas Syde of Worc. diocese, to t. of the A. & C. of St. Augustine's, Bristol.*

Richard Horlar of Broadwell, Worc. diocese, to t. of the P. & C. of Ivychurch.*

Robert de Venables of Coventry & Lichfield diocese, by l.d. to t. of the A. & C. of Hulton.

Richard de Swelle Inferiori, to t. of the monastery of St. Mary, Missenden.*

William atte Halle of Shenington, Worc. diocese, to t. of the house of Wroxton.

Robert Ward of Wyre Piddle (*Wyrpidele*), Worc. diocese, to t. of his patrimony.

John Clement of South Cerney, Worc. diocese, to t. of the prior & brethren of St. John's hospital, Lechlade.*

Adam Dod of Eatington (*Edyndon*), Worc. diocese, to t. of the P. & C. of Caldwell.*

William Hauthorn of Eatington, Worc. diocese, to t. of the P. & C. of Chacombe.*

William de Wollynton of Worc. diocese, to t. of St. Wulstan's hospital, Worcester.*

Priests: Religious

Br. William de Tymberhongle, *monk of Southwell*,[1] Coventry & Lichfield diocese, by l.d.

1 MS. *monachus de Southwell* (interlin.). But 'Sandwell' must have been intended. Cf. p. 236.

Br. William de Busseleye of
  Great Malvern.
Br. Thomas de Meston'.
Br. Robert de Glouc'.
Br. William Murimouth.
Br. Richard de Wylfreton.

Br. Peter de Wygorn'.
Br. Richard de Bromlegh.
Br. William Cauk.
Br. William Laȝharn.
Br. Hugh Berford.
Br. William de Mees.

Priests: Secular

John le Carpenter of Eatington,[1] Worc. diocese, to t. of the P. & C. of St. Frideswide's, Oxford.

Roger de Umfreston of Lincoln diocese, v. of St. Cross, Shrewsbury, by l.d.

William le Bakere of Grendon, Lincoln diocese, to t. of the P. & C. of Wroxton by l.d.

Henry Steyn of Lincoln diocese, to t. of the house & convent of Sulby (*Sulleby*), by l.d.

William le Gardener of Worc. diocese, to t. of the P. & C. of Amesbury.

Ds. Roger de Laneleye of Coventry & Lichfield diocese, r. of Preston-on-the-Weald Moors, to t. of his church.

William de Asshebourne of Coventry & Lichfield diocese, by l.d. to t. of the house of Ronton.*

William le Plomer of Bengeworth, Worc. diocese, to t. of the P. & C. of Wroxton.*

Geoffrey Crysp of Horsley, Worc. diocese, to t. of his patrimony.

Geoffrey son of Henry de Horseleye, to t. of the P. & C. of Bruton.

William le Vey of Syde, Worc. diocese, to t. of the A. & C. of St. Augustine's, Bristol.

John le Hopare of *Stannton*, to t. of the house of Cold Norton.*

John de Lech' of Coventry & Lichfield diocese, by l.d. to t. of the house of Trentham.

Edmund de Steventon of Coventry & Lichfield diocese, to t. of the house of Trentham.*

Roger atte Nelme of Dursley, Worc. diocese, to t. of patrimony.*

Thomas Brouwet of Little Comberton, to t. of the P. & C. of Cold Norton.

Richard de Hamslamp, v. of Kempsford, to t. of his vicarage.

John son of Robert de Benynton of Worc. diocese, to t. of patrimony.*

William atte Ȝate of Slimbridge, to t. of his patrimony.

John atte Were of Farmington, Worc. diocese, to t. of his patrimony.*

John de Neuwynham of Lincoln diocese, by l.d. to t. of the priory of Daventry &c.

John de Blockele, r. of Luffenham, Lincoln diocese, to t. of his church.

1 MS. *Odynton.* Cf. p. 243 n.1.

1070 *1 April 1346 Orders celebrated by the bishop in the chapel of Hartlebury Castle.*[1]

Subdeacons: Religious

Br. Hugh de Clone of the order of Minorites.
Br. Thomas de Wanertre, of the same order.

Subdeacon: Secular

Walter Lutulton of South Littleton, to t. of the A. & C. of Bordesley.

Deacon: Religious

Br. Robert Trillowe of the order of Preachers.

Deacons: Secular

John Enston of Winchcombe, v. of Hatherley, to t. of his vicarage.
Nicholas le Mey, to t. of the P. & C. of [St.] Frideswide's monastery, Oxford, which remains *penes registrum.*
Henry le Vischer of Gloucester, to t. of St. Bartholomew's hospital, Gloucester.*

Priests: Religious

Br. Thomas de F[?]elford of the order of Minorites.
Br. Thomas de Malmeshulle, monk of Winchcombe.

Priest: Secular [2]

Thomas Syde, to t. of the A. & C. of St. Augustine's, Bristol, which remains *penes registrum.*

1071 *15 April 1346 Orders celebrated by the bishop in Hartlebury parish church on Holy Saturday.*

Subdeacons: Secular

M. Richard de Elyndon of Salisbury diocese, to t. of the house of Merton in Oxford by l.d.
Walter Laurence, r. of Hope, Canterbury diocese, by l.d.
John Boreford of Stow, to t. of his patrimony.*

Deacons: Secular

M. Richard de Birmyngham of Idlicote, to t. of his church.
James son of John de Bysscheley of Worc. diocese, to t. of his patrimony.*

1 *Die Sabbati qua cantatur officium 'Scicientes'.*
2 MS. *presbiteri seculares.*

John de Northburgth, r. of Chesterton, Coventry & Lichfield diocese, by l.d.

Richard son of Nicholas de Etone of Warwick, our [*sic*] diocese, to t. of his patrimony.*

Priests: Religious

Br. William de Chedle of the order of Preachers.

Br. William Foleville, monk of Pershore.

Priests: Secular

M. John de Lychelade, r. of Ludgershall, Lincoln diocese, by l.d.

M. William Heghtredebury of Salisbury diocese, to t. of the house of Merton in Oxford by l.d.

Ds. John de Bokyngham, r. of Sutton Coldfield, Coventry & Lichfield diocese, by l.d.

Roger Palmere, deacon, to t. of M. John de Logardyn by the bishop's grace. From Hereford diocese.[1]

Henry le Visshere of Gloucester.

1072 *10 June 1346 Orders celebrated by the bishop in the conventual church of Tewkesbury on Saturday in Embertide.*

Acolytes: Religious

Br. Peter Roos ⎫
Br. Hugh Cleobur' ⎬ of the order of St. Augustine.

Br. John de Bretonia of the order of Preachers.

Br. Thomas Whitteneie, canon of Cold Norton, Lincoln diocese, by l.d.

Acolytes: [Secular]

John Shaterel of Uley.

John Harries of Throckmorton.

John de Calmondesden of North Cerney.

William Sweyn of Bibury.

Richard Hobkyns of Throckmorton.

Henry Taillour of Sherborne.

John Sweyn of Bibury.

John Sampson of Wick (*Wyk*).

Nicholas Stemene of Newbold Pacey.

Henry Colet of Birlingham.

John Botiller of Shipton.

Robert Faulor of Newbold Pacey.

Thomas de Sonnebury.

---

1 *de gracia domini Hereford' dioc.*

[*Acolytes: Secular continued.*]

Simon Jones of Toddington.
William Spellesbur' of Elmley.
Robert Upcote.
John Kittone of Maugersbury.
Geoffrey Herberd of Moreton [in-the-Marsh] (*Mortone*).
William Harryis of Maugersbury.
Walter Brok of Brailes.
Thomas de Pixstok, r. of Grendon, Coventry & Lichfield diocese, by l.d.
Henry Bonetonm.
John Polle.
William atte Ȝate.
Geoffrey Calwe of Charlecote.
Geoffrey de Garsinton of Bibury.
Roger de Doudeswelle.
William de Welford.
Richard Fremon of Slaughter.
John Simondes of Frampton-on-Severn.
Peter Lenyot of Upton-on-Severn.
William Machonn of Upton.
Thomas Amiger of Ampney Crucis.
John Wylcher of Severn Stoke.
William Maiel of Wick [by Pershore] (*Wyk*).
Thomas Grimbale of *grewe*.[1]
Henry Brut of Ampney.
Thomas Irisch of Fladbury.
Oliver Hoteknassh.
John Hymynton.
John Deiere of Dursley *ca. de Dis.* [*sic*].[2]
John Willy of Bibury.
Richard Hunte of Kineton (*Kyngton, exced' tamen* [*sic*]).
John Michel of Strensham.
William Aston of Sedgeberrow.
John Keys of Winchcombe.
John Boun of South Cerney.
William Monymouth of Gloucester.
Henry de Bristoll' of Fairford.
Walter Beteld of Piddle (*Pidele*).
John atte Halle of Sherborne.
William atte Broke of *Stannton*.
Richard Byge of Hawkesbury.
Richard de Muluere of Ampney.
Walter atte Hulle of Kempsford.

1 The scribe has written small 'g', but 'a' was probably intended for *Arewe* [Arrow].
2 Probably for 'chantry of Dursley'. See p. 258.

William Cole of Ampney.
Adam Dawe of Luddington.
Walter Thurkel of Powick.
Robert Gorge of Ampney.
John Hatterere of Besford.
William de Wolde of Stafford, Coventry & Lichfield diocese, by l.d.
Walter Stormy of Charlton [*Cherlenton*].
Thomas Greetere of Lench.
Thomas Coventr' of Eatington.
Thomas Michel of [Droit]wich.

Subdeacons: Religious

Br. Thomas de Bossedon of the order of Minorites.
Br. John de Cyrencestr' ⎫
Br. William de Haukesbury ⎬ monks of Kingswood.
Br. Thomas de Barton of the order of Preachers.
Br. John de Wolneye of the order of Minorites.
Br. William de Lega ⎫
Br. Geoffrey de Wasschebourne ⎬ monks of Hailes.
Br. Walter de Bachesouere, monk of Bruern.
Br. John de Castelton, canon of Cold Norton, Lincoln diocese, by l.d.
Br. John de la Sowthe, canon of Studley.
Br. William de Martherne ⎫
Br. Henry Strode ⎬ canons of St. Augustine's, Bristol.
Br. Thomas Marches of the order of St. Augustine.
Br. William de Foxcote ⎫
Br. Nicholas de Sterdesdene ⎬ monks of Gloucester.
Br. John de Compton ⎭
Br. John de Stone, monk of Merevale, Coventry & Lichfield diocese, by l.d.

Subdeacons: Secular

Richard de Sibford of Worc. diocese, to t. of the P. & C. of Wroxton.*
Robert Baner of Hatherop, Worc. diocese, to t. of the monastery of St. Mary, Keynsham.*
Richard Morewy of *Staunton*, Worc. diocese, to t. of Philip de Tame, prior of the hospital of St. John of Jerusalem in England.*
John son of Henry Lodebrok of Shenington, to t. of the P. & C. of Wroxton.*
Nicholas Dyngalt of Tysoe, Worc. diocese, to t. of the P. & C. of Caldwell, Lincoln diocese.
John son of Roger Hydemon of Aston sub-Edge, Worc. diocese, to t. of patrimony.

[*Subdeacons: Secular continued.*]

Thomas Pymme of Compton, Worc. diocese, to t. of the P. & C. of Wroxton.

Reginald le Fischare of Birlingham, to t. of St. Michael's hospital, Warwick.*

John le Clerk son of John le Clerk of Cowley (*Coueleye*), to t. of patrimony.*

William atte Watere of Ampney, to t. of the A. & C. of Godstow.

Richard Jones of Eatington, to t. of the A. & C. of Darley.*

William Lodynton of Compton, to t. of the P. & C. of Caldwell.*

Richard de la Hulle of Yardley, to t. of the A. & C. of Alcester.

William le Wodeward of Hanley, to t. of the P. & C. of Little Malvern.

John Wade of Coventry & Lichfield diocese, to t. of the A. & C. of Hulton.

William Diare of Cirencester, to t. of the P. & C. of St. Frideswide's, Oxford.

Robert Caperon of Horsley, Worc. diocese, to t. of the P. & C. of Bruton.*

John Edward, r. of Siddington, Worc. diocese, to t. of his church.*

Henry Symondes of Arlington (*Alrintone*), to t. of the A. & C. of Oseney.*

John Huwet [of] Bourton, to t. of the bishop's grace.

John Wyet of *Newenton*, by the bishop's wish.

Thomas son of Ralph de Inteberg of Warwick, to t. of the D. & C. of the collegiate church of St. Mary, Warwick, on the bishop's mandate.

Robert Gret Orle of Coventry & Lichfield diocese, by l.d. to t. of the P. & C. of Farewell.*

Robert Bate of Bishops Cleeve, to t. of the A. & C. of St. Augustine's monastery, Bristol.*

Adam Carles, r. of the third part of St. Nicholas', Warwick, to t. of his portion.*

John de Cheltenham of Worc. diocese, to t. of his patrimony, which on the oath of the dean of Pershore is worth 20s. a year and more.

John Wyget of Meon (*Mene*), to t. of the A. & C. of Alcester by the bishop's grace.

Deacons: Religious

Br. Thomas de Bannebur'   } canons of Wroxton, Lincoln diocese,
Br. Richard de Chirhull   }   by l.d.
Br. Thomas de Aston of the Cistercian order, from Bordesley.
Br. John de Pole[ye]   ⎫
Br. Robert de Weston   ⎬ monks of Merevale.
Br. John de Baxterleye   ⎪
Br. Thomas de Austele   ⎭

Br. Philip de Doune, monk of Combermere, Coventry & Lichfield diocese.

Br. Hugh de Saunderton ⎫
Br. Richard de Bensynton ⎬ canons of Cirencester.
Br. Robert de Wotton ⎭

Br. Hugh de Clone ⎫
Br. Roger de Writhtinton ⎬ of the order of Minorites.

Br. Thomas de Legh of the order of Minorites, from the Coventry convent.

Br. William de Steresdene ⎫
Br. Griffin Vaghan ⎬ of the order of Preachers.

Br. Robert de Stowe, monk of Bruern.

Br. Richard de Merewell, monk of Beaulieu, by l.d.

Deacons: Secular

Matthew Wodere of Worc. diocese, to t. of the P. & C. of Little Malvern.

Thomas Hyde of Aldsworth, Worc. diocese, to t. of the P. & C. of Llanthony Prima.

Elyas atte Crois of Minchinhampton, Worc. diocese, to t. of the P. & C. of Llanthony next Gloucester.

William Thorald of Warwick, r. of Ashow, Coventry & Lichfield diocese by l.d.

Adam de Bradewell of Worc. diocese, to t. of the prior of St. Mary's, Merton.

John son of William Wanere of Killingworth, Lincoln diocese, by l.d. of the A. & C. of Sulby.

John Boreuord of Stow, Worc. diocese, to t. of his patrimony.

John Colemon of Winchcombe, Worc. diocese, to t. of the A. & C. of Eynsham.

Richard Dragoun of [Droit]wich, to t. of patrimony.

John Fraunkelyn of Quinton, Worc. diocese, to t. of the A. & C. of Alcester.

William Whatcote of Tysoe, Worc. diocese, to t. of the P. & C. of Wroxton.

William Heyne of Tysoe, Worc. diocese, to t. of the P. & C. of Chacombe.

Robert Jay of Honington, Worc. diocese, to t. of the P. & C. of Bicester, Lincoln diocese.

Hugh atte Mulle of Ampney Crucis, Worc. diocese, to t. of the P. & C. of St. Oswald's, Gloucester.

Walter de Lutleton of South Littleton in the jurisdiction of Evesham, by l.d. to t. of the A. & C. of Bordesley.

John Cok of Cleeve, Worc. diocese, to t. of the A. & C. of Eynsham.

Thomas Derby of Bristol, Worc. diocese, to t. of the P. & C. of St. Peter & St. Paul's church, Taunton.

Priests: Religious

Br. Gilbert de Brailes of Wroxton, by l.d.
Br. Thomas de Sheynton ⎫
Br. Walter de Campeden ⎬ monks of Merevale, by l.d.
Br. Robert de Kerby ⎭
Br. Nicholas Costart, monk of Astley priory, Worc. diocese.
Br. John Croft of the order of Preachers.
Br. William Orle of the order of Minorites.
Br. John de Shipton, monk of Bruern.
Br. Richard de Pershore, canon of Cold Norton, Lincoln diocese, by l.d.
Br. Simon Evesham, canon of Studley.
Br. Richard de Wygorn'.
Br. William de Fechirby of the order of St. Augustine.
Br. Henry de Wotton ⎫
Br. John de Lech ⎬ monks of Gloucester.

Priests: Secular

Robert le Somenour of Windrush (*Wynrych*), Worc. diocese, to t. of his patrimony.*
Walter Averey of Adlestrop, Worc. diocese, to t. of the prior of Ivychurch.*
Richard son of Nicholas de Etone of Warwick, to t. of his patrimony.*
Richard Chantmond of Bishops Cleeve, to t. of patrimony.*
John Clement of South Cerney, to t. of the prior & brethren of St. John's hospital, Lechlade.
Simon Snow of Hanbury, Worc. diocese, to t. of the D. & C. of Hereford.*
Richard le Horlare of Broadwell, to t. of Ivychurch monastery.*
John de Odynton of Worc. diocese, to t. of the A. & C. of Oseney.*
Henry Haukeshert of Coventry & Lichfield diocese, to t. of the house of Trentham.*
William atte Halle of Shenington, to t. of the P. & C. of Wroxton.*
Adam Dod of Eatington, Worc. diocese, to t. of the P. & C. of Caldwell, Lincoln diocese.
John Sale of Moreton Daubeney, to t. of the A. & C. of St. James' outside Northampton.
John Stokwell of *Morton*, to t. of his patrimony.
James son of John Hobbes of Bushley (*Bischeleye*), to t. of his patrimony.
Robert Ward of Wyre Piddle, to t. of his patrimony.*
Adam Laurence of Pendock, to t. of the P. & C. of Llanthony Prima.
Henry Budel of Eccleshall, Coventry & Lichfield diocese, to t. of the P. & C. of Ronton by l.d.
Walter Turkedene, to t. of the A. & C. of Oseney

Robert de Swelle Inferiori, to t. of the A. & C. of Missenden.*

William de Wollynton, to t. of the master & brethren of St. Wulstan's hospital, Worcester diocese.

Nicholas Philippes of Southrop, to t. of St. John's hospital, Lechlade.*

Robert le Yunge of Coventry & Lichfield diocese, to t. of the house of Repton by l.d.

M. John de Northburgh of Coventry & Lichfield diocese, r. of Chesterton, by l.d.

Richard Webbester of Prescott, Coventry & Lichfield diocese, by l.d. to t. of the house of *Comberton.*[1]

John Enston of Winchcombe, perpetual v. of Hatherley parish church, Worc. diocese.

Thomas Cornyale of Coventry & Lichfield diocese, to t. of the house of Merevale.

John Taverner of Llandaff (*Land'*) diocese, by l.d. to t. of the A. & C. of Margam.

Thomas Mountestevene of Bristol, Worc. diocese, to t. of his patrimony.*

1073 *23 September 1346 Orders celebrated by the bishop in Stow parish church.*

Acolytes: Secular

Walter Bradewell.
Richard Bradewell.
William de Tatlesthorp.
Robert Lynham of Aylburton.
Nicholas Trentham of Tysoe.
Richard Hughe of Stanton.
William de Couleye.
Thomas de Ryndecumbe.
John atte Welle of Iccomb.
Elias Iccumbe.
John de Iccumbe.
Walter Leche of Stow.
William West of Chelmscote.
William Botyler of Farmington.
John Botyler of the same.
John Spyrie.
Ralph Templer of Broadwell.
Henry de Aston sub Egge.
John Brouwene of Rollright (*Roullandrych*), Lincoln diocese, by l.d.
Robert Nichol of Prestbury.

1 *Recte* Combermere.

21

[*Acolytes: Secular continued.*]

John Roys of Tysoe.
Thomas Pers of Chedworth.
William Harries of *Burton.*
John Hobbekynes of Stow.
Thomas le Roo of Farmington.
John de Weston, r. of Alderley, Coventry & Lichfield diocese, by l.d.
Thomas le Longe of Oddington.
John Skernyng' of Cirencester (*Cyr'*).
Thomas Benet.
John Colynes of Kempsford.
William Clyfford.
John London of Oxhill.
John Martyn of Bourton.
John Longeberg'.
Richard de Pynthrop'.
John Muluwart of Rissington.
Henry de Cheddeworth.
Elias de Weston.
Nicholas Haumond of Rissington.
Robert de Aston, r. of Wroxton, *de Marteldenan*[1] [*sic*], by l.d.
John Hassok of Norton Lindsey.
Thomas Aston.
John le Smyth of Barrington.
William Mathw of the same.
Kenelm Russel of Compton.
Geoffrey Stok of Ampney Crucis.
John Harryes of Coln St. Dennis.
John Payn of Thornbury.
Walter Dombelton.
John Dombelton.
John Haukyn of Oddington.
William Crem of Broadwell.
John le Roo of Farmington.
Edmund de Kyngton.
Adam Barth' of Llandaff diocese, by l.d.
Thomas de Kenemerton, warden (*custos*) of the chantry of Elmley
Castle, to t. of his chantry.
Walter Anketyl of *Horleye*, Coventry & Lichfield diocese, by l.d.
John Jones of Dodwell.
Roger Kyng' of Winchcombe.
William Medewey of Bristol.
Stephen Sloghthr'.
John Gyffart of Alderton.

1 Mitcheldean.

John Grayel of Slimbridge.
William Sissor of Slimbridge.
Thomas Caldecote.
Geoffrey de Bourton.
John Reod of Badminton.
Robert Cartere of Rissington.
William atte Mulne of Sherborne.
John Oxschulve.
Henry Abraham of Aston.
William de Alyncestr'.
John Barat of Beverstone.
John Paunteleye of Northleach.
Robert Navesby of Longborough[?] (*Longeb'*).

Acolytes: Religious

Br. Alan de Neuwton ⎫
Br. John de Bromhale ⎬ canons of Norton, Coventry & Lichfield
Br. William de Dutton ⎪ diocese, by l.d.
Br. Ralph de Dostok ⎭
Br. Peter Pendok ⎫
Br. Hugh de Leomunstrera ⎬ monks of Pershore.
Br. John Baleshale ⎪
Br. Geoffrey Somerton ⎭
Br. Thomas de Tame of the order of Carmelites.
Br. Thomas Freolond of the order of Preachers.
Br. John Sanborne, monk of Combe, Coventry & Lichfield diocese,
by l.d.
Br. Simon de Hosyntr' of the order of Minorites.
Br. Thomas de Coberlegh of the order of Carmelites.
Br. Stephen de Sutton of the order of Carmelites.
Br. John de Gloucestr' of the order of Minorites.
Br. Matthew de Euwyas, monk of Dieulacresse monastery, Coventry
& Lichfield diocese, by l.d.
Br. Roger de Hynham ⎫ canons of Kenilworth, Lincoln diocese
Br. John de Whytechurch ⎬ [*sic* for 'Coventry & Lichfield'],
⎭ by l.d.

Subdeacons: Religious

Br. Nicholas de Worthyn ⎫ monks of Shrewsbury, Coventry &
Br. Thomas de Lega ⎭ Lichfield diocese, by l.d.
Br. Thomas Pyk of the order of Carmelites.
Br. Thomas de Sobbury, monk of Kingswood, Worc. diocese.
Br. Thomas de Stone, monk of Dieulacresse, Coventry & Lichfield
diocese, by l.d.
Br. William de Merston ⎫ canons of Kenilworth, Coventry &
Br. Walter de Cherleton ⎭ Lichfield diocese, by l.d.

[*Subdeacons: Religious continued.*]

Br. Philip Hastyng' of the order of Minorites.

Br. John Mede of the order of Preachers.

Br. William Boclonde of the order of Preachers.

Br. John Rokele of the order of Preachers.

Br. William de Herberbury, monk of Combe, Coventry & Lichfield diocese, by l.d.

Br. Thomas de Whyteneye, canon of Cold Norton, Lincoln diocese, by l.d.

Subdeacons: Secular

William Swayn of Bibury, Worc. diocese, to t. of the A. & C. of Oseney.*

Robert Pardu of Snitterfield, to t. of the P. & C. of Studley.*

John le Dyȝare of Dursley, to t. of the perpetual chantry of St. Mary in Dursley parish church.

William Pynchepol of Windrush, Worc. diocese, to t. of his patrimony.*†

John son of William Dorne of Wick Rissington, Worc. diocese, to t. of the A. & C. of Eynsham.*

John Spaldyng of London diocese, to t. of the P. & C. of St. Frideswide's, Oxford.

Henry de Bourton of Worc. diocese, to t. of the P. & C. of St. Frideswide's, Oxford.

Ds. Edmund Rossel, r. of Peopleton, Worc. diocese, to t. of his church.

John Doukan of Cirencester, Worc. diocese, to t. of Br. Philip de Tame, prior of the hospital of St. John in England.

John Bykelonde of Worc. diocese, to t. of the house of Bordesley.*

Richard Flete of Holt, to t. of the P. & C. of Studley.

William Claynes of Worcester, to t. of the P. & C. of Kington.*

John Huwes of Blockley, to t. of the A. & C. of Eynsham.*

William Barbour of Pershore, to t. of his patrimony.†

William Fremon of Lighthorne, to t. of the P. & C. of Chacombe.*

Walter Clerk of Farmcote, to t. of the P. & C. of [St.] Frideswide's, Oxford.*

Matthew atte Ȝeate of Dursley, to t. of his patrimony.*†

John Adam of Honeybourne, to t. of the A. & C. of Oseney.

William Grafton of Eatington, to t. of the house of Wroxton.*

Simon Bakere of Wellesbourne, to t. of the P. & C. of Studley.*

Richard Crossun of Little Barrington, Worc. diocese, to t. of the A. & C. of Eynsham.

Richard Synteleye of Holt, to t. of his patrimony.†

Deacons: Religious

Br. William de Martene ⎱
Br. Henry de Strode   ⎰ canons of St. Augustine's, Bristol.

Br. John de Chastelton, monk [*sic*] of Cold Norton, Lincoln diocese, by l.d.

Br. Roger Barre of the order of Minorites.

Br. John de Melton of the order of Carmelites.

Br. Walter de Bachesouere, monk of Bruern, Lincoln diocese.

Br. Richard de Lynterworth, monk of Combe, Coventry & Lichfield diocese, by l.d.

Br. Nicholas de Ichynton ⎫
Br. Thomas de Bekynhull ⎬ canons of Maxstoke, Coventry & Lichfield diocese, by l.d.
Br. Roger de Byrmyngham ⎭

Br. William de Aston, monk of Stoneleigh, Coventry & Lichfield diocese, by l.d.

Br. John de Harscumbe of the order of Preachers.

Br. George de Morton, canon of Ashby, Lincoln diocese, by l.d.

Br. John Wolneye of the order of Minorites.

Br. John de Cirenc', monk of Kingswood.

Br. William de Haukesbury, monk of the same place.

Br. William de Bybury of the order of Preachers.

Br. John de la Southe, canon of Studley.

Deacons: Secular

Nicholas Dyngalt of Tysoe, to t. of the P. & C. of Caldwell, Lincoln diocese.*

John Stareton of Coventry & Lichfield diocese, to t. of the A. & C. of Stoneleigh by l.d.*

Robert Bate of Bishops Cleeve, Worc. diocese, to t. of the A. & C. of St. Augustine's, Bristol.

William atte Watre of Ampney Crucis, to t. of the A. & C. of Godstow.*

Richard Morewy of *Stanton*, Worc. diocese, to t. of the hospital of St. John of Jerusalem.

John Huwet of Bourton, to t. of the A. & C. of St. James outside Northampton.

Simon Potel of Maidenwell, Lincoln diocese, by l.d. to t. of the A. & C. of St. Mary de la Pré (*de Pratis*) outside Northampton.*

John son of Roger Hydemon of Aston sub-Edge, to t. of patrimony.†

Robert Caperon of Horsley, to t. of the P. & C. of Bruton (*Druton sic*).*

William le Wodewart of Hanley, to t. of the P. & C. of Little Malvern.*

William le Dyȝar of Cirencester, to t. of the P. & C. of St. Frideswide's monastery, Oxford.

John Bele of Prestbury, to t. of his patrimony.†

Richard Underwode of Farndon, Lincoln diocese, by l.d. to t. of the P. & C. of Daventry.*

[*Deacons: secular continued.*]

William Jolyf of Rollright, Lincoln diocese, to t. of the P. & C. of Wroxton by l.d.*

Richard Sibbeforde of Worc. diocese, to t. of the A. & C. of Wroxton by l.d.

William Lodyngton of Compton, to t. of the P. & C. of Caldwell.*

David Basselek of Llandaff diocese, to t. of the A. & C. of *Derlyma* by l.d.

John son of John le Clerk of Cowley, Worc. diocese, to t. of his patrimony.

Robert Baner of Hatherop, to t. of the A. & C. of Keynsham.*

Thomas Sibill of Woollashill, to t. of his patrimony.*

Henry Symont of Arlington (*Aluyrinton*), Worc. diocese, to t. of the A. & C. of Dorchester.*

John Wygot of Meon, to t. of the A. & C. of Alcester.*

John de Chyltenham, to t. of his patrimony.*

Richard de Leye, r. of Castle Eaton (*Eton Meysy*), Salisbury diocese, by l.d. to t. of his church.

Adam Carles, r. of a third part of St. Nicholas' church, Warwick, to t. of his part.

Thomas son of Ralph de Inteberg' of Warwick, to t. of the D. & C. of St. Mary's collegiate church, Warwick.

John Smyth of *Breulton*, Lichfield diocese, by l.d. to t. of the P. & C. of Daventry.

Robert le Hunte of Kineton (*Kyngton*), to t. of the prior of the hospital of St. John of Jerusalem.*

William de Penynton of Coventry & Lichfield diocese, to t. of the A. & C. of Lilleshall.*

John le Yonge of Breinton, Hereford diocese, to t. of the house of St. Bartholomew, Gloucester, by l.d.*

Priests: Religious

Br. Thomas de Lodebrok ⎫
Br. John de Stanton ⎪
Br. William de Steresden ⎬ all of the order of Preachers.
Br. John Rychard ⎭

Br. Ralph de Trentham ⎫ canons of Trentham, Coventry &
Br. Henry de Aston ⎬ Lichfield diocese, by l.d.

Br. Roger Wrightinton of the order of Minorites.

Br. Hugh de Clone of the same order.

Br. William de Cirenc' ⎫
Br. Robert de Stouwe ⎬ monks of Bruern, by l.d.

Br. Hugh de Beole, canon of Kenilworth, Coventry & Lichfield diocese, by l.d.

Br. Roger Clodeshal of the order of Minorites.

Br. Thomas de Couele, of the hospital of SS. James & John, Brackley, by l.d.

Br. Thomas de Aston, monk of Kingswood, Worc. diocese.

Br. William Keynesham of the order of Carmelites.

Br. Richard Boydel of the order of Preachers.

Br. Stephen de Alyncestr' ⎫
Br. John de Aston ⎭ monks of Bordesley.

Br. John Bradenham of the order of Minorites.

Br. Roger Wentebrigg ⎫
Br. John de Wotton ⎪
Br. John de Teynton ⎬ monks of Coventry, by l.d.
Br. John de Foxton ⎭

Br. Thomas de Bannebury ⎫ canons of Wroxton, Lincoln
Br. Richard de Cherchehulle ⎭ diocese, by l.d.

Priests: Secular

John Boreuorde of Stow, to t. of patrimony.*

Richard de Clyfford, r. of Dudleston, Coventry & Lichfield diocese, to t. of his church.

John Webbe of Gloucester, to t. of the A. & C. of Flaxley, Hereford diocese, by l.d.

Geoffrey Wygynton of Coventry & Lichfield diocese, by l.d. to t. of the house of Burton (*Bourton*).

William Hychekok of Holdfast, Worc. diocese, to t. of his patrimony.*

William Torald, r. of Ashow, Coventry & Lichfield diocese, by l.d.

Richard le Walkere of Ashow, Coventry & Lichfield diocese, to t. remaining in his diocesan's possession and by l.d.

Nicholas Baron of Stoneleigh, Coventry & Lichfield diocese, by l.d. to t. remaining in his diocesan's possession.

Thomas Cuby of Coventry & Lichfield diocese, by l.d. to t. of St. Frideswide's, Oxford.

John de Aston, v. of Runcorn, Coventry & Lichfield diocese, by l.d. to t. of his church.

Robert Solle of Radcot (*Rodecote*), Lincoln diocese, by l.d. to t. of the P. & C. of Wroxton.*

Hugh Greyby, r. of Ryton (*Ruyton*), Coventry & Lichfield diocese, by l.d. to t. of his church.

Nicholas Jordan of Sedgeberrow, Worc. diocese, to t. of his patrimony.

William Heyne of Tysoe, to t. of the P. & C. of Clattercote.*

Robert Jay of Honington, to t. of the P. & C. of Bicester.*

William Hauthorn of Eatington, to t. of the P. & C. of St. Frideswide's, Oxford.

Nicholas Mey of Bourton, to t. of St. Frideswide's monastery.

[*Priests: Secular continued.*]

Matthew Wodar' of Worcester, to t. of the P. & C. of Little Malvern.

Walter Luttelton of South Littleton in the vale of Evesham, to t. of the house of Bordesley.

Richard Dragon of [Droit]wich, to t. of patrimony.*

William de Wattecote, to t. of the P. & C. of Wroxton.

Richard Maysmor iuxta Glouc', to t. of St. Bartholomew's, Gloucester.*

William Batemon of Cubbington, Coventry & Lichfield diocese, to t. of the house of Stoneleigh by l.d.

John Frankeleyn of Quinton, Worc. diocese, to t. of the house of Alcester.

John Faukes of Quenington, to t. of the hospital of St. John of Jerusalem.*

Robert Corteys of Newport (*de Novo Burgo*), Llandaff diocese, to t. of the A. & C. of Caerleon (*Kalynn*) in that diocese, by l.d.

John Cok of Cleeve, to t. of the A. & C. of Eynsham.

Thomas Hyde of Aldsworth, Worc. diocese, to t. of the P. & C. of Llanthony Prima.

Adam Bradewell of Trimpley, Worc. diocese, to t. of the P. & C. of Merton.*

John Wylles of Worc. diocese, to t. of his patrimony.*

Walter Wyther of Eldersfield, to t. of the P. & C. [of Llanthony Prima] in Wales.

Lists of those ordained to the first tonsure

1074 *26 February* . . .
At Cirencester

Richard Faber of Tetbury.
William Stoke of South Cerney.
Richard Magerhugg.
Robert Baldwene of Siddington.
William de Sobbery.
William de Brentemersh.
John atte Зate of Siddington.
John Faber of Tetbury.
Thomas Peres of Cheltenham.
John de Elkeston.
John Hertushorn.
Richard de Aumeneye.
Thomas de Brakkel'.
Richard de Preston.
William de Clive.
John de Perschore.
Thomas de Bremusgrove.
John Pecok'.

William de Turkeden.
Thomas Faber of Ampney (*Almeneye*).
John de[?] Salle.
Robert Ragelane.

1075 *3 March* . . .
At Abbots Stanley

William Peddesmer.
John Hayward.
William de Claville.
John atte Mulle.
John Don' in Tounne.
William atte Bourne.
Henry de Duddebrugg'.
Thomas de Pagenhull.
Richard Abraham.
Roger le Hogg.
John de Couelee.
Robert Hockenale.

Richard Hokkenale.
Henry Spilman.
John Horn.
John Parker.
Henry Claville.
John, his brother.
Thomas le Clerk of Paganhill.
John Gorst.

1076 *25 January . . .*
At Wootton Wawen

John Someter of Eardiston.
William Bouwer and his
 brother, John.
Nicholas Muluwart.
John Schepessot'.
John Cok of Henley,
 illeg[itimate].
Richard Cok of Henley.
William Whythened.
John de Brome.
William de Cromhale.
William Treweman.
John Bertram.
Richard de Felde.
Thomas Muluwart of *Wotton.*
William Hyne.
John Herper [Hopper?].
John Scherman.
Simon de Aspele.
Richard de Bokkeston.
John Notehurste.
Henry, his brother.
John de Upton, illeg[itimate].
Roger Dawe of *Wotton.*
John Bryd of Claverdon
 (*Clardon*).

1077 *24 January . . .*
At Wroxall

Roger de Chetewynde.
Philip, his brother.
Roger de Wroxale,
 illeg[itimate].
Henry de Norton.
John Franceys.

1078 *27 January . . .*
At Warwick

John Luffe of Barford.
Richard de Wodelowe.
William Bannyng'.
John de Bristoll'.
Robert Taylour.
Robert Broun of Warwick.
John Cartere of Barford.
John Chauntour.
John Jacobz of *Hascleve.*
Thomas Morice.
William de Wolfreton.
John Porter.
Philip Goner.
John Somerville.
John Daywesone.
John Vincent of Warwick.
William Lyuet.
Robert Bron of Stratford.
John Gegge of Warwick.
John Mounfort.

1079 *7 February . . .*
At Quinton

William de Heyford.
John, his brother.
John Wyget.
John Geffe.
William Hikle.
John de Alvechirch.

1080 *9 February . . .*
At Great Compton

Henry Wolkare.
William le Hupner.
William Robert.
Richard Diconys.
Walter de Brayles.
Richard Durant of
 Wolford.
John Edde of Cherrington.
Robert Wilde of the same.
John Polyter.
John Bernhart of Brailes.
William Dychford of Wolford.

1081 *11 February . . .*
At Great Compton

William de Neubold.
William Rypyngale.
William Muluwart.
John Matken of Brailes.
Walter Taylour of Stourton.
John Heryng' of Tidmington
    (*Tydlyngton*).
Ralph Coupar' of Eatington.
William Betyn of Sutton
    (*Sotton*).
John Spiser[?] of Shipton.
Nicholas Hervy of Eatington.
John Monuyng' of Compton.
Robert Prestes of Eatington.
William Taylour of Compton.
Walter Mersch of Weston.
Laurence Willyes.

1082 *13 February . . .*

Richard Tommes of Oddington.
Thomas atte Mulne of
    Broadwell.
William Haptone of
    Longborough.
Henry atte Holdefeld.
Henry Leviot [Lemot?].
William Pykns.
John Godmon.
William Wybbe.
John Wybbe.
Richard Alexandr'.
Roger Schurp.
William Palfrey.
Roger Treyour.
John Oxschull.
John Sterygrom.
Simon Clericus.
Robert Scu[p?]tere.

1083 *17 March . . .*
At Shenington

William de Neuwynton.
William Caugeler.

John de Hogges.
John de Shutteforde.
William Sare.
William de Oxschull.

1084 *19 April 1345 At*
Tewkesbury, in the
monastery.

John atte Mulle.
John le Glasyare.
John Wyther.
John Rogers.
John Bakhous.
Walter Bredon.
Nicholas Atteberwe.

1085 *20 April 1345 At Llanthony*
next Gloucester, in the
conventual church.

John Walour.
John de Madesdon.
John Muleward.
John Sautemareys.
Richard de Longeney.
John le Welare.
John de Eldesfelde.
William Sawyare.
Laurence Lutleton.
John Cade.
William le Breware of
    Worcester.
John Granndon.
William Leytwene.
Richard atte Felde.
Walter Cade.
William Elmor' of Gloucester.
Richard Chiet [Cluet?].
Henry Glouc'.
Edward Pynon'.
John Marschal.
John Calwe.
John Gody.
William Syre.
Stephen Syre.
John Gryffyn.

John Kemele.
Richard Malmesbur'.
John Lavertone.
John atteWelle.
John Clyffort.
Richard Cornwayls.
John de Trynleye.
Gregory Kar[d?]nakare.
Richard de Dumbleton.
John Pendok.
William Ingelwyne.
John Drapare.
John atte Welde.

1086 *22 April 1345 At
Upton-on-Severn, in the
rectory.*

John Atteberwe.
Edmund Atteberwe.
Thomas le Botyler.
William le Botyler.
John le Wardroper.
John Chapmon.
William Wette.
Walter le Tayllour of Pendock.
Richard le Clerc.
John le Spencer.
John Stabold.
Robert Underhulle.
Godfrey le Masseger.
Richard le Prat.
Ralph Wasp.
Robert Attegrene.
John Gylmyn.
Simon de London.
Robert Emesyn.

1087 *22 May 1345 At Bredon*
Simon Armegrove of Painswick.
Henry Coterel of Croome.
John Waty of Besford.
Richard de la Lode.
John Calvestre.
Thomas Byke.
William Golafre of Longdon.

John son of Nicholas Richards
of Mickleton (*Muchelton*).
William Pendok of
Westmancote.
John Pendok of Westmancote
(*Westmo[co]te*).
John Payword.
Richard atte Nelme.
Robert Coterel.
Richard le Engelys of
Kemerton.
Thomas de Sawe.
William Ingram of Kemerton.
William Boveton.
Robert le Reve of Birlingham.
Richard Water.
Peter le Smyth of Rodmarton.
Stephen Gynnour of Rodmarton.
Stephen Rondelf.
Richard le Marschal of
Mickleton.
Robert le Bakere of Bredon.
John le Welare of Kempsey.
Richard le Barbour of
Tewkesbury.
William Kyng' of Forthampton,
disp[ensed].
William Ket of Buckland.
Henry le Cartar' of Little
Barrington.
Robert le Carpenter of Defford.
Robert Bernard of Baughton
(*Bokton*).
William Mason.
William Overbury of Wilmcote.
William Wyset of Powick.
William Corteys of Bredon,
disp[ensed].
Robert Merston of Tewkesbury.
John Dodde of Kempsey.
John Byrche of Woollashill.
John Fremon of Washbourne.
John Bracit [Brant?] of
Buckland.
Thomas Brant of Buckland.
John Leye of Worcester.

William Alblastre of
  Woodmancote.
John Baty of Holdfast.
Richard atte Brugge of
  Mathon.
John Guildyng' of Bredon.
John Taylour of Forthampton.
William Kyppyng' of Turkdean.
Walter Pleystede of
  Shurdington.
Henry Pleystede of
  Shurdington.
John Silattere of Pershore.
Robert Smethesende of
  Forthampton.
Robert Noteclive of Eckington.
Richard Home of Pershore.
John Colemon of Pirton.
William Crossom of Little
  Barrington.
John de Morton.
John atte Schepene of Mathon.
Thomas Herbard of Wick next
  Pershore (*Perchores Wyk*).
Henry Guildon of Guiting,
  disp[ensed].
William Besand of Aston.
William Stevene of Bushley
  (*Bisseleye*).
William Katel of Strensham.
William atte Schep' of Mathon.
John Sompter of Malvern.

1088 *7 July 1345 At Henbury in
  the bishop's chapel.*

William Coumbe.
Richard Shoppe.
John Botman.
John Cristofre.
Robert Roubrugh.
Robert Muleward.
Richard de Wolverton.
Hugh le Blount.
Robert de Sevenhampton.
John le Plasterer.

Richard le Marschal.
William Quellynge of Beckford.

1089 *25 July 1345 At Henbury in
  Salt Marsh.*

John Porter.
William Raymund.
Robert Raymund.
Thomas Long'.
Walter Long'.
William Vele.
John Haleway.
Robert Haleway.
John Hardy.
John Gosselyn.
John de Chew.
Henry Glovere.
Roger Tailoure.
Stephen Barry.
Edward Page.
John Vaumpway.
Thomas de Grauntbrigg'.
Walter de Pershore.
John Halayne.
Thomas Punchard.
Thomas Predye.
John Haukoc.
William Hoker.
Thomas le Webbe.
Robert Torner.
Robert Large.
John Scotte.
John Kent of Bristol.
Richard de Marscote.

1090 *1 August 1345 At Bristol,
  in the conventual church of
  St. Augustine.*

John Darras.
John Gonys.

1091 *10 August 1345 At Henbury*
John Sauekyn.
Randolph Beauver.

John Bastes.
Thomas Chiltenham.
Thomas Marchal.
Walter Hemyngton.
John Belethere.

1092 *3 July 1345 At Henbury in Salt Marsh, in the chapel of the [bishop's] manor.*

Walter atte Bergh of Nympsfield (*Nimiesfeld*).
William le Screveyn.
William Colomor.
Gilbert Walter.
Stephen Driestere.
Thomas de Toryton.
John Bosforde.

1093 *27 August 1345 At Henbury in Salt Marsh, in the chapel of the [bishop's] manor.*

Nicholas le Girdelere.
John de Rouburgh.
John Knyt.
Robert Vallet.
John Briggewater.
James Tilbȝ.
Walter Apperlere.
Walter Clement.
Thomas Carpunter.
John Carpunter.
Walter de Wertusburgh.
Ralph de Godeshall.

1094 *28 August 1345 At Henbury, in the [bishop's] chapel.*

William Grasmere.
John Fispayn.
John Hobbes.

1095 *14 . . . 1345 Withington*
William Aleyn.
Thomas Fortoye.
Henry Hale.

1096 *5 September 1345 At Cirencester, in the abbey.*

Thomas Caudeur.
Richard Russel.
John Muleward.
William Cerne.
Edmund Wyard dis[pensed].
John le Muleward of the Abbey (*de Abbathia*).
Henry Gorege.
Robert Hereward.
William Dosseles.
Thomas London'.
Thomas Foxcote.
Thomas Beaupeyne.

1097 *9 February 1346 At Hampton Bishop*

Richard Wilmot.
William Rouleye.
Nicholas Coupare.
William Crek'.

1098 *5 June 1346 At Hartlebury*

Aumary de Hulle.
John Howel.

1099 *27 July 1346 At Withington*

Robert de Yaneworth.
James Bisshop.
Robert le Poleter.
Richard Broun.
Henry Legger'.
John Harpour.

1100 *11 July 1346 At Olveston*

Aynolf de Brymsame.
William Marschale.
Thomas Royly.
John de Hayles.
William Trewbody.
Robert T(ur?)ygyne.
William Brox [Broy?].

1101 *9 July 1346 At Codrington*

Thomas Katour of West
  Littleton.
Thomas Padewell of Dodington.
John Coueleye of the same.

1102 *10 July*[1] *1346 At*
  Pucklechurch

John Mon of Doynton.
Peter Fraunceys of Doynton.
John Colemon.
Thomas, his brother.
William Hanecok.
John Lo(u?)ghton.
Henry Nichols.
[2]Gervase Treworgy of Exeter
  diocese, by l.d.
Richard de Fenton of Hereford
  diocese.

1103 *24 December 1346 At*
  Hartlebury

Thomas Clipuston.
William Dunleye.
Richard Mal.
Henry Stodleye.
Walter Hakern [Bakern?].
John Fayrmon.
William Spechusleye.
Hugh ye Ouschor.

1104 *5 September*[3] *1346 At*
  Horsley

Thomas Mayde.
John Broune *ger[manus]*.
William Spicer.
John Kynne.

1105 *5 September* . . . *At*
  Bibury

John Verne.
William Bruggio.

William Henri.
Nicholas Weston.
William Everard.
Henry Smythes.
John Pennebrugge.
John Carlton.
John M. . .con'.

1106 *13 June* . . . *At*
  Winchcombe

Nicholas Freman of
  Washbourne.
John Warde.
Richard Goldfinch.[4]
Henry Broun.
Henry Smith.
Thomas Lede, dis[pensed] by
  the abbot. [?][5]
Thomas Cock.
John Romusleye.
John Presbury.
Thomas Wych.
Simon Jay.
Brian Selers.
William Aldrinton.
Simon Stanewey.
John Deyare.
Thomas Branebi.

1107 *Trinity Sunday* . . *At Bredon*

Henry Millen.
Thomas Watrot'.
Walter Dech'.
William Rauele.
Nicholas Rameseye.
John Grene.
William Lokkesle.
John Talours.
John Freman.
John Bodi.
[The next 13 folios have been
lost.]

1 MS. *Ordines in crastino.*
2 The following two names are in the next column by themselves, but probably belong to
  this ordination.
3 *Festo Sancti Bertini.*   4 Added to the right of the column.   5 *Dis' per abb'.*

1108 *20 December 1348 Orders celebrated by the bishop in the chapel of Hartlebury Castle on the Saturday of Embertide in December.*[1]

Acolytes: Religious

Br. John Forest ⎫
Br. Roger Tendebur' ⎬ monks of Worcester.
Br. Thomas Croos ⎭

Acolytes: Secular

John Vey.	Richard Broun of
Thomas Adyneth.	Sherborne.
William Poti.	Thomas Edward.
William Long' of Hanbury	William Voul of Belbroughton.
(*Hambery*).	William Mabon.
John Stoke of Hanbury	Thomas Rycheyse.
(*Hambery*).	Robert Coueleye.
John son of Alan.	Maurice Wyth'.
Nicholas Bisshamton.	Henry atte Broke of *Kyngton*.

Subdeacon: Religious

Br. John de Pebmore of the order of Preachers.

Subdeacons: Secular

Thomas de Newelond of Salwarpe, r. of Wolverley, to t. of his church.
Walter son of Walter Rag' of Stow, to t. of the P. & C. of St. Frideswide's, Oxford.
Geoffrey de Aula of Cherrington,[2] Worc. diocese, to t. of the P. & C. of Studley.
William Veysy of Feckenham, to t. of patrimony.*
Philip Belynger of Astley, to t. of the P. & C. of Llanthony next Gloucester.
William atte Mulne of Sherborne, to t. of the A. & C. of Oseney.
John Bras of [Droit]wich, to t. of his patrimony.*
William Spende of Defford, to t. of patrimony.*
Hugh Trompe of Bromsgrove, to t. of patrimony.*
Ralph Hondekyn of Coughton, to t. of the P. & C. of Studley.
Thomas Dygon of Elmley, to t. of the A. & C. of Halesowen.
Henry Janne of Tachbrook, Coventry & Lichfield diocese, by l.d. to t. of the A. & C. of St. James' monastery outside Northampton.
John Payn, to t. of his patrimony.*

Deacons: Religious

Br. Peter Marcle *alias* Walssh ⎫
⎬ monks of Winchcombe.
Br. John Wytham ⎭

---

1 *Die Sabbati Quatuor Temporum mensis Decembris.*   2 MS. *Chiryton.*

Br. John Bretforton, canon of [Holy Sepulchre] Warwick.
Br. Thomas de la Peole, Minorite.[1]

Deacons: Secular

William Jones of Evenlode, to t. of the house of St. John the Evangelist, Cold Norton.
John de Barton in Hennemerssh, to t. of patrimony.
John son of John de Ynsale of Elmley Lovett, to t. of patrimony.
William de Willecote, to t. of the A. & C. of Polesworth.
William son of Henry atte Pole of Dudley, to t. of the prior & monks of the same given by copy (*dat[um] per copiam*).
John Hened' of Mathon, to t. of Evesham[2] monastery given by copy (*dat[um] per copiam*).
Walter Botild of Piddle (*Pidul'*), to t. of the P. & C. of Caldwell next Bedford given by copy (*dat[um] per copiam*).
John son of William Cissor, to t. of his patrimony.
John Budul', to t. of the house of Wombridge (*Wombrugg'*).
John Wake of Sheriffs Lench, to t. of patrimony.
John Hattere of Besford (*Bedeford*), to t. of patrimony.
Thomas Godman, to t. of his patrimony.
M. Clement de Weston, r. of St. Martin's Worcester.
Adam son of Roger de Oglot', to t. of his patrimony.
William Antony of Birmingham, Coventry & Lichfield diocese, to t. of the house of Henwood.*

Priests: Religious

Br. Richard de Stottesdon of the order of [St.] Augustine.
Br. John de Quynton.
Br. Richard de Duddeleye of the order from Halesowen [*sic*].
Br. Richard de Tanton ⎫ of the order from Cirencester, by l.d.
Br. John de Wytherleye ⎭   [*sic*].

Priests: Secular

Henry de Wodehous of Ombersley, to t. of patrimony.†
Robert de Briclampton of Worc. diocese, to t. of patrimony.
Simon Emmote of Blockley, to t. of the A. & C. of Medmenham.
Richard Wilkyn of Broadwell, to t. of the A. & C. of Oseney.
John Sweyn of Bibury, to t. of the P. & C. of St. Frideswide's, Oxford.
Richard son of Henry Beufys of Eastleach (*Estleuch*), to t. of the abbot of St. James' monastery outside Northampton.
Simon atte Mulne of Kempsey, to t. of his patrimony.*
William de Bradeweye, to t. of the P. & C. of Ivychurch.*
John Borewold of Kempsey, to t. of his patrimony.

1 MS. *minor*.
2 MS. *Evesham*, but cf. p. 275 where the reading is *Eynesham* (Eynsham).

John Spende of Defford, to t. of patrimony.*

Thomas son of Nicholas de Bermyngham of Dudley, to t. of the prior & monastery of the same.

William son of Richard Bonvyle of Great Compton, to t. of his patrimony.

Giles de Fenne of Belbroughton, to t. of patrimony.

William Colynes of Upper Quinton (*Over Quynton*), to t. of the A. & C. of Pershore.

Thomas atte Lowe, to t. of patrimony.

William Daukyns of Walsall, Coventry & Lichfield diocese, by l.d. to t.

Robert de Aldenham of Besford (*Bedford*), to t. of his patrimony.

John Royse of Tysoe, to t. of the P. & C. of Wroxton.

John Pistor of Stone, Coventry & Lichfield diocese, to t. of the house of Hulton.

William Grafton of Eatington, to t. of the P. & C. of Wroxton.

1109 *7 March 1349 Orders celebrated by the bishop in the chapel of Hartlebury Castle on the Saturday of Embertide in March.*[1]

Acolytes: Religious

Br. William Tancard of Thelsford (*Tewlesford*).

Br. Thomas Has ⎫
Br. William Fewareyn ⎬ Minorites.
Br. R. Bredok ⎭

Br. Edmund de Brantyngthrop ⎫ of Merevale Abbey.
Br. John de Belegrave ⎭

Acolytes: Secular

Robert Bartrem of Hanbury.

Thomas Chircheye of Moreton-in-Henmarsh.

Robert Mordak, r. of Winterbourne.

M. John de Balkeynton, by l.d. of [the bishop of] Hereford.

Walter de Stolstone.

Peter Payn of Sheriffs Lench.

William Sampsomp of Naunton (*Newynton*).

Thomas Cator of Pershore.

John Palmere of Bourton (*Bourton Coteswold*).

John Aude.

John Kyng' of Shurdington.

Thomas Lucas of Lechlade.

John Cassy of [Droit]wich.

Stephen Hathemare.

William Pleystede.

---

1 *Die Sabbati Quatuor Temporum mensis Marcii.*

22

[*Acolytes: Secular continued.*]

Thomas Hornere.

Richard de Pebmore.

Richard de Knytecote.

Richard de la Meere, r. of Holy Trinity church, Gloucester.

John Nicholes of Kidderminster.

John Wyshangere.

Richard Taylour.

Henry Watekote.

John Romayne of Lechlade.

John Lucas of Lechlade.

Richard Condycote.

Thomas Madeleye of Himbleton.

William Jankynes of Chesterton, Lincoln diocese, by l.d. to all holy orders.

John atte Lye of Rowell (*Roweleye*).

Thomas Passelade, r. of Rodmarton.

Thomas Dounton of Dormston.

John Ketell of *Kyngton*.

John Fayrmon of Hanbury next [Droit]wich.

Thomas Tyso of Brailes.

Subdeacons: Religious

Br. Thomas de Weston, monk of Stoneleigh.

Br. Walter Eyton of the order of Minorites.

Br. Walter Athelam of Tewkesbury monastery.

Br. William de Alcestr' of Lichfield diocese, from Merevale Abbey, by l.d.

Subdeacons: Secular

M. David de Milkesham, to t. of the vicarage of Berkeley church.

Henry Caldecote, to t. of patrimony.

Thomas Harry of Moreton (*Morton*), to t. of patrimony.

John Hayward of Moreton (*Morton*), to t. of patrimony.

William Blount, to t. of the P. & C. of Llanthony next Gloucester.

Thomas Gylberdes of Stoke Orchard (*Archerestoke*), to t. of the P. & C. of Llanthony next Gloucester.

William Harryes of *Burton*, to t. of his patrimony.

Adam Skyl of Halford, to t. of the P. & C. of Luffield.

William Bussh', to t. of patrimony worth 20s.

William Poughampton, to t. of the A. & C. of Halesowen (*Hales*).

Richard Sherley, to t. of his patrimony.

Thomas Irysch, to t. of patrimony.

John Graunt' of Ilmington, to t. of the A. & C. *de Novo Loco* [New Minster, Hyde], Winchester diocese.

Walter called 'le Clerk' of Quenington, to t. of his patrimony.

Henry son of Richard Guldecote, to t. of the A. & C. of Rocester in Dovedale.

Richard Lydeseye of Ilmington, to t. of the P. & C. of St. Mary's, Merton, Winchester diocese.

Thomas Blakemon, to t. of the P. & C. of Bruton (*Bruyuton*).

William Walcote, to t. of the P. & C. of Llanthony next Gloucester.

Henry Morys, to t. of his patrimony.

William Voul of Belbroughton, to t. of the prior & brethren of Holy Trinity hospital, Bridgnorth, by the bishop's grace.

Nicholas Moryce, to the bishop's t. (*ad titulum domini*).

John Goldeneye, to the bishop's t.

Henry de Penne of Kidderminster, by the bishop's grace.

Thomas Chesterton of Prestbury, to t. of the P. & C. of Llanthony next Gloucester.

Simon Jones of *Newynton Bovuton*, to t. of patrimony.

John Canon' of Gloucester, to t. of patrimony.

Thomas Conventr', to t. of the P. & C. of Trentham.

Richard Pynthrop, to t. of the A. & C. of Biddlesden.

William Corteys of Wolford, to t. of the P. & C. of St. Frideswide's, Oxford.

Simon of the Berewe, to t. of his patrimony.

William Boys of Withington (*Wythyndon*), to t. of five marks to be received annually from the hospital of St. John of Jerusalem.

John Boteller of Farmington (*Thormarton*), to t. of the P. & C. of Cold Norton.

Robert Escote, to t. of the A. & C. of Cirencester.

William Maldon of Stonehouse, to t. of the A. & C. of Elstow, *Lichfield*[1] diocese.

John Tilare of Gloucester, to t. St. Bartholomew's hospital, Gloucester by the bishop's grace.

John Hwet of Bishops Cleeve, to t. of the A. & C. of St. Augustine's, Bristol.

John Kynemaresforde, to t. of his grace from the apostolic see.

William Hayrun, to t. of the P. & C. of Caldwell next Bedford.

John le Vey, to t. of his chapel of Doynton.

William Harpour, to t. of St. Mary's chantry, Dursley.

William West of Chelmscote (*Chellescote*), to t. of the P. & C. of Caldwell next Bedford.

John Hope of Tetbury, to t. of the A. & C. of Keynsham.

Peter Bernard of Trimpley, to t. of the P. & C. of St. Mary's monastery, Merton, Winchester [diocese].

John Bradestoke [of] *Lanreryt*, Llandaff diocese, born in Worc. diocese.

1 MS. *Lich'*. *Recte Linc'* (Lincoln).

[Subdeacons: Secular continued.]

John Giffard of Bibury, to t. of the A. & C. of Oseney.

Henry Honynton, to t. of the A. & C. of Lesnes.

William de Sodbrok of Lincoln diocese, to t. of his grace from the apostolic see, by l.d.

Andrew de Fetherston of Lichfield diocese, to t. of the A. & C. of Lilleshall by l.d. Because his title lacks the common seal of that house, his letters of orders are kept back until such time as he bring the title with such seal.

Robert le Clerk of Marston, to t. of the P. & C. of [Holy Trinity] London.

Deacons: Religious

Br. John de Pedmore of the order of Preachers.

Br. Robert de Brayles, monk of Stoneleigh.

Deacons: Secular

William Veysy of Feckenham, to t. of patrimony.

Walter son of Walter Rag' of Stow, to t. of the house of St. Frideswide.

Geoffrey de Aula Chyryton,[1] to t. of the P. & C. of Studley.

William atte Mulne, to t. of the A. & C. of Oseney.

William Spende of Defford, to t. of patrimony.

Adam Toly of Brailes, to t. of the P. & C. of Caldwell.

William Walcote of Pershore, to t. of patrimony.

Hugh Trompe, to t. of patrimony.

Thomas son of John Whyther of Little Compton, to t. of the A. & C. of Eynsham.

John Bras, to t. of patrimony.

Ralph Hondekyn of Coughton, to t. of the P. & C. of Studley.

Henry Fylongeleye of Coventry diocese, by l.d. to t. of the house of Henwood.

William Melburne of Coventry diocese, by l.d. to t. of the house of Dieulacresse.

Ralph Cotene of Coventry diocese by l.d. to t. of the house of Gresley.

John Corteys, to t. of patrimony.

Richard son of Gilbert le Hunte of Kineton *(de in [sic] Kyngton)*, to t. of the P. & C. of Bicester.

Thomas Dygon, to t. of the A. & C. of Halesowen *(Hales)*.

Elyas Caves of Eycote, to t. of the A. & C. of St. Mary, Keynsham.

Gilbert Newemon of Woodstock, to t. of the house of Stoneleigh by l.d.

Roger Syde [of] Gloucester, to t. of patrimony.

Robert de Pubbesbury, r. of Meysey Hampton.

John of ye Naysshe of Fladbury, to t. of patrimony.

M. Thomas de Bynyngton, r. of Astbury, Coventry diocese by l.d.

1 *Sic.* This should read *de Aula de Chyryton* (Cherrington). Cf. p. 269.

Walter Page of Stourton, to t. of the P. & C. of Cold Norton.
William Clyfford, to t. of patrimony.
Philip Belyng', to t. of the P. & C. of Llanthony next Gloucester.
Thomas Neweland, r. of Wolverley, to t. of his church.

Priests: Religious

Br. Nicholas de Redyng', monk of Tewkesbury.
Br. John Rydel of Lichfield diocese, monk of Merevale, by l.d.
Br. Richard de Cornubia of the order of Preachers.
Br. John de Weston, monk of Stoneleigh.
Br. John Cholle ⎫
Br. William de Wynslowe ⎬ of the order of Minorites.
Br. Warin Longespy ⎭

Priests: Secular

Roger Mayel of Cheltenham, to t. of the A. & C. of Winchcombe.
William Jones of Evenlode, to t. of the house of St. John the Evangelist, Cold Norton.
Roger Tele of Hanley, to t. of patrimony.
William son of Henry atte Pole of Dudley, to t. of the prior & monks of Dudley.
Adam Oglot', to t. of patrimony by l.d.
Nicholas son of Alan de Duddeleye, to t. of the prior & monks of Dudley.
John son of William Tailor of *Acton*, to t. of patrimony.
William Wylcote of Stratford, to t. of the A. & C. of Polesworth.
Thomas Dyxeleye of Lichfield diocese, to t. of the monastery of Chester by l.d.
John Budell of Lichfield diocese, to t. of Wombridge by l.d.
William de Counston of Lichfield diocese, to t. of the house of Rocester by l.d.
William Welcombe, to t. of the A. & C. of Oseney.
Robert Knyght of Marston, to t. of the P. & C. of Holy Trinity, London.
John Barton of Henmarsh, to t. of patrimony.
John Gardiner of Kempsford, to t. of the P. & C. of Amesbury (*Aumbrosleye*).
John Wake, to t. of patrimony.
John Hatter', to t. of patrimony.
John Hened, to t. of the A. & C. of Eynsham.[1]
Walter Boteld, to t. of the P. & C. of Caldwell next Bedford.
William Antony of Lichfield diocese, by l.d. to t. of the house of Henwood.
John Insale, to t. of patrimony.
John Vynch of Churchdown (*Chircheton*), to t. of patrimony.

1 MS. *Eynesham*, but cf. p. 270 n.2.

[*Priests: Secular continued.*]

John atte Halle of Sherborne, to t. of the house of St. Botulph, Colchester.

Thomas de Wythwyk of Lichfield diocese, to t. of the A. & C. of Croxden, by l.d.

M. Clement de Weston, r. of St. Martin's, Worcester, to t. of his church.

1110 *28 March 1349 Orders celebrated by the bishop in the chapel of Hartlebury Castle.*[1]

Subdeacons: Religious

Br. John Foreste
Br. Roger de Temedebury } monks of Worcester.
Br. William Morton of the order of Preachers.

Subdeacons: Secular

Ralph de Endreby of Lincoln diocese, to t. of M. Henry de Neubold by l.d.

William de Perschor', to t. of the A. & C. of Oseney.

Henry son of Philip atte Chircheye of Iccomb, to t. of the house of Eynsham.

Thomas son of John de Hampton of Longborough, to t. of the A. & C. of Hailes.

Walter le Messag' of Wheatenhurst, to t. of the prior of St. Bartholomew's, Newbury, and of the fraternity of that house.

Philip atte Mulne of Chipping Campden (*Chepyngehampton*),[2] to t. of the prior & brethren of St. John the Baptist, Shrewsbury.

William le White of Forthampton, to t. of the A. & C. of Oseney.

John Ruyfeld of Coventry & Lichfield diocese, to t. of patrimony by l.d.

John Graunt of Wormington, to t. of patrimony.

Stephen Hathemare, to t. of the A. & C. of Gloucester, that is, to a good corrody in the priory of Stanley.

Thomas atte Pleystede of Badgeworth, to t. of the P. & C. of Usk.

John Wyshangre of Southam, to t. of the P. & C. of Llanthony.

Thomas Passelowe, r. of Rodmarton, to t. of his church.

William atte Welle of Fairford (*Fayruord*), to t. of the P. & C. of Llanthony.

John Hobkenes of Defford,[3] to t. of his patrimony.

John Samson of Childs Wickham, to t. of his patrimony.

1 *Die Sabbati qua cantatur officium 'Sitientes'.*
2 *Sic.* Cf. p. 337.
3 MS. *Defford.* Besford was probably intended, see pp. 337, 343.

Robert Coueleye, to t. of a certain annual rent of 40s. from the manor of Cam by grant of lord Thomas de Berkeleye.

Robert Mordak, r. of Winterbourne, to t. of his church.

Deacons: Secular

Richard Godefrey of Ronton, to t. of the house of Ronton.

Henry Moris, to t. of his patrimony.*

Thomas Irissh, to t. of patrimony.

Thomas Gilberdes of Stoke Orchard, to t. of the P. & C. of Llanthony.

Thomas Blakemon, to t. of the P. & C. of Bruton.

William de Sudbrok of Lincoln diocese, by l.d. to t. of his grace from the apostolic see.

William Voul of Belbroughton, to t. of the prior & brethren of Holy Trinity in Bridgnorth.

William Hayron of Compton Wyniates, to t. of the P. & C. of Caldwell next Bedford.

Adam Schyl of Halford (*Alford*), to t. of the P. & C. of Luffield.

Thomas Covyntr', to t. of the P. & C. of Trentham.

Henry Caldecote, to t. of patrimony.

Thomas Harry of Moreton (*Morton*), to t. of patrimony.

William Pounghampton, to t. of the A. & C. of Halesowen (*Hales*).

Richard Scherleye, to t. of patrimony.

William Corteys of Wolford, to t. of the P. & C. of St. Frideswide's.

Richard Lydeseye of Ilmington, to t. of the P. & C. of St. Mary's, Merton, Winchester diocese.

Robert Clerk of Marston, to t. of the P. & C. of Holy Trinity, London.

William West of Chelmscote, to t. of the P. & C. of Caldwell next Bedford.

William Harpour, to t. of St. Agnes' chantry, Dursley.

John Haywart of Moreton (*Morton*), to t. of patrimony.

William Boys of Withington, to t. of five marks' sterling from the hospital of St. John of Jerusalem.

John Hope of Tetbury, to t. of the A. & C. of Keynsham.

Thomas de Chesterton of Prestbury, to t. of the P. & C. of Llanthony.

Simon oye Berowe, to t. of his patrimony.

Peter Bernard of Trimpley, to t. of the P. & C. of the monastery of St. Mary, Merton, Winchester [diocese].

William Blount, to t. of the P. & C. of Llanthony.

William son of Richard Bussh of [Droit]wich, to t. of patrimony.

Henry Penne, to the bishop's title at the request (*per preces*) of Hugh de Cokeseye.

John Grant of Ilmington, to t. of the A. & C. *de Novo Loco* [New Minster, Hyde], Winchester diocese.

Henry son of Richard de Goldecote, to t. of the A. & C. of Rocester in Dovedale.

[*Deacons: Secular continued.*]

John Vey, r. of Doynton, to t. of his church.

John Huwet of Bishops Cleeve, to t. of the A. & C. of St. Augustine's, Bristol.

John de Kynmersford, to t. of his grace from the apostolic see.

M. David de Melkesham, perpetual v. of Berkeley, to t. of his vicarage.

Robert de Escote, to t. of the A. & C. of Cirencester.

Priests: Secular

Thomas Dygon, to t. of the A. & C. of Halesowen (*Hales*).

William Spende, to t. of his patrimony.

Philip Belynger, to t. of the P. & C. of Llanthony.

William Walcote of Pershore, to t. of his patrimony.

Hugh Trompe of Bromsgrove, to t. of his patrimony.

John Calewe of Elmley Lovett, to t. of the A. & C. of Halesowen (*Hales*).

Roger de Morton of Coventry & Lichfield diocese, by l.d. to t. of the house of Ronton (*Rompton*) which rests in the possession of his diocesan.

William Bagot of Coventry & Lichfield diocese, by l.d. to t. of the house of Lilleshall.

John Braჳ of [Droit]wich, to t. of his patrimony.

William de Melbourn' of Coventry & Lichfield diocese, to t. of the house of Dieulacresse by l.d.

Ralph Hondekyn of Coughton, to t. of the P. & C. of Studley.

Roger Syde of Gloucester, to t. of his patrimony.

Gilbert Neweman of Woodstock, Lincoln diocese, by l.d. to t. of the A. & C. of Stoneleigh.

M. Thomas de Bynynton, r. of Astbury, Coventry & Lichfield diocese, by l.d.

Robert de Pebbesbury, r. of Meysey Hampton, to t. of his church.

Roger Dissher of Stratford, to t. of the master & brethren of St. Michael's hospital, Warwick.

Elias Caues of Eycote, to t. of the A. & C. of Keynsham.

Thomas de Newelond of Salwarp, r. of Wolverley, to t. of his church.

IIII *29 March 1349 Orders celebrated on Passion Sunday.*[1]

Acolytes

Thomas de Walton of Coventry & Lichfield diocese, by l.d.

Richard de Knytcote of Worc. diocese.

Richard de Tisho.

1 *In capella de Hartlebury* above the next entry probably refers to this one as well.

John Wideford.
John Mal.
William le Ferour.

1112 *19 April 1349 Acolytes ordained on the first Sunday after Easter in Hartlebury chapel.*[1]

William Honte of Lighthorne.
John Lovekoc of Lighthorne.
William de Kenemersford.
Thomas de Legha, r. of St. Martin's, Eastleach.
Geoffrey Nanshog', r. of St. Bartholomew's, Newington [Bagpath] next Tetbury.

[Remaining two thirds of the folios left blank.]

Quire of Royal Writs
February 1339—April 1349
[Numbers 1113—1328]

1113 *16 February 1339 Westminster*

Writ of *fieri facias* received 26 March at Kempsey. The bishop has previously sequestrated ecclesiastical goods of Henry, parson of Kennet, Salisbury diocese,[2] executor of the testament of William de Hardenne, to the value of 20s., as he returned before the barons of the Exchequer on the morrow of St. Michael [i.e. 30 September]. From these and other goods, chattels and tenements of the said Henry he is to raise £7 7s. owed to Queen Isabella, the king's mother, for the verd cut down by William son of Walter de Boneclyve in Savernake forest, William's lands and tenements having passed to William de Hardenne and his heirs. The bishop is to have the money at the Exchequer in 15 days of Easter [i.e. 11 April] for payment to John de Baddeby for Isabella's use. Tested by J. de Shordych.

By the roll of Extracts of Pleas of the Forest before Robert de Ufford and his associates, justices itinerant in Wiltshire. Baddeby.

RETURN:

The bishop was unable to levy any money from the goods and ecclesiastical benefices of the parson of Kennet. On inspection of his

1 *In Dominica qua cantatur officium 'Quasi modo geniti'.*
2 In the margin: *Henricus nuper persona de Kenette nunc est rector ecclesie de Chotes* [Coates] *iuxta Cyrencestr'.*

predecessor's register[1] he found no sequestrated goods from which money could be raised.

1114 *27 February 1339 Westminster*

Writ of *fieri facias* received 27 March at Kempsey. From the ecclesiastical goods of John de Wyndesor, rector of *Bedyngdon*, the bishop is to raise £3 3s. 3½d. which the said John and M. Peter de Comton, lately parson of Corsley (*Cors'*), Salisbury diocese, acknowledged on 20 May 6 Edward III [1332] to be due to Queen Philippa, the king's consort, and which they ought to have paid at terms long past. The money is to be at the Exchequer on the morrow of the close of Easter [i.e. 5 April] for payment to John de Eston, Philippa's receiver. Other writs—the latest returnable on the morrow of St. Hilary [i.e. 14 January]—have neither been executed nor returned. Tested by R. de Sadyngton.

RETURN:

John de Wyndesor is not rector of *Bedynton* nor is there such a church in the diocese.[2]

1115 *20 March 1339 Berkhamstead*

Writ received 1 April at Spetchley. It is alleged that the abbots of St. Augustine's, Bristol, have been unaccustomed for some time past to attend the king's parliaments. Moreover, the present abbot, although he was not at the Westminster parliament of 12 Edward III [February 1338], in which the prelates and other magnates assembled granted a moiety of wool to the king, or at the Great Council held subsequently at Northampton [July 1338], where the method of levying such grant was determined, has been held liable for payment. He has discharged the sum due for the first year of the triennial tenth, half of that for the second year at the anticipated term agreed upon by the clergy in the convocation held at St. Bride's, London, on the morrow of St. Jerome [i.e. 1 October], and is likewise prepared to pay the other half of the tenth due for the second year, the remainder of the triennial tenth, and also the additional tenth granted at the above convocation. None the less, the collectors of wool and tenths appointed by the bishop have attempted to compel the abbot by distraints and ecclesiastical coercion to render the wool granted in the above parliament, for which he seeks remedy. In consideration of the above, the bishop is to exact only the remaining tenths—should the others have been discharged as alleged, to supersede the demand of the collectors for wool, and to relax any measures

1 That of Thomas de Hemenhale (1337–8).
2 Beddington, Winchester diocese?

taken against the abbot. Tested by Edward, duke of Cornwall and earl of Chester, custos of the realm. By the Council.

1116 *11 May 1339*[1] *Hartlebury*

Mandate to the cathedral prior. The bishop has received a writ of *certiorari* tested by the duke of Cornwall, custos of the realm, and dated 18 April from Berkhamstead, whereby he is directed to certify by the quindene of Trinity [i.e. 6 June] the amount of wool due from himself and others in the diocese [v. 1115], how much has been collected, what remains to be collected, to whom the collected wool has been delivered, and whether answer has been made for it to the king or not. The prior is to send details of those items which concern him by Trinity [23 May].

On the same date a similar mandate was directed to the abbot of Cirencester.

1117 *Undated*

Return of the above writ. At the time of the grant of wool the bishop had not been advanced to the see and so ought not to be burdened with payment. As for others in the diocese who are under obligation to pay, the prior of Worcester, collector in the Worcester archdeaconry, has received 157 stone from the abbot of Evesham, which remain in his possession, but nothing from the monasteries of Westminster, Reading and Winchcombe. The following quantities have still to be collected: from the abbot of Westminster, 68 st. 3½ lb.; the abbot of Reading, 19 st. 13½ lb.; the abbot of Winchcombe, 20 st. 8 lb.; against all of whom due execution has been made; and from the abbot of Evesham, 1 lb. The bishop has appointed the abbot of Cirencester collector in the Gloucester archdeaconry. He has received the following amounts, which are still in his possession: 43½ st. 5 lb. . . .; from the abbot of Malmesbury, 7½ st. 2 lb.; the abbot of Westminster, 5½ st. 3 lb.; the abbot of Winchcombe, 65 st. 2½ lb.; the abbot of Abingdon, 19½ st. 1 lb.; the bishop of Bath, 11½ st. (½?)lb.; the abbot of Cirencester, 92 st. 1½ lb.; the abbot of Gloucester 215 st. 2 lb.; the abbot of Glastonbury, 5 st.[2] The following have not yet paid: the abbot of Reading, 11 st. 1 lb.; the Hospitallers, for their spiritualities within the archdeaconry, 26 st.— their temporalities not being taxed the bishop is unable to answer for them. He has made due execution against those who have not paid,

1 *Die et anno supradictis.* In the mandate the writ is said to have arrived 11 May, but 6 May is the date given in the margin.
2 *xliii petras di. et v libras, de abbate de Malm' vii petras di. ii libras, de abbate Westm' v petras di. iii libras, de abbate de Wynch' lxv petras ii libras di., de abbate de Abyndon xix petras di. i libram, de episcopo Bath' xi petras di. di. libr', de abbate Cirenc' lxxxxii petras i libram et di., de abbate Glouc' ccxv petras ii libras, de abbate Glaston' v petras.*

except the abbot of Evesham whom he cannot coerce because of his immunity.

1118 *7 May 1339 Westminster*

Writ of *fieri facias* received 14 May at Bredon, the official of the archdeacon of Worcester being ordered to certify the bishop of its execution by St. Barnabas [11 June]. It appears from the Exchequer rolls that the prior of Worcester, collector of the triennial tenth in the archdeaconry of Worcester, is still burdened with the following sums for the second year: 10s. 8d. for Witley church, 5s. for Shrawley, 5s. 4d. for Spetchley, 6s. 8d. for Pirton, 16s. for Severn Stoke, 5s. 4d. for All Saints [Worcester], 24s. 8d. for Yardley, 24s. 8d. for Overbury with its chapels, 4s. 10½d. for Great Comberton, 8s. 8d. for Inkberrow, 4s. 2d. for [Flyford] Flavell, 4s. 4d. for North Piddle, 6s. 8d. for Feckenham, 4s. 10½d. for Hill Croome, 4s. 8d. for Croome Adam [Earls Croome], 22s. for Aston, 8s. 4d. for Coughton, 5s. 4d. for Barcheston, 20s. for Ilmington, 5s. 4d. for Oxhill, 6s. 8d. for Saintbury, 1¼d. for the prior of St. Sepulchre's portion in St. Nicholas', Warwick, 2½d. for that of the same in Haseley, 8d. for his portion in Snitterfield, 13s. 4d. for Snitterfield, 8s. 8d. for the abbot of Westminster's portion in St. Andrew's, Pershore, 2¼d. for his portion in Bourton, and 40s. for the archdeac[onry] of Worcester. The bishop is to see that the arrears are paid to the collector so that he can answer for them at the Exchequer. Any of the clergy who can produce acquittances are to appear at the Exchequer in 15 days of St. John the Baptist [i.e. 8 July], and the levying of the sums recorded therein is to be superseded meanwhile. Tested by R. de Sadyngton.

RETURN:

All those named in the writ later made satisfaction to the collector.

1119 *28 April 1339 Westminster*

Writ of *levari facias* received 26 May at Bredon. The bishop has previously sequestrated ecclesiastical goods of Robert de Hambury, formerly the king's chamberlain in North Wales, to the value of 10 marks [£6 13s. 4d.], as he returned on the morrow of St. Michael [i.e. 30 September 1338]. From these and other goods and chattels he is to levy £950 8s. 10d., being the remainder of Robert's account at the Exchequer for the issues of the Chamber during the latter half of the first year of the king's reign and the 6th and 7th years.[1] The money is to be at the Exchequer in 15 days of Trinity [i.e. 6 June]. Other writs, including one returnable many days ago, have not been executed. Tested by R. de Sadyngton.

1 The regnal years run from 25 January to 24 January 1327–8, 1332–3 and 1333–4.

RETURN:

The above writ, addressed to Thomas [de Hemenhale], was received 26 May 1329 [*sic*]. The bishop does not know what his predecessor did in the matter and is therefore unable to certify as to the writ's execution.

1120 *3 May 1339 Westminster*

Writ of *distringas* received 1 June at Bredon. The bishop is to distrain John de Stok' by his ecclesiastical goods and benefices, so that he come before the barons of the Exchequer on the morrow of St. John the Baptist [i.e. 25 June] to render account of the issues of all the priories, houses, lands, tenements and benefices of the alien religious, and of their goods and chattels, in the counties of Warwick and Leicester, from 1 July 11 Edward III [1337], the day he received custody of them. Tested by R. de Sadyngton.

RETURN:

John de Stoke has no goods in the diocese until the Autumn by which he can be distrained.

1121 *26 March 1339 Byfleet*

Writ received 7 June at Bredon. Because of his recent elevation to the episcopate the bishop is bound to pay an annual pension to one of the king's clerks until he can provide him with a suitable benefice. Robert de Kyngeston, the king's nominee, is to be given an appropriate pension and the bishop is to send an account of his response to this request by the bearer. Tested by Edward, duke of Cornwall [&c.]. [Cf. 56]. By writ of Privy Seal.

1122 *1 June 1339 Westminster*

Writ of *fieri facias* received 16 June at Bredon. The official of the archdeacon of Gloucester is to certify the bishop of its execution by St. Peter & St. Paul [29 June]. It appears from the Exchequer rolls that the abbot of Cirencester, collector of the triennial tenth in the Gloucester archdeaconry, is still burdened with the following sums for the first year: 12d. for the abbot of Margam's portion in Olveston church; 4s. for that of the abbot of Cormeilles in the same, 13s. 4d. for the prebend formerly held by Peter de Leycestre in Westbury church, 2s. 8d. for Tytherington church, 2s. 6d. for the prior of Bradenstoke's portion in Dodington church, 7s. 8d. for the rector of Tortworth, 5s. 4d. for the bishop of Worcester's portion in Down Ampney vicarage, and 8d. for that of M. Richard de Ware in Todenham church. The bishop is to see that the collector is paid without delay, unless any of the clergy can produce acquittances [&c. as in 1118 with the same term]. Tested by R. de Sadyngton.

RETURN:

The bishop has duly admonished those named in the writ to make payment and will continue to do so until the money has been rendered in full. He has been unable to find ecclesiastical goods of the prebendary of that prebend formerly held by Peter de Leycestre, nor can he be found in the diocese, so no action can be taken against him on this occasion.

1123 *9 March 1339 Guildford*

Writ of *supersedeas* received 18 May [*sic*] at Bredon. The prior and convent of Glastonbury have pleaded that although certain manors, lands and tenements have from ancient times been held by them separately from those of the abbot, both at times of vacancy and at other times, and like the other clergy they have duly discharged the various instalments of the tenths [as enumerated in 1115] and are prepared to pay the others as they fall due, they are being forced by distraints and ecclesiastical coercion to render the wool granted at the Westminster parliament [of February 1338], for which they seek remedy. If this be the case, the bishop is to relax his measures against the prior and convent. The abbot, should he be liable in accordance with the grant, is to render the wool. Tested by Edward, duke of Cornwall [&c.]. By the Council.

1124 *4 May 1339 Westminster*

Writ of *non omittas propter libertatem* addressed to the sheriff of Worcester. Notwithstanding the liberty of the bishop of Worcester in Oswaldslow, he is to enter and to distrain the tenants of certain tenements at Wast Hills which were held of the bishopric by Godfrey Giffard [bishop 1268–1302], as well as Hugh Fovard and William Brouning, sureties (*manucaptores*) for the relief of John Giffard, nephew and heir of Godfrey. They are to be brought (*habeas corpora eorum*) before the barons of the Exchequer in 15 days of Trinity [i.e. 6 June] to answer to the king together with the tenants of the manors of Norton sub-Edge and Weston sub-Edge in Gloucestershire, and of Boyton in Wiltshire, held in chief by Godfrey Giffard. The sheriff is to be there himself to receive judgement for not having executed a former writ returnable on the morrow of the close of Easter [i.e. 5 April]. Tested by R. de Sadyngton.

1125 *12 June 1339 Westminster*

Further writ received 24 June at Tewkesbury for the collection of arrears of a triennial tenth in the Gloucester archdeaconry [v. 1122].

The official of the archdeacon is to certify the bishop of its execution by 2 July. The abbot of Cirencester is still burdened with the following sums: 1s. 3d. for the abbot of Flaxley's portion in Brimpsfield church, 18s. 8d. for Tytherington church, 7s. 8d. for Tortworth, 14s. for Cromhall, 2s. 6d. for the prior of Bradenstoke's portion in Dodington church, 6s. 4d. for Aston Somerville church, 8d. for Richard de Ware's portion in Todenham church, 7s. 4d. for Todenham, 10s. for Frampton, 4s. 4d. for the portion of Frampton vicarage, 12d. for the abbot of Margam's portion in Olveston church, 24s. for Hatherop church, 8s. 8d. for the vicarage portion in the same, 5s. 4d. for the bishop of Worcester's portion in Down Ampney church, 6d. for that of the abbot of Chester in Campden church. The bishop is to see that the collector is paid without delay [&c. as in 1118 with the same term]. Tested by R. de Sadyngton.

1126 *13 July 1339*

Mandate to Ds. Stephen Baret and Ds. John de Stok', rectors respectively of Oddington and Saintbury. They are to certify the bishop by St. Michael [29 September] of their execution of a writ of *levari facias*, tested by Edward, duke of Cornwall [&c.], and dated 13 July from Berkhamstead, which was received 20 July at Bredon. John le Smale, prebendary of Studley in Ripon collegiate church, had acknowledged in the king's Chancery on 2 August last [1338] that he owed £540 to Simon [de Montacute], bishop of Ely [1337–45], of which he ought to have paid £180 at St. John the Baptist following [24 June 1339]. The bishop has been ordered to levy the latter sum from John's ecclesiastical goods and to have it at the Exchequer in 15 days of St. Michael [i.e. 13 November]. Accordingly, the commissaries are to sequestrate his goods at Blockley to that amount, and any who interfere with their sequestration are to incur greater excommunication *ipso facto*. The money levied is to be in the bishop's hands by St. Michael. A former commission to the dean of Blockley is revoked.

RETURN:

The bishop has sequestrated goods to the value of £30, for which he has not found purchasers.

1127 *12 June 1339 Berkhamstead*

Writ received 20 July at Bredon, its execution being committed to the prior of Worcester who is to certify the bishop of his having done so *expedito negocio*. The bishop is to deliver the wool collected in the diocese [v. 1116, 1117] both from himself and other prelates, abbots and priors, to the sheriff and other royal collectors, by means of indentures containing the number of sacks *in sortem patrie unde fuerint*.

The collectors are to have the wool carried to the port of London and there delivered to the collectors of the Customs. The bishop is to certify the Chancery as to the number of sacks, stone or cloves of wool. Tested by Edward, duke of Cornwall [&c.].

1128 *10 August 1339 Wick*

Mandate to the dean of [Droit]wich for the execution of a writ of *levari facias* received 8 August at Wick. The writ, tested by R. de Sadyngton and dated 16 June from Westminster, directs the bishop to raise £950 8s. 10d. from the goods of Robert de Hambury [as in 1119], the money to be at the Exchequer on the morrow of St. Michael [i.e. 30 September]. The dean is to sequestrate Robert's goods and to answer to the bishop by St. Matthew [21 September] for the sum levied from them.

RETURN:

The bishop did not execute this fully because of the arrival of a writ of *supersedeas* [1130].

1129 *5 July 1339 Westminster*

Writ of *fieri facias* received 7 August at Wick. The bishop is to raise four marks [£2 13s. 4d.] from the goods and chattels of Walter de Strattone, deceased, lately rector of Hatherop (*Hadhrop*), which are in the hands of his executors, this being part of a debt of 20 marks [£13 6s. 8d.] owed to Hugh le Despenser senior. The money is to be at the Exchequer on the morrow of St. Michael [i.e. 30 September] for payment to the king because of Despenser's forfeiture.

RETURN:

The bishop does not know who the executors of Walter de Stratton are, *nec vi[det]ur* [?] *hoc breve nobis directum.*

1130 *21 July 1339 Westminster*

Writ of *supersedeas* received 22 August at Alvechurch, the execution of which was committed to the dean of [Droit]wich. Because Robert de Hambury, lately chamberlain of North Wales, has now begun to account at the Exchequer for the issues of that Chamber and to 'prosecute' his allowances for the whole time he was in office, and has been given until three weeks of St. Michael [i.e. 20 October] to complete the process, the bishop is to delay his execution of the previous writ [1128] until that time and to relax any sequestration imposed. Tested by R. de Sadyngton.

1131 *15 August 1339 Windsor*

Writ requesting the prayers of the bishop and diocese for the success of the king's expedition to France. The bishop is asked to encourage the celebration of Masses, the setting forth of God's word, the holding of devout processions, fasts, vigils and almsgivings, with the king in mind. Tested by Edward, duke of Cornwall [&c.].[1]

1132 *25 August 1339 Windsor*

Writ summoning the bishop and representatives of the clergy of the diocese[2] to attend a parliament at Westminster on the quindene of St. Michael [i.e. 13 October] for the discussion of urgent business concerning the war and the state and defence of the realm and other of the king's lands. Tested by Edward, duke of Cornwall [&c.].

By the king himself, the custos, and the Council.

1133 *7 October 1339 Windsor*

Writ of *levari facias* received 30 October at [Droit]wich. The bishop has already signified that he has sequestrated goods of John le Smale to the value of £30 [1126]. From them and other goods of the said John he is to levy £180, to be delivered at the Exchequer on the quindene of St. Hilary [i.e. 27 January]. Tested by Edward, duke of Cornwall [&c.].

1134 *28 October 1339 Westminster*

Writ of *certiorari* received 15 November. The king wishes to know what dignities, prebends, churches, hospitals, chapels and other ecclesiastical benefices are held by aliens within the realm and in Wales, the names of the clergy possessing them, and of those who reside personally therein, as well as their true value, that is, how much more they are worth at the present time than their taxed value (*ultra taxam*). He also wishes to be informed of those benefices, the presentation or collation of which belongs to alien religious whose lands and possessions are in his hands because of the war with France, which have fallen vacant since 6 July 11 Edward III [1337], and of the persons who have been admitted to such, and at whose presentation or collation. The bishop is to certify the Chancery of his findings by St. Hilary [13 January]. Similar mandates were sent to each of the bishops in England and Wales. Tested by Edward, duke of Cornwall [&c.].

By the custos and the whole Council.

RETURN:

The bishop has consulted his register and made diligent enquiry. Such information as he has been able to discover is being sent with the writ.

---

1 Printed in Rymer, *Foedera* V, p. 121.
2 The *premunientes* clause specifies the prior of Worcester and the archdeacons in person, the chapter by one, and the clergy by two proctors.

23

1135 *10 December 1339 Hartlebury*

Mandate to the official [of the archdeacon] of Gloucester. He is to execute a writ of *venire facias* received 9 December and to certify the bishop of his having done so by the fifth day after Epiphany [i.e. 11 January]. The writ, tested by J. de Stonor and dated 10 November from Westminster, directs the bishop to make Henry de Forneaux appear before the justices in 15 days of St. Hilary [i.e. 27 January] to answer the plea of John Dygon of Wimborne Minster that he restore £18 2s. 9d. which he unjustly detains, the sheriff of Dorset having reported that he has no lay fee.

1136 *13 November 1339 Westminster*

Writ of *venire facias* against Robert Hasele, parson of Dyrham (*Duram*). He is to be made to appear before the justices in the octave of St. Hilary [i.e. 20 January] to answer the plea of Clement Tourtle of Bristol that he restore £10 which he owes him and unjustly detains, the sheriff of Gloucester having reported that he has no lay fee. Tested by J. de Stonor.

1137 *14 October 1339 Westminster*

Further writ of *fieri facias* against the executors of Walter de Stratton, received 25 December. The bishop is to have four marks [£2 13s. 4d.] at the Exchequer in the octave of St. Hilary [i.e. 20 January]. Tested by R. de Sadyngton. [v. 1129].

1138 *9 November 1339 Westminster*

Further writ of *venire facias* against Henry de Forneaux, parson of Slimbridge, received 4 January [cf. 1135]. The official of the archdeacon of Gloucester is to certify the bishop of its execution by the fifth day after St. Hilary [i.e. 18 January]. The writ directs the bishop to make the said Henry appear before the justices in 15 days of St. Hilary [i.e. 27 January] to answer the plea of Richard de Thornbury of Gloucestershire that together with John Mautravers senior and John de Glanville he restore £11 6s. 5d. which he owes and unjustly detains, the sheriff of Gloucester having reported that he has no lay fee. Tested by J. de Stonor.

1139 *22 February 1340 Westminster*

Writ of *certiorari* received 24 April at Alvechurch. The bishop is to inform the treasurer and barons of the Exchequer in 15 days of Easter [i.e. 30 April] as to whether the prioress of Wroxall has any spiritual goods in the diocese, and if so, their nature, whereabouts, value and how taxed. Tested by R. de Sadyngton.

RETURN:

The prioress has no spiritual goods in the diocese apart from the church of Hatton which is taxed at ten marks [£6 13s. 4d.].

1140 *5 July 1340 Westminster*

Writ of *certiorari* received 9 July. The king has been loaned all the money from the Cardinals' procurations for the current year until the date he has promised to repay it out of the proceeds of the biennial tenth granted by the clergy of the realm.[1] Accordingly, each prelate has been instructed to refund the sum provided by the procurations out of the tenth to be collected in his diocese [cf. 323]. The bishop is to inform the treasurer and barons of the Exchequer at the parliament to be held at Westminster [v. 137] of the amount of such procurations within his diocese, how much has been paid to him and by whose hand, and how much is still outstanding, and for what reason. The arrears are to be at the Tower on the morrow of St. Margaret [i.e. 21 July] at latest for livery to John de Flete, receiver of the procurations. Tested by R. de Sadyngton.

RETURN:

The writ was received after sunset on 9 July. The bishop [later] sent full information [v. infra].

1141 *12 July 1340 Tredington*

Certification of the above writ [1140 & cf. 16]. Having discussed the matter with his sub-collector, the abbot of Cirencester, the bishop signifies that the total of procurations in his diocese amounts to £184, of which he has received nothing at all. The sub-collector has received £176, half of which he has paid to the proctor of Bertrand, cardinal deacon of St. Mary in Aquiro, the other half being still in his possession.

1142 *16 April 1340 Westminster*

Writ for the collection of an additional tenth, received 29 June.[2] At the congregation of the clergy of Canterbury province which met on Friday the morrow of St. Juliana the Virgin[3] at the church of the Preaching Friars in London, a further tenth, additional to the triennial and annual tenths already conceded, and payable one third at the Nativity of St. John [24 June] and the remainder in

1 In fact it was only the York convocation which granted a biennial tenth.
2 Cf. Rymer & Sanderson, *Foedera* (1816–69), 2, ii, p. 1121.
3 In 1340 the morrow of St. Juliana fell on Thursday 24 February, but the morrow of St. Julianus, bishop and confessor on Friday 28 January. Stubbs (*Const. Hist.* 2, p. 381 n. 4) states that the convocation which granted this additional tenth met on 27 January.

equal instalments at the Purification [2 February 1341] and Nativity of St. John following, was granted subject to the concession of certain petitions touching the liberties of the Church. Of his special grace, and with the consent of his parliament at Westminster,[1] the king has conceded those petitions and has had letters patent drawn up confirming them.[2] The bishop is therefore to appoint collectors of this latest tenth without delay and to send their names to the Exchequer. Tested by the king (*me ipso*).   By the king and Council.

EXECUTION:

[The commissary] is to certify the bishop of his action in the matter by the Assumption [15 August]. Eastington, 29 June 1340.

1143 *18 October 1340 Westminster*

Further writ of *levari facias* against Robert de Hambury [cf. 1128, 1130] received 5 November. The dean of [Droit]wich is to certify the bishop of its execution by St. Edmund the archbishop [16 November]. The writ directs the bishop to levy £265 8s. 10d., part of a debt of £965 8s. 10d., the money to be at the Exchequer in 15 days of St. Martin [i.e. 25 November]. Tested by R. de Sadyngton.

RETURN:

The bishop has levied 20s. from the goods of Robert de Hambury, which he has sent to the Exchequer. He has not found other goods.

1144 *12 July 1340 Blockley*

Mandate [to the official of the Worcester archdeacon?][3] in response to a writ, tested by Edward, duke of Cornwall [&c.], and dated 28 June from Waltham Holy Cross, giving details of the naval victory of 24 June [Sluys] and requesting the prayers of the clergy of the diocese for the successful outcome of the royal expedition to Flanders. The bishop directs that the celebration of Masses, the holding of processions, the offering of prayers, and the performance of other works of piety be encouraged throughout the city and archdeaconry of Worcester and for that purpose grants a 40 days' indulgence.[4]

1 This met 29 March 1340. See 283.
2 *ita quod quasdam supplicaciones per clerum predictum nobis factas super diversis libertatibus et aliis tam pro decore et tranquillitate Anglicane ecclesie quam pro utilitate et prelatorum et aliorum virorum ecclesiasticorum obtinendis eisdem concedere curaremus, quibus quidem supplicacionibus de nostra speciali gracia ad honorem dei et ecclesie predicte ac profectum et quietem prelatorum et aliorum virorum ecclesiasticorum de assensu parliamenti nostri apud Westmonasterium ultimo tenti annuimus et litteras nostras patentes de libertatibus et aliis in eisdem contentis perpetuo duraturis fieri fecimus ut est moris.*
3 The opening phrases of the document have been omitted.
4 The writ is printed in Rymer, *Foedera* V, pp. 195-6, and the complete entry in Thomas, *Appendix* pp. 113-4.

1145 *20 September 1340 Andover*

Writ of *venire facias*. As the king wishes to be speedily informed of certain urgent matters touching his expedition, the bishop is to see that the collectors of the Cardinals' procurations in his diocese appear before the royal Council at Westminster in 15 days of St. Michael [13 October] and meanwhile is to supply their names. Tested by Edward, duke of Cornwall [&c.].[1]

1146 *Undated*

Reply to the above writ. The bishop has cited the abbot of Cirencester, sole collector in the diocese.

1147 *6 December 1340 Westminster*

Further writ of *levari facias* against Robert de Hambury [cf. 1143], received 25 December. The bishop is to raise £364 8s. 10d. from his goods, to be delivered at the Exchequer on the morrow of St. Hilary [i.e. 14 January]. Tested by R. de Sadyngton.

RETURN:

The bishop has had goods sequestrated to the value of 5 marks [£3 6s. 8d.], but so far has not found others. He has not yet had sufficient time to raise money from them.

1148 *16 November 1340 Westminster*

Writ of *venire facias* received 25 December against William le Freen, parson of St. Mary's, Witton by [Droit]wich. He is to be made to appear before the justices in the octave of St. Hilary [i.e. 20 January] to answer the plea of William de la Hulle of Bridgnorth that he restore 100s. which he unjustly detains, the sheriff of Worcester having reported that he has no lay fee. Tested by J. de Stonore.

RETURN:

The bishop has had William le Freen cited.

1149 *9 April 1341 Hartlebury parish church*

Memorandum that Ds. William le Freen, rector of St. Mary's, Witton by [Droit]wich, swore to indemnify the bishop for harm arising from the suit before the king's justices between himself and William de la Hulle. The sequestration imposed on his goods was relaxed and he was admonished under penalty of the law to reside in his church from St. Michael [29 September].

1 Printed in Rymer, *Foedera* V, pp. 204–5.

1150 *24 November 1340 Westminster*

Writ of *venire facias* against Thomas de Hompton, parson of Red-marley, received 17 January. He is to be made to appear before the justices on the morrow of the Purification [i.e. 3 February] to answer the plea of Reginald de Abbehale, kt., that he restore £20 which he unjustly detains, the sheriff of Gloucester having reported that he has no lay fee.

1151 *6 February 1341 Westminster*

Further writ of *levari facias* against Robert de Hambury, received 19 March, the dean of [Droit]wich being directed to certify its execution by Easter [8 April]. From the goods and chattels which he has already sequestrated to the value of 5 marks [v. 1147], and from other goods and ecclesiastical benefices of the above Robert, the bishop is to levy £364 8s. 10d., to be delivered at the Exchequer on the morrow of the close of Easter [i.e. 16 April]. Tested by R. de Sadyngton.

RETURN:

From the goods formerly sequestrated the bishop has raised 5 marks [£3 6s. 8d.] which he is sending to the Exchequer by Ds. John de Stok. Further goods he has been unable to find, apart from eight young oxen (*boviculi*) worth two marks [£1 6s. 8d.] which he has had sequestrated, but cannot at present raise money from them for lack of buyers.

1152 *4 May 1341 Westminster*

Further writ of *levari facias* against Robert de Hambury. From those goods valued at 7 marks [£4 13s. 4d.] which he has already se-questrated [1151], and from other goods, the bishop is to raise £364 8s. 10d., to be delivered at the Exchequer in 15 days of Trinity [i.e. 17 June]. Tested by R. de Sadyngton.

RETURN:

The bishop is sending 7 marks by John de Stok. He has not found other goods.

1153 *24 May 1341 Westminster*

Writ of *distringas*. The bishop is to distrain Robert de Hambury so that he appear before the barons of the Exchequer in 15 days of St. John the Baptist [i.e. 8 July] to render account of the issue of the Chamber of North Wales and of the escheatorship there. Tested by R. de Sadyngton. [cf. 1119, 1128, 1130].

RETURN:

Because the bishop has not been able to find any goods of the said Robert within the diocese he has distrained him by imposing sequestration on the future fruits, profits and obventions of his church of Stoke Prior.

1154 *16 June 1341 Westminster*

Further writ of *levari facias* against Robert de Hambury [cf. 1152–1153]. The bishop is to levy £359 15s. 6d. from his goods, to be delivered at the Exchequer on the morrow of St. Michael [i.e. 30 September]. Tested by R. de Sadyngton.

RETURN:

The bishop has sequestrated goods to the value of 10 marks [£6 13s. 4d.], but is unable to find more at present. He has not had time to raise money from them.

1155 *22 August 1341 Withington*

Memorandum that Ds. Henry Forneaux, rector of Slimbridge, swore before the bishop's special commissary *ad hoc*, M. H[ugh] de Penebrugg, to indemnify the bishop for expenses incurred in the king's court by reason of the suit between John Dygun of Wimborne Minster, Robert de Wodeford, and J. de Devenyssh, and himself. He also swore to leave fruits to the value of £10 and more in his rectory until after full discussion of the said expenses.

1156 *11 July 1341 Westminster*

Writ of *venire facias* against Henry de Hildesleye, parson of Alderley[?] (*Allerleye*). He is to be made to appear before the justices in 15 days of St. Michael [i.e. 13 October] to answer the plea of Maurice de Berkeley, kt., that he restore £29 11s. 6d. which he unjustly detains, the sheriff of Gloucester having reported that he has no lay fee. Tested by R. Hillary.

RETURN:

The bishop has had the above rector cited.

1157 *28 July 1341 Westminster*

Writ of *venire facias* against Robert, parson of Halford. He is to be made to appear before the justices in 3 weeks of St. Michael [i.e. 20 October] to answer the plea of the prior of Kenilworth that he restore £20, arrears of an annual rent of 5 marks [£3 6s. 8d.], the sheriff of Warwick having reported that he has no lay fee. Tested and returned as above [1156].

1158 *23 October 1341 Westminster*

Writ of *venire facias* against Thomas son of Thomas, parson of Rous Lench. He is to appear before the justices in the octave of St. Hilary [i.e. 20 January] to answer the plea of John, son of M. Richard Peore of Alcester, and of John de Aston, executors of the said Richard, that he restore 5 marks [£3 6s. 8d.] which he unjustly detains, the sheriff of Worcester having reported that he has no lay fee. Tested and returned as above [1156].

1159 *27 November 1341 Westminster*

Writ *de bastardia*. Before the king's justices Thomas Bernard has been seeking from Walter Hancokes two acres of land with appurtenances in Brailes of which a relative, Matilda [*Matill'*] la Clerkes, whose heir he is,[1] died seised in demesne as of fee. Thomas came into court and objected that Walter was no heir being a bastard, to which the latter responded that he was legitimate. Because cognition of such a cause belongs to the ecclesiastical forum, the bishop is to enquire as to the truth of the matter and to inform the justices. Tested by R. Hillary.

1160 *6 December 1341 Westminster*

Further writ of *levari facias* against Robert de Hambury. From those goods valued at 10 marks which he has already sequestrated [v. 1154], and from other goods, the bishop is to raise £359 15s. 6d., to be delivered at the Exchequer in 15 days of St. Hilary [i.e. 27 January]. Tested by R. de Sadyngton.

RETURN:

The bishop has sent 10 marks by Thomas de Evesham. He has not found other goods.

1161 *6 February 1342 Westminster*

Writ of *ne admittas* received 24 February at Hartlebury. The bishop is not to admit anyone to Batsford church, alleged to be vacant, the advowson of which is being disputed in the king's court between John Golafre and Walter de Hodynton. Tested by the king (*me ipso*).

1162 *6 February 1342 Westminster*

Writ of *venire facias* against Richard de Colewych, parson of Charfield. He is to be made to appear before the justices in 3 weeks of Easter [i.e. 21 April] to answer the plea of Walter le Marner, chaplain, and John de Puttelegh, executors of the will of Robert de

---

1 i.e. Thomas: *consanguinea predicti Thome cuius heres ipse est . . .*

Goldhull, and of John le Walsch and Isabella his wife, their co-executors, that he, together with Margaret formerly wife of Richard de Aston, the executors of the said Richard, restore to Peter de Veel and John de Melkesham £36 which they unjustly detain, the sheriff of Gloucester having reported to the justices in 15 days of St. Hilary [i.e. 27 January] that he has no lay fee. Tested by R. Hillary.

1163 *5 February 1342 Westminster*

Writ, received 26 February, informing the bishop of Roger Basset's recovery in the king's court against Ralph [de Ermenovilla], prior of Deerhurst, of the advowson of Little Compton in Henmarsh church, and directing him to admit Roger's presentee if suitable. Tested by R. Hillary.

1164 *22 January 1342 Morpeth*

Writ of *ne admittas* received 7 February. The bishop is not to admit anyone to the church of Little Compton in Henmarsh, alleged to be vacant, the advowson of which is being disputed in the king's court between Roger Basset of Sutton and Ralph [de Ermenovilla] prior of Deerhurst and M. Robert de Ikcumbe. Tested by the king (*me ipso*).

1165 *15 February 1342 Westminster*

A further writ of *ne admittas* concerning Little Compton church. No-one is to be admitted while the advowson is in dispute between the King and Roger Basset [cf. 1164]. Tested as above.

1166 *28 January 1342 Westminster*

Further writ of *levari facias* against Robert de Hambury [cf. 1160]. He is to levy £353 2s. 2d. out of a total debt of £865[1] 8s. 10d. the money to be delivered at the Exchequer on the morrow of the close of Easter [i.e. 8 April]. Tested by R. de Sadyngton.

1167 *13 April 1342 Westminster*

Further writ of *levari facias* against Robert de Hambury for the same sum, which is to be at the Exchequer on the morrow of Trinity [i.e. 3 June]. Tested as above.

1168 *7 May 1342 Westminster*

Writ of *venire facias* against John de Enefeld, merchant, received 29 May. He is to be made to appear before the justices on the morrow

1 *Recte* £965.

of St. John the Baptist [i.e. 25 June], to answer the plea of Thomas de Berkeley that he restore £20 which he unjustly detains, the sheriff of Gloucester having reported that he has no lay fee. Tested by R. Hillary.

RETURN:

The bishop has had John de Enefeld cited.

1169 *24 June 1342 Westminster*

Writ of *fieri facias* against Thomas de Hompton, parson of Redmarley. A sum of money [1] is to be delivered at the Exchequer on the morrow of St. Michael [i.e. 30 September]. Tested by R. de Sadyngton.

RETURN:

The bishop has levied 4 marks [£2 13s. 4d.] which he is sending by the bearer to the Exchequer for payment to John de Baddemy [*recte* Baddeby]. He has not found other goods on this occasion.

1170 *5 June 1342 Westminster*

Further writ of *levari facias* against Robert de Hambury [cf. 1166]. The bishop is to levy £353 2s. 2d. out of a total debt of £965 8s. 10d., the money to be delivered at the Exchequer on the morrow of St. Michael [i.e. 30 September]. Tested by R. de Sadyngton.

RETURN:

Goods have been sequestrated to the value of 10 marks [£6 13s. 4d.], but the bishop has been unable to raise money from them for lack of buyers. He has not found other goods.

1171 *12 August 1342*

A writ *pro pace*. [Duplicate of the writ *Terribilis in iudiciis* recited in 1045].

1172 *10 November 1342 Westminster*

Writ informing the bishop that the king has recovered against Roger Basset his presentation to the church of Little Compton, which is vacant. It is in the king's gift because the temporalities of Deerhurst priory are in his hands on account of the war with France. Tested by J. de Stonor'. [Cf. 1163-5].

---

1 The scribe missed out part of the writ which *mutatis mutandis* is the same as 1176 and 1177.

1173 *10 November 1342 Westminster*

Similar writ informing the bishop of the king's recovery of his presentation to the above church against Ralph [de Ermenovilla], prior of Deerhurst. Tested as above.

1174 *11 October 1342 Westminster*

Writ of *levari facias* against M. Robert de Wygorn', archdeacon of Worcester, received 3 January [1343] at Kempsey. From goods belonging to his archdeaconry and from his other ecclesiastical goods, the bishop is to levy £46 13s. 4d., arrears of the farm of Letcombe manor. The money is to be at the Exchequer on the morrow of St. Hilary [i.e. 14 January]. Tested by R. de Sadyngton.

RETURN:

The writ arrived late.

1175 *24 October 1342 Westminster*

Further writ of *levari facias* against Robert de Hambury, received 4 August at Kempsey. From those goods valued at 10 marks which he has already sequestrated [v. 1170], and from other goods, the bishop is to levy £353 2s. 2d., the money to be delivered at the Exchequer on the morrow of St. Hilary [i.e. 14 January]. Tested by R. de Sadyngton.

RETURN:

The bishop sent 10 marks [£6 13s. 4d.] and certified that he was unable to raise more during the current year or to proceed against Robert in other ways, he being in the king's service.

1176 *10 November 1342 Westminster*

Writ of *fieri facias* against Thomas de Hompton, parson of Redmarley, received 4 January. The bishop is to raise £27 6s. 8d. out of a debt of £530 14s. which Thomas de Hompton, Robert de Hompton, Henry son of John de Hereford of Frome, Walter Moton, William son of Ralph Hathewy and William son of William Hathewy, acknowledged before the barons of the Exchequer on 15 April 13 Edward III [1339] that they owed to Queen Isabella, and which they ought to have paid at terms long past. The money is to be at the Exchequer in 15 days of St. Hilary [i.e. 27 January] for payment to John de Baddeby, Isabella's receiver. Tested by R. de Sadyngton.

RETURN:

Apart from what was sent at the last term [1169] nothing can be levied from his goods until this year's fruits have been received.

1177 *24 April 1343 Westminster*

Further writ of *fieri facias* against Thomas de Hompton for livery of the same sum [v. 1176] in 15 days of Trinity [i.e. 22 June].

RETURN:

The bishop has found nothing among the goods of Thomas de Hompton from which money can be raised, nor will he be able to find anything before Autumn.

1178 *20 May 1343 Westminster*

Further writ of *levari facias* against M. Robert de Wygorn', archdeacon of Worcester, received 8 June [v. 1174]. The bishop is to have £46 13s. 4d. at the Exchequer on the morrow of St. John the Baptist [i.e. 25 June]. A writ returnable on the morrow of the close of Easter [i.e. 21 April] has been ignored. Tested by R. de Sadyngton.

RETURN:

Although diligent in the matter, the bishop cannot levy any money before the harvest.

1179 *7 August 1343 Henbury*

Letter to John de Stononere [*sic*] and his fellow justices. As it is expedient that the names of excommunicates should be known to all the faithful, lest they infect the Lord's flock, the bishop is notifying them that Roger Thwangton, merchant, is under sentence of greater excommunication.[1]

For this letter William de Chiltenham promised to indemnify the bishop.

1180 *23 June 1343 Westminster*

Writ of *supersedeas* for M. Robert de Wygorn'. As farmer of the abbot of Cluny's manor of Letcombe in Berkshire M. Robert is acquitted at the Exchequer of £70 which he owes to the king for arrears of the custody of that manor. The bishop is therefore not to execute the former mandate [1178] and is to relax any sequestration imposed. Tested by R. de Sadyngton.

1181 *26 June 1343 Westminster*

Further writ of *levari facias* against Robert de Hambury, received 15 September at Little Malvern. The bishop is to have £346 8s. 10d. [cf. 1175] at the Exchequer on the morrow of St. Michael [i.e. 30 September]. Tested as above.

1 *Postea mutata fuit hec forma ut supraadditur apud Wythindon vicesimo quinto die mensis Septembris eodem anno.* It probably became a letter *ad capiendum excommunicatum* as the marginal rubric states.

1182 *25 June 1343 Westminster*

Further writ of *fieri facias* against Thomas de Hompton, received on
the same day as the one above. The bishop is to have £37 6s. 8d.
[cf. 1176–7] at the Exchequer on the morrow of St. Michael [i.e.
30 September]. Tested as above.

1183 *Undated*

Return of the writ against Robert de Hambury [1181]. The bishop
has sequestrated all the goods and benefices of the said Robert
which he can find within the diocese, but is unable to raise the money
from them both because of their insufficiency and of the lack of
buyers. As soon as he can find purchasers he will send what money
he is able to raise to the Exchequer.

1184 *Undated*

Return of the preceding writ against Thomas de Hompton [1182].
The bishop has levied 100s. from goods received after the arrival of
the mandate, and is sending the whole of that sum. He is unable to
raise anything further from the goods on this occasion.

1185 *21 October 1343 Westminster*

Writ of *venire facias* against John de la Chambre, parson of Castle
Eaton,[1] received 5 November. He is to be made to appear before the
justices in the octave of St. Martin [i.e. 18 November] to answer the
plea of Walter Turk, citizen of London, that he restore £20 which he
unjustly detains, the sheriff of Middlesex having reported in 15 days
of St. Michael [i.e. 13 October] that he has no lay fee. Tested by
J. de Stonore.[2]

1186 *13 October 1343 Westminster*

Writ for the collection of arrears of a tenth in the Gloucester archdeaconry [cf. 1047], received 26 October at Stanton (*Stantone*). The
abbot of Winchcombe is still burdened with the following sums:
7s. 8d. for the precentor of Hereford and 24s. for the church of
Eastleach St. Martin. The bishop is to see that the collector is paid
without delay, but any of the clergy who can produce acquittances
are to appear at the Exchequer in 15 days of the Purification [i.e.
16 February], measures taken against them being stayed meanwhile
[cf. 1118]. Tested by W. de Stowe.

1187 *Undated*

Reply to a writ tested by Edward, duke of Cornwall [&c.], and
dated 22 January 1343 from Westminster. The prior of Great

1 *Eton Meysey.*
2 *Istuc dormit* is written in the margin. See 1201.

Malvern has intimated that as the bishop has appointed him collector within the diocese of the latest tenth granted by the clergy of Canterbury province [v. 1048] and he has no safe places in which to keep the money, his monastery being in a desolate spot (*loco solitudinis et vastitatis*) within Malvern chase and lacking suitable enclosure, the king may well be deprived of the proceeds by malefactors at large in that area. In consequence he has petitioned to be relieved of such collection. The truth of the prior's contention has been testified to before the king's Council and the bishop is accordingly directed to appoint another collector in his place. In reply the bishop argues that the prior of Great Malvern has long been accustomed to collect such tenths, that he and his helpers are consequently more expert than others, the registers are in his possession, and he knows the persons and churches concerned and the burdens incumbent upon them, and in any case has been appointed after due deliberation as being a knowledgeable person of substance, well suited to undertake the task. In case the pretended excuse of the monastery's isolation should weigh with the king, the bishop points out that he has allocated a place within the city of Worcester for the collector's use. Besides which, he understands that the prior has already collected tenths from some churches, so that if there were to be a change considerable confusion might result. He has certified the barons of the Exchequer of the prior's appointment, and the king will see that the petition was made more for the latter's relief than for the royal convenience and honour. He will therefore retain the prior's services despite the worthless arguments to the contrary.

1188 *Undated*

Reply to an undated writ of *certiorari* demanding information about Trimpley vicarage, when it last fell vacant, by whose death and in what manner, if anyone has been admitted or instituted or is at present in possession, and if so, the name of such person, and the time and manner of his gaining possession. The bishop has had his register carefully examined, but without result. By means of an enquiry and through public instruments which have been shown to him he has discovered that the vicarage fell vacant on 9 June 1340 with the death of Richard de Doudeswell, and that William Hyde of Aldsworth is now vicar and became so on 10 June in the same year by virtue of a grace of Pope Benedict XII, his acceptance of the benefice, collation by the executor of the grace, and by induction. The said Richard has held it from that time and is still in possession.

1189 *24 February 1343 Byfleet*

Writ summoning the bishop and representatives of the clergy of the diocese [as in 1132] to attend a parliament at Westminster on the

Monday after the quindene of Easter [i.e. 28 April]. Out of reverence for the pope and at the instance of his special nuncios, the cardinal bishops of Palestrina and Tusculum, a truce has been concluded with France [Malestroit: 19 January 1343] in the hope that an honourable peace may follow, for which purpose envoys have to be sent to the Holy See by the Nativity of St. John [24 June]. The parliament is being summoned to discuss this and other matters. Tested by Edward, duke of Cornwall [&c.]

1190 *4 March 1343 Westminster*

Writ countermanding payment from the proceeds of a tenth. Although £500 from the most recent tenth, payable at terms still to come [v. 1046–7], was assigned to the king's clerk, M. Paul de Monte Florum,[1] £200 to be paid at the first term and £300 at the second, and although the collectors deputed by the bishop have been instructed to make such payment and to receive tallies for the amount, the king no longer wishes it to be made and directs the bishop to order the collectors to gather the money for the tenth with all speed and to keep it pending further instructions. Should any of them pay money to M. Paul it will not be allowed to them in their account at the Exchequer. Tested by W. de Cusanc', the king's treasurer.

1191 *Undated*

Memorandum of the royal privileges granted to the bishop and his predecessors. An extract from the Great [Pipe] Roll of 16 Edward III[2] shows that the sheriff of Worcester accounted at the Exchequer for 10s. on account of the licence granted to Osbert Spelly and Agnes, his wife, for their tenements in Northwick by Worcester, and for 2d. for John de Fladbury, because he did not come. As they were all tenants of the bishop, the 10s. 2d. was paid to him in accordance with the royal writ enrolled among the Memoranda for the 14th year, Michaelmas term. There it is recorded that Edward II granted to Walter Reginald [Reynolds], formerly bishop of Worcester [1308–1313], that he and his successors should have the return of all writs in the lands of the bishopric, pleas *de vetito namii*, and the chattels of felons and fugitives, as well as the fines and amercements of all men and their tenants, to be levied for the bishop's use without hindrance of the king, justices, sheriffs [&c.]. The present king confirmed that charter and further granted to Simon [de Montacute], a later bishop [1333–7], that even if advantage had not been taken of such liberties in any particular case, he and his successors should

1 He had been engaged in Edward III's wool transactions. See *History* N.S., xxxvii (February 1952) no. 129, p. 21.
2 Exchequer year 29 September 1341—29 September 1342.

continue to enjoy them. The king has ordered that Bishop Wolstan is likewise to enjoy such liberties and payments.

1192 *22 April 1343 Hartlebury*

The bishop excuses himself from attendance at the parliament summoned for 28 April [1189] and appoints M. John de Severleye, his chancellor, and Ds. William de Salwarp, steward of his household (*nostri hospicii senescallum*), to act as proctors.

1193 *16 February 1343 Westminster*

Writ of *venire facias* against William de Bremesgrave, vicar of Inkberrow. He is to be made to appear before the justices a month from Easter [13 April] to answer the plea of John de Harddepire of Evesham that he restore 20 marks [£13 6s. 8d.] which he unjustly detains, the sheriff of Worcester having reported that he has no lay fee. Tested by J. de Stonore.

1194 *22 April 1343*

Appointment of proctors for parliament. [Duplicate of 1192].

1195 *20 July 1343 Clarendon*

Writ forbidding the admission of foreigners to benefices.[1] Papal provisions of alien persons to ecclesiastical benefices have become more excessive than usual, not only to the impoverishment of the realm and the lessening of divine worship within it, but also to the intolerable prejudice and disinheritance of the king and his subjects, and the curtailment of the right of patronage and advowson. Because of this, and at the urgent request of the community of the realm in his parliament which met on 28 April last [v. 1192], the king intends to curb the attempts of those who are striving to seize the advowsons and rights of the Crown. The bishop is forbidden to admit aliens or their proctors to benefices by reason of papal provisions, bulls or processes, or himself to provide them to such apostolic authority; to bring ecclesiastical sentences against those who resist aliens, or to do anything else prejudicial to the king's dignity and the right of patronage. Tested by the king (*me ipso*).

By the king and Council.

1196 *26 October 1343 Westminster*

Writ against Robert de Hambury received 11 November. The bishop has returned a writ of *levari facias* [1181] to the effect that he was unable to raise money from the sequestrated goods of the above

1 Cf. Rymer & Sanderson, *Foedera* (1816–69), 2, ii, p. 1230.

Robert for the time being [1183]. All such goods are to be offered for sale without delay and the required sum of £346 8s. 10d. levied from them, the money to be at the Exchequer in the octave of St. Martin [i.e. 18 November]. Robert's benefices are to remain under sequestration until the above debt is paid in full. Tested by W. de Stouwe.

RETURN:

The bishop has raised £4 13s. which he is sending to the Exchequer by Ds. John de Stok. He is unable to levy more from the goods.

1197 *4 November 1343 Westminster*

Writ for the collection of arrears of a tenth in the Worcester archdeaconry. The prior of Great Malvern [v. 1186–7] is still burdened with the following sums: £2 4s. for Aston church, 17s. 4d. for Suckley church, and 8s. 8d. for that of Bourton. The bishop is to see that the collector is paid without delay, but any of the clergy who can produce acquittances are to appear at the Exchequer in 15 days of St. Hilary [i.e. 27 January], measures taken against them being stayed meanwhile [cf. 1118]. Tested by W. de Stouwe.

1198 *14 November 1343 Westminster*

Writ *de bastardia* received 3 January at Hartlebury. In the king's court at Westminster Thomas Flory is claiming against John Joye 10 acres of land and 3 of meadow with appurtenances in Frampton-on-Severn as his right and inheritance by the seisin of one John Flory, his father, whose heir he alleges himself to be. John Joye came into court and objected that Thomas was no heir but a bastard. The bishop is to inform the justices of the truth of the matter [as in 1159]. Tested by J. de Stonore.

1199 *Undated*

Return of the above writ. The bishop signifies that an enquiry has found Thomas Flory to be legitimate.

1200 *8 December 1343 Westminster*

Writ of *supersedeas* for Robert de Hambury. The bishop is not to execute a former writ of *levari facias* [1196] and is to relax any sequestration imposed on Robert's goods. Tested by W. de Stowe.

1201 *3 December 1343 Westminster*

Writ of *venire facias* against John de la Chambre, parson of Castle Eaton,[1] received 13 January. He is to be made to appear before the

1 *Eton Meysey.* Cf. 1185.

justices in the octave of St. Hilary [i.e. 20 January] to answer the plea of Walter Turk, citizen of London, that he restore £20 [v. 1185]. Tested by J. de Stonore.

RETURN:

The church of Castle Eaton is not in the diocese, as the writ supposes. Consequently the bishop cannot make John de la Chambre appear.

1202 *14 November 1343*

Writ *de bastardia*. [Duplicate of 1198].

1203 *12 December 1343 Westminster*

Writ ordering the bishop to obey the ordinance prohibiting the bringing into England of any letters, bulls, processes [&c.], pre-judicial to the king and people, and forbidding their receipt without special licence, under pain of forfeiture. Tested by the king (*me ipso*).[1]

1204 *17 November 1343 Westminster*

Writ, received 31 January [1344], informing the bishop of the abbot of Halesowen's recovery in the king's court against John Botetourt of his presentation to the church of Clent, then vacant. He is to admit the abbot's presentee if suitable. Tested by J. de Stonore.

1205 *19 February 1343 Westminster*

Further writ of *fieri facias* against Thomas de Hompton, parson of Redmarley, received 16 March. The bishop is to have £32 6s. [cf. 1182] at the Exchequer on the morrow of the close of Easter [i.e. 21 April]. Tested by W. de Stowe.

1206 *Undated*

Return of the above writ. The bishop has been unable to find goods of the said Thomas and so can levy nothing before the harvest.

1207 *7 March 1344 Westminster*

Writ summoning the bishop to discuss, together with the prelates and others whom the king has ordered to be present, certain arduous and urgent affairs touching both the honour of God and the English church, and the welfare and safety of the realm. Tested by the king (*me ipso*).[2]

---

1 Printed in Wilkins, *Concilia* 2, p. 726.
2 The scribe omitted a phrase containing the date and place of the meeting. Cf. 1208.

1208 *Undated [1344]*

The bishop excuses himself from the Council (*tractatus*) summoned to Westminster for the quindene of Easter [i.e. 18 April] and appoints M. John de Thorsby, M. John de Severleye, and Ds. John de Stok, jointly and severally, as his proctors.

1209 *8 February 1344 Westminster*

Writ of *venire facias* against John de Rivers (*Ripariis*), received 7 April at Hartlebury. He is to be made to appear before the justices in 3 weeks of Easter [i.e. 25 April], to answer the plea of M. Elias of Saint Albans that he restore £56 18s. 6d. which he unjustly detains, the sheriff of Worcester having reported in the octave of St. Hilary [i.e. 20 January] that he has no lay fee. Tested by J. de Stonore.

1211 *1 May 1344 Hartlebury*

A second ordination of Tormarton chantry.[1] John de la Rivere, knight, has petitioned for the incorporation of Tormarton church as a perpetual *custodia* under the rule of a warden and with four chaplains, who are to celebrate Mass (*divina*) there in perpetuity, two clerks, one serving in the office of deacon, the other in that of subdeacon, and three choristers. He has asked the bishop to make provision for their offices and stipends in the following manner. The chaplains, clerks and choristers, clothed in white surplices and black almuces, are to come together daily in the church for the appointed Hours. They are to sing Matins and to celebrate three Masses: one, sung, of Our Lady; another, said, for the souls of the departed mentioned below; and the third, also sung, is to be the Mass of the day. On all days when according to the Sarum Use obsequies of the dead are to be performed in choir, they are to say them, prior to singing Vespers, for the souls of John de la Rivere, the founder, Margaret his wife, King Edward and Queen Philippa, Wolstan, bishop of Worcester, and John de Evesham, the cathedral prior—after their deaths, and for the souls of the founder's father and mother, his ancestors and descendants, patrons of the church, the benefactors of the chantry, the chaplains, and all the faithful departed. On the day of the founder's burial and of his anniversary, as on those of his father and mother and each of his descendants, patrons of the church, they are to perform obsequies and celebrate Mass for the departed. The warden is to make personal residence at his church and either he or one of the chaplains deputed for that purpose is to exercise the cure of souls. When the warden is present at the above offices he is to wear a white surplice and a fur or silk almuce according to the

1 The first part of this later ordination, which contains *inter alia* the mortmain licence, and the last part, which includes the penalty clauses, are materially as in 449 and have been omitted here.

season. As a mark of dignity he is to wear an over-tunic without openings (*supertunica clausa*), and when exercising the office of priest, a black furred cap, broad and round. He is to dispense stipends of 24s., 6s. and 40d. respectively, to each chaplain, clerk and chorister, and is to provide them with food and adequate accommodation in his house. He is to maintain one lamp continually burning in the chancel and other necessary lights, books, chalices, vestments and altar ornaments. For the support of this burden the founder has given oxen, horses and sheep to the value of £20. Each warden is to leave for his successor an equivalent amount in stock and money. For greater security the bishop decrees that the warden [&c.].[1]

1212 *3 May 1344 Hartlebury*

Union of the churches of Acton Turville and Tormarton. The warden and chaplains of Tormarton church, for which the bishop has lately provided a number of chaplains, clerks and other ministers, as is fully set out in his ordination [1211], have urged that their rents and profits are insufficient for the upkeep of themselves and the burdens incumbent on their church. They have therefore petitioned the bishop to unite Acton Turville church to that of Tormarton, it being in their patronage, as is evident from a charter of John de la Rivere, until recently the patron. The bishop, having enquired of trustworthy persons as to the truth of the above, and after careful discussion with the prior of Worcester, William de la Scherde, rector of Acton, and all others concerned, has declared, with their counsel and express consent, that the causes are true, sufficient and canonical, and thus reasonable and just, and that the union should be proceeded with on the grounds of urgent necessity and evident utility. Accordingly he unites and incorporates Acton church with that of Tormarton and appropriates it to the warden and chaplains.[2] On the death or cession of William de la Scherde it will be lawful for them to take possession; a suitable portion, to be assigned by the bishop or his successors, being reserved to a perpetual vicar who is to have the cure of souls. As indemnity for the loss suffered by the church of Worcester the chaplains on taking possession are to pay 6s. 8d. every Michaelmas [29 September] to the prior and convent.

1213 *Undated*

Ordination of the vicarage of Acton Turville. The bishop has appropriated Acton church to the perpetual warden of Tormarton parish church, with reservation of a suitable portion for a perpetual vicar [v. 1212]. The warden and chaplains are to have the tithes of

---

1 *mutatis mutandis* as in 449, *custos* and *custodia* being used in place of *rector* and *rectoria*.
2 . . . *ecclesiam de Acton . . . prefate ecclesie de Tormerton annectimus unimus incorporamus et concedimus in proprios usus vestros perpetuo possidendum* [*sic*].

corn and hay from the parish of Acton, together with the whole of the arable, meadow and other demesne land of the church, but with certain exceptions. The vicars are to have the hall and all the chambers, the kitchen, stable and the *pomarium*, commonly called *Orchart*, next to the hall, with free access to the same. They are also to have in each field of the vill of Acton five acres of arable land and one of hay meadow [*pratum falcabilis*] from the said demesne, together with the pasture appropriate for that amount of land according to the custom of the vill. In addition the vicars are to receive all other tithes, rents, profits and offerings, both greater and lesser, belonging to Acton church. The warden and chaplains are to sustain all ordinary and extraordinary burdens, except that of one silver mark [13s. 4d.] payable at Michaelmas [29 September] to the cathedral chapter as indemnity. This the vicars are to discharge. The latter are also to find lights, bread and wine for Mass [*divina*] in the same manner as the rectors were wont to do.

1214 *11 September 1344*

Royal presentation,[1] by reason of the vacancy of the bishopric, of Thomas de Baddeby, king's clerk, to the church of Tredington. Tested by the king (*me ipso*).

1215 [?] *October 1344*

Writ informing the bishop of the king's recovery against him of the presentation to Tredington church.[2]

1216 *20 April 1344 Westminster*

Writ summoning the bishop and representatives of the clergy of the diocese [as in 1132] to attend a parliament at Westminster on Monday after the octave of Trinity [i.e. 7 June]. Tested by the king (*me ipso*).

1217 *Undated*

The bishop excuses himself from attendance at the above parliament and appoints M. John de Thoresby, M. John de Severleye and Ds. John de Stok', jointly and severally, as his proctors.

1218 *27 April 1344 Stepney (Stebbenhethe)*

Mandate of Ralph [Stratford], bishop of London [1340–54], [in his capacity of dean of the Canterbury province]. He has received letters

1 *C.P.R.* 1343–45, p. 349.
2 *C.P.R.* 1343–45, p. 419. Only about half of the entry in the register is legible.

of the archbishop, dated 26 April from Lambeth, directing him to
execute a writ, tested by the king at Westminster on the 22nd,[1] for
summoning the clergy of the province to London. Accordingly he
directs the diocesan to appear in St. Paul's church on Monday the
morrow of Trinity [i.e. 31 May] and to cite representatives of the
clergy of his diocese to do likewise [as in 1043].[2]

1219 *10 May 1344 Acton Turville*

Certification by the official of the archdeacon of Gloucester of his
execution of the bishop's mandate, dated 3 May from Hartlebury,
for enquiry as to the annual value of Acton Turville church. He held
an enquiry in the above church on 10 May by means of the rectors
of Dyrham, Iron Acton, Dodington, Little Sodbury and Horton, the
vicars of Great Sodbury, Great Badminton and Wapley, the proctors
of other absent rectors and vicars, and Stephen Batyn, John atte
Welle, William Longe, William ate Welle, Thomas Hobbes and
John Edith, laymen, parishioners of Acton, all of whom were sworn
in forma iuris. The enquiry found as follows: the demesne land of
the church with the hay and the rectory house is worth 36s. in
common years, the assize rents amount to 8s.; in common years the
greater tithes of corn are worth £9, those of hay 12s., live and dead
mortuaries 6s. 8d., the tithe of wool and lambs, with the offerings,
lesser tithes, and everything else belonging to the altarage of the
church, 46s. 8d.; while the burdens to be sustained are 6s. 8d. for the
archdeacon of Gloucester's procuration at times of visitation, and
2s. a year for synodals.

1220 *20 May 1344 Blockley*

Letter to the archbishop in which the diocesan excuses himself from
personal attendance at the council summoned to London,[3] and
names the bearers, M. Thomas Euwyas, advocate in the Court of
Canterbury, and M. Thomas de Bradewell, as his proctors, jointly
or severally.

1221 *14 April 1344 Westminster*

Further writ of *fieri facias* against Thomas de Hompton, received
3 June at Blockley. The bishop is to have £32 6s. [cf. 1205] at the
Exchequer on the morrow of St. John the Baptist [i.e. 25 June].
Tested by W. de Stowe.

1 And received by the archbishop on the 25th.
2 A marginal sign refers to the entry concerning the appointment of proctors [1220].
3 *Procuratorium ad excusandum dominum episcopum a concilio archiepiscopi ne intersit* (rubric).
   A marginal sign refers back to 1218.

1222 *11 June 1344 Westminster*

Writ of *venire facias* against John de Ryvers, canon of Salisbury, parson of Hanbury, Coventry & Lichfield diocese, received 22 June at Blockley [cf. 1209]. He is to be made to appear before the justices in 15 days of St. John the Baptist [i.e. 8 July] to answer the plea of Richard de la Poule that he keep the agreement whereby he granted to him the fruits and profits of Hanbury church for a term of years, Robert [Wyville], bishop of Salisbury [1330–75], having come before the justices in the octave of Trinity [i.e. 6 June] and declared that John is a clerk beneficed in [Worcester] diocese.

1223 *12 July 1344 Westminster*

Further writ of *fieri facias* against Thomas de Hompton, received 3 August at Hartlebury. The bishop is to have £32 6s. [cf. 1221] at the Exchequer on the morrow of St. Michael [i.e. 30 September]. Tested by W. de Shareshull.

RETURN:

The bishop has had goods sequestrated to the value of 8 marks [£5 6s. 8d.], but has been unable to raise money from them for lack of buyers. He cannot find further goods on this occasion.

1224 *14 July 1344 Westminster*

Writ of *certiorari* received 12 September at Withington. The bishop is to inform the treasurer and barons of the Exchequer in the octave of St. Michael [i.e. 6 October] of the date of his institution of Peter Malet to Barnsley church, by reason of an exchange with Geoffrey atte Chirche for Spettisbury, Salisbury diocese, and also whether the said Geoffrey is native or a foreigner. Tested by W. de Schareshull.

RETURN:

Peter Malet was instituted 1 August 1343 [v. 431, 516]. The said Geoffrey is a native. This the bishop has discovered from his registers.

1225 *11 July 1344 Westminster*

Further writ of *venire facias* against John de Ryvers, canon of Salisbury and parson of Hanbury [Staffs.], received 19 September at Gloucester. He is to appear before the justices in the octave of St. Michael [i.e. 6 October] to answer a plea of Richard de la Poule [as in 1222], the sheriff of Berkshire having reported that he has no lay fee. Tested by J. de Stonore.

RETURN:

The bishop has had the above John cited.

1226 *16 July 1344 Westminster*

Writ of *venire facias*. The sheriff of London has returned at the Exchequer in 3 weeks of St. John the Baptist [i.e. 15 July] that M. Byndo de Bandinellis, rector of Suckley, has nothing in his bailiwick by which he can be attached, and that he is a clerk beneficed in [Worcester] diocese. The bishop is therefore to make him appear at Westminster on the morrow of St. Michael [i.e. 30 September] to answer the plea of the king and the prior of the alien house of Newent, proctor of the abbot of Cormeilles in England, that he render 32 marks [£21 6s. 8d.], arrears of an annual pension of 4 marks [£2 13s. 4d.], which he unjustly detains. The prior is under obligation to the king for this sum to the extent of his lands and possessions, which are in the royal hand and in the prior's custody in return for an annual farm. Tested by W. de Shareshull.

RETURN:

The bishop has been unable to find the above Byndo either in his church of Suckley or elsewhere in the diocese.

1227 *26 November 1344 Westminster*

Writ of *fieri facias* against William de Bremesgrave, vicar of Inkberrow, received 23 December at Hartlebury. The bishop is to have 20 marks [£13 6s. 8d.] before the justices in the octave of St. Hilary [i.e. 20 January] for payment to John de Hardepirie of Evesham, who has recovered them in the king's court [v. 1193]. He is to have a further 40s. there at the same term, being damages awarded for non-payment of the above debt. The sheriff of Worcester has reported that William is a clerk without lay fee. Tested by J. de Stonore.

RETURN:

The bishop has had goods sequestrated to the value of 60s., but for lack of buyers has not been able to raise any money on this occasion.

1228 *10 November 1344 Westminster*

Writ of *distringas* received 6 January at Hartlebury. The bishop is to distrain M. Peter Malet, rector of Barnsley, an alien clerk of the diocese [cf. the return of 1224], so that he appear before the barons of the Exchequer on the morrow of St. Nicholas [i.e. 7 December] to make satisfaction to the king for the fruits and profits of his church from 1 August 17 Edward III [1343], which, on account of the war with France, belong to the king. Tested by W. de Stowe.

RETURN:

The writ arrived late, that is 6 January, and so could not be executed on this occasion.

1229 *5 October 1344 Westminster*

Further writ of *fieri facias* against Thomas de Hompton, received 6 January [1345] at Hartlebury. The bishop is to have £27 6s. [cf. 1223] at the Exchequer in 15 days of St. Hilary [i.e. 27 January]. Tested by W. de Shareshull.

RETURN:

The bishop has not found any goods of the rector of Redmarley, nor will he be able to do so until next Autumn.

1230 *18 December 1344 Westminster*

Further writ of *distringas* against M. Peter Malet, received 6 January at Hartlebury. He is to be distrained by his ecclesiastical goods and benefices in such manner that neither he nor anyone else can meddle with them, so that he appear at the Exchequer on the morrow of St. Hilary [i.e. 14 January]. A previous writ [1228] was not returned on the morrow of St. Nicholas [i.e. 7 December].

RETURN:

The writ arrived late, that is 6 January, so the bishop could not do as he was ordered.

1231 *18 December 1344 Hoxne*

Writ for the collection of a tenth, received 6 January at Hartlebury. The clergy of the Canterbury province when they assembled at St. Paul's on 31 May last [v. 1218] granted a triennial tenth, the amount due for each year being payable in equal instalments at the Purification [2 February] and the feast of St. Barnabas [11 June]. Accordingly the bishop is to appoint collectors without delay and to send their names to the Exchequer. Tested by the king (*me ipso*).

1232 *Undated*

Reply to the above writ. The bishop has appointed the abbot of Tewkesbury and the prior of Studley as collectors in the archdeaconries of Gloucester and Worcester respectively. So as not to burden them excessively, he intends to depute other collectors for the second and third years, whose names he will send at the appropriate time.

1233 *20 January 1345 Westminster*

Further writ of *distringas* against M. Peter Malet, received 6 February at Hartlebury. The bishop is to distrain him by his ecclesiastical goods and benefices so that he appear before the barons of the Exchequer on the morrow of the close of Easter [i.e. 4 April], as the previous writ [1230] had not been delivered in time. Tested by W. de Shareshull.

RETURN:

M. Peter Malet has no ecclesiastical goods in the diocese by which he can be distrained, nor will have before harvest.

1234 *7 February 1345 Westminster*

Further writ of *fieri facias* against William de Brymesgrave, vicar of Inkberrow. The bishop is to have before the justices in 15 days of Easter [i.e. 10 April] the 60s. which he has already secured [v. 1227] and still retains. He is also to raise £10 6s. 8d., the remainder of a debt of 20 marks, and 40s.; such sums to be at Westminster at the same time for livery to John de Hardepirie of Evesham. Tested by J. de Stonore.

RETURN:

The bishop is sending the 60s. by Nicholas la Rok. Although he has made every effort, he has not so far been able to levy anything further from the vicar's goods.

1235 *30 January 1345 Westminster*

Writ of *venire facias* against John de Ryvers, lately parson of Hanbury [Staffs.], received 3 March at Hartlebury. He is to be made to appear before the justices in 15 days of Easter [i.e. 10 April] to answer the plea of Nicholas de Coleshulle, lately parson of Broughton, that he render 9 robes, arrears of an annual rent of one robe, which he unjustly detains, the sheriff[1] having reported in the octave of St. Hilary [i.e. 20 January] that he has no lay fee. Tested by J. de Stonore.

RETURN:

He has had the above John cited.

1236 *18 February 1345 Westminster*

Further writ of *fieri facias* against Thomas de Hompton, received 20 March at Hartlebury. The bishop is to have £32 6s. at the Ex-

1 The county is omitted. Cf. 1225.

chequer in 15 days of Easter [i.e. 10 April]. Tested by W. de Shareshull.

RETURN:

As 1229.

1237 *28 April 1345 Westminster*

Further writ of *fieri facias* against William de Brymesgrave. The bishop is to have 15 marks 6s. 8d. [£10 6s. 8d.] before the justices at Westminster on the morrow of St. John the Baptist [i.e. 25 June] for livery to John de Hardepirie [cf. 1234]. Tested by J. de Stonore.

RETURN:

Until the harvest the bishop can levy nothing more from William's goods than he has already sent.

1238 *15 April 1345 Westminster*

Further writ of *fieri facias* against Thomas de Hompton. The bishop is to have £32 6s. [v. 1236] at the Exchequer on the morrow of St. John [i.e. 25 June].

RETURN:

Until the harvest the bishop can levy nothing more than he has already sent.

1239 *12 February 1345 Westminster*

Writ of *levari facias* against Robert de Hambury, parson of Stoke Prior. On 23 August 14 Edward III [1340] Robert acknowledged in the king's Chancery that he owed £30 to Nicholas de Stratton, citizen of London, which he has not yet paid. The said Nicholas has chosen in accordance with the statute to have livery of all the chattels and half the land of Robert. The sheriff of Worcester, ordered to cite Robert to appear in the Chancery on the morrow of the Purification [i.e. 3 February] to show cause why this should not be done, has returned that he is a clerk, beneficed in the [Worcester] diocese, and without lay fee. The bishop is therefore to have the money in the chancery on the morrow of the Nativity of St. John [i.e. 25 June]. Tested by the king (*me ipso*).

RETURN:

As 1238.

1240 *9 July 1345 Westminster*

Writ of *fieri facias* against William de Bremysgrave, received 9 September at Withington. The bishop is to have £10 6s. 8d. before the justices in the octave of St. Michael [i.e. 6 October]. The bishop has been amerced for not having executed an earlier mandate [1237] and will be more heavily amerced unless he does so this time. Tested by J. de Stonore.

RETURN:

The bishop has had certain goods of the above William sequestrated. Because he cannot find buyers willing to have them he has not been able to raise any money, but will implement the mandate as soon as he can.

1241 *28 June 1345 Westminster*
Further writ of *fieri facias* against Thomas de Hompton [v. 1238]. The bishop is to have £32 6s. at the Exchequer on the morrow of St. Michael [i.e. 30 September]. Tested by W. de Shareshull.

RETURN:

The bishop has had sequestrated goods to the value of 6 marks [£4]. Because he cannot find buyers he has not raised any money on this occasion.

1242 *26 June 1345 Westminster*
Writ of *distringas* against M. Peter Malet, received 7 September. He is to be distrained by his goods so that he appear before the barons of the Exchequer on the morrow of St. Michael [i.e. 30 September], the bishop having returned that a previous writ [1230] arrived too late. Tested by W. de Shareshull.

RETURN:

The bishop has distrained M. Peter by imposing sequestration on all his ecclesiastical goods within the diocese.

1243 *12 August 1345* [*Westminster*]
Writ received 11 September at Withington for the collection of arrears of a triennial tenth in the Gloucester archdeaconry [v. 1231-2]. The abbot of Tewkesbury is still burdened with the following sums for the first year of the tenth: 4d. for the abbot of Bruern's portion in the church of Eastleach St. Andrew[1] [Eastleach Turville], 2s. 6d. for the abbot of Flaxley's portion in Brimpsfield church, 8d. for that of the abbot of Eynsham in Elkstone church, 2s. for his portion in Mickleton, 2s. 8d. for his portion in Quinton, 2s. 4d. for the prior of Bath's portion in Olveston, 1s. 4d. for his portion in Cold Ashton [*Cold Aston*], 3s. 4d. for the precentor of Hereford's portion in Sevenhampton church, 3s. 4d. for his portion in Prestbury, 2s. 6d. for the sacrist of Glastonbury's portion in

1 MS. *Lech Sancti Andree.*

Pucklechurch, 6s. 8d. for Nympsfield church, 5s. 4d. for the bishop's portion in Ampney (*Amen*'), and 1s. 4d. for that of Richard de Ware in Todenham church. The bishop is to see that the collector is paid without delay, but any of the debtors who can produce acquittances are to appear at the Exchequer on the morrow of St. Michael [i.e. 30 September], measures taken against them being stayed meanwhile [cf. 1118]. Tested by W. de Stouwe.

1244 *10 July 1345 Suthwyk*[1]

Further writ of *levari facias* against Robert de Hambury [v. 1239]. The bishop is to have £30 at the royal Chancery on the morrow of St. Martin [i.e. 12 November]. Tested by Lionel, the king's son, custos of England.

RETURN:

The bishop has had goods sequestrated to the value of 10 marks [£6 13s. 4d.], but for lack of buyers has not yet raised money from them.

1245 *15 June 1345 Westminster*

Writ informing the bishop of the king's decision in view of Philip de Valois' infringements of the truce [v. 1189] to mount an expedition against him, and asking that prayers, Masses [&c.] be offered for its success.[2]

1246 *11 September 1345 Withington*

Memorandum that in accordance with the above writ the archbishop sent a mandate *ad orandum pro pace*, and that the diocesan certified his execution of the same by letters dated 11 September from Withington.

1247 *18 December 1344 Hoxne*

Writ for the collection of a triennial tenth [duplicate of 1231], the execution of which was committed to the abbot of Tewkesbury and the prior of Studley.

1248 *20 December 1345 Hartlebury*

Memorandum that M. Peter Malet, rector of Barnsley, appeared in person before M. John de Severl[eye], the bishop's commissary, and swore on the Gospels to obey the mandates of the Church with respect to his contumacy, for which he had earlier been excommunicated in writing by M. Hugh de Penebrugg. After absolution he swore to indemnify the bishop for a certain royal writ and its

1 Apparently Southwick (Hants.). See Tout, *Chapters in Med. Admin. Hist.*, 3, p. 164, n.5.
2 Printed in Rymer, *Foedera* V, pp. 460–1.

possible consequences, under penalty of 20 marks [£13 6s. 8d.]. The bishop then relaxed the sequestration imposed on his goods and benefice.

1249 *12 July 1345 Westminster*

Writ of *venire facias* against M. Robert de Wyrcestr', parson of Claverdon.[1] The sheriff of Worcester has returned in 15 days of Trinity [i.e. 5 June] that Robert is a clerk without lay fee. The bishop is to make him appear before the barons of the Exchequer in 15 days of St. Michael [i.e. 13 October] to answer to the king and the prior of the alien house of Wootton for £14 18s. 8d., arrears of an annual pension of £3 14s. 8d., the prior being under obligation to the king [&c. as in 1226]. Tested by W. de Shareshull.

RETURN:

The bishop has had M. Robert cited.

1250 *25 October 1345 Westminster*

Writ of prohibition addressed to the bishop, his Official, and their commissaries. Richard le Porter of Clevelode after covenanting with William de Beauchamp senior, knight, that he would not sell, grant or lease his lands to anyone other than William, had broken the covenant by leasing certain tenements to someone else. Although covenants touching lay contract pertain to the king and Crown, the bishop at William's prosecution summoned Richard to answer in the Court Christian and held the plea contrary to the law and custom of the realm. He is forbidden to hear the suit and is to revoke any sentence of excommunication. Tested by the king (*me ipso*).

1251 *Undated*

Return of a writ of *levari facias* against Robert de Hambury [1244]. The bishop has levied ten marks [£6 13s. 4d.] which he is sending by the bearer. He is unable to levy more from the goods, nor does he think he will be able to this year.

1252 *3 December 1345 Westminster*

Writ for the appointment of a substitute collector of a triennial tenth [cf. 1231–2, 1243]. In response to a writ of 5 October last under the Great Seal for the appointment of collectors for the second and third years of the tenth, the bishop certified that he had deputed the abbot of Tewkesbury and the prior of Studley in the Gloucester and Worcester archdeaconries respectively. But because the abbot of

1 The church was attached to his archdeaconry of Worcester.

Tewkesbury is old and enfeebled, and he and his house are inadequate for the collection of the tenth and any arrears, and bearing in mind the bishop's own responsibility for any insufficiency, the king requires him to appoint another collector in the Gloucester archdeaconry and to certify the treasurer and barons of the Exchequer as to his name on the morrow of St. Hilary [i.e. 14 January]. Tested by W. de Edyngdon, the royal treasurer.

1253 *Undated*

Return of the above writ. The bishop has exonerated the abbot of Tewkesbury from his duties and appointed in his stead the abbot of St. Peter's, Gloucester, at least for the second year of the tenth.

1254 *8 November 1345 Westminster*

Further writ of *levari facias* against Robert de Hambury, lately Chamberlain of North Wales [v. 1196, 1200]. The bishop is to have £422 15s. 10d. at the Exchequer in the octave of St. Hilary [i.e. 20 January], this being the remainder of a debt of £922 15s. 10d. in Robert's account for the issues of the Chamber [v. 1119], which debt, like others in Wales, the king has granted to his son Edward. Tested by W. de Shareshull.

1255 *5 September 1348 Westminster*

Writ allowing the collection of the cardinals' procurations.[1] Although in accordance with an ordinance of parliament forbidding the payment of procuration to papal nuncios acting outside the realm, the king prohibited the levying of any such for Annibal, cardinal bishop of Tusculum, and Stephen, cardinal priest of the title of St. John & St. Paul, sent by the pope to France, in view of their services to him he has now granted special licence for collection to be made. The bishop is to permit this within his diocese. Tested by the king (*me ipso*).

1256 *13 October 1345 Westminster*

Further writ of *fieri facias* against Thomas de Hompton. From those goods which he has already sequestrated to the value of 6 marks [1241] and from other goods, the bishop is to have £37 6s. at the Exchequer in 15 days of St. Hilary [i.e. 27 January]. Tested by W. de Shareshull.

1257 *26 November 1345 Rockingham*

Writ summoning the bishop to a council (*colloquium et tractatus*). Because the king proposes to cross to France at the beginning of

1 The substance of the writ is as printed in Rymer, *Foedera* V, p. 635.

March, he wishes to discuss this and other matters with the prelates and magnates. Accordingly the bishop is to be at Westminster on the morrow of the Purification [i.e. 3 February]. Tested by the king (*me ipso*).

1258   *22 January 1346 Alvechurch*

The bishop excuses himself from the above council[1] and appoints M. John de Severleye and Ds. John de Stoke, jointly and severally, as his proctors.

1259   *12 February 1346 Westminster*

Writ for the citation of beneficed aliens. The king wishes to discuss matters concerning the safety and defence of the realm with all aliens beneficed in England, and with the proctors, farmers, and bailiffs of those so beneficed who are living abroad, and whose benefices are not yet in his hand. The bishop is to warn all such who can be found within his diocese to appear in person, under pain of total forfeiture, before the king and his council at London on Monday in the first week of Lent [i.e. 6 March], on which day he is to certify the king in Chancery as to their names. Tested by the king (*me ipso*).

1260   *Undated*

Return of the above. The bishop received the mandate after the ninth hour on 27 February,[2] and although it reached him too late, he wrote on the same day to the officials of the archdeacons with orders to execute it as quickly as possible. But they certified that they could not do so in the time allowed. The bishop hopes this will be evident, as he is always ready to do what is commanded on the king's behalf when it lies within his power.

1261   *8 December 1346 Westminster*

Writ of *certiorari*. On the part of M. Robert de Wygorn', archdeacon of Worcester, it has been represented that although he canonically holds the church of Claverdon, annexed to his archdeaconry by the gift of the king's progenitors, without any obligation of a pension, the prior of Wootton, claiming an annual pension of 5 marks 8s. [£3 14s. 8d.] for himself and his church of Wootton, has sued out various writs against him, for which he seeks remedy. The bishop is to inform the king in Chancery whether Claverdon church is burdened with a pension to the prior and church of Wootton, or not, and if so, then from what time, and in what manner. Tested by the king (*me ipso*).

1 Rubric: *Procuratorium ad excusandum dominum a parliamento pro predicto brevi.*
2 But the marginal rubric states that it was received 3 March at Hartlebury.

1262 *Undated*

Return of the above writ. The bishop has found in his register of taxes of ecclesiastical benefices that Claverdon is taxed according to Norwich at 6½ marks [£4 6s. 8d.],[1] to Stroud at 10 marks [£6 13s. 4d.],[2] and according to Vienne at 15⅓ marks [£10 6s. 8d.].[3] Besides which there is a vicarage portion of 6½ marks and the prior of Wootton's portion of 5 marks 8s. [£3 14s. 8d.].[4] From these findings it is not clear whether a pension ought to be paid, nor can it be so while the parties remain unheard. Long before the date of the writ a suit was pending in the consistory and still remains undecided. And so the cognition and decision of this matter lies with the bishop.[5]

1263 *30 January 1346 Westminster*

Further writ of *venire facias* against M. Robert de Wygorn', archdeacon of Worcester and parson of Claverdon [v. 1249]. He is to be made to appear before the justices in 3 weeks of Easter [i.e. 7 May] to answer the plea of the prior of Wootton that he render £22 8s., arrears of an annual rent of £3 14s. 8d., the sheriff of Warwick having returned in 15 days of St. Hilary [i.e. 27 January] that he is a clerk without lay fee. Tested by J. de Stonore.

RETURN:

The bishop has had the above Robert cited.

1264 *30 January 1346 Westminster*

Further writ of *venire facias* against M. Robert of Worcester [as in 1263 except that the sum claimed is £8].

RETURN:

As above.

1265 *3 February 1346 Westminster*

Further writ of *fieri facias* against Thomas de Hompton. From those goods which he formerly sequestrated to the value of 6 marks [1241] and from other goods which according to a return in 15 days of St. Hilary [i.e. 27 January] later came into his possession [1256: the

---

1 The Taxation of Norwich was named after Walter Suffield, bishop of that see. See Lunt, *The Valuation of Norwich* [1254], and Rose Graham, 'The Taxation of Pope Nicholas IV', in *English Ecclesiastical Studies*.

2 John de Strodes, canon of Shrewsbury, was one of the assessors of the tenth for the Holy Land [1276] in the diocese of Worcester. Lunt, *Papal Revenues in the Middle Ages* (1934), 2, pp. 173–4; *Financial Relations of the Papacy with England to 1327* (1939), pp. 318, 630.

3 A tenth was imposed by the Council of Vienne in 1311. See Lunt, *op. citatis*: 1, pp. 40, 243; 2, pp. 124–7; pp. 395–404.

4 The prior's portion is not mentioned in the Record Commission's *Taxatio* [1291].

5 *tam propter naturam cause quam propter huiusmodi litis dependenciam.*

25

return is lacking], the bishop is to have £47 6s. at the Exchequer on the morrow of the close of Easter [i.e. 24 April]. Tested by W. de Stowe.

RETURN:

The bishop has now raised the 6 marks. But[1] although after Hilary, and even lately, such goods as could be found were sequestrated, both because of lack of buyers and the paucity of goods no profit has come from the sequestration, nor will come before harvest if a priest is to be supported.

1266 *15 January 1346 Westminster*

Further writ of *levari facias* against Robert de Hambury. The 10 marks sent by the bishop [1251] were delivered to Nicholas de Stratton. He is to have the remaining 35 marks [£26 13s. 4d.: v. 1239] in the Chancery in 3 weeks of Easter [i.e. 7 May]. Tested by the king (*me ipso*).

RETURN:

The bishop has levied goods worth 5½ marks [£3 13s. 4d.], but cannot levy more before harvest.

1267 *18 May 1346 Westminster*

Further writ of *levari facias* against Robert de Hambury [v. 1254], received 29 May at Hartlebury. The bishop is to have £422 15s. 10d. at the Exchequer in the octave of St. John the Baptist [i.e. 1 July]. Tested by R. de Sadynton.

1268 *28 April 1346 Westminster*

Further writ of *fieri facias* against Thomas de Hompton, received 13 June at Bredon. From those goods worth 5 marks,[2] which according to his return of 24 April [v. 1265] he has already sequestrated, and from other goods, the bishop is to have £43 6s. at the Exchequer on the morrow of St. John the Baptist [i.e. 25 June]. Tested by R. de Sadynton.

1269 *30 July 1346 Windsor*

Writ summoning the bishop and representatives of the clergy of his diocese [as in 1132] to attend a parliament at Westminster on the Monday after the Nativity of St. Mary [i.e. 11 September] for the discussion of matters concerning the prosecution of the war, the

1 Marginal rubric: *Istud retornum decanus de Poywyk recepit et manucepit pro eo.*
2 *Recte* 6 marks. According to the return of 1265 [cf. 1241] the money had already been raised but not sent [v. 1271].

king's rights across the sea, and the state and defence of the realm.
Tested by Lionel, the king's son, custos of England.

1270 *3 August 1346 Windsor*

Writ giving details, in an attached schedule, of the good fortune
which followed the royal landing [12 July] at *Hogges* [St.-Vaast de la
Hougue] in Normandy, which the bishop is instructed to publish, and
asking that prayers and hosts be offered up, Masses celebrated, twice-
weekly processions held, and other placatory offices daily performed
for the king's continued success. Tested by Lionel, the king's son
[&c.].[1]

1271 *10 July 1346 Westminster*

Further writ of *fieri facias* against Thomas de Hompton [v. 1268].
The bishop is to have £43 6s. at the Exchequer on the morrow of St.
Michael [i.e. 30 September]. Tested by R. de Sadynton.

RETURN:

The bishop has levied 6 marks [£4] which he is sending by the
bearer. He is unable to levy more at present.

1272 *17 May 1346 Westminster*

Writ of *venire facias* against Richard Golafre, vicar of Ombersley. He
is to be made to appear before the justices in the octave of St. Michael
[i.e. 6 October] to answer the plea of the abbot of Evesham that he
render £10 which he owes and unjustly detains, the sheriff of
Worcester having reported that he is a clerk without lay fee. Tested
by J. de Stonore.

1273 *20 June 1346 Westminster*

Writ of *levari facias*. The bishop is to raise the following sums: from
the rector of Blockley for the second year of the triennial tenth of
11 Edward III [A.D. 1337], £3 13s. 4d., and for the tenth of 16
Edward III [1342], £3 13s. 4d.; from Robert de Hambury, rector of
Stoke Prior, as fine for transgression, 40s., and for contempt, 40s.
The money is to be at the Exchequer on the morrow of St. Michael
[i.e. 30 September]. Tested by R. de Sadynton.

1274 *28 June 1346 Westminster*

Writ of *venire facias* against John de Ryveris. He is to be made to
appear before the justices in the octave of St. Michael [i.e. 6 October]
to answer the plea of Peter Vanne, citizen and merchant of London,

1 Printed in Rymer & Sanderson, *Foedera* (1816–69) 3, i, p. 88.

that he render a reasonable account for the time that he acted as his receiver, the sheriff of Berkshire having returned in the octave of Trinity [i.e. 18 June] that he is a clerk without lay fee. Tested by J. de Stonore.

RETURN:

The writ arrived late and so could not be executed on this occasion.

1275 *3 July 1346 Westminster*

Further writ of *levari facias* against Robert de Hambury [v. 1267]. The bishop is to have £422 15s. 10d. at the Exchequer in the octave of St. Michael [i.e. 6 October]. Tested by R. de Sadyngton.

RETURN:
As above.

1276 *8 May 1346 Westminster*

Further writ of *levari facias* against Robert de Hambury. The 5½ marks sent by the bishop [v. 1266] were delivered to Nicholas de Stratton. He is to have the remaining 29½ marks [£19 6s. 8d.] in the Chancery on the Monday after St. Faith [i.e. 9 October]. Tested by the king (*me ipso*).

1277 *15 September 1346 Westminster*

Writ of *certiorari* [cf. 1134, 1259]. The king wishes to have the names of all aliens beneficed in the diocese, both cardinals and others, the description number and value of the benefices held by each of them, and details of those who reside and those who do not. The bishop is to send the information by the Monday after St. Edward the King [i.e. 19 March?] at latest. Tested by Lionel, the king's son [&c.].

1278 *13 November 1346 Westminster*

Writ of *venire facias* against Peter Gros, parson of Suckley. The sheriff of Worcester having returned in the quindene of St. Michael [i.e. 13 October] that Peter is a clerk without lay fee, he is to be made to appear at the Exchequer in 15 days of St. Hilary [i.e. 27 January] to answer to the king and the prior of the alien house of Newent, proctor of the abbot of Cormeilles, for 38 marks [£25 6s. 8d.], arrears of an annual pension of 4 marks [&c. as in 1226]. Tested by R. de Sadyngton.

RETURN:

The bishop has had the above Peter cited.

1279 *6 October 1346 Westminster*

Further writ of *fieri facias* against Thomas de Hompton. The bishop is to have £49 6s. at the Exchequer in 15 days of St. Hilary [i.e. 27 January]. Tested by R. de Sadyngton.

RETURN:

Until the harvest the bishop can levy nothing beyond the sum which he sent on 30 September last [v. 1271].

1280 *18 October 1346 Westminster*

Further writ of *levari facias* against Robert de Hambury [v. 1275]. The bishop is to have £422 15s. 10d. at the Exchequer of Prince Edward at Westminster on the morrow of St. Hilary [i.e. 14 January]. Tested by R. de Sadyngton.

1281 *10 October 1346 Westminster*

Writ of *levari facias*. From those goods of the rector of Blockley which according to his return of 30 September last [1273: return not given] he has already sequestrated, and from other goods, the bishop is to levy 10 marks [*sic*].[1] This sum, together with 60s. likewise levied from the sequestrated goods of Robert de Hambury for the payment of fines, is to be at the Exchequer on the morrow of St. Hilary [i.e. 14 January]. Tested by R. de Sadyngton.

RETURN:

The bishop is sending 6 marks [£4] levied from the goods of the rector of Blockley—all he can raise at present, together with 60s. from those of Robert [de Hambury].

1282 *9 November 1347 Westminster*

Writ of *certiorari*. The bishop is to inform the treasurer and barons of the Exchequer by the morrow of St. Hilary [i.e. 14 January] of the portions and pensions appropriated to the priory of Maxstoke. Tested by R. de Sadyngton.

1283 *30 January 1347 Westminster*

Further writ of *levari facias* against the rector of Blockley. The bishop is to have at the Exchequer on the morrow of the close of Easter [i.e. 9 April] £3 6s. 8d. of the £3 13s. 4d. owed by the rector for the second year of the tenth [v. 1273, 1281]. Tested by R. de Sadyngton.

RETURN:

The bishop has received a writ of later date than the present one and is enclosing a copy. Although it might have been possible to levy the money at one time he is unable to do so at present.

1 Said to comprise two sums of 73s. 4d., as in 1273.

1284 *16 February 1347 Westminster*

Writ of *venire facias* against Henry de Stanton, parson of Pillerton. He is to be made to appear before the justices in 15 days of Easter [i.e. 15 April] to answer the plea of Hugh de Cokeseye, M. William de Herewynton, Robert de Alruston, Roger de la Felde and Thomas de Sloughtr', executors of the testament of Adam de Herwynton, that he render £100 which he unjustly detains, the sheriff of Warwick having reported that he is a clerk without lay fee. Tested by J. de Stonore.

1285 *6 February 1347 Westminster*

Writ informing the bishop of John le Smale's recovery in the king's court against the abbot of St. Mary's, Tewkesbury, of the presentation to the church of St. Philip & St. Jacob, Bristol, which is vacant.

1286 *13 March 1347 Reading*

Writ of *certiorari*. The bishop is to certify the Chancery as to when and in what manner he or his predecessor, as commissary of Robert [Wyvill], bishop of Salisbury [1330–75], admitted M. Peter de Berkele to the prebend of Horton in Salisbury cathedral. Tested by Lionel, the king's son [&c.].

RETURN:

The bishop is sending all that he can discover about the matter in an attached schedule.

1287 *20 February 1347 Westminster*

Further writ of *levari facias* against Robert de Hambury. From those goods worth 11s. which he has already sequestrated [v. 1280], and from other goods, the bishop is to have £422 15s. 10d. at the Exchequer of Prince Edward in 15 days of Easter [i.e. 15 April]. Tested by R. de Sadyngton.

RETURN:

The bishop is sending 11s. by the bearer. He cannot raise more before the harvest.

1288 *6 February 1347 Westminster*

Writ of *supersedeas* for the rector of Blockley. The bishop is not to execute a former writ of *levari facias* [1283] and is to relax any sequestration imposed on the rector's goods. Tested by [William Edendon], bishop of Winchester [1346–66], the treasurer.

By the treasurer, because the church belongs to Cardinal [John] de Convenis and his proctor is to answer to the king for its farm under a certain form, as the treasurer records.

1289 *29 January 1347 Westminster*

Writ of *venire facias* against the abbot of Dore. He is to be made to appear before the justices in 3 weeks of Easter [i.e. 22 April] to answer the plea of John Rostele, executor of the testament of William de Rosteleye, clerk, and of William Archebaud and his wife Matilda, coexecutrix, that he render 50 marks [£33 6s. 8d.] which he unjustly detains, the sheriff of Gloucester having returned in 15 days of St. Hilary [i.e. 27 January] that he has no lay fee. Tested by J. de Stonore.

RETURN:

The abbot of Dore has nothing in the diocese except Duntisbourne church, where he has been cited.

1290 *15 April 1347 Reading*

Writ requesting a loan of wool. The king is sending his clerk, Henry de Haydok, with letters under his privy seal setting forth the state of the French war, the royal necessities, and the aid granted for their relief by the clergy and laity at the council last summoned to Westminster.[1] The bishop is asked to assist with a loan of wool and is to send details of what he intends to do by the above Henry. Tested by Lionel, the king's son [&c.].

1291 *12 April 1347 Reading*

Writ forbidding the collection of procurations on behalf of Annibal, cardinal bishop of Tusculum, and Stephen, cardinal priest of the title of St. John & St. Paul. Tested by Lionel, the king's son [&c.].[2]

1292 *14 May 1347 Reading*

Writ for the collection of a biennial tenth. The clergy of the Canterbury province in their last convocation at St. Paul's [16 October 1346] granted a biennial tenth. The bishop is to appoint collectors without delay. Tested by Lionel, the king's son [&c.].

1293 *30 May 1347 Hartlebury*

Form of commission for the collection of the above tenth in the Gloucester archdeaconry.[3]

---

1 This met 30 March 1347. The king obtained a loan of 20,000 sacks of wool from the merchants.
2 Printed in Rymer, *Foedera* V, pp. 558–9. Cf. 1255 above.
3 The abbot of St. Peter's, Gloucester, was the collector appointed (v. 1299). An interlineation gives the Purification [2 February] and St. Barnabas [11 June] as the terms appointed for the second year of the tenth.

1294 *20 April 1347 Westminster*

Writ of *venire facias* against Philip de Warle, lately parson of Clapton (*Clopton in le Welde*). He is to be made to appear before the justices in the octave of Trinity [i.e. 3 June] to answer the plea of Margery, formerly wife of William Herlisoun, that he render 8 marks [£5 6s. 8d.] which he owes and unjustly detains, the sheriff of London having returned in 15 days of Easter [i.e. 15 April] that he has no lay fee. Tested by J. de Stonore.

It was not returned because it arrived late.

1295 *6 February 1347 Westminster*

Writ of *supersedeas* for the rector of Blockley. [Duplicate of 1288.]

1296 *10 May 1347 Westminster*

Further writ of *levari facias* against Robert de Hambury [as in 1287]. The bishop is to have £422 15s. 10d. at the Exchequer of Prince Edward in the octave of St. John the Baptist [i.e. 1 July]. Tested by R. de Sadyngton.

RETURN:

He is sending 10s., but cannot levy more until the greater fruits have been received because of the other burdens which have to be supported.

1297 *14 June 1347 Reading*

Writ of *certiorari* received 20 June at Hartlebury. The bishop is to certify the Chancery as to who last presented to the vicarage of Leigh chapel next Deerhurst, by what title, when, and in what manner, and as to who was last admitted to the vicarage and at whose presentation or nomination. Tested by Lionel, the king's son [&c.].

RETURN:

The bishop has found in the register of his predecessor, Walter [Maidstone],[1] that the latter on 19 June 1316 admitted John de Cherleton at the presentation of the prior of Deerhurst and on the nomination of John de Pareys, lord of Leigh, and instituted him to the vicarage. He can find nothing further.

1298 *14 May 1347 Reading*

Writ for the collection of a biennial tenth.[2]

---

1 Bishop 1313–17.
2 A duplicate of 1292, except that this entry names the Assumption [15 August] and St. Martin [11 November] as terms for payment of the tenth in the first year.

1299 *12 July 1347 Hartlebury*

Return of the above writ. The bishop has appointed the prior of Studley and the abbot of St. Peter's, Gloucester, as collectors in the archdeaconries of Worcester and Gloucester respectively.

1300 *27 June 1347 Westminster*

Further writ of *fieri facias* against Thomas de Hompton [v. 1279]. The bishop is to have £60 at the Exchequer on the morrow of St. Michael [i.e. 30 September]. Tested by R. de Sadyngton.

1301 *16 July 1347 Westminster*

Writ of *levari facias* against Henry de Stredford. Because Henry is a clerk without lay fee beneficed at Overbury, the bishop is to levy £100 from the goods at his rectory and elsewhere in the diocese. This sum is part of a debt of £180, the remainder of £282 6s. 1½d. being exacted at the Exchequer under Henry's name and those of Robert de Longedon and Robert de Gatysby for arrears of the custody of the land and tenements of the abbot of Lyre prior to 16 Edward III [1342–3]. The £100 is to be at the Exchequer on the morrow of St. Michael [i.e. 30 September]. Tested by R. de Sadyngton.

1302 *3 July 1347 Westminster*

Further writ of *levari facias* against Robert de Hambury [v. 1296]. The bishop is to have £422 4s. 10d. at the Exchequer on the morrow of St. Michael [i.e. 30 September]. Tested by R. de Sadyngton.

1303 *9 November 1347*

Writ of *certiorari* concerning Maxstoke priory. [Duplicate of 1282.]

RETURN:

The churches of Tanworth, Aston Cantlow and Yardley are appropriated to the priory. The prior holds neither portions nor pensions within the diocese.

1304 *30 October 1347 Westminster*

Writ of *sequestrari facias*. Richard Auncell, rector of *Kyngesthorp*, Richard de Nessewyk, William Rysceby, John de Barton and Richard de Blythe, executors of the testament of Walter de Wytewang, lately treasurer of the wardrobe of the king's household, have given surety at the Exchequer for the rendering of the accounts of the said Walter and the payment of all arrears, in so far as the goods which belonged to him suffice. The king has accordingly granted them the administration of Walter's goods and chattels. The bishop is to sequestrate all such, whether in the deceased's prebend of *St. Nicholas*[1] in Westbury, or elsewhere, and to have them fairly priced. Details of the goods and their valuation are to be sent to the barons of the Exchequer in the octave of St. Hilary [i.e. 20 January]. Tested by R. de Sadyngton.

RETURN:

All the goods found at the above prebend and elsewhere in the diocese have been sequestrated and fairly valued at £10, which sum has been delivered to the executors.

1305 *25 October 1347 Westminster*

Writ of *fieri facias* against Walter, parson of Madresfield. The bishop is to have 13s. 4d. before the king, wherever he may be, in the octave of St. Hilary [i.e. 20 January] for payment to John de Ludynton and his associates, royal clerks, of the abbot of Pershore's gift. This sum is part of 10 marks' damages [£6 13s. 4d.] awarded to the abbot by reason of Walter's conviction for transgression *vi et armis*, the sheriff of Worcester having returned in the octave of St. Michael [i.e. 6 October] that he has no lay fee. Tested by W. de Thorp.

RETURN:

The bishop is sending 13s. 4d. by the bearer.

1306 *13 November 1347 Westminster*

Writ of summons to a parliament at Westminster on the morrow of St. Hilary [i.e. 14 January 1348]. The king wishes the bishop to know that it is being summoned, not in order to levy aids and tallages, but merely to provide justice for the injuries and grievances of the people. Tested by the king (*me ipso*).

1307 *11 October 1347 Westminster*

Further writ of *fieri facias* against Thomas de Hompton [v. 1300]. The bishop is to have £58, together with the 13s. 4d. already levied, at the Exchequer in 15 days of St. Hilary [i.e. 27 January]. Tested by R. de Sadyngton.

RETURN:

The bishop can raise nothing further until the harvest.

1308 *Undated*

Return of a writ of *levari facias* against Robert de Hambury [v. 1302]. The bishop can levy nothing at present nor will be able to do

1 *Sic.* This refers to the Nicholas de Wodeford (Goderynghill) prebend. See H. J. Wilkins, *Westbury College* (1917), pp. 65-66.

so before harvest, particularly as he has already sent to the Chancery—though late—the sum of 10 marks [£6 13s. 4d.] from this year's fruits for livery to Nicholas de Stratton.

1309 *31 October . . . la Grove*

Letter [in old French] from Elizabeth de Hastang requesting the bishop to empower the dean of St. Mary's, Warwick, to prove the will of her servant [*vadlet*], John de Denton, and to hear the account of his executor.

1310 *22 November 1347 Westminster*

Writ of *levari facias* against Peter Malet. The bishop is to have at the Exchequer on the morrow of St. Hilary [i.e. 14 January] the £5 3s. 7d. which Peter owes the king for arrears of his administration of the fruits of Spettisbury church. He failed to execute a writ returnable on the morrow of St. Michael [i.e. 30 September]. Tested by R. de Sadyngton.

RETURN:

The writ arrived so late that it could not be executed.

1311 *29 November 1347 Westminster*

Writ of *venire facias* against Philip de Warleigh, sometime parson of Albrighton. He is to be made to appear before the justices in the octave of St. Hilary [i.e. 20 January] to answer the plea of William de la Hull of Bridgnorth that he render 100s. which he owes and unjustly detains, the sheriff of Shropshire having reported that he has no lay fee. Tested by J. de Stonore.

1312 *15 February 1348 Westminster*

Further writ of *fieri facias* against Thomas de Hompton, received 27 March. The bishop is to have £58 and 13s. 4d. [as in 1307] at the Exchequer in 15 days of Easter [i.e. 4 May]. Tested by R. de Sadyngton.

RETURN:

The bishop is sending the 13s. 4d. but cannot levy more before the harvest.

1313 *28 January 1348 Westminster*

Further writ of *levari facias* against Peter Malet. The bishop is to have £5 3s. 7d. at the Exchequer on the morrow of St. Hilary [i.e.

14 January], a previous writ having arrived too late for execution [v. 1310]. Tested by R. de Sadyngton.

RETURN:

Peter Malet is rector of Marchergeryn, Llandaff diocese. Despite enquiry the bishop has not found any goods belonging to him.

1314 *5 October 1347 Westminster*

Further writ of *levari facias* against Robert de Hambury [v. 1302]. The bishop is to have £415 11s. 6d. at the Exchequer on the morrow of the close of Easter [i.e. 28 April]. Tested by R. de Sadyngton.

RETURN:

Before the harvest the bishop cannot raise anything more than what he sent immediately after Michaelmas.

1315 *30 January 1348 Westminster*

Further writ of *venire facias* against Philip de Warlegh [as in 1311]. He is to be made to appear before the justices in 15 days of Easter [i.e. 4 May]. Tested by J. de Stonore.

1316 *23 May 1348 Westminster*

Further writ of *levari facias* against Robert de Hambury, received 17 June at Bredon [v. 1314]. The bishop is to have £415 11s. 6d. at the Exchequer on the morrow of St. John the Baptist [i.e. 25 June]. Tested by R. de Sadyngton.

RETURN:

The bishop cannot levy more than he has already sent before the harvest.

1317 *21 May 1348 Westminster*

Further writ of *fieri facias* against Thomas de Hompton [v. 1312]. The bishop is to have £58 at the Exchequer on the morrow of St. John the Baptist [i.e. 25 June]. Tested by R. de Sadyngton.

RETURN:

As 1316.

1318 *28 May 1348 Westminster*

Writ of *certiorari*. The bishop is to certify the treasurer and barons of the Exchequer in 15 days of St. John the Baptist [i.e. 8 July] as to when and by what authority the churches of Tanworth, Aston

Cantlow and Yardley were appropriated to Maxstoke priory [v. 1303].

RETURN:

The church of Tanworth was appropriated 31 December 1340, that of Aston Cantlow 4 October 1345, and that of Yardley 3 May 1347, on the bishop's authority and in accordance with the law.[1]

1319 *30 June 1348 Westminster*

Further writ of *levari facias* against Robert de Hambury [v. 1316]. The bishop is to have £415 11s. 6d. at the Exchequer on the morrow of St. Michael [i.e. 30 September]. Tested by R. de Sadyngton.

1320 *4 July 1348 Westminster*

Further writ of *fieri facias* against Thomas de Hompton [v. 1317]. The bishop is to have £58 at the Exchequer on the morrow of St. Michael [i.e. 30 September]. Tested by R. de Sadyngton.

RETURN:

The bishop has levied 6 marks [£4] which he is sending by the bearer.

1321 *Undated*

Return of a writ against Robert de Hambury [1319]. The bishop has levied 10 marks [£6 13s. 4d.] which he is sending by John de Stok' the bearer. He is unable to levy more at present.

1322 *6 August 1348 Westminster*

Writ permitting the collection of the cardinals' procurations despite previous prohibition [v. 1255, 1291]. Tested by the king (*me ipso*).[2]

1323 *26 August 1348 Westminster*

Writ of *certiorari*. The bishop is to certify the Chancery as to when the church of Little Compton in Henmarsh fell vacant owing to the death of Bartholomew Fyz Waryn, Robert Walters of Iccomb entered upon it by virtue of a papal provision, and Roger Basset of Sutton presented a certain Henry Droys of Woolstone. Tested by the king (*me ipso*).

RETURN:

9 September 1348 Henbury

From his registers the bishop has discovered that Bartholomew FizWaren, sometime rector of Compton in Henmarsh, has been long

1 Cf. 1364.   2 Printed in Rymer, *Foedera* V, pp. 630–1.

dead. By his death the church fell vacant on 2[?] September 1341 and within three days Robert Walters entered upon it by means of an apostolic grace. In the same year Roger Basset presented Henry Drois.

1324 *20 November 1348 Westminster*

Writ summoning the bishop and representatives of the clergy of the diocese [as in 1132] to attend a parliament at Westminster on Monday after St. Hilary [i.e. 19 January 1349] for the discussion of the negotiations at Calais between the king's representatives, those of France, and those of the Count of Flanders, and for other urgent business. Tested by the king (*me ipso*).

1325 *1 January 1349 Westminster*

Writ postponing the above parliament until the quindene of Easter [i.e. 26 April] on account of the plague.[1]

1326 *15 October 1348 Westminster*

Further writ of *levari facias* against Robert de Hambury [v. 1319]. The bishop is to have £415 11s. 6d. at the Exchequer in 15 days of St. Hilary [i.e. 27 January]. Tested by R. de Sadyngton.

RETURN:

Before Michaelmas last the bishop received a similar writ [1319], in response to which he sent 10 marks by John de Stoke [1321]. He cannot raise more before harvest.

1327 *3 February 1349 Westminster*

Writ of *levari facias* against Elias Walteres of Iccomb. Walter acknowledged in the Chancery on 28 June 21 Edward III [1347] that he owed £10 to Philip de Alcestre, clerk, which he ought to have paid the following Michaelmas [29 September] and which still remains unpaid. The sheriff of Gloucester, ordered to cite him to appear in the octave of St. Hilary [i.e. 20 January 1349], has returned that he has no lay fee. The bishop is to have £10 in the Chancery on the quindene of Easter [i.e. 26 April] for livery to Philip. Tested by the king (*me ipso*).

1328 *18 April 1349 Westminster*

Further writ of *levari facias* against Elias Walteres [as above, but returnable in the octave of St. John, i.e. 1 July].

RETURN:

The bishop has found two marks [£1 6s. 8d.], 40 sheep[?], and three stone of wool, but no buyers so far.

1 Printed in Rymer, *Foedera* V, p. 655.

END OF FIRST VOLUME

Bransford Register
Volume 2

Memoranda Quire
June–August 1349
[Numbers 1329–1338]

Memoranda from 20 June 1349. [Rubric].

1329 *26 June 1349 Hartlebury*

Mandate to the prior of St. Bartholomew's, Gloucester. Celestra le Sherare of Gloucester has pleaded that Thomas de Wyneston of the same place received her as his wife *per verba de presenti*[1] and begot children by her, and that a matrimonial suit between them is pending in the Gloucester consistory. Despite this, and Celestra's open protest at the publication in St. Nicholas', Gloucester, of the banns between Thomas and Alice le Webbe, certain priests of that church have declared their intention of solemnising such marriage *de facto*—for they cannot do so *de iure*. The prior is to forbid the ministers of St. Nicholas, or other churches, to do this while the suit is pending in the consistory, under penalty of sentence of greater excommunication, which he is empowered to fulminate against contravenors of his injunction.

1330 *4 October 1342 Withington*

Commission[2] for M. John de Severleye, the chancellor, to enquire into, correct, and punish the crimes and excesses of the bishop's subjects, to take cognisance of all causes pertaining to his jurisdiction, both matrimonial and others, moved or to be moved, and to discuss and terminate such causes, with power of canonical coercion.

1331 *27 June 1349 Hartlebury*

Appointment [in Old French] of Richard de Bromwich as bailiff of the bishop's franchise of Oswaldslow.

---

1 For an exposition of the marriage law, see Pollock & Maitland, *History of English Law*, 2nd ed., 2, p. 390 *et seq.*
2 *Commissio generalis in omnibus causis et negociis.* Duplicated in 1365.

1332 *30 June 1349 Hartlebury*

Memorandum that Thomas atte Mulle of Stoke Prior had a similar letter for the above office under the bishop's seal *ad causas*.

1333 *2 July 1349 Hartlebury*

Special licence, until revoked, for John de Leominstria, monk of Worcester, to exercise the office of penitentiary[1] and to preach publicly within the diocese.

1334 *3 July 1349 Hartlebury*

Mandate to the prior and chapter of Worcester for the enforcement of ordinances made by the king and council.[2] The bishop has received a writ, tested by the king and dated 18 June from Westminster, requiring him to have published in churches and elsewhere the royal ordinances for the regulation of wages, and to direct rectors and vicars of such churches, their ministers, and other of his subjects, to admonish their parishioners to abide by them. He is also required to compel stipendiary chaplains, who are said to be unwilling to serve except for an excessive salary, to be content with the accustomed one, under pain of suspension and interdict. Accordingly the prior and convent are to publish the ordinances in the cathedral church and other places, in the presence of the clergy and people. All who openly or secretly oppose these measures are to be cited to appear before the bishop, wherever he may be in the diocese, on the fifth juridical day after citation.

Form of letter written to the commissary of the archdeacon of Worcester.[3] By virtue of his obedience and under penalty of greater excommunication, he is to have the ordinances published, even in the vulgar tongue, in all churches subject to him, in chapters, and other assemblies of clergy. He is also admonished under the above penalty and of suspension and interdict, and through him all rectors, vicars, other ministers and parishioners of his archdeaconry, to observe the ordinances and to compel stipendiary chaplains to serve for an appropriate salary.

A letter in the same form *mutatis mutandis* was sent to the official of the archdeacon of Gloucester.

1335 *25 July 1349 Hartlebury*

Commission for M. Henry de Neubold and M. Luke [de Herdebergh],[4] rectors of Weston-on-Avon and Honington respectively.

1 *corruptoribus monialium et fractoribus parcorum nostrorum dumtaxat exceptis.*
2 Printed in Rymer, *Foedera* V, pp. 693–5.
3 There is no break in the MS. entry at this point.
4 The scribe left a space for the name.

The bishop appropriated the parish church of Pillerton to the dean and canons of St. Mary's collegiate church, Warwick, so that on the death or cession of Henry, then rector, it would be lawful for them to take possession, there being reserved for the support of a vicar a suitable portion estimated at 12 marks [£8]. Such vicarage he ordained at that value, as is contained in his letters of appropriation. He now wishes to know the value of the church and of its portions, fruits and offerings. The commissaries are to go there in person and to hold an enquiry by a sworn body of trustworthy men with genuine knowledge of the matter. They are to send details of their findings under seal.

1336 *26 July 1349 Hartlebury*

Memorandum of the licence for John [Trilleck], bishop of Hereford [1344–60], to consecrate altars in the chapel of his manor at Prestbury within the diocese.

1337 *23 July 1349 Hartlebury*

Memorandum that the bishop confirmed the licence granted by Abbot William [of Sherborne] and the convent of Winchcombe for Br. John de Glouc', monk of that house, to visit the Roman Curia in lay clothes if necessary [*eciam in vestibus stragulatis seu aliis laicalibus si opportuerit*], and issued letters patent to that effect under his seal *ad causas*.

1338 *3 August 1349 Hartlebury*

Reply to letters of Prior Robert [Hathbrand] and the chapter of Christ Church, Canterbury. The bishop has received their commission, dated 17 July, empowering him by virtue of the prerogative of the church of Canterbury, which pertains to them *sede vacante*,[1] to insinuate, prove and approve [v. 8] the will of Sir Hugh le Despenser, knight, who at the time of his death held goods both in Canterbury and other dioceses of the province, to commit the administration of all such goods to the executors named therein, and to receive from them [an oath] that they will draw up a true inventory, make faithful administration, and render account when called upon.

---

1 *Cum ius recipiendi probaciones testamentorum personarum nobilium bona mobilia et immobilia tam in diocesi Cantuar' quam in diversis diocesibus Cantuar' provincie tempore sue mortis habencium, ac ius examinandi insinuandi et approbandi testamenta huiusmodi, necnon committendi in forma iuris executoribus testamentorum huiusmodi administracionem bonorum testamenta ipsa tangencium, audiendique compotum administracionis bonorum ad testamenta huiusmodi spectancium ac liberandi et acquietandi executores seu administratores bonorum ipsorum, ad priorem ecclesie nostre predicte qui pro tempore fuerit et eiusdem loci capitulum sede ibidem vacante nomine Cant' ecclesie iuxta prerogitivam ipsius ecclesie, de consuetudine laudabili et prescripta in dicta provincia usitata et observata . . . . . notorie pertinuerint et debeant pertinere.*
See Churchill, *Cant. Admin.* 1, p. 380 *et seq.*

26

He is required to send details of his process together with a copy of the will by the Assumption [15 August], after which date his power is to lapse. However, because the executors have not come to show him the will and to pursue the matter, nor have attempted to do so, he has been unable to implement the commission.

Quire of Ordinations
Celebrated in 1349
[Numbers 1339–1342]

1339 *11 April 1349 Orders celebrated by the bishop in the chapel of his castle at Hartlebury on Holy Saturday.*

Subdeacon: Religious
Br. William Tankard of the house of Thelsford.

Subdeacons: Unbeneficed
Roger in le Hurne of Winstone, to t. of the house of Oseney.
John Hope of Buckland, to t. of patrimony.
William Wager of Alveston, to t. of patrimony.
Walter son of William le Muleward of Hampton, to t. of the house of Thelsford.
Nicholas Gorwy of Fladbury, to t. of patrimony.
John Durling of Fairford, to t. of the house of Bradenstoke.
John Gamel of Stoke (*Stok'*), to t. of Ds. John de Stok.
Richard Gladiere of Tysoe, to t. of the house of Daventry.
Richard Calewe of Gloucester, to t. of the house of Llanthony by Gloucester.
Thomas Muleward of Charlecote, to t. of the house of Thelsford.
Thomas de Walton of Coventry & Lichfield diocese, by l.d. to t. of the house of Hulton.
John Perkyns of Westcote, to t. of the house of St. John, Lechlade.
John Bradeleye of Stoke (*Stok'*), to t. of Ds. John de Stok.
William Pendok', to t. of the house of Flaxley.
Thomas Boys of Alne, to t. of the house of Oseney.
Richard le Permenter of Kidderminster, to t. of John de Grafton and Roger de Bisshopesdon.
Roger Pyson of Haselor, to t. of patrimony.

Robert Kirkeby of Stow St. Edward [on-the-Wold], to t. of the house of Hailes.

John atte Brugg' son of John atte Brugg' of Holdfast, to t. of patrimony.

John Hobkyns of Whatcote, to t. of the house of St. James outside Northampton.

Deacon: Beneficed

Thomas Passeloue, r. of Rodmarton.

Deacons: Unbeneficed

Walter called 'Clerk' of Quenington, to t. of patrimony.

William Harrys of *Burton*, to t. of patrimony.

John Hobkyns of Besford, to t. of patrimony.

Philip atte Mulne of Chipping Campden, to t. of the house of St. John, Shrewsbury.

Thomas Hunte of Lighthorne, to t. of the house of Bordesley.

Walter le Messager of Wheatenhurst, to t. of the house of St. Bartholomew, Newbury.

Richard de Pynthorp, to t. of the house of Biddlesden.[1]

Thomas son of John de Hampton of Longborough, to t. of the house Hailes.

Henry son of Philip atte Chircheheye of Iccomb (*Hickombe*), to t. of the house of Eynsham.

John Sampson of Childs Wickham, to t. of patrimony.

John Giffard of Bibury, to t. of the house of Oseney.

William atte Well' of Fairford, to t. of the house of Dudston.

Stephen de Hathemer, to t. of the house of St. Peter, Gloucester.

William White of Forthampton, to t. of the house of Oseney.

Ralph de Endreby of Lincoln diocese, by l.d. to t. of the house of Alcester.

John Ruyfeld of Lichfield diocese, by l.d. to t. of patrimony.

John Boteler of Farmington, to t. of the house of Cold Norton.

Andrew Fetherston, to t. of the house of Lilleshall and of Ds. William de Shareshull.

John Wyshangre, to t. of the house of Llanthony next Gloucester.

Priests: Beneficed

M. Robert Pomit', r. of Aldington, by l.d. [of the abbot of Evesham].

William Harpor, to [t.] of the chantry of St. Mary, Dursley.

Priests: Unbeneficed

Thomas son of John Whyther of Little Compton, to t. of the house of Eynsham.

Thomas Iryssh of Fladbury, to t. of patrimony.

1 *Bytlesden.*

[*Priests: Unbeneficed continued.*]

Walter son of Walter Ragg' of Stow, to t. of the house of St. Frideswide, Oxford.

Henry Penne of Kidderminster, to t. of the bishop's grace.

Henry son of Richard de Goldecote, to t. of the house of Rocester in Dovedale.

William Poughampton, to t. of the house of Halesowen (*Hales*).

William Sodbrok', to t. of his grace [from the papacy].

Thomas Blakemon, to t. of the house of Bruton.

Thomas Gilberdes of Stoke Orchard, to t. of the house of Llanthony next Gloucester.

William Voul of Belbroughton, to t. of the hospital of Bridgnorth.

Henry Caldecote, to t. of patrimony.

Thomas Henr' of Moreton (*Mortone*), to t. of patrimony.

William Blount, to t. of the house of Llanthony next Gloucester.

William Boys of Withington, to t. of 5 marks [£3 6s. 8d.] to be received from the hospital of St. John of Jerusalem.

Robert Clerk' of Marston (*Mersshton*), to t. of the house of Holy Trinity, London.

William Bussh of *Wich*, to t. of patrimony.

William West of Chelmscote, to t. of the house of Caldwell.

Thomas Chesterton of Prestbury, to t. of the house of Llanthony next Gloucester.

John de Kymnesford, to t. of his grace [from the papacy].

John Hope, to t. of the house of Keynsham.

William Corteys of Wolford,[1] to t. of the house of St. Frideswide, Oxford.

John Grant of Ilmington, to t. of the New Place, Winchester.

Richard Lydeseye of Ilmington, to t. of the house of St. Mary, Merton.

Peter Bernard of Trimpley, to t. of the house of St. Mary, Merton.

John Huwet of Bishops Cleeve, to t. of the house of St. Augustine, Bristol.

Thomas Coventr', to t. of the house of Trentham.

Simon de la Berewe, to t. of patrimony.

John Hayward of Moreton Henmarsh, to t. of patrimony.

John atte Nassh of Fladbury, to t. of his inheritance.

1340 *31 May 1349 Orders celebrated by the bishop in the chapel of his castle at Hartlebury on the feast of Pentecost.*

Acolytes: Unbeneficed

Thomas Stok'.

Richard Ridere.

Roger Herton.

1 MS. *Welford*, apparently for *Wolford*. Cf. pp. 273, 277.

1341 *6 June 1349 Orders celebrated by the bishop in the same place [v. 1340] on the eve of Trinity Sunday.*

Acolytes: Religious

Br. William de Modeford of the house of Winchcombe.
Br. John Hay
Br. Nicholas Seynebury $\Big\}$ of the house of Pershore.

Acolyte: Beneficed

William, r. of Aston Somerville.

Acolytes: Unbeneficed

Thomas atte Mulne.
Thomas Cartere.
Richard de Mune.
Thomas le Peyntour.
John de Pylardynton.
John de Salford.
Richard Sygg'.
John de Warton.
John Scriveyn of Warwick.
Henry Trifelere of Kidderminster.
John Pylet of Elmley.
Thomas Broun of Wick (*Wyk'*).
Nicholas de Rotteleye of Coventry & Lichfield diocese, by l.d.
John de Paxford.
William Clyve.
Simon de Tredinton.
William Wolenton.
Richard de Piriton.
Richard Frere of Winchcombe.
Richard Averay of Minchinhampton.
Walter de Sonford.
Thomas Lucas of Dudley.
Walter Wygot of Buckland.
Hugh Dreu of Pegglesworth.
Nicholas Symecok' of South Cerney.
William de Bradeweye.
John de Eylworth.
John Dangervill.
Nicholas Wymbald.
John Heyward of *Beruhampton*.
Henry Leggare of Coln Rogers.
Thomas atte Leye of Rowley (*Rouleye*).

[*Acolytes: Unbeneficed continued.*]

Richard Wyke.
Robert de Enderdeby.
Nicholas Haket'.
William de Pylardynton.
Nicholas de Sodbury.
John de Alisestr'.
John Cade.
William Tayllour of Stourton.
John Wodeward of Hidcote.
William Ivelyn, by l.d.
Robert de Morton.
John de Bardesleye.
Richard Freman of Lighthorne.
Richard de Aston Canteloue.
Henry Brek' of Brailes.
John de Wotton.
Thomas Cokes of Studley.
William Frebern' of Bushley (*Bussheleye*).

Subdeacons: Beneficed

M. Thomas de Legh, r. of St. Martin's, Eastleach.
Thomas de Hampton, r. of Exhall.
M. Thomas ʒonge, r. of St. Stephen's, Bristol.
M. Roger le White, r. of Cold Ashton.
M. Robert de Southam, r. of Atherstone.
John Clerk' of Coberley, to t. of the perpetual chantry in St. Mary's, Coberley.
Simon Bullok', r. of St. Ewen's, Bristol.
Gilbert Derlyng', v. of Campden.

Subdeacons: Unbeneficed

John son of Walter Rottele of Tysoe, to t. of the house of Hurley.
Thomas le Cook' of Lechlade, to t. of the house of Lechlade.
William Pedemor of Kidderminster, at the request of John [?Joan] le Boys and John Beauchamp, for the order of subdeacon only.
John Kie of Powick, to t. of patrimony.
Thomas de Wynterton, to t. of the first chantry of Chelmscote chapel.
Simon le Heir of Barnsley, to t. of the house of Oseney.
Richard Wodeford of Broadwell, to t. of the house of St. Frideswide, Oxford.
Henry Banty of Great Barrington, to t. of the house of St. Frideswide, Oxford.

Simon son of William de Edmundescote of Tredington, to t. of the house of Wroxton.

William Stephenes of Witley (*Wytteleye*), to t. of patrimony.

Thomas de Lench, to t. of patrimony.

Nicholas de Whitwyk' of Coventry & Lichfield diocese, by l.d. to t. of patrimony.

Walter de Intlebur', to t. of the house of Kington (*Kyngton*).

Thomas Meysy, to t. of the house of Oseney.

Richard Suddelaye, to t. of the bishop's grace.

Thomas Warde of Little Wilmcote, to t. of St. John's hospital, Lichfield.

Richard Taylour of Cirencester, to t. of the house of Craswall.

Richard son of William atte Stok', to t. of the hospital of St. John of Jerusalem.

John de Kirkedal' of Coventry & Lichfield diocese, by l.d. to t. of St. John the Baptist's hospital, Lichfield.

John Starie, to t. of patrimony.

Philip de Colton of Coventry & Lichfield diocese, by l.d. to t. of the house of Leeds.

William Loveryng' of Farmington, to t. of the house of Llanthony next Gloucester.

Richard de Cotene of Coventry & Lichfield diocese, by l.d. to t. of the house of Gresley.

Henry Hadeleye of Ombersley, to t. of patrimony.

Thomas Stok', to t. of the bishop's grace.

Adam Pety of Hales[owen], to t. of the house of Halesowen (*Hales*).

Walter Rom of Fladbury, to t. of patrimony.

John Sampson of Wick-by-Pershore, to t. of patrimony.

William de Bradewas, to t. of patrimony.

Subdeacons: Religious

Br. John Lucas } of the house of Lechlade.
Br. John Malyns }

Br. Edward de Brantyngthorp } of the house of Merevale, Coventry
Br. John de Belgrave } & Lichfield diocese, by l.d.

Br. Roger de Eton of the house of Llanthony by Gloucester.

Br. Simon de Lye of the house of Winchcombe.

Br. John Strengesham } of the house of Pershore.
Br. Thomas de Pershore }

Deacons: Religious

Br. Thomas de Aston.

Br. William Tankard.

Br. Thomas de Cherlecote.

Br. Thomas de Weston of the house of Lilleshall, Coventry & Lichfield diocese, by l.d.

[*Deacons: Religious continued.*]

Br. William of Merevale, Coventry & Lichfield diocese, by [l.d.].
Br. Robert de Pakwode of the house of Maxstoke, Coventry & Lichfield diocese, by l.d.
Br. Thomas de Braunsford of the house of Malvern.
Br. John Bulleye ⎫
Br. John de Grafton ⎬ of the house of Llanthony by Gloucester.
Br. Walter Athelam.
Br. Roger Ledebury of the cathedral church of Worcester.

Deacons: Beneficed

M. Thomas de Aston, r. of St. Andrew's, Eastleach.
Robert Mordak', r. of Winterbourne.
Walter Clodsale, r. of Pedmore.
Thomas de Pykstok, r. of Grendon, Coventry & Lichfield diocese, by l.d.

Deacons: Unbeneficed

William Pershore, to t. of the house of Oseney.
Robert Pynson of Haselor, to t. of patrimony.
John Hope of Buckland, to t. of patrimony.
Richard Calewe of Gloucester, to t. of the house of Llanthony by Gloucester.
John atte Brugg' son of John atte Brugg' of Holdfast, to t. of patrimony.
William Pendok', to t. of the house of Flaxley (*Floxeleye*).
William Maldon of Stonehouse, to t. of the house of Elstow.
John Derlyng' of Fairford, to t. of the house of Bradenstoke.
Henry de Honyngton, to t. of the house of Lesnes.
Roger in le Hurne of Winstone, to t. of the house of Oseney.
Thomas Walton of Coventry & Lichfield diocese, to t. of the house of Hulton.
Richard de Shareshull, to t. of the house of Lilleshall.
John Perkynes of Westcote, to t. of the house of Lechlade.
Nicholas Gorwy of Fladbury, to t. of patrimony.
William son of William Abel of Coventry & Lichfield diocese, to t. of the house of Merevale.
John de Bradeleye of Coventry & Lichfield diocese, to t. of the house of St. John the Baptist next Stafford by l.d.
Robert de Kirkeby of Stow St. Edward, to t. of the house of Hailes.
John de Milverton, to t. of the house of Thelsford.
John Underhull of Bushbury (*Busbury*), Coventry & Lichfield diocese, by l.d.
William Godefray, to t. of the house of Rocester.

Walter le Meleward, to t. of the house of Thelsford.
Henry le Taillour of Lechlade, to t. of the house of Lechlade.

Priests: Religious

Br. Richard Wenlak' of the cathedral church of Worcester.
Br. Thomas de Wyk' of the house of Kingswood.
Br. Robert de Brailles of the house of Stoneleigh, Coventry & Lichfield diocese, by l.d.
Br. Robert atte Rudingge ⎱ of the house of Bordesley.
Br. Hugh de Sondford ⎰
Br. Thomas de Keleby of the house of Arbury, Coventry & Lichfield diocese, by l.d.
Br. Hugh de Weston of Shrewsbury ⎫
Br. William de Weston   ⎬ of the house of Lilleshall,
Br. Thomas de Bromleye   Coventry & Lichfield, diocese, by l.d.
Br. Adam de Bures   ⎭ ocese, by l.d.
Br. Peter de Pendok' of the house of Pershore.
Br. Thomas Mynsterworth of the house of Malvern.

Priests: Beneficed

Thomas Passelewe, r. of Rodmarton.
M. David de Milkesham, v. of Berkeley.
M. John de Lamley, r. of Hullasey chapel.

Priests: Unbeneficed

William de Mersshton, to t. of the house of Trentham (*Trengham*), by l.d.
William Hairon of Compton Wyniates, to t. of the house of Caldwell.
Walter Page of Stourton, to t. of the house of Cold Norton.
Philip atte Milne of Chipping Campden, to t. of the house of Shrewsbury.
Geoffrey de Aula of Cherrington,[1] to t. of the house of Studley.
Walter Messager, to t. of the house of St. Bartholomew, Newbury.
John Hobkyns of Besford, to t. of patrimony.
Adam Stille of Halford, to t. of the house of Luffield.
William White of Forthampton, to t. of the house of Oseney.
William son of John de Cotteleye, of Coventry & Lichfield diocese, by l.d. to t. of the house of Nuneaton.
Richard le Hunte of Kineton (*Magna Kyngton*), to t. of the house of Bicester.
Stephen Hathemere, to t. of the house of St. Peter, Gloucester.
John Ruyfeld of Coventry & Lichfield diocese, by l.d. to t. of patrimony.
William atte Well' of Fairford, to t. of the house of Llanthony by Gloucester.

1 MS. *Chiriton.*

344   THE REGISTER OF WOLSTAN DE BRANSFORD

[*Priests: Unbeneficed continued.*]
John Boteler of Farmington, to t. of the house of Cold Norton.
Richard de Mulverton of Coventry & Lichfield diocese, by l.d. to t. of the house of Studley.
Adam Toly, to t. of the house of Caldwell.
John Sampson of Childs Wickham, to t. of patrimony.
William Cot, to t. of the house of Missenden.
Ralph de Cotene of Coventry & Lichfield diocese, by l.d. to t. of the house of Gresley.

To the first tonsure

Memorandum that after the celebration of these orders the bishop conferred the first tonsure on John son of Richard de Mullecote of Evesham, in the jurisdiction of the abbot of Evesham, by l.d., and on Thomas Hogges of Wolverton (*Wolferton*).

1342 *22 July 1349 Acolytes ordained by the bishop in the chapel of Hartlebury Castle on the feast of St. Mary Magdalene.*

Acolyte: Religious
Br. John de Wygorn' of the house of Halesowen.

Acolyte: Beneficed
Richard de Lench Rondolf, r. of Rous Lench.

Quire of Royal Writs Directed to Bishop Thoresby
29 September 1350–8 May 1352
[Numbers 1344–1364]

[1364 is an interleaved fragment which is out of place.]

Royal writs from the feast of St. Michael 1350, the second year of the translation of John [Thoresby], bishop of Worcester.[1]

1344 *25 November 1350 Westminster*
Writ summoning Bishop John [Thoresby] and representatives of the clergy of the diocese [as in 1132] to attend a parliament (*colloquium et*

1 These properly belong to the next register in the series.

tractatus) at Westminster in the octave of the Purification [i.e. 9 February 1351]. Tested by the king (*me ipso*).

1345 — —*1350 Westminster*

Further writ of *fieri facias* against Thomas de Hompton [cf. 1176, 1320]. The bishop is to have 100 marks [£66 13s. 4d.] at the Exchequer on the morrow of the Purification [i.e. 3 February]. Tested by G. de Wylford.

1346 *8 November 1350 Westminster*

Writ of *venire facias* against John de Wyndesore, parson of Cleeve. He is to be made to appear before the justices in 15 days of St. Hilary [i.e. 27 January] to answer the plea of M. Robert de Chikwell, clerk, that he render £63 6s. 8d. which he owes and unjustly detains, the sheriffs of London having reported on the morrow of All Souls [i.e. 3 November] that he has no lay fee. Tested by J. de Stonore.

1347 *3 February 1351 Westminster*

Further writ of *levari facias* against Elias Walteres of Iccomb [as 1328, but returnable in 3 weeks of Easter, i.e. 8 May].

1348 *28 January 1351 Westminster*

Writ of *venire facias* against Hugh le Hayward, parson of Dunstall. He is to be made to appear before the justices in 3 weeks of Easter [i.e. 8 May] to answer the plea of Richard de Wylughby senior, kt., that he render £54 which he owes and unjustly detains, the sheriff of Leicester having reported in 15 days of St. Hilary that he has no lay fee. Tested by J. de Stonore.

1349 *22 February 1351 Westminster*

Writ of *certiorari*. The bishop is to certify the Chancery as to whether or not the church of Stratford on Avon is appropriated to the warden and chaplains of St. Thomas the Martyr's chapel, and if so, as to when this was done. Tested by the king (*me ipso*).[1]

1350 *10 May 1351 Westminster*

Further writ of *levari facias* against Elias Walteres of Iccomb [as 1328, 1347, but returnable the quindene of St. Michael, i.e. 13 October].

1 The church was appropriated by Bishop Montacute in 1336. Reg. Montacute 1, ff. 50r.–61v.

1351 *14 May 1351 Westminster*

Further writ of *venire facias* against Hugh le Hayward, parson of Dunstall [v. 1348]. He is to be made to appear before the justices in 15 days of Trinity [i.e. 26 June]. Tested by J. de Stonore.

1352 *24 May 1351 Westminster*

Further writ of *levari facias* against Thomas de Hompton [v. 1345]. The bishop is to have 100 marks [£66 13s. 4d.] at the Exchequer in 15 days of St. John the Baptist [i.e. 8 July]. Tested by G. de Wilford.

1353 *1 September 1351 Tower of London*

Writ of *certiorari*. The bishop is to send details of benefices held by aliens in the diocese by the quindene of St. Michael at latest [i.e. 13 October]. Tested by the king (*me ipso*). [Substantially as 1277.]

1354 *1 September 1351 Tower of London*

Writ for the collection of a tenth. The clergy of the Canterbury province in their last convocation in St. Paul's London [1 May], after hearing of the dangers threatening the Church and realm, granted a biennial tenth payable at four terms, St. Andrew [30 November] and the Nativity of St. John the Baptist [24 June] for the first year, and the Purification [2 February 1352] and the Nativity of St. John for the second, as is contained in the certificate sent by S[imon Islep], archbishop of Canterbury [1349–66]. The bishop is to appoint collectors and to send their names to the Chancery.

1355 *15 November 1351 Westminster*

Writ of summons [as 1344] to a parliament to be held at Westminster on Friday the feast of St. Hilary [13 January 1352]. Tested by the king (*me ipso*).

1356 *17 November 1351 Westminster*

Further writ of *levari facias* against Thomas de Hompton [as 1345 including the return day: cf. 1352].

1357 *7 March 1352 Westminster*

Writ of *certiorari*. The bishop is to certify the Chancery as to whether or not Joan, daughter and heiress of Brian de Hikelyng, deceased, who held of the king in chief, is married, and if so, when, where and to whom. Tested by the king (*me ipso*).

1358 *18 February 1352 Westminster*

Further writ of *levari facias* against Thomas de Hompton. The bishop is to have £100 [cf. 1352, 1356 &c.] at the Exchequer in 15 days of Easter. Tested by G. de Wilford.

1359 *16 April 1352 Westminster*

Writ of *levari facias* against M. Henry de Neubold, parson of Weston-on-Avon. Because M. Henry ought to have paid ten marks [£6 13s. 4d.] last Easter [8 April] to John de Codington, parson of Bottesford, and has still not done so, the bishop is to raise that sum from his goods and to have it at the Chancery on the morrow of the Ascension [i.e. 18 May]. Tested by the king (*me ipso*).

1360 *8 May 1352 Westminster*

Further writ of *levari facias* against Thomas de Hompton [v. 1358]. The bishop is to have £100 at the Exchequer in 15 days of St. Michael [i.e. 13 October] for livery to William de Walcote, Queen Isabella's receiver. Tested by G. de Wilford.

1361 *20 October 1352 Westminster*

Writ for the appointment of collectors for the second year of the biennial tenth [v. 1354], the conditions put forward by the clergy at the last parliament[1] having been met. Tested by the king (*me ipso*).

1362 *4 December 1352 Westminster*

Writ requiring the bishop to have John de Empyngham, clerk, inducted to the wardenship (*custodia*) of St. Wulstan's hospital, Worcester, which the king has granted him by reason of the recent vacancy of the see.

1363 *8 May 1352*

Further writ of *levari facias* against Thomas de Hompton. [Duplicate of 1360.]

1364 *31 December 1340 Worcester*

Fragment of MS. on which are written the last few lines of an appropriation document concerning Tanworth church with the prior & chapter's confirmatory clause [also dated as above]. On the verso are notes giving the dates of the Tanworth, Aston Cantlow and Yardley appropriations at 17 June 1340 [v. 160, 321, 325], 4 October 1345 [v. 750] and 3 May 1347 [v. 833, 838] respectively, together with the return of a writ [as in 1318 *q.v.*].

1 Parliament met 13 January and 16 August in 1352.

Register of The Bishop's Court of Audience
13 June–31 July 1349
[Numbers 1365–1376]

Register of causes held before the bishop or his commissaries in the Court of Audience from 13 June 1349. [Rubric]

1365 *4 October 1342*
Commission *ad causas et negocia* for M. John de Severleye. [Duplicate of 1330.]

1366 *18–27 June 1349 'Acta' in the parish church of Hartlebury before M. John de Severleye, the bishop's chancellor and commissary.*

18 June [Thursday]. Case of correction against William de Herthull of Belbroughton parish for withholding a mortuary. William appeared in person and swore to tell the truth with respect to a written article (*articulus*). He denied it. Monday was assigned for him to see the proofs to be produced on behalf of the office.

22 June [Monday]. William appeared as before and five witnesses were produced: Roger de Thelford, John Smyth of Bell (*Belne*), John de Thelford, Hugh Brentel of Bell and Henry atte Wode of Fairfield (*Foruelde*). These were sworn, examined, and their attestations published. Thursday was assigned for objection to them or their testimony, and in the event of nothing effectual being said, for the [accused] to show cause why he should not be pronounced perjured and under sentence of excommunication.

25 June [Thursday]. William alleged that three of the witnesses, Roger de Thelford, John Smyth and Hugh Brentel, were under sentence of greater excommunication, had been so at the time of their deposition, and that therefore their testimony was void. Saturday was assigned for proof of these exceptions.

27 June [Saturday]. William appeared as before. There being no proofs, the exceptions were rejected. John de Severleye pronounced sentence (*pronunciacio*).[1] In accordance with the Council of Oxford [1222] all who maliciously deprive the Church of her rights, or who infringe her liberty contrary to justice, thereby incur greater ex-

1 This included a recension of the charge or *articulus*.

communication [Lyndwood, *Const. Prov.*, p. 1]. William, by depriving the church and ministers of Belbroughton of a cow on 26 May 1349, fell under the Council's sentence. Later, after making satisfaction to God and the Church, he was absolved.

1367 *1 July 1349 'Acta' before M. John de Severleye, commissary, in the churchyard of Hartlebury parish church.*

Case against Ds. Stephen, rector of Shrawley, for incontinence with Margery, daughter of John de Hethe, lately wife of John de Farleye, and his parishioner. Stephen chose to appear in the above place rather than his own church—the place assigned, and denied the article, at least from the time of his correction. The 15th day was assigned for him to establish his correction and to purge himself with the sixth hand (*cum sexta manu*).[1]

16 July. The rector canonically purged himself.

1368 *13 July 1349 'Acta' before the commissary in Hartlebury church.*

Case against . . .[2] vicar of Ombersley, for incontinence with Agnes Crompe. The vicar appeared in person and alleged his own correction and the woman's death before correction. Monday after St. Kenelm [20 July] was assigned to him.

20 July 1349 'Acta' before the commissary in the same place.

The above vicar proved the woman's death but not his own correction.

1369 *u.s.*

Case against Thomas de Stretton, clerk, for incontinence with Isabella, wife of Thomas Malue of *Fipton*. Thomas appeared in person and confessed the article. As penance he was publicly to recite three psalters in his parish church during Mass, clothed in a surplice and with his hood thrown back. Afterwards the penance was reduced to one psalter, and that to be said secretly.

1370 *20 July 1349 'Acta' before the commissary in Hartlebury castle.*

Margery, sometime wife of John de Den', was accused of incontinence with Thomas de Den', John's brother. The woman appeared and confessed the article. As penance she was to receive three whippings round the church and three round the market place.

1 i.e. He swore himself and five compurgators also.
2 Gap in MS.

1371 *23 July 1349 'Acta' before the commissary in Hartlebury parish church.*

Case against Alexander de Luttelton, calling himself a brother of St. Wulstan's hospital, Worcester, by reason of a sentence of greater excommunication imposed on the bishop's authority. Alexander appeared in person and sought declaration of the sentence. He was declared to have incurred it for procuring the sale of corrodies, in particular one to John de Stodleye, without consulting the bishop and in defiance of his prohibition made under pain of excommunication. On the part of Alexander a written article was requested and a day for replying to the same. The following day was assigned for him to receive it, and Monday [27 July: v. 1373] for his response.

1372 *27 July 1349 'Acta' before the commissary in the same place.*
William Pechlyng was accused of incontinence with Felicia Bole. Both denied the article, the man alleging that 12 years had gone by [since the offence], the woman 10. Each claimed correction. Friday was assigned for them to establish such correction, and if successful, to purge themselves from that time with the eighth hand [i.e. 7 compurgators]. On that day [31 July] William failed to appear and was pronounced contumacious. He was declared to have failed in his proof and purgation and to be fully convicted of the crime.

The same was accused of incontinence with Isabella Lobery. Both denied the article, the man declaring on oath that he had not seen the woman before. Both were dismissed.

The same was accused of incontinence with Agnes Crompe. He alleged that she was his wife and Friday was assigned for him to prove this. On that day [31 July] he failed to appear, was pronounced contumacious, and declared to have failed in his proof.

1373 *u.s.*
Case against Alexander de Luttleton [v. 1371]. He appeared in person and put forward six exceptions, which were rejected, and one declinatory exception which so far as it concerned the foundation of St. Wulstan's hospital was sworn of malice [?].[1] Contestation of the article was made by denying the truth of the events as narrated, but with verbal protestation reserving appeal against the rejection of the exceptions. Friday [31 July: v. 1375] was assigned for further procedure.

1374 *u.s.*
Suit between John Heyne of Alcester, executor of the will of Isabella, relict of William Chyk' of Alcester, the plaintiff, and Ds. Robert

---

1 . . . *Alexandro personaliter comparente, propositis contra articulum sex excepcionibus . . . ac una excepcione declinatoria super qua quatenus concernit fundacionem domus hospitalis Sancti Wolstani Wyg'* [erasures] *de malicia iurato . . .*

atte Brugge of Alcester, chaplain, the defendant, who was alleged to have impeded the free administration of the deceased's goods. The parties came in person, contestation was made by denial [*negative*], and an oath *de calumpnia et de veritate dicenda* taken. Monday [3 August] was assigned for the plaintiff to prove his charge and for the defendant to see the proofs.

1375 *31 July 1349 'Acta' before the commissary in the same place.*
Case against Alexander de Luttelton [v. 1373]. He appeared in person as before. On the part of the office three witnesses were produced to prove the article: John called 'Goldsmyth' of [Droit]-wich, Henry le Boteler and Simon Panyter. These were sworn and a copy was requested of the warning previously given to Alexander and his brethren by the bishop's commissary, which was ordered to be received in the process.
Tuesday [4 August] was assigned for further procedure.

1376 *u.s.*
Suit between John Canoun of Worcester, executor of Alexander Raas, formerly the bishop's brewer, plaintiff, and Margery, daughter of William de Asshebarwe, defendant, who was alleged to have impeded the executor's administration by hiding and keeping back the deceased's goods. The parties appeared personally and the case was adjourned until Thursday [6 August].[1]

Quire of Institutions to Benefices, Elections to Monasteries, &c. For the Period 16 March—6 August 1349 [Numbers 1377—1568]

[Almost all the entries are to be found in the lists of appointments to religious houses and of institution to benefices which follow this section.]

1452 *16–17 June 1349 Hartlebury*
Confirmation of Br. Peter Warrewic's election as prior of the Holy Sepulchre, Warwick, following the amoval of Br. William de Witton.

1 The day of the bishop's death.

27

On Tuesday after St. Barnabas there appeared before the bishop in the chapel of Hartlebury castle Br. Peter, the elect, on his own behalf, and Br. John de Grete, canon of the house, as proctor of the convent, seeking confirmation of the election. The certificate of the dean of the Christianity of Warwick showed that there was no competitor, co-elect, or opponent of the election, and that general citation of any who might wish to raise objection had been made. After citation at the castle gates, the bishop precluded all such from bringing forward anything at a later stage. Subsequently the form of proxy and the election decree were exhibited, and also the commission to the compromisers, sealed with the common seal of the house, and the written petition of the elect—to which the proctor gave support in so far as it concerned the convent. Two instructors, the above Br. John de Grete and his fellow canon, Br. John de Bretfordeston, were produced, and also one witness, John called *de Keleswich*. After they had been admitted and sworn and their examination committed *viva voce* to M. John de Severleye, archdeacon of Worcester, there was an adjournment until the morrow. On that day [17 June] the elect and the proctor appeared as before, the attestations of the witnesses were delivered and published, and the parties asked whether they wished to propound anything further. They replied in the negative, and after discussion of the whole process, the bishop pronounced the election to have been canonically made and confirmed it. When the *Te Deum laudamus* had been chanted the prior elect and confirmed swore obedience to the bishop in the usual form and a letter was sent to M. Luke, rector of Honington, for his installation.

1484 *1 July 1349 Hartlebury*

Public instrument attesting the provision of William de Okleye, deacon, to Broadway rectory. The bishop having received letters of Clement VI [1342–52], under the form used for the beneficing of poor clerks, for the provision of William de Okleye to a benefice in the patronage of the abbot and convent of Pershore, deputed M. John de [la] Lowe, now deceased, at the time his official principal, as sub-executor of the grace. He expressly revokes such commission and by apostolic authority confers (*per pillii nostri tradicionem*) on William the parish church of Broadway, vacant by the death of the last rector, which falls within the terms of the grace and which William has accepted within the time allowed, but with reservation of the right to another benefice should the church lawfully belong to someone else. The bishop declares that he has committed his powers of further execution, and in particular, William's induction, to the archdeacon of Gloucester, his official, and the rural deans, rectors, vicars and chaplains of the archdeaconry. He has had the present instrument written out and published by William Aleyn, called *de Rothewell*, and has further strengthened it by appending his own seal. Present in the principal chamber of his castle during the process were M. John de Severleye, archdeacon of Worcester, and Richard de Okleye, clerk, witnesses to the above.

Subscription of William Aleyn, called *de Rothewell*, clerk of Lincoln diocese, notary public by apostolic authority and the bishop's scribe (*scriba*).

1504 *6–9 July 1349 Hartlebury*

Examination and confirmation of the election of John la Southe as prior of the Augustinian house at Studley. On the vacancy caused by the death of Br. Robert de Langedon, Br. John la Southe, canon of the house, was elected by way of scrutiny, the bishop's mandate for proclamation being directed to the abbot of Alcester. On 6 July 1349, before the ninth hour, the certificate of proclamation was delivered to M. John de Severleye, the bishop's special commissary, sitting *pro tribunali* in the chapel of the bishop's castle by virtue of a commission dated 6 July from Hartlebury.[1] The certificate showed that due citation had been made, but no-one appeared when summoned at the castle gates. Br. John, the elect, appeared in person, and Br. Thomas de Warr', a fellow canon, as proctor of the convent. The proxy and the election decree were exhibited, as well as two petitions for the confirmation of the election. The commissary then adjourned the session until after dinner. At that time the elect and the proctor appeared before the commissary in Hartlebury churchyard, and two instructors, the above Br. Thomas de War', and Br. John de Wrench, a fellow canon, were produced, together with one witness, John Barwe of Stratford-on-Avon, *literatus*. After they had been admitted, sworn and examined by means of articles put to them, their attestations were written down. As those cited did not appear, the commissary denied them further right of objection. When many things had been propounded and exhibited, and the bishop's register invoked as proof of the elect's orders, Wednesday [17 June] was assigned for further proceedings in Hartlebury parish church. On that day the parties appeared as before, the attestations were published, various instruments exhibited, and the business concluded with the consent of the parties. There followed discussion about the process, the elect and the proctor petitioning that the election decree should not be considered as a public instrument but merely as being proved by witnesses, and that the error in the words *indiccione tercia*[2] might be recalled. The petition was rejected as void and the commissary declared in a written document that the election had not been canonically made in accordance with the constitution

1 Which is recited in full.
2 ... *si et quatenus non est modo INDICCIO TERCIA.*

Quia propter[1] and that the canons had knowingly approved it. He therefore pronounced it null and deprived the canons of their right to elect on that occasion. Later, on 9 July, he appointed *iure devoluto* the above John la Southe as prior, and when the *Te Deum laudamus* had been chanted, the latter swore obedience to the bishop and a letter was written to the archdeacon of Worcester for his induction.

1537   *19 July 1349 Hartlebury*

Memorandum that on the authority of a licence granted by Roger [Northburgh], bishop of Coventry & Lichfield [1322–58], dated 30 June from Haywood, the diocesan received the profession of obedience made by Br. Robert Athereston, abbot of the Cistercian monastery of Stoneleigh, and gave him his blessing. After reading the profession, and as a sign of it, the abbot made a cross on the document with his own hand.

1568   *6 August 1349*

Memorandum that on the 6th day of August 1349, in the second year of the indiction, and the eighth of Clement VI's pontificate, at Hartlebury in the castle, the venerable father the lord Wolstan, by the grace of God bishop of Worcester, closed his last day.

END OF SECOND VOLUME

---

1 *Extra* 1, 6, c. 42.

Tables

TABLE I

TABLE I

Institutions to Benefices

For the most part memoranda of institutions are stereotyped and have therefore been omitted from the text. The essential details are recorded in the following table. In special cases, however, and always where exchanges are concerned, the relevant documents have also been summarised in the body of the edition, where fuller particulars can be found.

Abbreviations &c.

A.G. — archdeacon of Gloucester
A.W. — archdeacon of Worcester
ass. — assumed, or assumption
C.A.W. — commissary of the archdeacon of Worcester
chap. — chaplain (*capellanus*)
clk. — clerk (*clericus*)
D. — dean or, in vacancy column, death
Deany — deanery
e. — earl
exch. — exchange
Inqu. — inquisition (*inquisicio*) or enquiry. [This indicates that a mandate for enquiry into a vacancy was sent by the bishop. Unless otherwise noted it was directed to the inductor mentioned.]
iuratus — indicates that the person inducted took an oath of residence*
jurisd. (pec. jurisd.) — jurisdiction (peculiar jurisdiction)
O.A.G. — official of the archdeacon of Gloucester
O.A.W. — official of the archdeacon of Worcester
P.C. — perpetual chantry
Pr. — priory or prior

TABLE I   357

pr.   — proctor
pst.   — priest
R.   — Rectory
r.   — rector
res.   — resignation
u.s.   — ut supra
V.   — vicarage
v.   — vicar

* The phrase when given in full runs : *et vicarius perpetuus de continue residendo et personaliter ministrando in ea iuxta formam constitucionis domini Ottoboni edite in hac parte iuratus.*
Places of institution outside the diocese are in italics.

VOLUME I

Benefice	Date and place of institution	Person instituted	Former incumbent	Cause of vacancy	Patron	Inductor	Edition nos.
HANBURY R.	23 June 1339 *Stoneham* [1]	M. William de Herwynton, clk.[2]	M. John de Usk	Exch. for Portland R., Salisb. dioc.	Bp.	D. of Droitwich (26 June)	57–8, 197–9
BIBURY with chapels v.	30 Nov. 1339 Hartlebury	Br. Thomas de Mammesfeld, canon of Oseney, pst.			Oseney Abb.	Parish pst. of Bibury	98–9
BISHAMPTON R.	5 Apr. 1339 [Spetchley]	Thomas de Besford	Thomas de Abetot	Exch. [below]	Thomas de Somery		164
LEIGH, Cherkenhill portion R.	As above	Thomas de Abetot	Thomas de Besford	Exch. [above]	Pershore Abb.		164

[1] Bp. of Salisbury's certificate.
[2] He had appointed Adam le Boteler, clk, his proctor for the exchange (198).

Benefice	Date and place of institution	Person instituted	Former incumbent	Cause of vacancy	Patron	Inductor	Edition nos.
PIRTON R.	5 Apr. 1339 Spetchley	Nicholas de Drokensford, acol[1]			Thomas de Beauchamp, e. of Warwick	O.A.W.	165
COUGHTON V.	22 Apr. 1339 Hartlebury	John de Bishopeston, pst. *iuratus*[2]	Ralph de Staunton	Exch. [below]	Studley Pr.	O.A.W.	169–72
WORCESTER, St. Helen Chantry	As above	Ralph de Staunton, pst.	John de Bishopeston	Exch. [above]	r. of St. Helen's	r. of St. Helen's or his *locum tenens*	169–72
KEMERTON R.	30 Apr. 1339 u.s.	John de Holeweye, pst.	John de London	D.	John de Bures, kt., ld. of Boddington	O.A.G. & Inqu.	176–8
NORTH PIDDLE R.	29 Apr. 1339 u.s.	James de Plumstede, pst.	Thomas de Segrave	Res.	Lady Alice de Segrave	O.A.W.	181
RIPPLE Chantry	2 May 1339 u.s.	Walter Hatherich, pst.	John Hoghges, pst.		John Salemon, pst.	D. of Ripple jurisd. & Inqu.	179, 183
HARVINGTON [near Evesham] R.	5 May 1339	Robert de Wornesleye or Warsleye, pst.			Worcester Pr.	O.A.W. & Inqu. O.A.G. [*sic*]	175, 184
WORCESTER, St. Michael R.	29 May 1339 Bredon	Robert called 'Someri', pst.			Simon Crompe, sacrist of Worc. Cath.	O.A.W.	195
COLD ASTON V. [*alias* ASTON BLANK]	17 June 1339 u.s.	William called 'le Tippare', pst. *iuratus*.[3]	Robert Abraham	D.	Little Malvern Pr.	O.A.G.	196

TABLE I

359

GREAT COMBERTON R.	22 July 1339 u.s.	Robert de Amyas, pst.	Walter called 'le Mason'	Res.	Thomas de Beauchamp, e. of Warwick	O.A.W.	205
WORCESTER, St. Nicholas R.	11 Aug. 1339	Thomas de Faston, pst.[4]	William de Wygynton	Res.	Bp.	D. of Worcester	207
HATHEROP R.	22 Sept. 1339 Woodford[5]	John de Carlton pst.	M. Henry de Lodelow	Exch. for Laverstock V., Salisb. dioc.	St. Peter's Abb., Glouc.	O.A.G. (25 Sept.)	78, 212–3
OXHILL R.	14 Oct. 1339 Worcester	John Davy of Dodford			William de Kaynes, kt.	O.A.W.	217
KNIGHTWICK R.	16 Oct. 1339 Worcester[6]	M. John de Ullingwyk	William de Clyfford	Exch. [below]	Worcester Pr.	O.A.W.	218–9
COMBE BASKERVILLE R.	See above	William Clyfford	M. John de Ullingwyk	Exch. [above]	M. Philip de Ullingwyk	O.A.G. & Inqu.	218–9
MORETON DAUBENEY, Moiety R.	26 Oct. 1339 Clent.	Thomas de Goldlesdone, pst.			St. John's hosp., Warwick	O.A.W.	226
STRETTON-ON-FOSSE R.	10 Nov. 1339 Hampton Bishop	John de Wentebrygg, clk.	Henry de Schulton, pst.	Exch. for Southam R., Cov. & Lich. dioc.	John de Leycester	D. of Blockley	227

1 *Iuravit obedienciam in forma communi.* 2 Both this and the next institution were carried out by M. Hugh de Penebrugg *organum vocis domini constitutus.*
3 *prestito prius ab eo corporali iuramento de continua residencia facienda in eadem.*
4 . . . *presbitero et clerico suo* [i.e. of the bishop]. 5 Bp. of Salisbury's certificate.
6 The bp. carried out this institution himself and by a commission of the same date (219) directed the O.A.G. to enquire into the Combe Baskerville vacancy and, if appropriate, to institute and induct the presentee.

Benefice		Date and place of institution	Person instituted	Former incumbent	Cause of vacancy	Patron	Inductor	Edition nos.
CHURCH LENCH	R.	12 Nov. 1339 Warwick	Robert de More	Peter de Lench	Exch. for Chirton V., Salisb. dioc.	Thomas de Beauchamp, e. of Warwick	O.A.W.	228
BRISTOL, St. Werburgh	R.	26 Nov. 1339 Hartlebury	Thomas de Berwyk, pst.	John Leche	D.	Keynsham Abb.	O.A.G.	235
CLENT with ROWLEY Chapel	R.	3 Dec. 1339 u.s.	Nicholas Jobinol, pst.	John de Horsleye	Res.	John Botetourte	O.A.W.	236
LITTLE RISSINGTON	R.	7 Dec. 1339 u.s.	Thomas de Oxon, by his pr. M. Robert de Crassale	Thomas Marchal	D.	Oseney Abb.	O.A.G.	237
ALVECHURCH	R.	16 Dec. 1339 u.s.	Robert de Alne			Bp.	D. of Alvechurch (17 Dec.)	239
HALFORD	R.	30 Dec. 1339 u.s.	John Botoner, pst.			Bp.	O.A.W.[1] (19 Jan. 1340)	241
WORCESTER, St. Alban	R.	23 Jan. 1340 u.s.	Hugh Straddel of Gloucester	John de Merston	Exch. [below]	Evesham Abb.	O.A.W.	248
TIBBERTON	V.	As above	John de Merston, iuratus	Hugh de Straddel	Exch. [above]	Worcester Pr.	O.A.W.	248
WARNDON	R.	23 Jan. 1340 Hartlebury	Robert de Warmyndon, clk.	John de Aston	D.	Robert de Bracy	O.A.W.	249

TABLE I
361

Benefice	Date / place	Institutee	Predecessor	Cause	Patron	Note	Ref.
ROCK R. Chapel	14 Feb. 1340 Campden	Adam Boresford, pst.			Robert Muchegros, ld. of Woollashill	O.A.W.	254
DEERHURST R.	8 Feb. 1340 Winchcombe	Br. Ralph de Ermenovilla, Pr. of Deerhurst	Br. John de Vetolio, Pr. of Deerhurst	Recall on acc. of infirmity	Guy, abbot of St. Denis	D. of Winchcombe	256–8
TANWORTH R.	3 Apr. 1340 Hartlebury	Robert Wyk' of Packington, by his pr. John le Spencer, clk.			William de Clynton, e. of Huntingdon	O.A.W.	287
BREDON R.	24 Mar. 1340 Belvoir[2]	M. John de Orlton, by his pr. John de Beautr', clk.	M. John Trillek	Exch. for Witney R., Linc. dioc.	Bp.	r. of Strensham (1 Apr.)	114, 288
STRETTON-ON-FOSSE Chapel	27 Apr. 1340 Alvechurch	Roger Clonne, pst., by his pr. Henry de Shutyngton	John de Wentebrigg	Res.	John de Leycester	D. of Blockley jurisd.	303
BISHAMPTON, Chantry of St. Mary	28 Apr. 1340 u.s.	Henry de Kenewarton, pst.			Thomas de Somery	O.A.W.	304
DUMBLETON R.	30 Apr. 1340 u.s.	Walter de Aston, clk.	Walter de Poywyk	D.	Abingdon Abb.	D. of Campden	305

[1] The mandate was for Botoner's induction in the person of his proctor M. Thomas Bolvynch of Droitwich.
[2] Bp. of Lincoln's certificate received at Hartlebury 1 April.

Benefice	Date and place of institution	Person instituted	Former incumbent	Cause of vacancy	Patron	Inductor	Edition nos.
TANWORTH R.	3 May 1340 Alvechurch	William de Coton of Eardiston	Robert de Pakynton	D.	Maxstoke Pr.	O.A.W.	306
TORMARTON R.	3 May 1340 u.s.	John de Astweyt		Exch. for Brightwalton R., Salisb. dioc.		D. of Hawkesbury & Bitton Inqu. O.A.G.	126, 307
PERSHORE, St. Andrew V.	4 May 1340 u.s.	John de Bradewas, pst. iuratus	Richard de Upton	Res.	Pershore Abb.	O.A.W.	308
LITTLE SODBURY R.	11 May 1340 Worcester	William de Cerston, pst.	(1)		Jordan Bishop	O.A.G.	311
WARWICK, St. James R.	18 May 1340 Bredon	Philip Bosse of Besford, pst.	J.	D.	Adam de Herwynton, *vice et nomine* the e. of Warwick	O.A.W.	312
LOWER SWELL V.	31 May 1340 Codrington	Roger de Colecote, pst. iuratus	Walter de Stowe	D.	Notley Abb.	O.A.G.	314
SALWARPE R.	2 June 1340 Pucklechurch	William de Triswell, pst. by his pr. J.	Walter de Remmesbury	D.	Adam de Herwynton [&c. as 312]	O.A.W.	316
DROITWICH, St. Andrew R.	8 June 1340[2] Henbury	William Beste, pst.			Prior of Deerhurst	O.A.W. & Inq.	319

TABLE I   363

POWICK	v.	17 June 1340 u.s.	John le Porter of Hartlebury, *iuratus.*			Great Malvern Pr.	O.A.W.	320
SUCKLEY	R.	19 June 1340³	John de Weston		Exch. for Little Gransden R., Ely dioc.		O.A.W.	324
DAGLING- WORTH	R.	14 July 1340 Tredington	Ivo de Edenham, chap.			Godstow Abb.	O.A.G.	330
CAMPDEN	v.	17 July 1340 Blockley	Robert de Radeford, chap. *iuratus.*			St. Werburgh's Abb., Chester	O.A.G.	331
TORMARTON	R.	20 July 1340 u.s.	William de Tormarton, clk.		D.	Dionisia de la River	O.A.G.	332
GRAFTON, [TEMPLE]	v.	21 July 1340 u.s.	Henry de Lygthurn, *iuratus.*	Thomas de Donynton	D.	Philip de Thame, Pr. of St. John of Jerusalem	O.A.W.	333

¹ On 3 July 1339 the bp. had directed the O.A.G. to enquire into a vacancy at Little Sodbury, Jordan of Sodbury having presented John de Bretonia, pst. (220). The latter's institution is not recorded.
² Date of commission for the O.A.W. to enquire into the vacancy and to institute and induct the presentee should the enquiry find for him. Cf. nos. 810–12, which show that he was instituted.
³ Date of mandate for O.A.W. to induct, sent after the diocesan's receipt of the Bp. of Ely's certificate.

Benefice	Date and place of institution	Person instituted	Former incumbent	Cause of vacancy	Patron	Inductor	Edition nos.
COBERLEY. Chantry at St. Mary's altar	21 July 1340 Blockley	Walter de Bradeweye, pst.	Newly founded		Thomas de Berkeley, kt., ld. of Coberley, the founder	r. of Coberley	334
LITTLE RISSINGTON R.	3 Aug. 1340 Hartlebury	Thomas de Ippewell	Thomas de Oxon	Exch. for Wood Eaton R., Linc. dioc.	Oseney Abb.	A.G. or O.	340
OXHILL R.	6 Aug. 1340 u.s.	John de Baynton	John Davy of Dodford	Exch. for Dodford V., Linc. dioc.	William de Kaynes, kt.	O.A.W.	341
WORCESTER, St. Helen R.	11 Sept. 1340 Bosbury[1]	Richard called 'Clerk' by his pr. William de Kentles	Roger de Stanford of Worc.	Exch. for Rock R., Heref. dioc.	Bp.	D. of Worcester (12 Sept.)	348
WARWICK, Colleg. Deanv. church of St. Mary	16 Sept. 1340 Hartlebury	Robert de Endredeby, pst.	M. Thomas Lench of [Droit]wich	Exch. for Congreve preb. in colleg. church of St. Michael, Penkridge [Cov. & Lich. dioc.]	Thomas de Beauchamp, e. of Warwick	O.A.W.	349

TABLE I   365

Benefice	Date and place	Clerk instituted	Last incumbent	Cause	Patron	By	Page
WESTON-ON-AVON R.	28 Oct. 1340 Alvechurch	M. Hugh de Penebrugg, pst.	Richard	D.	Bp.		357
WOLVERTON R.	5 Nov. 1340 u.s.	Robert de Hertyndon, clk.	Robert de Alne	D.	William Musard	O.A.W.	359
KIDDER-MINSTER v.	20 July 1340[2] Kidderminster	John de la Doune, pst. *iuratus.*	M. John de Karsleye	D.	Maiden Bradley hosp.	O.A.W.	369
WHATCOTE R.	24 Nov. 1340 Hartlebury	Thomas de la Morhall, first tons.	Ralph de Snelleston	D.	John de la Morhall	O.A.W.	372
HAWLING R.	6 Dec. 1340 u.s.	Richard de Billesleye, pst.	Robert Belde of Stratford	Exch. [below]	Winchcombe Abb.	O.A.G.	378
GREAT BARRINGTON v.	As above	Robert Belde of Stratford, pst. *iuratus.*	Richard de Billesleye	Exch. [above]	Llanthony Pr. by Glouc.	O.A.G.	378
CHURCHILL R. [near Kidderminster]	11 Dec. 1340 Hartlebury	William de la More of *Chitteleye,* acol.	M. John de Suckeleye	Res.	Giles de Bastenhall of Suckley.	O.A.W.	379
NAUNTON R.	17 Dec. 1340 u.s.	M. John Botoner, pst.[3]	[Robert Marny]	Exch. [below]	Bp.	D. of Stow	381, 383
HALFORD R.	17 Dec. 1340 u.s.	Robert Marny of Bishops Cleeve, clk.[4]	[M. John Botoner]	Exch. [above]	Bp.	D. of Kineton	382–3

1 Bp. of Hereford's certificate.
2 Institution by O.A.W. as bp.'s special commissary. *Inspeximus* and confirmation by bp. dated 19 November.
3 *eumque per anuli sui tradicionem investivit.*
4 *ipsumque per anuli sui tradicionem investivit.*

Benefice	Date and place of institution	Person instituted	Former incumbent	Cause of vacancy	Patron	Inductor	Edition nos.
WOOTTON WAWEN R.	2 Jan. 1341	Br. John de Silvaneto[1]	Br. John de Lotoveris	Res.	Peter de Lonuceio Alerynelni[?] for John, abb. of Conches	O.A.W.	384
WORCESTER, St. Clement R.	15 Jan. 1341 Hartlebury	Reginald de Baldenhale, clk.			Worc. Cath. Pr.	O.A.W.	387
LOWER SWELL V.	16 Jan. 1341 u.s.	John Crowe *iuratus*	Roger Colicote	Exch. for Earley, St. Nicholas' chapel, Salisb. dioc.	Notley Abb.	A.G. or C.	388
HARTLEBURY R.	19 Jan. 1341 u.s.	M. Hugh de[2] Penebrugg, pst.	William de Lugwardyn	D.	Bp.	M. John Botoner, comm. *ad hoc.*	389
WESTON-ON-AVON R.	20 Jan. 1341 u.s.	M. Henry de[3] Neubold, pst.	M. Hugh de Penebrugg	Res.	Bp.	M. Richard Maiel, r. of Preston-on-Stour	390
LIGHTHORNE R.	22 Jan. 1341 u.s.	Richard de Leukenor, pst.	William de Schell'	D.	Adam de Herwynton, *vice et nomine* the e. of Warwick	D. of Kineton[4]	391

TABLE I 367

CROMHALL R.	30 Jan. 1341 u.s.	Richard de Stratton, pst.	Robert de Walsned	Res.	William de Wanton, kt., ld. of Cromhall	A.G. or C.	392
BISHAMPTON R.	2 Mar. 1341 u.s.	Geoffrey de Welneford, clk., by his pr. M. John Vannpage	M. Thomas de Besford	D.		O.A.W.	393
LECHLADE, St. Laurence v.	3 [Mar.] 1341 u.s.	William Poty, pst. iuratus	John	D.	St. John's hosp., Lechlade	A.G. or O. or C.	394
LITTLE SODBURY R.	16 Apr. 1341 Tewkesbury	Thomas Bisshop, pst.	William de Cofton	Res.	Jordan Bisshop, ld. of Sodbury	A.G. or O. or C.	399
BITTON v.	9 May 1341 Hartlebury	Nicholas Franceys, pst. iuratus	John de Strengeston	Res.	Edmund de Remmesbury	A.G. or O. or C.	402
TURKDEAN v.	26 May 1341 u.s.	John le Walker of Arlington, pst. iuratus	John Felice	D.	Oseney Abb.	A.G. or O.	403
HAMPTON BISHOP [HAMPTON LUCY] R.	18 June 1341 Hampton	M. Robert de Chigewell, clk., canon of London, by his pr. M. John Botoner	M. Walter de Morton	D.	Bp.	Warden of Stratford chantry	410

28

1 Instituted *ad ecclesiam et prioratum.*   2 *ipsumque per tradicionem anuli sui investivit.*   3 As n. 2 above.   4 *salvo iure archidiaconi Wyg' in hac parte.*

Benefice	Date and place of institution	Person instituted	Former incumbent	Cause of vacancy	Patron	Inductor	Edition nos.
WESTON MAUDUIT Chapel	21 June 1341 Blockley	Adam de Sodyngton,[1] pst.	Thomas de Dorsynton Parva	D.	William de Careswell, kt.	M. Henry de Neubold, r. of Weston-on-Avon	411
GLOUCESTER, St. Aldate R.	29 June 1341 u.s.	Henry de Wygemore	William Wyring	Exch. for Little Cowarne R. Heref. dioc.	Deerhurst Pr.	A.G. or O.	413
SUCKLEY R.	29 July 1341 Withington	John de Flete		Exch. for wardenship of *Sydingburne-brok* hosp., London dioc.[2]	King on acc. of temps. of Newent Pr. [alien]	O.A.W.	416
ODDINGLEY R.	13 Aug. 1341 Bredon	M. Alan de Suthlyngton, pst.	John de Caumpeden	D.	King	r. of St. Helen's, Worcester	426
WARWICK, St. Nicholas portion R.	24 Aug. 1341 Withington	Philip de Sapercote, pst.	Ralph	D.	Adam de Herwynton, preb. of St. Mary's, Warwick	O.A.W.	427
TANWORTH V.	25 Aug. 1341 u.s.	Robert de Folwode, pst. iuratus			Maxstoke Pr.	O.A.W.	428

TABLE I

369

	R./V.	Date			D.		
BARNSLEY	R.	2 Sept. 1341 u.s.	Geoffrey ate Cherche of Gt. Waltham, pst., by his pr. William de Preston, r. of Hethe, Linc. dioc.	Thomas le Heyer	D.	Humphrey de Bohun, e. of Hereford & Essex	D. of Bibury, warden of the exempt. jurisd.	431
WOLFORD	V.	4 Sept. 1341 u.s.	Robert Garoun of Ospringe, pst. *iuratus*	Peter	D.	Robert de Trenge, warden of the scholars of Merton, Oxford	O.A.W.	434
BREDON	R.	8 Sept. 1341 u.s.	M. John de la[3] Lowe, Prof. of Civil Law, pst.	M. John de Orlton	D.	Bp.	M. Henry de Neubold, r. of Weston	435
MINCHIN- HAMPTON, Chantry of St. Mary		5 Oct. 1341 Alvechurch	Thomas de Chalkford, pst., by his pr. Robert de Southam[4]			William de Prestebury, r. of Minchin- hampton	D. of Stonehouse	437
HOLT	V.	7 Oct. 1341 u.s.	Henry de Gretford, pst. *iuratus*	Henry de Birlyngham	D.	Thomas Powys, r. of Holt	O.A.W.	438

[1] Instituted as perpetual chaplain.
[2] St. John the Baptist [near Brentwood, Essex].
[3] *ipsumque investivit per anuli sui tradicionem.*
[4] *de residendo et cotidie celebrando cum onere personaliter ministrandi in ea iuratum.*

Benefice	Date and place of institution	Person instituted	Former incumbent	Cause of vacancy	Patron	Inductor	Edition nos.
PUCKLE-CHURCH R.	11 Oct. 1341 Alvechurch	Ralph de la Rode, by his pr. M. John de Midelton	M. Richard Praers	Exch. for Hodnet R., Cov. & Lich. dioc.	Bp. of Bath	O.A.G.	439
FROCESTER V.	12 Oct. 1341 u.s.	Henry de Wygemor, iuratus	William le Heyberar	Exch. [below]	St. Peter's Abb., Glouc.	O.A.G.	440
GLOUCESTER, St. Aldate R.	As above	William le Heyberar	Henry de Wygemor	Exch. [above]	Pr. of Deerhurst	O.A.G.	440
MARTLEY R.	12 Oct. 1341 Alvechurch	David Maynard	M. John de Northwode	Res.	King on acc. of temps. of Cormeil-les Abb. [alien]	O.A.W.	441
FECKENHAM V.	21 Oct. 1341 Hartlebury	John ate Greneburgh iuratus	Stephen de Grene,	Exch. [below]	King on acc. of temps. of Lyre Abb. [alien]	O.A.W.	442
STANTON R.	As above	Stephen de Greneburgh	John ate Grene	Exch. [above]	Winchcombe Abb.	O.A.G.	442
WARWICK, Colleg. Canon. church & preb. of St. Mary	14 Nov. 1341 Hartlebury	Henry de Stonelegh, by his pr. Edmund de Haselegh	Richard Grages of *Barwe.*	D.	Thomas de Beauchamp, e. of Warwick	D. of St. Mary Warwick for install.	443

TABLE I   371

Church		Date	Instituted	Predecessor	Cause	Patron		No.
HULLASEY Chapel	R.	2 Dec. 1341 u.s.	M. John de Lamel', acol. by his pr. M. Nicholas de Markeleye	Walter de Lamel'	Res.	Walter de Cirencester	O.A.G.	444
SALWARPE	R.	12 Dec. 1341 u.s.	Robert de Clypston, by his pr. Thomas de Laxton[1]	William de Tyreswell	D.	Thomas de Beauchamp, e. of Warwick	O.A.W.	445
HALFORD	R.	17 Dec. 1341 u.s.	John Bate of Cleeve (Clyve)				D. of Kineton	446
WORCESTER, St. Martin	R.	25 Dec. 1341 u.s.	Clement de Weston, clk., by his pr. M. Hugh de Penebrugg	Richard	D.	Worcester Cath. Pr.	O.A.W.	447
HARNHILL	R.	2 Feb. 1342 u.s.	Geoffrey de Weston, pst.	Alexander	D.	Henry de Harnhill, kt.	O.A.G.	452
NYMPSFIELD	R.	25 Feb. 1342 u.s.	Peter de Strode, chap.			Gloucester Abb.	O.A.G.	453
STRETTON-ON-FOSSE Chapel	R.	2 Mar. 1342 u.s.	Thomas de Barnak, chap.			Walter de Leycester, clk.	O.A.G.	454
WINSTONE	R.	18 Mar. 1342 u.s.	Thomas Stephans of Edgeworth			John de Alspathe, ld. of Winstone	O.A.G.	455

[1] Immediately afterwards, M. John de la Lowe, the Official of Worcester, on the bp.'s authority warned the rector in the person of his proctor to reside in his church the following Easter under penalty of the law. Present were M. Thomas Lench and John Hulle of [Droit]wich. R. Marny.

Benefice	Date and place of institution	Person instituted	Former incumbent	Cause of vacancy	Patron	Inductor	Edition nos.
DITCHFORD[1] FRARY　R.	20 Mar. 1342 Hartlebury	Nicholas Wandelard, chap.			John de Brayles of Ditchford	O.A.[W]	456
WARWICK, St. James　R.	20 Mar. 1342 u.s.	Walter de Ulnehale, chap.			Thomas de Beauchamp, e. of Warwick	O.A.W.	457
BATSFORD　R.	29 Mar. 1342 u.s.	Richard Weolegh of Broad Campden, chap.			Thomas Golafre, pst.	O. of the exempt jurisd. of Blockley[2]	458
FILTON　R.	6 Apr. 1342 u.s.	Elyas de Filton, chap.			Elys de Filton	O.A.G.	459
HAMPTON BISHOP　V.	16 Mar. 1342	Richard de Wykyngeston, subd., *iuratus*		D.	Robert de Chikwell, r. of Hampton	O.A.W.	460
GLOUCESTER, St. Owen　V.	13 Apr. 1342 u.s.	Simon Tankard *iuratus*	Richard de Hatherleye	Exch. [below]	Llanthony Pr. by Glouc.	O.A.G.	461
GLOUCESTER, St. Mary in the South　R.	As above	Richard de Hatherleye	Simon Tankard	Exch. [above]	Llanthony Pr. by Glouc.	O.A.G.	461
WORCESTER, St. Clement　R.	25 Apr. 1342 Hartlebury	Thomas, son of Robert Aleyn of [Droit]wich, clk.			Worcester Cath. Pr.	O.A.W.	462

TABLE I
373

Benefice	Date of institution	Person instituted	Vacated by	Cause	Patron		Page
HAMPTON BISHOP V.	8 May 1342	Richard Thoky, pst. *iuratus*	[v. 460]	D.	Robert de Chikwell, r. of Hampton	O.A.W.	463
WOOLSTONE R.	29 May 1342 Tetbury	Thomas Neuwynham	William de Newynham	Res.	King on acc. of temps. of Deerhurst Pr. [alien]	O.A.G.	464
HALFORD R.	28 Mar. 1342 Worcester	Robert Marny of Bishops Cleeve, deac., by his pr. M. John Botiner	John Bate	Res.	Bp.	O.A.W.	465
DUNTISBOURNE ABBOTS R.	3 Aug. 1342 Fladbury	William de Pillardynton, chap.	Thomas de Maydyn-nyston	Res.	St. Peter's Abb., Glouc.	O.A.G.	475
GLOUCESTER, St. Mary in the South R.	8 Sept. 1342 Hartlebury	Simon Tankart, pst.[3]			Llanthony Pr. by Glouc.	O.A.G.	477
HILL CROOME R.	12 Sept. 1342 u.s.	Henry in the Hale of Broadwas, pst.	Henry atte Nayssch	Exch. [below]	Joan, formerly wife of John de Willynton, kt.	O.A.W.	478
WESTON BIRT R.	As above	Henry atte Nayssch of Alcester, pst.	Henry in the Hale	Exch. [above]	Pershore Abb.	O.A.G.	479
GLOUCESTER, St. Owen v.	20 Sept. 1342 Gloucester	William Petyt of Gloucester, pst. *iuratus*	[v. 461]		Llanthony Pr. by Glouc.		481

1 The scribe incorrectly wrote *Wychford* through this entry.
2 *Dictus pater scripsit iurisdiccionis exemple sue de Blockelegh officiali pro ipsius induccione.*
3 He had exchanged this benefice for Gloucester, St. Owen, the previous April (461).

Benefice	Date and place of institution	Person instituted	Former incumbent	Cause of vacancy	Patron	Inductor	Edition nos.
PERSHORE, St. Andrew v.	21 Sept. 1342 Gloucester	Roger Baret, pst. *iuratus*			Pershore Abb.		482
ELMLEY CASTLE P.C. Chapel	20 Oct. 1342	M. William de Kenemerton[1]	William de Hampton	Exch. for Flamstead, Linc. dioc.			484
PRESTON v.	23 Oct. 1342	John de Harpele *iuratus*		Exch. for Chilcombe, Salisb. dioc.			486
ABBOTS MORTON R.	8 Nov. 1342 Upton Warren	Nicholas de Poywek[2]	M. John de Walcot	D.	Evesham Abb.	O.A.W.	487–8
ABBOTS LENCH Chapel [Fladbury parish] v.	27 Nov. 1342 Hartlebury	John Enche of Throckmorton, pst. *iuratus*	William Blenche, pst.	Res.	William de Everdone, r. of Fladbury, at nomination of John le Bruyn		489
YATE R.	25 Nov. 1342	Thomas de Weston in Gorrdene, chap.	Robert de Wylynton	D.	Ralph de Wylynton, kt.		490
EATINGTON v.	4 Feb. 1343 Hampton Bishop	Hugh de Knytcote, chap. *iuratus*			Kenilworth Pr.	O.A.W.	495
BADMINTON v.	21 Jan. 1343 Arrow	Walter le Cook, chap. *iuratus*			Lilleshall Abb.	O.A.[G.]	496

TABLE I

375

SEVERN STOKE R.	24 Mar. 1343 Alvechurch	Thomas de Custon, clk. of York dioc., by his pr. Nicholas de Poywek	Robert de Clifford, kt.	O.A.W.	497
WORCESTER, St. Michael R.	7 Mar. 1343 Withington	Henry de Pyrie, chap.	Richard Colis, sacrist of Worc. Cath. Pr.	O.A.W.	499
DIDMARTON R.	18 Feb. 1343	Peter de Besilles, clk.	John Turpyn	O.A.G.	500
BRISTOL, St. Stephen R.	3 Apr. 1343 Bredon	M. Hugh de Monyngton, clk.	Glastonbury Abb.	O.A.G.	501
CLIFTON by Bristol R.	28 Apr. 1343 Hartlebury	Matthew de Eorlestok, pst.	John de Senlo (*Sancto Laudo*)	O.A.G.	502
WHICHFORD R.	1 May 1343 u.s.	John Payn, pst.	John Mouhon, kt.	O.A.W.	503
WESTON SUB-EDGE R.	7 May 1343 u.s.	Henry de Ingelby, clk., by his pr. William Catgaut	King as cust. of lands & heir of John Gyffard, dcd.	O.A.G.	504
STRATTON by Cirencester v.	25 May 1343 u.s.	Stephen de Croppethorn pst. *iuratus*	John de Cirencester, r. of Stratton	O.A.G.	505

1 *et iuramentum corporale prestitit cum onere residendi si ad hoc teneatur per registrum domini episcopi.*
2 But Henry Coleman, of whose institution there is no trace, was (or claimed to be) rector, resigning 7 November 1342 because he had been newly instituted to Wolverley (488). There is likewise no record of this latter institution.

Benefice	Date and place of institution	Person instituted	Former incumbent	Cause of vacancy	Patron	Inductor	Edition nos.
NORTHFIELD with COFTON R. Chapel	24 June 1343 Henbury	John de Wyclifford-brugg, pst.	John [Ch]astelyn	Res.	Dudley Pr.	O.A.W.	509, 515
BARNSLEY R.	1 Aug. 1343 u.s.	M. Peter Malet, by his pr. Nicholas Hogges		Exch. for Spettisbury R., Salisb. dioc.	Humphrey de Bohun, e. of Essex		516
WITHINGTON R.	29 Aug. 1343 Hartlebury	M. William called 'Loveryng,' of Northleach, by his pr. John de Lech		Exch. for Woodchurch, Cant. dioc.	Bp.		517
WESTON SUB-EDGE R.	10 Oct. 1343 Withington	John de Codynton, pst. by his pr. John Porter of Codynton	Henry de Ingelby	Res.	King on acc. of minority of heir of John Giffard of Weston	O.A.G.	518
WARWICK, St. Nicholas, 3rd portion R.	19 Sept. 1343 Bishops Cleeve	William Iweyn, acol.., of Pershore	William de Wygorn	D.	John de Walcote	D. of Xtianity of Warwick	519
BRISTOL, St. Stephen R.	8. Nov. 1343 Hartlebury	Walter le Whyte of Bristol	Hugh de Monyngton	Res.[1]	Glastonbury Abb.	O.A.G.	520

TABLE I 377

				D.				
BRIMPSFIELD	V.	8 Nov.[2] 1343 u.s.	William de Hildesleye iuratus	D.	John de Prestbury	Roger de Haketo, Pr. of Brimpsfield	O.A.G. & Inqu.	524–5
BOXWELL	R.	26 Apr. 1343 Wiveliscombe[3]	M. Thomas de la Felde, pst.	Exch. for Oake R., Bath & Wells dioc.	M. Roger de Middeltone	St. Peter's Abb., Glouc.	Inqu. O.A.G.	562–3
CLENT with ROWLEY Chapel	R.	10 Sept. 1343 London[4]	M. John de Northwell, clk.	Exch. for Kingswinford R., Cov. & Lich. dioc.	Nicholas Jobinol		O.A.W.	568–9
RIPPLE	R.	15 Oct. 1343 Potterne[5]	John de Ryvers, preb. of Netherbury in Salisb. Cath.	Exch. for preb. of Netherbury in Salisb. Cath.	Robert de Burton	Bp.	O.A.G.	570
STONE	V.	25 Nov. 1343 Eaton[6]	John de Uppynton iuratus	Exch. for Kinlet V., Heref. dioc.	John de Portes		O.A.W. & Inqu.	575
ROCK [Chapel]	R.	9 Oct. 1345 Hartlebury	Richard de Wollashull, son of the patron			Robert Muchegros, ld. of Woollashill	O.A.W.	591

1 In accordance with *Si beneficia, Extra: De prebendis* (*Sext* 3, 4, c. 20).
2 As the enquiry into the vacancy was held on 27 November, this should probably be the 28th.
3 Bp. of Bath & Wells' certificate.
4 Bp. of Coventry & Lichfield's certificate.
5 Bp. of Salisbury's certificate.
6 Bp. of Hereford's certificate.

Benefice	Date and place of institution	Person instituted	Former incumbent	Cause of vacancy	Patron	Inductor	Edition nos.
BROOM R.	5 Nov. 1345 Hartlebury	Roger de Weston subtus Luʒerd, pst.			Brewood Pr.	O.A.W.	592
COMPTON WYNIATES R.	20 Dec. 1343 u.s.	M. Thomas de Clypston, clk.	John Suvasayle	D.	Thomas de Parva Compton in le Wyndʒate	O.A.W.	593
DUNTISBOURNE [ABBOTS] R.	22 Feb. 1344 u.s.	Walter de Retford	William de Pillardynton	Exch. for White Staunton R., Bath & Wells dioc.	St. Peter's Abb., Glouc.	O.A.G.	598, 606
PAINSWICK V.	5 Mar. 1344[1] u.s.	Adam de Halle, deac.			Llanthony Pr. by Glouc.	Institutors [v. note] Inqu. O.A.G.	601
BRIMPSFIELD V.	17 Feb. 1344 u.s.	William de Hildesleye iuratus	William de Hildesleye[2]	Res.	King on acc. of temps. of Brimpsfield Pr. [alien]	O.A.G.	604–5
WORCESTER, St. Alban R.	2 Mar. 1344 u.s.	William, son of William Hodynton of Worcester, clk.	Hugh de Straddel, alias 'of Gloucester'	Res.[3]	Evesham Abb.	O.A.W.	607

TABLE I

379

	R.				D.			
HINDLIP	R.	24 Mar. 1344 u.s.	William de Rothewelle, pst., by his pr. John de Chalveston, clk.	Richard	D.	Thomas de Beauchamp, e. of Warwick	O.A.W.	609
STRETTON-ON-FOSSE Chapel	R.	22 Dec. 1343 u.s.	William de Askeby		Exch. for Sutton V., Linc. dioc.	Roger Hillary, kt.	D. of pecul. jurisd. of Blockley	610
STOKE GIFFORD	R.	12 Feb. 1344 u.s.	Robert de Vyfhyde, chap.			Bp.		612
BISLEY, 2nd portion	R.	25 Mar. 1344 u.s.	John Boyloun, clk.		(4)	Humphrey de Bohun, e. of Hereford	O.A.G.	618
CLENT with ROWLEY Chapel	R.	22 Mar. 1344 Burton by Beverley[5]	William de Northwell, by his pr. William de Rutton, clk. of York dioc.	John de Northwell, canon of Southwell	Exch.[6] for Owston R., York dioc.	Halesowen Abb.	O.A.W. [31 Mar.] & Inqu. C.O.A.W.	619–20
WARWICK, Colleg. church of St. Mary Compton Mordack preb.		10 Apr. 1344 Hartlebury	John de Bukyngham, acol.	Adam de Herwynton	D. on 31 Mar.	Thomas de Beauchamp, e. of Warwick	O.A.W.	621

1 Commission for the prior of St. Bartholomew's, Glouc., the dean of that place, the abbot of St. Peter's, Glouc., and the prior of St. Oswald's there, to admit, institute and induct the presentee should the O.A.G.'s enquiry find for him. ² See 524–5, 594, 605. This could be a re-presentation.
3 . . . prout per quoddam instrumentum publicum cuiusdam Johannis de Wallens' Lincolniensis diocesis publici auctoritate apostolica notarii signo et subscripcione suis signatum apparebat.
4 The vacancy began 28 February. 5 Abp. of York's certificate, received at Hartlebury 31 March.
6 Of Clent with Rowley and Northwell prebend in Southwell.

Benefice		Date and place of institution	Person instituted	Former incumbent	Cause of vacancy	Patron	Inductor	Edition nos.
IPSLEY	R.	14 Apr. 1344 Hartlebury	John, son of Nicholas Geraud of Stratford, clk.	Roger de Haukesbury	D. on 25 Dec.	John Huband, kt.	O.A.W.	622
SHELL Chapel by Hanbury	R.	8 May 1344 u.s.	Richard Bertram	John Bernard	D.	Roger de Butterleye, ld. of Shell	M. William de Herwynton, r. of Hanbury	625
ASTON SOMERVILLE	R.	5 May 1344 u.s.	John de Aston, clk.	Alan Jankens or Janekynes	Res.	Geoffrey de Aston Somervill	O.A.G. & Inqu.	Cf. 623–4, 627
ACTON TURVILLE	V.	2 July 1344 Alvechurch	William ate Scherde, pst. iuratus			William Edward, warden of chantry of Tormarton church	O.A.G.	632
WHICHFORD	R.	9 June 1344 Blockley	Baldwin de Mohun, pst.	John Payn of Miltecombe	Res.	John de Mohun, kt.	O.A.W.	633
LEIGH, Cherkenhill portion	R.	2 June 1344 u.s.	William de Limbergh, pst.	Thomas de Abetot	Exch. [below]	Pershore Abb.	O.A.W.	634
ODDINGTON	R.	6 June 1344 Blockley	Thomas de Abetot	William de Limbergh	Exch. [above]	M. Robert de Nassington, precentor of St. Peter's Cath., York	O.A.G.	635

TABLE I 381

					D.		O.A.G.	
LITTLETON	R.	14 July 1344 Alvechurch	John de Batesford, clk.	Nicholas de Bondeston		Malmesbury Abb.	O.A.G.	636
SHELL Chapel by Hanbury	R.	16 July 1344 u.s.	John called 'le Meyr' of [Droit]wich as 'perpetual administrator'	Richard Bartelam	Res. [12 July]	Roger de Butterleye	M. William de Herwynton, r. of Hanbury	637–8
SHELL Chapel	R.	22 July 1344 u.s.	William called 'le Chyld' as perp. administrator, by his pr. Robert Payn	John le Meyr	Exch. [below]	Roger de Butterleye	u.s.[1]	639–41
WITTON [by Droitwich], St. Peter	v.	As above	John le Meyr pst., *iuratus*	William 'le Chyld'	Exch. [above]	Studley Pr.	O.A.W.[2]	639–41 *et seq.*
EASTLEACH ST. MARTIN (*alias* 'Burithorp')	R.	3 Aug. 1344 Hartlebury	M. Robert Marny of Bishops Cleeve	Edmund de Snypston	Exch. [below]	Great Malvern Pr.		646
HALFORD	R.	As above	Edmund de Snypston	M. Robert Marny	Exch. [above]	Bp.		646
WORCESTER, St. Clement	R.	12 Aug. 1344 Hartlebury	John de Curdewalle	Thomas Aleyn	Exch. for Mamble V., Heref. dioc.	Worcester Cath. Pr.	O.A.W. Inqu. O.A. Shropshire	647–9, 654–656

[1] *per modum et formam quarundam inquisicionum ex utraque parte captarum et in hac parte factarum.*

[2] See note 1 above.

Benefice	Date and place of institution	Person instituted	Former incumbent	Cause of vacancy	Patron	Inductor	Edition nos.
PEDMORE R.	30 July 1344 Alvechurch	Walter, son of Thomas de Clodeshale, clk.	William de Brangtr'	D.	Walter de Clodeshale & his son Richard	O.A.W.	650
SIDDINGTON by Cirencester R.	24 Aug.[1] 1344 Withington	Ralph de Brantyngham, clk.			King on acc. of temps. of Monmouth Pr. [alien]	O.A.G. & Inqu.	652
SHELL Chapel R.	31 July 1344 Hartlebury	Richard Bartlem, son of Richard Bartlem of Shell, as perp. warden	William le Schyld	Res. [30 July]		M. William de Herwynton	642–3, 653
WHICHFORD R.	10 Sept. 1344 Withington	John de Harewell, clk.	Baldwin de Mohun	Ass. Fording-bridge R., Winch. dioc.[2]	John de Mohun, kt.	O.A.W.	657
HASELOR R.	19 Apr. 1345 Tewkesbury	William de Southam, pst.			William de Meldon, ld. of Haselor	O.A.W.	663
STAUNTON by Corse R.	7 Sept. 1345 Blockley	John de Underhulle, pst.			John de Seymour (Sancto Mauro) & Thomas de Underhull, lds. of Staunton	O.A.W.	664

TABLE I   383

KINGTON 29	R.	14 July 1345 Henbury	Richard de Dovyrdale, pst.[3]		Hugh de Cokeseye	O.A.W.	665
BINTON	R.	17 Dec. 1345 Hartlebury	Bartholomew de Wynecote, pst.		William de Wynecote, ld. of Binton	O.A.W.	666
LITTLETON	R.	15 Oct. 1344 Bredon	Robert Maunser, pst.		Malmesbury Abb.	O.A.G.	671
RIPPLE Chantry		10 Sept. 1344 Withington	Nicholas Rondulf, pst.		John Salemon	D. of exempt jurisd. of Ripple	672
MISERDEN	R.	6 Nov. 1344 Buckden[4]	John de Bymbrok	Exch. for Shoby, Linc. dioc.	King on acc. of heir of Edmund, e. of Kent	O.A.G. (10 Nov.) & Inqu.	674–5
ODDINGLEY	R.	1 Nov. 1344 Hartlebury	Geoffrey de Cattone, first tons.		King	r. of St. Helen's, Worcester	678
BROADWAS Chantry in St. Mary's Chapel		12 Dec. 1344 u.s.	Richard Letyce of Campden, chap.	Thomas de Colne Rogeri, pst.[5] Res.	M. John de Bradewas, [founder]	O.A.W.	682

[1] Commission for the O.A.G. to enquire into the vacancy with power to institute and induct the presentee.

[2] *Et nichilominus quidam M. Radulphus de Brayles clericus, procurator dicti Baldewini ad resignandum omne ius que habuit in dicta ecclesia de Wycheford, renunciavit et resignavit.*

[3] *Iuravitque idem dominus Ricardus tactis sacrosanctis evangeliis quod salvabit dominum episcopum indempnem si contingat ipsum dominum episcopum inbrigari occasione ipsius ecclesie.*

[4] Bp. of Lincoln's certificate.

[5] Thomas of Coln Rogers and Walter of Broadwas were the first chaplains of the chantry (684).

384 TABLE I

Benefice	Date and place of institution	Person instituted	Former incumbent	Cause of vacancy	Patron	Inductor	Edition nos.
BROADWAS Chantry [The other chaplaincy]	21 Dec. 1344 Hartlebury	Walter le Taverner of Broadwas, pst.	Walter [de Bradewas]	Res.	M. John de Bradewas	O.A.W.	683
ASTON CANTLOW v.	21 Dec. 1344 Auckland[1]	Thomas de Normanton	Antony Fossour	Exch. for Bedlington V., Durham dioc.		O.A.W.	685
HINDLIP R.	3 Dec. 1344 Hartlebury	Simon de Calveston, pst. by his pr. John de Calveston, clk.				O.A.W.	687
BREADSTONE, St. P.C. Michael's Chapel	30 Sept. 1344 u.s.	Henry de Twyford, chap.			Thomas de Bradeston, kt.	O.A.G.	688
WARWICK, Preb. Colleg. church of St. Mary	24 Dec. 1344 u.s.	William Derby, pst.	Richard de Pacwode	D.	Thomas de Beauchamp, e. of Warwick	O.A.W.	689
SUCKLEY R.	22 Dec. 1344 u.s.	M. Peter Gros of Worcester, clk.	Byndo de Bandinellis	Res.	King on acc. of Newent Pr. [alien]	O.A.W.	690

TABLE I

385

				D.			
HONINGTON R.	12 Jan. 1345 u.s.	M. Luke de Herdeburgh, acol.	Edmund Bornham		William, Pr. of St. Mary's, Coventry	O.A.W. Inqu.[2]	691
BREDICOT R.	28 Feb. 1345 u.s.	Matthew de Bromleye, pst.				O.A.W.	702
CHARFIELD R.	2 Mar. 1345 u.s.	Robert Boune, pst., of Hanslope				O.A.G.	703
CLENT with ROWLEY Chapel V.	1 Apr. 1345 u.s.	John Andreu, pst. *iuratus*			Halesowen Abb.	O.A.W.	716
BECKFORD V.	8 Apr. 1345 u.s.	Geoffrey Pynel of Weston, deac. *iuratus*			King on acc. of Beckford Pr. [alien]	O.A.G.	717
INKBERROW (Attached Preb. to Hereford Cath. canonry)	30 Mar. 1345 u.s.	M. John de Lech, by his pr. M. William de Lech	John de la Chambre, of Hereford	Exch. for Maple-durham with Petersfield chapel, Winch. dioc.	Bp. of Hereford	O.A.W.	719–20
SOUTH LUFFENHAM R. Linc. dioc.[3]	26 Apr. 1345 u.s.	John de Blockeleygh, by his pr. William de Sotton			Thomas de Beauchamp, e. of Warwick	Inqu.	721

[1] Bp. of Durham's certificate.
[2] Probably by O.A.W. MS.: *prout cavit inquisicio in hac parte capta.*
[3] On the authority of the bp. of Lincoln's mandate dated 23 April from Buckden.

Benefice	Date and place of institution	Person instituted	Former incumbent	Cause of vacancy	Patron	Inductor	Edition nos.
ODDINGLEY R.	30 Apr. 1345 Hartlebury	John de Irford, clk., by pr.				r. of St. Helen's, Worcester	722
SPETCHLEY R.	20 Apr. 1345 u.s.	William atte Halle, pst.			William de Everley	O.A.W.	723
BARCHESTON R.	8 May 1345 u.s.	Roger Chastelion, clk.	Gilbert	Ass. Woodborough R., Salisb. dioc.	Alexander de Bercheston	O.A.W.	724
ASTON CANTLOW R.	14 Sept. 1345 Withington	Adam de Overton, pst., by his pr. M. Luke de Herdeburgh	William Savage, clk.	Res.		O.A.W.	742, 743
WARWICK, St. Peter R.	1 Aug. 1345 St. Aug.'s Abb., Bristol	M. Thomas called 'Bolewynch' of [Droit]wich,			Bp. *iure devoluto*	O.A.W. Rob. de Staverton, port. of St. Nicholas, Warwick, John de Tyso, par. pst. of Billesley	744–5

TABLE I   387

SIDDINGTON R.	11 Feb. 1348 Hartlebury	Richard Northcrek, in minor orders, by his pr. William, r. of Charborough			King on acc. of Monmouth Pr. [alien]		752
WORCESTER, St. Swithin R.	24 Jan. 1346 *Liddington*[1]	William de Preston	Philip de Gosynton	Exch. for Hethe R., Linc. dioc.			754–5
BROCKWORTH v.	18 Mar. 1347 Hartlebury	M. William de Besford, by pr., *iuratus*		Exch. [below]		O.A.G.	756
[FLYFORD] FLAVELL R.	(2)		M. William de Besford	Exch. [above]			756
DEERHURST R.	17 Feb. 1346 Cropthorne	Br. John Godelli, monk of St. Denis	Br. Thomas Garculi	Res.	Giles, abb. of St. Denis	O.A.G.	759–62
NORTHFIELD with COFTON R. Chapel	3 Jan. 1346 Hartlebury	Roger de Bereford, pst.	John de Wytlesford-brugg		Thomas, Pr. of Dudley	O.A.W.	763–4
WARWICK, St. Nicholas R. 3rd portion	12 Jan. 1346 u.s.	Adam Carles, first tons.			John de Bokyngham	O.A.W.	765
SPERNALL R.	23 Dec. 1345 u.s.	Nicholas atte Sale, pst.	John de Walton	Exch. [below]		O.A.W.	766

1 Bp. of Lincoln's commission empowering the diocesan to carry out the exchange. There is no specific record of institution but Philip de Gosynton resigned on 29 January (755).
2 Institution not specifically recorded.

Benefice	Date and place of institution	Person instituted	Former incumbent	Cause of vacancy	Patron	Inductor	Edition nos.
STUDLEY V.	23 Dec. 1345 Hartlebury	John de Walton *iuratus*	Nicholas atte Sale	Exch. [above]		O.[A.W.]	767
CHURCH LENCH R.	5 Mar. 1346 u.s.	John called 'le Bor'	Robert atte More	Exch. [below]		O.A.W.	768
DODDERHILL V.	As above	Robert atte More *iuratus*	John called 'le Bor'	Exch. [above]		O.[A.W.]	769
SIDDINGTON R.	7 Apr. 1346 Hartlebury	John Edwart	Ralph de Brantyngham	Res. (2 Apr.) Ass. Kirkby Thore, Carlisle dioc.	King	O.A.G.	770-1
PERSHORE, St. Edburgh's Abb.	12 Apr. 1346 u.s.	John de la Feld, pst.	Newly founded		Exors. of Adam de Herwynton	D. of Pershore	775-6
Harvington Chantry in Nave		John de Dyclesdon, pst.	Newly founded				
PEOPLETON R.	20 June 1346 Bredon	Edmund Russhel, acol.			John Russhel, ld. of Peopleton	O.A.W.	777
BRISTOL, St. Philip & St. Jacob R.	22 May 1346 Hartlebury	Richard le[1] Smale, clk.			John le Smale, his brother	O.A.G.	795

TABLE I   389

WAPLEY	V.	22 July 1346 Henbury	John Permayn, pst. *iuratus*		St. Aug.'s Abb., Bristol	O.A.G.	797
ELMLEY CASTLE Chapel	P.C.	23 July 1345 u.s.	Thomas, son of John le Erl of Kemerton, first tons.[2]	M. William de Kenemerton Res.	Thomas de Beauchamp, e. of Warwick	O.A.W.	805
STONE Chapel	V.	29 Sept. 1345 Blockley	Richard Ussel, pst. *iuratus*		Richard de Bromhull, r. of Chaddesley	O.A.W.	806
DROITWICH, St. Andrew	R.	16 Nov. 1346 Hartlebury	Walter de la Brok	William le Beste Exch. for Marden, Heref. dioc.		O.A.W. & Inqu.	810–12
SHIPTON OLIFFE	R.	28 June 1346 Bredon	Thomas Frankeleyn of Driffield		Ralph de Doudyswell	O.A.G.	813
KEMPSEY	V.	19 Jan. 1347 Hartlebury	William Rok, pst. *iuratus*			O.A.W.	814
DIDMARTON	R.	18 Jan. 1347 u.s.	Thomas Percehay, in minor orders		John Turpyn	O.A.G.	815
YARDLEY	R.	28 Feb. 1347 u.s.	Adam de Overton, pst.		Maxstoke Pr.	O.A.W.	816

[1] iuravit se soluturum expensas faciendas nomine dicti venerabilis patris et pro eodem patre si contingat in futurum eundem patrem occasione illius ecclesie inbrigari. Testibus magistro Henrico de Neubold et Radulpho clerico suo.
[2] Instituted as 'rector' of the chapel and chantry.

Benefice	Date and place of institution	Person instituted	Former incumbent	Cause of vacancy	Patron	Inductor	Edition nos.
HAMPTON R.	23 Sept. 1346 Blockley	Simon de Geynesburgh, by his pr. William Curteys	Nicholas Janyny	Exch. for Sparham R., Norwich dioc.			819, 824–5
KNIGHTWICK R.	26 Jan.[1] 1347 Hartlebury	M. Philip Drym, pst., by his pr. Adam called 'Botyler'	M. Philip de Ullyngwyk	Exch. for Ullingswick R., Heref. dioc.	Worcester Cath. Pr.	O.A.W.	826–7
KEMERTON R.	21 Jan. 1347 Wick by Worcester	William de Coleford, clk.			Thomas Beauchamp, e. of Warwick	O.A.G.	829
ROWINGTON, St. Laurence v.	15 Oct. 1347 Alvechurch	John Draper called 'Thacham' pst. iuratus	Gilbert de Aston	Res.	Reading Abb.	O.A.W.	839–40
WINSTONE R.	14 Mar. 1348 Towcester[2]	John de Rideswell	Thomas de Eggesworth	Exch. for Broadwell R., Linc. dioc.	John de Allespath	O.A.G. (25 Mar.) & Inqu.	842–3

TABLE I 391

EDGEWORTH R.	21 Feb.[3] 1348	John Duffeld, pst., by his pr. John de Drayton		Bp. *iure devoluto*	O.A.G.	844
DAGLING-WORTH R.	28 Nov.[4] 1347 Hartlebury	Robert de Upthon	Exch. for Oving R., Linc. dioc.		O.A.G.	845–7
SHENINGTON R.	18 Dec. 1347	John Gerad or Jerad	Exch. for Sherston R. Salisb. dioc.	John Borgh	O.A.G.	850–1
COMPTON GREENFIELD Chapel	29 Oct. 1347 Hartlebury	Robert Astmede, clk.		Maurice de Berkeley	O.A.G.	852
YARDLEY V.	2[9?] Nov. 1347 u.s.	John Somery, pst. *iuratus*		Maxstoke Pr.	O.A.W.	853
DYRHAM R.	27 Nov. 1347 Wick	Robert Hardewyk, chap.		Roger Cantok	O.A.G.	854
STAUNTON by Corse R.	12 Jan. 1348 Hartlebury	John Pyrie, pst.		Robert de Staunton, ld. of Staunton	O.A.W.	856

[1] But the bp. of Hereford certified (25 January) that he had instituted Drym in accordance with the diocesan's commission for effecting an exchange.

[2] Bp. of Lincoln's certificate.

[3] Collated 6 February, instituted 21st.

[4] A later entry (855) gives 29 November as the date of instiution to both Oving and Daglingworth.

Benefice	Date and Place of institution	Person instituted	Former incumbent	Cause of vacancy	Patron	Inductor	Edition nos.
MEYSEY HAMPTON R.	19 Jan. 1348 Hartlebury	Robert de Pubbesbury, clk.			Lord Thomas Seymour, kt.	O.A.G.	857
PRESTON V.	4 Jan. 1348 Ramsbury[1]	Robert Douwale, by his pr. iuratus	John Harpele	Exch. for Winkfield V., Salisb. dioc.		O.A.G. (15 Jan.)	858, 865, 869–70
KIDDER-MINSTER, Chantry of St. Mary in a chapel in the churchyard	4 Mar. 1348 Hartlebury	William Baroun, pst.[2]					863
COMPTON WYNIATES R.	19 Feb. 1348 u.s.	Robert le Ferour, by his pr. William Rothewell	M. Thomas de Clypston	Exch. for Great Ponton, Linc. dioc.	Thomas de Compton in le Wynʒate	O.A.W.	866–868, 876
TORTWORTH R.	12 Apr. 1348 u.s.	John de Stokes	M. Peter FilzWaryn	Exch. for Lytchett Matravers R., Salisb. dioc.		O.A.G.	871, 872–874
MORETON & WHADDON Preb. (attached to Hereford Cath. canonry)	28 Aug. 1348[3] Henbury	M. William de Herwynton, pst.	M. Richard de Chaddesley	D.	Bp. of Hereford	O.A.G. & D. of Glouc.	875

TABLE I   393

Benefice		Date	Incumbent	Patron		No.
PINNOCK	R.	3 June 1348 Hartlebury	Henry de Overe Etyndon	William de Clynton, e. of Huntingdon	O.A.G.	877
POWICK	V.	17 Jan. 1349 u.s.	John de Longeneye, pst. *iuratus*	Great Malvern Pr.	O.A.W.	878
YATE	R.	16 Nov. 1348 u.s.	Robert Ewyas, pst.	Henry de Wylynton, kt. Notley Abb.	O.A.G.	880
LOWER SWELL	V.	10 Jan. 1349 u.s.	John de Wytchirche		O.A.G.	881
PRESTON	V.	23 Jan. 1349 u.s.	Robert Stevenus of *Eschakeburne*, pst. *iuratus*	Cirencester Abb.	O.A.G.	882
STRATTON	[R.]	16 Dec. 1348[4] u.s.	William atte Broke	John Cirencester, ld. of Stratton	O.A.G.	883
STRATTON	V.	23 Jan. 1349 u.s.	Simon de Southcerneye *iuratus*	John de Cirencester, r. of Stratton	O.A.G.	884
HORTON (attached to Salisbury Cath. canonry)	Preb.	12 July 1347[5] u.s.	William de Farlegh, clk., by his pr. Richard de Hyde	King on acc. of vac. of Salisbury bpric.	O.A.G.	886–8

[1] Bp. of Salisbury's certificate.
[2] *cum onere continue celebrandi missam de Beata Virgine in eadem ... Iuravitque idem Willelmus quod debito modo obediret vicario de Kydermunstr' qui pro tempore fuerit et quod occasione illius cantarie huiusmodi vicario non dampnificaret.*
[3] Date of mandate for induction in response to the bp. of Hereford's commission.
[4] If the dates are correct William atte Broke should be the patron in 884. Cf. 505, 1541.
[5] Mandate for induction in response to the commission of the vicars-general of the bp. of Salisbury.

TABLE I

Benefice	Date and place of institution	Person instituted	Former incumbent	Cause of vacancy	Patron	Inductor	Edition nos.
COMBE R. BASKERVILLE	10 July 1347 *Wellington*[1]	M. John Stilligo	William de Clyfford	Exch. for Sparkford R., Bath & Wells dioc.		O.A.G. (15 July) & Inqu.	889–90
BARNSLEY R.	9 Sept. 1347 *Tintern*[2]	Nicholas Hogges[3]	Peter Malet	Exch. for Marchergeryn R., Llandaff dioc.	Humphrey de Bohun, e. of Hereford & Essex		895–6
COBERLEY, St. Giles. Chantry of St. Mary	24 Sept. 1347 Withington	Henry Averay, pst.[4]	Newly founded		Lord Thomas de Coberleye		898
GLOUCESTER ARCHDEACONRY	7 Apr. 1348 Hartlebury Castle	Richard de Ledebury, by his pr. Thomas de Ledebury	Roger de Breynton[5]	Exch. for Doddington, Ely dioc.	Bp.	Prior & sacrist of Worc. Cath.	901–2, 904
LEIGH v. Chapel in Deerhurst parish	6 July 1347 Hartlebury	William Heron, pst.			King on acc. of temps. of Deerhurst Pr. [alien], at nom. of Matilda, lady of Leigh		914

TABLE I

395

SWINDON	R.	14 Oct. 1348 u.s.	Thomas LeWyn, pst.	Robert Moryn, ld. of Swindon	O.A.G.	915
MINCHIN-HAMPTON, Chantry of St. Mary		19 Oct. 1348 u.s.	Peter de Avenynge, pst.	Bp. for this turn	O.A.G.	916
BISLEY	v.	21 Jan. 1349 u.s.	Roger Solstan of Stanford on Teme, *iuratus*	Richard Clavyle, r. of 1st port. of Bisley	O.A.G.	917
ALMONDSBURY	v.	20 Jan. 1349 u.s.	Thomas de Syde, *iuratus*	St. Aug.'s Abb., Bristol	O.A.G.	918
BRISTOL, St. Stephen	R.	13 Dec. 1348 u.s.	M. Thomas le Yonge by his pr. M. Walter de Hull	Glastonbury Abb.	O.A.G.	919
FRAMPTON COTTERELL	R.	13 Dec. 1348 u.s.	Thomas Braȝ, pst.	Henry de Wylynton, kt.	O.A.G.	920
CLIFTON	R.	13 Dec. 1348 u.s.	John Blank, pst.	John de Senlo (*Sancto Laudo*), kt.	O.A.G.	921
TORMARTON, Chantry of St. Mary		13 Dec. 1348 u.s.	William de la Scherde, pst., as warden[6]		O.A.G.	922

[1] Bp. of Bath & Wells' certificate. [2] Bp. of Llandaff's certificate.

[3] *prestitit canonicam obedienciam prout moris est et iuramentum corporale de salvando dominum indempnem pro exitibus de xv solidis currentibus versus Petrum Malet.*

[4] *iuratum quod ordinaciones dicti domini Thome super statu cantarie predicte quatenus te concernunt fideliter observabis et facies quatenus in te est ab aliis observari, quodque continue residebis ibidem in loco et manso pro te et aliis capellanis ac tuis et eorum successoribus pro dicta cantaria ordinatis et per dictum dominum Thomam edificatis. . . .*

[5] Cf. 19. [6] *cum onere personaliter ministrandi in ea iuratum ad observandum omnia onera eidem cantarie incumbencia iuxta ordinacionem dicte cantarie.*

Benefice	Date and place of institution	Person instituted	Former incumbent	Cause of vacancy	Patron	Inductor	Edition nos.
GLOUCESTER, Holy Trinity R.	2 Dec. 1348 Wick	Richard atte More, clk.			King	O.A.G.	923
DOYNTON Chapel	19 Dec. 1348 Hartlebury	John le Veye, clk.			John Tracy, kt., ld. of Doynton	O.A.G.	924
RIPPLE Chantry. alia pars	4 Jan. 1349 u.s.	Henry called 'le Muleward', chap.	Henry Thomas, chap.		John Hardes or Hardres, chap. of the chantry	John de Ryvers, r. of Ripple	925, 971 Cf. 972
STAVERTON V.	4 June 1348 Bredon	William de Baggesouere, iuratus	William Heritage	Exch. for Clifford V., Heref. dioc.		O.A.G.	947–949
BRISTOL, Chantry in St. Augustine's Abb.	14 Nov. 1348 Hartlebury	William de Tormarton, chap.[1]				D. of Bristol & —, the bp.'s penitentiary	951
DROITWICH, St. Andrew R.	30 July 1348 Withington	John de Rondeleshām	Walter de la Broke	Exch. for Tarrington V., Heref. dioc.		O.A.W.	953–5
CHERRINGTON R.	25 Oct. 1348 Hartlebury	M. John, son of Nicholas Gerond of Stratford	Leonard Lucy	Exch. [below]	William de Lucy, kt.	O.A.W.	955
IPSLEY R.	30 Oct. 1348 u.s.	Leonard Lucy	M. John	Exch. [above]		O.A.W.	956

TABLE I 397

Benefice	Date	Incumbent	Predecessor	Cause	Patron		No.
DOWDESWELL R.	19 Dec. 1348 u.s.	Richard Erchebaud,² pst.			John de Dowdeswell		957
RIPPLE, Salemon Chantry	4 Nov. 1348 u.s.	John de Hard(r)es, chap.	Walter Hatherich, chap.	D.	Bp. for this turn		958, 970
TORTWORTH R.	22 Dec. 1348 u.s.	Osbert Lyrlyng, pst.			Peter de Veel, kt.	O.A.G.	959
BRISTOL, St. Peter R.	23 Dec. 1348 u.s.	John de Wolfrynton, pst.			Tewkesbury Abb.	O.A.G.	960
WINTERBOURNE R.	21 Dec. 1348 u.s.	Robert Murdak, clk.			Thomas de Bradeston	O.A.G.	961
ODDINGLEY R.	7 Dec. 1348 u.s.	John Malteyn, pst.			John de Beauchamp	r. of St. Helen's, Worcester	962
BRISTOL, St. Augustine v. the Less	7 Nov. 1348 u.s.	John Besford, pst. iuratus			St. Aug.'s³ Abb., Bristol	O.A.G.	963
IRON ACTON R.	20 Nov. 1348 u.s.	Reginald Mareschal, pst.			John de Acton, kt.	O.A.G.	964
ALDERLEY Chapel (Arle)	20 Jan. 1349 u.s.	Nicholas Perkyn, pst.			John Chausy, ld. of Alderley	O.A.G.	965

¹ prestititque iuramentum corporale de continuo residendo in eadem et eidem cantarie iuxta formam et eius artacionem deserviendum, prout ordinacio sua inde confecta exigit et requirit.

² Iuravitque tactis sacrosanctis evangeliis coram magistro Johanne de Severle cancellario domini se soluturum unam pensionem annuam quadraginta solidorum sterlingorum nomine ecclesie sue predicte rectori ecclesie de Wythindon qui pro tempore fuerit sibi et ecclesie sue de iure debitam sicut in inquisicione in hoc casu capta expresse cavetur quod in tanto ecclesie parochiali de Wythyndon ecclesia de Doudeswell pensionaria reperitur.

³ Also termed minoris in the MS.

TABLE I

Benefice	Date and place of institution	Person instituted	Former incumbent	Cause of vacancy	Patron	Inductor	Edition nos.
WAPLEY V.	20 Jan. 1349 Hartlebury	Thomas Fox, pst.			St. Aug.'s Abb., Bristol	O.A.G.	966
BRISTOL, St. Nicholas V.	20 Jan. 1349 u.s.	John de Betton, pst. *iuratus*			St. Aug.'s Abb., Bristol	O.A.G.	967
BRISTOL, St. Mary *in Foro* [le-Port] R.	20 Jan. 1349 u.s.	William called 'Taverner', pst.			Keynsham Abb.	O.A.G.	968
RIPPLE Chantry	4 Jan. 1349 u.s.	Henry called 'le Muleward'	Henry Thomas		John de Hardres Bp. for this turn		971
	20 Feb. 1349 u.s.	William Phelipps, pst.	John Hardes or Hardres				972
MARTIN [HUSSINGTREE] R.	17 Dec. 1348 *Whitbourne*[1]	Robert Morys of Worcester	Robert Payne	Exch. for Lindridge V., Heref. dioc.	Walter de Pyrie	Inqu. O.A.W.	973
SISTON, St. Mary R.	3 Mar. 1349 Hartlebury	John de Ingleby, pst.			Peter Corbet, kt, ld. of Siston	O.A.G.	974
BRISTOL, St. Philip & St. Jacob R.	31 Jan. 1349	John de Wydecombe, pst.			Tewkesbury Abb.	O.A.G.	975
DUNTISBOURNE V.	20 Feb. 1349 Hartlebury	Roger Whipp, pst. *iuratus*			Dore Abb.	O.A.G.	976
CROMHALL R.	19 Feb. 1349 u.s.	John Brasyer de Trelyngg, pst.			Thomas de Wanton, son of William de Wanton	O.A.G.	977

TABLE I   399

Benefice	Date	Person	Patron		No.
RENDCOMBE, R.	20 Feb. 1349 u.s.	Walter Frylond, by his pr.	Ralph, Baron Stafford	O.A.G.	978
NEWPORT Chapel P.C.	18 Feb. 1349 u.s.	John Runston		(2)	979
RODMARTON R.	20 Feb. 1349 u.s.	Thomas Passelowe, clk.	Roger Burdon of Rodmarton	O.A.G.	980
CROOME, EARLS (SIMOND) R.	21 Feb. 1349 u.s.	Gregory de Lynton, pst.[3]	Thomas de Beauchamp, e. of Warwick	O.A.W.	982
BRISTOL, St. Ewen R.	30 Jan. 1349 u.s.	John de Byssheleye, pst.	Thomas, abbot of Tewkesbury	O.A.G.	983
TOCKINGTON, Chapel of St. Nicholas	18 Feb. 1349 u.s.	Simon de Hylegh, pst.	William de Gylden, ld. of Olveston	O.A.G.	984
ASTON SOMERVILLE R.	13 Feb. 1349 u.s.	Alan Jankyns, pst.	John Somervyle	O.A.G.	985
ASTON SOMERVILLE R.	5 Mar. 1349 u.s.	William de Aston, clk.	John Somervyle	O.A.G.	986
BRISTOL, St. Nicholas v.	12 Mar. 1349 u.s.	William de Tormerton, pst. iuratus	St. Aug.'s Abb., Bristol	O.A.G.	987
BOXWELL R.	20 Feb. 1349 u.s.	Roger de Herton, clk.	St. Peter's Abb., Glouc.	O.A.G.	988

30

[1] Bp. of Hereford's certificate.   [2] *sine inquisicione aliqua ex gracia domini.*   [3] Under oath to pay the portion of 20s. due to the rector of Ripple.

Benefice	Date and place of institution	Person instituted	Former incumbent	Cause of vacancy	Patron	Inductor	Edition nos.
TORMARTON, Chantry of St. Mary	5 Mar. 1349 Hartlebury	John le Botyler, pst., bro. of Thomas le Botyler of Upton, kt.[1]			John de la Ryvere, kt.	O.A.G.	989
BADMINTON v.	5 Mar. 1349 u.s.	Adam Fetherston, pst. *iuratus*			Henry, abbot of Lilleshall	O.A.G.	990
RIPPLE Chantry	13 Mar. 1349 u.s.	Walter de Leobury, pst.	William Phelip, chap.		Henry Masoun, chap.	r. of Ripple	991
WARWICK, Colleg. Preb. church of St. Mary	4 Feb. 1349 u.s.	Thomas Basset, pst.	M. John de Bulkynton		Thomas de Beauchamp, e. of Warwick	Thomas Rower	992
BRISTOL, St. Laurence R.	16 Mar. 1349 u.s.	Thomas de Quenyngton, pst.			Henry de Fayrford, & William de Prestcote, chap.	O.A.G.	993
GLOUCESTER, St. Owen v.	19 Mar. 1349 u.s.	John Northwych, pst. *iuratus*			Llanthony Pr. by Glouc.	O.A.G.	994
BRISTOL, St. Stephen, Richard le Whyte Chantry	18 Mar. 1349 u.s.	Thomas Myncy, pst.			Mayor of Bristol[2]	O.A.G.	995
idem. P.C.	22 Feb. 1349 u.s.	William Corry, pst.			Mayor of Bristol	O.A.G.	996

TABLE I　　401

VOLUME TWO[3]

Benefice	Date and place of institution	Person instituted	Former incumbent	Cause of vacancy	Patron	Inductor	Edition nos.
BRISTOL, St. Stephen. Whyte chantry at St. Katherine's altar[5]	16 Mar. 1349 Hartlebury	Robert Pyk pst.[4]	Newly founded			O.A.G. & Inqu.	1377
BITTON (Prebendal to v. Salisbury Cathedral)	16 Mar. 1349 u.s.	John de Alta Ripa, pst. iuratus	Nicholas Fraunceys	D.	Walter Waleys, canon of Salisbury	O.A.G. & Inqu.	1378
EASTLEACH, R. St. Martin	20 Mar. 1349 u.s.	M. Thomas de Legh, acol.	M. Robert	D.	Great Malvern Pr.	O.A.G. & Inqu.	1379
BRISTOL, St. Ewen R.	20 Mar. 1349 u.s.	Simon Bullok, acol.	James	D.	Tewkesbury Abb.	O.A.G. & Inqu.	1380

[1] Instituted as warden.

[2] tunc vacantem per denunciacionem prioris et fratrum Kalendarum Bristoll' ac per maiorem ville dicto patri presentatum.

[3] Rubric: Admissiones instituciones collaciones et prefecciones clericorum et aliorum in beneficiis ecclesiasticis facte per venerabilem patrem dominum Wolstanum dei gracia Wygorn' episcopum a sextodecimo die mensis Marcii anno domini millesimo CCCmo. quadragesimo octavo et consecracionis dicti patris decimo.

[4] Newly founded for the souls of M. Thomas le White, lately rector of Cold Ashton, his father and mother, brothers, sisters, and for those of all the faithful departed.

[5] iuratus cum onere personaliter ministrandi in eadem secundum ordinacionem dicte cantarie prout ordinacio ipsius cantarie ad officium suum pertinens exigit et requirit.

Benefice	Date and place of institution	Person instituted	Former incumbent	Cause of vacancy	Patron	Inductor	Edition nos.
BERKELEY V.	28 Mar. 1349 Hartlebury	M. David de Milkesham, subd. *iuratus*	Matthew	D.	St. Augustine's Abb., Bristol	O.A.G. & Inqu.	1381
MATSON R.	1 Apr. 1349 u.s.	Henry de Kinemersford, pst.	Walter	D.	St. Peter's Abb., Glouc.	O.A.G. & Inqu.	1382
EXHALL R.	3 Apr. 1349 u.s.	Thomas de Hampton, acol.	John de Pershore	D.	Kenilworth Pr.	O.A.W. & Inqu.	1383
KEMPSEY V.	5 Apr. 1349 u.s.	Nicholas Bacoun, pst. *iuratus*	William le Rok	D.	Giles Lovet, r. of Kempsey	O.A.W. & Inqu.	1384
CHERRINGTON R.	21 Apr. 1349 u.s.	John le Warner of Rowington, pst.	M. John, son of Nicholas Geronde	D.	William Lucy, kt., ld. of Cherrington	O.A.W. & Inqu.	1385
FULBROOK R.	22 Apr. 1349 u.s.	Simon le Bakere of Wellesbourne, pst.	John Wodecok	D.	Simon de Geynesbury, r. of Hampton	O.A.W. & Inqu.	1386
STRATFORD P.C. Sub-wardenship of the chapel of St. Thomas the Martyr	22 Apr. 1349 u.s.	John Saucer, pst.	William	D.	Bishop Warden of the chapel	D. of Xtianity of Warwick & Inqu.	1387

TABLE I   403

Place		Date	Incumbent		Successor	Patron	Authority	Year
WARWICK, St. Michael	R.	22 Apr. 1349 u.s.	Robert, son of John in le Gate of Enderby, clk.	D.	Thomas Rower	D. of colleg. church of St. Mary, Warwick, Henry de Stonleye & William de Derby, canons & prebendaries of the same	O.A.W. & Inqu.	1388
SHERBORNE	V.	22 Apr. 1349 u.s.	John Bakere, pst. *iuratus*	D.	Nicholas de la More	Br. Philip de Thame, Pr. of St. John of Jerusalem	O.A.W. & Inqu.	1389
TWYNING	R.	23 April 1349 u.s.	John Somery, pst.	D.	M. William de Bosco	Winchcombe Abb.	O.A.W. [*sic*] & Inqu.	1390
PEOPLETON	R.	23 Apr. 1349 u.s.	William de Westcote, pst.			John Russel, ld. of Peopleton	O.A.W. & Inqu.	1391
STRENSHAM	R.	23 Apr. 1349 u.s.	Edward Russel, pst.	D.	Robert Russel	Agnes Russel, widow, lady of the manor & vill of Strensham	O.A.W. & Inqu.	1392
SYDE	R.	29 Apr. 1349 u.s.	Robert de Coueleye, subd.	D.	John	Thomas de Berkeley, kt.	O.A.G. & Inqu.	1393
TYTHERING-TON	V.	30 Apr. 1349 u.s.	Robert de Difford, pst. *iuratus*	D.	Christopher	Llanthony Pr. by Glouc.	O.A.G. & Inqu.	1394

Benefice	Date and place of institution	Person instituted	Former incumbent	Cause of vacancy	Patron	Inductor	Edition nos.
NORTH CERNEY R.	30 Apr. 1349 Hartlebury	M. John de Asshebourn, acol.	Robert	D.	Ralph, Baron Stafford, ld. of Tonbridge	O.A.G. & Inqu.	1395
RENDCOMBE R.	1 May 1349 u.s.	John de Rothewell, acol.	Walter Frelond	Res. by pr. Richard atte Boure	Ralph, Baron Stafford	O.A.G. & Inqu.	1396
WASPERTON V.	2 May 1349 u.s.	Roger Patthelowe, pst. iuratus	Richard	D.	Simon de Geynesbrugh, r. of Hampton Bishop	Guardian (per. . gardianum) of chapel of St. Thomas the Martyr, Stratford & Inqu.	1397
MINCHIN-HAMPTON Chantry of St. Mary	3 May 1349 u.s.	Peter de Asshewell, chap.			William de Prestbury, r. of Minchinhampton	O.A.G. & Inqu.	1398
WITTON [by Droitwich], v. St. Peter	3 May 1349 u.s.	Thomas Cassy of [Droit]wich iuratus	John Gerard	D.	Studley Pr.	O.A.W. & Inqu.	1399
COLN ST. ALDWYN V.	4 May 1349 u.s.	David de Quenyngton, pst. iuratus	John de Lenchewyk	D.	St. Peter's Abb., Glouc.	O.A.G. & Inqu.	1400

TABLE I   405

Place	Date	Name	Cause	Predecessor	Source	Patron	Year
HAGLEY R.	4 May 1349 u.s.	William Humon of Dudley, pst.	Res.	Robert de Haggeley	O.A.W. & Inqu.	Edmund, ld. of Hagley	1401
ROWELL V. or ROEL	5 May 1349 u.s.	John Dod, chap. *iuratus*	D.	William	O.A.G. & Inqu.	Winchcombe Abb.	1402
UPPER SWELL (*Swell maior*) R.	5 May 1349 u.s.	John de Iccombe, acol.	D.	Robert	O.A.G. & Inqu.	Evesham Abb.	1403
STAVERTON, Chantry of St. Mary	7 May 1349 u.s.	William Derveshal, pst.			O.A.G. & Inqu.	Thomas Prykke of Staverton	1404
OLDBURY Chapel R.	8 May 1349 u.s.	Nicholas Loret, chap.	D.	Richard	O.A.G. & Inqu.	Nicholas Bordon, ld. of Oldbury	1405
BRISTOL, Chantry in St. Augustine's Abb.	8 May 1349 u.s.	Stephen le Bakare, pst.			D. of Bristol *nulla inquisicione premissa*	Thomas de Berkeley, kt.	1406
WELLES-BOURNE V.	12 May 1349 u.s.	John de Ansty, pst. *iuratus*	D.	Peter de Salle	O.A.W. & Inqu.	Kenilworth Pr.	1407
WARWICK, Colleg. Preb. Church of St. Mary	12 May 1349 u.s.	Robert de Gersyndon, chap.		William de Derby	Robert de Staverton, r. of 3rd portion in St. Nicholas, Warwick & Inqu.	Thomas de Beauchamp	1408

Benefice	Date and place of institution	Person instituted	Former incumbent	Cause of vacancy	Patron	Inductor	Edition nos.
GRAFTON V. [TEMPLE]	14 May 1349 Hartlebury	Walter de Allesle, pst. iuratus	John Saucer	Ass. sub-wardenship of St. Thomas' chapel, Stratford	Br. Philip de Thame, Pr. of St. John of Jerusalem	O.A.W. & Inqu.	1409
CLAVERDON V.	14 May 1349 u.s.	Thomas Person of Rowington, chap. iuratus	John de Feckenham	D.	M. Robert [of Worcester], archd. of Worc.	O.A.W. & Inqu.	1410
POWICK V.	15 May 1349 u.s.	William called 'Faber' of Sutton, chap. iuratus	John de Longeneye	D.	Great Malvern Pr.	O.A.W. & Inqu.	1411
CHURCHILL R. [by Worcester]	16 May 1349 u.s.	Richard Shirreve of Morton Underhill, pst.	Richard Spelly	D.	Hawisia, lady of Churchill	O.A.W. & Inqu.	1412
WORCESTER ARCHDEACONRY	22 May 1349 u.s.	M. John de Severley, clk.[1]			Bp.	Pr. of Worcester to install	1413
HARTPURY V.	23 May 1349 Kempsey	Philip Hobberewe, pst. iuratus	Richard	D.	St. Peter's Abb., Glouc.	O.A.G. & Inqu.	1414

TABLE I 407

OLD SODBURY	v.	24 May 1349 Ripple	Ralph de Enderby, deac. *iuratus*	Henry	D.	Br. Richard Colys, sacrist of Worc. Cath. Pr.	O.A.G. & Inqu.	1415
COLD ASHTON	R.	24 May 1349 u.s.	Roger le White, acol.	John Wodere	D.	Bath Cath. Pr.	O.A.G. & Inqu.	1416
PUCKLE-CHURCH	R.	24 May 1349 u.s.	John Power, deac. by his pr. Nicholas de Pontesbury	Ralph	D.	Ralph, Bp. of Bath & Wells	O.A.G. & Inqu.	1417
WORCESTER, St. Helen Chantry		25 May 1349 Kempsey	John de Quynton, chap.	Ralph	D.	M. Walter de Merston, r. of St. Helen's	O.A.W. & Inqu.	1418
MISERDEN	R.	26 May 1349 Hartlebury	John de Grimesby, pst.	Roger	D.	King	O.A.G. & Inqu.	1419
SAPPERTON	R.	26 May 1349 u.s.	Thomas atte Gotere of Broad Rissington, pst.	Thomas	D.	Walter de Lisle, ld. of Sapperton	O.A.G. & Inqu.	1420
WORCESTER, All Saints	R.	26 May 1349 u.s.	Ralph Kersover, pst.	Peter de Penebrok	D.	Worc. Cath. Pr.	O.A.W. & Inqu.	1421
HATHEROP	R.	27 May 1349 u.s.	Thomas Torel, pst.	John	D.	St. Peter's Abb., Glouc.	O.A.G. & Inqu.	1422
ODDINGTON	R.	28 May 1349 u.s.	John de Helewelle, pst.	Thomas	D.	M. Robert de Patryngton, Prof. of Sacred Theology, Precentor of York Cath.	O.A.G. & Inqu.	1423

1 *teque per pillei nostri tradicionem investimus canonice de eodem.*

Benefice	Date and place of institution	Person instituted	Former incumbent	Cause of vacancy	Patron	Inductor	Edition nos.
ELMLEY CASTLE v.	28 May 1349 Hartlebury	Walter Thoury of Elmley, pst. *iuratus*	William de Lench	D.	Thomas de Kenemerton, warden or master of the chapel & chantry of E.C.	O.A.W. & Inqu.	1424
LONG COMPTON v.	28 May 1349 u.s.	William le Fullare of *Roydon*, pst. *iuratus*	Adam	Res. on ass. of High Easter V., London dioc.		O.A.W. & Inqu.	1425
WALTON D'EIVILLE Chapel P.C.	28 May 1349 u.s.	Robert de Bannebury, chap.	Simon de Walton	D.	Kenilworth Pr.	O.A.W. & Inqu.	1426
FLADBURY v.	28 May 1349 u.s.	Richard de Weston, pst. *iuratus*	Richard	D.	John de Brailles, r. of Fladbury	O.A.W. & Inqu.	1427
CHERRINGTON R.	28 May 1349 u.s.	John de Geydon, pst.	John Warner	D.	William de Lucy, kt.	O.A.W. & Inqu.	1428
DAGLING-WORTH R.	28 May 1349 u.s.	Thomas atte Barre of Shutford	Robert	D.	Godstow Abb.	O.A.G. & Inqu.	1429
NORTHLEACH v.	28 May 1349 u.s.	Adam le White, chap. *iuratus*	John	D.	St. Peter's Abb., Glouc.	O.A.G. & Inqu.	1430

TABLE I 409

	Date	Presentee	Cause	Predecessor	Patron	Authority	Year
BIRTSMORTON R.	28 May 1349 u.s.	Hugh Pershore of Campden, chap.	D.	William de Borstall	Richard Ruyhale	C.A.W. & Inqu.	1431
COUGHTON V.	29 May 1349 u.s.	John Grenhull, pst. *iuratus*	D.	John de Bisshopesdon	Studley Pr.	C.A.W. & Inqu.	1432
BECKFORD V.	29 May 1349 u.s.	Henry de Grafton, chap. *iuratus*	D.	Geoffrey	King	O.A.G. & Inqu.	1433
MICKLETON R.	29 May 1349 u.s.	John called 'le Mercer', of Pershore, chap.	D.	William	Eynsham Abb.	O.A.G. & Inqu.	1435
RISSINGTON (*Broderispndon*) R.	1 June 1349 u.s.	William de Welneford, chap.	D.	Robert	Walter de Lisle	O.A.G. & Inqu.	1436
ATHERSTONE R.	5 June 1349 u.s.	M. Robert de Southam, acol.	D.	M. William de Asshedon	Tewkesbury Abb.	C.A.W.	1438
HILLSLEY Chapel	5 June 1349 u.s.	Nicholas Wynebald, clk.	D.	Richard	William de Chyltenham Bp.	O.A.G. & Inqu.	1439
HENBURY in SALT MARSH V.	6 June 1349 u.s.	Walter de Lynhale, chap. *iuratus*					1440
BILLESLEY R.	9 June 1349 u.s.	Roger de Conyngesby, clk.	Ass. archdv. of Worc.	M. John de Severleye	John Trussel of *Kybblesdon*	C.A.W. & Inqu.	1441
ALCESTER R.	9 June 1349 u.s.	John le Dekene, of Alcester, pst.	D.	John de Codestone	Pr. of St. Mary & St. John the Baptist, Cookhill	D.¹ of Warwick & Inqu.	1442

1 Of Christianity.

Benefice	Date and place of institution	Person instituted	Former incumbent	Cause of vacancy	Patron	Inductor	Edition nos.
HASELOR	R. 9 June 1349 Hartlebury	John Guldune of *Langeford*, clk.	William de Southam	D.	William Meldon of *Langeford*	C.A.W. & Inqu.	1443
WARWICK, St. Nicholas 3rd portion	R. 9 June 1349 u.s.	Robert, son of John in the Gate of Enderby, acol.	Robert de Staverton	D.	D. of St. Mary's colleg. church, Warwick. (Robert de Enderdeby)	C.A.W. & Inqu.	1444
TODENHAM	R. 11 June 1349 u.s.	Philip de Alyncester, pst.	William	D.	King on acc. of vacancy of Westminster Abb.	O.A.G. & Inqu.	1445
ASTON SUB-EDGE	R. 12 June 1349 u.s.	M. William de Besford, pst.	Thomas	D.	John Flemyng' of Aston sub-Edge	O.A.G. & Inqu.	1446
SHIPTON SOLLARS (*Shipton Chaunflour*), St. Mary	R. 12 June 1349 u.s.	William de Overbury, clk	Richard Solers	D.	John Solers	O.A.G. & Inqu.	1447
HADZOR	R. 11 June 1349 u.s.	Richard Haldeford, pst.	Giles de Rudyngg'	D.	Thomas Cassy	D. of Droitwich & Inqu.	1448

TABLE I 411

Benefice	Date				Patron		Year
SPETCHLEY R.	14 June 1349 u.s.	John de Specheleye, pst.	William de Halle	D.	Alice de Specheleye, lady of Spetchley	C.A.W. & Inqu.	1449
LECKHAMPTON R.	16 June 1349 u.s.	William de Blechesden, pst.	William	D.	John Giffard of Leckhampton	O.A.G. & Inqu.	1450
STRATFORD, Wardenship P.C. of chapel of St. Thomas the Martyr	16 June 1349 u.s.	M. John Geraud of Stratford[1]			Bp.	M. Henry [de] Neubold & M. Henry de Aumbresle, rectors of Weston & Welford resp.	1451
GLOUCESTER, St. Mary in the South R.	18 June 1349 u.s.	William Heyberare of Gloucester, pst.	Simon	D.	Llanthony Pr. by Glouc.	O.A.G. & Inqu.	1453
RUSHOCK V.	18 June 1349 u.s.	William de Aston Episcopi, pst. iuratus	Robert Crok	D.	Richard de Bromhull, r. of Chaddesley Corbett	C.A.W. & Inqu.	1454
FROCESTER V.	19 June 1349 u.s.	Richard Arnald, chap. iuratus	Henry	D.	St. Peter's Abb., Glouc.	O.A.G. & Inqu.	1456
NORTH PIDDLE R.	19 June 1349 u.s.	William Walys, pst.	James	D.	John de Segrave, kt.	C.A.W. & Inqu.	1457

1 *ipsumque per pillui sui tradicionem investivit canonice de eadem. Iuratusque de tenendo et observando quatenus in eo est ordinacionem dicte capelle iuxta disposicionem fundatoris, et de obediendo episcopo suisque successoribus et eorum ministris in licitis et canonicis mandatis . . . .*

Benefice	Date and place of institution	Person instituted	Former incumbent	Cause of vacancy	Patron	Inductor	Edition nos.
UPTON SNODSBURY R.	19 June 1349 Hartlebury	Thomas de Yevele, pst.	Roger de la Felde	D.	Great Malvern Pr.	C.A.W. & Inqu.	1458
WASPERTON V.	21 June 1349 u.s.	Henry Diconum of *Wykyngeston*, pst. *iuratus*	Roger de Pathelowe	D.	Simon de Geynesburgh, r. of Hampton Bishop	Warden & sub-ward. of St. Thomas the Martyr chant., Stratford. Inqu. by John, the sub-warden	1459
CLIFFORD R.	21 June 1349 u.s.	John de Wynchecomb, chap.			St. Peter's Abb., Glouc.	M. Henry de Newebold, the bp.'s sequestrator[1]	1460
ALVESTON V.	21 June 1349 u.s.	Walter le Hopper le [de?] *Fulbrok*, chap. *iuratus*	Philip	D.	Simon de Geynesburgh, r. of Hampton Bishop	As in no. 1459 above	1461
OVER Chantry	21 June 1349 u.s.	William Wyxy, chap.	William	D.	William de Syde	D. of Bristol. Inqu. by O.A.G.	1462
ACTON BEAUCHAMP R.	23 June 1349 u.s.	William Fallo, chap.	Nicholas	D.	Thomas de Beauchamp, e. of Warwick	C.A.W. & Inqu.	1463

TABLE I 413

WELLAND v.	25 June 1349 u.s.	Thomas Neel of Rodbourne, pst. *iuratus*			Great Malvern Pr. at nomination of r. of Bredon	C.A.W. & Inqu.	1464
BISLEY v.	25 June 1349 u.s.	Edmund de Elcomb, pst. *iuratus*	D.	Roger	Richard Clavyll, portionist of the 1st port. of Bisley church	O.A.G. & Inqu.	1465
COWLEY R.	25 June 1349 u.s.	Nicholas de Puriton, pst.	D.	Walter	Pershore Abb.	O.A.G. & Inqu.	1466
ALDERMINSTER v.	25 June 1349 u.s.	Henry de Goldicote, pst. *iuratus*			Pershore Abb.	C.A.W.[2]	1467
RIPPLE, Chantry of John Salemon of Ripple	25 June 1349 u.s.	John Stabald, chap.[3]	D.	William de Lebur' [Ledbury]	Henry Machoun, chap. of the chantry	Parish chap.[4] of Ripple	1468
COBERLEY, Chantry of St. Mary	26 July [*sic*] 1349 u.s.	John Clerk, subd.	D.	Walter	Thomas de Coberleye, kt.	O.A.G. & Inqu.	1469
TARDEBIGGE v.	26 [June] 1349 u.s.	Walter de Ulnehal', pst. *iuratus*	D.	Warren (*Warinus*)	Bordesley Abb.	C.A.W. & Inqu.	1470

1 *nulla inquisicione premissa, quia de vacacione dicte ecclesie, iure patronatus, meritis persone presentate, et aliis consuetis articulis inquirendis episcopo constabat ad plenum.*
2 *nulla inquisicione premissa, quia tam de vacacione dicte ecclesie, quam aliis articulis in ea parte debitis et consuetis episcopo constabat ad plenum.*
3 Admitted *de gracia speciali domini episcopi.*
4 *nulla inquisicione* [&c. as in no. 1460 n.].

Benefice	Date and place of institution	Person instituted	Former incumbent	Cause of vacancy	Patron	Inductor	Edition nos.
MINCHIN-HAMPTON R.	26 [June] 1349 Hartlebury	John de Henton, pst., by his pr. John de Middelton literatus	William	D.	King, on acc. of temps. of Caen (Came) Abb. [alien][1]	O.A.G. & Inqu.	1471
CHEDWORTH V.	26 [June] 1349 u.s.	Hugh de Ouston, pst. iuratus	John	D.	King	O.A.G. & Inqu.	1472
MEYSEY HAMPTON R.	26 [June] 1349 u.s.	Richard Pillisgate, clk.	Robert	D.	Thomas Seymour, kt.	O.A.G. & Inqu.	1473
DOWN AMPNEY V.	27 June 1349 u.s.	William Walsshe, pst. iuratus	John	D.	Philip de Thame, Pr. of St. John of Jerusalem	O.A.G. & Inqu.	1474
EXHALL R.	28 June 1349 u.s.	Roger Mayel, pst.	Thomas de Hampton	D.	Kenilworth Pr.	C.A.W. & Inqu.	1475
BIDFORD V.	28 June 1349 u.s.	Robert Owayn, chap. iuratus	Henry	D.	Kenilworth Pr.	C.A.W. & Inqu.	1476
MATSON R.	28 June 1349 u.s.	Walter de Mareys, pst. by his pr. John Dikkeleye, clk.	Henry	D.	St. Peter's Abb., Glouc.	O.A.G. & Inqu.	1477
COLD ASTON V. [alias ASTON BLANK]	27 June 1349 u.s.	Thomas de Hanewell, pst. iuratus	William	D.	Little Malvern Pr.	O.A.G. & Inqu.	1478

TABLE I   415

Place	Date	Person instituted	Predecessor	Reason	Patron	Authority	Year
COMPTON IN HENMARSH [LITTLE COMPTON] R.	28 June 1349 u.s.	John Paty, pst. by his pr. John Paty, clk.	Philip de Alcestr'	Res.	King on acc. of temps. of St. Denis [alien]	O.A.G. & Inqu.	1479
OLDBERROW R.	29 June 1349 u.s.	Nicholas de Hampstede, pst.	Thomas Warr' [Warwick]	D.	Evesham Abb.	C.A.W. & Inqu.	1480
NORTH CERNEY R.	29 June 1349 u.s.	Robert de Asshebourn, pst.	M. John de Asshebourn	Res.	Ralph, Baron Stafford, ld. of Tonbridge	O.A.G. & Inqu.	1481
SLAUGHTER R.	30 June 1349 u.s.	Thomas de Lokeryngg', pst.	Thomas	D.	Richard atte Well of Upper Slaughter	O.A.G. & Inqu.	1482
DRY MARSTON R.	30 June 1349 u.s.	Roger Basset, clk.			Coventry Cath. Pr.	O.A.G.[2]	1483
BROADWAY R.	1 July 1349 u.s.	William de Okleye, poor clk., deac.		D.	Bp. as exec. of papal prov. to a benefice in patronage of Pershore Abb.	A.G. & O.A.G. & clergy of archdy.	1484
BATSFORD R.	1 July 1349 u.s.	William Folebrok of Churchill, pst.	Richard Wele	D.	John Golafre, kt.	D. of pecul. jurisd. of Blockley	1485

31

1 Benedictine nunnery of Holy Trinity.
2 *nulla inquisicione premissa quia constabat episcopo de articulis consuetis in ea parte inquirendis ad plenum.*

Benefice	Date and place of institution	Person instituted	Former incumbent	Cause of vacancy	Patron	Inductor	Edition nos.
MICKLETON R.	2 July 1349 Hartlebury	John, son of John Wylee of Chipping Campden, clk.	John	D.	Eynsham Abb.	O.A.G. & Inqu.	1486
BUCKLAND R.	1 July 1349 u.s.	M. Roger de Middilton, pst.	John	D.	St. Peter's Abb., Glouc.	O.A.G. & Inqu.	1487
LITTLE WORMINGTON, Holy Trinity R.	1 July 1349 u.s.	Robert de Clipston, clk.	John	D.	Robert de Bodenham	O.A.G. & Inqu.	1488
STANTON R.	2 July 1349 u.s.	Walter de Shirbourn, pst.	Stephen	D.	Winchcombe Abb.	O.A.G. & Inqu.	1489
CHILDS WICKHAM V.	2 July 1349 u.s.	John de Colishull in Ardena, pst. *iuratus*	William	D.	Bordesley Abb.	O.A.G. & Inqu.	1490
PEBWORTH V.	2 July 1349 u.s.	Robert de Cherlenton, pst. *iuratus*		D.	Alcester Abb.	O.A.G. & Inqu.	1491
BEL-BROUGHTON R.	2 July 1349 u.s.	John Aaron, pst.	William de Wolwardel' [Wolverley]	D.	Eleanor de Suydleye [Sudeley]	C.A.W. & Inqu.	1492
HAGLEY R.	2 July 1349 u.s.	William de Belne, clk.	William de Duddesleye	D.	Edmund de Haggele	C.A.W. & Inqu.	1493 Cf. 1401

TABLE I

417

						Bp.	
KEMPSEY, Chantry of St. Mary	3 July 1349 u.s.	William de Harpedale of Long Itchington			v. of Kempsey		1495
HOLT	v. 5 July 1349 u.s.	William Alwy, chap. *iuratus*	Henry de Grutford	D.	M. Thomas Powys, r. of Holt	C.A.W. & Inqu.	1496
ASTLEY	v. 5 July 1349 u.s.	John Maudyt, pst. *iuratus*			King on acc. of temps. of Astley Pr. [alien]	C.A.W. & Inqu.	1497
WITLEY	R. 5 July 1349 u.s.	Walter de Malleye, pst.	M. Richard de la Felde	D.	Hugh de Cokeseye	C.A.W. & Inqu.	1498
WORCESTER, St. Michael	R. 6 July 1349 u.s.	John de Lemustre, pst.	John de Wynchecomb	Ass. Clifford church [v. 1460]	Richard Colys, sacrist of Worc. Cath. Pr.	D. of Worc. Inqu. by C.A.W.	1499
BREDICOT	R. 6 July 1349 u.s.	Elias de Herforton, chap.	Matthew	D.	William Dufford, ld. of Bredicot	C.A.W. & Inqu.	1500
WILLERSEY	R. 7 July 1349 u.s.	William Founteneye, pst.	John	D.	Evesham Abb.	O.A.G. & Inqu.	1501
BUTLERS MARSTON	v. 7 July 1349 u.s.	Philip de Warmyngton, chap. *iuratus*	John de Adbrycton	D.	Alcester Abb.	C.A.W. & Inqu.	1502

Benefice	Date and place of institution	Person instituted	Former incumbent	Cause of vacancy	Patron	Inductor	Edition nos.
BROCKWORTH v.	7 July 1349 Hartlebury	John Colet of Besford, pst. *iuratus*	William de Besford	Res.	Llanthony Pr. by Glouc.	O.A.G. & Inqu.	1503
GLOUCESTER, St. Aldate R.	10 July 1349 u.s.	Griffin de Berches, chap.	William Heyberare	Res.	King on acc. of temps. of Deerhurst Pr. [alien]	O.A.G. & Inqu.	1505
POWICK v.	10 July 1349 u.s.	William le Bakare of Rock, chap. *iuratus*	William	D.	Great Malvern Pr.	C.A.W. & Inqu.	1506
LONGDON v.	10 July 1349 u.s.	John de Oxhull, chap. *iuratus*			King on acc. of vacancy of Westminster Abb.	C.A.W. & Inqu.	1507
LEIGH Kymenhale portion R.	10 July 1349 u.s.	Walter de Morton, pst.	William	D.	Pershore Abb.	C.A.W. & Inqu.	1508
GREAT MALVERN v.	10 July 1349 u.s.	Nicholas le Smythes of Powick, pst. *iuratus*	John de Bredon	D.	Great Malvern Pr.	C.A.W. & Inqu.	1509
YARDLEY v.	11 July 1349 u.s.	John Calunden, pst. *iuratus*	John de Wotton	Res.	Maxstoke Pr.	C.A.W. & Inqu.	1510

TABLE I   419

OZLEWORTH R.	11 July 1349 u.s.	William de Broughton, pst.	D.	Richard	St. Peter's Abb., Glouc.	O.A.G. & Inqu.	1511
BEOLEY v.	14 July 1349 u.s.	Nicholas de Fladbury, pst. *iuratus*	D.	Hugh	Alcester Abb.	C.A.W. & Inqu.	1513
CHADDESLEY [CORBETT] R.	15 July 1349 u.s.	John de Boys, acol.	D.	Richard de Bromhull	Robert de Boys	C.A.W. & Inqu.	1514
BROADWAS, Chantry of M. John de Bradewas	16 July 1349 u.s.	John Partrich, chap.	D.	Walter le Taverner	Br. John [of Evesham], pr. of Worc.	r. of Broadwas[1]	1515
BRISTOL, St. Philip & St. Jacob R.	16 July 1349 u.s.	Nicholas de Usk, pst.		John	Tewkesbury Abb.	O.A.G. & Inqu.	1516
MARSHFIELD v.	16 July 1349 u.s.	Peter Hale of Washbourne, pst. *iuratus*	D.	Richard	Tewkesbury Abb.	O.A.G. & Inqu.	1517
SEZINCOTE IN HENMARSH Church or Chapel R.	16 July 1349 u.s.	John de Hedyndon, clk.	D.	William de Rodeston	John de Walyngford, ld. of Sezincote	D. of exempt jurisd. of Blockley & Inqu.	1518
OLDBURY Chapel R.	16 July 1349 u.s.	Edward Beaufrere, chap.	D.	Nicholas	Nicholas Bordon, ld. of Oldbury	O.A.G. & Inqu.	1519

[1] *nulla inquisicione premissa quia de vacacione, iure patronatus, meritis persone presentate, et aliis articulis consuetis et debitis in hac parte constabat ad plenum.*

Benefice	Date and place of institution	Person instituted	Former incumbent	Cause of vacancy	Patron	Inductor	Edition nos.
WARWICK, St. Nicholas 3rd portion	R. 17 July 1349 Hartlebury	Richard de Braundeston, chap. by his pr. Simon de Blockele, clk.	Adam Carles	Res.	John de Bukyngham, prebr. of Compton preb. in colleg. church of St. Mary, Warwick	C.A.W. & Inqu.	1520
DRIFFIELD	V. 17 July 1349 u.s.	Thomas Frankeleyn of Driffield, chap. iuratus	John	D.	Cirencester Abb.	O.A.G. & Inqu.	1521
WARWICK, St. James	R. 17 July 1349 u.s.	Robert Sotemay, pst.	Walter	Ass. V. of Tardebigge [v. 1470]	Thomas de Beauchamp, e. of Warwick	C.A.W. & Inqu.	1522
ASTON CANTLOW	V. 17 July 1349 u.s.	Nicholas de Sheldon, pst. iuratus	Thomas de Normanton	D.	Maxstoke Pr.	C.A.W. & Inqu.	1523
TANWORTH	V. 17 July 1349 u.s.	Richard le Gardiner, pst. iuratus	Robert de Fulwode	D.	Maxstoke Pr.	C.A.W. & Inqu.	1524
FULBROOK	R. 17 July 1349 u.s.	John Wyrgeyn, pst.	Simon le Bakere	D.	Simon de Geynesburgh, r. of Hampton Bishop	C.A.W. & Inqu.	1525

TABLE I   421

Benefice	Date	Presentee		Cause	Patron / Predecessor	Authority	Year
WARWICK, St. Laurence R.	17 July 1349 u.s.	Adam Coriate of Warwick, pst.	William de Walshe	D.	John de Bukyngham, prebr. of Compton preb. in colleg. church of St. Mary, Warwick	C.A.W. & Inqu.	1526
WARWICK, Colleg. Preb. Church of St. Mary	17 July 1349 u.s.	John de Clebury, clk., by his pr. Robert Sotemay, pst.	Thomas Basset	D.	Thomas de Beauchamp, e. of Warwick	C.A.W. & Inqu.	1527
WORCESTER, St. Swithin. Chantry founded by Robert Batel	17 July 1349 u.s.	John Smyth	Henry David	D.	John de Tewkesbury, r. of St. Swithin	C.A.W. & Inqu.	1528
PRESTON v.	17 July 1349 u.s.	Robert Polton of Latton, pst. *iuratus*	Robert	Res.	Cirencester Abb.	O.A.G. & Inqu.	1529
WORCESTER, St. Nicholas R.	17 July 1349 u.s.	Nicholas de Poywyk, pst.	John de Wynchecomb	Ass. Clifford church [v. 1460]¹	Bp.	r. of St. Helen	1530
SPERNALL Chapel R.	18 July 1349 u.s.	John de Grenhulle of Evesham, pst.	Nicholas atte Ʒale	D.	Cookhill Pr.	C.A.W. & Inqu.	1531

¹ This would seem to be an error, unless John of Winchcombe was a pluralist. He is also said to have resigned St. Michael's, Worcester, because of his institution to Clifford [v. 1499]. The register has no record of his institution to either of these Worcester churches.

Benefice	Date and place of institution	Person instituted	Former incumbent	Cause of vacancy	Patron	Inductor	Edition nos.
EYFORD R.	19 July 1349 Hartlebury	William le Sclattere of Winch[combe], chap.	Simon	D.	John Beysyn	O.A.G. & Inqu.	1532
WELLESBOURNE V.	19 July 1349 u.s.	John de Clynes, pst.	John Ansty	D.	Kenilworth Pr.	C.A.W. & Inqu.	1533
LITTLE BARRINGTON V.	19 July 1349 u.s.	John Wynchestr', pst.	William	D.	Llanthony Pr. by Glouc.	O.A.G. & Inqu.	1534
HINDLIP R.	19 July 1349 u.s.	Robert de Wythindon, clk.	Simon de Chalveston	D.	Thomas de Salewarp	C.A.W. & Inqu.	1535
DITCHFORD FRARY R. Church or Chapel	19 July 1349 u.s.	John Bacheler, pst.	Nicholas	Ass. V. of Leek Wootton, Cov. & Lichf. dioc.	John de Brailles, ld. of Ditchford	C.A.W. & Inqu.	1536
MORTON [BAGOT] R.	20 July 1349 u.s.	Thomas Pal', pst.	Richard	D.	Kenilworth Pr.	C.A.W. & Inqu.	1538
ASTON BISHOP Chapel. V. [WHITE LADIES ASTON]	20 July 1349 u.s.	Osbert Priour of Claines, pst. iuratus	Hugh de Claines	D.	Whiston Pr.	C.A.W. & Inqu.	1539
BARFORD R.	21 July 1349 u.s.	Walter Roos, acol.	Adam Inwys	D.	Evesham Abb.	C.A.W. & Inqu.	1540

TABLE I 423

STRATTON v.	21 July 1349 u.s.	Richard called 'le Taillour' of Alkerton, pst. *iuratus*	Simon	D.	William atte Brok', r. of Stratton	O.A.G. & Inqu.	1541
STONE v.	23 July 1349 u.s.	William Fayting', pst. *iuratus*	Richard de Sheldesl'	D.	John Boys, r. of Chaddesley Corbett	C.A.W. & Inqu.	1542
[FLYFORD] FLAVELL R.	24 July 1349 u.s.	John Harly, pst.	John de London	D.	Joan, relict of John Besford	C.A.W. & Inqu.	1543
INKBERROW v.	24 July 1349 u.s.	Thomas de Foxton of *Thirneby*, pst. *iuratus*	William Welykempt	D.	Richard de la Felde	C.A.W. & Inqu.	1544
STRENSHAM R.	24 July 1349 u.s.	Stephen de Duddeleye, pst.	Edward Russell	D.	King	C.A.W. & Inqu.	1545
ABBOTS LENCH v.	24 July 1349 u.s.	John de Budiford, pst. *iuratus*	John Inch'	D.	John de Brailles r. of Fladbury, at nomination of John Bruyn	C.A.W. & Inqu.	1546
ROUS LENCH R.	24 July 1349 u.s.	Richard, son of William Wylmyn of Rous Lench	Thomas, son of Thomas ld. of R. L.	D.	Richard de Lench Rondulf	C.A.W. & Inqu.	1547
SIDDINGTON R.	25 July 1349 u.s.	Richard Patty, pst.	Roger[1]	D.	King on acc. of temps. of Monmouth Pr. [alien]	O.A.G. & Inqu.	1548

1 *Richard* Northcrek was instituted in 1348. See p. 387.

Benefice	Date and place of institution	Person instituted	Former incumbent	Cause of vacancy	Patron	Inductor	Edition nos.
DOWDESWELL [R.]	25 July 1349 Hartlebury	John le Yonge, pst.[1]	Robert[2]	D.	William de Clynton, e. of Huntingdon	O.A.G. & Inqu.	1549
HATHEROP R.	25 July 1349 u.s.	John Wateres of Coln, pst.	Nicholas[3]	D.	St. Peter's Abb., Glouc.	O.A.G. & Inqu.	1550
SHIPTON OLIFFE R.	26 July 1349 u.s.	Thomas Fraunceys of Pegglesworth, clk.	Thomas Frankeleyn	Ass. V. of Driffield [v. 1521]	Christine, lady of Shipton O.	O.A.G. & Inqu.	1551
FECKENHAM V.	28 July 1349 u.s.	M. Nicholas de Lodelowe, pst. iuratus			King on acc. of temps. of Lyre Abb. [alien]	C.A.W. & Inqu.	1552
PEDMORE R.	29 July 1349 u.s.	Hugh Cordewan, pst.	Walter de Clodeshale	D.	Richard de Clodeshale	C.A.W. & Inqu.	1553
CLENT with ROWLEY Chapel V.	29 July 1349 u.s.	John Bugging', pst. iuratus	John Andreu	D.	Halesowen Abb.	C.A.W. & Inqu.	1554
WINDRUSH V.	1 Aug. 1349 u.s.	John Dod of Fairford, pst.	Robert	D.	Llanthony Pr. by Glouc.	O.A.G. & Inqu.	1555
NOTGROVE R.	1 Aug. 1349 u.s.	William de Attelberwe, clk.	Walter	D.	Thomas de Beauchamp, e. of Warwick	C.A.W. & Inqu.	1556

TABLE I 425

					Ass.		O.A.G. & Inqu.	
BOXWELL	R.	1 Aug. 1349 u.s.	John de Berewyk, pst.	M. Roger de Horton	Ass. Chipping Norton church, Linc. dioc.	St. Peter's Abb., Glouc.	O.A.G. & Inqu.	1557
ALDERTON	R.	3 Aug. 1349 u.s.	Robert Wympol pst.	John Serle	Res. [v. 1559]	Lady Elizabeth le Despenser	O.A.G. & Inqu.	1558
GRAFTON FLYFORD (*Grafton sub Flavel*)	R.	3 Aug. 1349 u.s.	John Serle, pst.	Roger de Grafton	D.	John de Grafton	C.A.W. & Inqu.	1559
DROITWICH [WITTON], St. Mary	R.	4 Aug. 1349 u.s.	Richard Peperwhich, pst.	William le Freen	D.	Thomas Cassy of [Droit]wich	C.A.W. & Inqu.	1560
GRIMLEY with HALLOW Chapel	V.	4 Aug. 1349 u.s.	John de Hatherleye, pst. *iuratus*	Alexander de Stodleye	D.	Worc. Cath. Pr.	C.A.W. & Inqu.	1561
NAUNTON ON [COTS]WOLD	R.	4 Aug. 1349 u.s.	M. William Aleyn, called 'de Rothewell', acol.	John Botyner	Ass. V. of Wisbech, Ely dioc.	Bp.	John de Rippon, chap. of the bp.	1562
HALFORD	R.	4 Aug. 1349 u.s.	John de Rippon, chap.	Roger	D.	Bp.	M. Henry de Newebold & Robert del Hull of Withington	1563

1 In the presence of M. John de Severley, archd. of Worcester, Ds. John Waters of Coln, r. of Hatherop, and M. William Aleyn, called 'of Rothwell', clk. of Lincoln dioc., he swore to pay annually to the r. of Withington the 50s. pension due to Withington church from that of Dowdeswell.
2 But *Richard* Erchebaud was instituted in 1348. See p. 397.
3 But *Thomas* Torel had been instituted only two months previously. See 1422.

TABLE I

Benefice	Date and place of institution	Person instituted	Former incumbent	Cause of vacancy	Patron	Inductor	Edition nos.
BLOCKLEY V. (creatam de novo)	4 Aug. 1349 Hartlebury	John Bavent, chap. iuratus			Bp.	John de Rippon, chap.	1564
SOUTH CERNEY V.	4 Aug. 1349 u.s.	Thomas Lech, pst. iuratus	Robert	D.	St. Peter's Abb., Glouc.	O.A.G. & Inqu.	1565
WITHINGTON R.	6 Aug.[1] 1349 u.s.	M. William Aleyn, called 'de Rothewell', acol.	William de Lech	D.	Bp.	O.A.G. & clergy of diocese[2]	1566
NAUNTON ON [COTS]WOLD R.	6 Aug. 1349 u.s.	Richard, son of John le Taylour of Leckhampton, acol.	M. William Aleyn	Inst. to Withington [v. 1566]	Bp.	As above[3]	1567

1 *statim post ortum solis eiusdem diei. The next institution took place immediate post.*
2 *Scriptum est officiali archidiaconi Glouc' ac omnibus et singulis decanis, rectoribus, vicariis et capellanis, ac clericis aliis quibuscumque per Wygorn' diocesem constitutis pro eius induccione comiunctim et divisim et cuilibet eorum insolidum.*
3 *Scriptum est eisdem personis modo consimili pro eius induccione.*

TABLE 2 427

TABLE 2

The Appointment of Heads of Religious Houses

Place	House	Office	Person promoted	Other details	Episcopal process	Date	Edition nos.
ASTLEY	Ben. Pr. dependent on St. Taurin, Evreux	Prior	Ralph de Valle	Presented by A. & C. of St. Taurin	Inst.	18 Apr. 1341	400
			William Provot		Inst.	5 June 1343	506
			Hugh de Valle	Wm. Provot recalled on acc. of infirmity	Inst.	18 June 1349	1455[1]
BILLESWICK, BRISTOL	Hosp. of St. Mark alias Gaunt's	Master	John de Stokelonde	Amoval of Ralph de Tetbury who had gone on pilgrimage	Confirm. of election	27 Apr. 1346	781 sqq., 793–4 Cf. 75–7
BRISTOL	Aug. Abb.	Abbot	Ralph de Assch	D. of John Snow [elected 1332: Reg. Orleton I, ff. 40v–41r]	Confirm. of election	31 July 1341	419
BRISTOL	Aug. N. St. Mary Magdalene	Prioress	Matilda de Luttelton		App.mt.	27 May 1349	997

1 Printed in Nash, *Worcs.* 2, p. 48.

Place	House	Office	Person promoted	Other details	Episcopal process	Date	Edition nos.
COOKHILL	Cist. N.	Prioress	Christine Durvassal	Election by way of scrutiny on d. of Pss. Sarah quashed by bp.	App[mt.]	29 May 1349	1434[1]
DEERHURST	Ben. Pr. dependent on St. Denis	Prior	Ralph de Ermenovilla	Recall owing to infirmity of John de Vitolio [prior since 1329]	Inst. in acc. with composition to parish church only	8 Feb. 1340	256-7
			Thomas Garculi	App[d.] 1344 on Ralph's amoval [*V.C.H. Gloucs.* 2, p. 105]. Resigned (under pressure?) 26 Nov. 1345	[App[mt.] not in register]		759-60 Cf. 663
			John Godelli		Inst. in acc. with comp.	17 Feb. 1346	759-61
LONGBRIDGE by Berkeley	Hosp.	Warden	Thomas de Baldene, pst.	William Barneby exchanged it for wardenship of St. Mary's chapel, Norton, York dioc.	Collation for this turn	12 July 1339	204
	Chapel or Hosp.	Rector or warden	Robert atte Nelme, pst.	Presented by Thomas de Berkeley, kt. No enquiry into vacancy because bp. fully acquainted with the facts	Inst. Mandate for induct. to v. of Berkeley	14 July 1349	1512

TABLE 2   429

House	Order	Office	Name		Circumstance	Date	Refs
PERSHORE	Ben. Abb.	Abbot	Thomas de Pyriton	William de Herwynton [abbot since 1307: *Reg. Geynsb.* p. 30] res. 26 Sept. 1340	Appmt. after quashing double election	[14 Nov.] 1340	351–3, 366 sqq.
PINLEY	Cist. N.	Prioress	Amicia de Hynton		Confirm. of election	21 Aug. 1342	485
STUDLEY	Aug. Pr.	Prior	John la South	D. of Robert de Langedon	Appmt. after quashing election	9 July 1349	1504
TEWKESBURY	Ben. Abb.	Abbot	Thomas de Legh	D. of John de Cotes [elected 1328: *V.C.H. Gloucs.* 2, p. 65]	Confirm. & declaration of election	10 Sept. 1347	926 sqq.
WARWICK	Aug. Pr. St. Sepulchre	Prior	Peter Warwick	Amoval of William de Wilton[2]	Confirm. of election	17 June 1349	1452
WARWICK	Hosp. of St. John	Master or Warden	Philip de Besford	Res. of Henry Bobbi	Confirm. of election	23 Feb. 1344	527, 579, 602
		Master	John de Alyncestre, junior		Appmt. following res. owing to defective election	26 May 1349	1002

1 Printed in Nash, *Worcs.* 2, p. 16.
2 Or 'Witton'.

Place	House	Office	Person promoted	Other details	Episcopal process	Date	Edition nos.
WARWICK	Hosp. of St. Michael	Master or warden	William de Knytcote	Presented by Thomas de Beauchamp, e. of Warwick	Inst.	10 Sept. 1343	523, 574
			Nicholas de Southam of Warwick	Present. as above on d. of Wm. de Knytcote	Inst.	4 June 1349	1437
WHISTON or WHITSTONES (in Claines)	Cist. N.	Prioress	Agnes de Monynton	D. of Juliana de Power	Appmt.	3 July 1349	1494[1]
WINCH-COMBE	Ben. Abb.	Abbot	William de Sherborne	Richard de Iddebury [abbot since 1315: *V.C.H. Glouc.* 2, p. 72] res. 22 Mar. 1340	Appmt. after quashing election	26 Apr. 1340	284, 295 sqq.
WOOTTON WAWEN	Ben. Pr. dependent on Conches, Normandy	Prior	John de Silvaneto	Res. of John de Lotoveris	Inst.	2 Jan. 1341	384
WORCESTER	Ben. Cath. Pr.	Prior	Simon le Botiler	Elevation of Wolstan de Bransford to episcopate	Appmt. from 7 nominees in acc. with composition	13 Apr. 1339	38 sqq., 92–3

TABLE 2 431

		Simon Cromp	D. of Simon le Botiler	App^mt. as above	6 Nov. 1339	229
WORCESTER Hosp. of St. Oswald	Master or preceptor	John de Evesham	D. of Simon Cromp, 10 Apr. 1340	App^mt. as above	[22] Apr. 1340	290 sqq.
WORCESTER Hosp. of St. Wulstan	Preceptor	William de Salopia		App^mt.	6 May 1349	1003
		Peter Fraunceys	Robert de Merston deprived by bp. [*C.P.L.* 1342–62, p. 70]	App^mt.	18 June 1341	408–9
WROXALL Ben. N.	Prioress	Isabella de Fokerham	Res. of Agnes de Broy	App^mt. at convent's request	25 Oct. 1339	279, 281

1 Printed in Nash, *Worcs.* I, p. 217.

32

TABLE 3

Letters Dimissory

The usual form in the register is as follows:

Frater Wolstanus [&c] dilecto nobis in Christo . . . *diacono* Wygorn' diocesis salutem et graciam salvatoris. Tue devocionis precibus inclinati, ut a quocumque episcopo catholico ordinis sui execucionem habente qui tibi sacras manus imponere voluerit ad *ordinem presbiteratus* licite valeas promoveri, dumtamen titulum sufficientem exhibueris, non obstante quod de dicta diocesi oriundus [*or* beneficiatus] existis, aliudque canonicum tibi non obsistat, tibi et ordinatori tuo tenore presencium licenciam concedimus specialem. In cuius rei testimonium sigillum nostrum presentibus duximus apponendum. Dat' [&c.]

But for the most part such licences are recorded as highly abbreviated memoranda. The essential details are given in the following list.

Date and place	Name and description	Order	Licence for Order(s) of:	Edition nos.
16 Feb. 1339 London	John Lovenhull of Twyning	deac.	pst.	9
19 Feb. 1339 u.s.	Richard de Billesleye	acol.	subd. & deac.	10
19 Feb. 1339 u.s.	Thomas de Pyriton, r. of Dursley	deac.	pst.	11
19 Feb. 1339 u.s.	Richard Solers, r. of Shipton Sollars' chapel	subd.	deac.	12 (Cf. 15)
21 Feb. 1339 Hillingdon	Richard de Haveresham, r. of Severn Stoke[1]	deac.	pst.	13
2 Mar. 1339 u.s.	Roger de Middeltone, r. of Boxwell	acol.	all holy	14
2 Mar. 1339 u.s.	Richard Solers, r. of Shipton Sollars		pst.	15 (Cf. 12)
3 Apr. 1339 [Spetchley]	John de Hanley	first tons.	all higher	162
9 July 1342	John Anketil of Ampney		all minor	472
24 Mar. 1343 Alvechurch	Thomas de Custon, clk. of York dioc., r. of Severn Stoke		all holy	498

[1] Ratifying a licence previously issued by the bishop as prior exercising the jurisdiction *sede vacante*. This licence is not in the R.S.V.

TABLE 3   433

Date and place	Name and description	Order	Licence for Order(s) of:	Edition nos.
22 Jan. 1344 Hartlebury	Thomas Payn of *Hontyngthrop*	subd.	deac. & pst.	529
24 Oct. 1343 Withington	John Robert of *Stanton*		subd.	546
18 Sept. 1343 Bishops Cleeve	Nicholas Wymond of Cirencester	deac.	pst.	547
12 Jan. 1545 Hartlebury	Luke de Herdebergh	acol.	all holy	550
13 Jan. 1345	John de Aston, r. of Aston Somerville		all holy	551
8 Dec. 1344 Hartlebury	Richard née Ralph	subd.	deac. & pst.	553
8 Dec. 1344 u.s.	William de Draycote, clk.		all holy	554
8 July 1343	John Billynges of *Lech'*, clk.		all minor not recd.	557
14 Dec. 1344 Hartlebury	John de Harewell, r. of Whichford	subd.	deac.	558
9 Oct. 1344	Simon de Cherlynton	acol.	subd.	561
23 Jan. 1344	William Wygeput of Cirencester	deac.	pst.	584
16 Sept. 1343	William Wette of Great Rissington	acol.	all holy	586
1 Apr. 1344 Hartlebury	M. Thomas de Clypston	acol.	subd.	589
6 Mar. 1344 u.s.	William Roberd of South Littleton	acol.	all holy	603
12 Mar. 1344	Robert le Kene of Northway	acol.	subd.	613
17 Feb. 1344 Hartlebury	Robert the clerk (*clericus*) of Tetbury	acol.	all holy	616
17 Sept. 1343 Bredon	William Boter of Longdon (*Langedon*)	acol.	subd. & deac.	617
7 May 1344 Tewkesbury	John Grey of Stanley	acol.	all holy	626
19 May 1344 Hartlebury	John le Mareschal of Barton in Henmarsh		all holy	631

Date and place	Name and description	Order	Licence for Order(s) of:	Edition nos.
21 Aug. 1344 Withington	Thomas Cok of Kempsford	acol.	all holy	651
1 Nov. 1344 Hartlebury	Geoffrey de Cattone	first tons.	acol. & all major	678
28 Jan. 1345 u.s.	John de Oxon, r. of St. Andrew's, Worcester	first tons.	all minor & major	686
12 Jan. 1345 u.s.	M. Luke de Herdebergh, r. of Honington	acol.	all holy	694
13 Jan. 1345	John de Aston, r. of Aston Somerville	acol.	all holy	695
9 May 1343	Robert de Bourton	subd.	deac. & pst.	697
7 Sept. 1344 Withington	Henry Kynny of Fairford	acol.	all holy	698
28 Nov. 1344 Hartlebury	John Boner	deac.	pst.	699
20 Feb. 1345 u.s.	William called 'Pyk' of Ampney St. Peter	acol.	all holy not recd.	700
7 Mar. 1345 u.s.	John de Harewell, r. of Whichford	deac.	pst.	707
1 Mar. 1345	John Edden	deac.	pst.	711
2 Mar. 1345	John Jones of Down Ampney	deac.	pst.	712
2 Mar. 1345	John de Wolfrynton		all minor & major	713
25 May 1345 Bredon	Simon le Mariner of Eldersfield	subd.	deac. & pst.	727
12 Aug. 1345 Henbury	Richard son of Gilbert Magot of Kempsford	acol.	subd.	731
19 July 1345 u.s.	Roger Payn	acol.	all holy	734
20 Aug. 1345 u.s.	Robert de la More	acol.	all holy	737
23 Aug. 1345	James Ondeslowe	deac.	pst.	738
3 May 1345 Hartlebury	Walter, son of William Rogers of Broadway	acol.	all holy	740
26 Mar. 1345 u.s.	Richard, son of John Batyn of Swell	acol.	subd.	758
11 Dec. 1345 u.s.	Simon de Cherleton	subd.	all holy not recd.	796

TABLE 3   435

Date and place	Name and description	Order	Licence for Order(s) of:	Edition nos.
16 Sept. 1346 Withington	Nicholas Janyny, calling himself r. of Hampton Bishop		pst.[1]	798
3 Oct. 1345 Blockley	Gydicunte de Pillardynton	acol.	all holy	799
12 June 1346 Winchcombe	John Radeford of Sherborne	subd.	deac. & pst.	800
12 Mar. 1346 Hartlebury	William de Ʒerdel'	acol.	all holy	802
7 Sept. 1345 Withington	William Fabre of Ampney Crucis	acol.	subd.	804
21 May 1345 Bredon	William de Lodynton, *literatus*		all holy not recd.	807
4 Oct. 1346 Withington	Elias Canes of Eycote	acol.	subd. *et non ultra*	808
22 Apr. 1347 Hartlebury	Walter atte Hulle, clk.		acol. & all holy	809
19 July 1347 u.s.	William Smyth of Ampney Crucis	subd.	deac. & pst.	830
26 Feb. 1348 u.s.	William de Bradeweye		all holy	859
2 Mar. 1348 u.s.	John atte Halle of Sherborne		all holy	860
3 Mar. 1348	William Jordan		subd.	861
12 Mar. 1348	Henry Penne of Stratford-on-Avon	acol.	subd.	862
4 May 1348 Hartlebury	Robert de Haytfeld, r. of Coln St. Dennis		all holy	864
8 Aug. 1348 Withington	William Monfort of Aston-on-Carrant	acol.	all holy	908
22 May 1349	John de Chiltenham of Winchcombe	acol.	all holy	981
	Walter Henore of Little Rissington	acol.	all holy	
14 Mar.[1344]	Nicholas de Chiltenham		first tons.	1016
30 Mar. 1339	John called 'Le Longe' of Fairford	acol.	all holy	1022

[1] *cum ad eum recipiendum per ordinatorem tuum literatura moribus et etate inventus fueris idoneus, sibique titulum sufficientem exhibueris et aliud canonicum non obsistat.*

Date and place	Name and description	Order	Licence for Order(s) of:	Edition nos.
11 Mar. 1340	William de Weston Robert Westhrop of Cherrington	deac. subd.	pst. deac. & pst.	1023
1 May 1339 Hartlebury	Thomas, son of Philip le Mareschal of Longborough	acol.	subd.	1026
1 June 1339 Bredon	John de Thornbury		first tons.	1027
22 June 1339 Bredon	Thomas, son of Thomas called 'Bryd' of Malmesbury		all minor	1028
14 July 1339	John son of Henry Hewet of Northwick		all minor	1029
8 Aug. 1339 Wick by Worcester	Roger de Stanforde		all minor & major	1030
11 Sept. 1339 Hartlebury	William Budel of Marston Meysey & Walter Budel of the same		pst.	1031
11 Sept. 1339 u.s.	Walter de Caunpeden		subd. & deac.	1032
14 Sept. 1339 u.s.	John Goffe of Stow	deac.	pst.	1033
3 Nov. 1339 Pershore	John de Chiryton	deac.	pst.	1034
6 Nov. 1339 Honington	Alexander son of John Stappe of Honington		all holy	1035
4 Dec. 1339 Hartlebury	Br. John Groete Br. John de Lyndeweye, Br. Richard de Heny-feld, clk., canons of St. Augustine's Abb., Bristol		all holy	1036
13 Dec. 1339 u.s.	Br. John de Lyndeweye, canon of St. Augustine's Abb., Bristol		acol.	1037
16 Feb. 1340 Broadwell	William le Palmere of Sezincote		first tons.	1038

TABLE 3   437

Date and place	Name and description	Order	Licence for Order(s) of:	Edition nos.
(16 Feb. 1340 Broadwell)	John de Rotcote of Longborough Richard son of Henry de Langebergh		(first tons.)	(1038)
18 Feb. 1340 Great Barrington	John Kyng of Winchcombe	first tons.	all minor & major	1039
19 Feb. 1340 u.s.	John Gorgan & William, his brother german, *literati*		first tons.	1040
23 Feb. 1340 Chedworth	Stephen ate Halle of Kings Weston	subd.	deac.	1041
28 Apr. 1344 Hartlebury	Richard le Walkere of Swell	acol.	all holy	1210
30 July 1349 u.s.	Henry Baldewene, clk.		all minor not recd. & all holy	1343

TABLE 4

Analysis of Licences for absence from ecclesiastical benefices

LICENCES FOR STUDY

Granted to:	Duration	Edition nos.
1 Rector of Clent	1 yr.	161
2 Rector of St. Andrew's, Worcester	6 mths.	166
3 Rector of Pirton	1 yr.	167
4 Rector of St. Swithin's, Worcester	1 yr.	173
5 Rector of Miserden (and to farm)	1 yr.	186, 193
6 Dean of Warwick	1 yr.	190
7 Rector of Pucklechurch	1 yr.	194
8 Rector of Tortworth	1 yr.	210
9 Rector of Horton	1 yr.	216
10 Rector of St. Andrew's, Worcester	1 yr.	220

Granted to:	Duration	Edition nos.
11 Rector of Sapperton (and to farm)	2 yrs.	221
12 Rector of Hanbury	1 yr.	222
13 Rector of Billesley	1 yr.	223
14 Rector of Dorsington	1 yr.	224
15 Rector of Evenlode (and to farm)	1 yr.	225
16 Rector of Little Rissington	1 yr.	238
17 Rector of Cherrington (Wa.)	1 yr.	250
18 Rector of Tortworth	1 yr.	345
19 Rector of Coln St. Dennis	2 yrs.	350
20 Rector of Horton	2 yrs.	355
21 Rector of Clifford	1 yr.	358
22 Rector of St. Andrew's, Worcester	2 yrs.	363
23 Rector of [St. Michael's, Gloucester]	2 yrs.	364
24 Rector of [Whatcote]	1 yr.	373
25 Rector of Daglingworth (and to farm)	1 yr.	396
26 Rector of Hawling (and to farm)	1 yr. 5 mths.	401
27 Rector of Bishampton	5 yrs.	433
28 Rector of St. Martin's, Worcester (and to farm)	2 yrs.	448
29 Rector of Kymenhale portion in Leigh (and to farm)	3 yrs.	507
30 Rector of St. Stephen's, Bristol	1 yr.	508
31 Rector of Halford	1 yr.	528
32 Rector of Barnsley	2 yrs.	543
33 Rector of Winstone	1 yr.	544
34 Rector of Withington	2 yrs.	585
35 Rector of [Compton Wyniates]	1 yr.	589
36 Rector of Quinton		615
37 Rector of Pedmore	1 yr.	705
38 Rector of Honington	3 yrs.	709
39 Rector of Suckley	2 yrs.	710
40 Rector of Broadwell	1 yr.	718, 757
41 Rector of Nympsfield (and to farm)	4 yrs.	736
42 Rector of [Eastleach St. Andrew]	1 yr.	801
43 Rector of Pedmore	1 yr.	849
44 Rector of Kemerton	1 yr.	910
45 Rector of Eastleach		1015

62 yrs. 11 mths.

LICENCES FOR ABSENCE

Granted to:	Duration	Edition nos.
1 Rector of Bredon	5 yrs.	191
2 Rector of St. Michael's, Gloucester	1 yr.	192

TABLE 4   439

Granted to:	Duration	Edition nos.
3 Rector of Lasborough		208
4 Rector of Weston-on-Avon	2 yrs.	211
5 Rector of St. Martin's, Worcester (and to farm)	3 yrs	234
6 Rector of Eckington (and to farm)	3 yrs.	278
7 Rector of Rodmarton	2 yrs.	313
8 Rector of Salwarpe	1 yr.	317
9 Rector of Miserden (and to farm)	1 yr.	327
10 Rector of Alcester	1 yr.	335
11 Rector of Bagendon (and to farm)	1 yr.	337
12 Rector of Acton Turville (and to farm)	2 yrs.	343
13 Rector of Billesley	1 yr.	344
14 Rector of Fulbrook	2 yrs.	346
15 Rector of Weston Birt	1 yr.	356
16 Rector of Wickwar	8 mths.	385
17 Rector of St. Swithin's, Worcester (and to farm)	1 yr.	398
18 Rector of Miserden (and to farm)	1 yr.	424
19 Rector of Billesley	2 yrs.	429
20 Rector of Coln St. Dennis	2 yrs.	436
21 Rector of [Ripple] and to farm	1 yr.	474
22 Rector of Pucklechurch	1 yr.	480
23 Vicar of Tirley	7 wks.	493
24 Rector of Severn Stoke	1 yr.	498
25 Rector of Hampton Bishop	2 yrs.	514
26 Rector of [Coln] St. Dennis	1 yr.	548
27 Rector of Pillerton (and to farm)	3 yrs.	552, 696
28 Rector of Churchill	2 yrs.	559
29 Rector of Miserden	1 yr.	614
30 Rector of St. Werburgh's, Bristol	1 yr.	732, 739
31 Rector of Coln St. Dennis	2 yrs.	741
32 Rector of St. Andrew's, Worcester	1 yr.	820
33 Rector of Abbots Morton	1 yr.	821
34 Rector of Cam	2 yrs.	909

51 yrs 8 mths. 7 wks.

LICENCES TO ATTEND PROMINENT PERSONS

Granted to:	For attendance upon:	Duration	Edition nos.
1 Rector of Fretherne	John de Sapy, kt.	1 yr.	168
2 Rector of St. Stephen's, Bristol	Abbess of Shaftesbury	1 yr.	201

	Granted to:	For attendance upon:	Duration	Edition nos.
3	Rector of Stow	William de Everdone, r. of Fladbury	1 yr.	209
4	Rector of St. Michael's, Worcester	Isabella de Clare	1 yr.	215
5	Rector of Harvington	Prior of Worcester	1 yr.	233
6	Rector of Pirton (and to farm)	M. John de Gaddesdene	1 yr. 8 mths.	246
7	Rector of Littleton	Abbot of Malmesbury	1 yr.	263
8	Rector of Shipton Moyne	Robert Selymon, kt.	1 yr. 4 mths.	315
9	Rector of St. Andrew's, Droitwich	Hugh le Despenser		336
10	Rector of Haresfield	Thomas Charlton, Bp. of Hereford	2 yrs.	338
11	Rector of St. Helen's, Worcester	Thomas Charlton, Bp. of Hereford	2 yrs.	338
12	Rector of Fretherne	John de Sapy, kt.	1 yr.	339
13	Rector of Dyrham (and to farm)	Prior of Lewes in Ct. of Canterbury	2 yrs.	342
14	Rector of St. Stephen's, Bristol	Abbess of Shaftesbury	11 mths.	360
15	Rector of Didmarton	Prior of Bath	1 yr.	380
16	Rector of Badminton	Earl of Lancaster	1 yr.	395
17	Rector of Boxwell	Abbot of Cirencester	1 yr.	423
18	Rector of Twyning	Bp. of Chichester	indef.	510
19	Rector of Miserden (and to farm)	Bp. of Durham	2 yrs.	522
20	Rector of Whichford	Hugh of Audley, e. of Gloucester	1 yr.	706, 708
21	Rector of Broughton Hackett	John Handlowe, kt.	1 yr.	803

23 yrs. 11 mths.

TABLE 4   441

LICENCES TO FARM BENEFICES

Granted to:	Duration	Edition nos.
1 Rector of Miserden (and to study)	1 yr.	186, 193
2 Rector of Witley	2 yrs.	202
3 Rector of Sapperton (and to study)	2 yrs.	221
4 Rector of Evenlode (and to study)	1 yr.	225
5 Rector of St. Martin's, Worcester (and to be absent)	3 yrs.	234
6 Rector of Pirton (and to attend)	1 yr. 8 mths.	246
7 Rector of Daylesford	3 yrs.	252
8 Rector of Hatherop	1 yr.	265
9 Rector of Eckington (and to be absent)	3 yrs.	278
10 Dean of Warwick (for his deanery)	1 yr.	309
11 Rector of Miserden (and to be absent)	1 yr.	327
12 Rector of Bagendon (and to be absent)	1 yr.	337
13 Rector of Dyrham (and to attend)	2 yrs.	342
14 Rector of Acton Turville (and to be absent)	2 yrs.	343
15 Rector of Daglingworth (and to study)	1 yr.	396
16 Rector of St. Swithin's, Worcester (and to be absent)	1 yr.	398
17 Rector of Hawling (and to study)	1 yr. 5 mths.	401
18 Rector of Miserden (and to be absent)	1 yr.	424
19 Rector of St. Martin's, Worcester (and to study)	2 yrs.	448
20 Rector of [Ripple] (and to be absent)	1 yr.	474
21 Rector of Barford	1 yr.	483
22 Rector of Kymenhale portion in Leigh (and to study)	3 yrs.	507
23 Rector of Bredon (for Cutsdean Chapel)	3 yrs.	545
24 Rector of Pillerton (and to be absent)	3 yrs.	552, 696
25 Rector of Barford	2 yrs.	588
26 A. & C. of Gloucester (for South Cerney R.)	3 yrs.	590
27 Rector of Churchill	3 yrs.	704
28 Rector of Nympsfield (and to study)	4 yrs.	736
29 Rector of St. Michael's, Worcester	1 yr.	831
30 Abbot of Chester (for Campden R.)	3 yrs.	892

58 yrs. 1 mth.

TABLE 5
Numerical Details of Ordinations

The list of ordinations is by no means complete. For 1342 there is only one ordination record and perhaps part of another. Some lists for 1344 are missing, others are incomplete. All the lists for 1347, apart from that of 18 February—a very small one—and all save one for 1348, have been lost. Other extant lists are incomplete, this fact being indicated in the table by an asterisk.

Ordinations were commonly held on Saturdays of the *Quatuor Tempora* or four seasons of Embertide. These followed the first Sunday in Lent, Pentecost, the Exaltation and St. Lucy respectively. The bishop also held regular ordinations on Holy Saturday and the eve of Passion Sunday, and irregularly at other times.

Ordinations to the first tonsure (1006, 1007, 1020, 1021, 1074–1107) have been omitted.

Abbreviations:

R. – Regular clergy
S. – Secular clergy
T. – Total

Date	Season	Place	Acolytes			Subdeacons			Deacons			Priests			Totals	Edition no.
			R.	S.	T.	R.	S.	T.	R.	S.	T.	R.	S.	T.		
1339																
27 Mar.	Holy Saturday	Kempsey ch.	4	3	7	4	1	5	4	8	12	4	10	14	38	1004
22 May	Eve of Trinity (Sat. in Embertide)	Tewkesbury abb.	7	146	153	18	102	120	20	113	133	?	54*	54	460*	1008
1340																
1 Apr.	Saturday, Eve of Passion Sunday	Kidderminster	0	28	28	0	28	28	0	12	12	3	30	33	101	1009
15 Apr. [1342?]	Holy Saturday	Alvechurch ch.	0	0	0	0	1	1	0	1	1	3	0	3	5	1010
Undated			?	?	?	?	3*	3	13	31	44	22	29	51	98*	1042

TABLE 5   443

Date	Occasion	Place														Total	No.
1342 21 Dec.	Saturday in Embertide after St.Lucy	Hartlebury ch.	4	5	9	6	9	15	5	9	14	8	12	20	58	1049
1343 8 Mar.	Saturday in the 1st week of Lent (Embertide)	Cheltenham ch.	5	28	33	12	10	22	8	12	20	9	20	29	104	1050
9 Mar.	2nd Sunday in Lent	Withington, bp.'s chapel	2	0	2	0	0	0	0	0	0	0	0	0	2	1068
29 Mar.	Saturday, Eve of Passion Sunday	Bredon, bp.'s chapel	0	6	6	5	3	8	6	3	9	1	1	2	25	1051
12 Apr.	Holy Saturday	Hartlebury ch.	0	0	0	0	3	3	1	3	4	1	3	4	11	1052
7 June	Eve of Trinity (Sat. in Embertide)	Hartlebury ch.	5	14	19	4	8	12	4	10	14	7	11	18	63	1053
20 Sept.	Saturday in Embertide after the Exaltation	Bishops Cleeve ch.	5	17	22	13	15	28	11	14	25	11	28	39	114	1054
20 Dec.	Saturday in Embertide after St. Lucy	Hartlebury ch.	1	6	7	9	?	9*	?	?	?	?	?	?	16*	1055
1344 20 Mar.	Saturday, Eve of Passion Sunday	Hartlebury, bp.'s chapel	0	0	0	0	4	4	1	0	1	0	2	2	7	1056
3 Apr.	Holy Saturday	Hartlebury ch.	1	2	3	0	4	4	0	5	5	1	1	2	14	1057
9 May	Rogation Sunday	Hartlebury	3	0	3	0	0	0	0	0	0	0	0	0	3	560
29 May	Eve of Trinity (Sat. in Embertide)	Campden ch.	16	24	40	11	21	32	6	30	36	?	?	?	108*	1058

Date	Season	Place	Acolytes			Subdeacons			Deacons			Priests			Totals	Edition no.
			R.	S.	T.	R.	S.	T.	R.	S.	T.	R.	S.	T.		
[1344?] 18 Dec.[?]			?	?	?	?	5	5	8	12	20	14	9	23	48*	1059
1345 6 Feb.	Quinquagesima Sunday	Hartlebury, bp.'s chapel	0	3	3	0	0	0	0	0	0	0	0	0	3	692
19 Feb.	Saturday in the 1st week of Lent (Embertide)	Hartlebury ch.	5	12	17	9	15	24	2	13	15	3	13	16	72	1060
20 Feb.	2nd Sunday in Lent	Hartlebury	0	1	1	0	0	0	0	0	0	0	0	0	1	701
12 Mar.	Saturday, Eve of Passion Sunday	Hartlebury, bp.'s chapel	0	0	0	3	3	6	7	7	12	3	5	8	26	1061
26 Mar.	Holy Saturday	Hartlebury ch.	0	0	0	0	7	7	2	2	4	0	6	6	17	1063
27 Mar.	Easter Day	Hartlebury, bp.'s chapel	0	3	3	0	0	0	0	0	0	0	0	0	3	1062
21 May	Saturday in Embertide after Pentecost	Tewkesbury abb.	6	62	68	9	31	40	9	20	29	19	20	39	176	1064
24 Sept.	Saturday in Embertide after the Exaltation	Campden ch.	1	13	14	4	16	20	1	18	19	6	21	27	80	1066
17 Dec.	Saturday in Embertide after St. Lucy	Hartlebury, bp.'s chapel	0	0	0	9	6	15	11	9	20	1	6	7	42	1067
1346 11 Mar.	Saturday in the 1st week of Lent (Embertide)	Hartlebury ch.	4	23	27	11	20	31	11	22	33	12	22	34	125	1069

Date	Feast	Place													Total	No.
1 Apr.	Saturday, Eve of Passion Sunday	Hartlebury bp.'s chapel	0	0	0	2	1	3	1	3	4	2	1	3	10	1070
15 Apr.	Holy Saturday	Hartlebury ch.	0	0	0	0	3	3	0	4	4	2	5	7	14	1071
10 June	Saturday in Embertide after Pentecost	Tewkesbury abb.	4	65	69	17	27	44	18	17	35	14	28	42	190	1072
23 Sept.	Saturday in Embertide after the Exaltation	Stow ch.	18	75	93	13	22	35	18	30	48	25	31	56	232	1073
1347 18 Feb.	Quadragesima Sunday		0	2	2	0	0	0	0	0	0	0	0	0	2	1065
1348 20 Dec.	Saturday in Embertide after St. Lucy	Hartlebury, bp.'s chapel	3	15	18	1	13	14	4	15	19	5	20	25	76	1108
1349 7 Mar.	Saturday in the 1st week of Lent (Embertide)	Hartlebury, bp.'s chapel	6	34	40	4	49	53	2	27	29	7	25	32	154	1109
28 Mar.	Saturday, Eve of Passion Sunday	Hartlebury, bp.'s chapel	0	0	0	3	18	21	0	35	35	0	18	18	74	1110
29 Mar.	Passion Sunday		0	6	6	0	0	0	0	0	0	0	0	0	6	1111
11 Apr.	Holy Saturday	Hartlebury, bp.'s chapel	0	0	0	1	20	21	0	20	20	0	31	31	72	1339
19 Apr.	Quasimodo Sunday	Hartlebury, bp.'s chapel	0	5	5	0	0	0	0	0	0	0	0	0	5	1112
31 May	Whit Sunday	Hartlebury bp.'s chapel	0	3	3	0	0	0	0	0	0	0	0	0	3	1340

TABLE 5

TABLE 5

Date	Season	Place	Acolytes			Subdeacons			Deacons			Priests			Totals	Edition no.
			R.	S.	T.	R.	S.	T.	R.	S.	T.	R.	S.	T.		
1349 6 June	Eve of Trinity (Sat. in Embertide)	Hartlebury, bp.'s chapel	3	51	54	8	37	45	11	26	37	12	23	35	171	1341
22 July	St Mary Magdalene	Hartlebury, bp.'s chapel	1	1	2	0	0	0	0	0	0	0	0	0	2	1342
			104	653	757	176	505	681	182	531	713	195	485	680	2831	

TABLE 6   447

TABLE 6

Licences for Oratories

Date of licence	Location of oratory	Beneficiary	Duration	Edition no.
30 Mar. 1339	*Walbrok* in Halesowen parish	John de Honesworth	2 yrs.	25
10 Apr. 1339	Naunton Beauchamp	Thomas de Newynton		37
7 May 1339	Broadway	Henry de Bradeweye	*quociens sibi placuerit*	47
29 July 1339	Woodcroft and Charlton	John de Cheltenham	2 yrs.	68
1 Aug. 1339	Whitefield and Admington	William de Adelmynton	3 yrs.	69
1 Aug. 1339	Wood Bevington	Emma Wilkynes		70
11 Sept. 1339	Westbury[?], in his prebendal house	M. John de Trilleck, r. of Bredon		82
11 Sept. 1339	Hill and Hollybed	Robert de Longedon	1 yr.	83
7 Oct. 1339	Prinknash	Abbot of St. Peter's, Gloucester		95
9 Jan. 1340	St. Augustine's abbey, Bristol, and Berkeley castle	Ds. William de Syde		240
13 Jan. 1340	*Hilyngwyk*	Margaret, widow of Richard Bikerton		247
8 Feb. 1340	Alderton	John Besemancel		251
14 Feb. 1340	Badminton and Weston sub-Edge	Thomas Boteller, kt.	2 yrs.	255
3 Mar. 1340	Minchinhampton and Down Hatherley	John de Anseleye, kt.		267
5 Mar. 1340	Uley	Simon Basset, kt.		270
6 Mar. 1340	Daneway (*Deneweye*) in Bisley parish	Henry de Clyfford and his wife, Matilda	2 yrs.	271
6 Mar. 1340	Alderton	Margery Bartram	2 yrs.	272
7 Mar. 1340	......	Robert Dabitot		273
8 Mar. 1340	Uley (6 priests)	Maurice de Berkeley	2 yrs.	274
8 Mar. 1340	......	Henry de Brocworth		275
8 Mar. 1340	Brockworth	William de Mathesdene	2 yrs.	276
11 Mar. 1340	Longdon and Hollybed in Castle Morton parish [?]	Robert de Longedon	2 yrs.	277
10 May 1340	Blakeley	John Huwet of Rowley		310
26 June 1341	Dumbleton and Wormington	Walter Dastyn, kt.		412
29 Aug. 1341	Billesley	Warin Trussel, kt., and his wife, Matilda	2 yrs.	430

Date of licence	Location of oratory	Beneficiary	Duration	Edition no.
2 June 1342	*Schrigg* in Pucklechurch parish	Thomas de Shyrigg	until revoked	466
2 June 1342	. . . . . .	Walter Whyt and his wife, Isabella	during illness	468
14 June 1342	Pucklechurch	William de Cheltenham	until revoked	467
15 June 1342	Bristol	Roger Tortele and his wife, Juliana		470
28 June 1342	St. Chloe (*Senkeleye*)	William de Tedyrhynton	until revoked	471
2 June 1343	Lapworth	Hugh de Brandeston		511
2 June 1343	Morton Foliot	Thomas de Morton Folet	until revoked	512
16 June 1343	Southam in Bishops Cleeve parish	Thomas de Aumondisham		513
6 Aug. 1343	Parish of St. Nicholas, Bristol	John Horncastel	until revoked	1017
7 Aug. 1343	*La Lee* manor in Henley parish	Roger de Lemesey, kt.	until revoked	1018
18 Sept. 1343	Salford	Agnes Austyn of Salford		587
19 Oct. 1343	Cheltenham parish	Eleanor, widow of John de Chyltenham		549
17 July 1345	Crookbarrow in parish of St. Peter, Worcester	Edmund Hakelute, his wife, and M. Thomas de Hakelute	1 yr.	728
19 July 1345		Elias de Filton and his wife, Emma	until revoked	729
16 Aug. 1345	Kings Weston in Henbury parish	William de Syde		730
26 Aug. 1345	*Uphovere*	John Uphovere	during infirmity	733

TABLE 7   449

TABLE 7

The Pagination and Binding of the Register

(See the introduction, p. i *et seq.*)

PAGINATION—VOLUME ONE

Numeration: Original (Roman)	Additional (Arabic)	Corrected (including lost folios
i	1	
iii [1]	2	
iii	3	
iv	4	

The numbers then advance *pari passu* until fo. 81.

lxxxi	81	
lxxxiii [2]	82	83

The Roman numerals continue one in advance of the Arabic until fo. cxiiii (113).

cxiiii	113	
cxv	115	

The numbers then advance *pari passu* until fo. 121.

cxxi	121	
cxxii	121	

The Roman numerals continue one in advance of the Arabic until fo. cxxix (128).

cxxix	128	
Omitted [3]	129	130
cxxx	130	131

The numbers then advance *pari passu* but one below the true folio number until fo. cxliiii (144).

cxliiii	144	145
Illegible	145	146
cxlv	146	147
cxlvi	147	148

In the register as at present bound there is a gap until fo. ccxviii which, as the Arabic numerals continue straight on, is also numbered 148. Assuming that there were no further errors in the Roman numerals this folio should have been numbered 220. Some of the intervening folios have been bound after volume two but are inserted here in their proper place.[4]

cxlvii	47	149

---

[1] *Recte* ii.

[2] There was a fo. lxxxii as the last sentence on fo. lxxxi v. is incomplete and not continued on the folio numbered lxxxiii. Moreover, two stubs follow fo. lxxxi (81), on the first of which are traces of writing.

[3] The verso of this folio has an entry continued on fo. cxxx, so it is in its correct place. The scribe when numbering the folios must have turned over two leaves at once.

[4] Their present order is given below. While separated from the register many folios were lost and others became disarranged.

Numeration: Original (Roman)	Additional (Arabic)	Corrected (including lost folios)
cxlviii	48	150
cxlix	34	151
cl	35	152
Four folios missing.		
clv	39	157
clvi	40	158
clvii [1]	49	159
clviii	50	160
Twelve folios missing.		
clxxi	12	173
clxxii	13	174
clxxiii	14	175
clxxiiii	15	176
clxxv	16	177
clxxvi	17	178
clxxvii	18	179
clxxviii	19	180
clxxix [2]	?	181 ?
Two folios missing.		
clxxxii	43	184
clxxxiii	44	185
Two folios missing.		
clxxxvi [4]	82	188
clxxxvii	62	189
clxxxviii	63	190
clxxxix	64	191
clxxxx	65	192
clxxxxi	67 (sic)	193
clxxxxii	68	194
clxxxxiii	69	195
clxxxxiiii	70	196
clxxxxv	71	197
clxxxxvi	72	198
clxxxxvii(?)	73	199
clxxxxviii	74	200
Thirteen folios missing.		
ccxii	77	214

[1] No such number can be traced now, but the subject matter shows that this folio should precede fo. clviii.

[2] This number is very faint, but the folio was part of the sheet containing fo. clxxxvi. This sheet was probably the outside one of a quire of 4 sheets which contained ff. clxxxii and clxxxiii as the centre sheet. The remainder of the quire has been lost.

[3] This folio has been put back in its proper order. It formed part of a quire the remaining two sheets of which are now in the wrong place. See the previous note.

[4] This folio is considerably torn and faded. This fact, and its Arabic number 82, indicate that it was at one time the outside folio of the detached leaves and followed ccxv 80 (Arabic 81 is missing).

TABLE 7   451

Numeration: Original (*Roman*)	*Additional* (*Arabic*)	*Corrected* (*including lost folios*)
ccxiii	78	215
ccxiiii	79	216
ccxv	80	217

The next two folios are missing. The remainder are correctly bound in volume one.

ccxviii	148	220

Both sets of numbers increase uniformly until:

ccxxiiii	154	226
ccxxv	156 (*sic*) [1]	227

Both sets again increase uniformly until:

ccli	182	253
ccliii [2]	183	254
ccliiii	184	255

Fo. cclv (185) is missing.

cclvi	186	257
cclvii	187	258

PAGINATION–VOLUME 2

The first folio is numbered i (Roman) and 2 (Arabic). The Roman numerals, which are small, cease at v (6). This suggests that they represent a temporary foliation of a loose gathering. The Arabic numerals continue until the final folio (19).

Present order of the folios bound after Volume 2

cxlvii	47
[&c. as in the above list]	
clxxviii	19
clxxxii	43
clxxix (?)	?
clxxxvii	62
clxxxviii	63
[&c. as above]	
clxxxxviii	74
clxxxvi	82
clxxxiii	44
ccxii	77
[&c. as above]	
ccxv	80 (last folio)

[1] Although the scribe made a slip and wrote ccvi for ccxxvi (157).

[2] It seems probable that there never was a fo. cclii.

BINDING–VOLUME 1

Quires	Folios	Details (See Table 8)
1	12 (6 sheets)	Flyleaf to folio 11
2	10 (5 sheets)	fo. 12 to fo. 21
3	4 (3 sheets)	fo. 22 to fo. 25. 2 folios removed
4	13 (7 sheets)	fo. 26 to fo. 38. 1 folio removed. Fragment of MS. between ff. 28 and 29
5	9 (5 sheets)	fo. 39 to fo. 47. 1 folio removed
6	12 (6 sheets)	fo. 48 to fo. 59
7	8 (4 sheets)	fo. 60 to fo. 67
8	8 (4 sheets)	fo. 68 to fo. 75
9	6 (4 sheets)	fo. 76 to fo. 81. 2 folios removed
10	12 (6 sheets)	fo. 82 to fo. 93 (lxxxxiiii)
11	12 (6 sheets)	fo. 94 to fo. 105 (cvi)
12	12 (6 sheets)	fo. 106 to fo. 118 (cxviii)
13	10 (5 sheets)	fo. 119 to fo. 127 (cxxviii)
14	12 (6 sheets)	fo. 128 to fo. 139 (cxxxix)
15	8 (4 sheets)	fo. 140 to fol 147 (cxlvi) fo. 147 (cxlvi). Verso blank
16	12 (6 sheets)	fo. 148 to fo. 160 (ccxxix)
17	10 (5 sheets)	fo. 161 to fo. 170 (ccxxxix)
18	14 (7 sheets)	fo. 171 to fo. 184 (ccliiii)
Two separate folios have been added at this point.		
	2	ff. 186 (cclvi) and 187 (cclvii). No folio 185
Total	186	

BINDING—VOLUME 2

Odd folios	2	ff. 2 and 3 (i and ii)
1	4 (2 sheets)	fo. 4 to fo. 7
Odd folios	2	ff. 8 and 9
2	8 (4 sheets)	fo. 10 to fo. 17
Odd folios	2	ff. 18 and 19
Total	18	

Folios bound after Volume 2 (properly belonging to vol. 1)

1	8 (4 sheets)	fo. 47 (cxlvii) to fo. 50 (clviii)
2	8 (4 sheets)	fo. 12 (clxxi) to fo. 19 (clxxviii)
3	16 (8 sheets)	fo. 43 (clxxxii) to fo. 44 (clxxxiii)
4	4 (2 sheets)	fo. 77 (ccxii) to fo. 80 (ccxv)
Total	36	

TABLE 8   453

TABLE 8

Collation of MS. Folios and Edition Numbers

The folio numbers have been omitted from the text, but they can be readily found from the following table. The register has a double numeration, Arabic and Roman (see the introduction, p. i *et seq.*). Where these coincide only the Arabic numbers are given; where they differ, both Arabic and Roman are set out. After fo. 147 al. cxlvi the Roman numerals precede the Arabic because of the latter's disorder.

MS. folio	Edition nos.	MS. folio	Edition nos.
Fly-leaf verso	1–4	19 v.	139–142
1 recto	5–10	20 r.	142–147
1 verso	11–17	20 v.	147–152
2 r. iii	17–18	21 r.	153
2 v. iii	18–19	21 v.	153
3 r.	19–23	22 r.	153
3 v.	24–27	22 v.	153–154
4 r.	27–31	23 r.	154
4 v.	32–37	23 v.	154–157
5 r.	38–40	24 r.	158–159
5 v.	40–45	24 v.	159–160
6 r.	45–50	25 r.	160
6 v.	51–57	25 v.	160
7 r.	58–61	26 r.	161–171
7 v.	62–66	26 v.	171–178
8 r.	67–73	27 r.	178–183
8 v.	74–78	27 v.	183–194
9 r.	78–81	28 r.	195–201
9 v.	82–88	28 v.	202–211
10 r.	89	29 r.	211–216
10 v.	90–94	Attached	
11 r.	94–98	portion of MS.	217
11 v.	98–101	29 r. (cont.)	218–222
12 r.	102	29 v.	223–228
12 v.	102–104	30 r.	228–232
13 r.	105–107	30 v.	232–240
13 v.	108	31 r.	241–243
14 r.	108–111	31 v.	244–245
14 v.	112–116	32 r.	246–253
15 r.	116	32 v.	254–257
15 v.	117	33 r.	258–266
16 r.	117	33 v.	267–275
16 v.	117–118	34 r.	276–281
17 r.	119	34 v.	282–286
17 v.	120–121	35 r.	287–289
18 r.	122–126	35 v.	290–292
18 v.	126–133	36 r.	292–296
19 r.	134–138	36 v.	296–299

MS. folio	Edition nos.	MS. folio	Edition nos.
37 r.	299–303	60 v.	531–532
37 v.	304–312	61 r.	532–533
38 r.	313–318	61 v.	533–535
38 v.	318	62 r.	535–540
39 r.	318–321	62 v.	541–554
39 v.	321–324	63 r.	555–561
40 r.	325	63 v.	562–564
40 v.	325	64 r.	565–568
41 r.	326–329	64 v.	568–571
41 v.	329–335	65 r.	572–574
42 r.	336–341	65 v.	575–576
42 v.	341–348	66 r.	577–580
43 r.	348–351	66 v.	580–581
43 v.	351–360	67 r.	581–583
44 r.	361–364	67 v.	583–592
44 v.	365–366	68 r.	593–595
45 r.	366–368	68 v.	595–597
45 v.	368–374	69 r.	597–598
46 r.	374–379	69 v.	599–602
46 v.	380–388	70 r.	602
47 r.	388–395	70 v.	603–608
47 v.	396–402	71 r.	609–617
48 r.	403–407	71 v.	618–619
48 v.	408–416	72 r.	619–623
49 r.	416–418	72 v.	623–627
49 v.	419–424	73 r.	627–633
50 r.	425–431	73 v.	634–640
50 v.	432–439	74 r.	640–643
51 r.	439–442	74 v.	644–649
51 v.	443–448	75 r.	649–654
52 r.	449	75 v.	654–657
52 v.	449	76 r.	658
53 r.	450	76 v.	658
Attached portion of MS.	451	77 r.	659
53 v.	452–459	77 v.	659
54 r.	460–464	78 r.	660
54 v.	465–477	78 v.	660
55 r.	478–484	79 r.	660–661
55 v.	485–488	79 v.	661
56 r.	488–492	80 r.	661–662
56 v.	493–499	80 v.	663–667
57 r.	500–504	81 r.	668–669
57 v.	505–514	81 v.	669–670
58 r.	515–518	82 r. lxxxiii	671–675
58 v.	519–523	82 v. lxxxiii	676–680
59 r.	524–525	83 r. lxxxiiii	681
59 v.	526–529	83 v. lxxxiiii	681–683
60 r.	530–531	84 r. lxxxv	684
		84 v. lxxxv	684

TABLE 8   455

MS. folio	Edition nos.	MS. folio	Edition nos.
85 r. lxxxvi	684	108 v. cix	834
85 v. lxxxvi	684–687	109 r. cx	834
86 r. lxxxvii	688–699	109 v. cx	834–835
86 v. lxxxvii	700–713	110 r. cxi	835
87 r. lxxxviii	714–718	110 v. cxi	835
87 v. lxxxviii	719–722	111 r. cxii	836
88 r. lxxxix	723–734	111 v. cxii	836–837
88 v. lxxxix	735	112 r. cxiii	837–838
89 r. lxxxx	735	112 v. cxiii	838–840
89 v. lxxxx	735–742	Attached	
90 r. lxxxxi	743–745	portion of MS.	841
90 v. lxxxxi	746	113 r. cxiiii	842–844
91 r. lxxxxii	747–749	113 v. cxiiii	845–850
91 v. lxxxxii	750	No folio 114	
92 r. lxxxxiii	750–752	(Arabic)	
92 v. lxxxxiii	753–758	115 r. cxv	851–855
93 r. lxxxxiiii	759–761	115 v. cxv	855–858
93 v. lxxxxiiii	762–767	116 r.	859–865
94 r. lxxxxv	768–772	116 v.	866–868
94 v. lxxxxv	773–774	117 r.	869–871
95 r. lxxxxvi	775–777	117 v.	871–875
95 v. lxxxxvi	778–779	118 r.	875–879
96 r. lxxxxvii	779–780	118 v.	880–884
96 v. lxxxxvii	781	119 r.	885
97 r. lxxxxviii	781	119 v.	885–887
97 v. lxxxxviii	781–782	120 r.	888–890
98 r. lxxxxix	782–783	120 v.	891–894
98 v. lxxxxix	784–786	121 r. cxxi	895–897
99 r. c	786	121 v. cxxi	898–901
99 v. c	786–788	121 r. (bis) cxxii	902–905
100 r. ci	788–790	121 v. cxxii	906
100 v. ci	790–792	122 r. cxxiii	906
101 r. cii	792	122 v. cxxiii	906
101 v. cii	792–796	123 r. cxxiiii	906
102 r. ciii	797–809	123 v. cxxiiii	906
102 v. ciii	810–811	124 r. cxxv	906
103 r. ciiii	811–816	124 v. cxxv	906
103 v. ciiii	817–818	125 r. cxxvi	906–907
104 r. cv	818–821	125 v. cxxvi	907
Attached		126 r. cxxvii	907–910
portion of MS.	822	126 v. cxxvii	911–915
104 v. cv	823–826	127 r. cxxviii	916–919
105 r. cvi	826–831	127 v. cxxviii	920–925
105 v. cvi	832–833	128 r. cxxix	926–927
106 r. cvii	834	128 v. cxxix	927–929
106 v. cvii	834	129 r. (caret)	930–932
107 r. cviii	834	129 v. (caret)	933–934
107 v. cviii	834	130 r.	934–935
108 r. cix	834	130 v.	936–937

MS. folio		Edition nos.	MS. folio		Edition nos.
131 r.		938–939	clvii(?) r.	49	1020–1021
131 v.		940	clvii(?) v.	49	1021
132 r.		940	clviii r.	50	1021–1025
132 v.		940–941	clviii v.	50	1026–1041
133 r.		941	clxxi r.	12	1042
133 v.		941	clxxi v.	12	1042
134 r.		941	clxxii r.	13	1042–1043
134 v.		941	clxxii v.	13	1043
135 r.		941	clxxiii r.	14	1043–1044
135 v.		941	clxxiii v.	14	1044
136 r.		942	clxxiiii r.	15	1044–1045
136 v.		942	clxxiiii v.	15	1045–1046
137 r.		943	clxxv r.	16	1046–1048
137 v.		943–944	clxxv v.	16	1048–1049
138 r.		945	clxxvi r.	17	1049
138 v.		945	clxxvi v.	17	1050
139 r.		945	clxxvii r.	18	1050
139 v.		946–949	clxxvii v.	18	1051–1052
140 r.		950–951	clxxviii r.	19	1053
140 v.		952–954	clxxviii v.	19	1054
141 r.		954–961	clxxix r.	caret	1054
141 v.		962–968	clxxix v.	caret	1054–1055
142 r.		969	clxxxii r.	43	1056–1057
142 v.		969	clxxxii v.	43	1058
143 r.		969	clxxxiii r.	44	1058
143 v.		970–971	clxxxiii v.	44	1058
144 r.		972–973	clxxxvi r.	82	1059
144 v.		974–981	clxxxvi v.	82	1060
145 r.		982–988	clxxxvii r.	62	1060–1062
145 v.		989–994	clxxxvii v.	62	1063–1064
146 r.		995–998	clxxxviii r.	63	1064
146 v.		999–1001	clxxxviii v.	63	1064
147 r. cxlvi		1002–1003	clxxxix r.	64	1064–1066
147 v. cxlvi		Blank	clxxxix v.	64	1066
			clxxxx r.	65	1066–1067
(Rearranged folios, at present bound after volume 2)			clxxxx v.	65	1067–1068
			clxxxxi r.	67	1069
cxlvii r.	47	1004–1007	clxxxxi v.	67	1069
cxlvii v.	47	1008	clxxxxii r.	68	1069
cxlviii r.	48	1008	clxxxxii v.	68	1069–1070
cxlviii v.	48	1008	clxxxxiii r.	69	1070–1072
cxlix r.	34	1008	clxxxxiii v.	69	1072
cxlix v.	34	1008	clxxxxiiii r.	70	1072
cl r.	35	1008	clxxxxiiii v.	70	1072
cl v.	35	1008	clxxxxv r.	71	1072–1073
clv r.	39	1009	clxxxxv v.	71	1073
clv v.	39	1009	clxxxxvi r.	72	1073
clvi r.	40	1010–1018	clxxxxvi v.	72	1073
clvi v.	40	1019	clxxxxvii r.	73	1074–1083

TABLE 8　　　　　　　457

MS. folio		Edition nos.
clxxxxvii v.	73	1084–1089
clxxxxviii r.	74	1089–1099
clxxxxviii v.	74	1100–1107
ccxii r.	77	1108
ccxii v.	77	1108–1109
ccxiii r.	78	1109
ccxiii v.	78	1109
ccxiiii r.	79	1109
ccxiiii v.	79	1110
ccxv r.	80	1110
ccxv v.	80	1110–1112
ccxviii r.	148	1113–1115
ccxviii v.	148	1115–1116
Attached portion of MS.		1117
ccxviii v.) (contd.)	148	1118
ccxix r.	149	1118–1120
ccxix v.	149	1120–1122
ccxx r.	150	1123–1124
ccxx v.	150	1124–1126
ccxxi r.	151	1127–1130
ccxxi v.	151	1130–1133
ccxxii r.	152	1133–1135
ccxxii v.	152	1135–1138
ccxxiii r.	153	1139–1141
ccxxiii v.	153	1142–1143
ccxxiiii r.	154	1144
ccxxiiii v.	154	1145–1148
ccxxv r.	156	1148–1152
ccxxv v.	156	1153–1156
cc(xx)vi r.	157	1157–1159
cc(xx)vi v.	157	1160–1163
ccxxvii r.	158	1164–1167
ccxxvii v.	158	1168–1170
ccxxviii r.	159	1171–1173
ccxxviii v.	159	1174–1177
ccxxix r.	160	1178–1182
ccxxix v.	160	1183–1186
ccxxx r.	161	1187–1188
ccxxx v.	161	1188–1190
ccxxxi r.	162	1190–1192
ccxxxi v.	162	1193–1195
ccxxxii r.	163	1196–1197
ccxxxii v.	163	1198–1201
ccxxxiii r.	164	1202–1205
ccxxxiii v.	164	1206–1210
ccxxxiiii r.	165	1211

MS. folio		Edition nos.
ccxxxiiii v.	165	1211
ccxxxv r.	166	1212–1213
ccxxxv v.	166	1213–1215
ccxxxvi r.	167	1216–1218
ccxxxvi v.	167	1218
ccxxxvii r.	168	1219–1220
ccxxxvii v.	168	1220–1223
ccxxxviii r.	169	1223–1226
ccxxxviii v.	169	1227–1229
ccxxxix r.	170	1230–1233
ccxxxix v.	170	1234–1237
ccxl r.	171	1237–1240
ccxl v.	171	1241–1243
ccxli r.	172	1243–1245
ccxli v.	172	1245–1248
ccxlii r.	173	1249–1251
ccxlii v.	173	1252–1255
ccxliii r.	174	1256–1258
ccxliii v.	174	1259–1261
ccxliiii r.	175	1262–1265
ccxliiii v.	175	1265–1266
ccxlv r.	176	1267–1270
ccxlv v.	176	1270–1273
ccxlvi r.	177	1274–1276
ccxlvi v.	177	1276–1279
ccxlvii r.	178	1279–1282
ccxlvii v.	178	1283–1286
ccxlviii r.	179	1287–1289
ccxlviii v.	179	1290–1291
ccxlix r.	180	1291–1294
Attached portion of MS.		1295
ccxlix v.	180	1296–1298
ccl r.	181	1298–1301
ccl v.	181	1302–1304
ccli r.	182	1305–1307
Attached portion of MS.	r.	1308
	v.	1309
ccli v.	182	1310–1312
ccliii r.	183	1313–1315
ccliii v.	183	1316–1318
ccliiii r.	184	1319–1321
ccliiii v.	184	1322–1323
cclvi r.	186	1324–1325
cclvi v.	186	1326–1328
cclvii r.	187	1328

VOLUME 2		MS. folio	Edition nos.
MS. folio	Edition nos.	10 v.	1387–1399
2 r.	1329–1334	11 r.	1399–1411
2 v.	1334	11 v.	1412–1423
3 r.	1334–1338	12 r.	1423–1436
3 v.	1338	12 v.	1436–1449
4 r.	1339–1341	13 r.	1449–1455
4 v.	1341	13 v.	1455–1464
5 r.	1341–1343	14 r.	1464–1473
5 v.	1344–1347	14 v.	1474–1484
6 r.	1348–1352	15 r.	1484–1489
6 v.	1353–1356	15 v.	1490–1496
7 r.	1357–1361	16 r.	1496–1504
7 v.	1362	16 v.	1504–1506
Portion of MS.		17 r.	1507–1518
between ff. 4 & 5	1363	17 v.	1518–1529
Portion of MS.		18 r.	1529–1539
between ff. 6 & 7	1364	18 v.	1539–1550
8 r.	1365–1366	19 r.	1550–1561
8 v.	1367–1374	19 v.	1561–1568
9 r.	1374–1376		
10 r.	1377–1386	END OF VOLUME 2	

Appendix of
Original Documents

A note on the transcription of documents

The scribes of the Worcester registers in some respects allowed themselves considerable latitude. Thus 'p' and 'b' are often interchangeable, as in 'publicare' (puplicare), so too are 'm' and 'n' in certain cases (imperpetuum, inperpetuum), 'c' and 's' (cituato, situato), 'd' and 't' (sicud, sicut), 'e' and 'i' (deaconi, diaconi), 'y' and 'i' (Wygorn', Wigorn') &c. An 'h' may be added, as in 'inibi' (inhibi), or omitted, as in 'heres' (eres). No rule appears to have been observed with regard to the duplication of medial consonants. Thus we find 'ellectus' and 'electus', 'littera' and 'litera' &c. Other variations include the insertion of a 'c' in exercendum (excercendum), 'sumptibus' written as 'sumptubus' and the not infrequent use of the present infinitive active where we might expect the passive form, or of the indicative rather than the subjunctive mood ('sunt' instead of 'sint', 'fuerunt' for 'fuerint').

'Excercicium' is often rendered 'excercium'; 'infra' is sometimes used with the ablative, and 'in' with the accusative or ablative indifferently. It is often difficult to extend the enigmatic 'prox' of the MS. and 'proximo' seems to have been used as an adverb rather than 'proxime'. It is clear that 'c' was written in many cases where we might expect 't', as in 'circumspeccio', 'eleccio' &c. It is difficult if not impossible to distinguish 'v' and 'u', so modern practice has been followed in this respect. With regard to 'i' and 'j', the latter has been used in the case of proper nouns 'Johannes', 'dies Jovis' &c. In general, scribal peculiarities of construction and spelling have been preserved and only an occasional 'sic' has been inserted to point the more unusual of these.

One cannot be certain about the use of gerunds and gerundives. The evidence suggests that the scribes were not dogmatic about the matter and sometimes used either in entries having the same form. In extending the enigmatic *end* or *and* of the MS. the gerund has been preferred except where there is an indication that such was not the scribe's intention.

With punctuation, the rule has been to follow that of the MS. as far as possible, only adding or emending to establish the sense of a passage. The irregular use of capitals in the MS. has not been adopted.

Additional words, the extension of more doubtful contractions, the editorial '&c.', as well as other emendations have been enclosed within brackets in the usual way.

Dates have been rendered in the New Style.

APPENDIX OF ORIGINAL DOCUMENTS

Chantries

154 *5 July 1340* Inspeximus *and confirmation of Thomas de Berkeley of Coberley's ordination of a chantry in the church of St. Giles there.*

ORDINACIO CANTARIE BEATE MARIE DE CUBBERLEGH.

Universis sancte matris ecclesie filiis ad quorum noticiam presentes littere pervenerint, frater Wolstanus permissione divina Wygorn' episcopus, salutem in domino sempiternam. Noverit universitas vestra quod litteras nobilis viri domini Thome de Berkeleye de Cobberleye recepimus, inspeximus et vidimus diligenter, tenorem qui sequitur continentes: Christi fideles noverint universi quod ego Thomas de Berkel' de Coberl', attendens secundum apostolum quod omnes stabimus ante tribunal Christi[1] in magni et extremi iudicii examine, recepturi pro eo quod in corpore gessimus secundum merita vel demerita, gaudium vel merorem, volensque diem messionis extreme operibus misericordie quantum possum utiliter prevenire, et illud in terris seminare intuitu eternorum quod reddente domino cum multiplicato fructu recolligere valeam cum gloria in futuro, et de temporalium bonorum meorum usibus sic disponere ut michi ad adminicula spiritualium subsidia prosint in celestibus et in terris grata prestent proximis alimenta. Quapropter, de consensu et per cartam domini nostri domini Edwardi tercii regis Anglie illustris, cuius carte tenor inferius continetur, ordinavi et ordino per presentes unam perpetuam cantariam ad altare Beate Virginis in ecclesia Sancti Egidii de Cobberleye per capellanum ydoneum celebrandam, quam de terris meis dominicis, redditibus et proventibus manerii mei de Cobberl', ac bonis aliis, fundavi pariter et dotavi. Tenor vero carte domini nostri, domini Edwardi regis supradicti, talis est:[2] Edwardus dei gracia rex Anglie, dominus Hibernie, et dux Aquitanie, omnibus ad quos presentes littere pervenerint, salutem. Licet de communi concilio regni nostri statutum sit quod non liceat viris religiosis seu aliis ingredi feodum alicuius, ita quod ad manum mortuam deveniat, sine licencia nostra et capitalis domini de quo res illa immediate tenetur: volentes tamen dilecto et fideli nostro Thome de Berkel' de Cobberl' graciam facere specialem, concessimus et licenciam dedimus pro nobis et heredibus nostris quantum in nobis est eidem Thome, quod ipse unum mesuagium, duo tofta, quatuor virgatas terre et duas marcatas redditus cum pertinenciis in Cobberl' dare possit et assignare cuidam capellano divina in honore Beate Marie Virginis pro anima ipsius Thome et animabus antecessorum suorum et omnium fidelium defunctorum in ecclesia Sancti Egidii de Cobberleye singulis diebus celebraturo, habenda et tenenda eidem

---

1 Romans xiv, 10.
2 *C.P.R.* 1334–38, p. 268.

capellano et successoribus suis capellanis divina in ecclesia predicta sicut predictum est celebraturis imperpetuum. Et eidem capellano quod ipse predicta mesuagium, tofta, terram et redditum cum pertinenciis a prefato Thoma recipere possit et tenere sibi et successoribus suis predictis imperpetuum sicut predictum est, tenore presencium similiter licenciam dedimus specialem. Nolentes quod predictus Thomas vel heredes sui, aut prefatus capellanus seu successores sui, racione predicti per nos vel heredes nostros inde occasionentur in aliquo seu graventur: salvis tamen capitalibus domini[s] feodi illius serviciis inde debitis et consuetis. In cuius rei testimonium has litteras nostras fieri fecimus patentes. Teste me ipso apud Wodestok' xxiii$^{mo.}$ die Maii anno regni nostri x$^{mo.}$[1] Et ut circa premissa ordinacionis mee modus et devocionis affectus vobis cerenius[2] illucescant carte mee formam sub tenore qui sequitur duxi presentibus inserendam, cuius est eciam tenor talis: Sciant presentes et futuri quod ego Thomas de Berkel' de Cubberlegh dedi, concessi et hac presenti carta mea confirmavi pro me et heredibus meis imperpetuum domino Waltero de Bradeweye capellano et successoribus suis capellanis perpetuo singulis diebus missam Beate Marie Virginis et missas de Sancta Trinitate, de Sancto Spiritu et Sancto Johanne Baptista, prout inferius continetur, pro me in vita mea, et anima mea post mortem meam, patris et matris ac aliorum parentum meorum, necnon pro animabus omnium fidelium defunctorum cantaturis seu celebraturis[3] in ecclesia Sancti Egidii de Cubberlegh ad altare Beate Marie Virginis eiusdem ecclesie, unum mesuagium, duo tofta, quatuor virgatas terre et duas marcatas annui redditus cum pertinenciis in Cubberl' exeuntes, videlicet, de tenemento Willelmi Clocleford unam marcam, et de tenemento Walteri le Walkar unam marcam, percipiendo dictas duas marcas a dictis tenentibus et heredibus suis ad quatuor anni terminos equales et usuales, cum wardis, maritagiis, escaetis, sectis curiarum et herietis cum acciderit [sic] et cum omnibus aliis pertinenciis suis, habenda et tenenda omnia predicta mesuagium, tofta, terram et redditus cum omnibus pertinenciis suis[4] ut predictum est predicto Waltero de Bradeweye capellano et successoribus suis capellanis missas ut premittitur in ecclesia predicta ad altare predictum celebraturis[5] seu cantaturis de capitalibus dominis feodi illius per servicium debitum et consuetum libere, quiete, bene et in pace imperpetuum. Et ego vero predictus Thomas et heredes mei predicta[6] ad altare predictum celebraturis contra omnes warentizabimus, aquietabimus et defendemus imperpetuum. In cuius rei testimonium huic carte sigillum meum est

1 1336.
2 *Rectius* 'serenius'.
3 MS. 'celebratur*us*'.
4 'habenda—suis' interlineated.
5 The scribe wrote 'celebraturus' as above but deleted one of the minims by subpunctuation.
6 It seems that the scribe omitted a line at this point owing to the recurrence of 'predicta'. Cf. pp. 482, 491.

appensum. Dat' apud Cubberlegh die Dominica proxima ante festum Sancti Martini episcopi et confessoris,[1] anno regni regis Edwardi tercii post Conquestum xi. Hiis testibus: domino Waltero tunc rectore ecclesie de Cobberl', Johanne Delkeston, Henrico de Brocworth, Johanne Lohaut, Willelmo de Solers, et aliis. Ad quam quidem cantariam predictum dominum Walterum capellanum venerabili in Christo patri domino Wolstano dei gracia Wygorn' episcopo presentavi et per ipsum ad eandem admitti, institui, et corporaliter induci in eadem sicut decet capellanum perpetuum procuravi, sicque toto vite mee tempore quociens ipsam cantariam vacare contigerit domino Wygorn' episcopo qui pro tempore fuerit[2] presbiterum ydoneum presentabo, ac eciam post decessum meum heredes mei domini de Cubberl' predicta consimiliter presentabunt. Et si[3] ego vel heredes mei predicti presentare omisero vel omiserint per mensem a tempore vacacionis huiusmodi cantarie, volo et ordino quod rector ecclesie de Cubberlegh ad eandem tunc presentet, qui si forte per mensem dimiserit vel negligens fuerit in presentando, quo casu episcopus Wygorn' qui pro tempore fuerit sede plena, vel ipsa vacante prior Wygorn', ipsam cantariam conferat suo iure. Ac volo et ordino quod dicti domini Walteri successores capellani in dictam cantariam[4] residenciam faciant personalem et cotidie celebrent et ministrent iuxta ordinacionem subscriptam, et de hoc faciendo in institucione sua coram ordinariis ad sancta dei evangelia prestent corporaliter iuramentum prout fragilitas humane condicionis permittet. In quibus residencia et celebracione si defecerint continuo per quindenam illi ad quos spectat presentacio seu collacio presentent seu conferant sine mora, nisi forte iusta causa et racionabilis fuerit absentandi vel cessandi auctoritate ordinaria approbanda vel reprobanda prout viderit expedire. Quodque predicti Walteri successores capellani singuli temporibus suis [sint] in ecclesia parochiali singulis diebus festivis, et in festis novem leccionum, in matitunis[5] missa et vesperis presentes et cum aliis ministrent, nisi ex causis legitimis fuerint inpediti. Et quod singulis diebus quibus artati sunt per ordinale de usu Sar' dicant officium mortuorum pro animabus subscriptis. Diebus vero dominicis singulis ebdomadis per annum missam de Sancta Trinitate; diebus vero Jovis missam de Sancto Spiritu; diebus vero Martis missam de Sancto Johanne Baptista; ceteris vero diebus in singulis ebdomadis missam de Sancta Virgine; in ecclesia predicta ad altare predictum pro salubri statu meo dum vixero, et cum carnis debitum exsolvero pro anima mea, patris matris parentum meorum, cunctorumque benefactorum

---

1 9 November 1337. The feast falls on the 11th.
2 The MS. has 'in' here. Perhaps 'unum' was intended.
3 'si' interlineated.
4 Accusative *sic*. Probably an error. In 735, another ordination which follows this one closely, the ablative is correctly used.
5 *Recte* 'matutinis'.

dicte cantarie, omniumque fidelium animabus celebrent, vel si legitime impediti fuerint, faciant per alios celebrari, nisi infirmitate vel aliqua inevitabili causa fuerint perturbati. In omnibus autem missis quas dicturi sunt, hoc precipio firmiter observari, quod pro me Thoma superstite dicant collectam que sic incipit: OMNIPOTENS SEMPITERNE DEUS MISERERE FAMULO TUO THOMA &c., et post mortem meam collectam que sic incipit: OMNIPOTENS SEMPITERNE DEUS CUI NUNQUAM SINE SPE MISERICORDIE SUPPLICATUR &c., nomen meum exprimentes in eadem. Dicere autem teneantur prefatus presbiter et successores sui presbiteri imperpetuum singulis annis post mortem meam in die obitus mei officium mortuorum cum novem psalmis et novem leccionibus et totidem responsoriis pro anima mea, et quod a nullo recipiant pecuniam pro divino officio celebrando, sed porcione per me eis assignata penitus sint contenti. Quod si quis eorum secus egerit et super hoc convictus fuerit, amoveatur et loco sui alius subrogetur. Si quis autem eorum ad tantam etatem sive infirmitatem devenerit quod personaliter non poterit missas[1] celebrare, dicat privatas oraciones quas poterit et singulis septimanis faciat duas missas, unam videlicet pro animabus predictorum, et aliam de Sancta Maria, celebrari, et propter etatem vel infirmitatem huiusmodi nullatenus amoveatur. Et quod heredes mei predicta omnia supervideant et curent et procurent, quod secundum ordinacionem meam in huiusmodi cantaria ad honorem dei et pro me et anima mea et animabus omnium fidelium defunctorum laudabiliter serviatur. Et quod domos [sic], edificia et clausure dicte cantarie congrue sustententur, ne pro defectu cooperture vel alias corruant vel deficiant per negligenciam capellani; et si casu fortuito per ignem, ventum, vel alio modo inopinato, aut propter vetustatem, edificia huiusmodi ruere contingat, vel alias sine culpa capellani quovismodo fueri[n]t deteriorata, volo, ordino, et heredes meos et assignatos dominos de Cubberl' onero quantum possum, quod ipsi heredes et assignati huiusmodi edificia de proprio meremio suo et sumptibus suis edificent et emendant, ne pro defectu eorum huiusmodi cantaria in animarum periculum negligetur. Et quod episcopus loci diocesanus in suis visitacionibus et aliis temporibus cum voluerit de premissis omnibus inquirat, et si quos defectus invenerit in premissis deficientes puniat condecenter, et capellanos delinquentes amoveat si quantitas delicti exegerit eorundem. Et quia volo quod hec mea ordinacio rata et firma imperpetuum perseveret, ex parte dei patris omnipotentis et Beate Marie Virginis et omnium sanctorum sub interminacione divini iudicii in die ultionis precipio ne quis meus heres, consanguineus vel affinis seu quevis [sic] alius, cuiuscumque condicionis vel status existat, hanc ordinacionem meam, ad honorem dei omnipotentis et pro salute anime mee, parentum et benefactorum meorum factam, aliqualiter

1 MS. 'missarum'.

34

impediat vel impugnet vel eam in aliquibus articulis suis quovismodo infringat. In quorum omnium testimonium sigillum meum presentibus est appensum. Hiis testibus: domino Waltero tunc rectore ecclesie de Cubberlegh, Johanne Delkeston, Henrico de Brocworth, Johanne Lovat, Willelmo de Solers, et aliis. Dat' apud Cubberlegh die Dominica proxima ante festum Sancti Martini episcopi et confessoris anno regni regis Edwardi tercii post Conquestum xi^{mo.}[1] Nos frater Wolstanus episcopus supradictus, laudabile propositum et pium desiderium domini Thome de Berkel' de Cubberl' predicti quo ad fundacionem, dotacionem et ordinacionem cantarie de qua in dictis litteris plenius continetur, merito commendantes, huiusmodi cantariam, ipsiusque fundacionem, dotacionem et ordinacionem quantum in nobis est auctoritate nostra ordinaria approbamus, ratificamus et ex certa sciencia confirmamus. Inhibemus eciam omnibus et singulis subditis nostris ne fundacionem, dotacionem, et ordinacionem supradictas aliquo modo maliciose infringant, capellanos-ve[2] dicte cantarie in suis iuribus et porcionibus percipiendis impediant seu perturbant[3] animo iniurando, sub pena excommunicacionis sentencie maioris, quam contraveniens quilibet in hac parte merito poterit formidare. In quorum omnium testimonium sigillum nostrum fecimus hiis apponi. Dat' apud Blockel' v^{to.} die Julii, anno domini millesimo ccc^{mo.}·xl^{mo.} et nostre consecracionis secundo, ac regni regis Edwardi tercii post Conquestum xiiii^{mo.}

834 *24 September 1347* Inspeximus *of Thomas de Berkeley of Coberley's later foundation for three priests who are likewise to serve in the church of St. Giles at Coberley.*

ORDINACIO CANTARIE DE CUBYRLEYE.

Universis sancte matris ecclesie filiis presentem ordinacionem visuris vel audituris, Thomas de Berkeleye de Cubberleye, salutem in domino sempiternam. Christi fideles noverint universi quod ego Thomas antedictus attendens [&c. as in 154 above—proximis alimenta;] . . . in honore sanctissime Trinitatis patris et filii et Spiritus Sancti ac beatissime dei genetricis semperque virginis Marie et Sancti Egidii abbatis et confessoris omniumque sanctorum dei, de consensu et licencia excellentissimi principis et domini nostri domini Edwardi dei gracia regis illustris Anglie et Francie, necnon rectoris ecclesie parochialis de Cubberl' predicta, ac eciam omnium aliorum quorum interest vel interesse poterit in futurum, et per cartam eiusdem domini nostri regis predicti cuius tenor talis est: Edwardus [&c. as in 154—tenetur;] . . . per finem tamen quem dilectus et fidelis noster Thomas de Berkeleye de Cubberleye fecit nobiscum concessimus et licenciam dedimus pro nobis et heredibus

---

1 9 November 1337.   2 've' interlineated above 'ut' crossed out.   3 *Recte* 'perturbent'

nostris quantum in nobis est eidem Thome quod ipse tresdecim mesuagia, duo tofta, triginta et quatuor virgatas terre et duas acras bosci cum pertinenciis in Cubberleye dare possit et assignare tribus capellanis divina pro salubri statu ipsius Thome dum vixerit et anima eius cum ab hac luce migraverit ac animabus antecessorum suorum et omnium fidelium defunctorum in ecclesia Sancti Egidii de Cubberleye singulis diebus iuxta ordinacionem in hac parte faciendam celebraturis, habenda et tenenda eisdem capellanis et successoribus suis capellanis divina in ecclesia predicta singulis diebus in forma predicta celebraturis imperpetuum. Et eisdem capellanis quod ipsi predicta mesuagia tofta terram et boscum cum pertinenciis a prefato Thoma recipere possint et tenere sibi et successoribus suis predictis imperpetuum sicut predictum est tenore presencium similiter licenciam dedimus specialem. Nolentes [&c. as in 154— fecimus patentes.] Teste me ipso apud Turrim London' decimo septimo die Marcii, anno regni nostri Anglie decimo nono, regni vero nostri Francie sexto.[1] Ad divini cultus augmentum feci, ordinavi et ordino perpetuam cantariam trium presbiterorum Christo iugiter famulancium in ecclesia Sancti Egidii de Cubberleye Wygorn' diocesis, pro salubri statu meo et Johanne uxoris mee dum vixerimus, et animarum nostrarum requie cum ab hac luce migraverimus, et pro animabus antecessorum et heredum meorum dicteque cantarie benefactorum, et omnium fidelium defunctorum, per custodem presbiterum et duos capellanos ydoneos eidem adiunctos celebrandam, quam de terris meis dominicis, boscis et proventibus manerii mei de Cubberleye predicta et aliis bonis meis fundavi pariter et dotavi. Et ut circa premissa ordinacionis mee modus et devocionis affectus vobis clarius illucescant carte mee formam sub tenore qui sequitur duxi inserendam. Sciant presentes et futuri quod ego Thomas de Berkeleye de Cubberleye dedi, concessi, et hac presenti carta mea confirmavi pro me et heredibus meis, ad honorem dei et gloriose virginis Marie matris sue Sanctique Egidii et omnium sanctorum dei, dilecto michi in Christo domino Henrico Averay[2] capellano custodi cantarie Beate Marie de Cubberley Wygorn' diocesis et omnibus suis successoribus capellanis secularibus dicte cantarie custodibus pro se et aliis duobus capellanis eidem domino Henrico Averay capellano custodi et successoribus suis capellanis secularibus dicte cantarie custodibus adiungendis, ac per eundem Henricum Averay et suos successores predictos sustentandis, in ecclesia Sancti Egidii de Cubberleye predicta divina singulis diebus pro salubri statu meo dum vixero et anima mea cum ab hac luce migravero et animabus antecessorum meorum et omnium fidelium defunctorum iuxta ordinacionem meam in hac parte faciendam celebraturis, tresdecim mesuagia, duo tofta, triginta et quatuor

1 *C.P.R.* 1343–45, p. 449 (17 March 1345). By fine of 40 marks.
2 Blank spaces were left and this name filled in afterwards both here and below.

virgatas terre et duas acras bosci cum pertinenciis in Cubberleye, videlicet illud mesuagium et tres virgatas terre cum suis pertinenciis, que tenementa vocantur *Eldresfeldeslond*, et unum toftum et tres virgatas terre cum suis pertinenciis, que tenementa vocantur *Baillifslond*, et unum mesuagium et duas virgatas terre cum suis pertinenciis que Thomas Jannes tenet in bondagio, et unum mesuagium et duas virgatas terre cum suis pertinenciis que Willelmus Lutesone tenet in bondagio, et unum mesuagium et unum toftum et tres virgates terre cum suis pertinenciis que Robertus Jannes tenet in bondagio, et unum mesuagium et duas virgatas terre cum suis pertinenciis que Alicia Willes tenet in bondagio, et unum mesuagium et duas virgates terre cum suis pertinenciis que Thomas le Holdare tenet in bondagio, et unum mesuagium et duas virgatas terre cum suis pertinenciis que Thomas Elyot tenet in bondagio, et unum mesuagium et duas virgatas terre cum suis pertinenciis que Philippus Jones tenet in bondagio, et unum mesuagium et duas virgatas terre cum suis pertinenciis que Thomas Jones tenet in bondagio, et unam virgatam terre cum suis pertinenciis quam Johannes Fyppes tenet in bondagio, et duas virgatas terre cum suis pertinenciis que Thomas Murival tenet in bondagio, et unum mesuagium et duas virgatas terre cum suis pertinenciis que Johannes Colynes tenet in bondagio, et unum mesuagium et duas virgatas terre cum suis pertinenciis que Henricus le Muleward tenet in bondagio, et unum mesuagium et duas virgatas terre cum suis pertinenciis que Ricardus Jones tenet in bondagio, et unum mesuagium et duas virgatas terre cum suis pertinenciis que Henricus Brouning tenet in bondagio, simul cum predictis Thoma, Willelmo, Roberto, Alicia, Thoma, Thoma, Philippo, Thoma, Johanne, Thoma, Johanne, Henrico, Ricardo et Henrico, ac cum omnibus bonis et catallis et sequelis suis, que et quas dicte cantarie et capellanis eiusdem qui pro tempore fuerint successive de consensu omnium quorum interest concurrentibus omnibus que de iure requiruntur in hac parte pro tempore perpetuo assignavi intuitu caritatis, habenda et tenenda omnia predicta mesuagia, tofta, terras et boscum, ut in croftis, viis, semitis, boscis, pascuis et pasturis, ac cum omnibus aliis suis ubique pertinenciis simul cum predictis Thoma [&c. as above—sequelis suis,] . . . predicto domino Henrico Averay capellano et omnibus successoribus suis pro se et aliis duobus capellanis eidem domino Henrico Averay capellano et successoribus suis capellanis successive adiungendis, ac per eundem dominum Henricum Averay et successores suos in eadem cantaria capellanos sustendandis, iuxta ordinacionem meam inde faciendam divina singulis diebus in ecclesia predicta pro salubri statu meo et Johanne uxoris mee dum vixerimus, et pro animarum nostrarum requie cum ab hac luce migraverimus, necnon pro animabus predictorum celebraturis seu cantaturis, libere, quiete, bene et in pace imperpetuum. Et ego vero predictus Thomas et heredes mei omnia predicta mesuagia, tofta, terras et boscum cum omnibus suis pertinenciis simul cum predictis Thoma, [&c. as above—Henrico,] . . . et cum omnibus bonis et catallis suis ac sequelis suis predicto domino Henrico Averay capellano et successoribus suis capellanis pro se et aliis duobus capellanis [&c.— sustentandis,] in forma predicta divina singulis diebus in prefata ecclesia celebraturis seu cantaturis contra quoscumque warantizabimus, acquietabimus et imperpetuum defendemus. In cuius rei testimonium huic presenti carte sigillum meum apposui. Hiis testibus: domino Johanne Giffard de Lecamptone, domino Thoma Botiler, militibus, domino Willelmo rectore ecclesie de Hampton Monialium, domino Waltero rectore ecclesie de Cubberley, Johanne de Elkeston et aliis. Dat' apud Cubberl' &c. Ad dictam vero ordinacionem meam super premissa faciendam Christi nomine primitus invocato procedo in hunc modum: In primis volo et ordino quod dictus dominus Henricus Averay presbiter secularis sit custos predicte cantarie perpetuus ad presentacionem meam per venerabilem patrem Wygorn' episcopum institutus in eadem et eius auctoritate inductus qui in eadem cantaria secum habeat duos seculares capellanos ydoneos per me dum vixero ibidem ponendos. Item volo et ordino quod postea quoscienscumque [sic] et quandocumque dictam cantariam per mortem vel cessionem custodis eiusdem seu alio quovis modo vacare contigerit unus capellanorum dicte cantarie qui magis ydoneus et sufficiens fuerit iuxta eius discrecionem ad quem illa vice pertinet presentacio, et nullus alius quam unus eorum, per me dum vixero et post mortem meam per rectorem ecclesie de Cubberl' predicta qui pro tempore fuerit, ipsaque ecclesia vacante, per priorem Minoris Malvernie vel suppriorem et conventum eiusdem loci illo prioratu vacante, episcopo Wygorn' qui pro tempore fuerit infra mensem a tempore vacacionis dicte vicarie continue numerandum sede plena presentetur, vel illi ad quem spectat beneficiorum institucio vice eiusdem episcopi dicta sede vacante, per eundem sine difficultate quacumque admittendus et instituendus, ipsisque infra dictum mensem non presentantibus, episcopus Wygorn' qui pro tempore fuerit sede plena, vel ipsa vacante ille ad quem beneficiorum spectat ut premittitur collacio, dictam cantariam illa vice conferat suo iure uni ut predicitur dictorum capellanorum. Quorum si neuter infra mensem ut predicitur conferat a tempore iuris sibi adquisiti in hac parte, tunc archiepiscopus Cantuarie sede plena, vel prior Sancte Trinitatis Cantuar' dicta sede vacante, uni dictorum capellanorum illa vice suo iure modo conferat supradicto, salvo semper iure dictis rectori, priori, suppriori et conventui Malvernie predicte suis temporibus ut predicitur ad dictam cantariam alias cum vacaverit iuxta formam ordinacionis mee predicte libere presentandi. Volo eciam et ordino quod idem custos tam in institucione sua coram ipsum instituente quam in induccione sua coram ipsum inducente ac

rectore ecclesie de Cubberl' predicta et suis parochianis si interesse
voluerint, iuramentum prestet corporale, quod ordinaciones meas
super statu dicte cantarie quatenus ipsum concernunt fideliter
observabit, et faciet quatenus in eo est ab aliis observari, et continue
residebit ibidem in loco et manso pro eodem et aliis capellanis
predictis suisque successoribus in dicta cantaria ordinatis per me et
edificatis, quos locum et mansum *Bevalee* de cetero vocandos ordino
et nominandos, nisi ipsum pro negociis dicte cantarie necessario
oporteat abesse, quodque iura dicte cantarie manutenebit et
defendet pro suo posse; alioquin institucio huiusmodi non teneat
ipso iure. Qui quidem custos sic institutus, inductus et iuratus
liberam et legitimam habeat administracionem et disposicionem
terrarum tenementorum et rerum omnium ad dictam cantariam et
custodiam eiusdem ubique pertinencium seu spectancium quovis
modo presencium et futurorum. Item volo et ordino quod predictus
custos duos secum habeat capellanos ydoneos castos et honestos,
scientes, valentes et volentes in cantaria predicta divinum officium
facere celebrari, et adimplere competenter iuxta ordinacionem
meam infrascriptam, secum continue morantes, quos idem custos de
bonis dicte cantarie dum in eadem deserviunt in esculentis et
poculentis competenter et honeste sustentet, videlicet pane de
frumento per medium stricti cribi cribato, et servicia[1] bona, videlicet
sex lagenis de meliori de uno buscello boni bras[iati] ordei factis, una
cum legumine, ac diebus non festivis uno ferculo in prandio et alio
in cena, binis simul comedentibus, ministrando, diebus vero festivis
et solempnibus eisdem duo fercula ministrentur, ita tamen quod due
partes primi ferculi sint de carnibus salsis et de instauro domus
predicte, et tercia pars de carnibus recentibus;[2] et idem volo ceteris
diebus quibus a carnibus abstinent in exhibendis piscibus observari,
secundum vero ferculum in diebus festivis non sit sumptuosum sed
simplex et competens ut decenter vivere possint; et ultra id utrique
eorum duas marcas sterlingorum per equales porciones ad festa
Annunciacionis Beate Marie et Beati Petri ad Vincula pro vestitu,
superpelliciis et omnibus aliis eorum necessariis annuatim persolvat.
Qui quidem capellani dicto custodi et suis successoribus subsint et
in admissione sua corporaliter sibi et domui sue iurent fidelitatem et
eidem custodi obedienciam quod sibi in mandatis licitis et honestis
pareant et intendant, quos duos capellanos idem custos post mortem
meam prout sibi melius videbitur expedire assumat et eos ex causa
racionabili et non alias amoveat ut inferius ordinabitur. Residuum
vero bonorum dicte cantarie sub debito iuramenti sui prestiti, deductis
expensis predictis et aliis expensis suis necessariis et familie sue quam
habeat necessariam et non onerosam, iuxta discrecionem a deo sibi
datam convertat in utilitatem cantarie predicte seu pertinencium ad
eandem, nec testetur aliqualiter de eisdem. Item volo et ordino quod

1 For 'cervisia'.   2 MS. 'recensibus'.

dictus custos pro se et dictis duobus capellanis inveniat in ecclesia predicta vinum et lumen eis necessarium in celebracione divinorum. Item volo et ordino quod dicti custos et capellani eorumque successores imperpetuum liberum habeant ingressum in prefatam ecclesiam de Cubberl' temporibus competentibus pro divinorum celebracione et ministracione et hostii nove capelle per me constructe penes se habeant clavem. Item volo et ordino quod nec predictus custos nec capellani seu aliquis eorum curam habens seu administracionem bonorum cantarie predicte quocumque casu emergente eciam si de omni vel maioris partis eorum voluntate processerit et consensu terras, prata, tenementa, res, redditus, boscum, possessiones aut alia iura quecumque ad eandem cantariam quomodolibet spectancia sive pertinencia alienet in feodum nec dimittat ad terminum vite vel annorum, exceptis dumtaxat domibus, reddittualibus et bondagiis que liceat eidem ad terminum dimittere iuxta formam et modum consuetum ad utilitatem cantarie supradicte. Neque eciam corrodium aliquid vel liberacionem aliquam seu pensionem alicui vendat donet vel concedat nec aliquod aliud onus imponat quovismodo sub pena excommunicacionis maioris. Et si dictus custos inventus fuerit incestus, adulter, luxuriosus, inhabilis vel indignus, statim per episcopum Wygorn' qui pro tempore fuerit eiusve commissarium sede plena, vel priorem et conventum Wygorn' dicta sede vacante per processum summarium ex officio mero seu instancia partis simpliciter de plano, sine strepitu et figura iudicii totaliter amoveatur perpetuo a dicta custodia, et alius sufficiens et ydoneus custos loco sui secundum formam premissam instituatur in eadem, appellacione, in integrum restitucione, querela et omni alio iuris remedio eidem omnino interdictis in hac parte. Volo eciam et ordino quod tociens quociens dictorum capellanorum aliquis notabiliter incestus, adulter, criminosus vel culpabilis aut alias insufficiens communiter contrarius vel negligens inventus fuerit notorie, prefatus custos illum absque more dispendio amoveat iuxta sue beneplacitum voluntatis et alium sacerdotem ydoneum etate, sciencia et moribus loco ipsius ponere vel subrogare infra mensem teneatur ad celebrandum divina in ecclesia predicta. Quibus eciam subrogatis de esculentis et poculentis et aliis debeat ut premittitur ministrari. Et si aliquis dictorum capellanorum cesserit et decesserit seu aliquo modo amotus fuerit, predictus custos infra[1] unum mensem proximo tunc sequentem subroget sacerdotem ydoneum cessante legitimo impedimento sub pena privacionis a custodia predicta, quam penam ipsum custodem si hoc non fecerit incurrere volo et ordino ipso facto, ac alius capellanorum predictorum ydoneus et sufficiens ut premittitur ad dictam cantariam presentetur et instituatur in eadem, appellacione, restitucione in integrum, querela et omni alio iuris remedio eidem omnino interdictis. Et ne per magnum tempus missarum celebracio in dicta cantaria differatur,

[1] 'Infra' interlineated.

volo et ordino ut statim post lapsum dicti mensis infra quem dictus custos de capellano vel capellanis ydoneis ut est dictum non providerit, liceat rectori ecclesie de Cubberl' qui pro tempore fuerit, et ipsa ecclesia vacante priori Minoris Malvernie in loco capellani vel capellanorum amoti vel amotorum quovis modo cedencium vel decedencium alium vel alios ydoneum vel ydoneos subrogare qui procurentur et recipiant ut est superius ordinatum, salvo alias iure dicto custodi et successoribus suis cum opus fuerit de capellanis ydoneis providere. Item volo et ordino quod prefati custos et capellani et eorum successores tonsuram gerant decentem, ita quod aures habeant patulas, largamque coronam, et vestibus utantur de una secta, videlicet de blueto puro vel modicum mixto aut russeto non nimis albo, nec nimis nigro, cum supertunica clausa et talari sicut decet, ferialibus tamen diebus et alias in laboribus uti possunt cursioribus semper tamen clausis, ita quod precium ulne non excedat duos solidos. Item volo et ordino quod custos et capellani predicti sint honeste mutuo conversantes prout sacerdotalem condecet gravitatem, et simul habitent, simul in una mensa comedant et iaceant prout in eorum loco et manso predictis est ordinatum, proviso tamen quod alique mulieres infra mansum eorundem nullatenus morentur vel eisdem infra hospicium suum deserviant in futurum. Item volo et ordino quod dicti custos et capellani cotidie dicant devociori modo quo poterunt simul matutinas et omnes alias horas canonicas distincte, tractim, et devote, et in loco ubi conveniencius et devocius dicere possunt; diebus tamen dominicis et aliis festivis in ecclesia parochiali predicta in superpelliciis, cum nota vel sine nota, prout cum rectore eiusdem concorditer convenire poterint pro libito sue voluntatis, nisi laudabilis et racionabilis causa eos vel eorum aliquem probabiliter excuset in aliquo premissorum, matutinas eciam et omnes alias horas Beate Marie Virginis, ac PLACEBO, DIRIGE, et commendacionem cotidie similiter insimul dicant vel saltim duo modis et locis supradictis iuxta usum ecclesie Sar' nisi ut supra eorum aliquis excusetur. Item volo et ordino quod singulis diebus cessante legitimo impedimento missam celebret eorum quilibet tam custos quam alii capellani, videlicet, unus eorum de dicta gloriosa semperque virgine Maria[1] matre domini nostri Jhesu Christi et singulis diebus sabbati cum nota in capella contigua dicte ecclesie per me constructa vel alibi in ecclesia predicta si conveniencius fieri poterit, alius vero de die cum recommendacione status et animarum predictarum, tercius vero de requiem [sic] pro salubri statu meo et Johanne uxori[s] mee dum vixerimus et animarum nostrarum requie cum ab hac luce migraverimus et animarum antecessorum et heredum meorum dicteque cantarie benefactorum et omnium fidelium defunctorum in ecclesia predicta iuxta ordinacionem dicti custodis et sine preiudicio rectoris et ecclesie supra-

1 MS. 'Marie'.

dictorum. Item volo et ordino quod predicti custos et capellani postquam diem meum clausero extremum imperpetuum anniversarium meum singulis annis cum solempni pulsacione campanarum in ecclesia predicta solempniter faciant cum nota, videlicet die precedenti post vesperas PLACEBO et DIRIGE cum nota, et in crastino videlicet die anniversarii mei missam cum nota honestiori et solempniori modo quo poterunt celebrent in communi. Eodem vero modo per omnia observent anniversarium patris mei dicteque Johanne uxoris mee post mortem suam, et nunc de cetero Johanne prioris uxoris mee defuncte. Item volo et ordino quod tam custos quam capellani predicti singuli singulis diebus post matutinas et horas canonicas dicant pro fidelibus defunctis psalmum DE PROFUNDIS cum PATER NOSTER ac AVE et oracionibus consuetis, hiisque finitis quando et prout eum concernit dicat eorum quilibet: ANIMA DOMINI THOME FUNDATORIS NOSTRI ET ANIME UXORIS SUARUM PARENTUM ET HEREDUM BENEFACTORUMQUE NOSTRORUM ET OMNIUM FIDELIUM DEFUNCTORUM PER DEI MISERICORDIAM IN PACE REQUIESCANT. Eadem per omnia dicat quilibet post missam suam celebratam, et unus eorum singulis diebus post gracias deo redditas qui eas dixerit in mensa. Item, volo et ordino quod dicti capellani astringantur et eorum quilibet astringatur in sua admissione quod ipse officium suum quatenus ad eum pertinet iuxta formam presentis ordinacionis mee bene et fideliter faciet et exequetur, iuraque et libertates cantarie predicte manutenebit et defendet iuxta suum posse quodque in eadem cantaria continuam residenciam faciat [sic] personalem. Si vero aliquis custos qui pro tempore fuerit senio vel morbo continuo fuerit impeditus quominus officio suo incumbencia valeat adimplere, volo et ordino quod prefatus rector qui pro tempore fuerit seu prior Minoris Malvernie in forma predicta unum coadiutorem de capellanis predictis loci diocesano presentet et presentatus huiusmodi per eundem diocesanum deputetur custodi predicto qui iuxta ordinacionem predictam in omnibus officium custodis agere valeat et exercere et de dicta custodia suo periculo compotum in communi reddere teneatur, et pro tempore quo ipse custos coadiutore ut premittitur indiguerit, habeat servientem competentem cui necessaria de bonis dicte cantarie volumus ministrari, et si facultates dictorum bonorum suppetant admittatur alius sacerdos durante impedimento dicti custodis ad celebrandum terciam missam ne dicta cantaria in eadem diminucionem paciatur. Et quia capellani predicti et eorum singuli, si bene se gesserint ac fideles [habiles?][1] honesti fuerint et casti, erunt ut perpetui, si contingat ipsorum aliquem fore debilem, cecum vel senio confractum aut alias morbo perpetuo vel continuo impeditum quominus missam suam et aliud sibi incumbens officium peragere

---

1 The MS. has '*h'ites*'.

valeat et non habeat unde competenter sustentari, custos qui pro tempore fuerit victum eidem invenire teneatur; de salario vero suo et aliis bonis dicte cantarie loco ipsius et eciam aliorum quorumcumque sic ut premittitur infirmorum vel impeditorum alii capellani ydonei subrogentur, qui huiusmodi infirmorum et impeditorum vices in omnibus iuxta ordinacionem premissam volueri[n]t et valeant adimplere. Volo eciam et ordino quod nullus custos in dicta cantaria institutus possit per procuratorem in corporalem possessionem eiusdem induci, nisi in adipiscenda possessione corporali dicte cantarie presens existat, in quam per eum ad quem pertinuerit corporaliter inducatur. Et statim post induccionem antequam de bonis seu rebus ad predictam cantariam spectantibus administret, in presencia rectoris ecclesie de Cubberl' qui pro tempore fuerit et dictorum capellanorum plenum fidele et perfectum conficiat inventarium de calicibus, libris, vestimentis, ornamentis et aliis rebus quibuscumque pro divinis obsequiis ibidem ordinatis seu alia existentibus et de omnibus nominibus debitorum si que sunt et de quantitatibus debitorum ac eciam de omnibus et singulis vasis argenteis stagneis ereis et aliis utensilibus et rebus de bonis quibuscumque ac eciam de equis, bobus, affris et iumentis, vaccis, ovibus, porcis, et alio instauro quocumque, carrettis, carrucis et aliis rebus quibuscumque ibidem vel alibi inventis vel existentibus ad dictam cantariam quovis modo pertinentibus seu assignatis vel in posterum assignandis; quod inventarium indentura tripartita scribatur, cuius indenture habeat rector predictus unam partem et custos aliam et terciam predicti capellani, quorum bonorum nichil omnino alienetur, elongetur, destruatur seu aliqualiter amoveatur sub districti examinis interminacione, sed pocius dictus custos ut fidelis dispensator et prudens talentum sibi traditum per suam industriam modis quibus poterit licitis dictisque capellanis auxiliantibus augeat et multiplicet, nichil sibi de huiusmodi facultatibus seu bonis retinendis, vel si eum quocumque casu inde migrare contigerit secum aliquid deferendo seu in detrimentum cantarie predicte quicquam aliis conferendo, sed omnia in utilitatem dicte cantarie integraliter convertendo sub interminacione predicta; ceteri vero presbiteri qui se ut deberent fraudem ut premittitur facientibus non opponunt, pro tempore quo premissa sine debita contradiccione permiserint, nichil percipiant de stipendiis sibi constitutis. Item, volo et ordino quod dicto custode cedente vel decedente seu quovis modo privato a dicta cantaria seu remoto, omnes fructus et proventus ad prefatam cantariam huiusmodi vacacionis tempore provenientes vel qualitercumque pertinentes in usus cantarie predicte integraliter convertantur et legitima administracio quorumcumque bonorum et rerum ad dictam cantariam spectancium sit ipso iure ad ipsius cantarie presbiterum qui in ea diucius deserviverit ac laudabiliter se gesserit et honeste devoluta, donec novus custos in eiusdem cantarie possessionem corporalem personaliter inductus inventarium fecerit ut est supradictum. Volo eciam et ordino quod sequestrator seu quicumque alius minister ordinarii cuiuscumque vel alterius de bonis seu rebus cantarie predicte vel aliqua parte eorundem racione vacacionis vel alia causa quacumque quocumque colore quesito se nullatenus intromittat. Item, volo et ordino quod vacante dicta cantaria capellanus eius administrator de administracione nullatenus se intromittat antequam de bonis dicte cantarie inventarium secundum modum fecerit supradictum. Postquam autem administrare ceperit, ille ad quem tempore vacacionis huiusmodi est administracio devoluta omnia huiusmodi vacacionis tempore ad ipsam cantariam obveniencia et de ipsa qualitercumque proveniencia et expensas tempore vacacionis per ipsum factas plenarie et distincte redigat in scripturam, ipsamque scripturam liberet custodi predicto infra mensem post induccionem eiusdem custodis et compotum inde plenarie reddat eidem custodi iuramento corporali prius prestito ab eodem de fideli compoto reddendo de receptis quibuscumque et expensis per ipsum factis. Item cum a crapula et ebrietate omnes et precipue dei ministros deceat abstinere, cum ebrietas tam mentis inducat exilium quam libidinis provocet incentivum, volo et ordino quod custos et capellani predicti qui pro tempore fuerint tabernas non frequentent, et ut occasionem ipsas frequentandi non habeant prohibeo districte ne ad domos aliquorum dicti capellani frequenter accedant sine custodis licencia petita et obtenta. Et si custos qui pro tempore fuerit vel aliquis dictorum capellanorum transgressor istius ordinacionis in aliquo sui articulo inventus fuerit tanquam periurus puniatur et a cantaria supradicta eo ipso imperpetuum amoveatur, nullo sibi remedio in hac parte profuturo; idemque observetur si custos memoratus vel aliquis dictorum capellanorum dicte cantarie bonorum dilapidator inveniatur. Et ne fundacio, dotacio et ordinacio predicte seu illa que presentibus sunt incerta [1] oblivioni tradantur aut aliqualis ignorancia premissorum in hac parte pretendatur, volo et ordino quod hec dicta mea presens fundacio, dotacio et ordinacio singulis annis imperpetuum certis terminis, videlicet in singulis quinque vigiliis festorum Beate Marie Virginis et in vigilia Nativitatis Beati Johannis Baptiste, in ecclesia de Cubberl' in presencia dictorum custodis et capellanorum per aliquem eorundem distincte perlegatur. Ordino insuper quod custos qui pro tempore fuerit in singulis diebus Veneris proximis post lecturam huiusmodi ordinacionum mearum ante prandium ambos capellanos convocet in loco honesto et contra eas venientes vel aliquam earundem seu alias se minus bene habentes corripiat, corrigat, castiget et puniat canonice secundum demerita eorundem. Et ut presentes littere meam voluntatem et ordinacionem continentes vim perpetuitatis obtineant, volo et ordino ad maiorem securitatem et perpetuam rei memoriam has litteras meas sub sigillo

1 MS. 'inserta'.

meo et sub sigillis eorum qui eis in hac parte auctoritatem prestare voluerint quadruplari, quarum una penes dictum custodem et successores suos dicte cantarie custodes, alia penes rectorem ecclesie de Cubberl' predicta et successores suos in eadem rectores, tercia penes priorem et conventum Minoris Malvernie, et quarta penes episcopum Wygorn' et suos successores inhibi episcopos remaneat in futurum fideliter conservanda. Et quia volo quod hec mea fundacio, dotacio et ordinacio rata et firma imperpetuum perseveretur, ex parte dei omnipotentis patris et filii et Spiritus Sancti et Beati Marie virginis gloriose et omnium sanctorum dei ac sub interminacione divini iudicii in die ulcionis hortor, moneo et precipio ne quis meus eres, consanguineus, affinis vel amicus seu quivis alius cuiuscumque condicionis vel status existat, hanc meam ordinacionem [ad honorem] dei omnipotentis et pro salute anime mee et pro animabus antecessorum meorum et omnium fidelium defunctorum factam aliqualiter impedeat [sic], perturbet vel impugnet aut in aliquibus articulis suis premissis quovis modo infringere contendat. In quorum &c. Hiis t[estibus] &c. Dat' apud Wythyndon' vicesimo quarto die mensis Septembris anno domini MCCCXLVII, et nostre consecracione nono.

449 *Undated* [1341?] *Letters patent of the diocesan's ordination of a chantry founded by John de la Riviere in Tormarton church.*[1]

APPROPRIACIO ECCLESIE DE THORMERTON.

Universis presentes litteras inspecturis frater Wolstanus permissione divina Wygorn' episcopus, salutem in omnium salvatore. Inter preclara divine laudis obsequia unum de precipuis arbitramur, ut ecclesiam sanctam dei cuius in parte nobis commissa regimini licet inmeriti presidemus novo semper fetu multiplici et nova studeamus prole digne ministrancium in divinis quatenus est nobis possibile fecundare, ut multiplicatis in domo domini ministris devotis intercessoribus assiduis et inmaculatis eorundem sacrificiis cum devocione debita frequencius recensitis alma mater ecclesia ipso deo rectore et duce temporibus pacificis gubernetur et ex multiplicato[2] meritorum semine fructum in suis membris centesimum[3] premiorum ad diem retribucionis extreme valeat germinare. Sane dilectus filius noster dominus Johannes de la Rivere miles, dominus de Tormerton nostre diocesis et ecclesie parochialis ville eiusdem patronus, ad honorem omnipotentis dei et pie genitricis eiusdem virginis gloriose,[4] de consensu domini Willelmi rectoris ipsius ecclesie qui nunc est et

1 The whole entry is crossed out, *vacat* being written in the margin. It is complementary rather than contradictory to the other ordination (1211) which follows.
2 1211 has 'multiplici'.
3 1211 has 'consensuum' which does not make sense. 'Centuplum' may have been intended. Cf. the parable of the sower, Luke viii, 8.
4 1211 lacks 'virginis gloriose'.

aliorum quorum interest, volens in eadem ecclesia cultum augmentare divinum ac presbiterorum et aliorum ministrancium in divinis numerum propagare, nobis humiliter supplicavit, quatenus assignatis et appropriatis in forma iuris eidem ecclesie et eius rectori[1] inperpetuum per eundem pro subscriptis omnibus[2] supportandis uno mesuagio et duobus carucatis terre arabilis cum pertinenciis in parochia de Tormerton predicta, de quibus in cartis excellentissimi principis domini Edwardi dei gracia regis Anglie illustris tercii post Conquestum ac domini capitalis ville predicte et dicti militis plenius continetur, quatuor capellanos preter rectorem ecclesie predicte in perpetuum divina celebraturos ibidem, necnon duos clericos, unum videlicet in diaconatus et alium in subdiaconatus officio servientes, qui clerici continue ministerio ecclesie deserviant antedicte, et de nocte iaceant in eadem, ac tres choristas, et omnium predictorum stipendia et officia in forma que sequitur disponere curaremus. Ita videlicet quod omni die profesto seu alio simplici non solempni in ecclesia sive extra mane hora matutinali iuxta temporis diversitatem unus de clericis antedictis unam longam pulsacionem cum una campana faciat ad matutinas pulsare. Deinde bono interposito intervallo, secunda fiat pulsacio cum altera campana quasi medie longitudinis pulsacionis prioris. Ac deinde interposito spacio quasi brevi, cum duabus campanis tercia pulsacio fiat brevis. In cuius pulsacionis terminacione quatuor capellani, clerici et choriste predicti sint in cancello ipsius ecclesie modo et forma descriptis inferius ad psallendum matutinas parati. Diebus vero festivalibus et solempnibus in ecclesia, qui tamen laycis[3] nequaquam pro feriatis seu festivalibus sunt induti, fiat ut premittitur cum una campana prima pulsacio bene longa. Deinde interposito intervallo prout supra, secunda pulsacio brevior cum duabus fiat campanis. Ac postmodum tercia cum duabus campanis fiat eciam sicut supra. Diebus quoque dominicis et aliis festivis per totam parochiam clericis et laycis indifferenter indutis, fiant tres pulsaciones cum duabus campanis sub eadem proporcione longitudinis que prefertur et cum similibus intervallis; modoque consimili pulsetur ad vesperas cum distinccione festivorum et profestorum dierum consimili et cum similibus intervallis. Quibus pulsacionibus finitis, statim quatuor capellani, clerici et choriste predicti constituti in ecclesia predicta ut prefertur parati singulis diebus albis superpelliciis et nigris almiciis induti matutinas cum nota et omnes horas canonicas cum nota vel sine nota prout eis videbitur expedire, preterquam in maioribus festis in quibus dicantur cum nota. Item unam missam de Beata Virgine cum nota et tribus collectis, una de Beata Virgine, alia pro vivis, tercia pro defunctis. Et aliam missam pro defunctis sine nota pro animabus subscriptis cum tribus collectis, prima pro defunctis, secunda de

1 1211 lacks 'et eius rectori'.   2 1211 has 'oneribus'.
3 For 'layci' (laici)? The precise meaning of this phrase is obscure. See below.

pace, tercia pro vivis. Ad terciam missam de die cum tribus solempniter [sic] collectis, una de die, alia pro vivis, tercia pro defunctis cum nota solempniter faciant celebrari, nec ante matutinale missarum et horarum canonicarum completum ministerium prefati capellani, clerici seu choriste absque causa necessaria exeant aut discurrant nec habitum suum predictum deponant. Omnibus autem diebus quibus iuxta usum ecclesie Sar' exequia mortuorum celebrantur in choro, in terminacione prime pulsacionis ad vesperas capellani clerici seu choriste predicti in habitu suo predicto in ecclesia predicta confestim parati faciant sine nota modo debito exequias mortuorum pro animabus dicti domini Johannis fundatoris huiusmodi cantarie et domine Margarete uxoris eiusdem cum de hac luce subtracti fuerint ac animabus patris et matris omniumque antecessorum et successorum dictorum militis, memorate ecclesie patronorum aliorumque benefactorum cantarie, dictorum capellanorum et omnium fidelium defunctorum, ac subsequenter statim finita tercia pulsacione ad vesperas inchoent et perficiant vesperas et completorium omni die cum nota. Die vero deposicionis ac die anniversario dicti fundatoris, uxoris sue, patris et matris predictorum, necnon cuiuslibet futuri successoris eiusdem ecclesie predicte patroni, fiant exequie et misse defunctorum, solempniter cum ix leccionibus, nisi in paschali tempore, cum capis et tunica et cum nota. Pulsetur similiter cum una campana diu [1] et prolixe ignitegium cum [2] sero. Item in singulis festivitatibus Beate Virginis et precipue in festo Assumpcionis eiusdem cum solempnitate celebri quantum possint in eiusdem gloriose virginis laudem gloriam et honorem divinum officium studeant adimplere. Dies vero anniversarios dicti militis, patris, matris, uxoris et omnium successorum suorum patronorum ecclesie predicte, cum missis et exequiis solempnibus teneantur quociens accidere contigerit ipsos observare. Rector vero ecclesie predicte qui pro tempore fuerit teneatur ad residensiam personalem ac per se et capellanos predictos vel unum ex eis quem ad id deputaverit curam ipsius ecclesie in spiritualibus excercere, et cum ipsum rectorem in prefatis officiis contigerit interesse albo superpellicio et almicio nigro furrato vel cendellato iuxta diversitatem temporis induatur. Idem quoque rector prefatis capellanis necnon clericis et choristis exhibeat stipendia sua iuxta cuiuslibet gradus decenciam competencia et honesta prout inter ipsum rectorem et quemlibet de capellanis, clericis et choristis predictis poterit conveniri, ita tamen quod stipendia competencia pro ministris huiusmodi competentibus sufficiencia debeant merito reputari et insufficiencia stipendiorum non sit occasio insufficientes habendi ministros. Item teneatur rector predictus omnia vestimenta et cetera ornamenta altaris et precipue quinque paria vestimentorum ad magnum altare, unum videlicet indi coloris pro diebus profestis sine capa et tunicis, et unum par rubei

1 MS. 'die'.   2 For 'omni'?

coloris cum capa et tunicis pro festo Pasche et solempnis [sic] festivitatibus apostolorum et martirorum. Item unum par viridis coloris cum capa et tunicis pro festis Natalis Domini ac festivitatibus solempnibus confessorum. Item unum par albi coloris cum capa et tunicis pro quinque festivitatibus virginis gloriose et aliis solempnioribus festis virginum beatarum. Item unum par nigri coloris pro anniversariis et deposicionum diebus fundatorum cantarie predicte et aliorum de quibus superius est expressum. Item tria paria vestimentorum in capella Beate Virginis, unum videlicet albi coloris sine capa et tunicis pro missis Beate Virginis in diebus profestis, aliud par similiter albi coloris precii carioris pro diebus dominicis et aliis festis communibus, tercium nigri coloris pro missa de defunctis. Item duo paria vestimentorum pro duobus altaribus in navi ecclesie, unum videlicet pro altari Beate Anne et aliud pro altari Beati Joachym, pro capellanis non intitulatis ad missas predictas[1] missas ibidem[2] volentibus celebrare, cum manutergiis et pannis altarium predictorum. Item unam capsam deauratum in qua una crux aurea cum quadam particula de lingno [sic] crucis dominice et unum vas cristallinum cum quadam particula zone Beate Virginis et cetere diverse reliquie continentur. Item duos moros argeniteos deauratos pro capis. Item tres calices cum tribus paribus corporalium, duo missalia, duo gradalia et duo portiphoria cum nota. Item decem superpellicia, decem almicia. Que omnia una cum pluribus aliis ornamentis diversis prefatus miles dicte ecclesie contulit sub salva custodia suo periculo custodiri, ipsisque vestimentis libris calicibus et ceteris ornamentis demum deficientibus vetustate alia subrogari, pro quo specialiter onere supportando miles prefatus centum arietes dicto rectori donavit, ita quod quilibet rector ecclesie predicte cedens vel decedens tot capita arietum suo successori relinquat ex quarum [sic] fructu onus specialiter supportetur. Item teneatur rector predictus in cancello ipsius ecclesie unam lampadem ardentem continue invenire ac omni anno in die Parasceve quamdiu vixerit idem miles, post eiusdem vero decessum die anniversarii sui, teneatur idem rector centum pauperibus videlicet cuilibet unum panem precii unius oboli et unum allec in dicti militis et omnium predictorum memoriam perpetuam erogare. Nos igitur super premissis cum patrono et rectore predictis necnon cum ceteris quorum interest habito diligenti tractatu et cause cognicione premissa, attendentes eadem ad humani lapsus remedium animarum quoque salutem et altissimo cedere ad honorem, de consilio nobis assidencium peritorum, invocata Spiritus Sancti gracia, de ipsorum patroni et rectoris consensu expresso, rectoriam et rectores ecclesie predicte[3] qui pro tempore fuerint successive, necnon capellanos cantarie, clericos et choristas predictos, sub forma premissa fore previdimus et decernimus

1 As it stands the phrase does not make sense. Perhaps 'ad altaria predicta' was intended.
2 'dem' interlineated.   3 'custodiam et custodes perpetuos ecclesie predicte' in 1211.

auctoritate nostra ordinaria in perpetuum ordinandos et tenore presencium ordinamus. Adicientes de consensu expresso dictorum patroni et rectoris pro ipsis et eorum successoribus in futurum, quod dictus rector [1] pro tempore suo necnon quilibet eius successor futurus in ecclesia antedicta in admissione sua ad rectoriam [2] eandem iuret tactis per eundem corporaliter sacrosanctis [evangeliis] [3] se omnia et singula premissa circa invencionem capellanorum, clericorum et choristarum huiusmodi et eorum stipendia prelibata necnon circa sustentacionem in cantaria huiusmodi lampadis, vestimentorum, vasorum, et aliorum ornamentorum invencionem, reparacionem atque custodiam, ac omnia et singula premissa fideliter servaturum sub pena centum solidorum ecclesie cathedrali Wyg', centum solidorum Wygorn' episcopo, centum solidorum archidiacono Glouc', ac centum solidorum patrono ecclesie de Tormerton predicte qui pro tempore fuerunt, a rectore [4] qui premissis contraire presumpserit quociens [5] in aliquo eorundem defecerit persolvendam, ad quam quidem penam sub forma premissa solvendam omnes rectores [6] qui pro tempore fuerunt [7] ecclesie predicte in eorum admissione astringi volumus et decernimus iuramenti vinculo corporalis. Proviso nichilominus specialiter quod rata manente pene commissione predicte contra eum quem incidere contigerit in eandem si in substituendo loco deficientis vel amoti capellano, clerico seu chorista, rector [8] qui pro tempore fuerit quocumque colore quesito per mensem nec[g]ligens fuerit aut remissus, loci diocesanus aut officialis Wygorn' qui pro tempore fuerit capellanum, clericum seu choristam in loco amoti vel deficientis huiusmodi substituant competenter. Capellani vero clerici et choriste predicti si divinum sub forma premissa servicium [9] adimplere seu eidem interesse [10] non curaverint et super hoc convicti fuerint, pro modo culpe per ordinarium loci graviter puniantur. Et nichilominus a serviciis suis amoveantur omnino, si hoc exposcat eorum negligencia sive culpa, et alii in eorum loco per rectorem [11] loci vel ob eius defectum per eos de quibus premittitur ydonei [12] subrogentur, qui implere velint et valeant efficaciter quod incumbit. Et ut rector predictus liberius ut premittitur residere et capellani predicti officia sua diligencius valeant adimplere, volumus et eciam ordinamus quod rector aut capellani predicti in servis[io] vel obsequio domini seu patroni ecclesie predicte aut alicuius alterius aliunde nullatenus occupentur. Quam quidem ordinacionem nostram patronus et rector predicti pro se et successoribus suis auctoritate nostra et decreto intercedentibus emologarunt et appro-

1 'custos' in 1211.
2 'custodiam' in 1211.
3 Also omitted in 1211.
4 'custode' in 1211.
5 'quocienscumque' in 1211.
6 'custodes' in 1211.
7 'fuerint' in 1211.
8 'custos' in 1211.
9 'serviencium' [sic] in 1211.
10 'intendere' in 1211.
11 'custodem' in 1211.
12 'ydoneis' [sic] in 1211.

barunt expresse et nos eam auctoritate nostra pontificali tenore presencium communimus perpetuis temporibus duraturam: salvis nobis et successoribus nostris ecclesie nostre Wygorn', priori et capitulo eiusdem ecclesie sede vacante, ac archidiacono nostro Glouc' et aliis nostris ministris canonica obediencia, procuracionibus et pentecostalibus consuetis ac aliis omnibus nobis ecclesie priori capitulo archidiacono et ministris nostris predictis racionabiliter debitis ac eciam consuetis. In quorum omnium testimonium sigillum nostrum una cum sigillis dictorum patroni et rectoris presentibus litteris sunt appensa.[1]

1211 *1 May 1344 Letters patent of the later ordination of a chantry at Tormarton (cf. 449 above).*

ORDINACIO CANTARIE DE TORMERTON

Universis [&c. with slight verbal differences as in 449] . . . continetur, dictam ecclesiam sub nomine perpetue custodie et sub regimine custodis intitulandi in ea perpetuo incorporandam et quatuor capellanos in perpetuum divina celebraturos ibidem ac duos clericos, unum videlicet in diaconatus et alium in subdiaconatus officio servientes, ac tres choristas, et omnium predictorum stipendia et officia in forma que sequitur disponere curaremus.[2] Ita videlicet quod quatuor capellani, clerici et choriste predicti convenientes cotidie in ecclesia antedicta superpelliciis albis et nigris almiciis induti horis debitis, matutinas cum nota [dicant]:[3] item unam missam de Beate Virgine cum nota et aliam missam[4] pro defunctis sine nota pro animabus subscriptis ac terciam missam de die cum nota faciant solempniter celebrari. Omnibus autem diebus quibus iuxta usum ecclesie Sar' exequie mortuorum solent celebrari in choro, capellani clerici et choriste predicti ante vesperas cum nota, sicut de matutinis premittitur, celebrandas faciant in ecclesia predicta sine nota modo debito exequias mortuorum pro animabus dicti domini Johannis fundatoris huius[5] cantarie et domine Margarete uxoris eiusdem, necnon domini Edwardi regis supradicti et domine Philippe uxoris sue, domini Wolstani dei gracia Wyg' episcopi et domini Johannis de Evesham' prioris ecclesie cathedralis Wyg' cum de hac luce subtracti fuerunt, ac animabus patris et matris omniumque antecessorum et successorum dicti militis memorate ecclesie patronorum aliorumque benefactorum dicte cantarie, dictorum capellanorum, et omnium fidelium defunctorum. Die vero deposicionis ac die anniversario dicti fundatoris et uxoris sue, patris et matris predictorum, necnon cuiuslibet futurorum successorum eiusdem ecclesie predicte patroni, fiant pro animabus ipsorum exequie et missa solempniter de

1 'est appensum' in 1211.   2 're' interlineated.
3 Cf. 449.   4 A second 'et aliam missam' crossed out.
5 MS. 'huiusmodi'.

35

defunctis. Custos vero ecclesie predicte qui pro tempore fuerit teneatur ad residenciam personalem apud ipsam ecclesiam faciendum ac per se et capellanos predictos vel unum ex eis quem ad hoc deputaverit curam ipsius ecclesie in spiritualibus exercere, et cum ipsum custodem in prefatis officiis contigerit interesse albo superpellicio et almicio nigro furrato vel sendellato iuxta diversitatem temporis induatur. Idem quoque custos dignitatis nomine senceatur et in signum sue dignitatis utatur supertunica clausa et cum sacerdotis officio personaliter fungitur utatur eciam pillio nigro lato rotundo furrato. Ipsis quoque capellanis clericis et choristis exhibeat[1] stipendia sua iuxta cuiuslibet gradus decenciam competencia et honesta, videlicet victualia sua et hospicia competencia in domo ipsius custodis ac dictis capellanis videlicet cuilibet eorum viginti quatuor solidos sterlingorum, clericis quoque singulis sex solidos, cuilibet eciam choriste quadraginta denarios. Item teneatur custos predictus unam lampadem in cancello dicte ecclesie ardentem continuo ac alia sufficiencia luminaria, libros, calices, vestimenta, et altaris ornamenta cetera invenire, pro quo specialiter onere supportando miles prefatus instaurum animalium, videlicet boum, equorum et ovium ad valorem viginti librarum sterlingorum, prefato rectori donavit; ita quod quilibet custos ecclesie predicte cedens vel decedens tantummodo instauri vel pecunie numerate suo successori relinquerit, ex cuius proveniente onus prefatum specialiter supportetur. Nos igitur super premissis cum patrono et rectore predictis necnon omnibus ceteris quorum interest habito diligenti tractatu [&c. as in 449] . . . presentibus litteris est appensum.[2] Dat' apud Hertlebury primo die mensis Maii anno domini mcccxliiii, et consecracionis nostre sexto.

658 *5 July 1343*[3] *Episcopal confirmation of William de Syde's ordination of a chantry in the church of Our Lady, Syde.*

SYDE   CANTARIA IN ECCLESIA BEATE MARIE DE SYDE.

Christi fideles noverint universi quod ego Willelmus de Syde attendens secundum apostolum [&c. as in 154—disponere] . . . ut michi ad subsidia spiritualia prosint in celestibus et in terris proximis grata prestent alimenta. Qua propter de consensu et per cartam domini nostri domini Edwardi tercii post Conquestum regis Anglie illustris cuius carte tenor inferius continetur ordinavi et ordino per presentes unam perpetuam cantariam in ecclesia parochiali Beate Marie semper virginis de Syde Wygorn' diocesis per capellanum ydoneum celebrandam, quam de terris redditibus et tenementis meis

1 'dispendia' crossed out.
2 The slight verbal difference between the two entries is noted in 449 above.
3 The ordination is dated 20 June 1343.

in Syde et aliis bonis meis fundavi pariter et dotavi. Tenor vero carte domini nostri domini Edwardi regis supradicti talis est: Edwardus [&c. as in 154—teneatur] . . . de gracia tamen nostra speciali concessimus et licenciam dedimus pro nobis et heredibus nostris quantum in nobis est Willelmo de Syde quod ipse unum mesuagium, duas virgates terre et unam acram bosci cum pertinenciis in Syde que de nobis non tenentur ut dicitur, dare possit et assignare cuidam capellano divina singulis diebus in ecclesia de Syde celebraturo, habenda et tenenda eidem capellano et successoribus suis capellanis divina singulis diebus in ecclesia predicta celebraturis inperpetuum. Et eidem capellano quod ipse mesuagium terram et boscum predicta cum pertinenciis a prefato Willelmo recipere possit et retinere sibi et successoribus suis predictis sicut predictum est, tenore presencium similiter licenciam dedimus specialem. Nolentes quod idem Willelmus seu heredes sui aut predictus capellanus [&c. as in 154—patentes]. Teste me ipso apud Westmonasterium quinto die Maii anno regni nostri Anglie decimo septimo, regni vero nostri Francie quarto.[1] Et ut circa premissa ordinacionis mee modus et devocionis affectus vobis serenius illucescat, carte mee formam sub tenore qui subsequitur duxi presentibus inserendam cuius est tenor talis: Sciant presentes et futuri quod ego Willelmus de Syde dedi concessi et hac presenti carta mea confirmavi pro me et heredibus meis inperpetuum domino Radulpho Cole capellano et successoribus suis capellanis perpetuo singulis diebus in ecclesia parochiali Beate Marie semper virginis de Syde divina de predicta Beata Maria semper virgine pro salubri statu meo dum vixero et pro salubri statu domini Thome domini de Berkelee, domini Mauricii de Berkelee, et domini Mauricii de Berkelee,[2] domini Johannis Mautravers, domini Reginaldi de Cobham, domine Johanne uxoris eius, Ricardi de Cestre, Willelmi de Chiltenham, et omnium consanguineorum amicorum et benefactorum meorum et omnium aliorum quorum debitor sum et pro anima mea cum ab hac luce migravero et pro animabus omnium supradictorum cum diem clauserint extremum, ac eciam pro animabus patris mei et matris mee, fratrum, sororum, et omnium consanguineorum meorum et animabus domini Johannis Gyffard, domine Margarete Gyffard, domine Margarete de Berkelee, domini Johannis de Wylinton, domine Johanne uxoris eius, et omnium amicorum et benefactorum meorum et omnium aliorum quorum debitor sum, ac omnium fidelium defunctorum, celebraturis, unum mesuagium, duas virgatas terre et unam acram bosci cum pertinenciis in Syde, habenda et tenenda omnia predicta mesuagium, terram et boscum cum pertinenciis ut predictum est prefato domino Radulpho capellano et successoribus suis capellanis in ecclesia predicta celebraturis inperpetuum. Et ego predictus Willelmus et heredes mei

---

1 C.P.R. 1343–45, p. 32: 5 May 1343.
2 Thomas de Berkeley had a brother and a son named Maurice.

omnia predicta mesuagium, terram et boscos cum pertinenciis
prefato domino Radulpho capellano et successoribus suis capellanis
divina singulis diebus in ecclesia predicta in forma supradicta
celebraturis contra omnes homines warantizabimus et defendemus
inperpetuum. Ad quam quidem cantariam predictum dominum
capellanum venerabili in Christo patri domino Wolstano dei gracia
Wygorn' episcopo presentavi, ac per ipsum ad eandem admitti,
institui et corporaliter induci in eadem sicut capellanum decet
perpetuum procuravi, sicque toto vite mee tempore quociens ipsam
cantariam vacare contigerit, domino Wygorn' episcopo qui pro
tempore fuerit sede plena, vel priori Wygorn' ipsa vacante, unum
capellanum idoneum ad eandem cantariam presentabo et post
mortem meam dominus de Berkelee qui pro tempore fuerit consimili
modo inperpetuum presentabit. Et si ego in vita mea a tempore
vacacionis dicte cantarie aut dominus de Berkelee qui pro tempore
fuerit post mortem meam capellanum idoneum presentare omisero
vel omiserit per mensem, volo et ordino quod abbas Sancti Augustini
Bristoll' qui pro tempore fuerit ad eandem cantariam capellanum
idoneum presentet illa vice. Et si forte per mensem omiserit vel in
presentando necligens fuerit, volo et ordino quod episcopus Wygorn'
qui pro tempore fuerit sede plena, aut prior Wygorn' ipsa vacante,
ipsam cantariam capellano idoneo conferat illa vice. Salvis tamen
michi dum vixero et domino de Berkelee qui pro tempore fuerit post
mortem meam cum dictam cantariam alias vacare contigerit iure et
privilegio presentandi ad eandem iuxta modum et formam prenominatos. Ac volo et ordino quod predictus dominus Radulphus
capellanus et successores sui capellani in dicta cantaria residenciam
faciant personalem et quod cotidie celebrent et ministrent iuxta
ordinacionem meam prescriptam et subscriptam. In quibus residencia et celebracione si continue defecerint per quindenam ille ad
quem dicte cantarie pertinet presentacio capellanum idoneum loco
ipsius sic a residencia et celebracione cessantis presentet sine mora,
nisi forte iusta et racionabilis causa fuerit absentandi vel a celebracione cessandi auctoritate ordinaria approbanda et reprobanda. Et
volo et ordino quod predictus dominus Radulphus capellanus et
successores sui capellani in dicta ecclesia parochiali sint cotidie ad
missam matutinas et horas cum aliis eiusdem ecclesie ministris
cantantes et ministrantes, nisi legitimis causis fuerint impediti, et
quod singulis diebus devote dicant officium mortuorum pro animabus
omnium supradictorum videlicet PLACEBO et DIRIGE cum commendacione, et quod in singulis missis suis dicant pro me et pro omnibus
supradictis vivis collectam DEUS QUI CARITATIS DONA cum secreto et
postcommunione pertinentibus, et pro animabus supradictorum
collectam FIDELIUM DEUS vel OMNIPOTENS SEMPITERNE DEUS CUI
NUNQUAM SINE SPE cum secreto et postcommunione pertinentibus, et
quod singulis annis post mortem meam in diem anniversarii mei

dicant pro anima mea plenarie officium mortuorum cum missa in crastino et sic annuatim die anniversarii mei faciant inperpetuum. Et volo et ordino quod a nullo pecuniam nec aliquod pro divino officio celebrando accipiant set de porcione per me eis assignata omnino sint contenti, et quod nulli homini deserviant set soli deo in spiritualibus et sibi ipsis in honestis et necessariis temporalibus, et quod caste et honeste vivant, ad mercata neque ad tabernas accedant nisi ex causis necessariis, nec de mercimoniis illicitis ullo modo se intromittant, et quod ludibria et spectacula illicita et congregaciones inhonestas omnino fugiant. Volo eciam et ordino quod capellanus predicte cantarie qui pro tempore fuerit de supradicta porcione pro dicte cantarie sustentacione per me ut premittitur assignata et ordinata alicui ad firmam [non] dimittat nisi ad terminum annorum et hoc ad verum valorem et de assensu meo dum vixero et domini de Berkel' qui pro tempore fuerit post mortem meam. Et si forte contra formam predictam aliquod inde dimiserit, volo et ordino quod ille capellanus per quem huiusmodi dimissio facta fuerit statim amoveatur, et quod ex tunc bene liceat michi in vita mea et domino de Berkel' qui pro tempore fuerit post mortem meam porciones sic dimissas seisire et retinere in quorumcumque manu devenerint quousque alius idoneus capellanus ad eandem cantariam presentetur admittatur et legitime in eadem instituatur, cui ego in vita mea, seu dominus de Berkelee qui pro tempore fuerit post mortem meam, dictas porciones sic dimissas et ob hanc causam seisitas et retentas reddamus et iuxta tenorem huiusmodi carte reddere teneamur. Ac volo et ordino quod edificia clausure et omnia alia ad dictam cantariam pertinencia per predictum dominum Radulphum capellanum et successores suos capellanos congrue inperpetuum sustententur et gubernentur, ne pro defectu sustentacionis corruant et periclitentur. Et quia volo quod predicta cantaria et omnia ad ipsam spectancia ad honorem dei et sanctissime Marie semper virginis omniumque sanctorum inperpetuum utilius et decensius sustententur, predicto domino Radulpho capellano dedi et liberare feci de bonis meis ad valenciam quatuordecim librarum decem et octo solidorum et decem denariorum, videlicet unum equum et duos boves precii xxx s. et iiii^{xx} et decem multones precii vi li. xv s., vii acras seminatas cum frumento precii xxi s., xi acras seminatas cum ordio precii xxvii s. vid., vii acras seminatas cum dragio precii xiiii s., xii acras seminatas cum avena precii xviii s., et in denariis quatuor marcas. Quare volo et ordino quod predictus dominus Radulphus capellanus et successores sui capellani post eorum decessum per visum domini de Berkel' qui pro tempore fuerit capellano succedenti bona et catalla tam in denariis quam in aliis rebus ad predicte summe valenciam dimittant, et quod predictus dominus de Berkel' qui pro tempore fuerit cum omni diligencia de anno in annum supervidere faciat quod capellanus dicte cantarie sic se in rebus et negocio dictam cantariam tangentibus gerat et habeat, quod predictam ordinacionem meam in omnibus valeat adimplere. Et ad omnia predicta tenenda et observanda in forma supradicta, volo et ordino quod quilibet capellanus dicte cantarie qui pro tempore fuerit in eius institucione coram ordinario corporale prestet sacramentum prout fragilitas humane condicionis permittet. Et ut predicte ordinacionis mee modus omnibus in futurum appareat evidenter et memorie futurorum specialiter recommendetur, volo et ordino quod capellanus dicte cantarie qui pro tempore fuerit faciat annuatim inperpetuum in supradicta ecclesia in festo Assumpcionis Beate Marie ad missam vel alio tempore quando melius viderit expedire hoc presens instrumentum coram omni populo puplicare.[1] Et si dicte cantarie capellanus qui pro tempore fuerit ad tantam etatem seu infirmitatem pervenerit, quod personaliter non poterit missam celebrare, dicat cotidie oracionem dominicam et alias oraciones privatas cum PLACEBO, DIRIGE, et commendacione, septem psalmos[2] et quindecim cum letania pro me et omnibus aliis supradictis vivis et defunctis, ita quod conscienciam suam servet illesam, et singulis septimanis per capellanum idoneum faciat duas missas celebrari, videlicet unam de Sancta Maria pro me et omnibus supradictis vivis, et aliam pro animabus omnium supradictorum defunctorum; et tamen propter etatem inexcusabilem seu infirmitatem non amoveatur. Et volo et ordino quod loci dyocesanus aut eius in hac parte vicarius in suis visitacionibus et aliis temporibus inquirat et inquirere faciat si predicta cantaria et omnia ad ipsam spectancia secundum modum et formam ordinacionis mee supradicte gubernentur, exequantur et observentur. Et si quos defectus notabiles seu crimina turpia invenerit, delinquentem secundum delicti sui exigenciam corrigat et puniat condecenter, ne propter inmundiciam predicta cantaria labescat in futurum. In quorum omnium testimonium presentibus sigillum meum apposui. Hiis testibus, domino Thoma de Berkelee de Cubberleye, domino Johanne de Acton, Waltero de Cirencestr', Johanne de Elkeston, Thoma de la Mare de Rendecombe, Johanne de Alspath, Thoma de Berton de Eycote, et aliis. Dat' apud Syde vicesimo die Junii anno regni regis Edwardi supradicti decimo septimo.

Nos igitur frater Wolstanus permissione divina Wygorn' episcopus, laudabile propositum et pium desiderium predicti domini Willelmi de Syde quo ad fundacionem dotacionem et ordinacionem dicte cantarie de qua superius plenius continetur merito comendantes, huiusmodi cantariam ipsiusque fundacionem dotacionem et ordinacionem quantum in nobis est auctoritate nostra ordinaria approbamus ratificamus et ex certa sciencia confirmamus. Inhibemus eciam omnibus et singulis subditis nostris ne fundacionem dotacionem et

1 *Rectius* 'publicari'.
2 MS. 'spalm'.

ordinacionem supradictas aliquo modo infringant seu infringere procurent, capellanum eiusdem cantarie in suis iuribus et porcionibus percipiendis animo iniuriandi impediant seu perturbent, sub pena excommunicacionis sentencie maioris. In quorum omnium testimonium sigillum nostrum hiis fecimus apponi. Dat' apud Heortlebur' [*sic*] quinto die Julii anno domini millesimo ccc^{mo} quadragesimo tercio, et consecracionis nostre quinto.

Et nos frater Johannes prior et capitulum ecclesie cathedralis Wygorn', predictas donaciones, concessiones, dotaciones, litteras et assignaciones, approbacionem, ratificacionem et confirmacionem supradicti venerabilis patris nostri sicut rite et canonice fieri dinoscuntur, ratas habentes et gratas, omni iure Wygorn' ecclesie semper salvo, tenore presencium approbamus et confirmamus. In cuius rei testimonium sigillum nostrum commune presentibus fecimus apponi. Dat' in capitulo nostro Wygorn' decimo die Julii anno domini millesimo ccc^{mo}. quadragesimo tercio.

660 *20 June 1343* *Episcopal confirmation of William de Syde's ordination of a chantry in St. Maurice's chapel, Newport, in Berkeley parish, which is to be served by two chaplains.*[1]

NEWEPORT.

Christi fideles noverint universi [&c. as in 658—inferius continetur,] ordinavi et ordino per presentes unam perpetuam cantariam in capella Sancti Mauricii de Neweport Wygorn' diocesis per duos capellanos idoneos celebrandam, quam de terris redditibus et tenementis meis in Berkel', Wotton, Alkynton, et Hulle iuxta Berkelee, ac bonis meis aliis fundavi pariter et dotavi. Tenor vero carte [&c.] . . . Willelmo de Syde quod ipse duo mesuagia, duas virgatas terre, et centum solidatas redditus cum pertinenciis in Berkelee, Wotton, Alkynton et Hulle iuxta Berkelee, que de nobis non tenentur, ut dicitur, dare possit et assignare duobus capellanis divina singulis diebus in capella de Neweport celebraturis, habenda et tenenda eisdem capellanis et successoribus suis capellanis divina singulis diebus in capella predicta celebraturis inperpetuum. Et eisdem capellanis quod ipsi mesuagia, terram et redditum predicta cum pertinenciis a prefato Willelmo recipere possint et tenere sibi et successoribus suis predictis sicut predictum est, tenore presencium similiter licenciam dedimus specialem. Nolentes quod idem Willelmus seu heredes sui aut predicti capellani vel successores sui racione statuti predicti per nos vel heredes nostros inde occasionentur

---

1 For the most part this ordination follows that of Syde verbatim, but because at Newport there was provision for a second chaplain, 'ut dicte capelle custodem' (& *mutatis mutandis* for oblique cases) follows the usual 'capellanum idoneum'.

[&c.] . . . quarto.[1] Et ut circa premissa [&c.] . . . talis: Sciant
presentes et futuri quod ego Willelmus de Syde dedi, concessi et hac
presenti carta mea confirmavi pro me et heredibus meis inperpetuum
domino Roberto de Sodynton capellano custodi capelle Sancti
Mauricii de Neweport et successoribus suis capellanis custodibus et
uni alii capellano perpetuo singulis diebus in predicta capella pro
salubri statu meo dum vixero ac pro salubri statu domini Thome
[&c.] . . . Willelmi de Chiltenham, Roberti Groundy, et omnium
amicorum et benefactorum meorum [&c.—celebraturis,] . . . duo
mesuagia, duas virgatas terre, et centum solidatas redditus cum
pertinenciis in Berkelee, Wotton, Alkynton et Hulle iuxta Berkel',
habenda et tenenda predicta mesuagia, terram et redditum cum
pertinenciis ut predictum est predicto domino Robert capellano dicte
capelle custodi et successoribus suis capellanis eiusdem capelle
custodibus et uni alii capellano divina singulis diebus in capella
predicta celebraturis ut predictum est inperpetuum. Et ego predictus
Willelmus et heredes mei omnia predicta mesuagia, terram et
redditum cum pertinenciis prefato domino Roberto capellano dicte
capelle custodi et successoribus suis capellanis eiusdem capelle
custodibus et uni alii capellano secundario divina singulis diebus in
predicta capella ut predictum est celebraturis contra omnes gentes
warantizabimus et inperpetuum defendemus. Ad quam quidem
cantariam predictum dominum Robertum capellanum dicte capelle
custodem sub nomine custodis venerabili in Christo patri domino
Wulstano dei gracia Wygorn' episcopo presentavi, ac per ipsum ad
eandem admitti institui et corporaliter induci in eadem sicut decet
capellanum perpetuum procuravi, et unum alium capellanum
secundarium ibidem ordinavi, sicque [&c.] . . . unum capellanum
idoneum ut predicte capelle custodem ad eandem cantariam
presentabo [&c. *mutatis mutandis* as in 658—prenominatos.] Ac volo
et ordino quod dictus dominus Robertus capellanus dicte capelle
custos et successores sui capellani eiusdem capelle custodes et alius
capellanus secundarius in dicta cantaria residenciam faciant
personalem, et quod cotidie celebrent et ministrent iuxta ordinacionem subscriptam. In quibus residencia et celebracione si ambo vel
alter eorum continue defecerint vel defecerit per quindenam, ille ad
quam dicte cantarie pertinet presentacio unum capellanum idoneum
seu capellanos idoneos loco ipsorum seu ipsius sic a celebracione
cessancium vel cessantis presentet sine mora, nisi forte iusta causa et
racionabilis fuerit absentandi vel a celebracione cessandi auctoritate
ordinaria approbanda vel reprobanda. Et volo et ordino quod
predictus dominus Robertus capellanus dicte capelle custos et
successores sui capellani dicte capelle custodes et alius capellanus
secundarius sint in ecclesia parochiali de Berkel' cum aliis ministris
eiusdem ecclesie cantantes et ministrantes, videlicet die[bus]

1 *C.P.R.* 1343–45, p. 23: 5 May 1343.

Natalis Domini, Epiphanie, ad matutinas et missam; diebus Purificacionis, Cynerum, Ramis Palmarum, ad missam; Cene Domini,
Parasceves, vigilia Pasche et in die Pasche, ad matutinas et missam;
in vigilia et in die Pentecostes ad missam; et in omnibus aliis festis in
quibus de iure vel de consuetudine eiusdem ecclesie parochiani offere
tenentur, nisi ex causis legitimis fuerint inpediti, et quod singulis
diebus devote dicant officium mortuorum pro animabus omnium
supradictorum, videlicet PLACEBO et DIRIGE cum commendacione, et quod in singulis missis suis dicant pro me et pro supradictis
amicis et benefactoribus meis et pro omnibus aliis vivis quorum
debitor sum collectam DEUS QUI CARITATIS DONA cum secreto et
postcommunione pertinentibus, et pro animabus omnium superius
nominatorum ac omnium amicorum et benefactorum meorum
et aliorum quorum debitor sum et omnium fidelium defunctorum collectam FIDELIUM DEUS vel OMNIPOTENS SEMPITERNE DEUS CUI
NUNQUAM SINE SPE cum secreto et postcommunione pertinentibus,
et quod singulis annis post mortem meam in die anniversarii mei
dicant plenarie pro anima mea officium mortuorum cum missa in
crastino, et sic die anniversarii mei annuatim faciant inperpetuum.
Et volo et ordino quod a nullo [&c.—temporalibus,] . . . et quod caste
et honeste simul vivant simul habitent et comedant et in uno manso
cubent absque inconvenienti personarum distinccione, et quod ad
mercata neque ad tabernas nisi ex causis necessariis accedant nec de
mercimoniis illicitis ullo modo se intromittant, et quod ludibria et
spectacula illicita et congregaciones inhonestas fugiant. Et quia volo
quod tam iter agentes quam agri cultores et alii operarii ad honorem
omnipotentis dei cotidie missam audiant, volo et ordino quod unus
predictorum duorum capellanorum qui pro tempore fuerint pro dis-
posicione dicti capellani custodis mane et alius capellanus circa
horam terciam in estate et circa horam sextam in yeme cotidie celebrent nisi forte inexcusabilis causa eos excusat. Et volo et ordino quod
capellanus dicte capelle custos et successores sui capellani eiusdem
capelle custodes capellano secundario qui pro tempore fuerit in victu,
vestitu et aliis necessariis sicut sibi ipsis inveniant et ministrent. Ac
volo et ordino quod capellanus dicte capelle custos qui pro tempore
fuerit omnium rerum ad dictam cantariam spectancium principalem
curam habeat et administracionem, ita tamen quod unanimi
consilio operentur et faciant. Volo eciam et ordino quod post
decessum vel recessum capellani secundarii custos dicte capelle qui
pro tempore fuerit alium capellanum idoneum loco capellani
decedentis vel recedentis de assensu meo dum vixero et domini de
Berkel' qui pro tempore fuerit post mortem meam infra mensem
prox[ime] sequentem provideat et sibi in socium admittat. Et volo et
ordino quod capellanus dicte capelle custos qui pro tempore fuerit de
supradicta porcione pro sustentacione dicte cantarie per me ut
premittitur assignata alicui ad firmam [non] dimittat nisi ad

terminum annorum et hoc ad verum valorem et de assensu meo dum vixero et domini de Berkel' qui pro tempore fuerit post decessum meum. Et si forte inde contra formam predictam aliquid dimiserit, volo et ordino quod ille capellanus per quem huiusmodi dimissio facta fuerit statim amoveatur, et quod ex tunc bene liceat michi in vita mea et domino de Berkel' qui pro tempore fuerit post decessum meum omnia predicta terram et tenementa sic dimissa seisire et retinere in quorumcumque manus devenerint quousque alius capellanus ut dicte capelle custos presentetur, admittatur et legitime instituatur, cui ego dum vixero seu dominus de Berkel' qui pro tempore fuerit post mortem meam dicta terram et tenementa sic dimissa et ob hanc causam seisita et retenta reddamus et iuxta tenorem huius carte reddere teneamur. Ac volo et ordino quod predicta capella et eiusdem ornamenta et omnia alia eidem necessaria, domus, edificia, clausure, et omnia alia ad dictam cantariam pertinentes per dicte capelle custodem qui pro tempore fuerit congrue inperpetuum et honeste sustententur, ne pro defectu sustentacionis alias corruant et periclitentur per necgligenciam et defectum dicti custodis. Et quia volo quod predicta cantaria et omnia ad ipsam spectancia ad honorem dei et sanctissime Marie semper virginis omniumque sanctorum inperpetuum utilius et decencius sustententur, predicto Roberto capellano dicte capelle custodi de bonis meis dedi et liberare feci ad valenciam decem et septem librarum sex solidorum et octo denariorum, videlicet tria iumenta precii viginti et quatuor solidorum, sex boves precii quatuor librarum, decem et octo acras terre seminatas cum frumento precii sexaginta et duodecim solidorum, quatuordecim acras seminatas cum fabis precii triginta et quinque solidorum, unam acram seminatam cum dragio precii duorum solidorum, decem et octo acras seminatas cum avena precii viginti et septem solidorum, et in denariis numeratis pro salario eiusdem capellani dicte capelle custodis et socii sui capellani pro anno proximo futuro octo marcas. Quare volo et ordino quod predictus dominus Robertus dicte capelle custos et successores sui capellani eiusdem capelle custodes post eorum decessum vel recessum capellano dicte capelle custodi succedenti bona et catalla tam in denariis quam in aliis rebus ad supradicte summe valenciam per visum domini de Berkel' qui pro tempore fuerit dimittant, et quod predictus dominus de Berkel' qui pro tempore fuerit supervideat et cum omni diligencia supervidere faciat quod capellanus dicte capelle custos qui pro tempore fuerit in rebus et negociis ad dictam cantariam spectantibus sic se habeat et gerat quod predictam ordinacionem meam in omnibus valeat adimplere. Et ad omnia predicta in omnibus facienda tenenda et in forma supradicta observanda, volo et ordino quod prefatus dominus Robertus capellanus custos et successores sui capellani eiusdem capelle custodes in eorum institucione coram ordinario ad sancta dei evangelia corporale prestent iuramentum prout fragilitas humane condicionis permittet. Et volo et ordino quod dicte capelle custos qui pro tempore fuerit annuatim inperpetuum faciat hoc presens instrumentum in festo Omnium Sanctorum in predicta ecclesia de Berkel' de verbo in verbum coram omni populo recitare et puplicare. Et si forte dicte capelle custos qui pro tempore fuerit ad tantam etatem seu infirmitatem pervenerit, quod personaliter non poterit missam celebrare, dicat cotidie oracionem dominicam et alias privatas oraciones quas poterit cum PLACEBO, DIRIGE et commendacione, septem spalmos [sic] et quindecim cum letania pro me dum vixero et omnibus supradictis vivis dum vixerint et anima mea cum ab hac luce migravero et animabus omnium supradictorum, ita quod conscienciam suam servet illesam, et singulis septimanis loco suo faciat duas missas videlicet unam pro salubri statu meo dum vixero vel pro anima mea cum ab hac luce migravero, et aliam de Sancta Maria pro animabus omnium supradictorum, per capellanum idoneum celebrari, et tamen propter etatem inexcusabilem seu infirmitatem inevitabilem non amoveatur, et quod loci dyocesanus in suis visitacionibus et aliis temporibus aut eius in hac parte vicarius diligenter inquirat et inquirere faciat si predicta cantaria et omnia ad ipsam spectancia secundum modum et formam ordinacionis mee predicte in omnibus exequantur, gubernentur et observentur. Et si quod defectus notabiles veluti dilapidacionem bonorum et substancie dictorum capellanorum vel crimen incontinencie aut aliquod aliud enorme invenerit, delinquentem seu delinquentes in hac parte secundum delicti exigenciam corrigat, puniat seu totaliter amoveat, ne propter eorum necgligenciam vel vite et morum inmundiciam predicta cantaria labescat et corruat in futurum. In quorum omnium testimonium presentibus sigillum meum apposui. Hiis testibus, dominis Thoma de Bradeston, Johanne de Acton, Petro Corbet, Simone Basset militibus, Johanne le Sergeant et aliis. Dat' apud Berkel' vicesimo die Junii anno regni regis Edwardi supradicti decimo septimo.

[The bishop and the prior and chapter of Worcester append their confirmation and approval verbatim as in 658.]

735 *30 June 1345 Episcopal confirmation of Thomas de Berkeley's ordination of a chantry at Over.*

ORDINACIO CANTARIE DE OVERE.

Universis sancte matris ecclesie filiis ad quorum noticiam presentes littere pervenerint frater Wolstanus permissione divina Wygorn' episcopus, salutem in domino sempiternam. Noverit universitas vestra quod nos litteras nobilis militis domini Thome domini de Berkelee recepimus, inspeximus et vidimus diligenter, tenorem qui sequitur continentes: Christi fideles noverint universi quod ego Thomas de Berkelee filius Mauricii de Berkelee chivaler attendens [&c. as in 154—alimenta.] . . . Quapropter de consensu et per cartam domini nostri domini Edwardi tercii post Conquestum regis Anglic illustris cuius carte tenor inferius continetur, ordinavi et ordino per presentes unam perpetuam cantariam in capella Sancti Jacobi de Ovr' Wygorn' diocesis per capellanum ydoneum celebrandam quam de terris meis dominicis, redditibus et proventibus manerii mei de Ovr' ac bonis aliis fundavi pariter et dotavi. Tenor vero carte domini nostri domini Edwardi regis supradicti talis est. Edwardus [&c. as in 154—salutem]. Sciatis quod de gracia nostra speciali concessimus et licenciam dedimus pro nobis et heredibus nostris quantum in nobis est dilecto et fideli nostro Thome de Berkelee quod ipse unum mesuagium et duas virgatas terre cum pertinenciis in Ovr', que de nobis non tenentur in capite ut dicitur, dare possit et assignare cuidam capellano divina singulis diebus in capella de Ovr' pro anima ipsius Thome et anima Margarete que fuit uxor predicti Thome iam defuncte, necnon animabus omnium fidelium defunctorum celebraturo, habenda et tenenda eidem capellano et successoribus suis capellanis divina singulis diebus in capella predicta pro animabus predictis celebraturis in perpetuum, et eidem capellano quod ipse mesuagium et terram predicta cum pertinenciis a prefato Thoma recipere possit et tenere sibi et successoribus suis capellanis divina singulis diebus in capella predicta pro animabus predictis celebraturis inperpetuum[1] sicut predictum est, tenore presencium similiter licenciam dedimus specialem, statuto de terris et tenementis ad manu[m] mortuam ńon ponendis edito non obstante. Nolentes quod predictus Thomas vel heredes sui aut prefatus capellanus seu successores sui racione statuti predicti per nos vel heredes nostros inde occasionentur in aliquo seu graventur: salvis tamen capitalibus dominis feodi illius serviciis inde[2] debitis et consuetis. In cuius rei testimonium has litteras nostras fieri fecimus patentes. Teste me ipso apud Westmonasterium duodecimo die Marcii anno regni nostri Anglie decimo nono, regni vero nostri Francie sexto.[3] Et ut [&c. as in 154—talis.] . . . Sciant presentes et futuri quod ego Thomas de Berkelee filius Mauricii de Berkelee chivaler dedi concessi et hac presenti carta mea confirmavi pro me et heredibus meis imperpetuum domino Willelmo de Cope de Tettebur' capellano et successoribus suis capellanis perpetuo singulis diebus in capella Sancti Jacobi de Ovre divina pro salubri statu meo dum vixero et anima mea cum ab hac luce migravero, necnon pro animabus Margarete quondam uxoris mee, patris et matris mee ac aliorum parentum et amicorum meorum, ac eciam pro animabus omnium fidelium defunctorum pro quibus orare teneor, necnon pro animabus omnium fidelium

1 'et eidem — inperpetuum' interlineated.
2 'inde' interlineated.   3 C.P.R. 1343–45, p. 442: 12 March 1345.

defunctorum, celebraturis, unum mesuagium et duas virgatas terre cum pertinenciis in Over', habenda et tenenda omnia predicta mesuagium et terram ut predictum est predicto domino Willelmo capellano et successoribus suis capellanis in capella predicta divina singulis diebus celebraturis ut predictum est imperpetuum. Et ego vero predictus Thomas et heredes mei predicta mesuagium et duas virgatas terre cum pertinenciis suis prefato domino Willelmo capellano et successoribus suis capellanis divina singulis diebus in capella predicta celebraturis ut predictum est contra omnes homines warantizabimus acquietabimus et defendemus imperpetuum. In cuius omnium testimonium huic presenti carte sigillum meum est appensum. Dat' apud Berkelee vicesimo die Maii anno regni regis Edwardi tercii a Conquestu decimo nono. Ad quam quidem cantariam predictum dominum Willelmum [&c. as in 154— presentabo], ac eciam heredes mei predicti consimiliter presentabunt. Et si ego vel heredes mei predicti presentare omisero vel omiserint per mensem a tempore vacacionis huiusmodi cantarie volo et ordino quod abbas Sancti Augustini Bristoll' qui pro tempore fuerit ad eandem presentet illa vice, nisi forte per mensem dimiserit vel negligens fuerit in presentando, in quo casu episcopus Wygorn' qui pro tempore fuerit sede plena, vel ipsa vacante prior Wygorn', ìpsam cantariam conferat sine mora: salvis michi et heredibus meis alias cum dictam cantariam vacare contigerit iure et privilegio presentacionis supradicte iuxta modum et formam prenotatos. Ac volo et ordino quod dictus dominus Willelmus [&c. as in 154—viderit expedire,] . . . quodque predicti dominus Willelmus capellanus et successores sui capellani temporibus suis sint in ecclesia parochiali de Almundesbur' ad matutinas et missas, videlicet diebus Natalis Domini, Epiphanie, Purificacionis Beate Marie, diebus Cinerum ad missam, Cene Domini, Parasceves, vigilia Pasche et in die Pasche, vigilia Penthecostes et in die Penthecostes,[1] et cum aliis cantent et ministrent nisi ex causis legitimis fuerint impediti; et quod singulis diebus dicant officium mortuorum, videlicet PLACEBO et DIRIGE cum commendacione pro animabus predictis; et quod in singulis missis suis pro me et aliis parentibus et benefactoribus vivis dicant collectam DEUS QUI CARITATIS DONA cum secreto et postcommunione, et pro amicis parentibus et benefactoribus meis defunctis collectam FIDELIUM DEUS vel OMNIPOTENS SEMPITERNE DEUS CUI NUNQUAM SINE SPE cum secreto et postcommunione. Prefati autem capellanus et successores sui capellani singulis annis post mortem meam in die obitus mei plenarie dicant pro anima mea officium mortuorum cum missa in crastino et sic faciant annuatim die anniversarii mei imperpetuum. Et quod a nullo pecuniam vel aliquod aliud accipiant pro divino

---

1 Something has gone wrong with the phrasing here, and it may be compared with p. 616.

officio celebrando sed de porcione per me eis assignata sint contenti: quod si quis eorum secus egerit et super hoc convictus fuerit statim amoveatur et loco suo alius capellanus ydoneus sine mora subrogetur. Si quis autem eorum ad tantam etatem sive infirmitatem pervenerit quod personaliter non poterit missam celebrare, dicat privatas oraciones suas quas poterit ita quod conscienciam suam servet illesam, et singulis septimanis faciat duas missas, videlicet unam pro salubri statu meo dum vixero et pro animabus predictis et aliam de Sancta Maria per capellanum ydoneum celebrari; et tamen propter etatem inexcusabilem seu infirmitatem inevitabilem non amoveatur. Et quod heredes mei predicti omnia supervideant curent et procurent quod secundum ordinacionem huiusmodi cantaria ad honorem dei et pro anima mea et animabus predictis laudabiliter in forma predicta serviatur. Et quod dicta capella, domus, edificia, clausura et omnia alia dicte cantarie necessaria congrue sustententur et inveniantur per predictum capellanum et successores suos capellanos, ne pro defectu cooperture alias corruant vel deficiant per negligenciam capellani qui pro tempore fuerit. Et si casu fortuito[1] per ignem ventum vel per alium modum inopinatum huiusmodi edificia ruere contingat sine culpa capellani, quo huiusmodi fuerint deteriorata, vel quod ornamenta capelle per latrones furentur et apportentur, volo et onero heredes et assignatos meos quantum possum quod ipsi huiusmodi defectus sumptubus suis propriis reedificent, emendent et supleant, ne pro defectu eorum huiusmodi cantaria in animarum periculum negligetur. Et quod nec dictus capellanus nec successores sui capellani de dicta porcione alicui tradant nisi ad terminum vite et ad verum valorem et hoc de assensu meo seu heredum meorum: quod si fecerint tunc bene licebit michi et heredibus meis in tenementis sic dimissis ad quorumcunque manus devenerint ingredi et retinere quousque alius capellanus instituatur, cui ego seu heredes mei dictam terram sic dimissam reddemus et iuxta tenorem huiusmodi carte reddere teneamur. Et quod loci diocesanus aut suus in hac parte vicarius in suis visitacionibus et aliis temporibus de premissis omnibus ac eciam aliis defectubus et criminibus inhonestis diligenter inquirat seu inquirere faciat: et si quos defectus notabiles et inhonestos invenerit delinquentem capellanum secundum delicti sui exigenciam puniat condecenter. Et quia volo quod hac mea ordinacio rata et firma imperpetuum preservetur ex parte dei patris omnipotentis et Beate Marie semper virginis et omnium sanctorum sub interminacione divine iudicii in die ultionis, precipio ne quis heres meus consanguineus vel affinis seu quivis alius cuiuscunque condicionis vel status existat hanc ordinacionem meam ad honorem dei omnipotentis et pro saluti anime mee parentum et benefactorum meorum factam aliqualiter impediat, inpugnet vel eam in aliqualibus articulis quovismodo infringat vel infringere procuret. In quorum

1 MS. 'fortituto'.

omnium testimonium sigillum meum presentibus est appensum. Hiis testibus: dominis Mauricio de Berkelee, domino de Iweleye fratre meo; Mauricio de Berkeleye filio meo, Thoma de Bradeston, Simone Basset, Petro Corbet, militibus, et aliis. Nos igitur frater Wolstanus Wyg' episcopus supradictus laudabile prepositum et pium desiderium domini Thome de Berkelee quo ad fundacionem [&c. as in 154—apponi.] Dat' apud Bredone secundo Kalen' Junii anno domini MCCCXLV, et consecracionis nostre septimo.

835 *11 October 1346 Letters patent of the ordination of Abbot Hereward's chantry in Cirencester Abbey.*

ORDINACIO CANTARIE BEATE MARIE IN CAPELLA MONASTERII CIRENC'.

Sancte matris ecclesie filiis, nos frater Wolstanus miseracione divina Wygorn' episcopus notum facimus universis, quod nuper dum monasterium Beate Marie Cirenc' nostre diocesis visitavimus iure nostro pro parte religiosi viri fratris Willelmi Herward' dicti loci abbatis coram nobis in domo capitulari eiusdem monasterii presentibus tunc ibidem fratre Reginaldo de Schypton[1] priore ac conventu dicti monasterii fuerat allegatum, quod idem Willelmus abbas dictum monasterium ante sue creacionis tempus et tunc onere debitorum multiplici depressum paterne solicitudinis providencia relevavit, ac conventualem ecclesiam ipsius monasterii variis tunc iminentibus ruinis notoriis subiectam reparari et in magna sui parte de novo construi ac utiliter fecerat roborari, domos insuper nedum utiles sed necessarias tam infra ipsius cepta monasterii quam extra in maneriis et locis ad idem spectantibus monasterium magnifice fecit exstrui gravibus sumptibus et labore, necnon iura et libertates que in fundacione dicti monasterii a regibus Anglie ac aliis liberaliter eidem donata et concessa fuerant et alia iura varia que dicto monasterio competunt de consuetudine antiqua, per quosdam ipsi monasterio instinctu diabolico nequiter invidentes tam suorum predecessorum quam suis temporibus calumpniata et graviter impugnata, procuravit et fecit cum effusivis expensis sua laboriosa diligencia confirmari, et quedam in carta fundacionis eiusdem monasterii contente, que aliquorum oppinione sue iudicio reputabantur dubia seu obscura, procuravit et gravibus sumptibus inpetravit ad perpetuam firmitatem lucide declarari. Preterea dictus abbas quendam annuum redditum quatuor librarum et alium redditum sexaginta solidorum predicte monete[2] sterlingorum . . . . .[3] predicte

1 'de Schypton' interlineated.
2 'quatuor—monete' interlineated above 'quinque marcarum et duorum denariorum' crossed out.
3 'et alium redditum quinquaginta sex solidorum et septum denariorum' crossed out.

monete,[1] necnon et alium annuum redditum triginta[2] solidorum[3] sterlingorum sua industria noviter adquisivit, ac dictum redditum quatuor librarum[4] in divini cultus augmentum capelle beate virginis dei matris in ecclesia dicti monasterii constructe, redditum vero sexaginta[5] [solidorum] ad uberiorem procuracionem cotidianam fratrum dicti monasterii et ipsorum ampliorem quietem pitanciarie predicti monasterii, ac redditum triginta solidorum[6] ad latiorem provisionem pauperum ad ipsum monasterium in dies confluencium eiusdem monasterii elemosinarie suo consenciente conventu perpetualiter assignavit, que asseruit esse publica et notoria et ea se optulit legitime probaturum. Unde per partem dicti abbatis tunc petitum fuerat coram nobis ut docto de premissis sufficienter sicut ipsius huiusmodi operum exhibicio frequenti et cotidiano patet ac perpetuo patebit aspectui, sic eius memoria ex hoc prout convenit retenta districcius in speciali recommendacione inter ipsius monasterii confratres presentes et posteros deo in sancta religione servituros ibidem perpetim habeatur, et super hoc paretur securitas perpetuo duratura. Nos siquidem talium[7] narratorum examinavimus cum ea qua potuimus diligencia omnem veritatem et ea tam per exhibicionem litterarum seu[8] cartarum regiarum et rerum aliarum inspeccionem oculatam quam per alia documenta legitima invenimus esse vera. Demum idem abbas pro parte sua et prior ac conventus predicti pro sua parte super premissis in nos compromiserant et se super eis mox nostris arbitrio, diffinicioni, ordinacioni, dicto seu laudo, nostra potestate ordinaria nobis salva, in hac parte se submiserant et nostrum spoponderant arbitrium servaturos sub hac forma: In dei nomine amen. Nos Willelmus abbas et Reginaldus prior monasterii Beate Marie Cyrenc' ipsiusque loci conventus Wygorn' diocesis. Super narratis, allegatis, et petitis huiusmodi, que pro repetitis hic et nunc habemus et in nostra presenti submissione haberi volumus recitata, nos arbitrio, diffinicioni, ordinacioni, dicto seu laudo reverendi patris et domini Wolstani dei gracia Wygorn' episcopi nostri diocesani pure, sponte, simpliciter et absolute alte et basse submittimus, et nos ipsius super premissis arbitrium, ordinacionem, diffinicionem, dictum et laudum in virtute obediencie ad quam ex professione astringimur et sub nostrarum animarum periculis promittimus servaturos, salvo [sic] dicto patri sua super hiis ordinaria potestate. Petito postmodum ab utraque parte cum instancia ut super hiis arbitrari, ordinare, diffinire, dicere ac laudare ad per-

1 The scribe omitted to cross out this remnant of the original entry.
2 'viginti quinque' crossed out.
3 'sterlingorum' interlineated and 'et trium denariorum' crossed out.
4 'quinque marcarum et duorum denariorum' crossed out.
5 'quinquaginta sex solidorum et vii denariorum' crossed out.
6 'viginti quinque' crossed out, 'solidorum' repeated, and 'et trium denariorum' crossed out.
7 Altered from 'taliter'.
8 'tam' crossed out.

petuam rei memoriam vellemus, demum tractatum super premissis omnibus et singulis inter nos et predictos abbatem ac priorem et conventum aliosque iuris peritos tunc nobis assistentes diligentem et solempnem habuimus et fecimus frequentem, ac arbitrandi, ordinandi, diffiniendi, dicendi et laudandi onus in nos suscepimus, salva semper nobis nostra in hac parte ordinaria potestate. Unde nos religiosa et pia vota predicti abbatis favore prosequentes benigne, estimantesque fore iustum ut sibi pro temporalibus perpetuo duraturis comodis per ipsum prefato monasterio inpensis multimode digna premiorum merita compensentur, dei nomine[1] invocato, super premissis arbitramur, ordinamus, diffinimus, dicimus et laudamus tam nostra potestate ordinaria quam virtute submissionis predicte, quod capellanus secularis in cantu convenienter edoctus in cappela [sic] Beate Marie virginis predicti monasterii diebus singulis misse de Beata Virgine genetrice dei Maria celebrande indutus superpellicio intersit et in eadem missa cantando et alias ministrando deserviat reverenter. Et quod post missam Beate Virginis in dicta capella in dies celebratam idem capellanus immediate pro predicto abbate ac eius statu quam diu in humanis egerit et pro anima sua cum ab hac luce migraverit necnon pro statu salubri fratrum et canonicorum dicti monasterii presencium et futurorum et pro anima fundatoris eiusdem ac pro animabus regum Anglie ac benefactorum dicti monasterii et pro domino nostro rege ac regina et eorum liberis, pro animabus insuper patris et matris abbatis predicti et aliorum omnium Christi fidelium defunctorum singulis diebus missam celebret ad altare capelle predicte. Arbitramur insuper, ordinamus, diffinimus, dicimus et laudamus, quod quivis canonicus custos capelle Beate Marie virginis predicti monasterii qui erit pro tempore de bonis eiusdem capelle per dictum abbatem collatis seu assignatis ut premittitur celebraturo capellano huiusmodi de habitacione conpetenti pro ipso infra septa dicti monasterii necnon de in [sic] esculentis poculentis et indumentis ac necessariis aliis usque ad summam quatuor marcarum et dimidie sterlingorum inclusive annuatim valituris debeat providere ac eciam ministrare; quodque prefato abbate ab hac luce subtracto dies anniversarius eiusdem solempniter a fratribus seu canonicis dicti monasterii qui erunt ibidem perpetuo celebretur, sicut anniversarii dies Henrici Ade et Ricardi olim dicti monasterii abbatum solent seu consueverunt celebrari, ac quod singulis annis in festo Assumpcionis Beate Virginis dicto abbate superstite ipsius monasterii elemosinarius qui erit pro tempore pauperibus ad elemosinariam eiusdem confluentibus de bonis officio suo assignatis ut est dictum distribucionem ad summam viginti sex solidorum et octo denariorum[2] valituram ultra consuetam

---

1 'amen' crossed out.
2 MS. originally 'quinque solidorum' but 'quinque' has been crossed out and 'sex' and 'et octo denariorum' interlineated.

distribucionem solitam ibi fieri facere teneatur. Eodem vero abbate defuncto elemosinarius huiusmodi die anniversarii prefati abbatis distribucionem consimilis quantitatis ultra solitum modum illuc distribuendi huiusmodi pauperibus annuatim facere perpetuo sit astrictus. Pitansiarius siquidem prefati monasterii qui erit inposterum, pro assignacione suo facta officio ut premittitur, singulis annis dum idem abbas vixerit in festo Assumpciacionis[1] Beate Marie virginis unam pitanciam valoris viginti[2] solidorum[3] sterlingorum ad usum conventus dumtaxat provideat et ministret. Ita videlicet quod de dicta denariorum summa singulis canonicis et confratribus die huiusmodi unam quartam vini distribuat et ministret; et quod de dicta summa non expensum in vino[4] superesse contigerit in esculentorum pitancia convertatur. Post obitum vero abbatis predicti diebus singulis anniversariis eiusdem consimilis pitancia vini et victualium ad valorem predictam in forma descripta superius per pitanciarium qui erit illuc inposterum conventui antedicto perpetuo ministretur. Premissis subsequentur dictis abbati priori et conventui clarius intimatis et ad eorum noticiam sufficienter deductis, idem abbas prior et conventus nostris arbitrio, diffinicioni, dicto et laudo huiusmodi de ac super premissis adquieverunt pacifice ac ea emologarunt, approbarunt, ratificarunt pariter et acceptarunt, et eisdem pro se ac suis successoribus consenserunt expresse, seque premissa per nos taliter arbitrata, ordinata et diffinita promiserunt pro se suisque successoribus fideliter servaturos. Inhibemus igitur sub pena excommunicacionis maioris ne quis vel qui subditorum nostrorum arbitrium, ordinacionem, diffinicionem, dictum et laudum nostra predicta quovismodo infringat aut procuret infringi clam vel palam, opere, consilio sive facto, seu ipsius cantarie capellanum[5] qui erit in ea pro tempore in suis percipiendis predictis porcionibus, vel custodem quemcumque capelle Beate Virginis, elemosinariumve aut pitanciarium predictos in prestacione, distribucione, solucione ac satisfaccione premissorum seu agnicione dictorum onerum ascriptorum eisdem et continuacione perpetua eorundem impediat in toto vel in parte seu perturbet, aut inpedimentum prestet super hiis, aut ea vel eorum aliqua inpedientibus det consilium auxilium vel favorem. Nos vero abbas ac prior et conventus predicti arbitrium, ordinacionem, diffinicionem, dictum et laudum predicta rite, recte ac racionabiliter promulgata, facta gesta seu interposita quantum ad nos coniunctim vel divisim attinet approbamus et acceptamus ac eisdem pro nobis et successoribus nostris adquiessimus et libenti animo consentimus, nosque promittimus ea fideliter[6] servaturos, et in premissorum testimonium nos tangencium,

1 *Sic*. Interlineated above 'Annunciacionis' crossed out.
2 'sexdecim' crossed out.   3 'et septem denariorum' crossed out.
4 'in vino' interlineated.
5 MS. 'cappelanum' with the first 'p' cancelled by subpunctuation.
6 'fideliter' interlineated.

nostrum sigillum commune presentibus duximus apponendum. Ceterum, ut premissa per nos episcopum supradictum arbitrata, ordinata et diffinita tam utiliter tamque pie ac laudabiliter acta, gesta et ordinata devocius ac cum maiori caritate fervencius observentur inposterum, singulis parochianis nostris de peccatis suis vere penitentibus et contritis ac aliis, quorum diocesani hanc nostram indulgenciam ratam habuerint et acceptam, qui ad premissa in aliquo amplianda quicquam de bonis suis a deo sibi collatis contulerint seu ad ea observanda et peragenda fideliter et integraliter curam fecerint seu adhibuerint diligenciam, vel ad supportandum et continuandum antedicta consilium, auxilium prebuerint aut favorem, et qui pro salubri statu dicti abbatis dum vixerit seu pro ipsius anima cum ab hac luce migraverit devote oraverint et oracionem dominicam cum salutacione angelica dixerint mente pia, quadraginta dies indulgencie concedimus per presentes. Ratificamus insuper omnes indulgencias in hac parte seu pro premissis concessas et imposterum concedendas. In quorum omnium testimonium nos Wygorn' episcopus memoratus nostrum sigillum fecimus hiis apponi. Dat' quo ad nos episcopum antedictum apud Blockelegh' undecimo die mensis Octobris anno domini mcccxlvi, et nostre consecracionis octavo.

906 *27 February 1346 Letters patent of the ordination of Adam de Herwynton's chantry in Pershore Abbey.*

ORDINACIO CANTARIE DOMINI ADE DE HERWYNTON.

Universis sancte matris ecclesie filiis, frater Wolstanus permissione divina Wyg', salutem in eo qui est omnium vera salus. Inter omnia que curam nostram cotidiana meditacione solicitant precipuum habemus in votis ut in diocesi quam deus nobis[1] credidit gubernandam ortodoxe fidei cultus nostris temporibus augeatur et precipue in missarum celebracionibus in quibus venerabile sacramentum corporis Christi salvatoris nostri deo patri tam pro vivis quam pro mortuis immolatur, in quo vite suffragium consequimur et salutis. Hoc est inquam memoriale dulcissimum, sacrosanctissimum et eciam salutiferum in quo gratam recensemus memoriam, in quo a malo retrahimur et confortamur in bono et ad virtutum et graciarum proficimus incrementa. Sane dominus Adam de Herwynton condicionem humane fragilitatis attendens et qualiter omni creature tam sublimi quam humili presentis appareat vite finis cupiensque diem messionis extreme pietatis operibus prevenire, confidens eciam quod oracionum suffragia ad dei misericordiam implorandum inter alia pietatis opera multum prosunt, de bonis sibi a deo collatis unam perpetuam cantariam duorum presbiterorum secularium in ecclesia conventuali de Perschor' nostre diocesis erigere disposuit, qui pro

---

1 'nobis' interlineated.

anima nobilis viri domini Guidonis de Bello Campo nuper comitis
Warr' ac pro animabus dicti domini Ade patris et matris eiusdem
aliorumque parentum et benefactorum suorum, ac omnium fidelium
defunctorum, ac pro salute nobilis viri domini Thome comitis Warr'
domineque Katerine uxoris eiusdem dicti loci comitisse, dum
superstites fuerint, ac pro animabus ipsorum post eorum obitum,
singulis diebus domino offerent vitulos labiorum dumtamen ad hoc
accederent nostri auctoritas et consensus. Proposita siquidem coram
nobis dilectorum filiorum tam abbatis[1] et conventus monasterii
Beate Marie et Sancte Edburge virginis de Pershor' nostre diocesis
quam domini Ade de Herwynton eiusdem diocesis unanimis peticio
continebat, quod cum idem dominus Adam quasdam terras et
tenementa in villa de Persora et in campis eiusdem sitas cum
pertinenciis ad valorem decem librarum sterlingorum annui redditus
eisdem abbati et conventui contulerat perpetuo possidendas ut una
cantaria perpetua duorum presbiterorum secularium pro anima
dicti domini Guidonis et pro anima eiusdem domini Ade, ac
parentum et benefactorum suorum, necnon pro animabus omnium
fidelium defunctorum ac pro salute nobilis viri domini Thome
comitis Warr' domineque Katerine uxoris eiusdem dicti loci
comitisse, dum superstites fuerint, ac pro animabus ipsorum post
eorum obitum, sumptibus dictorum religiosorum ad altare quod in
navi ecclesie conventualis supradicte ex parte australi eiusdem est
situatum in quadam capella in qua corpus dicti domini Ade iam
quiescit humatum, erigeretur et crearetur, ac singulis annis uno die
per totum conventum predictum anniversarium solempne pro
anima prefati domini Ade celebraretur, eidem abbati et monachis
tam pro dicta cantaria quam pro anniversario suprascripto in-
cumbentibus oneribus universis ad creacionem et ordinacionem
cantarie ac anniversarii predictorum procedere curaremus. Protinus
insuper [pro] sustentacione anniversarii perpetuo celebrandi Hugo
de Cokeseye, magister Willelmus de Herwynton, Robertus de
Alvreston, Rogerus de la Felde et Thomas de Sloghtre, executores
testamenti et ultime voluntatis dicti domini Ade centum quadraginta
et tres marcas sterlingorum eisdem abbati et conventui contulerunt,
quam pecuniam iidem abbas et conventus ad perpetuo subeundum
onus anniversarii supradicti a supradictis executoribus solidam
receperunt et in utilitatem sui monasterii converterunt. Ac predicti
abbas et monachi omnes et singuli gratanter supradicta eis donata
recipientes ad sustentacionem cantarie predicte ac anniversarii
supradicti omnia onera pro collacione supradictarum terrarum ac
supradicte pecunie eis facta gratanter supportare perpetuo
disponentes ac se et eorum quemlibet necnon ipsorum ecclesiam et
abbatiam de Persora obligacionis vinculo perpetuo astringentes per
suas patentes litteras sigillo illorum communi signatas, ac dicto

1 'abbatis' interlineated.

domino Ada ante perfeccionem premissorum viam universe carnis ingresso supradicti executores testamenti et ultime voluntatis dicti domini Ade ad tam salubriter incepta et animarum saluti prospera perpetuo roboranda per suas patentes litteras sigillis eorundem[1] munitas, nostris voluntati, dicto, laudo, arbitrio, ordinacioni, decreto, condempnacioni et sentencie cuicumque pure, sponte, simpliciter et absolute submittentes et coram nobis constituti nos requisiverunt humiliter et devote quatinus dignaremur submissiones suas huiusmodi admittere et de premissis prout nobis visum fuerit salubriter ordinare. Tenor vero submissionis dictorum religiosorum virorum talis est:[2] Noverint universi has litteras inspecturi quod nos frater Thomas permissione divina abbas monasterii Beate Marie et Sancte Edburge virginis de Persora et eiusdem loci conventus a bone memorie Ada de Herwynton nuper defuncto quasdam terras et tenementa cum pertinenciis in villa de Persora et in campis eiusdem sitas *le Porters* nuncupatas ad valorem decem librarum annui redditus recepimus et habemus perpetuo possidendas ut una cantaria perpetua duorum presbiterorum secularium qui celebrarent pro anima bone memorie nobilis viri domini Guidonis de Bello Campo comitis Warr' nuper defuncti ac pro anima dicti domini Ade ac pro salute nobilis viri Thome comitis Warr' domineque Katerine uxoris eiusdem dicti loci comitisse dum superstites fuerint ac pro animabus ipsorum post eorum obitum, ac pro animabus patris et matris dicti domini Ade aliorumque parentum et benefactorum suorum erigeretur et crearetur in navi ecclesie antedicte in quadam capella ex parte australi dicte navis in qua corpus dicti Ade traditum est ecclesiastice sepulture. Recepimus insuper et habemus centum quadraginta et tres marcas per manus executorum dicti domini Ade in usus nostros et monasterii nostri utiliter conversas ad celebrandum unum anniversarium singulis annis imperpetuum pro anima dicti domini Ade in die obitus sui, ita quod omnia et singula onera supradicte cantarie et anniversarii incumbencia pro collacione et recepcione dictarum terrarum et pecunie antedicte quas nos recepisse et habuisse fatemur imperpetuum subiremus. Unde nos predicti abbas et conventus sencientes supradicta nobis collata dicto monasterio nostro et nobis fore lucrosa et sufficiencia pro supradictis oneribus imperpetuum subeundis, quantum ad ordinacionem predictorum cantarie et anniversarii per vos venerabilem patrem dominum Wolstanum dei gracia Wygorn' episcopum diocesanum nostrum faciendam, vestris voluntati, dicto, laudo, arbitrio, ordinacioni, decreto, condempnacioni ac sentencie cuicumque pure, sponte, simpliciter et absolute nos submittimus per presentes, paternitatem vestram rogantes quatinus ad ordinacionem supradictorum cantarie et anniversarii ac supportacionem onerum eisdem incumbencium velitis procedere et iuxta id

1 Interlineated above 'illorum' crossed out.
2 The following letters patent are duplicated in 773.

quod vestre paternitati visum fuerit iuxta submissionem nostram supradictam salubriter ordinare. In quorum omnium testimonium sigilla nostra presentibus sunt appensa. Dat' apud Persor' in capitulo nostro die Sabbati proxima post festum Sancti Mathie apostoli anno domini MCCCXLV.[1] Tenor autem submissionis dictorum executorum talis est:[2] Noverint universi has litteras inspecturi quod nos Hugo de Cokeseye, Willelmus de Herwynton, Robertus de Alvreston, Rogerus de la Felde et Thomas de Sloughtr' executores testamenti seu ultime voluntatis bone memorie domini Ade de Herwynton nuper defuncti quantum ad ordinacionem cuiusdam cantarie perpetue pro anima nobilis viri domini[3] Guidonis de Bello Campo nuper comitis Warr', pro anima domini Ade de Herwynton [&c. as above— benefactorum suorum] . . . in navi ecclesie conventualis de Persora erigende et creande ac cuiusdam anniversarii pro anima eiusdem domini Ade singulis annis in perpetuum in die obitus sui celebrandi ac quo ad imposicionem onerum supradictorum cantarie et anniversarii incumbencium per vos et venerabilem patrem dominum Wolstanum dei gracia Wyg' episcopum diocesanum nostrum faciendam [&c. as above—sunt appensa.] . . . Et quia sigilla nostra pluribus sunt incognita sigillum officii officialis Wyg' presentibus apponi procuravimus. Et nos officialis Wyg' ad personalem rogatum executorum sigillum officii nostri presentibus apposuimus. Dat' apud Broedon xxvi[to.][4] die mensis Februarii anno domini MCCCXLV[to.] Nos igitur frater Wolstanus Wyg' episcopus supradictus, piam intencionem dicti domini Ade executorumque suorum merito advertentes, attendentes eciam quam sit meritorium tam pro vivis quam pro defunctis erga deum suffragia procurare, prefatis peticioni et requisicioni favorabiliter annuentes dictas submissiones ad effectum supradictum admittimus et eciam acceptamus. Et quia premissa inquisicione et examinacione diligenti comperimus dictas terras et tenementa per prefatum dominum dominum Adam religiosis predictis ut prefertur sic data ad predictam cantariam et sustentacionem presbiterorum qui ministrabunt eidem ac supradictam summam pecunie per supradictos executores eisdem abbati et conventui ad anniversarium ut premittitur perpetuo inveniendum ac pro omnibus oneribus predictorum sustentandis fore sufficiencia, ac considerato situ dicte abbatie dictas terras et tenementa ipsis religiosis in inmensum utilia et lucrosa, ad ordinacionem dicte cantarie ac anniversarii supradicti virtute submissionum predictarum de consensu dictorum religiosorum et ipsius domini Ade ad hoc dum vixit adhibito per eundem ac executorum suorum predictorum et de consilio iuris peritorum nobis assistencium, invocato dei nomine,

1　25 February 1346.
2　The executors' submission is duplicated in 774.
3　'H' cancelled by subpunctuation.
4　27 February in 774.

procedimus[1] in hunc modum:[2] In primis ordinamus creamus et erigimus unam perpetuam cantariam duorum presbiterorum secularium in ecclesia conventuali de Persora ad altare quod situatum est[3] in navi ecclesie conventualis predicte ex parte australi in quadam capella in qua corpus dicti domini traditum est ecclesiastice sepulture pro anima nobilis viri [&c. as above] . . . benefactorum suorum ac omnium fidelium defunctorum, statuentes quod illi duo presbiteri singulis diebus ad altare predictum circa horam primam missas duas de defunctis celebrent specialiter pro anima dicti domini Ade et aliis animabus supradictis nisi forsan in festis maioribus de officio diei celebrare voluerint et tunc pro animabus ipsis commemoracionem faciant specialem, quodque singulis diebus inibi dicant pro anima dicti domini Ade specialiter ac pro ceteris animabus suprascriptis plenum officium mortuorum. Volumus eciam et ordinamus quod illi duo presbiteri litteris patentibus supradictorum executorum infra spacium duorum mensium a tempore ordinacionis nostre presentis ad dictam cantariam primo, et postea quociens particulariter vel in toto eam vacare contigerit infra unius mensis spacium ab ipsius vacacione continue numerandum litteris patentibus supradictorum religiosorum vel maioris partis eorundem, nobis et successoribus nostris legitime presententur; qui si ydonei ad huiusmodi cantariam inveniantur sine difficultate admittentur ac instituantur et inducantur canonice in eadem. In qua quidem institucione ipsos et eorum utrumque ad conservandum omnia et singula in presenti nostra ordinacione contenta cessante[4] impedimento legitimo corporali astringi volumus et decernimus iuramento. Decernimus eciam et statuimus ordinando, quod predictis duobus presbiteris in dicta cantaria ut supra premittitur institutis eorumque successoribus universis de bonis et facultatibus eiusdem monasterii per dictos religiosos singulis annis novem marce argenti in festo Natalis Domini, Annunciacionis Beate Marie, Nativitatis Sancti Johannis Baptiste et Sancti Michaelis, per equales porciones absque retardacione, diminucione seu remissione quacumque pro eorum sustentacione persolvantur. Volumus eciam et statuimus quod dicti duo presbiteri in una et eadem domo que ad opus eorum infra mesuagium quod vocatur *le Porters* in Persora est constructa ad eandem mensam perpetuo conversentur, cuius domus reparacio ac eciam sustentacio predictis abbati et conventui pertineant infuturum. Prefati nichilominus abbas et conventus pro tempore existentes presbiteris predictis pro animabus predictis celebrantibus libros, calicem, vestimenta, luminaria, cereos, panem et vinum in celebracione missarum supradictarum[5] omniaque alia pro eadem cantaria necessaria

1 'procedimus' interlineated.
2 An early 16th century copy of part of these ordinances is bound in the register after fo. 95.
3 'est' interlineated.   4 MS. 'censante'.   5 'supradictarum' interlineated.

inperpetuum subministrent. Volumus insuper statuimus et ordinamus, quod, abbas et conventus predicti singulis annis imperpetuum pro anima predicti domini Ade in die obitus sui[1] videlicet ultimo die mensis Marcii solempne celebrent anniversarium quodque quilibet monachus eiusdem abbatie in missis suis inter animas benefactorum suorum cunctis futuris temporibus de anima dicti domini Ade habeat memoriam visceribus compassivis. Et ut ad hec non solummodo metu imposicionis presentis ordinacionis coarcentur, quin pocius ad actum tam meritorium percepcione commodi invitentur[2] volumus et eciam ordinamus quod in anniversario pro anima dicti domini Ade ut prefertur singulis annis prefato ultimo die mensis Marcii celebrando inter monachos predicte domus quadraginta solidi sterlingorum annuatim de bonis eiusdem monasterii pro porcionibus equalibus distribuantur: ita tamen quod abbas et prior dicte domus prout in aliis distribucionibus recipiunt de dictis quadraginta solidis uberiores capiant porciones. Et ne, quod absit, dicta cantaria et anniversarium[3] per fluxum temporis necgligantur, seu quicquam in elusionem presentis ordinacionis nostre per indevotos religiosos aliquos retrahatur, minutetur [sic] aut fraudulenter seu perperam in hac parte aliquid[4] detrahatur, premissa omnia onera et singula invenienda, subeunda, sustenenda et perpetuo supportanda prefatis abbati et conventui eorumque successoribus ac ecclesie et abbatie suis de Persora predicta, quorum ut comperimus interest specialiter ut gaudeant dictis terris et tenementis sicut premittitur in hac causa receptis, imponimus per decretum. Et ad ea supportanda dictos abbatem et conventum eorumque successores ac abbatiam et ecclesiam eorum supradictas, presentibus magistris Johanne de la Lowe, Willelmo de Adelmynton, domino Johanne de Rypon capellano, Johanne de Aula de Persora, fratrem Robertum de Lutleton dictorum religiosorum procuratorem ad hoc legitime et specialiter constitutum ac procuratorio nomine comparentem coram nobis pro eisdem ac predictos abbatem et totum conventum in persona eiusdem conde[m]pnamus sentencialiter et diffinitive ex certa sciencia in hiis scriptis sub pena maioris excommunicacionis, quam abbatem, priorem, subpriorem, celerarium et omnes maiores dicte domus qui nunc sunt et qui erunt pro tempore qui contra premissa vel eorum aliqua quecumque preiudicialia attemptare presumpserint, moram-ve culpam seu offensam contraxerint seu impedimentum notabile directe vel indirecte, clam vel palam, scienter prestiterint incurrere volumus ipso facto punicione canonica iuxta qualitatem delicti[5] sui moderanda[6] ipsi conventui nichilominus iminente. Et si, quod absit, cantaria predicta per maliciam abbatis vel alicuius religiosi dicte abbatie per spacium

1 'sui' interlineated.   2 MS. 'imitentur'.
3 'ct anniversarium' interlineated.   4 'aliquid' interlineated.
5 MS. 'dilecti'.   6 'moderanda' interlineated.

octo dierum cessare contigerit, volumus et ordinamus quod predicti
religiosi nomine pene quociens eam sic cessare contigerit in triginta
solidos sterlingorum elemosine nostre seu successorum nostrorum qui
pro tempore fuerint applicandos efficaciter obligentur. Insuper ut
presens nostra ordinacio firmiori munimine roboretur ac execucione
salubri perhenniter tueatur, adiciendo statuimus quod in visitacionibus nostris et successorum nostrorum in dicta abbatia exercendis
per nos vel successores nostros seu alium in hac parte deputandum a
nobis vel ab eis, necnon alias cum clamore referente visum fuerit
expedire, viis et modis licitis a[1] religiosis personis eiusdem abbatie,
eciam iuramento ab eis exacto, de prefatis cantaria et anniversario
aliorumque premissorum onerum eisdem incumbencium supporta-
cione eorumque circumstanciis congruis speciali diligencia veritas
inquiratur. Et ut ipsa nostra ordinacio prelibata perpetuam obtineat
roboris firmitatem, volumus et statuimus ordinando quod abbas iam
presidens prefato monasterio ac prior et monachi eiusdem et singuli
qui nunc sunt iuramentum prestent corporale quod per eos non
stabit quominus predicta cantaria ac anniversarium predictum iuxta
tenorem presentis ordinacionis nostre inviolabiliter observentur;
quin pocius quod quantum in eis est eadem facient firmiter observari,
ac quod a quocumque quem[2] futuris temporibus recipi continget in
monachum et in fratrem dicti monasterii in professione sua idem
receipient [sic] iuramentum. Tenor vero mandati[3] procuratoris
dictorum religiosorum de quo supra fit mencio talis est:[4] Universis
pateat per presentes quod nos frater Thomas permissione divina
abbas monasterii Beate Marie et Sancte Edburge virginis de Persora
et eiusdem loci conventus dilectum nobis in Christo Robertum de
Lutleton commonachum nostrum et confratrem verum et legitimum
ordinamus, constituimus et facimus procuratorem, dantes et con-
cedentes eidem potestatem specialem et mandatum generale
quandam submissionem per nos factam voluntati, laudo, dicto,
arbitrio, ordinacioni, decreto, condempnacioni ac sentencie cuicumque venerabilis patris domini Wolstani dei gracia Wyg' episcopi
diocesani nostri quo ad ordinacionem cuiusdam cantarie perpetue
in quadam capella in navi ecclesie nostre conventualis ex parte
australi situata in qua corpus domini Ade de Herwynton traditum
est ecclesiastice sepulture, pro anima nobilis viri Guidonis de Bello
Campo nuper comitis Warr' [&c. as above—benefactorum
suorum,] . . . per dictum venerabilem patrem erigende et creande
eidem venerabili patri nomine nostro presentandi, ac quamcumque
conde[m]pnacionem virtute dicte submissionis nostre per eundem
patrem in personis nostris faciendam subeundi, ipsamque ordinacionem audiendi, recipiendi et eidem consenciendi, omniaque alia
et singula faciendi et expediendi que in premissis necessaria fuerint

1 MS. 'ac'. 2 Interlineated above 'a' cancelled by subpunctuation.
3 'dicti' crossed out. 4 The following appointment is duplicated in 772.

vel eciam oportuna: ratum et gratum habituri quicquid per dictum procuratorem nostrum actum seu gestum fuerit in hac parte. In cuius rei testimonium sigilla nostra presentibus sunt appensa. Dat' Persor' in capitulo nostro quinto Kalen' Marcii anno domini MCCCXLV$^{to.1}$

In quorum omnium testimonium nos frater Wolstanus permissione divina episcopus supradictus sigillum nostrum fecimus hiis apponi. Dat' apud Bredon' vicesimo septimo die mensis Februarii anno domini MCCCXLV$^{to.}$ et nostre consecracionis septimo.

Register of the bishop's Court of Audience

1365–1376 Proceedings before M. John de Severleye between 13 June and 31 July 1349.

REGISTRUM CAUSARUM ET NEGOCIORUM IN AUDIENCIA CURIA VENERABILIS PATRIS DOMINI WOLSTANI DEI GRACIA WYGORN' EPISCOPI TAM CORAM IPSO DOMINO EPISCOPO QUAM COMMISSARIIS SUIS MOTORUM A TERCIODECIMO DIE MENSIS JUNII ANNO DOMINI MILLESIMO CCC$^{mo.}$ XLIX$^{no.}$ CONSECRACIONIS DICTI PATRIS UNDECIMO, INDICCIONIS SECUNDA, PONTIFICATUS SANCTISSIMI PATRIS ET DOMINI DOMINI CLEMENTIS DIVINA PROVIDENCIA PAPE VI$^{ti.}$ ANNO OCTAVO.

COMMISSIO AD CAUSAS ET NEGOCIA. Frater Wolstanus permissione divina Wyg' episcopus dilecto filio magistro Johanni de Severleye cancellario nostro, salutem graciam et benediccionem. Ad inquirendum, corrigendum et puniendum crimina quecumque et excessus quorumcumque subditorum nostrorum, necnon ad cognoscendum in causis quibuscumque ad nostram iurisdiccionem sive nocionem qualitercumque spectantibus, tam matrimonialibus quam aliis, motis seu movendis, et ad ipsas causas discuciendum et fine debito terminandum, vobis de cuius^{2} discrecione fidelitate et industria plenam in domino fiduciam optinemus, vices nostras committimus cum cohercionis canonice cuiuslibet potestate. Dat' apud Wythendon quarto die Octobris anno domini millesimo quadragesimo secundo et consecracionis nostre quarto.

ACTA. ACTA IN ECCLESIA PAROCHIALI DE HERTLEBUR' CORAM VENERABILI VIRO MAGISTRO JOHANNE DE SEVERLEYE CANCELLARIO ET COMMISSARIO DICTI PATRIS UT PREMITTITUR SUPRADICTO XVIII DIE MENSIS JUNII ANNO DOMINI MILLESIMO

---

1 25 February 1346.
2 A second 'de cuius' cancelled by subpunctuation.

ccc$^{mo.}$ xlix$^{no.}$, INDICCIONIS SECUNDA, PONTIFICATUS SANCTIS-
SIMI PATRIS ET DOMINI, DOMINI CLEMENTIS DIVINA PRO-
VIDENCIA PAPE VI$^{ti.}$ ANNO OCTAVO.

HERTHULL. In negocio correccionis contra Willelmum de Herthull de parochia ecclesie de Belne Broghton occasione detencionis sive spoliacionis[1] cuiusdam mortuarii eidem ecclesie debiti ut pretenditur, ex officio dicti patris moto, dicto Willelmo personaliter comparente et iurato de veritate dicenda super quodam articulo in scriptis redacto, quo negato, ad videndum probaciones in ea parte ex parte dicti officii producendas et ulterius faciendum in dicto negocio quod est iustum datus est die Lune loco quo supra.

HERTHULL. Quo die, videlicet xxii$^{do.}$ mensis Junii, anno, indiccione, pontificatu et loco predictis, coram dicto commissario dicto Willelmo ut prius personaliter comparente, productis quinque testibus, videlicet Rogero de Thelford, Johanne Smyth de Belne, Johanne de Thelford, Hugone Brentel de Belne et Henrico atte Wode de Foruelde, quibus iuratis examinatis ac eorum attestacionibus publicatis, ad dicendum contra testes et eorum dicta et in eo eventu quo nichil effectuale dixerit in ea parte, ad proponendum causam racionabilem si quam habeat quare periurus pronunciari et in sentenciam excommunica-cionis maioris incidisse nominatim publicari non debeat, datus est dies Jovis proximo futurus loco quo prius.

HERTHULL. Quo die, videlicet xxv$^{to.}$ dicti mensis [&c. as above] ... comparente, dicit idem Willelmus asserendo quod tres testes producti contra eum sunt maioris excommunicacionis sentencia involuti, videlicet Rogerus de Thelford, Johannes Smyth de Belne et Hugo Brentel, et fuerunt tempore deposicionis eorum per processus ecclesiasticos habitos contra eos, ideo testimonium eorum nullum. Et ad probandum excepciones huiusmodi in forma iuris et ulterius faciendum in negocio quod est iustum datus est dies Sabbati loco quo prius.

HERTHULL. Quo die, videlicet xxvii$^{do.}$ dicti [mensis] [&c. as above] ... comparente, nullis probacionibus propositis, sed reiectis excepcionibus tanquam non probatis, nichilque dicto seu proposito quare ad pronunciacionem procedi non debeat, pronunciatum fuerat in dicto negocio in hunc modum:[2] IN DEI NOMINE AMEN. Nos Johannes de Severleye clericus, venerabilis patris domini Wolstani dei gracia Wyg' episcopi commissarius generalis, rimato processu contra Willelmum de Herthull in negocio spoliacionis cuiusdam herieti prout in articulo contra eum proposito habito,[3] cuius tenor est talis: IN DEI NOMINE AMEN.[4] Nos frater Wol-stanus permissione divina Wyg' episcopus tibi Willelmo de Herthull de parochia de Belne Broghton nostre diocesis dicimus proponimus et obicimus, ad correccionem anime tue procedentes,

1 'sive spoliacionis' interlineated. 2 'PRONUNCIACIO' in margin.
3 'habito' interlineated. 4 'ARTICULUS' in margin.

quod licet omnes illi et singuli qui maliciose ecclesiam suo iure privare presumunt, seu qui contra iusticiam libertatem ecclesiasticam infringere seu perturbare contendunt, sint maioris excommunicacionis sentencia in concilio Oxon' provide lata dampnabiliter involuti;[1] tu tamen post publicacionem et artacionem dicti concilii die vicesimo sexto mensis Maii anno domini MCCCXLIX[no.] in villa de Beln' Broghton predicta iura et libertates ecclesiasticas ausu sacrilego perturbare et infringere contendisti et actualiter infregisti ac nequiter perturbasti, dictam maioris excommunicacionis sentenciam incurrendo, pro eo et ex eo quod tu dictis die et loco maliciose et contra iusticiam quandam vaccam, in cuius possessione iusta et dominio ecclesia de Belne Broghton prelati et ministri eiusdem tunc extiterunt sine fraude, ausu sacrilego cepisti abduxisti et ipsis iunctis contractasti, prefatam ecclesiam necnon prelatos et ministros eiusdem iure et libertate eorum temere spoliando. Quare, probatis in hac parte probandis seu quovis alio modo detectis, intendimus ad correccionem anime tue, et ut dicta ecclesia conservetur indempnis, contra te procedere statuere et diffinire secundum quod exigunt canonice sancciones, protestantes nos velle alias istam materiam in meliorem formam redigere si sit opus, iuris beneficio semper salvo. Quia invenimus intencionem dicti officii sufficienter probatam ipsum in sentenciam excommunicacionis maioris latam in ea parte in concilio Oxon' incidisse pronunciamus. Postmodum vero[2] a dicta sentencia excommunicacionis maioris in forma iuris fuerat absolutus satisfacto primitus deo et ecclesie contra quam deliquit.

ACTA CORAM MAGISTRO JOHANNE DE SEVERLEYE COMMISSARIO &C. IN CIMITERIO ECCLESIE PAROCHIALIS DE HERTLEBUR' PRIMO DIE JULII ANNO DOMINI MCCCXLIX, INDICCIONIS SECUNDA [&C.].

SHRAVELEYE. In negocio moto contra dominum Stephanum rectorem ecclesie de Shraveleye occasione criminis dampnate incontinencie inter ipsum et Margeriam filiam Johannis de Hethe nuper uxorem Johannis de Farlye parochianam suam[3] commisse ut dicitur, dicto Stephano, dicto loco de consensu suo, non obstante quod in dicta ecclesia locus fuerat assignatus eidem, personaliter comparente, obiectoque sibi articulo huiusmodi, quo negato, a tempore saltem correccionis sue, ad docendum de huiusmodi correccione et ad purgandum se a tempore correccionis pretense cum sexta manu, datus est dies xv a dicto primo die Julii continue numerandos si iur[idicus] sit alioquin proximo die iuridico tunc sequente in ecclesia de Hertlebur' supradicta. Quo die, videlicet xvi[mo.] dicti mensis anno [&c.] . . . et loco predictis, rector canonice se purgavit.

1 Council of Oxford, 1222.   2 'HERTHULL ABSOLUCIO' in margin.
3 'parochianam suam' interlineated.

ACTA IN ECCLESIA DE HERTLEBUR' CORAM DICTO COMMISSARIO XIII^{mo.} DIE MENSIS JULII ANNO [&C.] . . . PREDICTIS.

OMBRESLEYE. In negocio contra . . .[1] vicarium de Ombresleye occasione incontinencie inter ipsum et Agnetem Crompe ut dicitur moto, dicto vicario personaliter comparente allegat se correctum et mulierem ipsam mortuam ante correccionem. Ideo datus est sibi dies Lune proximo post festum Sancti Kenelmi ad ostendendum suam correccionem et probandum mortem mulieris predicte loco predicto.

ACTA CORAM DICTO COMMISSARIO XX^{mo.} DIE JULII ANNO [&C.] . . . PREDICTIS.

OMBRESLEYE. In negocio contra vicarium de Ombresleye &c. Idem vicarius probavit mortem mulieris de qua agitur, sed correccionem suam nequaquam.

STRETTON. In negocio contra Thomam de Stretton clerico racione incontinencie cum Isabella uxore Thome Malue de Fipton commisse ut dicitur moto, dictus Thomas personaliter comparens confessus fuit articulum huiusmodi, et iniunctum est sibi pro penitencia quod dicat publice in ecclesia sua parochiali inter missarum solemnia tria psalteria, indutus superpellicio, deposito capucio. Postmodum remissum fuit sibi de huiusmodi penitencia, videlicet quod dicat nisi unum psalterium, et hoc secrete.

ACTA CORAM DICTO COMMISSARIO EISDEM ANNO INDICCIONE MENSE DIE ET PONTIFICATU IN CASTRO EPISCOPALI DE HERTLEBUR'.

DEN'. Margeria quondam uxor Johannis de Den' notatur super incontinencia cum Thoma de Den' fratre eiusdem Johannis.[2] Mulier comparavit et fatetur articulum, et iniunctum est sibi pro penitencia tres fustigaciones circa ecclesiam et tres circa mercatum.

ACTA CORAM DICTO COMMISSARIO IN ECCLESIA PAROCHIALI DE HERTLEBUR' XXIII DIE MENSIS JULII ANNO, INDICCIONE ET PONTIFICATU PREDICTIS.

CONTRA QUENDAM FRATREM HOSPITALIS SANCTI WOLSTANI WYG'. In negocio contra Alexandrum de Luttelton[3] se pretendentem confratrem hospitalis Sancti Wolstani Wyg', occasione cuiusdam sentencie excommunicacionis maioris in ipsum auctoritate domini episcopi Wyg' suis exigentibus demeritis late, moto; dicto Alexandro personaliter comparente, petitaque per partem ipsius declaracione sentencie huiusmodi, declaratum fuit quod idem Alexander dicta sentencia extitit innodatus, eo quod alias auctoritate dicti domini episcopi sub pena excommunicacionis maioris late una cum aliis confratribus suis fuerat legitime monitus ne corrodia aliqua aliquibus personis venderent episcopo inconsulto, huiusmodi corrodia contra

1 Space left in MS.   2 'Thoma—Johannis' added beneath.
3 'de Luttelton' interlineated.

prohibicionem huiusmodi vendi nichilominus temere procuravit, et unum precipue cuidam Johanni de Stodleye, sentenciam sic latam dampnabiliter incurrendo. Super cuius sentencie declaracione pars dicti Alexandri articulum in scriptis peciit sibi edi, et diem ad respondendum eidem articulo. Demum ad recipiendum articulum huiusmodi, crastina dies, et ad respondendum eidem, dies Lune, loco predicto, prefixus extitit et eciam assignatus. Postmodum die assignata in castro de Hertlebur' recepit articulum supradictum in scriptis.

ACTA CORAM DICTO COMMISSARIO XXVII^mo· DIE MENSIS JULII ANNO INDICCIONE PONTIFICATU ET LOCO PREDICTIS.

PECHLYNG'. Willelmus Pechlyng notatur super incontinencia cum Felicia Bole; qui comparentes fatentur articulum, vir videlicet quod xii anni sunt elapsi, mulier vero quod decem, et ambo allegant correcciones; ad probandum huiusmodi correcciones in forma iuris, et in casu quo doceant de correccionibus huiusmodi ad purgandum se ab illo tempore cum viii manu, datus est dies Veneris loco predicto. Quibus die et loco, ipso Willelmo licet preconizato diuciusque expectato nullo modo comparente pronunciatus est contumax et in pena contumacie huiusmodi pronunciatum est ipsum tam defecisse in probacione quam in purgacione et de crimine plenius convictum fuisse.

Idem notatur super incontinencia cum Isabella Lobery. Vir et mulier comparentes negant articulum, et vir dicit in virtute iuramenti prestiti se nunquam vidisse eam ante illud tempus. Ideo tam ipse quam mulier dimissi.

Idem notatur super incontinencia cum Agnete Crompe. Vir comparens allegat mulierem uxorem suam: ad hoc probandum dies Veneris est sibi prefixus loco quo supra. Quibus die et loco, dicto Willelmo preconizato diuciusque expectato et nullo modo comparente pronunciatus est contumax, et in pena contumacie sue huiusmodi pronunciatum est ipsum defecisse in probacione.

LUTTELTON. In negocio contra Alexandrum de Luttelton &c. moto:[1] dicto Alexandro personaliter comparente, propositis contra articulum sex excepcionibus, quibus reiectis, ac una excepcione declinatoria super qua quatenus concernit fundacionem domus hospitalis Sancti Wolstani Wyg' . . .[2] de malicia iurato, facta que contestacione ad articulum negative, dicendo narrata prout narrantur vera non esse, ideo processus in ea parte contra eundem Alexandrum fieri non debere, cum protestacione tamen prius facta de non recedendo ab appellacione occasione reieccionum excepcionum predictarum interposita verbaliter, et salva sibi materia iustificandi in eventu, ad . . .[3] faciendum ulterius et recipiendum in dicto negocio quod est iustum datus est dies Veneris loco predicto.

ALYNCESTRE. In causa seu negocio que vel quod inter Johannem

---

1 See above.   2 Erasures in the MS.   3 Further erasures.

Heyne de Alyncestr' executorem testamenti Isabelle relicte Willelmi Chyk' de Alyncestr' defuncti cui administracio bonorum eiusdem defuncti in forma iuris ut dicitur est commissa, actorem ex parte una, et dominum Robertum atte Brugge de Alyncestr' capellanum, reum ex altera, eo quod idem Robertus dictum Johannem executorem, quominus in ipsis bonis libere administrare valeat ut deberet, impedit seu impedire procurat iniuste, verti speratur: partibus huiusmodi personaliter comparentibus, liteque negative contestata, et iurato de calumpnia et de veritate dicenda hincinde, ad probandum intencionem suam, parti actrici, parti vero ree ad videndum probaciones huiusmodi, et utrique parti ulterius faciendum quod est iustum, datus est dies Lune, loco predicto.

ACTA CORAM DICTO COMMISSARIO ULTIMO DIE MENSIS JULII ANNO, INDICCIONE ET PONTIFICATU PREDICTIS.

LUTTELTON. In negocio contra Alexandrum de Luttelton &c. moto: ipso Alexandro ut prius personaliter comparente, productis ex parte officii tribus testibus ad probandum articulum, videlicet Johanne dicto Goldsmyth de Wych, Henrico le Boteler, et Simone le Panyter, quibus in forma iuris iuratis, petitaque copia monicionis alias contra ipsum Alexandrum et confratres suos per commissarium domini episcopi facte, qua in processu recipienda decreta, ad ponendum et supradicto producendum ulteriusque faciendum in dicto negocio quod est iustum, datus est dies Martis loco quo supra.

CANOUN DE WYRCESTR'. In causa seu negocio que seu quod inter Johannem Canoun de Wyrcestr' executorem Alexandri Raas nuper braciatoris domini episcopi Wyg' defuncti, cui administracio bonorum ipsius defuncti in forma iuris auctoritate ipsius domini episcopi est commissa, actorem ex parte una, et Margeriam filiam Willelmi de Asshebarwe partem ream ex altera, eo quod idem Margeria dictum executorem, quominus in ipsius bonis libere administrare valeat ut deberet temere impedit, seu impediri procurat, bona ipsius defuncti occultando et detinendo iniuste, vertitur vertive speratur, partibus ipsis personaliter comparentibus continuatus est iste dies cum die Jovis proximo futuro loco predicto ad idem.

Injunctions to a Monastery

116 *Undated* [?1340] *Injunctions sent to the abbot and convent of St. Augustine's, Bristol, after the bishop's visitation [19–20 June 1340].*

INIUNCCIONES FACTE ABBATI ET CONVENTUI SANCTI AUGUSTINI BRISTOLL'.

Frater Wolstanus &c. religiosis viris abbati et conventui Sancti Augustini Bristoll' nostre diocesis, salutem graciam et benediccionem.

Cum ad morum emendacionem et ad corrigendum subditorum excessus visitacionis officium sit salubriter institutum, ea que nuper apud vos visitantes comperimus corrigenda deserere nolumus sicut nec possumus incorrecta, vestre igitur obediencie mittimus articulos in scriptura presenti contentos vobis sub eiusdem virtute firmiter iniungentes quatenus eos curetis perficere et inviolabiliter observare.

In primis[1] quod cum secundum utriusque iuris veritatem parum sit statuta condere nisi sit qui ea tueatur, et melior sit obediencia quam victima,[2] mandamus ne quis vestrum canonicus claustralis iuvenis vel annosus claustrum exire presumat absque prelati sui seu custodis ordinis licencia petita et obtenta: quod si quis contrarium attemptare presumpserit per tres dies immediate sequentes claustrum non exeat sed in eodem sedeat psalterium perdicendo.

Item cum in execucione operis divini negligencia sit graviter arguenda, mandamus quod quilibet vestrum quem iusta causa absencie non excusat singulis horis nocturnis et diurnis missis et capitulo intersit: et si quis vestrum de cetero ab eisdem nisi ex causa legitima per prelatum capituli querenda et approbanda abstinere presumpserit per totidem dierum spacium per quot predicta commiserint [sic] claustrum omnino non exeant [sic], vel si officiarii fuerint tot psalteria dicere vel tot disciplinas suscipere iuxta prelati arbitrium qui tunc capitulum tenuerit regulariter compellatur [sic].

Item cum secundum utriusque iuris statutum revelator consilii iudicetur infidelis, inhibemus ne quis vestrum consilium capituli vestri cuivis seculari revelet[3] ullo modo: quod si quis repertus fuerit culpabilis in hac parte omni privetur officio et a tractatu capituli ut infamis[4] et proditor tamdiu segregetur quamdiu prelato et fratribus visum fuerit expedire.

Item cum secundum doctrinam evangelii si quis offerens munus ad altare recordatus fuerit fratrem suum aliquid habere contra eum prius debeat reconciliari fratri suo et demum munus altari offere,[5] inhibemus districte ne quis vestrum de cetero vilipendat fratres suos nec ad rixas seu iurgia provocet ullo modo, et ne quis qui fratrem suum offenderit convicio vel facto ad altare accedat nisi prius reconcilietur fratri suo: quod si quis contra predicta attemptare presumpserit per tres sextas ferias immediate sequentes pane servisia et leguminibus tantummodo sit contentus, et si residivaverit domino abbati et eciam priori penam predictam aggravare licebit contra eum.

Item quia teste veritate pluribus implicatus negociis minorem singulis valeat opem dare, mandamus quatenus frater obedienciarius qui misse maiori inscribitur conventum sequatur cotidie durante

---

1 The original is not paragraphed.   2 1 Samuel 15,22.
3 MS. 'relevet'.   4 MS. 'infanis'.
5 Matthew 5, 23–4.

ebdomada sua et si officium habuerit aliquem fidelem sibi substituat qui vices sui officii fideliter impleat quousque finita ebdomada sua ad officium suum implendum revertatur.

Item cum legere et non intellegere neglectui ascribitur, ideo ut fratres domus vestre per excercicium melius intelligant quod ore proferunt, mandamus quod in labore et in quavis alia licita et regulari locucione lingua latina vel gallica loquantur fratres de cetero sub pena per prelatum prudenter moderanda.

Premissos articulos cum penarum suarum adieccione nichil novi statuendos vestre caritati transmittimus observandos, sed pro salute animarum vestrarum ad statuta et iniuncciones per visitatores vestri capituli generalis vobis factas vestras consciencias affectuosius excitamus.

Item cum pauperes Christi debita porcione nusquam sint fraudendi[1] et eam non conveniat nimis augeri, vobis mandamus quatenus elemosina in domo vestra per elemosinarium qui pro tempore fuerit integre colligatur et fideliter distribuatur iuxta constituciones sanctorum patrum editas in hac parte.

Item cum domus dei quam decet sanctitudo non debeat patere ruinis, mandamus quod sacrista domus vestre qui pro tempore fuerit ecclesiam vestram decenter faciat cooperiri, eo quod huiusmodi onus a sacristis domus vestre agnosci consuevit ab antiquo.

Ceterum dilecti ad nostrarum iniunccionum observacionem vos non astringimus per excommunicacionum sentencias prout a quibusdam visitatoribus antea vidimus esse factam. Volentes obviare periculis animarum sperantesque quod sufficere debeat pena arbitraria vel ordinaria per nos absque dubio in contemptores si qui fuerint infligenda. Nec volumus ista vice vobis correctorem aut commissarium perficere alienum, tum quia magis volumus latere vestros defectus et crimina quam patere, tum eciam quia invenimus apud vos laudato altissimo multa plura que commendacione quam que correccione sint digna. Has nostras iniuncciones volumus et mandamus semel saltem in anno legi in capitulo coram vobis. Faciat vos altissimus vestre religionis capere dignos fructus. Dat' &c.

Miscellaneous Entries

323 *30 May 1340 Private letter from Archbishop John Stratford advising the bishop to retain a portion of the royal tenth to compensate for the intended diversion of part of the cardinals' procurations to the king's use.*

LITTERA PRIVATA ARCHIPISCOPI QUE FUIT RECEPTA APUD ESTYNTON PENULTIMO DIE JUNII IN FESTO APOSTOLORUM PETRI ET PAULI UNA [CUM] CARTA DOMINI REGIS DE

---

1 *Rectius* 'fraudandi'.

LIBERTATIBUS ECCLESIE ANGLIE ET UNA CUM BREVI DOMINI
REGIS PRO DECIMA LEVANDA EISDEM PER CLERUM CONCESSA.
Frater karissime. Circa reformacionem status ecclesie Anglie
operaciones nostras et studia dirigentes, cartam domini nostri regis
Anglie de amplioribus libertatibus eidem concessis, quam idem
dominus noster rex per harum baiulum vobis mittit, non sine magnis
laboribus impetravimus, sicut erat in ultima convocacione cleri
nostre Cantuar' provincie per nos facta[1] unanimiter ordinatum:
unde vestram fraternitatem in domino exhortamur ut cartam
huiusmodi in vestra cathedrali ecclesia sub salva custodia faciatis
reponi ut ecclesia anglicana futuris temporibus sua gaudeat uberius
libertate. Ad hec audivimus a nonnullis quod dictus noster rex
procuraciones cardinalium instantis anni sibi ex mutuo intendit
accipere a manibus collectorum, eciam si resistant, quod nobis et
vobis ceterisque nostris suffraganeis in grave preiudicium verisimiliter
redundabit. Nos una cum dicto nostro rege sic deliberavimus ista
vice quod de decima persolvenda eidem tantum retineatur in
manibus collectorum huiusmodi quantum de procuracionibus ipsis
recipitur nomine dicti regis, unde dictis cardinalibus possit debite
responderi et periculum imminens caucius evitari: quod per vos
fieri consulimus et hortamur. Ad ecclesie sancte regimen vos
conservet altissimus ut optamus. Script' apud Lamht' xxx die Maii.

837 27 *February* 1347 Inspeximus *of Bishop Mauger's confirmation of
the grant of Standish manor to the almonry at
Gloucester Abbey. The diocesan mitigates the
penalty imposed by his predecessor and regulates the
payments from the manor.*

ORDINACIO ET CONCESSIO ELEMOSINARIE DE MANERIO DE
STANDYSCH IN ARCHIDIACONATU GLOUCESTR'.
Universis presentes litteras inspecturis frater Wolstanus permissione
divina Wygorn' episcopus, salutem graciam et benediccionem
divinam. Litteras bone memorie Maugerii dei gracia Wygorn'
episcopi [1200–1212] predecessoris nostri nos inspexisse noveritis in
hec verba. Omnibus sancte matris ecclesie filiis ad quos presens
scriptum pervenerit Maugerius dei gracia Wygorn' episcopus
eternam in domino salutem. Ad universitatis vestre noticiam
volumus pervenire, dilectum filium nostrum Thomam abbatem
Glouc' ad monicionem et peticionem nostram et tocius conventus
Glovernie restituisse deo et elemosinarie Glou' in usus pauperum
Christi totum manerium de Stanedissh' cum omnibus pertinenciis
suis scilicet in decimis et redditibus et omnibus proventibus inperpetuum, salvis celerario Glovernie[2] antiquis assisis tam in
anniversario abbatis Serlonis quam in brasio. Ita quod elemosinarius

1 This had met 27 January 1340.
2 'in usus—Glovernie' interlineated.

qui pro tempore fuerit habebit plenam et integram disposicionem eiusdem manerii et convertet illud in usus pauperum prout melius secundum deum viderit expedire, nec umquam licebit alicui in alios usus illud manerium in toto vel in parte transferre nisi in magna necessitate et de communi consilio tocius conventus. Salvis tam predicto Thome abbati quam omnibus successoribus suis duabus marcis annis singulis ad Natale Domini et aliis duabus ad Pascha de eodem manerio ab elemosinario ad privatas elemosinas eiusdem abbatis faciendis imperpetuum percipiendis. Quod ne processu temporis possit infirmari, presenti scripto sigillo nostro munito confirmavimus. Data a nobis ad peticionem predictorum abbatis et conventus Glouc' excommunicacionis sentencia in eos qui hanc concessionem infirmare presumunt, nisi de magna necessitate ut supradictum est et de consilio tocius conventus. Facta est autem hec concessio anno ab incarnacione domini MCCII in capitulo Glouc' in die Sancte Marie Magdalen'[1] Hiis testibus: memorato venerabili patre nostro M[augerio] dei gracia Wygorn' episcopo, Roberto eadem gracia abbate Wynchelec' et multis aliis. Nos siquidem advertentes quod non sit in dei ecclesia quam excommunicacio maior pena, et quod homines in presenciarum [sic] fragiliores et debiliores ac ad peccandum proniores sunt solito, et antiquus hostis versutus religiosis precipue qui perfecciores esse deberent aliis et solebant plus invidet, ipsosque sepius optantes plus sapere quam oportet ultra quam alios in nimiam curiositatis subtilitatem et simplicitatem seducit et ipsius consciencias facit sepissime indiscretas, dictam excommunicacionis sentenciam in dictis litteris comprehensam de consensu expresso religiosorum virorum domini Ade dei gracia abbatis monasterii Sancti Petri Glouc' ordinis Sancti Benedicti nostre Wygorn' diocesis et eiusdem loci conventus auctoritate inmutamus et revocamus omnino et aliam penam equiorem loco subrogamus ipsius. Statuentes et in virtute sancte obediencie dictis religiosis viris firmiter iniungentes, quatenus tota assisa ab antiquo debita et consueta de manerio suo predicto de Stanedissh' singulis septimanis per elemosinarium subelemosinario liberetur, sine diminucione per subelemosinarium pauperibus fideliter eroganda, videlicet pro assisa panis coci in pane furnito quinque busshelli frumenti cum quarta parte unius busshelli per septimanam, que se in toto anno extendet ad triginta quatuor quarteria et quinque busshellos frumenti; et pro assisa panis fulberti in pane furnito quatuor quarteria et unus busshelus de pols' per septimanam, que in toto anno se extendat ad ducenta quatuordecim et dimidium quarterium de pols'. Item statuimus et in virtute obediencie ut prius iniungimus quod dictus elemosinarius liberet et donet annuatim nonaginta virgas panni lanei triginta pauperibus contra Natale inter eos equaliter parciendas videlicet cuilibet eorum tres virgas.

1 22 July.

Et si elemosinarius qui pro tempore fuerit preter necessitatem predictam in liberando vel subelemosinarius in errogando ut premittitur in nostra seu successorum nostrorum visitacione seu alias modo legitimo necgligentes inventi fuerint vel remissi, quod absit, volumus et de ipsorum religiosorum expresso consensu et assensu statuimus et ordinamus quod pro huiusmodi defectu in visitacionibus vel alias ut premissum est in hac parte comperto, centum solidi sterlingorum de bonis dictorum religiosorum nomine pene in usus fabrice ecclesie nostre cathedralis Wygorn' convertendi plenarie persolvantur. Ad quam penam in eventum predictum quociens contigerit persolvendam, dictos religiosos viros in personam magistri Willelmi de Bergeveny clerici et procuratoris eorundem procuratoremque suum predictum in personis dominorum suorum predictorum ad peticionem ipsorum et de ipsorum expresso consensu et assensu condempnamus diffinitive et sentencialiter in hiis scriptis. In quorum omnium testimonium parti huius littere indentate penes ipsos religiosos remanenti sigillum nostrum duximus apponendum, parti vero penes nos remanenti sigillum suum dicti religiosi apposuerunt commune. Dat' quo ad nos apud Hertlebury die Lune proxima post festum Sancti Mathie apostoli anno domini MCCCXLVI^to.; et quo ad religiosos viros dominos abbatem et conventum predictos apud Glouc' die Jovis proxima post festum Sancti Mathie predictum anno domini supradicto.[1]

905 *Undated* [1180 X 1184] *Endowment of St. Katherine's chapel, Campden, during Bishop Baldwin's episcopate.*

ORDINACIO CANTARIE CAPELLE BEATE KATERINE DE CAMPEDEN' QUE EST SUB CERA IN THESAURO ECCLESIE CATHEDRALIS WYGORN'.

Notum sit tam presentibus quam futuris quod ego Gondevill' dedi concessi et[2] pro salute anime mee et antecessorum meorum tres hidas terre in villa de Westynton' cum omnibus pertinenciis suis liberas et quietas ab omni seculari accioni et servicio capelle Beate Virginis Katerine quam ego fundavi in curia mea de Campedene imperpetuam[3] et puram elemosinam, scilicet dimidiam hidam terre quam Willelmus Ailwy tenet, et virgatam terre quam Hardyng' tenet, et virgatam quam Levi tenet, et virgatam quam Aluered tenet Huerel [sic], et virgatam quam Willelmus Collyng' tenet, et virgatam quam Walterus filius Gunnild' tenet, et virgatam quam Aluered' filius Radulphi tenet, et virgatam quam Willelmus filius Walteri tenet, et virgatam quam Auerd' filius H(er?)urb' tenet, et virgatam quam Amfridus filius suus[4] tenet, et virgatam quam Gaufridus

1 26 February and 1 March 1347.
2 Something has been omitted here, probably 'hac presenti carta mea confirmavi'.
3 For 'in perpetuam'.
4 MS. Amfrid' fil' suam [sic]. An alternative rendering would be 'Amfrida filia sua'.

Hathe tenet, et duo mesuagia in villa de Campeden ante portam curie mee scilicet a mesuagio Serlonis usque ad dominicum Hereberti, salvis decimis matri ecclesie pertinentibus. Constitui eciam consilio et assensu clericorum et laicorum duos presbiteros in eadem capella ministrantes, ita quod unus presbiter habeat in prebendam hidam et dimidiam et alter hidam et dimidiam ex hiis tribus[1] hidis predictis reddendo matri ecclesie unam libram incensi annuatim. Actum[2] est hoc in presencia Baldewini episcopi Wygorn' per voluntatem Osmundi persone; ita quod predicta capella plenam libertatem habeat. Dedi eciam matri ecclesie predicte manerii de Campeden' pro hac concessione decimas quatuor molendinorum eiusdem manerii quas antea non habuerat imperpetuam elemosinam. Presentacio vero capellanorum predicte capelle ad heredes meos pertinebit. Qui cum episcopo fuerint presentati et ab eo instituti fidelitatem[3] iurare debeat [sic] persone matris ecclesie quod nichil de oblacionibus vel decimis vel aliis rebus ad ius matris ecclesie pertinentibus contra utilitatem persone usurpabunt. Iurare debent eciam residenciam ibi nisi licencia episcopi aut voluntate domini aliquando pro honesta causa permittatur abesse ad tempus vel in brevi reversuri. Nec licebit heredibus meis alios presentare quam presbiteros qui predicte capelle assidue deserviant et propriis personis. Hiis testibus: Baldewyno episcopo Wygorn', Simone Luvel' archidiacono, Ricardo Luvel, Willelmo filio Roberti Osmund' de Campeden', Willelmo de Baton', Radulpho de Welneford, Alueredo, Willelmo Caperon, Ricardo, Eustachio de Horsynton; Roberto, Willelmo, Andrea fratribus; Roberto marescallo, Rogero coco, Roberto Waleys, Gilberto, Gilberto clerico, Ada clerico, Galfrido Hibernensi et aliis &c.

1 MS. 'tres'.   2 MS. 'Auctum'.
3 For 'fideliter'?

A Note on the Index of Persons and Places

Place names have been rendered in modern form, except when they constitute part of a personal name, the principal MS. readings being italicised within brackets. Places which cannot be identified with certainty are given in Italic capitals. Where a place is outside the Worcester diocese, the name of the diocese in which it lies is added, if mentioned in the text, otherwise the name of the county is supplied. Religious houses in other dioceses are listed with the appropriate county as well as the usual abbreviations to indicate rank and order. Warwickshire houses in Coventry & Lichfield diocese are entered with indication of both county and diocese.

It is more difficult to devise a satisfactory uniform system for personal names. To modernise them, so far as this is possible, might be to obscure consistent variants and make reference from the text less easy. There has been amalgamation of names generally spelled the same way or with minor litteral differences (e.g. Aston, Astone), while more individual variants have been indexed separately with appropriate cross-references (e.g. Asschton, Aysschton, and Asshton, Asshedon). Exceptional spellings (e.g. Aysschton) are listed alphabetically with a cross-reference to the full entry under the regular form. Name-places have likewise been kept in their MS. form with such amalgamation as seems necessary. In both categories entries are grouped under the most common form (where spellings are not wholly idiosyncratic), although occasionally when the modern form occurs in the MS. or is to be found in the introduction this has been used instead (e.g. Worcester rather than Wygorn').

The Diocese of Worcester in the XIVth Century

Boundaries

Diocese

Archdeaconry

Deanery

Peculiars

Deaneries — BRISTOL

Episcopal Manors — ○ Ripple

Miles

0 _____ 10

N

COVENTRY
&
LICHFIELD
DIOCESE

Halesowen

Clent

Kidderminster

KIDDERMINSTER

Alvechurch

DROITWICH

Warwick

Dodderhill Hanbury

Droitwich

Claverdon

WORCESTER

Hallow

WARWICK

Hampton Bp.

Broadwas

Alcester

Stratford

Worcester

Spetchley

PERSHORE

Kineton

Powick

Kempsey

Malvern

Pershore

KINETON

POWICK

EVESHAM

Evesham

Campden

Tredington

Ripple

Bredon

CAMPDEN

Longdon

Blockley

Tewkesbury

BLOCKLEY

Deerhurst

Hailes

Winchcombe

Stow

WINCHCOMBE

Cheltenham

STOW

CHURCHDOWN

Gloucester

Llanthony

Coberley

Withington

GLOUCESTER

Syde

CIRENCESTER

BIBURY

Bibury

Barnsley

FAIRFORD

Cirencester

STONEHOUSE

Fairford

Berkeley

Dursley

DURSLEY

HEREFORD DIOCESE

LINCOLN DIOCESE

SALISBURY DIOCESE

HAWKESBURY
&
BITTON

BRISTOL

Tormarton

Henbury

Westbury

Bristol

Bitton

BATH
& WELLS
DIOCESE

Based on Ordnance Survey Map.

Index of Persons and Places

Abbreviations:

A. & C., abbot and convent; Abb., abbey; abb., abbot; abp., archbishop; abss., abbess; acol., acolyte; adv., advowson; approp., appropriation; archd(y.), archdeacon(ry); Aug. (Fr.), Augustinian (friar); Beds., Bedfordshire; Ben., Benedictine; bp., bishop; Br. [title], brother (*frater*); bro., brother; Bucks., Buckinghamshire; C., convent; *c., circa*; can(s.), canon(s); Cant., Canterbury; cath., cathedral; celebr., celebrated (or Orders); ch(s.), church(es); chant(s.), chantry, chantries; chap., chapel; chapl., chaplain; Ches., Cheshire; Chich., Chichester; Cist., Cistercian; clk., clerk; Clun., Cluniac; co., county; colleg. ch., collegiate church; convoc., convocation; Cov. & Lich., Coventry and Lichfield; dau., daughter; deac., deacon; deany., deanery; dedic., dedication; Derbys., Derbyshire; dioc., diocese; doc(s.), document(s); Dors., Dorset; e., earl; Ess., Essex; exchd., exchanged (of benefices); exor., executor; fam., family; fl., *floruit*; Flints., Flintshire; Fr. Preacher, Dominican (Preaching) friar; Gilb., Gilbertine; Gl., Gloucestershire; Glam., Glamorgan; Heref., Hereford(shire); hosp. hospital; jurisd., jurisdiction; kt., knight; Kts. Hosp., Knights Hospitallers; Leics., Leicestershire; ld., lord; Linc., Lincoln; m. (mks.), monk (monks); M., Master (Magister); man., manor; Mon., Monmouthshire; N., Nunnery; Norf., Norfolk; Northants., Northamptonshire; ob., *obit.*, offic., official; orat., oratory; ord., ordained; ordin., ordination (of vicarage); pap. prov., papal provision; par., parish; pec., peculiar; Pembs., Pembrokeshire; port., portion; Pr., Priory; pr., prior; preb(s.), prebend(s); preby., prebendary; precept., preceptor; precepty., preceptory; Premonst., Premonstratensian; pss., prioress; pst., priest; r., rector; rect., rectory; recd., received; reg., register; Salisb., Salisbury; Salop., Shropshire; Som., Somerset; Staffs., Staffordshire; subd., subdeacon; Suff., Suffolk; Surr., Surrey; Suss., Sussex; v., vicar; val., valuation; vic., vicarage; visit., visitation; w., wife; Wa., Warwickshire; ward., warden; wid., widow; Wilts., Wiltshire; Winch., Winchester; Wo., Worcestershire; Yorks., Yorkshire.

* According to W. E. Lunt, *Financial Relations of the Papacy with England 1327–1534*,
pp. 636–639, Androin de la Roche was prior of St. Seine.

BATY, John, of Holdfast, 266
BATYN:
John, 210
John, of Swell, 434
Richard, son of John, 434
Stephen, 308
BAUDINTON, BAUDYNTON:
Philip de, 201
William de, 181
BAUGHTON (*Bokton*), 265
BAVENT, John, v. of Blockley, 426
BAWET, Henry, 199
BAXTER, Roger le, of Wixhill, 231
BAXTERLEYE, John de, m. of Merevale, 242, 252
BAYEUX DIOCESE (*Baioc'*), 211, 214, 216
BAYLYF, BAILLIF:
John, 162, 164, 166
William, of Norton by Bredon, 188
William le, William son of, 185
BAYNGROVE:
John, of Aston Somerville, 186
Thomas de, 183
BAYNTON, John de, v. of Dodford (Linc. dioc.), r. of Oxhill, 71, 364
BAYONNE DIOCESE (*Baionens'*), 208, 216 n. 1
BEALE:
John, of Longdon, 185, 193
Walter, 198; *and see* Bele
BEAUCHAMP:
fam., 10 n. 2
Alice [de Tony], w. of Walter ld. of Powick, 173
Giles de, son of Walter ld. of Powick, 173
Guy de, e. of Warwick (1298–1315), xli n. 1, 156, 493
John de, kt., younger bro. of Thomas e. of Warwick, ld. of Beoley & Yardley, 33, 340, 397
Katherine, w. of Thomas e. of Warwick, 156, 498
Petronilla, dau. of Walter ld. of Powick, 173
Thomas de, son of Guy, e. of Warwick (1329–69), xli n. 1, xliii, 44, 53, 92, 100, 101, 105, 122, 156, 197, 358–360, 362, 366, 370–372, 379, 384, 385, 389, 390, 399, 400, 412, 420, 421, 424, 430, 498
Walter de, ld. of Powick (ob. 1303), 173, 175

Walter de, son of Walter ld. of Powick, 173
William de, senior, kt. (son of Walter), ld. of Powick & Clevelode, 173, 316
William de, m. of Pershore, 158
BEAUFRERE, Edward, r. of Oldbury, 419
BEAULIEU [?] (*Beauli*) Hants., Cist. Abb., 253
BEAUPEYNE, Thomas, 267
BEAUTR', John de, 61, 361
BEAUVER, Randolph, 266
BEBINGTON, William de, abb. of St. Werburgh's Chester, 153 n. 1, *and see* Chester
BECKFORD (*Beckeford, Bekeford*), 186, 189, 203, 210, 238, 266
ch. of, 28, 95
v., vic. of, 107, 385, 409
BECKFORD, Aug. Pr., 385
BECKEFORD, William de, r. of Holy Trinity, Bristol, 8
BEDDINGTON[?] (*Bedyngton*), Winch. dioc., 280 n. 2
BEDEL, John le, of Marston Meysey, 186
BEDESTON, BUDESTON [Biddestone, Wilts.], Walter de, m. of Malmesbury, 226, 237
BEDEWYNDE, Walter de, r. of Ripple, 173
BEDFORD, *see* Caldwell
BEDLINGTON, Durham dioc., 120, 384
BEDMINSTER (*Bedmynstre*), Bath & Wells dioc., hosp. of St. Katherine near, 133
BEGGERESCY, 20
BEGGE(S)WORTH, M. Walter de, r. of Mathon, 159, 238
BEGWORTH, Walter, Carmelite, 203
BEK, Thomas, bp. of Lincoln (1342–47), 115, 128
BEKKEFORD, Adam de, m. of Little Malvern, 147
BEKYNHULL, Thomas de, can. of Maxstoke, 259
BELAMY, M. Thomas, r. of Broadwell, 120, 122, 128, 232
BELBROUGHTON (*Bellebrocton, Belne Brocton*), 269, 271, 273, 277, 338, 348–349
ch., r., rect. of, 18, 22, 94, 349, 416, 505 *et seq.*
BELDE, Robert, of Stratford, v. of Great Barrington, 77, 365

38

D

* Only in one case, noted in the text,
    does *Tormerton* occur. Elsewhere
    Thormerton is invariably used. Un-
    fortunately the scribe sometimes
    wrote *Thormerton* for Tormarton, so
    identification cannot always be
    certain.

40

KILLINGWORTH (*Kyllingworth*), Linc. dioc., 229

KILWORTH, NORTH (*Kenelingworth rabat3*), Linc. dioc., 229

KINEMERSFORD, KYNEMARESFORD, KYMMESFORD, KNYMERSFORD:
Henry de, r. of Matson, 402, 414
John, 273, 278, 338
Richard, of Longdon, v. of Marshfield, 228, 230, 236, 242
William de, 279; *and see* Kempsford.

KINETON (*Kyngton, Kyngton fori*) (*Magna Kyngton*), 250, 260, 274, 343
dean, deany. of, 9, 12, 19, 22, 35, 77, 366, 371
v. of, 221, 225; *and see* Kington

KINGS NORTON (*Norton, Kyngesnorton*), 182, 183, 187, 215, 216, 232
chap. of, 18, 94

KINGS STANLEY (*Stanleye Regis*), ch., r. of, 29, 36; *and see* Abbots Stanley, Leonard Stanley

KINGS SUTTON (*Kyngessutton*), Linc. dioc., 221

KINGS WESTON, in Henbury (*Kynges-Weston*), 123, 437, 448

KINGSCOTE (*Kyngescote*), 59; chap. of, 29, 31

KINGSCOTE, KYNGESCOTE:
Adam de, father of Reginald, 203, 213
Adam, son of Reginald de, 203, 213
Reginald, son of Adam de, 203, 213
William, 201

KINGSTON SEYMOUR (*Kyngeston Semor*), Bath & Wells dioc., 238

KINGSWINFORD (*Kynggessweneford*), r. of, 99, 377; *and see* Northwell

KINGSWOOD (*Kyngeswode*), Cist. Abb., 5, 178, 202, 203, 211, 213, 224, 237
mks. of, 234, 251, 257, 259, 261, 343

KINGTON (*Kyngton*), Wilts., Ben. N., 183, 203, 213, 258, 341

KINGTON (*Kyngton*), Wo., r. of, 383

KINGTON or KINETON (*q.v.*) (*Kyngton*), 190, 269, 272

KINGTON or KYNETON, nr. Wotton, Gl. (*Kynton*), 233

KINLET (*Kynlet*), Heref. dioc., v., vic. of, 101, 377

KINLEY (*Kynleye*), sec. college of, 29

KINNERSLEY (*Kynardesleye*), Heref. dioc., 180

KINWARTON (*Kynwarton*), 23

KINYTEL, Master J., of Droitwich, 75

KIRKBY THORE (*Kyrkeby Thore*), Carlisle dioc., 129, 388

KIRKEBY, Robert, of Stow, 337, 342

KIRKEDAL, John de, of Cov. & Lich. dioc., 341

KITTONE, John, of Maugersbury, 250

KNIGHTWICK (*Knyhtwyk*), ch., r., rect. of, 52, 128, 359, 390

KNYGHT, Robert, of Marston, 275

KNYT:
John, ord. to first tons., 267
John, of Adlestrop, 208

KNYTCOTE, KNYTECOTE:
Hugh de, 374
Richard de, 272, 278
William de, ward. of St. Michael's hosp., Warwick, 92, 100, 430

KOK, John le, *see* Cok

KOKES, William, *see* Cokes

KRONNOK, William, of South Cerney, 187

KYARD, Nicholas, 133

KYBBLESDON, 409

KYDE, Richard, of Heref. dioc., 184

KYDERMUSTR', Richard de, *see* Kiddermunstre

KYLLESBY, William de, 118

KYLPEK, John, m. of St. Peter's, Gloucester, 168

KYMENHALE, port. of in Leigh ch., 418, 438, 441

KYMMESFORD, KYNEMARESFORD, *see* Kinemersford

KYNG, KYNG', KYNGES:
Henry, of Winchcombe, 129, 213, 214, 217
John, acol., 180
John, of Shurdington, 271
John, of Winchcombe, 211, 216, 437
Philip, of Winchcombe, 213
Roger, layman, 87
Roger, of Winchcombe, 256
William, of Forthampton, 265

KYNGESCOTE, William, *see* Kingscote

KYNGESTHORP [Kingston?], 327

KYNGESTON [error for Kington, Wilts. *q.v.*], 213

KYNGESTON, Robert de, King's clk., 11, 34, 283

KYNGTON:
Edmund de, 256
John de, 198

KYNIOT:
John, of Shell, 182, 202

Merston, Mersston(e), Merhston: (cont.)
Robert de, preceptor of St. Wulstan's hosp., Worcester, xlvii, 431
Simon de, bro. of St. John's hosp., Warwick, 93, 101
Thomas de, 125
M. Walter de, r. of St. Helen's, Worcester, 179, 407
William de, subd., 184
William de, pst. 343
William de, can. of Kenilworth, 258
MERSTON BOTELER, Walter de, 234
MERTHYR (*Merthyr*), Llandaff dioc., r. of, 218 n. 2, 219
MERTON (*Merton*), Surr., Aug. Pr. of St. Mary, 245, 253, 262, 273, 277, 338
MERTON COLLEGE, Oxford, 178, 214, 226, 236, 248, 249, 369
MESSAGER, MASSEGER:
Godfrey le, 265
Walter le, of Wheatenhurst, 276, 337, 343
MESTON, Br. Thomas de, 247
METKE, John, of Chirton (Salisb. dioc.), 188
MEY, Nicholas le, of Bourton, 248, 261
MEYR, John le, administrator of Shell chap., v. of St. Peter's, Witton, 108, 381
MEYSEY HAMPTON (*Hampton Meysy, Hampton Meysi*), 187, 213, 274, 278
r., rect. of, 392, 414
MEYSY, Thomas, 341
MICHEL, MICEL:
John, of Strensham, 197, 250
Thomas, of Droitwich, 251
William, ord. to first tons., 198
William, of Marlcliff, 220
MICKLETON (*Mukilton, Mikelton, Muchelton*), 222, 223, 265, 314
r., rect. of, 416
v., vic. of, 409
MIDDELMOR, John de, 16
MIDELTON, MIDELTONE, MIDDELTON(E), MIDDILTON:
John de, *literatus*, 414
M. John de, 370
M. Robert de, 226
M. Roger de, r. of Boxwell, 82, 377, 432; r. of Buckland, 416
William, 201

MIDDLEHAM (*Midelham*), York dioc., 214
MIDDLESEX, sheriff of, 299
MILBORNE (*Muleborn*), Salisb. dioc., 151
MILDENHALE, Martin de, of Norwich dioc., 179
MILE:
John, 190
Thomas, 217
MILKESHAM, M. David de, *see* Melkesham
MILLEN, Henry, 268
MILTECOMBE [Milcombe, Oxon.?], 380
MILVERTON, John de, 342
MINCHINHAMPTON (*Hampton Monialium*), 59, 224, 230, 253, 339
chant. of B.V.M. in, 160, 369, 395, 404
ch. of, 29
man. of, 59
orat. in, 59, 447
r., rect. of, 140, 369, 414
MINSTERWORTH (*Monstruworth*), Heref. dioc., 193
MINSTREWORTHE, Laurence de, 212; *and see* Munstreworth, Mynsterworth
MISERDEN (*Musardere*), ch. of, 48, 49
r., rect. of, 69, 82, 92, 106, 115, 383, 407, 437, 439, 440, 441; *and see* Brescy, William
MISSENDEN (*Messenden*), Bucks., Aug. Abb., 240, 246, 255, 344
MITCHELDEAN (*Marteldenan*), 256
MITTON (*Mutton*), ch. of, 94
MODEFORD, William de, m. of Winchcombe, 339
MOGGE, Thomas, of Defford, 180, 229, 231, 232
MOHUN, MOUHON:
Baldwin de, r. of Whichford, 90, 116, 380, 382
John de, kt., 90, 375, 380, 382
MOLENDINARIUS, William, of Rowington, 183
MON, John, of Doynton, 268
MONDEVILLA, Nicholas de, subprior of St. Denis, 129
MONFORT, MOUNFORT, *see* Mountford
MONIASSCH, Ralph, 212
MONK:
John, 201
William, 199

Morton (cont.)
Simon de, 197
Walter de, r. of Hampton, 80, 367
Walter de, r. of Kymenhale port.
in Leigh, 418
William de, ord. to first tons., 197
William de, Fr. Preacher, 276
MORTON FOLET, Thomas de, 91, 448
MORYCE, MORYS, MOREYS, MORICE,
MORIS:
Henry, deac., 273, 277
Henry, r. of Daylesford, 56
John, 229
Nicholas, m. of Worcester, 16, 62,
115
Richard, m. of Worcester, 139
Robert, of Worcester, r. of Martin
Hussingtree, 398
Robert, of Worcester, v. of Lind-
ridge, Heref. dioc., 109, 176
Thomas, 263
William, subd., 192
William, pst., 210
MORYN, Robert, ld. of Swindon, 395
MOSARD, Elias, of Strensham, 220
MOSE, William, m. of Worcester, 104
MOTON, Walter, 297
MOTTISFONT (*Montesfrounte*), Hants.,
Aug. Pr., 183
MOUNSEREL, William, m. of Bruern,
189
MOUNTESTEVENE, Thomas, of Bristol,
236, 255
MOUNTFORD, MOUNDFORD, MONFORT,
MOUNFORT:
John, 263
Peter de, kt., 61
William, of Aston-on-Carrant, 233,
345
MOY, Nicholas le, 235
MUCH WENLOCK PRIORY, *see* Wenlock
MUCHEGROS, Robert, ld. of Wool-
lashill, 361, 377
—Richard, his son., 377
MUCHELDEVERE, Walter, r. of Cam.
159
MUCHILNEYE, John de, m. of Wor-
cester, 8
MUKELTON, Robert, m. of Fountains,
189
MULCOTE, Helias de, 198
MULEWARD, MULLEWARD:
Henry de, chant. pst. of Ripple, 396
Henry le, layman, 140, 466
John, ord. to first tons., 264

John, ord. to first tons., 267
John, of Castlett (*Catheslade*), 238
John, of Chaddesley (*Chaddesle*), 229
John, of Cowley, 187
John, of Shirley, ord. to first tons.,
199
John, of Southrop, 183
John le, from Cirencester abb., ord.
to first tons., 267
John le, of Lechlade, 179
Richard, 200
Robert, 266
Thomas, ord. to first tons., 199
Thomas, of Charlecote, 336
Walter, son of William le, 336
William, ord. to first tons., 199
William, ord. to first tons., 201
William, of Windrush, 233
William le, of Hampton, 336; *and
see* Meleward, Muluwart
MULLE:
John, ord. to first tons., 262
John, ord. to first tons., 264
John atte, chant. pst. of Wortley,
176
John atte, of *Wilmeston*, 244
Hugh atte, of Ampney Crucis, 235,
253
Thomas atte, of Stoke Prior, xxvii,
334
MULLECOTE:
John, son of Richard de, 344
Richard de, of Evesham, 344
MULNE:
Philip atte, of Campden, 276, 337,
343
Simon atte, of Kempsey, 270
Thomas atte, 339
Thomas atte, of Broadwell, ord. to
first tons., 264
William atte, of Sherborne, 257,
269, 274
MULTONE, Resus de, 178
MULUERE, Richard de, of Ampney,
250
MULUWART:
John, of Rissington, 256
Thomas, 263
William, 264; *and see* Muleward
MULVERTON, Richard de, 344
MUMHAM, Thomas de, 200
MUNE, Richard de, 339
MUNEDE, Andrew, m. of St. Peter's,
Gloucester, 168
MUNKES, Robert, 199

* There is also a Quinton in Wo. and some name-places may refer to it.

T

* There is some danger of confusion with Farmington *q.v.*

3

Z

Subject Index

This is not intended to be a complete analysis of the entries in the Calendar, but to provide a means of finding the principal items. It has been arranged with administrative detail particularly in mind, and should be used in conjunction with the synopsis preceding the introduction.

A

ACQUITTANCES:
  for bp.'s receiver (M. John le Botoner), 96, 97
  for bp.'s sequestrator and corrector (M. Henry de Neubold), 160
  for clk. of bp.'s household (John de Chalveston), 96–97
  for indemnity by reason of appropriation, 34, 38, 42, 115–116, 154
ALIENS,
  writs concerning:
    certiorari with respect to eccles. benefices held by, 287; *certiorari* with respect to the names of aliens and the value of their benefices, 322; *distringas* against r. of Barnsley, 310 *and see* Index of Persons & Places *s.v.* Malet, M. Peter; for the citation of beneficed aliens, 318; forbidding their admission to benefices, 302
ALMS, EPISCOPAL:
  obligation to pay money towards, 2
APPARITORS,
  appointments of: Dursley deanery, 17; Pershore deanery, 10; Powick deanery, 17
  revocation of appointments in Glouc. archdy., 10
APPOINTMENTS AND ELECTIONS OF HEADS OF RELIGIOUS HOUSES, 427–431
APPROPRIATION OF CHURCHES, xlii–xlv,
  Acton Turville [Tormarton chant.], 306; Aston Cantlow [Maxstoke Pr.], 127; Campden [St. Werburgh's, Chester], 69–70; Clent [Halesowen Abb.], 116–117; Gt.

Badminton [Lilleshall Abb.], 86–87; Moreton Daubeney moiety [St. John's hosp., Warwick], 24–25; Pillerton [Warwick colleg. ch.], 335; Tanworth [Maxstoke Pr.], 66–67; Yardley [Maxstoke Pr.], 140, 147;
  induction of A. & C. of Evesham to Ombersley rect., 72
  pensions due to bp. on acc. of approp., 34, 38, 40, 42, 43, 44, 103, 115–116, 117, 154
  returns of writs of *certiorari* concerning churches approp. to Maxstoke Pr., 327, 330–331, 347
ARCHDEACONRIES, xiv, xvi–xvii
ARCHDEACONS, xvii
  of Gloucester,
    commission to install abb. of Winchcombe, 64
  of Worcester,
    commission to secure (with others) anticipation of dates for payment of a 10th, 130
    writs concerning: *levari facias*, 297, 298; *supersedeas*, 298; *venire facias*, 316, 319
  of Gloucester & Worcester,
    commissions: to enquire into the detention of Bp. Hemenhale's goods, 2; to summon the clergy to a diocesan assembly, 4
  and see Index of Persons & Places *s.v.* Breynton, M. Roger de; Ledbury, M. Richard de; Worcester, M. Robert of
ARCHDEACONS' OFFICIALS, xvii
  of Gloucester,
    certificates of execution of mandates: for citation of opponents of Tewkesbury election, 162;

Archdeacons' Officials (cont.)

for enquiry into vacancy of Aston Somerville rect., 106, into value of Acton Turville ch., 308, into value of Gt. Badminton rect., 87; for summoning clergy to undergo visitation, 94–95

commissions: to cite dean of Campden for failure to execute a mandate, 6; to declare revocation of commissions to penitentiaries, 10; to enquire into dilapidations at Cold Aston vic., 11–12; to enquire into vacancies of benefices, 46, 47, 50, 52; to execute writs—of *fieri facias*, 283, 288, of *venire facias*, 288; to induct to an episcopal ch. in Worc. archdy., 100; to institute presentee to a benefice after enquiry, 52, 105

of Worcester,

certificates of execution of mandates: for citation of co-elect of Pershore, 73, 74; for enquiry into vacancy of St. Andrew's, Droitwich, 136

commissions: to cite opponents of election at Pershore, 73–74, of election at Pinley, 89; to collect ¼d in £ from ecclesiastical benefices, 102; to enquire into vacancies of benefices, 66, 93; to execute writ for arrears of 10th, 282; to execute writ giving details of the victory of Sluys and requesting that thanksgiving be made, 290; to induct prior of Astley, 78, 90; to induct prior of Wootton Wawen, 77; to induct and install pss. of Wroxall, 60; to install abb. of Pershore, 76; to install prior of Worcester, 63; to summon clergy to undergo visitation, 17–18, 94

of Gloucester & Worcester jointly,

commissions: to collect the cardinals' procurations, 102; to execute a writ for citation of beneficed aliens, 318; to publish council ordinances for the regulation of wages at the time of the Black Death, 334

B

BENEFICES, xxxii *et seq.*

absence from, xxxii–xxxiii, 437–441

coadjutors: (*iconomus*) for Deerhurst par. ch., 113–114; for r. of Frampton Cotterell, 9, 35; for r. of Oldbury, 42; for r. of St. Helen's, Worcester, 152–153; for v. of Turkdean, 35

dilapidations: at Cold Aston vic., 11–12; because of fire at Nympsfield rect., 124–125

enquiries into vacancies of benefices or reasons for their exchange:

outside the diocese: held by clergy of Weston deany., Hereford dioc. (Tarrington), 172–173; by offic. of archd. of Dorset (Lytchett Matravers), 151; by offic. of archd. of Lincoln (Gt. Ponton), 150; by offic. of archd. of Norwich (Sparham), 137–138; by offic. of archd. of Shropshire (Mamble), 109; by offic. of archd. of Wiltshire (Sherston), 149

within the diocese, 356–426 (*s.v.* 'Inqu.'), held by officials of archds. of Gloucester & Worcester, 14, 33, 34, 46, 47, 50, 52, 66, 93, 106, 136–137, 149, 176, 377 n. 2 *and see* Archdeacons' officials

enquiries into value: Acton Turville rect., 308; Gt. Badminton rect., 87; Pillerton rect., 335

exchanges, xxxiii–xxxiv

appointment of proctors to effect, 49, 108, 114–115

commissions for: execution of, 11, 49, 50, 51, 53, 56, 61, 64, 68, 70–71, 71, 72, 76–77, 77–78, 80, 83, 83–84, 84, 87, 91, 91–92, 98, 99, 99–100, 106, 108, 115, 120, 122, 136–137, 137–138, 139, 148, 149, 149–150, 152, 153, 154, 170–171, 175–176, 309; issued to the bp. by other ordinaries, 104, 109, 115, 128, 136, 138, 148, 149, 149–150, 151, 154, 170, 387 n. 1; issued by the bp. to other

priory appointments:

sacrist, 54

tumbaries at shrine of SS. Oswald & Wulfstan, 104, 176

temporal officers, xxvi–xxviii

bailiff of Oswaldslow (Thomas le Somery, Richard de Bromwich, Thomas atte Mulle), 99, 333, 334

bailiff of Stratford & Hampton manors (Adam de Styventon), 6

constable of Hartlebury castle (Penebrugg, Hugh de), 6–7

custos of bp.'s house in the Strand (William de Netherton), 37

grantee of fruits of Hillingdon ch. (Thomas de Evesham), 37

steward of lands in Gloucestershire (William de Cheltenham), xxvi, 13

steward of lands in Warwickshire & Worcestershire (Peter de Groete), xxvii, 7

ORDINATIONS, xlviii–xlix, 177–279, 336–344

numerical details of, 442–446

P

PAPAL CURIA:

appointment of proctors, 55

appointment of proctors to prosecute the bp.'s case against Philip le Yonge, 55

PAPAL PENITENTIARY:

see Index of Persons & Places *s.v.* Gaucelinus, bp. of Albano

PAPAL PRIVILEGES:

enabling bp. to grant licences in accordance with *Super cathedram*, 67

enabling bp. to select two Worcester monks for attendance at the Schools, 139

for Malmesbury Abb., 237

PAPAL PROVISION:

bp. as sole executor of bull in favour of John Rich delegates his powers, 5

bp. as sole executor of bull in favour of Robert Waltres delegates his powers to sub-executors, 36

process of, concerning Broadway rect. (William de Okleye), 352–

353 *cf.* 415

writ forbidding the admission of foreigners to benefices and deploring the increase of papal provision, 302, 304

writ of *certiorari* regarding provision to Little Compton (Robert Walters or Waltres) and return thereof, 331, 332

writ of *certiorari* regarding provision to Trimpley vic., 300

writ requiring obedience to an ordinance against bringing bulls into the country, 304

and see Title

PARLIAMENTS AND COUNCILS:

February 1338 Westminster, 280

July 1338 Northampton, 280

January 1340 Westminster (app. of proctors), 24

March 1340 Westminster (app. of proctors), 61

July 1340 Westminster (app. of proctors), 36

April 1343 Westminster, 301, 302 (app. of proctors, 302)

April 1344 Westminster, 304 (app. of proctors, 305)

June 1344 Westminster, 307 (app. of proctors, 307)

February 1346 Westminster, 317–318 (app. of proctors, 318)

September 1346 Westminster, 320–321

January 1348 Westminster, 328

January 1349 Westminster, 332*

April 1349 [postponement], 332

February 1351 Westminster, 344–345

PENSIONS, granted by the bp.:

100s. to king's clk. on account of bp.'s elevation, 11, 34, 283; 100s. to abp.'s crucifer on account of bp.'s consecration, 24; 5 marks to William de Asteleye, 17; 10 marks to M. John de Lech, 26; 10 marks to M. Richard de Thormerton, 96; 10 marks to bp.'s steward in Gloucs. (William de Cheltenham), 13

and see Grants of land and rent

PILGRIMAGE:

to shrine of Our Lady at Walsingham, 69, of St. James [at Compostella], 15

* In the event this assembly never met. The *Handbook of British Chronology* (1961) does not record this summons or the next one.

list of monks: Pershore, 158; St. Peter's, Gloucester, 168; Tewkesbury, 161–162

patrons: consent to election of abb. of Tewkesbury, 160–161; licence to hold an election at Tewkesbury, 160–161; notification to Qu. Philippa of election at St. Augustine's Abb., Bristol, 164

penalty imposed on canon of Holy Sepulchre, Warwick—relaxation of, 148

provision for a retired abbot of Winchcombe, 65–66

proxy for foundation of chantry in Pershore Abb., 130

resignation of heads: letters asking leave to resign, 25 (Winchcombe), 72 (Pershore); acceptance of, 61 (Winchcombe)

temporalities: letter for release of, 64

RURAL DEANERIES, xvii–xviii

RURAL DEANS:

commissions and mandates to deans of:

Bristol: to cite opponents of election at St. Mary's, Billeswick, 132 (certificate), 135; to induct pss. of St. Mary Magdalene's, Bristol, 176; to institute and induct (with others) to vic. of Painswick, 105

Campden: to cite opponents of election of abb. of Winchcombe, 62, 63 (certificate); to relax sequestration, 50

Cirencester: to enforce payment of episcopal fees for reconciliation, 19

Droitwich: to execute writs of *levari facias*, 286, 292, of *supersedeas*, 292; to induct to Hanbury ch., 49

Dursley: to admonish parishioners of Eastington not to attend Mass elsewhere, 35–36

Gloucester: to claim criminous clerks from the lay justices, 16, 38, 39; to induct to prebend of Moreton & Whaddon, 151

Hawkesbury and Bitton: to induct to Tormarton rect., 64

Kidderminster: to cite r. of Clent and admonish him to make residence, 36

Kineton: to cite a layman in *ex officio* suit, 9; to claim criminous clerks from the lay justices, 19, 35; to examine witnesses for the r. of Dry Marston's purgation, 12; to induct r. of Halford, 77

Pershore: to cite those guilty of faults at visitation, 23, 95; to excommunicate those guilty of defamation, 14; to exercise r. of Ripple's jurisdiction with respect to an intestate, 47

Stonehouse: to restore to v. of Tetbury the fruits of his benefice, 17

Stow: to examine reasons for taking vow of chastity (certificate), 137; to induct to Naunton rect., 77; to secure criminous clerks from the lay justices, 9

Warwick: to denounce laymen removing candles at the Purification, 104; to induct warden of St. Michael's hosp., Warwick, 92; to make citation in a charge of assault, 9; to secure criminous clerks from the lay justices, 35; to sequestrate the goods of a benefice, 126

Winchcombe: to cite opponents of purgation, 20; to induct prior of Deerhurst to cure of Deerhurst parish ch., 57

Worcester: to allow use of St. Oswald's churchyard for burial at time of Black Death, 176; to induct to St. Helen's, Worcester, 72; to pronounce sacrilegious persons excommunicate, 9–10; to pronounce excommunicate all failing to observe Broadwas chantry ordinances, 120

seals of appended to documents for greater authenticity: Bristol, 81, 132, 134; Droitwich, 91, 107, 108; Pershore, 158; Stow, 137; Tredington, 90; Warwick, 43; Worcester, 89

T

TAXATION, vii, 1

Papal: assessments of Norwich, Stroud and Vienne, 319

Taxation (cont.)
  Tenths:
    episcopal appointment of col-
      lectors: for 10th of 1342,
      abb. of Winchcombe (Gl.
      archdy.), pr. of Gt. Malvern
      (Wo. archdy.), 207; for first
      year of triennial 10th of 1344,
      abb. of Tewkesbury (Gl.
      archdy.), pr. of Studley (Wo.
      archdy.), 311, 315, abb. of St.
      Peter's, Gloucester, as sub-
      stitute for abb. of Tewkesbury,
      316–317; for biennial 10th of
      1346, abb. of St. Peter's,
      Gloucester (Gl. archdy.), pr.
      of Studley (Wo. archdy.), 327,
      form of commission for collec-
      tion of above biennial 10th, 325
    royal writs: for collection of trien-
      nial 10th of 1337 [mention of],
      37, of arrears in Gl. archdy., 3–4,
      6, 37, 283–285, of arrears in Wo.
      archdy., 282; for collection of
      additional 10th of 1340, 289–290;
      for anticipation of dates of pay-
      ment of 10th of 1342, 206–207;
      countermanding instruction for
      payment of above 10th to M.
      Paul de Monte Florum, 301; for
      collection of arrears of 10th of
      [1342] in Gl. archdy., 299; for
      collection of arrears of 10th of
      [1342] in Wo. archdy., 303; for
      collection of triennial 10th of
      1344, 311, 315, and cf. 130, of
      arrears in Gl. archdy., 314–315;
      for collection of biennial 10th of
      1346, 325, 326; for collection of
      second year of biennial 10th of
      1351, 346, 347; for appointment
      of substitute for abb. of Tewkes-
      bury in Gl. archdy., 316–317
    commission to A. & C. of Ciren-
      cester to proceed against those
      who had failed to pay the
      triennial 10th of 1337 in Gl.
      archdy., 37
    commission to sequestrator for
      execution of writ (1339) for col-
      lection of arrears, 3–4
    mandate for citation of dean of
      Campden for failure to execute
      the sequestrator's order for col-
      lection of arrears, 6

    payments of 10th made by the
      abbots of St. Augustine's, Bristol,
      280
    request by prior of Gt. Malvern to
      be relieved of duty of collection,
      299–300
    Wool: grant of a moiety of the crop
      (1338), 280, 281, 281–282, 285–
      286; writ of *certiorari* requiring
      details of collection of wool, 281;
      writ of *supersedeas* for the relaxa-
      tion of measures against the abb.
      of Glastonbury for non-payment,
      284; writ of *supersedeas* for the
      relaxation of measures against
      the abb. of St. Augustine's,
      Bristol, in view of his not having
      been present at the parliament
      which made the grant, 280–281;
      writ requesting a loan of wool
      (1347), 325
TITLE FOR ORDINATION:
    of 5 marks granted by lord of
      manor of Bredicot, 122
    of papal grace, 273, 277, 278, 338
      (*bis*)
    and see Canon Law *s.v.* obligation of
      bps. to support those ordained
      without sufficient title

                    V

VICARAGES, xlv–xlvi
    ordinations of: Acton Turville,
      306–307; Campden, 103; Gt.
      Badminton, 43; Tanworth, 43–
      45, 68; Wellesbourne, 171
    re-ordination of: Kidderminster,
      39–41
    acquittance for 13s. 4d. paid in
      accordance with Tanworth vicar-
      age ordination, 42
VISITATION, xxviii–xxxii
    itineraries: Gloucester archdy.
      (1340), 28–32; Worcester archdy.
      (1339), 18, 21–23, (1342), 94,
      (1345), 127–128
    proceedings arising from, xxx–xxxii
      commission to accept resignation
      of Tytherington vic., 104–105;
      commissions to carry out cor-
      rections following visitation,
      23–24, 95, 99; enquiry into